THE THREE APOLOGIES
OF
G.K. CHESTERTON

HERETICS, ORTHODOXY
&
THE EVERLASTING MAN

Mockingbird Press
www.mockingbirdpress.com
info@mockingbirdpress.com

Ordering Information:
Quantity sales. Special discounts are available on quantity purchases by corporations, associations, and others. For details, contact the publisher at the email address above.

Publisher's Cataloging-In-Publication Data

Chesterton, Gilbert Keith
The Three Apologies of G.K. Chesterton / Gilbert Keith Chesterton;
Chesterton, G.K., 1874-1936

ISBN-13: 978-1-946774-30-9
ISBN-10: 1-946774-30-8

1. Christianity, 2. Apologetics, I. G.K. Chesterton. II. The Three Apologies of G.K. Chesterton

BR1-1725 / BT1095-1255

THE AUTHOR

Gilbert Keith Chesterton was born in London, England on the 29th of May, 1874. Though he considered himself a mere "rollicking journalist," he was actually a prolific and gifted writer in virtually every area of literature. A man of strong opinions and enormously talented at defending them, his exuberant personality nevertheless allowed him to maintain warm friendships with people—such as George Bernard Shaw and H. G. Wells—with whom he vehemently disagreed.

Chesterton had no difficulty standing up for what he believed. He was one of the few journalists to oppose the Boer War. His 1922 "Eugenics and Other Evils" attacked what was at that time the most progressive of all ideas, the idea that the human race could and should breed a superior version of itself. In the Nazi experience, history demonstrated the wisdom of his once "reactionary" views.

His poetry runs the gamut from the comic 1908 "On Running After One's Hat" to dark and serious ballads. During the dark days of 1940, when Britain stood virtually alone against the armed might of Nazi Germany, these lines from his 1911 Ballad of the White Horse were often quoted:

> I tell you naught for your comfort,
> Yea, naught for your desire,
> Save that the sky grows darker yet
> And the sea rises higher.

Though not written for a scholarly audience, his biographies of authors and historical figures like Charles Dickens and St. Francis of Assisi often contain brilliant insights into their subjects. His Father Brown mystery stories, written between 1911 and 1936, are still being read and adapted for television.

His politics fitted with his deep distrust of concentrated wealth and power of any sort. Along with his friend Hilaire Belloc and in books like the 1910 "What's Wrong with the World" he advocated a view called "Distributionism" that was best summed up by his expression that every man ought to be allowed to own "three acres and a cow." Though not known as a political thinker, his political influence has circled the world. Some see in him the father of the "small is beautiful" movement and a newspaper article by him is credited with provoking Gandhi to seek a "genuine" nationalism for India rather than one that imitated the British.

Heretics belongs to yet another area of literature at which Chesterton excelled. A fun-loving and gregarious man, he was nevertheless troubled in his adolescence by thoughts of suicide. In Christianity he found the answers to the dilemmas and paradoxes he saw in life. Other books in that same series include his 1908 Orthodoxy (written in response to attacks on this book) and his 1925 The Everlasting Man. Orthodoxy is also available as electronic text.

Chesterton died on the 14th of June, 1936 in Beaconsfield, Buckinghamshire, England. During his life he published 69 books and at least another ten based on his writings have been published after his death. Many of those books are still in print. Ignatius Press is systematically publishing his collected writings.

CONTENTS

ORTHODOXY - *Continued*

THE EVERLASTING MAN

THE EVERLASTING MAN - *CONTINUED*

HERETICS

by

G. K. Chesterton

[1905]

To My Father

HERETICS

by

G. K. Chesterton

[1905]

To My Father

INTRODUCTORY REMARKS ON THE IMPORTANCE OF ORTHODOXY

Nothing more strangely indicates an enormous and silent evil of modern society than the extraordinary use which is made nowadays of the word "orthodox." In former days the heretic was proud of not being a heretic. It was the kingdoms of the world and the police and the judges who were heretics. He was orthodox. He had no pride in having rebelled against them; they had rebelled against him. The armies with their cruel security, the kings with their cold faces, the decorous processes of State, the reasonable processes of law—all these like sheep had gone astray. The man was proud of being orthodox, was proud of being right. If he stood alone in a howling wilderness he was more than a man; he was a church. He was the centre of the universe; it was round him that the stars swung. All the tortures torn out of forgotten hells could not make him admit that he was heretical. But a few modern phrases have made him boast of it. He says, with a conscious laugh, "I suppose I am very heretical," and looks round for applause. The word "heresy" not only means no longer being wrong; it practically means being clear-headed and courageous. The word "orthodoxy" not only no longer means being right; it practically means being wrong. All this can mean one thing, and one thing only. It means that people care less for whether they are philosophically right. For obviously a man ought to confess himself crazy before he confesses himself heretical. The Bohemian, with a red tie, ought to pique himself on his orthodoxy. The dynamiter, laying a bomb, ought to feel that, whatever else he is, at least he is orthodox.

It is foolish, generally speaking, for a philosopher to set fire to another philosopher in Smithfield Market because they do not agree in their theory of the universe. That was done very frequently in the last decadence of the Middle Ages, and it failed altogether in its object. But there is one thing that is infinitely more absurd and unpractical than burning a man for his philosophy. This is the habit of saying that his philosophy does not matter, and this is done universally in the twentieth century, in the decadence of the great revolutionary period. General theories are everywhere contemned; the doctrine of the Rights of Man is dismissed with the doctrine of the Fall of Man. Atheism itself is too theological for us to-day. Revolution itself is too much of a system; liberty itself is too much of a restraint. We will have no generalizations. Mr. Bernard Shaw has put the view in a perfect epigram: "The golden rule is that there is no golden rule." We are more and more to discuss details in art, politics, literature. A man's opinion on tramcars matters; his opinion on Botticelli matters; his opinion on all things does not

1

matter. He may turn over and explore a million objects, but he must not find that strange object, the universe; for if he does he will have a religion, and be lost. Everything matters—except everything.

Examples are scarcely needed of this total levity on the subject of cosmic philosophy. Examples are scarcely needed to show that, whatever else we think of as affecting practical affairs, we do not think it matters whether a man is a pessimist or an optimist, a Cartesian or a Hegelian, a materialist or a spiritualist. Let me, however, take a random instance. At any innocent tea-table we may easily hear a man say, "Life is not worth living." We regard it as we regard the statement that it is a fine day; nobody thinks that it can possibly have any serious effect on the man or on the world. And yet if that utterance were really believed, the world would stand on its head. Murderers would be given medals for saving men from life; firemen would be denounced for keeping men from death; poisons would be used as medicines; doctors would be called in when people were well; the Royal Humane Society would be rooted out like a horde of assassins. Yet we never speculate as to whether the conversational pessimist will strengthen or disorganize society; for we are convinced that theories do not matter.

This was certainly not the idea of those who introduced our freedom. When the old Liberals removed the gags from all the heresies, their idea was that religious and philosophical discoveries might thus be made. Their view was that cosmic truth was so important that every one ought to bear independent testimony. The modern idea is that cosmic truth is so unimportant that it cannot matter what any one says. The former freed inquiry as men loose a noble hound; the latter frees inquiry as men fling back into the sea a fish unfit for eating. Never has there been so little discussion about the nature of men as now, when, for the first time, any one can discuss it. The old restriction meant that only the orthodox were allowed to discuss religion. Modern liberty means that nobody is allowed to discuss it. Good taste, the last and vilest of human superstitions, has succeeded in silencing us where all the rest have failed. Sixty years ago it was bad taste to be an avowed atheist. Then came the Bradlaughites, the last religious men, the last men who cared about God; but they could not alter it. It is still bad taste to be an avowed atheist. But their agony has achieved just his—that now it is equally bad taste to be an avowed Christian. Emancipation has only locked the saint in the same tower of silence as the heresiarch. Then we talk about Lord Anglesey and the weather, and call it the complete liberty of all the creeds.

But there are some people, nevertheless—and I am one of them—who think that the most practical and important thing about a man is still his view of the universe. We think that for a landlady considering a lodger, it is important to know his income, but still more important to know his philosophy. We think that for a general about to fight an enemy, it is important to know the enemy's numbers, but still more important to know the enemy's philosophy. We think the question is not whether the theory of the cosmos affects matters, but whether in the long run, anything else affects them. In the fifteenth century men cross-examined and tormented a man because he preached some immoral attitude; in the nineteenth century we feted and flattered Oscar Wilde because he preached such an attitude, and then broke his heart in penal servitude because he carried it out. It may be a question which of the two methods was the more cruel; there can be no kind of question which was the more ludicrous. The age of the Inquisition has not at least the disgrace of having produced a society which made an idol of the very same man for preaching the very same things which it made him a convict for practising.

Now, in our time, philosophy or religion, our theory, that is, about ultimate things, has been driven out, more or less simultaneously, from two fields which it used to occupy. General ideals used to dominate literature. They have been driven out by the cry of "art for art's sake." General ideals used to dominate politics. They have been driven out by the cry of "efficiency," which may roughly be translated as "politics for politics' sake." Persistently for the last twenty years the ideals of order or liberty have dwindled in our books; the ambitions of wit and eloquence have dwindled in our parliaments. Literature has purposely become less political; politics have purposely become less literary. General theories of the relation of things have thus been extruded from both; and we are in a position to ask, "What have we gained or lost by this extrusion? Is literature better, is politics better, for having discarded the moralist and the philosopher?"

When everything about a people is for the time growing weak and ineffective, it begins to talk about efficiency. So it is that when a man's body is a wreck he begins, for the first time, to talk about health. Vigorous organisms talk not about their processes, but about their aims. There cannot be any better proof of the physical efficiency of a man than that he talks cheerfully of a journey to the end of the world. And there cannot be any better proof of the practical efficiency of a nation than that it talks constantly of a journey to the end of the world, a journey to the Judgment Day and the New Jerusalem. There can be no stronger sign of a coarse material health than the tendency to run after high and wild ideals; it is in the first exuberance of infancy that we cry for the moon. None of the strong men in the strong ages would have understood what you meant by working for efficiency. Hildebrand would have said that he was working not for efficiency, but for the Catholic Church. Danton would have said that he was working not for efficiency, but for liberty, equality, and fraternity. Even if the ideal of such men were simply the ideal of kicking a man downstairs, they thought of the end like men, not of the process like paralytics. They did not say, "Efficiently elevating my right leg, using, you will notice, the muscles of the thigh and calf, which are in excellent order, I—" Their feeling was quite different. They were so filled with the beautiful vision of the man lying flat at the foot of the staircase that in that ecstasy the rest followed in a flash. In practice, the habit of generalizing and idealizing did not by any means mean worldly weakness. The time of big theories was the time of big results. In the era of sentiment and fine words, at the end of the eighteenth century, men were really robust and effective. The sentimentalists conquered Napoleon. The cynics could not catch De Wet. A hundred years ago our affairs for good or evil were wielded triumphantly by rhetoricians. Now our affairs are hopelessly muddled by strong, silent men. And just as this repudiation of big words and big visions has brought forth a race of small men in politics, so it has brought forth a race of small men in the arts. Our modern politicians claim the colossal license of Caesar and the Superman, claim that they are too practical to be pure and too patriotic to be moral; but the upshot of it all is that a mediocrity is Chancellor of the Exchequer. Our new artistic philosophers call for the same moral license, for a freedom to wreck heaven and earth with their energy; but the upshot of it all is that a mediocrity is Poet Laureate. I do not say that there are no stronger men than these; but will any one say that there are any men stronger than those men of old who were dominated by their philosophy and steeped in their religion? Whether bondage be better than freedom may be discussed. But that their bondage came to more than our freedom it will be difficult for any one to deny.

The theory of the unmorality of art has established itself firmly in the strictly artistic classes. They are free to produce anything they like. They are free to write a "Paradise Lost" in which Satan shall conquer God. They are free to write a "Divine Comedy" in which heaven shall be under the floor of hell. And what have they done? Have they produced in their universality anything grander or more beautiful than the things uttered by the fierce Ghibbeline Catholic, by the rigid Puritan schoolmaster? We know that they have produced only a few roundels. Milton does not merely beat them at his piety, he beats them at their own irreverence. In all their little books of verse you will not find a finer defiance of God than Satan's. Nor will you find the grandeur of paganism felt as that fiery Christian felt it who described Faranata lifting his head as in disdain of hell. And the reason is very obvious. Blasphemy is an artistic effect, because blasphemy depends upon a philosophical conviction. Blasphemy depends upon belief and is fading with it. If any one doubts this, let him sit down seriously and try to think blasphemous thoughts about Thor. I think his family will find him at the end of the day in a state of some exhaustion.

Neither in the world of politics nor that of literature, then, has the rejection of general theories proved a success. It may be that there have been many moonstruck and misleading ideals that have from time to time

4

perplexed mankind. But assuredly there has been no ideal in practice so moonstruck and misleading as the ideal of practicality. Nothing has lost so many opportunities as the opportunism of Lord Rosebery. He is, indeed, a standing symbol of this epoch—the man who is theoretically a practical man, and practically more unpractical than any theorist. Nothing in this universe is so unwise as that kind of worship of worldly wisdom. A man who is perpetually thinking of whether this race or that race is strong, of whether this cause or that cause is promising, is the man who will never believe in anything long enough to make it succeed. The opportunist politician is like a man who should abandon billiards because he was beaten at billiards, and abandon golf because he was beaten at golf. There is nothing which is so weak for working purposes as this enormous importance attached to immediate victory. There is nothing that fails like success.

And having discovered that opportunism does fail, I have been induced to look at it more largely, and in consequence to see that it must fail. I perceive that it is far more practical to begin at the beginning and discuss theories. I see that the men who killed each other about the orthodoxy of the Homoousion were far more sensible than the people who are quarrelling about the Education Act. For the Christian dogmatists were trying to establish a reign of holiness, and trying to get defined, first of all, what was really holy. But our modern educationists are trying to bring about a religious liberty without attempting to settle what is religion or what is liberty. If the old priests forced a statement on mankind, at least they previously took some trouble to make it lucid. It has been left for the modern mobs of Anglicans and Nonconformists to persecute for a doctrine without even stating it.

For these reasons, and for many more, I for one have come to believe in going back to fundamentals. Such is the general idea of this book. I wish to deal with my most distinguished contemporaries, not personally or in a merely literary manner, but in relation to the real body of doctrine which they teach. I am not concerned with Mr. Rudyard Kipling as a vivid artist or a vigorous personality; I am concerned with him as a Heretic—that is to say, a man whose view of things has the hardihood to differ from mine. I am not concerned with Mr. Bernard Shaw as one of the most brilliant and one of the most honest men alive; I am concerned with him as a Heretic— that is to say, a man whose philosophy is quite solid, quite coherent, and quite wrong. I revert to the doctrinal methods of the thirteenth century, inspired by the general hope of getting something done.

Suppose that a great commotion arises in the street about something, let us say a lamp-post, which many influential persons desire to pull down. A grey-clad monk, who is the spirit of the Middle Ages, is approached upon the matter, and begins to say, in the arid manner of the Schoolmen, "Let us first of all consider, my brethren, the value of Light. If Light be in itself good—" At this point he is somewhat excusably knocked down. All the people make a rush for the lamp-post, the lamp-post is down in ten minutes, and they go about congratulating each other on their unmediaeval practicality. But as things go on they do not work out so easily. Some people have pulled the lamp-post down because they wanted the electric light; some because they wanted old iron; some because they wanted darkness, because their deeds were evil. Some thought it not enough of a lamp-post, some too much; some acted because they wanted to smash municipal machinery; some because they wanted to smash something. And there is war in the night, no man knowing whom he strikes. So, gradually and inevitably, to-day, to-morrow, or the next day, there comes back the conviction that the monk was right after all, and that all depends on what is the philosophy of Light. Only what we might have discussed under the gas-lamp, we now must discuss in the dark.

ON THE NEGATIVE SPIRIT

Much has been said, and said truly, of the monkish morbidity, of the hysteria which as often gone with the visions of hermits or nuns. But let us never forget that this visionary religion is, in one sense, necessarily more wholesome than our modern and reasonable morality. It is more wholesome for this reason, that it can contemplate the idea of success or triumph in the hopeless fight towards the ethical ideal, in what Stevenson called, with his usual startling felicity, "the lost fight of virtue." A modern morality, on the other hand, can only point with absolute conviction to the horrors that follow breaches of law; its only certainty is a certainty of ill. It can only point to imperfection. It has no perfection to point to. But the monk meditating upon Christ or Buddha has in his mind an image of perfect health, a thing of clear colours and clean air. He may contemplate this ideal wholeness and happiness far more than he ought; he may contemplate it to the neglect of exclusion of essential THINGS he may contemplate it until he has become a dreamer or a driveller; but still it is wholeness and happiness that he is contemplating. He may even go mad; but he is going mad for the love of sanity. But the modern student of ethics, even if he remains sane, remains sane from an insane dread of insanity.

The anchorite rolling on the stones in a frenzy of submission is a healthier person fundamentally than many a sober man in a silk hat who is walking down Cheapside. For many such are good only through a withering knowledge of evil. I am not at this moment claiming for the devotee anything more than this primary advantage, that though he may be making himself personally weak and miserable, he is still fixing his thoughts largely on gigantic strength and happiness, on a strength that has no limits, and a happiness that has no end. Doubtless there are other objections which can be urged without unreason against the influence of gods and visions in morality, whether in the cell or street. But this advantage the mystic morality must always have—it is always jollier. A young man may keep himself from vice by continually thinking of disease. He may keep himself from it also by continually thinking of the Virgin Mary. There may be question about which method is the more reasonable, or even about which is the more efficient. But surely there can be no question about which is the more wholesome.

I remember a pamphlet by that able and sincere secularist, Mr. G. W. Foote, which contained a phrase sharply symbolizing and dividing these two methods. The pamphlet was called BEER AND BIBLE, those two very noble things, all the nobler for a conjunction which Mr. Foote, in his stern old Puritan way, seemed to think sardonic, but which I confess to thinking appropriate and charming. I have not the work by me, but I remember that Mr. Foote dismissed very contemptuously any attempts to deal with the problem of strong drink by religious offices or intercessions, and said that a picture of a drunkard's liver would be more efficacious in the matter of temperance than any prayer or praise. In that picturesque expression, it seems to me, is perfectly embodied the incurable morbidity of modern ethics. In that temple the lights are low, the crowds kneel, the solemn anthems are uplifted. But that upon the altar to which all men kneel is no longer the perfect flesh, the body and substance of the perfect man; it is still flesh, but it is diseased. It is the drunkard's liver of the New Testament that is marred for us, which we take in remembrance of him.

Now, it is this great gap in modern ethics, the absence of vivid pictures of purity and spiritual triumph, which lies at the back of the real objection felt by so many sane men to the realistic literature of the nineteenth century. If any ordinary man ever said that he was horrified by the subjects discussed in Ibsen or Maupassant, or by the plain language in which they are spoken of, that ordinary man was lying. The average conversation of average men throughout the whole of modern civilization in every class or trade is such as Zola would never dream of printing. Nor is the habit of writing thus of these things a new habit. On the contrary, it is the Victorian prudery and silence which is new still, though it is already dying. The tradition of calling a spade a spade starts very early in our literature and comes down very late. But the truth is that the ordinary honest man, whatever vague account he may have given of his feelings, was not either disgusted or even annoyed at the candour of the moderns. What disgusted him, and very justly, was not the presence of a clear realism, but the absence of a clear idealism. Strong and genuine religious sentiment has never had any objection to realism; on the contrary, religion was the realistic thing, the brutal thing, the thing that called names. This is the great difference between some recent developments of Nonconformity and the great Puritanism of the seventeenth century. It was the whole point of the Puritans that they cared nothing for decency. Modern Nonconformist newspapers distinguish themselves by suppressing precisely those nouns and adjectives which the founders of Nonconformity distinguished themselves by flinging at kings and queens. But if it was a chief claim of religion that it spoke plainly about evil, it was the chief claim of all that it spoke plainly about good. The thing which is resented, and, as I think, rightly resented, in that great modern literature of which Ibsen is typical, is that while the eye that can perceive what are the wrong things increases in an uncanny and devouring clarity, the eye which sees what things are right is growing mistier and mistier every moment, till it goes almost blind with doubt. If we compare, let us say, the morality of the DIVINE COMEDY with the morality of Ibsen's GHOSTS, we shall see all that modern ethics have really done. No one, I imagine, will accuse the author of the INFERNO of an Early Victorian prudishness or a Podsnapian optimism. But Dante describes three moral instruments— Heaven, Purgatory, and Hell, the vision of perfection, the vision of improvement, and the vision of failure. Ibsen has only one—Hell. It is often said, and with perfect truth, that no one could read a play like GHOSTS and remain indifferent to the necessity of an ethical self- command. That is quite true, and the same is to be said of the most monstrous and material descriptions of the eternal fire. It is quite certain the realists like Zola do in one sense promote morality—they promote it in the sense in which the hangman promotes it, in the sense in which the devil promotes it. But they only affect that small minority which will accept any virtue of courage. Most healthy people dismiss these moral dangers as they dismiss the possibility of bombs or microbes. Modern realists are indeed Terrorists, like the dynamiters; and they fail just as much in their effort to create a thrill. Both realists and dynamiters are well-meaning people engaged in the task, so obviously ultimately hopeless, of using science to promote morality.

I do not wish the reader to confuse me for a moment with those vague persons who imagine that Ibsen is what they call a pessimist. There are plenty of wholesome people in Ibsen, plenty of good people, plenty of happy people, plenty of examples of men acting wisely and things ending well. That is not my meaning. My meaning is that Ibsen has throughout, and does not disguise, a certain vagueness and a changing attitude as well as a doubting attitude towards what is really wisdom and virtue in this life—a vagueness which contrasts very remarkably with the decisiveness with which he pounces on something which he perceives to be a root of evil, some convention, some deception, some ignorance. We know that the hero of GHOSTS is mad, and we know why he is mad. We do also know that Dr. Stockman is sane; but we do not know why he is sane. Ibsen does not profess to know how virtue and happiness are brought about, in the sense that he professes to know how our modern sexual tragedies are brought about. Falsehood works ruin in THE PILLARS OF SOCIETY, but truth works equal ruin in THE WILD DUCK. There are no cardinal virtues of Ibsenism. There is no ideal man of Ibsen. All this is not only admitted, but vaunted in the most valuable and thoughtful of all the eulogies upon Ibsen, Mr. Bernard Shaw's QUINTESSENCE OF IBSENISM. Mr. Shaw sums up Ibsen's teaching in the phrase, "The golden rule is that there is no golden rule." In his eyes this absence of an enduring and positive ideal, this absence of a permanent key to virtue, is the one great Ibsen merit. I am not discussing now with any fullness whether this is so or not. All I venture to point out, with an increased firmness, is that this omission, good or bad, does leave us face to face with the problem of a human consciousness filled with very definite images of evil, and with no definite image of good. To us light must be henceforward the dark thing—the thing of which we cannot speak. To us, as to Milton's devils in Pandemonium, it is darkness that is visible. The human race, according to religion, fell once, and in falling gained knowledge of good and of evil. Now we have fallen a second time, and only the knowledge of evil remains to us.

A great silent collapse, an enormous unspoken disappointment, has in our time fallen on our Northern civilization. All previous ages have sweated and been crucified in an attempt to realize what is really the right life, what was really the good man. A definite part of the modern world has come beyond question to the conclusion that there is no answer to these questions, that the most that we can do is to set up a few notice-boards at places of obvious danger, to warn men, for instance, against drinking themselves to death, or ignoring the mere existence of their neighbours. Ibsen is the first to return from the baffled hunt to bring us the tidings of great failure.

Every one of the popular modern phrases and ideals is a dodge in order to shirk the problem of what is good. We are fond of talking about "liberty"; that, as we talk of it, is a dodge to avoid discussing what is good. We are fond of talking about "progress"; that is a dodge to avoid discussing what is good. We are fond of talking about "education"; that is a dodge to avoid discussing what is good. The modern man says, "Let us leave all these arbitrary standards and embrace liberty." This is, logically rendered, "Let us not decide what is good, but let it be considered good not to decide it." He says, "Away with your old moral formulae; I am for progress." This, logically stated, means, "Let us not settle what is good; but let us settle whether we are getting more of it." He says, "Neither in religion nor morality, my friend, lie the hopes of the race, but in education." This, clearly expressed, means, "We cannot decide what is good, but let us give it to our children."

Mr. H.G. Wells, that exceedingly clear-sighted man, has pointed out in a recent work that this has happened in connection with economic questions. The old economists, he says, made generalizations, and they were (in Mr. Wells's view) mostly wrong. But the new economists, he says, seem to have lost the power of making any generalizations at all. And they cover this incapacity with a general claim to be, in specific cases, regarded as "experts", a claim "proper enough in a hairdresser or a fashionable physician, but indecent in a philosopher or a man of science." But in spite of the refreshing rationality with which Mr. Wells has indicated this, it must also be said that he himself has fallen into the same enormous modern error. In the opening pages of that excellent book MANKIND IN THE MAKING, he dismisses the ideals of art, religion, abstract morality, and the rest, and says that he is going to consider men in their chief function, the function of parenthood. He is going to discuss life as a "tissue of births." He is not going to ask what will produce satisfactory saints or satisfactory heroes, but what will produce satisfactory fathers and mothers. The whole is set forward so sensibly that it is a few moments at least before the reader realises that it is another example of unconscious shirking. What is the good of begetting a man until we have settled what is the good of being a man? You are merely handing on to him a problem you dare not settle yourself. It is as if a man were asked, "What is the use of a hammer?" and answered, "To make hammers"; and when asked, "And of those hammers, what is the use?" answered, "To make hammers again". Just as such a man would be perpetually putting off the question of the ultimate use of carpentry, so Mr. Wells and all the rest of us are by these phrases successfully putting off the question of the ultimate value of the human life.

The case of the general talk of "progress" is, indeed, an extreme one. As enunciated today, "progress" is simply a comparative of which we have not settled the superlative. We meet every ideal of religion, patriotism, beauty, or brute pleasure with the alternative ideal of progress—that is to say, we meet every proposal of getting something that we know about, with an alternative proposal of getting a great deal more of nobody knows what. Progress, properly understood, has, indeed, a most dignified and legitimate meaning. But as used in opposition to precise moral ideals, it is ludicrous. So far from it being the truth that the ideal of progress is to be set against that of ethical or religious finality, the reverse is the truth. Nobody has any business to use the word "progress" unless he has a definite creed and a cast-iron code of morals. Nobody can be progressive without being doctrinal; I might almost say that nobody can be progressive without being infallible—at any rate, without believing in some infallibility. For progress by its very name indicates a direction; and the moment we are in the least doubtful about the direction, we become in the same degree doubtful about the progress. Never perhaps since the beginning of the world has there been an age that had less right to use the word "progress" than we. In the Catholic twelfth century, in the philosophic eighteenth century, the direction may have been a good or a bad one, men may have differed more or less about how far they went, and in what direction, but about the direction they did in the main agree, and consequently they had the genuine sensation of progress. But it is precisely about the direction that we disagree. Whether the future excellence lies in more law or less law, in more liberty or less liberty; whether property will be finally concentrated or finally cut up; whether sexual passion will reach its sanest in an almost virgin intellectualism or in a full animal freedom; whether we should love everybody with Tolstoy, or spare nobody with Nietzsche;—these are the things about which we are actually fighting most. It is not merely true that the age which has settled least what is progress is this "progressive" age. It

11

is, moreover, true that the people who have settled least what is progress are the most "progressive" people in it. The ordinary mass, the men who have never troubled about progress, might be trusted perhaps to progress. The particular individuals who talk about progress would certainly fly to the four winds of heaven when the pistol-shot started the race. I do not, therefore, say that the word "progress" is unmeaning; I say it is unmeaning without the previous definition of a moral doctrine, and that it can only be applied to groups of persons who hold that doctrine in common. Progress is not an illegitimate word, but it is logically evident that it is illegitimate for us. It is a sacred word, a word which could only rightly be used by rigid believers and in the ages of faith.

ON MR. RUDYARD KIPLING AND MAKING THE WORLD SMALL

There is no such thing on earth as an uninteresting subject; the only thing that can exist is an uninterested person. Nothing is more keenly required than a defence of bores. When Byron divided humanity into the bores and bored, he omitted to notice that the higher qualities exist entirely in the bores, the lower qualities in the bored, among whom he counted himself. The bore, by his starry enthusiasm, his solemn happiness, may, in some sense, have proved himself poetical. The bored has certainly proved himself prosaic.

We might, no doubt, find it a nuisance to count all the blades of grass or all the leaves of the trees; but this would not be because of our boldness or gaiety, but because of our lack of boldness and gaiety. The bore would go onward, bold and gay, and find the blades of grass as splendid as the swords of an army. The bore is stronger and more joyous than we are; he is a demigod—nay, he is a god. For it is the gods who do not tire of the iteration of things; to them the nightfall is always new, and the last rose as red as the first.

The sense that everything is poetical is a thing solid and absolute; it is not a mere matter of phraseology or persuasion. It is not merely true, it is ascertainable. Men may be challenged to deny it; men may be challenged to mention anything that is not a matter of poetry. I remember a long time ago a sensible sub-editor coming up to me with a book in his hand, called "Mr. Smith," or "The Smith Family," or some such thing. He said, "Well, you won't get any of your damned mysticism out of this," or words to that effect. I am happy to say that I undeceived him; but the victory was too obvious and easy. In most cases the name is unpoetical, although the fact is poetical. In the case of Smith, the name is so poetical that it must be an arduous and heroic matter for the man to live up to it. The name of Smith is the name of the one trade that even kings respected, it could claim half the glory of that arma virumque which all epics acclaimed. The spirit of the smithy is so close to the spirit of song that it has mixed in a million poems, and every blacksmith is a harmonious blacksmith.

Even the village children feel that in some dim way the smith is poetic, as the grocer and the cobbler are not poetic, when they feast on the dancing sparks and deafening blows in the cavern of that creative violence. The brute repose of Nature, the passionate cunning of man, the strongest of earthly metals, the wierdest of earthly elements, the unconquerable iron subdued by its only conqueror, the wheel and the ploughshare, the sword and the steam-hammer, the arraying of armies and the whole legend of arms, all these things are written, briefly indeed, but quite legibly, on the visiting-card of Mr. Smith. Yet our novelists call their hero "Aylmer Valence," which means nothing, or "Vernon Raymond," which means nothing, when it is in their power to give him this sacred name of Smith— this name made of iron and flame. It would be very natural if a certain hauteur, a certain carriage of the head, a certain curl of the lip, distinguished every one whose name is Smith. Perhaps it does; I trust so. Whoever else are parvenus, the Smiths are not parvenus. From the darkest dawn of history this clan has gone forth to battle; its trophies are on every hand; its name is everywhere; it is older than the nations, and its sign is the Hammer of Thor. But as I also remarked, it is not quite the usual case. It is common enough that common things should be poetical; it is not so common that common names should be poetical. In most cases it is the name that is the obstacle. A great many people talk as if this claim of ours, that all things are poetical, were a mere literary ingenuity, a play on words. Precisely the contrary is true. It is the idea that some things are not poetical which is literary, which is a mere product of words. The word "signal-box" is unpoetical. But the thing signal-box is not unpoetical; it is a place where men, in an agony of vigilance, light blood-red and sea-green fires to keep other men from death. That is the plain, genuine description of what it is; the prose only comes in with what it is called. The word "pillar-box" is unpoetical. But the thing pillar-box is not unpoetical; it is the place to which friends and lovers commit their messages, conscious that when they have done so they are sacred, and not to be touched, not only by others, but even (religious touch!) by themselves. That red turret is one of the last of the temples. Posting a letter and getting married are among the few things left that are entirely romantic; for to be entirely romantic a thing must be irrevocable. We think a pillar-box prosaic, because there is no rhyme to it. We think a pillar-box unpoetical, because we have never seen it in a poem. But the bold fact is entirely on the side of poetry. A signal-box is only called a signal-box; it is a house of life and death. A pillar-box is only called a pillar-box; it is a sanctuary of human words. If you think the name of "Smith" prosaic, it is not because you are practical and sensible; it is because you are too much affected with literary refinements. The name shouts poetry at you. If you think of it otherwise, it is because you are steeped and sodden with verbal reminiscences, because you remember everything in Punch or Comic Cuts about Mr. Smith being drunk or Mr. Smith being henpecked. All these things were given to you poetical. It is only by a long and elaborate process of literary effort that you have made them prosaic.

Now, the first and fairest thing to say about Rudyard Kipling is that he has borne a brilliant part in thus recovering the lost provinces of poetry. He has not been frightened by that brutal materialistic air which clings only to words; he has pierced through to the romantic, imaginative matter of the things themselves. He has perceived the significance and philosophy of steam and of slang. Steam may be, if you like, a dirty by-product of science. Slang may be, if you like, a dirty by-product of language. But at least he has been among the few who saw the divine parentage of these things, and knew that where there is smoke there is fire—that is, that wherever there is the foulest of things, there also is the purest. Above all, he has had something to say, a definite view of things to utter, and that always means that a man is fearless and faces everything. For the moment we have a view of the universe, we possess it.

Now, the message of Rudyard Kipling, that upon which he has really concentrated, is the only thing worth worrying about in him or in any other man. He has often written bad poetry, like Wordsworth. He has often said silly things, like Plato. He has often given way to mere political hysteria, like Gladstone. But no one can reasonably doubt that he means steadily and sincerely to say something, and the only serious question is, What is that which he has tried to say? Perhaps the best way of stating this fairly will be to begin with that element which has been most insisted by himself and by his opponents—I mean his interest in militarism. But when we are seeking for the real merits of a man it is unwise to go to his enemies, and much more foolish to go to himself.

Now, Mr. Kipling is certainly wrong in his worship of militarism, but his opponents are, generally speaking, quite as wrong as he. The evil of militarism is not that it shows certain men to be fierce and haughty and excessively warlike. The evil of militarism is that it shows most men to be tame and timid and excessively peaceable. The professional soldier gains more and more power as the general courage of a community declines. Thus the Pretorian guard became more and more important in Rome as Rome became more and more luxurious and feeble. The military man gains the civil power in proportion as the civilian loses the military virtues. And as it was in ancient Rome so it is in contemporary Europe. There never was a time when nations were more militarist. There never was a time when men were less brave. All ages and all epics have sung of arms and the man; but we have effected simultaneously the deterioration of the man and the fantastic perfection of the arms. Militarism demonstrated the decadence of Rome, and it demonstrates the decadence of Prussia.

And unconsciously Mr. Kipling has proved this, and proved it admirably. For in so far as his work is earnestly understood the military trade does not by any means emerge as the most important or attractive. He has not written so well about soldiers as he has about railway men or bridge builders, or even journalists. The fact is that what attracts Mr. Kipling to militarism is not the idea of courage, but the idea of discipline. There was far more courage to the square mile in the Middle Ages, when no king had a standing army, but every man had a bow or sword. But the fascination of the standing army upon Mr. Kipling is not courage, which scarcely interests him, but discipline, which is, when all is said and done, his primary theme. The modern army is not a miracle of courage; it has not enough opportunities, owing to the cowardice of everybody else. But it is really a miracle of organization, and that is the truly Kiplingite ideal. Kipling's subject is not that valour which properly belongs to war, but that interdependence and efficiency which belongs quite as much to engineers, or sailors, or mules, or railway engines. And thus it is that when he writes of engineers, or sailors, or mules, or steam-engines, he writes at his best. The real poetry, the "true romance" which Mr. Kipling has taught, is the romance of the division of labour and the discipline of all the trades. He sings the arts of peace much more accurately than the arts of war. And his main contention is vital and valuable. Every thing is military in the sense that everything depends upon obedience. There is no perfectly epicurean corner; there is no perfectly irresponsible place. Everywhere men have made the way for us with sweat and submission. We may fling ourselves into a hammock in a fit of divine carelessness. But we are glad that the net-maker did not make the hammock in a fit of divine carelessness. We may jump upon a child's rocking-horse for a joke. But we are glad that the carpenter did not leave the legs of it unglued for a joke. So far from having merely preached that a soldier cleaning his side-arm is to be adored because he is military, Kipling at his best and clearest has preached that the baker baking loaves and the tailor cutting coats is as military as anybody.

Being devoted to this multitudinous vision of duty, Mr. Kipling is naturally a cosmopolitan. He happens to find his examples in the British Empire, but almost any other empire would do as well, or, indeed, any other highly civilized country. That which he admires in the British army he would find even more apparent in the German army; that which he desires in the British police he would find flourishing, in the French police. The ideal of discipline is not the whole of life, but it is spread over the whole of the world. And the worship of it tends to confirm in Mr. Kipling a certain note of worldly wisdom, of the experience of the wanderer, which is one of the genuine charms of his best work.

The great gap in his mind is what may be roughly called the lack of patriotism—that is to say, he lacks altogether the faculty of attaching himself to any cause or community finally and tragically; for all finality must be tragic. He admires England, but he does not love her; for we admire things with reasons, but love them without reasons. He admires England because she is strong, not because she is English. There is no harshness in saying this, for, to do him justice, he avows it with his usual picturesque candour. In a very interesting poem, he says that—

"If England was what England seems"

—that is, weak and inefficient; if England were not what (as he believes) she is—that is, powerful and practical—

"How quick we'd chuck 'er! But she ain't!"

He admits, that is, that his devotion is the result of a criticism, and this is quite enough to put it in another category altogether from the patriotism of the Boers, whom he hounded down in South Africa. In speaking of the really patriotic peoples, such as the Irish, he has some difficulty in keeping a shrill irritation out of his language. The frame of mind which he really describes with beauty and nobility is the frame of mind of the cosmopolitan man who has seen men and cities.

"For to admire and for to see,
For to be'old this world so wide."

He is a perfect master of that light melancholy with which a man looks back on having been the citizen of many communities, of that light melancholy with which a man looks back on having been the lover of many women. He is the philanderer of the nations. But a man may have learnt much about women in flirtations, and still be ignorant of first love; a man may have known as many lands as Ulysses, and still be ignorant of patriotism.

Mr. Rudyard Kipling has asked in a celebrated epigram what they can know of England who know England only. It is a far deeper and sharper question to ask, "What can they know of England who know only the world?" for the world does not include England any more than it includes the Church. The moment we care for anything deeply, the world—that is, all the other miscellaneous interests—becomes our enemy. Christians showed it when they talked of keeping one's self "unspotted from the world;" but lovers talk of it just as much when they talk of the "world well lost." Astronomically speaking, I understand that England is situated on the world; similarly, I suppose that the Church was a part of the world, and even the lovers inhabitants of that orb. But they all felt a certain truth—the truth that the moment you love anything the world becomes your foe. Thus Mr. Kipling does certainly know the world; he is a man of the world, with all the narrowness that belongs to those imprisoned in that planet. He knows England as an intelligent English gentleman knows Venice. He has been to England a great many times; he has stopped there for long visits. But he does not belong to it, or to any place; and the proof of it is this, that he thinks of England as a place. The moment we are rooted in a place, the place vanishes. We live like a tree with the whole strength of the universe.

The globe-trotter lives in a smaller world than the peasant. He is always breathing, an air of locality. London is a place, to be compared to Chicago; Chicago is a place, to be compared to Timbuctoo. But Timbuctoo is not a place, since there, at least, live men who regard it as the universe, and breathe, not an air of locality, but the winds of the world. The man in the saloon steamer has seen all the races of men, and he is thinking of the things that divide men—diet, dress, decorum, rings in the nose as in Africa, or in the ears as in Europe, blue paint among the ancients, or red paint among the modern Britons. The man in the cabbage field has seen nothing at all; but he is thinking of the things that unite men—hunger and babies, and the beauty of women, and the promise or menace of the sky. Mr. Kipling, with all his merits, is the globe-trotter; he has not the patience to become part of anything. So great and genuine a man is not to be accused of a merely cynical cosmopolitanism; still, his cosmopolitanism is his weakness. That weakness is splendidly expressed in one of his finest poems, "The Sestina of the Tramp Royal," in which a man declares that he can endure anything in the way of hunger or horror, but not permanent presence in one place. In this there is certainly danger. The more dead and dry and dusty a thing is the more it travels about; dust is like this and the thistle-down and the High Commissioner in South Africa. Fertile things are somewhat heavier, like the heavy fruit trees on the pregnant mud of the Nile. In the heated idleness of youth we were all rather inclined to quarrel with the implication of that proverb which says that a rolling stone gathers no moss. We were inclined to ask, "Who wants to gather moss, except silly old ladies?" But for all that we begin to perceive that the proverb is right. The rolling stone rolls echoing from rock to rock; but the rolling stone is dead. The moss is silent because the moss is alive.

The truth is that exploration and enlargement make the world smaller. The telegraph and the steamboat make the world smaller. The telescope makes the world smaller; it is only the microscope that makes it larger. Before long the world will be cloven with a war between the telescopists and the microscopists. The first study large things and live in a small world; the second study small things and live in a large world. It is inspiriting without doubt to whizz in a motor-car round the earth, to feel Arabia as a whirl of sand or China as a flash of rice-fields. But Arabia is not a whirl of sand and China is not a flash of rice-fields. They are ancient civilizations with strange virtues buried like treasures. If we wish to understand them it must not be as tourists or inquirers, it must be with the loyalty of children and the great patience of poets. To conquer these places is to lose them. The man standing in his own kitchen-garden, with fairyland opening at the gate, is the man with large ideas. His mind creates distance; the motor-car stupidly destroys it. Moderns think of the earth as a globe, as something one can easily get round, the spirit of a schoolmistress. This is shown in the odd mistake perpetually made about Cecil Rhodes. His enemies say that he may have had large ideas, but he was a bad man. His friends say that he may have been a bad man, but he certainly had large ideas. The truth is that he was not a man essentially bad, he was a man of much geniality and many good intentions, but a man with singularly small views. There is nothing large about painting the map red; it is an innocent game for children. It is just as easy to think in continents as to think in cobble-stones. The difficulty comes in when we seek to know the substance of either of them. Rhodes' prophecies about the Boer resistance are an admirable comment on how the "large ideas" prosper when it is not a question of thinking in continents but of understanding a few two-legged men. And under all this vast illusion of the cosmopolitan planet, with its empires and its Reuter's agency, the real life of man goes on concerned with this tree or that temple, with this harvest or that drinking-song, totally uncomprehended, totally untouched. And it watches from its splendid parochialism, possibly with a smile of amusement, motor-car civilization going its triumphant way, outstripping time, consuming space, seeing all and seeing nothing, roaring on at last to the capture of the solar system, only to find the sun cockney and the stars suburban.

MR. BERNARD SHAW

In the glad old days, before the rise of modern morbidities, when genial old Ibsen filled the world with wholesome joy, and the kindly tales of the forgotten Emile Zola kept our firesides merry and pure, it used to be thought a disadvantage to be misunderstood. It may be doubted whether it is always or even generally a disadvantage. The man who is misunderstood has always this advantage over his enemies, that they do not know his weak point or his plan of campaign. They go out against a bird with nets and against a fish with arrows. There are several modern examples of this situation. Mr. Chamberlain, for instance, is a very good one. He constantly eludes or vanquishes his opponents because his real powers and deficiencies are quite different to those with which he is credited, both by friends and foes. His friends depict him as a strenuous man of action; his opponents depict him as a coarse man of business; when, as a fact, he is neither one nor the other, but an admirable romantic orator and romantic actor. He has one power which is the soul of melodrama—the power of pretending, even when backed by a huge majority, that he has his back to the wall. For all mobs are so far chivalrous that their heroes must make some show of misfortune—that sort of hypocrisy is the homage that strength pays to weakness. He talks foolishly and yet very finely about his own city that has never deserted him. He wears a flaming and fantastic flower, like a decadent minor poet. As for his bluffness and toughness and appeals to common sense, all that is, of course, simply the first trick of rhetoric. He fronts his audiences with the venerable affectation of Mark Antony—

> "I am no orator, as Brutus is;
> But as you know me all, a plain blunt man."

It is the whole difference between the aim of the orator and the aim of any other artist, such as the poet or the sculptor. The aim of the sculptor is to convince us that he is a sculptor; the aim of the orator, is to convince us that he is not an orator. Once let Mr. Chamberlain be mistaken for a practical man, and his game is won. He has only to compose a theme on empire, and people will say that these plain men say great things on great occasions. He has only to drift in the large loose notions common to all artists of the second rank, and people will say that business men have the biggest ideals after all. All his schemes have ended in smoke; he has touched nothing that he did not confuse. About his figure there is a Celtic pathos; like the Gaels in Matthew Arnold's quotation, "he went forth to battle, but he always fell." He is a mountain of proposals, a mountain of failures; but still a mountain. And a mountain is always romantic.

There is another man in the modern world who might be called the antithesis of Mr. Chamberlain in every point, who is also a standing monument of the advantage of being misunderstood. Mr. Bernard Shaw is always represented by those who disagree with him, and, I fear, also (if such exist) by those who agree with him, as a capering humorist, a dazzling acrobat, a quick-change artist. It is said that he cannot be taken seriously, that he will defend anything or attack anything, that he will do anything to startle and amuse. All this is not only untrue, but it is, glaringly, the opposite of the truth; it is as wild as to say that Dickens had not the boisterous masculinity of Jane Austen. The whole force and triumph of Mr. Bernard Shaw lie in the fact that he is a thoroughly consistent man. So far from his power consisting in jumping through hoops or standing on his head, his power consists in holding his own fortress night and day. He puts the Shaw test rapidly and rigorously to everything that happens in heaven or earth. His standard never varies. The thing which weak-minded revolutionists and weak-minded Conservatives really hate (and fear) in him, is exactly this, that his scales, such as they are, are held even, and that his law, such as it is, is justly enforced. You may attack his principles, as I do; but I do not know of any instance in which you can attack their application. If he dislikes lawlessness, he dislikes the lawlessness of Socialists as much as that of Individualists. If he dislikes the fever of patriotism, he dislikes it in Boers and Irishmen as well as in Englishmen. If he dislikes the vows and bonds of marriage, he dislikes still more the fiercer bonds and wilder vows that are made by lawless love. If he laughs at the authority of priests, he laughs louder at the pomposity of men of science. If he condemns the irresponsibility of faith, he condemns with a sane consistency the equal irresponsibility of art. He has pleased all the bohemians by saying that women are equal to men; but he has infuriated them by suggesting that men are equal to women. He is almost mechanically just; he has something of the terrible quality of a machine. The man who is really wild and whirling, the man who is really fantastic and incalculable, is not Mr. Shaw, but the average Cabinet Minister. It is Sir Michael Hicks-Beach who jumps through hoops. It is Sir Henry Fowler who stands on his head. The solid and respectable statesman of that type does really leap from position to position; he is really ready to defend anything or nothing; he is really not to be taken seriously. I know perfectly well what Mr. Bernard Shaw will be saying thirty years hence; he will be saying what he has always said. If thirty years hence I meet Mr. Shaw, a reverent being with a silver beard sweeping the earth, and say to him, "One can never, of course, make a verbal attack upon a lady," the patriarch will lift his aged hand and fell me to the earth. We know, I say, what Mr. Shaw will be, saying thirty years hence. But is there any one so darkly read in stars and oracles that he will dare to predict what Mr. Asquith will be saying thirty years hence?

The truth is, that it is quite an error to suppose that absence of definite convictions gives the mind freedom and agility. A man who believes something is ready and witty, because he has all his weapons about him. He can apply his test in an instant. The man engaged in conflict with a man like Mr. Bernard Shaw may fancy he has ten faces; similarly a man engaged against a brilliant duellist may fancy that the sword of his foe has turned to ten swords in his hand. But this is not really because the man is playing with ten swords, it is because he is aiming very straight with one. Moreover, a man with a definite belief always appears bizarre, because he does not change with the world; he has climbed into a fixed star, and the earth whizzes below him like a zoetrope. Millions of mild black-coated men call themselves sane and sensible merely because they always catch the fashionable insanity, because they are hurried into madness after madness by the maelstrom of the world.

People accuse Mr. Shaw and many much sillier persons of "proving that black is white." But they never ask whether the current colour-language is always correct. Ordinary sensible phraseology sometimes calls black white, it certainly calls yellow white and green white and reddish-brown white. We call wine "white wine" which is as yellow as a Blue-coat boy's legs. We call grapes "white grapes" which are manifestly pale green. We give to the European, whose complexion is a sort of pink drab, the horrible title of a "white man"—a picture more blood-curdling than any spectre in Poe.

Now, it is undoubtedly true that if a man asked a waiter in a restaurant for a bottle of yellow wine and some greenish-yellow grapes, the waiter would think him mad. It is undoubtedly true that if a Government official, reporting on the Europeans in Burmah, said, "There are only two thousand pinkish men here" he would be accused of cracking jokes, and kicked out of his post. But it is equally obvious that both men would have come to grief through telling the strict truth. That too truthful man in the restaurant; that too truthful man in Burmah, is Mr. Bernard Shaw. He appears eccentric and grotesque because he will not accept the general belief that white is yellow. He has based all his brilliancy and solidity upon the hackneyed, but yet forgotten, fact that truth is stranger than fiction. Truth, of course, must of necessity be stranger than fiction, for we have made fiction to suit ourselves.

So much then a reasonable appreciation will find in Mr. Shaw to be bracing and excellent. He claims to see things as they are; and some things, at any rate, he does see as they are, which the whole of our civilization does not see at all. But in Mr. Shaw's realism there is something lacking, and that thing which is lacking is serious.

Mr. Shaw's old and recognized philosophy was that powerfully presented in "The Quintessence of Ibsenism." It was, in brief, that conservative ideals were bad, not because They were conservative, but because they were ideals. Every ideal prevented men from judging justly the particular case; every moral generalization oppressed the individual; the golden rule was there was no golden rule. And the objection to this is simply that it pretends to free men, but really restrains them from doing the only thing that men want to do. What is the good of telling a community that it has every liberty except the liberty to make laws? The liberty to make laws is what constitutes a free people. And what is the good of telling a man (or a philosopher) that he has every liberty except the liberty to make generalizations. Making generalizations is what makes him a man. In short, when Mr. Shaw forbids men to have strict moral ideals, he is acting like one who should forbid them to have children. The saying that "the golden rule is that there is no golden rule," can, indeed, be simply answered by being turned round. That there is no golden rule is itself a golden rule, or rather it is much worse than a golden rule. It is an iron rule; a fetter on the first movement of a man.

But the sensation connected with Mr. Shaw in recent years has been his sudden development of the religion of the Superman. He who had to all appearance mocked at the faiths in the forgotten past discovered a new god in the unimaginable future. He who had laid all the blame on ideals set up the most impossible of all ideals, the ideal of a new creature. But the truth, nevertheless, is that any one who knows Mr. Shaw's mind adequately, and admires it properly, must have guessed all this long ago.

For the truth is that Mr. Shaw has never seen things as they really are. If he had he would have fallen on his knees before them. He has always had a secret ideal that has withered all the things of this world. He has all the time been silently comparing humanity with something that was not human, with a monster from Mars, with the Wise Man of the Stoics, with the Economic Man of the Fabians, with Julius Caesar, with Siegfried, with the Superman. Now, to have this inner and merciless standard may be a very good thing, or a very bad one, it may be excellent or unfortunate, but it is not seeing things as they are. It is not seeing things as they are to think first of a Briareus with a hundred hands, and then call every man a cripple for only having two. It is not seeing things as they are to start with a vision of Argus with his hundred eyes, and then jeer at every man with two eyes as if he had only one. And it is not seeing things as they are to imagine a demigod of infinite mental clarity, who may or may not appear in the latter days of the earth, and then to see all men as idiots. And this is what Mr. Shaw has always in some degree done. When we really see men as they are, we do not criticise, but worship; and very rightly. For a monster with mysterious eyes and miraculous thumbs, with strange dreams in his skull, and a queer tenderness for this place or that baby, is truly a wonderful and unnerving matter. It is only the quite arbitrary and priggish habit of comparison with something else which makes it possible to be at our ease in front of him. A sentiment of superiority keeps us cool and practical; the mere facts would make, our knees knock under as with religious fear. It is the fact that every instant of conscious life is an unimaginable prodigy. It is the fact that every face in the street has the incredible unexpectedness of a fairy-tale. The thing which prevents a man from realizing this is not any clear-sightedness or experience, it is simply a habit of pedantic and fastidious comparisons between one thing and another. Mr. Shaw, on the practical side perhaps the most humane man alive, is in this sense inhumane. He has even been infected to some extent with the primary intellectual weakness of his new master, Nietzsche, the strange notion that the greater and stronger a man was the more he would despise other things. The greater and stronger a man is the more he would be inclined to prostrate himself before a periwinkle. That Mr. Shaw keeps a lifted head and a contemptuous face before the colossal panorama of empires and civilizations, this does not in itself convince one that he sees things as they are. I should be most effectively convinced that he did if I found him staring with religious astonishment at his own feet. "What are those two beautiful and industrious beings," I can imagine him murmuring to himself, "whom I see everywhere, serving me I know not why? What fairy godmother bade them come trotting out of elfland when I was born? What god of the borderland, what barbaric god of legs, must I propitiate with fire and wine, lest they run away with me?"

The truth is, that all genuine appreciation rests on a certain mystery of humility and almost of darkness. The man who said, "Blessed is he that expecteth nothing, for he shall not be disappointed," put the eulogy quite inadequately and even falsely. The truth "Blessed is he that expecteth nothing, for he shall be gloriously surprised." The man who expects nothing sees redder roses than common men can see, and greener grass, and a more startling sun. Blessed is he that expecteth nothing, for he shall possess the cities and the mountains; blessed is the meek, for he shall inherit the earth. Until we realize that things might not be we cannot realize that things are. Until we see the background of darkness we cannot admire the light as a single and created thing. As soon as we have seen that darkness, all light is lightening, sudden, blinding, and divine. Until we picture nonentity we underrate the victory of God, and can realize none of the trophies of His ancient war. It is one of the million wild jests of truth that we know nothing until we know nothing.

Now this is, I say deliberately, the only defect in the greatness of Mr. Shaw, the only answer to his claim to be a great man, that he is not easily pleased. He is an almost solitary exception to the general and essential maxim, that little things please great minds. And from this absence of that most uproarious of all things, humility, comes incidentally the peculiar insistence on the Superman. After belabouring a great many people for a great many years for being unprogressive, Mr. Shaw has discovered, with characteristic sense, that it is very doubtful whether any existing human being with two legs can be progressive at all. Having come to doubt whether humanity can be combined with progress, most people, easily pleased, would have elected to abandon progress and remain with humanity. Mr. Shaw, not being easily pleased, decides to throw over humanity with all its limitations and go in for progress for its own sake. If man, as we know him, is incapable of the philosophy of progress, Mr. Shaw asks, not for a new kind of philosophy, but for a new kind of man. It is rather as if a nurse had tried a rather bitter food for some years on a baby, and on discovering that it was not suitable, should not throw away the food and ask for a new food, but throw the baby out of window, and ask for a new baby. Mr. Shaw cannot understand that the thing which is valuable and lovable in our eyes is man—the old beer-drinking, creed-making, fighting, failing, sensual, respectable man. And the things that have been founded on this creature immortally remain; the things that have been founded on the fancy of the Superman have died with the dying civilizations which alone have given them birth. When Christ at a symbolic moment was establishing His great society, He chose for its corner-stone neither the brilliant Paul nor the mystic John, but a shuffler, a snob a coward—in a word, a man. And upon this rock He has built His Church, and the gates of Hell have not prevailed against it. All the empires and the kingdoms have failed, because of this inherent and continual weakness, that they were founded by strong men and upon strong men. But this one thing, the historic Christian Church, was founded on a weak man, and for that reason it is indestructible. For no chain is stronger than its weakest link.

MR. H.G. WELLS AND THE GIANTS

We ought to see far enough into a hypocrite to see even his sincerity. We ought to be interested in that darkest and most real part of a man in which dwell not the vices that he does not display, but the virtues that he cannot. And the more we approach the problems of human history with this keen and piercing charity, the smaller and smaller space we shall allow to pure hypocrisy of any kind. The hypocrites shall not deceive us into thinking them saints; but neither shall they deceive us into thinking them hypocrites. And an increasing number of cases will crowd into our field of inquiry, cases in which there is really no question of hypocrisy at all, cases in which people were so ingenuous that they seemed absurd, and so absurd that they seemed disingenuous.

There is one striking instance of an unfair charge of hypocrisy. It is always urged against the religious in the past, as a point of inconsistency and duplicity, that they combined a profession of almost crawling humility with a keen struggle for earthly success and considerable triumph in attaining it. It is felt as a piece of humbug, that a man should be very punctilious in calling himself a miserable sinner, and also very punctilious in calling himself King of France. But the truth is that there is no more conscious inconsistency between the humility of a Christian and the rapacity of a Christian than there is between the humility of a lover and the rapacity of a lover. The truth is that there are no things for which men will make such herculean efforts as the things of which they know they are unworthy. There never was a man in love who did not declare that, if he strained every nerve to breaking, he was going to have his desire. And there never was a man in love who did not declare also that he ought not to have it. The whole secret of the practical success of Christendom lies in the Christian humility, however imperfectly fulfilled. For with the removal of all question of merit or payment, the soul is suddenly released for incredible voyages. If we ask a sane man how much he merits, his mind shrinks instinctively and instantaneously. It is doubtful whether he merits six feet of earth. But if you ask him what he can conquer—he can conquer the stars. Thus comes the thing called Romance, a purely Christian product. A man cannot deserve adventures; he cannot earn dragons and hippogriffs. The mediaeval Europe which asserted humility gained Romance; the civilization which gained Romance has gained the habitable globe. How different the Pagan and Stoical feeling was from this has been admirably expressed in a famous quotation. Addison makes the great Stoic say—

"'Tis not in mortals to command success;

But we'll do more, Sempronius, we'll deserve it."

But the spirit of Romance and Christendom, the spirit which is in every lover, the spirit which has bestridden the earth with European adventure, is quite opposite. 'Tis not in mortals to deserve success. But we'll do more, Sempronius; we'll obtain it.

And this gay humility, this holding of ourselves lightly and yet ready for an infinity of unmerited triumphs, this secret is so simple that every one has supposed that it must be something quite sinister and mysterious. Humility is so practical a virtue that men think it must be a vice. Humility is so successful that it is mistaken for pride. It is mistaken for it all the more easily because it generally goes with a certain simple love of splendour which amounts to vanity. Humility will always, by preference, go clad in scarlet and gold; pride is that which refuses to let gold and scarlet impress it or please it too much. In a word, the failure of this virtue actually lies in its success; it is too successful as an investment to be believed in as a virtue. Humility is not merely too good for this world; it is too practical for this world; I had almost said it is too worldly for this world.

The instance most quoted in our day is the thing called the humility of the man of science; and certainly it is a good instance as well as a modern one. Men find it extremely difficult to believe that a man who is obviously uprooting mountains and dividing seas, tearing down temples and stretching out hands to the stars, is really a quiet old gentleman who only asks to be allowed to indulge his harmless old hobby and follow his harmless old nose. When a man splits a grain of sand and the universe is turned upside down in consequence, it is difficult to realize that to the man who did it, the splitting of the grain is the great affair, and the capsizing of the cosmos quite a small one. It is hard to enter into the feelings of a man who regards a new heaven and a new earth in the light of a by-product. But undoubtedly it was to this almost eerie innocence of the intellect that the great men of the great scientific period, which now appears to be closing, owed their enormous power and triumph. If they had brought the heavens down like a house of cards their plea was not even that they had done it on principle; their quite unanswerable plea was that they had done it by accident. Whenever there was in them the least touch of pride in what they had done, there was a good ground for attacking them; but so long as they were wholly humble, they were wholly victorious. There were possible answers to Huxley; there was no answer possible to Darwin. He was convincing because of his unconsciousness; one might almost say because of his dulness. This childlike and prosaic mind is beginning to wane in the world of science. Men of science are beginning to see themselves, as the fine phrase is, in the part; they are beginning to be proud of their humility. They are beginning to be aesthetic, like the rest of the world, beginning to

27

spell truth with a capital T, beginning to talk of the creeds they imagine themselves to have destroyed, of the discoveries that their forbears made. Like the modern English, they are beginning to be soft about their own hardness. They are becoming conscious of their own strength—that is, they are growing weaker. But one purely modern man has emerged in the strictly modern decades who does carry into our world the clear personal simplicity of the old world of science. One man of genius we have who is an artist, but who was a man of science, and who seems to be marked above all things with this great scientific humility. I mean Mr. H. G. Wells. And in his case, as in the others above spoken of, there must be a great preliminary difficulty in convincing the ordinary person that such a virtue is predicable of such a man. Mr. Wells began his literary work with violent visions— visions of the last pangs of this planet; can it be that a man who begins with violent visions is humble? He went on to wilder and wilder stories about carving beasts into men and shooting angels like birds. Is the man who shoots angels and carves beasts into men humble? Since then he has done something bolder than either of these blasphemies; he has prophesied the political future of all men; prophesied it with aggressive authority and a ringing decision of detail. Is the prophet of the future of all men humble? It will indeed be difficult, in the present condition of current thought about such things as pride and humility, to answer the query of how a man can be humble who does such big things and such bold things. For the only answer is the answer which I gave at the beginning of this essay. It is the humble man who does the big things. It is the humble man who does the bold things. It is the humble man who has the sensational sights vouchsafed to him, and this for three obvious reasons: first, that he strains his eyes more than any other men to see them; second, that he is more overwhelmed and uplifted with them when they come; third, that he records them more exactly and sincerely and with less adulteration from his more commonplace and more conceited everyday self. Adventures are to those to whom they are most unexpected—that is, most romantic. Adventures are to the shy: in this sense adventures are to the unadventurous.

Now, this arresting, mental humility in Mr. H. G. Wells may be, like a great many other things that are vital and vivid, difficult to illustrate by examples, but if I were asked for an example of it, I should have no difficulty about which example to begin with. The most interesting thing about Mr. H. G. Wells is that he is the only one of his many brilliant contemporaries who has not stopped growing. One can lie awake at night and hear him grow. Of this growth the most evident manifestation is indeed a gradual change of opinions; but it is no mere change of opinions. It is not a perpetual leaping from one position to another like that of Mr. George Moore. It is a quite continuous advance along a quite solid road in a quite definable direction. But the chief proof that it is not a piece of fickleness and vanity is the fact that it has been upon the whole in advance from more startling opinions to more humdrum opinions. It has been even in some sense an advance from unconventional opinions to conventional opinions. This fact fixes Mr. Wells's honesty and proves him to be no poseur. Mr. Wells once held that the upper classes and the lower classes would be so much differentiated in the future that one class would eat the other. Certainly no paradoxical charlatan who had once found arguments for so startling a view would ever have deserted it except for something yet more startling. Mr. Wells has deserted it in favour of the blameless belief that both classes will be ultimately subordinated or assimilated to a sort of scientific middle class, a class of engineers. He has abandoned the sensational theory with the same honourable gravity and simplicity with which he adopted it. Then he thought it was true; now he thinks it is not true. He has come to the most dreadful conclusion a literary man can come to, the conclusion that the ordinary view is the right one. It is only the last and wildest kind of courage that can stand on a tower before ten thousand people and tell them that twice two is four.

Mr. H. G. Wells exists at present in a gay and exhilarating progress of conservativism. He is finding out more and more that conventions, though silent, are alive. As good an example as any of this humility and sanity of his may be found in his change of view on the subject of science and marriage. He once held, I believe, the opinion which some singular sociologists still hold, that human creatures could successfully be paired and bred after the manner of dogs or horses. He no longer holds that view. Not only does he no longer hold that view, but he has written about it in "Mankind in the Making" with such smashing sense and humour, that I find it difficult to believe that anybody else can hold it either. It is true that his chief objection to the proposal is that it is physically impossible, which seems to me a very slight objection, and almost negligible compared with the others. The one objection to scientific marriage which is worthy of final attention is simply that such a thing could only be imposed on unthinkable slaves and cowards. I do not know whether the scientific marriage-mongers are right (as they say) or wrong (as Mr. Wells says) in saying that medical supervision would produce strong and healthy men. I am only certain that if it did, the first act of the strong and healthy men would be to smash the medical supervision.

The mistake of all that medical talk lies in the very fact that it connects the idea of health with the idea of care. What has health to do with care? Health has to do with carelessness. In special and abnormal cases it is necessary to have care. When we are peculiarly unhealthy it may be necessary to be careful in order to be healthy. But even then we are only trying to be healthy in order to be careless. If we are doctors we are speaking to exceptionally sick men, and they ought to be told to be careful.

But when we are sociologists we are addressing the normal man, we are addressing humanity. And humanity ought to be told to be recklessness itself. For all the fundamental functions of a healthy man ought emphatically to be performed with pleasure and for pleasure; they emphatically ought not to be performed with precaution or for precaution. A man ought to eat because he has a good appetite to satisfy, and emphatically not because he has a body to sustain. A man ought to take exercise not because he is too fat, but because he loves foils or horses or high mountains, and loves them for their own sake. And a man ought to marry because he has fallen in love, and emphatically not because the world requires to be populated. The food will really renovate his tissues as long as he is not thinking about his tissues. The exercise will really get him into training so long as he is thinking about something else. And the marriage will really stand some chance of producing a generous-blooded generation if it had its origin in its own natural and generous excitement. It is the first law of health that our necessities should not be accepted as necessities; they should be accepted as luxuries. Let us, then, be careful about the small things, such as a scratch or a slight illness, or anything that can be managed with care. But in the name of all sanity, let us be careless about the important things, such as marriage, or the fountain of our very life will fail.

Mr. Wells, however, is not quite clear enough of the narrower scientific outlook to see that there are some things which actually ought not to be scientific. He is still slightly affected with the great scientific fallacy; I mean the habit of beginning not with the human soul, which is the first thing a man learns about, but with some such thing as protoplasm, which is about the last. The one defect in his splendid mental equipment is that he does not sufficiently allow for the stuff or material of men. In his new Utopia he says, for instance, that a chief point of the Utopia will be a disbelief in original sin. If he had begun with the human soul—that is, if he had begun on himself—he would have found original sin almost the first thing to be believed in. He would have found, to put the matter shortly, that a permanent possibility of selfishness arises from the mere fact of having a self, and not from any accidents of education or ill-treatment. And the weakness of all Utopias is this, that they take the greatest difficulty of man and assume it to be overcome, and then give an elaborate account of the overcoming of the smaller ones. They first assume that no man will want more than his share, and then are very ingenious in explaining whether his share will be delivered by motor-car or balloon. And an even stronger example of Mr. Wells's indifference to the human psychology can be found in his cosmopolitanism, the abolition in his Utopia of all patriotic boundaries. He says in his innocent way that Utopia must be a world-state, or else people might make war on it. It does not seem to occur to him that, for a good many of us, if it were a world-state we should still make war on it to the end of the world. For if we admit that there must be varieties in art or opinion what sense is there in thinking there will not be varieties in government? The fact is very simple. Unless you are going deliberately to prevent a thing being good, you cannot prevent it being worth fighting for. It is impossible to prevent a possible conflict of civilizations, because it is impossible to prevent a possible conflict between ideals. If there were no longer our modern strife between nations, there would only be a strife between Utopias. For the highest thing does not tend to union only; the highest thing, tends also to differentiation. You can often get men to fight for the union; but you can never prevent them from fighting also for the differentiation. This variety in the highest thing is the meaning of the fierce patriotism, the fierce nationalism of the great European civilization. It is also, incidentally, the meaning of the doctrine of the Trinity.

But I think the main mistake of Mr. Wells's philosophy is a somewhat deeper one, one that he expresses in a very entertaining manner in the introductory part of the new Utopia. His philosophy in some sense amounts to a denial of the possibility of philosophy itself. At least, he maintains that there are no secure and reliable ideas upon which we can rest with a final mental satisfaction. It will be both clearer, however, and more amusing to quote Mr. Wells himself.

He says, "Nothing endures, nothing is precise and certain (except the mind of a pedant).... Being indeed!—there is no being, but a universal becoming of individualities, and Plato turned his back on truth when he turned towards his museum of specific ideals." Mr. Wells says, again, "There is no abiding thing in what we know. We change from weaker to stronger lights, and each more powerful light pierces our hitherto opaque foundations and reveals fresh and different opacities below." Now, when Mr. Wells says things like this, I speak with all respect when I say that he does not observe an evident mental distinction. It cannot be true that there is nothing abiding in what we know. For if that were so we should not know it all and should not call it knowledge. Our mental state may be very different from that of somebody else some thousands of years back; but it cannot be entirely different, or else we should not be conscious of a difference. Mr. Wells must surely realize the first and simplest of the paradoxes that sit by the springs of truth. He must surely see that the fact of two things being different implies that they are similar. The hare and the tortoise may differ in the quality of swiftness, but they must agree in the quality of motion. The swiftest hare cannot be swifter than an isosceles triangle or the idea of pinkness. When we say the hare moves faster, we say that the tortoise moves. And when we say of a thing that it moves, we say, without need of other words, that there are things that do not move. And even in the act of saying that things change, we say that there is something unchangeable.

31

But certainly the best example of Mr. Wells's fallacy can be found in the example which he himself chooses. It is quite true that we see a dim light which, compared with a darker thing, is light, but which, compared with a stronger light, is darkness. But the quality of light remains the same thing, or else we should not call it a stronger light or recognize it as such. If the character of light were not fixed in the mind, we should be quite as likely to call a denser shadow a stronger light, or vice versa If the character of light became even for an instant unfixed, if it became even by a hair's-breadth doubtful, if, for example, there crept into our idea of light some vague idea of blueness, then in that flash we have become doubtful whether the new light has more light or less. In brief, the progress may be as varying as a cloud, but the direction must be as rigid as a French road. North and South are relative in the sense that I am North of Bournemouth and South of Spitzbergen. But if there be any doubt of the position of the North Pole, there is in equal degree a doubt of whether I am South of Spitzbergen at all. The absolute idea of light may be practically unattainable. We may not be able to procure pure light. We may not be able to get to the North Pole. But because the North Pole is unattainable, it does not follow that it is indefinable. And it is only because the North Pole is not indefinable that we can make a satisfactory map of Brighton and Worthing.

In other words, Plato turned his face to truth but his back on Mr. H. G. Wells, when he turned to his museum of specified ideals. It is precisely here that Plato shows his sense. It is not true that everything changes; the things that change are all the manifest and material things. There is something that does not change; and that is precisely the abstract quality, the invisible idea. Mr. Wells says truly enough, that a thing which we have seen in one connection as dark we may see in another connection as light. But the thing common to both incidents is the mere idea of light—which we have not seen at all. Mr. Wells might grow taller and taller for unending aeons till his head was higher than the loneliest star. I can imagine his writing a good novel about it. In that case he would see the trees first as tall things and then as short things; he would see the clouds first as high and then as low. But there would remain with him through the ages in that starry loneliness the idea of tallness; he would have in the awful spaces for companion and comfort the definite conception that he was growing taller and not (for instance) growing fatter.

And now it comes to my mind that Mr. H. G. Wells actually has written a very delightful romance about men growing as tall as trees; and that here, again, he seems to me to have been a victim of this vague relativism. "The Food of the Gods" is, like Mr. Bernard Shaw's play, in essence a study of the Superman idea. And it lies, I think, even through the veil of a half-pantomimic allegory, open to the same intellectual attack. We cannot be expected to have any regard for a great creature if he does not in any manner conform to our standards. For unless he passes our standard of greatness we cannot even call him great. Nietszche summed up all that is interesting in the Superman idea when he said, "Man is a thing which has to be surpassed." But the very word "surpass" implies the existence of a standard common to us and the thing surpassing us. If the Superman is more manly than men are, of course they will ultimately deify him, even if they happen to kill him first. But if he is simply more supermanly, they may be quite indifferent to him as they would be to another seemingly aimless monstrosity. He must submit to our test even in order to overawe us. Mere force or size even is a standard; but that alone will never make men think a man their superior. Giants, as in the wise old fairy-tales, are vermin. Supermen, if not good men, are vermin.

"The Food of the Gods" is the tale of "Jack the Giant-Killer" told from the point of view of the giant. This has not, I think, been done before in literature; but I have little doubt that the psychological substance of it existed in fact. I have little doubt that the giant whom Jack killed did regard himself as the Superman. It is likely enough that he considered Jack a narrow and parochial person who wished to frustrate a great forward movement of the life-force. If (as not unfrequently was the case) he happened to have two heads, he would point out the elementary maxim which declares them to be better than one. He would enlarge on the subtle modernity of such an equipment, enabling a giant to look at a subject from two points of view, or to correct himself with promptitude. But Jack was the champion of the enduring human standards, of the principle of one man one head and one man one conscience, of the single head and the single heart and the single eye. Jack was quite unimpressed by the question of whether the giant was a particularly gigantic giant. All he wished to know was whether he was a good giant—that is, a giant who was any good to us. What were the giant's religious views; what his views on politics and the duties of the citizen? Was he fond of children—or fond of them only in a dark and sinister sense? To use a fine phrase for emotional sanity, was his heart in the right place? Jack had sometimes to cut him up with a sword in order to find out. The old and correct story of Jack the Giant-Killer is simply the whole story of man; if it were understood we should need no Bibles or histories. But the modern world in particular does not seem to understand it at all. The modern world, like Mr. Wells is on the side of the giants; the safest place, and therefore the meanest and the most prosaic. The modern world, when it praises its little Caesars, talks of being strong and brave: but it does not seem to see the eternal paradox involved in the conjunction of these ideas. The strong cannot be brave. Only the weak can be brave; and yet again, in practice, only those who can be brave can be trusted, in time of doubt, to be strong. The only way in which a giant could really keep himself in training against the inevitable Jack would be by continually fighting other giants ten times as big as himself. That is by ceasing to be a giant and becoming a Jack. Thus that sympathy with the small or the defeated as such, with which we Liberals and Nationalists have been often reproached, is not a useless sentimentalism at all, as Mr. Wells and his friends fancy. It is the first law of practical courage. To be in the weakest camp is to be in the strongest school. Nor can I imagine anything that would do humanity more good than the advent of a race of Supermen, for them to fight like dragons. If the Superman is better than we, of course we need not fight him; but in that case, why not call him the Saint? But if he is merely stronger (whether physically, mentally, or morally stronger, I do not care a farthing), then he ought to have to reckon with us at least for all the strength we have. It we are weaker than he, that is no reason why we should be weaker than ourselves. If we are not tall enough to touch the giant's knees, that is no reason why we should become shorter by falling on our own. But that is at bottom the meaning of all modern hero-worship and celebration of the Strong Man, the Caesar the Superman. That he may be something more than man, we must be something less.

Doubtless there is an older and better hero-worship than this. But the old hero was a being who, like Achilles, was more human than humanity itself. Nietzsche's Superman is cold and friendless. Achilles is so foolishly fond of his friend that he slaughters armies in the agony of his bereavement. Mr. Shaw's sad Caesar says in his desolate pride, "He who has never hoped can never despair." The Man-God of old answers from his awful hill, "Was ever sorrow like unto my sorrow?" A great man is not a man so strong that he feels less than other men; he is a man so strong that he feels more. And when Nietszche says, "A new commandment I give to you, 'be hard,'" he is really saying, "A new commandment I give to you, 'be dead.'" Sensibility is the definition of life.

I recur for a last word to Jack the Giant-Killer. I have dwelt on this matter of Mr. Wells and the giants, not because it is specially prominent in his mind; I know that the Superman does not bulk so large in his cosmos as in that of Mr. Bernard Shaw. I have dwelt on it for the opposite reason; because this heresy of immoral hero-worship has taken, I think, a slighter hold of him, and may perhaps still be prevented from perverting one of the best thinkers of the day. In the course of "The New Utopia" Mr. Wells makes more than one admiring allusion to Mr. W. E. Henley. That clever and unhappy man lived in admiration of a vague violence, and was always going back to rude old tales and rude old ballads, to strong and primitive literatures, to find the praise of strength and the justification of tyranny. But he could not find it. It is not there. The primitive literature is shown in the tale of Jack the Giant-Killer. The strong old literature is all in praise of the weak. The rude old tales are as tender to minorities as any modern political idealist. The rude old ballads are as sentimentally concerned for the underdog as the Aborigines Protection Society. When men were tough and raw, when they lived amid hard knocks and hard laws, when they knew what fighting really was, they had only two kinds of songs. The first was a rejoicing that the weak had conquered the strong, the second a lamentation that the strong had, for once in a way, conquered the weak. For this defiance of the statu quo, this constant effort to alter the existing balance, this premature challenge to the powerful, is the whole nature and inmost secret of the psychological adventure which is called man. It is his strength to disdain strength. The forlorn hope is not only a real hope, it is the only real hope of mankind. In the coarsest ballads of the greenwood men are admired most when they defy, not only the king, but what is more to the point, the hero. The moment Robin Hood becomes a sort of Superman, that moment the chivalrous chronicler shows us Robin thrashed by a poor tinker whom he thought to thrust aside. And the chivalrous chronicler makes Robin Hood receive the thrashing in a glow of admiration. This magnanimity is not a product of modern humanitarianism; it is not a product of anything to do with peace. This magnanimity is merely one of the lost arts of war. The Henleyites call for a sturdy and fighting England, and they go back to the fierce old stories of the sturdy and fighting English. And the thing that they find written across that fierce old literature everywhere, is "the policy of Majuba."

CHRISTMAS AND THE AESTHETES

The world is round, so round that the schools of optimism and pessimism have been arguing from the beginning whether it is the right way up. The difficulty does not arise so much from the mere fact that good and evil are mingled in roughly equal proportions; it arises chiefly from the fact that men always differ about what parts are good and what evil. Hence the difficulty which besets "undenominational religions." They profess to include what is beautiful in all creeds, but they appear to many to have collected all that is dull in them. All the colours mixed together in purity ought to make a perfect white. Mixed together on any human paint-box, they make a thing like mud, and a thing very like many new religions. Such a blend is often something much worse than any one creed taken separately, even the creed of the Thugs. The error arises from the difficulty of detecting what is really the good part and what is really the bad part of any given religion. And this pathos falls rather heavily on those persons who have the misfortune to think of some religion or other, that the parts commonly counted good are bad, and the parts commonly counted bad are good.

It is tragic to admire and honestly admire a human group, but to admire it in a photographic negative. It is difficult to congratulate all their whites on being black and all their blacks on their whiteness. This will often happen to us in connection with human religions. Take two institutions which bear witness to the religious energy of the nineteenth century. Take the Salvation Army and the philosophy of Auguste Comte.

The usual verdict of educated people on the Salvation Army is expressed in some such words as these: "I have no doubt they do a great deal of good, but they do it in a vulgar and profane style; their aims are excellent, but their methods are wrong." To me, unfortunately, the precise reverse of this appears to be the truth. I do not know whether the aims of the Salvation Army are excellent, but I am quite sure their methods are admirable. Their methods are the methods of all intense and hearty religions; they are popular like all religion, military like all religion, public and sensational like all religion. They are not reverent any more than Roman Catholics are reverent, for reverence in the sad and delicate meaning of the term reverence is a thing only possible to infidels. That beautiful twilight you will find in Euripides, in Renan, in Matthew Arnold; but in men who believe you will not find it—you will find only laughter and war. A man cannot pay that kind of reverence to truth solid as marble; they can only be reverent towards a beautiful lie. And the Salvation Army, though their voice has broken out in a mean environment and an ugly

shape, are really the old voice of glad and angry faith, hot as the riots of Dionysus, wild as the gargoyles of Catholicism, not to be mistaken for a philosophy. Professor Huxley, in one of his clever phrases, called the Salvation Army "corybantic Christianity." Huxley was the last and noblest of those Stoics who have never understood the Cross. If he had understood Christianity he would have known that there never has been, and never can be, any Christianity that is not corybantic.

And there is this difference between the matter of aims and the matter of methods, that to judge of the aims of a thing like the Salvation Army is very difficult, to judge of their ritual and atmosphere very easy. No one, perhaps, but a sociologist can see whether General Booth's housing scheme is right. But any healthy person can see that banging brass cymbals together must be right. A page of statistics, a plan of model dwellings, anything which is rational, is always difficult for the lay mind. But the thing which is irrational any one can understand. That is why religion came so early into the world and spread so far, while science came so late into the world and has not spread at all. History unanimously attests the fact that it is only mysticism which stands the smallest chance of being understood of the people. Common sense has to be kept as an esoteric secret in the dark temple of culture. And so while the philanthropy of the Salvationists and its genuineness may be a reasonable matter for the discussion of the doctors, there can be no doubt about the genuineness of their brass bands, for a brass band is purely spiritual, and seeks only to quicken the internal life. The object of philanthropy is to do good; the object of religion is to be good, if only for a moment, amid a crash of brass.

And the same antithesis exists about another modern religion—I mean the religion of Comte, generally known as Positivism, or the worship of humanity. Such men as Mr. Frederic Harrison, that brilliant and chivalrous philosopher, who still, by his mere personality, speaks for the creed, would tell us that he offers us the philosophy of Comte, but not all Comte's fantastic proposals for pontiffs and ceremonials, the new calendar, the new holidays and saints' days. He does not mean that we should dress ourselves up as priests of humanity or let off fireworks because it is Milton's birthday. To the solid English Comtist all this appears, he confesses, to be a little absurd. To me it appears the only sensible part of Comtism. As a philosophy it is unsatisfactory. It is evidently impossible to worship humanity, just as it is impossible to worship the Savile Club; both are excellent institutions to which we may happen to belong. But we perceive clearly that the Savile Club did not make the stars and does not fill the universe. And it is surely unreasonable to attack the doctrine of the Trinity as a piece of bewildering mysticism, and then to ask men to worship a being who is ninety million persons in one God, neither confounding the persons nor dividing the substance.

But if the wisdom of Comte was insufficient, the folly of Comte was wisdom. In an age of dusty modernity, when beauty was thought of as something barbaric and ugliness as something sensible, he alone saw that men must always have the sacredness of mummery. He saw that while the brutes have all the useful things, the things that are truly human are the useless ones. He saw the falsehood of that almost universal notion of to-day, the notion that rites and forms are something artificial, additional, and corrupt. Ritual is really much older than thought; it is much simpler and much wilder than thought. A feeling touching the nature of things does not only make men feel that there are certain proper things to say; it makes them feel that there are certain proper things to do. The more agreeable of these consist of dancing, building temples, and shouting very loud; the less agreeable, of wearing green carnations and burning other philosophers alive. But everywhere the religious dance came before the religious hymn, and man was a ritualist before he could speak. If Comtism had spread the world would have been converted, not by the Comtist philosophy, but by the Comtist calendar. By discouraging what they conceive to be the weakness of their master, the English Positivists have broken the strength of their religion. A man who has faith must be prepared not only to be a martyr, but to be a fool. It is absurd to say that a man is ready to toil and die for his convictions when he is not even ready to wear a wreath round his head for them. I myself, to take a corpus vile, am very certain that I would not read the works of Comte through for any consideration whatever. But I can easily imagine myself with the greatest enthusiasm lighting a bonfire on Darwin Day.

That splendid effort failed, and nothing in the style of it has succeeded. There has been no rationalist festival, no rationalist ecstasy. Men are still in black for the death of God. When Christianity was heavily bombarded in the last century upon no point was it more persistently and brilliantly attacked than upon that of its alleged enmity to human joy. Shelley and Swinburne and all their armies have passed again and again over the ground, but they have not altered it. They have not set up a single new trophy or ensign for the world's merriment to rally to. They have not given a name or a new occasion of gaiety. Mr. Swinburne does not hang up his stocking on the eve of the birthday of Victor Hugo. Mr. William Archer does not sing carols descriptive of the infancy of Ibsen outside people's doors in the snow. In the round of our rational and mournful year one festival remains out of all those ancient gaieties that once covered the whole earth. Christmas remains to remind us of those ages, whether Pagan or Christian, when the many acted poetry instead of the few writing it. In all the winter in our woods there is no tree in glow but the holly.

The strange truth about the matter is told in the very word "holiday." A bank holiday means presumably a day which bankers regard as holy. A half-holiday means, I suppose, a day on which a schoolboy is only partially holy. It is hard to see at first sight why so human a thing as leisure and larkiness should always have a religious origin. Rationally there appears no reason why we should not sing and give each other presents in honour of anything—the birth of Michael Angelo or the opening of Euston Station. But it does not work. As a fact, men only become greedily and gloriously material about something spiritualistic. Take away the Nicene Creed and similar things, and you do some strange wrong to the sellers of sausages. Take away the strange beauty of the saints, and what has remained to us is the far stranger ugliness of Wandsworth. Take away the supernatural, and what remains is the unnatural.

And now I have to touch upon a very sad matter. There are in the modern world an admirable class of persons who really make protest on behalf of that antiqua pulchritudo of which Augustine spoke, who do long for the old feasts and formalities of the childhood of the world. William Morris and his followers showed how much brighter were the dark ages than the age of Manchester. Mr. W. B. Yeats frames his steps in prehistoric dances, but no man knows and joins his voice to forgotten choruses that no one but he can hear. Mr. George Moore collects every fragment of Irish paganism that the forgetfulness of the Catholic Church has left or possibly her wisdom preserved. There are innumerable persons with eye-glasses and green garments who pray for the return of the maypole or the Olympian games. But there is about these people a haunting and alarming something which suggests that it is just possible that they do not keep Christmas. It is painful to regard human nature in such a light, but it seems somehow possible that Mr. George Moore does not wave his spoon and shout when the pudding is set alight. It is even possible that Mr. W. B. Yeats never pulls crackers. If so, where is the sense of all their dreams of festive traditions? Here is a solid and ancient festive tradition still plying a roaring trade in the streets, and they think it vulgar. if this is so, let them be very certain of this, that they are the kind of people who in the time of the maypole would have thought the maypole vulgar; who in the time of the Canterbury pilgrimage would have thought the Canterbury pilgrimage vulgar; who in the time of the Olympian games would have thought the Olympian games vulgar. Nor can there be any reasonable doubt that they were vulgar. Let no man deceive himself; if by vulgarity we mean coarseness of speech, rowdiness of behaviour, gossip, horseplay, and some heavy drinking, vulgarity there always was wherever there was joy, wherever there was faith in the gods. Wherever you have belief you will have hilarity, wherever you have hilarity you will have some dangers. And as creed and mythology produce this gross and vigorous life, so in its turn this gross and vigorous life will always produce creed and mythology. If we ever get the English back on to the English land they will become again a religious people, if all goes well, a superstitious people. The absence from modern life of both the higher and lower forms of faith is largely due to a divorce from nature and the trees and clouds. If we have no more turnip ghosts it is chiefly from the lack of turnips.

OMAR AND THE SACRED VINE

A new morality has burst upon us with some violence in connection with the problem of strong drink; and enthusiasts in the matter range from the man who is violently thrown out at 12.30, to the lady who smashes American bars with an axe. In these discussions it is almost always felt that one very wise and moderate position is to say that wine or such stuff should only be drunk as a medicine. With this I should venture to disagree with a peculiar ferocity. The one genuinely dangerous and immoral way of drinking wine is to drink it as a medicine. And for this reason, If a man drinks wine in order to obtain pleasure, he is trying to obtain something exceptional, something he does not expect every hour of the day, something which, unless he is a little insane, he will not try to get every hour of the day. But if a man drinks wine in order to obtain health, he is trying to get something natural; something, that is, that he ought not to be without; something that he may find it difficult to reconcile himself to being without. The man may not be seduced who has seen the ecstasy of being ecstatic; it is more dazzling to catch a glimpse of the ecstasy of being ordinary. If there were a magic ointment, and we took it to a strong man, and said, "This will enable you to jump off the Monument," doubtless he would jump off the Monument, but he would not jump off the Monument all day long to the delight of the City. But if we took it to a blind man, saying, "This will enable you to see," he would be under a heavier temptation. It would be hard for him not to rub it on his eyes whenever he heard the hoof of a noble horse or the birds singing at daybreak. It is easy to deny one's self festivity; it is difficult to deny one's self normality. Hence comes the fact which every doctor knows, that it is often perilous to give alcohol to the sick even when they need it. I need hardly say that I do not mean that I think the giving of alcohol to the sick for stimulus is necessarily unjustifiable. But I do mean that giving it to the healthy for fun is the proper use of it, and a great deal more consistent with health.

The sound rule in the matter would appear to be like many other sound rules—a paradox. Drink because you are happy, but never because you are miserable. Never drink when you are wretched without it, or you will be like the grey-faced gin-drinker in the slum; but drink when you would be happy without it, and you will be like the laughing peasant of Italy. Never drink because you need it, for this is rational drinking, and the way to death and hell. But drink because you do not need it, for this is irrational drinking, and the ancient health of the world.

For more than thirty years the shadow and glory of a great Eastern figure has lain upon our English literature. Fitzgerald's translation of Omar

Khayyam concentrated into an immortal poignancy all the dark and drifting hedonism of our time. Of the literary splendour of that work it would be merely banal to speak; in few other of the books of men has there been anything so combining the gay pugnacity of an epigram with the vague sadness of a song. But of its philosophical, ethical, and religious influence which has been almost as great as its brilliancy, I should like to say a word, and that word, I confess, one of uncompromising hostility. There are a great many things which might be said against the spirit of the Rubaiyat, and against its prodigious influence. But one matter of indictment towers ominously above the rest—a genuine disgrace to it, a genuine calamity to us. This is the terrible blow that this great poem has struck against sociability and the joy of life. Some one called Omar "the sad, glad old Persian." Sad he is; glad he is not, in any sense of the word whatever. He has been a worse foe to gladness than the Puritans.

A pensive and graceful Oriental lies under the rose-tree with his wine-pot and his scroll of poems. It may seem strange that any one's thoughts should, at the moment of regarding him, fly back to the dark bedside where the doctor doles out brandy. It may seem stranger still that they should go back to the grey wastrel shaking with gin in Houndsditch. But a great philosophical unity links the three in an evil bond. Omar Khayyam's wine-bibbing is bad, not because it is wine-bibbing. It is bad, and very bad, because it is medical wine-bibbing. It is the drinking of a man who drinks because he is not happy. His is the wine that shuts out the universe, not the wine that reveals it. It is not poetical drinking, which is joyous and instinctive; it is rational drinking, which is as prosaic as an investment, as unsavoury as a dose of camomile. Whole heavens above it, from the point of view of sentiment, though not of style, rises the splendour of some old English drinking-song—

> "Then pass the bowl, my comrades all,
> And let the zider vlow."

For this song was caught up by happy men to express the worth of truly worthy things, of brotherhood and garrulity, and the brief and kindly leisure of the poor. Of course, the great part of the more stolid reproaches directed against the Omarite morality are as false and babyish as such reproaches usually are. One critic, whose work I have read, had the incredible foolishness to call Omar an atheist and a materialist. It is almost impossible for an Oriental to be either; the East understands metaphysics too well for that. Of course, the real objection which a philosophical Christian would bring against the religion of Omar, is not that he gives no place to God, it is that he gives too much place to God. His is that terrible theism which can imagine nothing else but deity, and which denies altogether the outlines of human personality and human will.

> "The ball no question makes of Ayes or Noes,
> But Here or There as strikes the Player goes;
> And He that tossed you down into the field,
> He knows about it all—he knows—he knows."

A Christian thinker such as Augustine or Dante would object to this because it ignores free-will, which is the valour and dignity of the soul. The quarrel of the highest Christianity with this scepticism is not in the least that the scepticism denies the existence of God; it is that it denies the existence of man.

In this cult of the pessimistic pleasure-seeker the Rubaiyat stands first in our time; but it does not stand alone. Many of the most brilliant intellects of our time have urged us to the same self-conscious snatching at a rare delight. Walter Pater said that we were all under sentence of death, and the only course was to enjoy exquisite moments simply for those moments' sake. The same lesson was taught by the very powerful and very desolate philosophy of Oscar Wilde. It is the carpe diem religion; but the carpe diem religion is not the religion of happy people, but of very unhappy people. Great joy does, not gather the rosebuds while it may; its eyes are fixed on the immortal rose which Dante saw. Great joy has in it the sense of immortality; the very splendour of youth is the sense that it has all space to stretch its legs in. In all great comic literature, in "Tristram Shandy" or "Pickwick", there is this sense of space and incorruptibility; we feel the characters are deathless people in an endless tale.

It is true enough, of course, that a pungent happiness comes chiefly in certain passing moments; but it is not true that we should think of them as passing, or enjoy them simply "for those moments' sake." To do this is to rationalize the happiness, and therefore to destroy it. Happiness is a mystery like religion, and should never be rationalized. Suppose a man experiences a really splendid moment of pleasure. I do not mean something connected with a bit of enamel, I mean something with a violent happiness in it—an almost painful happiness. A man may have, for instance, a moment of ecstasy in first love, or a moment of victory in battle. The lover enjoys the moment, but precisely not for the moment's sake. He enjoys it for the woman's sake, or his own sake. The warrior enjoys the moment, but not for the sake of the moment; he enjoys it for the sake of the flag. The cause which the flag stands for may be foolish and fleeting; the love may be calf-love, and last a week. But the patriot thinks of the flag as eternal; the lover thinks of his love as something that cannot end. These moments are filled with eternity; these moments are joyful because they do not seem momentary. Once look at them as moments after Pater's manner, and they become as cold as Pater and his style. Man cannot love mortal things. He can only love immortal things for an instant.

Pater's mistake is revealed in his most famous phrase. He asks us to burn with a hard, gem-like flame. Flames are never hard and never gem-like—they cannot be handled or arranged. So human emotions are never hard and never gem-like; they are always dangerous, like flames, to touch or even to examine. There is only one way in which our passions can become hard and gem-like, and that is by becoming as cold as gems. No blow then has ever been struck at the natural loves and laughter of men so sterilizing as this carpe diem of the aesthetes. For any kind of pleasure a totally different spirit is required; a certain shyness, a certain indeterminate hope, a certain boyish expectation. Purity and simplicity are essential to passions— yes even to evil passions. Even vice demands a sort of virginity.

Omar's (or Fitzgerald's) effect upon the other world we may let go, his hand upon this world has been heavy and paralyzing. The Puritans, as I have said, are far jollier than he. The new ascetics who follow Thoreau or Tolstoy are much livelier company; for, though the surrender of strong drink and such luxuries may strike us as an idle negation, it may leave a man with innumerable natural pleasures, and, above all, with man's natural power of happiness. Thoreau could enjoy the sunrise without a cup of coffee. If Tolstoy cannot admire marriage, at least he is healthy enough to admire mud. Nature can be enjoyed without even the most natural luxuries. A good bush needs no wine. But neither nature nor wine nor anything else can be enjoyed if we have the wrong attitude towards happiness, and Omar (or Fitzgerald) did have the wrong attitude towards happiness. He and those he has influenced do not see that if we are to be truly gay, we must believe that there is some eternal gaiety in the nature of things. We cannot enjoy thoroughly even a pas-de-quatre at a subscription dance unless we believe that the stars are dancing to the same tune. No one can be really hilarious but the serious man. "Wine," says the Scripture, "maketh glad the heart of man," but only of the man who has a heart. The thing called high spirits is possible only to the spiritual. Ultimately a man cannot rejoice in anything except the nature of things. Ultimately a man can enjoy nothing except religion. Once in the world's history men did believe that the stars were dancing to the tune of their temples, and they danced as men have never danced since. With this old pagan eudaemonism the sage of the Rubaiyat has quite as little to do as he has with any Christian variety. He is no more a Bacchanal than he is a saint. Dionysus and his church was grounded on a serious joie-de-vivre like that of Walt Whitman. Dionysus made wine, not a medicine, but a sacrament. Jesus Christ also made wine, not a medicine, but a sacrament. But Omar makes it, not a sacrament, but a medicine. He feasts because life is not joyful; he revels because he is not glad. "Drink," he says, "for you know not whence you come nor why. Drink, for you know not when you go nor where. Drink, because the stars are cruel and the world as idle as a humming-top. Drink, because there is nothing worth trusting, nothing worth fighting for. Drink, because all things are lapsed in a base equality and an evil peace." So he stands offering us the cup in his hand. And at the high altar of Christianity stands another figure, in whose hand also is the cup of the vine. "Drink" he says "for the whole world is as red as this wine, with the crimson of the love and wrath of God. Drink, for the trumpets are blowing for battle and this is the stirrup-cup. Drink, for this my blood of the new testament that is shed for you. Drink, for I know of whence you come and why. Drink, for I know of when you go and where."

THE MILDNESS OF THE YELLOW PRESS

There is a great deal of protest made from one quarter or another nowadays against the influence of that new journalism which is associated with the names of Sir Alfred Harmsworth and Mr. Pearson. But almost everybody who attacks it attacks on the ground that it is very sensational, very violent and vulgar and startling. I am speaking in no affected contrariety, but in the simplicity of a genuine personal impression, when I say that this journalism offends as being not sensational or violent enough. The real vice is not that it is startling, but that it is quite insupportably tame. The whole object is to keep carefully along a certain level of the expected and the commonplace; it may be low, but it must take care also to be flat. Never by any chance in it is there any of that real plebeian pungency which can be heard from the ordinary cabman in the ordinary street. We have heard of a certain standard of decorum which demands that things should be funny without being vulgar, but the standard of this decorum demands that if things are vulgar they shall be vulgar without being funny. This journalism does not merely fail to exaggerate life—it positively underrates it; and it has to do so because it is intended for the faint and languid recreation of men whom the fierceness of modern life has fatigued. This press is not the yellow press at all; it is the drab press. Sir Alfred Harmsworth must not address to the tired clerk any observation more witty than the tired clerk might be able to address to Sir Alfred Harmsworth. It must not expose anybody (anybody who is powerful, that is), it must not offend anybody, it must not even please anybody, too much. A general vague idea that in spite of all this, our yellow press is sensational, arises from such external accidents as large type or lurid headlines. It is quite true that these editors print everything they possibly can in large capital letters. But they do this, not because it is startling, but because it is soothing. To people wholly weary or partly drunk in a dimly lighted train, it is a simplification and a comfort to have things presented in this vast and obvious manner. The editors use this gigantic alphabet in dealing with their readers, for exactly the same reason that parents and governesses use a similar gigantic alphabet in teaching children to spell. The nursery authorities do not use an A as big as a horseshoe in order to make the child jump; on the contrary, they use it to put the child at his ease, to make things smoother and more evident. Of the same character is the dim and quiet dame school which Sir Alfred Harmsworth and Mr. Pearson keep. All their sentiments are spelling-book sentiments—that is to say, they are sentiments with which the pupil is already respectfully familiar. All their wildest posters are leaves torn from a copy-book.

Of real sensational journalism, as it exists in France, in Ireland, and in America, we have no trace in this country. When a journalist in Ireland wishes to create a thrill, he creates a thrill worth talking about. He denounces a leading Irish member for corruption, or he charges the whole police system with a wicked and definite conspiracy. When a French journalist desires a frisson there is a frisson; he discovers, let us say, that the President of the Republic has murdered three wives. Our yellow journalists invent quite as unscrupulously as this; their moral condition is, as regards careful veracity, about the same. But it is their mental calibre which happens to be such that they can only invent calm and even reassuring things. The fictitious version of the massacre of the envoys of Pekin was mendacious, but it was not interesting, except to those who had private reasons for terror or sorrow. It was not connected with any bold and suggestive view of the Chinese situation. It revealed only a vague idea that nothing could be impressive except a great deal of blood. Real sensationalism, of which I happen to be very fond, may be either moral or immoral. But even when it is most immoral, it requires moral courage. For it is one of the most dangerous things on earth genuinely to surprise anybody. If you make any sentient creature jump, you render it by no means improbable that it will jump on you. But the leaders of this movement have no moral courage or immoral courage; their whole method consists in saying, with large and elaborate emphasis, the things which everybody else says casually, and without remembering what they have said. When they brace themselves up to attack anything, they never reach the point of attacking anything which is large and real, and would resound with the shock. They do not attack the army as men do in France, or the judges as men do in Ireland, or the democracy itself as men did in England a hundred years ago. They attack something like the War Office—something, that is, which everybody attacks and nobody bothers to defend, something which is an old joke in fourth-rate comic papers. just as a man shows he has a weak voice by straining it to shout, so they show the hopelessly unsensational nature of their minds when they really try to be sensational. With the whole world full of big and dubious institutions, with the whole wickedness of civilization staring them in the face, their idea of being bold and bright is to attack the War Office. They might as well start a campaign against the weather, or form a secret society in order to make jokes about mothers-in-law. Nor is it only from the point of view of particular amateurs of the sensational such as myself, that it is permissible to say, in the words of Cowper's Alexander Selkirk, that "their tameness is shocking to me." The whole modern world is pining for a genuinely sensational journalism. This has been discovered by that very able and honest journalist, Mr. Blatchford, who started his campaign against Christianity, warned on all sides, I believe, that it would ruin his paper, but who continued from an honourable sense of intellectual responsibility. He discovered, however, that while he had undoubtedly shocked his readers, he had also greatly advanced his newspaper. It was bought—first, by all the people who agreed with him and wanted to read it; and secondly, by all the people who disagreed with him, and wanted to write him letters. Those letters were voluminous (I helped, I am glad to say, to swell their volume), and they were generally inserted with a generous fulness. Thus was accidentally discovered (like the steam-engine) the great journalistic maxim—that if an editor can only make people angry enough, they will write half his newspaper for him for nothing.

Some hold that such papers as these are scarcely the proper objects of so serious a consideration; but that can scarcely be maintained from a political or ethical point of view. In this problem of the mildness and tameness of the Harmsworth mind there is mirrored the outlines of a much larger problem which is akin to it.

The Harmsworthian journalist begins with a worship of success and violence, and ends in sheer timidity and mediocrity. But he is not alone in this, nor does he come by this fate merely because he happens personally to be stupid. Every man, however brave, who begins by worshipping violence, must end in mere timidity. Every man, however wise, who begins by worshipping success, must end in mere mediocrity. This strange and paradoxical fate is involved, not in the individual, but in the philosophy, in the point of view. It is not the folly of the man which brings about this necessary fall; it is his wisdom. The worship of success is the only one out of all possible worships of which this is true, that its followers are foredoomed to become slaves and cowards. A man may be a hero for the sake of Mrs. Gallup's ciphers or for the sake of human sacrifice, but not for the sake of success. For obviously a man may choose to fail because he loves Mrs. Gallup or human sacrifice; but he cannot choose to fail because he loves success. When the test of triumph is men's test of everything, they never endure long enough to triumph at all. As long as matters are really hopeful, hope is a mere flattery or platitude; it is only when everything is hopeless that hope begins to be a strength at all. Like all the Christian virtues, it is as unreasonable as it is indispensable.

It was through this fatal paradox in the nature of things that all these modern adventurers come at last to a sort of tedium and acquiescence. They desired strength; and to them to desire strength was to admire strength; to admire strength was simply to admire the statu quo. They thought that he who wished to be strong ought to respect the strong. They did not realize the obvious verity that he who wishes to be strong must despise the strong. They sought to be everything, to have the whole force of the cosmos behind them, to have an energy that would drive the stars. But they did not realize the two great facts—first, that in the attempt to be everything the first and most difficult step is to be something; second, that the moment a man is something, he is essentially defying everything. The lower animals, say the men of science, fought their way up with a blind selfishness. If this be so, the only real moral of it is that our unselfishness, if it is to triumph, must be equally blind. The mammoth did not put his head on one side and wonder whether mammoths were a little out of date. Mammoths were at least as much up to date as that individual mammoth could make them. The great elk did not say, "Cloven hoofs are very much worn now." He polished his own weapons for his own use. But in the reasoning animal there has arisen a more horrible danger, that he may fail through perceiving his own failure. When modern sociologists talk of the necessity of accommodating one's self to the trend of the time, they forget that the trend of the time at its best consists entirely of people who will not accommodate themselves to anything. At its worst it consists of many millions of frightened creatures all accommodating themselves to a trend that is not there. And that is becoming more and more the situation of modern England. Every man speaks of public opinion, and means by public opinion, public opinion minus his opinion. Every man makes his contribution negative under the erroneous impression that the next man's contribution is positive. Every man surrenders his fancy to a general tone which is itself a surrender. And over all the heartless and fatuous unity spreads this new and wearisome and platitudinous press, incapable of invention, incapable of audacity, capable only of a servility all the more contemptible because it is not even a servility to the strong. But all who begin with force and conquest will end in this.

The chief characteristic of the "New journalism" is simply that it is bad journalism. It is beyond all comparison the most shapeless, careless, and colourless work done in our day.

I read yesterday a sentence which should be written in letters of gold and adamant; it is the very motto of the new philosophy of Empire. I found it (as the reader has already eagerly guessed) in Pearson's Magazine, while I was communing (soul to soul) with Mr. C. Arthur Pearson, whose first and suppressed name I am afraid is Chilperic. It occurred in an article on the American Presidential Election. This is the sentence, and every one should read it carefully, and roll it on the tongue, till all the honey be tasted.

"A little sound common sense often goes further with an audience of American working-men than much high-flown argument. A speaker who, as he brought forward his points, hammered nails into a board, won hundreds of votes for his side at the last Presidential Election."

I do not wish to soil this perfect thing with comment; the words of Mercury are harsh after the songs of Apollo. But just think for a moment of the mind, the strange inscrutable mind, of the man who wrote that, of the editor who approved it, of the people who are probably impressed by it, of the incredible American working-man, of whom, for all I know, it may be true. Think what their notion of "common sense" must be! It is delightful to realize that you and I are now able to win thousands of votes should we ever be engaged in a Presidential Election, by doing something of this kind. For I suppose the nails and the board are not essential to the exhibition of "common sense;" there may be variations. We may read—

"A little common sense impresses American working-men more than high-flown argument. A speaker who, as he made his points, pulled buttons off his waistcoat, won thousands of votes for his side." Or, "Sound common sense tells better in America than high-flown argument. Thus Senator Budge, who threw his false teeth in the air every time he made an epigram, won the solid approval of American working-men." Or again, "The sound common sense of a gentleman from Earlswood, who stuck straws in his hair during the progress of his speech, assured the victory of Mr. Roosevelt."

There are many other elements in this article on which I should love to linger. But the matter which I wish to point out is that in that sentence is perfectly revealed the whole truth of what our Chamberlainites, hustlers, bustlers, Empire-builders, and strong, silent men, really mean by "commonsense." They mean knocking, with deafening noise and dramatic effect, meaningless bits of iron into a useless bit of wood. A man goes on to an American platform and behaves like a mountebank fool with a board and a hammer; well, I do not blame him; I might even admire him. He may be a dashing and quite decent strategist. He may be a fine romantic actor, like Burke flinging the dagger on the floor. He may even (for all I know) be a sublime mystic, profoundly impressed with the ancient meaning of the divine trade of the Carpenter, and offering to the people a parable in the form of a ceremony. All I wish to indicate is the abyss of mental confusion in which such wild ritualism can be called "sound common sense." And it is in that abyss of mental confusion, and in that alone, that the new Imperialism lives and moves and has its being. The whole glory and greatness of Mr. Chamberlain consists in this: that if a man hits the right nail on the head nobody cares where he hits it to or what it does. They care about the noise of the hammer, not about the silent drip of the nail. Before and throughout the African war, Mr. Chamberlain was always knocking in nails, with ringing decisiveness. But when we ask, "But what have these nails held together? Where is your carpentry? Where are your contented Outlanders? Where is your free South Africa? Where is your British prestige? What have your nails done?" then what answer is there? We must go back (with an affectionate sigh) to our Pearson for the answer to the question of what the nails have done: "The speaker who hammered nails into a board won thousands of votes."

Now the whole of this passage is admirably characteristic of the new journalism which Mr. Pearson represents, the new journalism which has just purchased the Standard. To take one instance out of hundreds, the incomparable man with the board and nails is described in the Pearson's article as calling out (as he smote the symbolic nail), "Lie number one. Nailed to the Mast! Nailed to the Mast!" In the whole office there was apparently no compositor or office-boy to point out that we speak of lies being nailed to the counter, and not to the mast. Nobody in the office knew that Pearson's Magazine was falling into a stale Irish bull, which must be as old as St. Patrick. This is the real and essential tragedy of the sale of the Standard. It is not merely that journalism is victorious over literature. It is that bad journalism is victorious over good journalism.

It is not that one article which we consider costly and beautiful is being ousted by another kind of article which we consider common or unclean. It is that of the same article a worse quality is preferred to a better. If you like popular journalism (as I do), you will know that Pearson's Magazine is poor and weak popular journalism. You will know it as certainly as you know bad butter. You will know as certainly that it is poor popular journalism as you know that the Strand, in the great days of Sherlock Holmes, was good popular journalism. Mr. Pearson has been a monument of this enormous banality. About everything he says and does there is something infinitely weak-minded. He clamours for home trades and employs foreign ones to print his paper. When this glaring fact is pointed out, he does not say that the thing was an oversight, like a sane man. He cuts it off with scissors, like a child of three. His very cunning is infantile. And like a child of three, he does not cut it quite off. In all human records I doubt if there is such an example of a profound simplicity in deception. This is the sort of intelligence which now sits in the seat of the sane and honourable old Tory journalism. If it were really the triumph of the tropical exuberance of the Yankee press, it would be vulgar, but still tropical. But it is not. We are delivered over to the bramble, and from the meanest of the shrubs comes the fire upon the cedars of Lebanon.

The only question now is how much longer the fiction will endure that journalists of this order represent public opinion. It may be doubted whether any honest and serious Tariff Reformer would for a moment maintain that there was any majority for Tariff Reform in the country comparable to the ludicrous preponderance which money has given it among the great dailies. The only inference is that for purposes of real public opinion the press is now a mere plutocratic oligarchy. Doubtless the public buys the wares of these men, for one reason or another. But there is no more reason to suppose that the public admires their politics than that the public admires the delicate philosophy of Mr. Crosse or the darker and sterner creed of Mr. Blackwell. If these men are merely tradesmen, there is nothing to say except that there are plenty like them in the Battersea Park Road, and many much better. But if they make any sort of attempt to be politicians, we can only point out to them that they are not as yet even good journalists.

THE MOODS OF MR. GEORGE MOORE

Mr. George Moore began his literary career by writing his personal confessions; nor is there any harm in this if he had not continued them for the remainder of his life. He is a man of genuinely forcible mind and of great command over a kind of rhetorical and fugitive conviction which excites and pleases. He is in a perpetual state of temporary honesty. He has admired all the most admirable modern eccentrics until they could stand it no longer. Everything he writes, it is to be fully admitted, has a genuine mental power. His account of his reason for leaving the Roman Catholic Church is possibly the most admirable tribute to that communion which has been written of late years. For the fact of the matter is, that the weakness which has rendered barren the many brilliancies of Mr. Moore is actually that weakness which the Roman Catholic Church is at its best in combating. Mr. Moore hates Catholicism because it breaks up the house of looking-glasses in which he lives. Mr. Moore does not dislike so much being asked to believe in the spiritual existence of miracles or sacraments, but he does fundamentally dislike being asked to believe in the actual existence of other people. Like his master Pater and all the aesthetes, his real quarrel with life is that it is not a dream that can be moulded by the dreamer. It is not the dogma of the reality of the other world that troubles him, but the dogma of the reality of this world.

The truth is that the tradition of Christianity (which is still the only coherent ethic of Europe) rests on two or three paradoxes or mysteries which can easily be impugned in argument and as easily justified in life. One of them, for instance, is the paradox of hope or faith—that the more hopeless is the situation the more hopeful must be the man. Stevenson understood this, and consequently Mr. Moore cannot understand Stevenson. Another is the paradox of charity or chivalry that the weaker a thing is the more it should be respected, that the more indefensible a thing is the more it should appeal to us for a certain kind of defence. Thackeray understood this, and therefore Mr. Moore does not understand Thackeray. Now, one of these very practical and working mysteries in the Christian tradition, and one which the Roman Catholic Church, as I say, has done her best work in singling out, is the conception of the sinfulness of pride. Pride is a weakness in the character; it dries up laughter, it dries up wonder, it dries up chivalry and energy. The Christian tradition understands this; therefore Mr. Moore does not understand the Christian tradition.

For the truth is much stranger even than it appears in the formal doctrine of the sin of pride. It is not only true that humility is a much wiser and more vigorous thing than pride. It is also true that vanity is a much

53

wiser and more vigorous thing than pride. Vanity is social—it is almost a kind of comradeship; pride is solitary and uncivilized. Vanity is active; it desires the applause of infinite multitudes; pride is passive, desiring only the applause of one person, which it already has. Vanity is humorous, and can enjoy the joke even of itself; pride is dull, and cannot even smile. And the whole of this difference is the difference between Stevenson and Mr. George Moore, who, as he informs us, has "brushed Stevenson aside." I do not know where he has been brushed to, but wherever it is I fancy he is having a good time, because he had the wisdom to be vain, and not proud. Stevenson had a windy vanity; Mr. Moore has a dusty egoism. Hence Stevenson could amuse himself as well as us with his vanity; while the richest effects of Mr. Moore's absurdity are hidden from his eyes.

If we compare this solemn folly with the happy folly with which Stevenson belauds his own books and berates his own critics, we shall not find it difficult to guess why it is that Stevenson at least found a final philosophy of some sort to live by, while Mr. Moore is always walking the world looking for a new one. Stevenson had found that the secret of life lies in laughter and humility. Self is the gorgon. Vanity sees it in the mirror of other men and lives. Pride studies it for itself and is turned to stone.

It is necessary to dwell on this defect in Mr. Moore, because it is really the weakness of work which is not without its strength. Mr. Moore's egoism is not merely a moral weakness, it is a very constant and influential aesthetic weakness as well. We should really be much more interested in Mr. Moore if he were not quite so interested in himself. We feel as if we were being shown through a gallery of really fine pictures, into each of which, by some useless and discordant convention, the artist had represented the same figure in the same attitude. "The Grand Canal with a distant view of Mr. Moore," "Effect of Mr. Moore through a Scotch Mist," "Mr. Moore by Firelight," "Ruins of Mr. Moore by Moonlight," and so on, seems to be the endless series. He would no doubt reply that in such a book as this he intended to reveal himself. But the answer is that in such a book as this he does not succeed. One of the thousand objections to the sin of pride lies precisely in this, that self-consciousness of necessity destroys self-revelation. A man who thinks a great deal about himself will try to be many-sided, attempt a theatrical excellence at all points, will try to be an encyclopaedia of culture, and his own real personality will be lost in that false universalism. Thinking about himself will lead to trying to be the universe; trying to be the universe will lead to ceasing to be anything. If, on the other hand, a man is sensible enough to think only about the universe; he will think about it in his own individual way. He will keep virgin the secret of God; he will see the grass as no other man can see it, and look at a sun that no man has ever known. This fact is very practically brought out in Mr. Moore's "Confessions." In reading them we do not feel the presence of a

clean-cut personality like that of Thackeray and Matthew Arnold. We only read a number of quite clever and largely conflicting opinions which might be uttered by any clever person, but which we are called upon to admire specifically, because they are uttered by Mr. Moore. He is the only thread that connects Catholicism and Protestantism, realism and mysticism—he or rather his name. He is profoundly absorbed even in views he no longer holds, and he expects us to be. And he intrudes the capital "I" even where it need not be intruded—even where it weakens the force of a plain statement. Where another man would say, "It is a fine day," Mr. Moore says, "Seen through my temperament, the day appeared fine." Where another man would say "Milton has obviously a fine style," Mr. Moore would say, "As a stylist Milton had always impressed me." The Nemesis of this self-centred spirit is that of being totally ineffectual. Mr. Moore has started many interesting crusades, but he has abandoned them before his disciples could begin. Even when he is on the side of the truth he is as fickle as the children of falsehood. Even when he has found reality he cannot find rest. One Irish quality he has which no Irishman was ever without—pugnacity; and that is certainly a great virtue, especially in the present age. But he has not the tenacity of conviction which goes with the fighting spirit in a man like Bernard Shaw. His weakness of introspection and selfishness in all their glory cannot prevent him fighting; but they will always prevent him winning.

ON SANDALS AND SIMPLICITY

The great misfortune of the modern English is not at all that they are more boastful than other people (they are not); it is that they are boastful about those particular things which nobody can boast of without losing them. A Frenchman can be proud of being bold and logical, and still remain bold and logical. A German can be proud of being reflective and orderly, and still remain reflective and orderly. But an Englishman cannot be proud of being simple and direct, and still remain simple and direct. In the matter of these strange virtues, to know them is to kill them. A man may be conscious of being heroic or conscious of being divine, but he cannot (in spite of all the Anglo-Saxon poets) be conscious of being unconscious.

Now, I do not think that it can be honestly denied that some portion of this impossibility attaches to a class very different in their own opinion, at least, to the school of Anglo-Saxonism. I mean that school of the simple life, commonly associated with Tolstoy. If a perpetual talk about one's own robustness leads to being less robust, it is even more true that a perpetual talking about one's own simplicity leads to being less simple. One great complaint, I think, must stand against the modern upholders of the simple life—the simple life in all its varied forms, from vegetarianism to the honourable consistency of the Doukhobors. This complaint against them stands, that they would make us simple in the unimportant things, but complex in the important things. They would make us simple in the things that do not matter—that is, in diet, in costume, in etiquette, in economic system. But they would make us complex in the things that do matter—in philosophy, in loyalty, in spiritual acceptance, and spiritual rejection. It does not so very much matter whether a man eats a grilled tomato or a plain tomato; it does very much matter whether he eats a plain tomato with a grilled mind. The only kind of simplicity worth preserving is the simplicity of the heart, the simplicity which accepts and enjoys. There may be a reasonable doubt as to what system preserves this; there can surely be no doubt that a system of simplicity destroys it. There is more simplicity in the man who eats caviar on impulse than in the man who eats grape-nuts on principle. The chief error of these people is to be found in the very phrase to which they are most attached—"plain living and high thinking." These people do not stand in need of, will not be improved by, plain living and high thinking. They stand in need of the contrary. They would be improved by high living and plain thinking. A little high living (I say, having a full sense of responsibility, a little high living) would teach them the force and meaning of the human festivities, of the banquet that has gone on from the beginning of the world. It would teach them the historic fact that the

56

artificial is, if anything, older than the natural. It would teach them that the loving-cup is as old as any hunger. It would teach them that ritualism is older than any religion. And a little plain thinking would teach them how harsh and fanciful are the mass of their own ethics, how very civilized and very complicated must be the brain of the Tolstoyan who really believes it to be evil to love one's country and wicked to strike a blow.

A man approaches, wearing sandals and simple raiment, a raw tomato held firmly in his right hand, and says, "The affections of family and country alike are hindrances to the fuller development of human love;" but the plain thinker will only answer him, with a wonder not untinged with admiration, "What a great deal of trouble you must have taken in order to feel like that." High living will reject the tomato. Plain thinking will equally decisively reject the idea of the invariable sinfulness of war. High living will convince us that nothing is more materialistic than to despise a pleasure as purely material. And plain thinking will convince us that nothing is more materialistic than to reserve our horror chiefly for material wounds.

The only simplicity that matters is the simplicity of the heart. If that be gone, it can be brought back by no turnips or cellular clothing; but only by tears and terror and the fires that are not quenched. If that remain, it matters very little if a few Early Victorian armchairs remain along with it. Let us put a complex entree into a simple old gentleman; let us not put a simple entree into a complex old gentleman. So long as human society will leave my spiritual inside alone, I will allow it, with a comparative submission, to work its wild will with my physical interior. I will submit to cigars. I will meekly embrace a bottle of Burgundy. I will humble myself to a hansom cab. If only by this means I may preserve to myself the virginity of the spirit, which enjoys with astonishment and fear. I do not say that these are the only methods of preserving it. I incline to the belief that there are others. But I will have nothing to do with simplicity which lacks the fear, the astonishment, and the joy alike. I will have nothing to do with the devilish vision of a child who is too simple to like toys.

The child is, indeed, in these, and many other matters, the best guide. And in nothing is the child so righteously childlike, in nothing does he exhibit more accurately the sounder order of simplicity, than in the fact that he sees everything with a simple pleasure, even the complex things. The false type of naturalness harps always on the distinction between the natural and the artificial. The higher kind of naturalness ignores that distinction. To the child the tree and the lamp-post are as natural and as artificial as each other; or rather, neither of them are natural but both supernatural. For both are splendid and unexplained. The flower with which God crowns the one, and the flame with which Sam the lamplighter crowns the other, are equally of the gold of fairy-tales. In the middle of the wildest fields the most rustic child is, ten to one, playing at steam-engines. And the only spiritual or philosophical objection to steam-engines is not that men pay for them or work at them, or make them very ugly, or even that men are killed by them; but merely that men do not play at them. The evil is that the childish poetry of clockwork does not remain. The wrong is not that engines are too much admired, but that they are not admired enough. The sin is not that engines are mechanical, but that men are mechanical.

In this matter, then, as in all the other matters treated in this book, our main conclusion is that it is a fundamental point of view, a philosophy or religion which is needed, and not any change in habit or social routine. The things we need most for immediate practical purposes are all abstractions. We need a right view of the human lot, a right view of the human society; and if we were living eagerly and angrily in the enthusiasm of those things, we should, ipso facto, be living simply in the genuine and spiritual sense. Desire and danger make every one simple. And to those who talk to us with interfering eloquence about Jaeger and the pores of the skin, and about Plasmon and the coats of the stomach, at them shall only be hurled the words that are hurled at fops and gluttons, "Take no thought what ye shall eat or what ye shall drink, or wherewithal ye shall be clothed. For after all these things do the Gentiles seek. But seek first the kingdom of God and His righteousness, and all these things shall be added unto you." Those amazing words are not only extraordinarily good, practical politics; they are also superlatively good hygiene. The one supreme way of making all those processes go right, the processes of health, and strength, and grace, and beauty, the one and only way of making certain of their accuracy, is to think about something else. If a man is bent on climbing into the seventh heaven, he may be quite easy about the pores of his skin. If he harnesses his waggon to a star, the process will have a most satisfactory effect upon the coats of his stomach. For the thing called "taking thought," the thing for which the best modern word is "rationalizing," is in its nature, inapplicable to all plain and urgent things. Men take thought and ponder rationalistically, touching remote things—things that only theoretically matter, such as the transit of Venus. But only at their peril can men rationalize about so practical a matter as health.

SCIENCE AND THE SAVAGES

A permanent disadvantage of the study of folk-lore and kindred subjects is that the man of science can hardly be in the nature of things very frequently a man of the world. He is a student of nature; he is scarcely ever a student of human nature. And even where this difficulty is overcome, and he is in some sense a student of human nature, this is only a very faint beginning of the painful progress towards being human. For the study of primitive race and religion stands apart in one important respect from all, or nearly all, the ordinary scientific studies. A man can understand astronomy only by being an astronomer; he can understand entomology only by being an entomologist (or, perhaps, an insect); but he can understand a great deal of anthropology merely by being a man. He is himself the animal which he studies. Hence arises the fact which strikes the eye everywhere in the records of ethnology and folk-lore—the fact that the same frigid and detached spirit which leads to success in the study of astronomy or botany leads to disaster in the study of mythology or human origins. It is necessary to cease to be a man in order to do justice to a microbe; it is not necessary to cease to be a man in order to do justice to men. That same suppression of sympathies, that same waving away of intuitions or guess-work which make a man preternaturally clever in dealing with the stomach of a spider, will make him preternaturally stupid in dealing with the heart of man. He is making himself inhuman in order to understand humanity. An ignorance of the other world is boasted by many men of science; but in this matter their defect arises, not from ignorance of the other world, but from ignorance of this world. For the secrets about which anthropologists concern themselves can be best learnt, not from books or voyages, but from the ordinary commerce of man with man. The secret of why some savage tribe worships monkeys or the moon is not to be found even by travelling among those savages and taking down their answers in a note-book, although the cleverest man may pursue this course. The answer to the riddle is in England; it is in London; nay, it is in his own heart. When a man has discovered why men in Bond Street wear black hats he will at the same moment have discovered why men in Timbuctoo wear red feathers. The mystery in the heart of some savage war-dance should not be studied in books of scientific travel; it should be studied at a subscription ball. If a man desires to find out the origins of religions, let him not go to the Sandwich Islands; let him go to church. If a man wishes to know the origin of human society, to know what society, philosophically speaking, really is, let him not go into the British Museum; let him go into society.

This total misunderstanding of the real nature of ceremonial gives rise to the most awkward and dehumanized versions of the conduct of men in rude lands or ages. The man of science, not realizing that ceremonial is essentially a thing which is done without a reason, has to find a reason for every sort of ceremonial, and, as might be supposed, the reason is generally a very absurd one—absurd because it originates not in the simple mind of the barbarian, but in the sophisticated mind of the professor. The teamed man will say, for instance, "The natives of Mumbojumbo Land believe that the dead man can eat and will require food upon his journey to the other world. This is attested by the fact that they place food in the grave, and that any family not complying with this rite is the object of the anger of the priests and the tribe." To any one acquainted with humanity this way of talking is topsy-turvy. It is like saying, "The English in the twentieth century believed that a dead man could smell. This is attested by the fact that they always covered his grave with lilies, violets, or other flowers. Some priestly and tribal terrors were evidently attached to the neglect of this action, as we have records of several old ladies who were very much disturbed in mind because their wreaths had not arrived in time for the funeral." It may be of course that savages put food with a dead man because they think that a dead man can eat, or weapons with a dead man because they think that a dead man can fight. But personally I do not believe that they think anything of the kind. I believe they put food or weapons on the dead for the same reason that we put flowers, because it is an exceedingly natural and obvious thing to do. We do not understand, it is true, the emotion which makes us think it obvious and natural; but that is because, like all the important emotions of human existence it is essentially irrational. We do not understand the savage for the same reason that the savage does not understand himself. And the savage does not understand himself for the same reason that we do not understand ourselves either.

The obvious truth is that the moment any matter has passed through the human mind it is finally and for ever spoilt for all purposes of science. It has become a thing incurably mysterious and infinite; this mortal has put on immortality. Even what we call our material desires are spiritual, because they are human. Science can analyse a pork-chop, and say how much of it is phosphorus and how much is protein; but science cannot analyse any man's wish for a pork-chop, and say how much of it is hunger, how much custom, how much nervous fancy, how much a haunting love of the beautiful. The man's desire for the pork-chop remains literally as mystical and ethereal as his desire for heaven. All attempts, therefore, at a science of any human things, at a science of history, a science of folk-lore, a science of sociology, are by their nature not merely hopeless, but crazy. You can no more be certain in economic history that a man's desire for money was merely a desire for money than you can be certain in hagiology that a saint's desire for God was merely a desire for God. And this kind of vagueness in the primary phenomena of the study is an absolutely final blow to anything in the nature of a science. Men can construct a science with very few instruments, or with very plain instruments; but no one on earth could construct a science with unreliable instruments. A man might work out the whole of mathematics with a handful of pebbles, but not with a handful of clay which was always falling apart into new fragments, and falling together into new combinations. A man might measure heaven and earth with a reed, but not with a growing reed.

As one of the enormous follies of folk-lore, let us take the case of the transmigration of stories, and the alleged unity of their source. Story after story the scientific mythologists have cut out of its place in history, and pinned side by side with similar stories in their museum of fables. The process is industrious, it is fascinating, and the whole of it rests on one of the plainest fallacies in the world. That a story has been told all over the place at some time or other, not only does not prove that it never really happened; it does not even faintly indicate or make slightly more probable that it never happened. That a large number of fishermen have falsely asserted that they have caught a pike two feet long, does not in the least affect the question of whether any one ever really did so. That numberless journalists announce a Franco-German war merely for money is no evidence one way or the other upon the dark question of whether such a war ever occurred. Doubtless in a few hundred years the innumerable Franco-German wars that did not happen will have cleared the scientific mind of any belief in the legendary war of '70 which did. But that will be because if folk-lore students remain at all, their nature will be unchanged; and their services to folk-lore will be still as they are at present, greater than they know. For in truth these men do something far more godlike than studying legends; they create them.

There are two kinds of stories which the scientists say cannot be true, because everybody tells them. The first class consists of the stories which are told everywhere, because they are somewhat odd or clever; there is nothing in the world to prevent their having happened to somebody as an adventure any more than there is anything to prevent their having occurred, as they certainly did occur, to somebody as an idea. But they are not likely to have happened to many people. The second class of their "myths" consist of the stories that are told everywhere for the simple reason that they happen everywhere. Of the first class, for instance, we might take such an example as the story of William Tell, now generally ranked among legends upon the sole ground that it is found in the tales of other peoples. Now, it is obvious that this was told everywhere because whether true or fictitious it is what is called "a good story;" it is odd, exciting, and it has a climax. But to suggest that some such eccentric incident can never have happened in the whole history of archery, or that it did not happen to any particular person of whom it is told, is stark impudence. The idea of shooting at a mark attached to some valuable or beloved person is an idea doubtless that might easily have occurred to any inventive poet. But it is also an idea that might easily occur to any boastful archer. It might be one of the fantastic caprices of some story-teller. It might equally well be one of the fantastic caprices of some tyrant. It might occur first in real life and afterwards occur in legends. Or it might just as well occur first in legends and afterwards occur in real life. If no apple has ever been shot off a boy's head from the beginning of the world, it may be done tomorrow morning, and by somebody who has never heard of William Tell.

This type of tale, indeed, may be pretty fairly paralleled with the ordinary anecdote terminating in a repartee or an Irish bull. Such a retort as the famous "je ne vois pas la necessite" we have all seen attributed to Talleyrand, to Voltaire, to Henri Quatre, to an anonymous judge, and so on. But this variety does not in any way make it more likely that the thing was never said at all. It is highly likely that it was really said by somebody unknown. It is highly likely that it was really said by Talleyrand. In any case, it is not any more difficult to believe that the mot might have occurred to a man in conversation than to a man writing memoirs. It might have occurred to any of the men I have mentioned. But there is this point of distinction about it, that it is not likely to have occurred to all of them. And this is where the first class of so-called myth differs from the second to which I have previously referred. For there is a second class of incident found to be common to the stories of five or six heroes, say to Sigurd, to Hercules, to Rustem, to the Cid, and so on. And the peculiarity of this myth is that not only is it highly reasonable to imagine that it really happened to one hero, but it is highly reasonable to imagine that it really happened to all of them. Such a story, for instance, is that of a great man having his strength swayed or thwarted by the mysterious weakness of a woman. The anecdotal story, the story of William Tell, is as I have said, popular, because it is peculiar. But this kind of story, the story of Samson and Delilah of Arthur and Guinevere, is obviously popular because it is not peculiar. It is popular as good, quiet fiction is popular, because it tells the truth about people. If the ruin of Samson by a woman, and the ruin of Hercules by a woman, have a common legendary origin, it is gratifying to know that we can also explain, as a fable, the ruin of Nelson by a woman and the ruin of Parnell by a woman. And, indeed, I have no doubt whatever that, some centuries hence, the students of folk-lore will refuse altogether to believe that Elizabeth Barrett eloped with Robert Browning, and will prove their point up to the hilt by the unquestionable fact that the whole fiction of the period was full of such elopements from end to end.

Possibly the most pathetic of all the delusions of the modern students of primitive belief is the notion they have about the thing they call anthropomorphism. They believe that primitive men attributed phenomena to a god in human form in order to explain them, because his mind in its sullen limitation could not reach any further than his own clownish existence. The thunder was called the voice of a man, the lightning the eyes of a man, because by this explanation they were made more reasonable and comfortable. The final cure for all this kind of philosophy is to walk down a lane at night. Any one who does so will discover very quickly that men pictured something semi-human at the back of all things, not because such a thought was natural, but because it was supernatural; not because it made things more comprehensible, but because it made them a hundred times more incomprehensible and mysterious. For a man walking down a lane at night can see the conspicuous fact that as long as nature keeps to her own course, she has no power with us at all. As long as a tree is a tree, it is a top-heavy monster with a hundred arms, a thousand tongues, and only one leg. But so long as a tree is a tree, it does not frighten us at all. It begins to be something alien, to be something strange, only when it looks like ourselves. When a tree really looks like a man our knees knock under us. And when the whole universe looks like a man we fall on our faces.

PAGANISM AND MR. LOWES DICKINSON

Of the New Paganism (or neo-Paganism), as it was preached flamboyantly by Mr. Swinburne or delicately by Walter Pater, there is no necessity to take any very grave account, except as a thing which left behind it incomparable exercises in the English language. The New Paganism is no longer new, and it never at any time bore the smallest resemblance to Paganism. The ideas about the ancient civilization which it has left loose in the public mind are certainly extraordinary enough. The term "pagan" is continually used in fiction and light literature as meaning a man without any religion, whereas a pagan was generally a man with about half a dozen. The pagans, according to this notion, were continually crowning themselves with flowers and dancing about in an irresponsible state, whereas, if there were two things that the best pagan civilization did honestly believe in, they were a rather too rigid dignity and a much too rigid responsibility. Pagans are depicted as above all things inebriate and lawless, whereas they were above all things reasonable and respectable. They are praised as disobedient when they had only one great virtue—civic obedience. They are envied and admired as shamelessly happy when they had only one great sin—despair.

Mr. Lowes Dickinson, the most pregnant and provocative of recent writers on this and similar subjects, is far too solid a man to have fallen into this old error of the mere anarchy of Paganism. In order to make hay of that Hellenic enthusiasm which has as its ideal mere appetite and egotism, it is not necessary to know much philosophy, but merely to know a little Greek. Mr. Lowes Dickinson knows a great deal of philosophy, and also a great deal of Greek, and his error, if error he has, is not that of the crude hedonist. But the contrast which he offers between Christianity and Paganism in the matter of moral ideals—a contrast which he states very ably in a paper called "How long halt ye?" which appeared in the Independent Review—does, I think, contain an error of a deeper kind. According to him, the ideal of Paganism was not, indeed, a mere frenzy of lust and liberty and caprice, but was an ideal of full and satisfied humanity. According to him, the ideal of Christianity was the ideal of asceticism. When I say that I think this idea wholly wrong as a matter of philosophy and history, I am not talking for the moment about any ideal Christianity of my own, or even of any primitive Christianity undefiled by after events. I am not, like so many modern Christian idealists, basing my case upon certain things which Christ said. Neither am I, like so many other Christian idealists, basing my case upon certain things that Christ forgot to say. I take historic Christianity with all its sins upon its head; I take it, as I would take Jacobinism, or Mormonism, or any other mixed or unpleasing human

64

product, and I say that the meaning of its action was not to be found in asceticism. I say that its point of departure from Paganism was not asceticism. I say that its point of difference with the modern world was not asceticism. I say that St. Simeon Stylites had not his main inspiration in asceticism. I say that the main Christian impulse cannot be described as asceticism, even in the ascetics.

Let me set about making the matter clear. There is one broad fact about the relations of Christianity and Paganism which is so simple that many will smile at it, but which is so important that all moderns forget it. The primary fact about Christianity and Paganism is that one came after the other. Mr. Lowes Dickinson speaks of them as if they were parallel ideals— even speaks as if Paganism were the newer of the two, and the more fitted for a new age. He suggests that the Pagan ideal will be the ultimate good of man; but if that is so, we must at least ask with more curiosity than he allows for, why it was that man actually found his ultimate good on earth under the stars, and threw it away again. It is this extraordinary enigma to which I propose to attempt an answer.

There is only one thing in the modern world that has been face to face with Paganism; there is only one thing in the modern world which in that sense knows anything about Paganism: and that is Christianity. That fact is really the weak point in the whole of that hedonistic neo-Paganism of which I have spoken. All that genuinely remains of the ancient hymns or the ancient dances of Europe, all that has honestly come to us from the festivals of Phoebus or Pan, is to be found in the festivals of the Christian Church. If any one wants to hold the end of a chain which really goes back to the heathen mysteries, he had better take hold of a festoon of flowers at Easter or a string of sausages at Christmas. Everything else in the modern world is of Christian origin, even everything that seems most anti-Christian. The French Revolution is of Christian origin. The newspaper is of Christian origin. The anarchists are of Christian origin. Physical science is of Christian origin. The attack on Christianity is of Christian origin. There is one thing, and one thing only, in existence at the present day which can in any sense accurately be said to be of pagan origin, and that is Christianity.

The real difference between Paganism and Christianity is perfectly summed up in the difference between the pagan, or natural, virtues, and those three virtues of Christianity which the Church of Rome calls virtues of grace. The pagan, or rational, virtues are such things as justice and temperance, and Christianity has adopted them. The three mystical virtues which Christianity has not adopted, but invented, are faith, hope, and charity. Now much easy and foolish Christian rhetoric could easily be poured out upon those three words, but I desire to confine myself to the two facts which are evident about them. The first evident fact (in marked contrast to the delusion of the dancing pagan)—the first evident fact, I say, is that the pagan virtues, such as justice and temperance, are the sad virtues, and that the mystical virtues of faith, hope, and charity are the gay and exuberant virtues. And the second evident fact, which is even more evident, is the fact that the pagan virtues are the reasonable virtues, and that the Christian virtues of faith, hope, and charity are in their essence as unreasonable as they can be.

As the word "unreasonable" is open to misunderstanding, the matter may be more accurately put by saying that each one of these Christian or mystical virtues involves a paradox in its own nature, and that this is not true of any of the typically pagan or rationalist virtues. Justice consists in finding out a certain thing due to a certain man and giving it to him. Temperance consists in finding out the proper limit of a particular indulgence and adhering to that. But charity means pardoning what is unpardonable, or it is no virtue at all. Hope means hoping when things are hopeless, or it is no virtue at all. And faith means believing the incredible, or it is no virtue at all.

It is somewhat amusing, indeed, to notice the difference between the fate of these three paradoxes in the fashion of the modern mind. Charity is a fashionable virtue in our time; it is lit up by the gigantic firelight of Dickens. Hope is a fashionable virtue to-day; our attention has been arrested for it by the sudden and silver trumpet of Stevenson. But faith is unfashionable, and it is customary on every side to cast against it the fact that it is a paradox. Everybody mockingly repeats the famous childish definition that faith is "the power of believing that which we know to be untrue." Yet it is not one atom more paradoxical than hope or charity. Charity is the power of defending that which we know to be indefensible. Hope is the power of being cheerful in circumstances which we know to be desperate. It is true that there is a state of hope which belongs to bright prospects and the morning; but that is not the virtue of hope. The virtue of hope exists only in earthquake and, eclipse. It is true that there is a thing crudely called charity, which means charity to the deserving poor; but charity to the deserving is not charity at all, but justice. It is the undeserving who require it, and the ideal either does not exist at all, or exists wholly for them. For practical purposes it is at the hopeless moment that we require the hopeful man, and the virtue either does not exist at all, or begins to exist at that moment. Exactly at the instant when hope ceases to be reasonable it begins to be useful. Now the old pagan world went perfectly straightforward until it discovered that going straightforward is an enormous mistake. It was nobly and beautifully reasonable, and discovered in its death-pang this lasting and valuable truth, a heritage for the ages, that reasonableness will not do. The pagan age was truly an Eden or golden age, in this essential sense, that it is not to be recovered. And it is not to be recovered in this sense again that, while we are certainly jollier than the pagans, and much more right than the pagans, there is not one of us who can, by the utmost stretch of energy, be so sensible as the pagans. That naked innocence of the intellect cannot be recovered by any man after Christianity; and for this excellent reason, that every man after Christianity knows it to be misleading. Let me take an example, the first that occurs to the mind, of this impossible plainness in the pagan point of view. The greatest tribute to Christianity in the modern world is Tennyson's "Ulysses." The poet reads into the story of Ulysses the conception of an incurable desire to wander. But the real Ulysses does not desire to wander at all. He desires to get home. He displays his heroic and unconquerable qualities in resisting the misfortunes which baulk him; but that is all. There is no love of adventure for its own sake; that is a Christian product. There is no love of Penelope for her own sake; that is a Christian product. Everything in that old world would appear to have been clean and obvious. A good man was a good man; a bad man was a bad man. For this reason they had no charity; for charity is a reverent agnosticism towards the complexity of the soul. For this reason they had no such thing as the art of fiction, the novel; for the novel is a creation of the mystical idea of charity. For them a pleasant landscape was pleasant, and an unpleasant landscape unpleasant. Hence they had no idea of romance; for romance consists in thinking a thing more delightful because it is dangerous; it is a Christian idea. In a word, we cannot reconstruct or even imagine the beautiful and astonishing pagan world. It was a world in which common sense was really common.

My general meaning touching the three virtues of which I have spoken will now, I hope, be sufficiently clear. They are all three paradoxical, they are all three practical, and they are all three paradoxical because they are practical. it is the stress of ultimate need, and a terrible knowledge of things as they are, which led men to set up these riddles, and to die for them. Whatever may be the meaning of the contradiction, it is the fact that the only kind of hope that is of any use in a battle is a hope that denies arithmetic. Whatever may be the meaning of the contradiction, it is the fact that the only kind of charity which any weak spirit wants, or which any generous spirit feels, is the charity which forgives the sins that are like scarlet. Whatever may be the meaning of faith, it must always mean a certainty about something we cannot prove. Thus, for instance, we believe by faith in the existence of other people.

But there is another Christian virtue, a virtue far more obviously and historically connected with Christianity, which will illustrate even better the connection between paradox and practical necessity. This virtue cannot be questioned in its capacity as a historical symbol; certainly Mr. Lowes Dickinson will not question it. It has been the boast of hundreds of the champions of Christianity. It has been the taunt of hundreds of the opponents of Christianity. It is, in essence, the basis of Mr. Lowes

Dickinson's whole distinction between Christianity and Paganism. I mean, of course, the virtue of humility. I admit, of course, most readily, that a great deal of false Eastern humility (that is, of strictly ascetic humility) mixed itself with the main stream of European Christianity. We must not forget that when we speak of Christianity we are speaking of a whole continent for about a thousand years. But of this virtue even more than of the other three, I would maintain the general proposition adopted above. Civilization discovered Christian humility for the same urgent reason that it discovered faith and charity—that is, because Christian civilization had to discover it or die.

The great psychological discovery of Paganism, which turned it into Christianity, can be expressed with some accuracy in one phrase. The pagan set out, with admirable sense, to enjoy himself. By the end of his civilization he had discovered that a man cannot enjoy himself and continue to enjoy anything else. Mr. Lowes Dickinson has pointed out in words too excellent to need any further elucidation, the absurd shallowness of those who imagine that the pagan enjoyed himself only in a materialistic sense. Of course, he enjoyed himself, not only intellectually even, he enjoyed himself morally, he enjoyed himself spiritually. But it was himself that he was enjoying; on the face of it, a very natural thing to do. Now, the psychological discovery is merely this, that whereas it had been supposed that the fullest possible enjoyment is to be found by extending our ego to infinity, the truth is that the fullest possible enjoyment is to be found by reducing our ego to zero.

Humility is the thing which is for ever renewing the earth and the stars. It is humility, and not duty, which preserves the stars from wrong, from the unpardonable wrong of casual resignation; it is through humility that the most ancient heavens for us are fresh and strong. The curse that came before history has laid on us all a tendency to be weary of wonders. If we saw the sun for the first time it would be the most fearful and beautiful of meteors. Now that we see it for the hundredth time we call it, in the hideous and blasphemous phrase of Wordsworth, "the light of common day." We are inclined to increase our claims. We are inclined to demand six suns, to demand a blue sun, to demand a green sun. Humility is perpetually putting us back in the primal darkness. There all light is lightning, startling and instantaneous. Until we understand that original dark, in which we have neither sight nor expectation, we can give no hearty and childlike praise to the splendid sensationalism of things. The terms "pessimism" and "optimism," like most modern terms, are unmeaning. But if they can be used in any vague sense as meaning something, we may say that in this great fact pessimism is the very basis of optimism. The man who destroys himself creates the universe. To the humble man, and to the humble man alone, the sun is really a sun; to the humble man, and to the humble man alone, the sea is really a sea. When he looks at all the faces in the street, he does not only realize that men are alive, he realizes with a dramatic pleasure that they are not dead.

I have not spoken of another aspect of the discovery of humility as a psychological necessity, because it is more commonly insisted on, and is in itself more obvious. But it is equally clear that humility is a permanent necessity as a condition of effort and self-examination. It is one of the deadly fallacies of Jingo politics that a nation is stronger for despising other nations. As a matter of fact, the strongest nations are those, like Prussia or Japan, which began from very mean beginnings, but have not been too proud to sit at the feet of the foreigner and learn everything from him. Almost every obvious and direct victory has been the victory of the plagiarist. This is, indeed, only a very paltry by-product of humility, but it is a product of humility, and, therefore, it is successful. Prussia had no Christian humility in its internal arrangements; hence its internal arrangements were miserable. But it had enough Christian humility slavishly to copy France (even down to Frederick the Great's poetry), and that which it had the humility to copy it had ultimately the honour to conquer. The case of the Japanese is even more obvious; their only Christian and their only beautiful quality is that they have humbled themselves to be exalted. All this aspect of humility, however, as connected with the matter of effort and striving for a standard set above us, I dismiss as having been sufficiently pointed out by almost all idealistic writers.

It may be worth while, however, to point out the interesting disparity in the matter of humility between the modern notion of the strong man and the actual records of strong men. Carlyle objected to the statement that no man could be a hero to his valet. Every sympathy can be extended towards him in the matter if he merely or mainly meant that the phrase was a disparagement of hero-worship. Hero-worship is certainly a generous and human impulse; the hero may be faulty, but the worship can hardly be. It may be that no man would be a hero to his valet. But any man would be a valet to his hero. But in truth both the proverb itself and Carlyle's stricture upon it ignore the most essential matter at issue. The ultimate psychological truth is not that no man is a hero to his valet. The ultimate psychological truth, the foundation of Christianity, is that no man is a hero to himself. Cromwell, according to Carlyle, was a strong man. According to Cromwell, he was a weak one.

The weak point in the whole of Carlyle's case for aristocracy lies, indeed, in his most celebrated phrase. Carlyle said that men were mostly fools. Christianity, with a surer and more reverent realism, says that they are all fools. This doctrine is sometimes called the doctrine of original sin. It may also be described as the doctrine of the equality of men. But the essential point of it is merely this, that whatever primary and far-reaching moral dangers affect any man, affect all men. All men can be criminals, if tempted; all men can be heroes, if inspired. And this doctrine does away altogether with Carlyle's pathetic belief (or any one else's pathetic belief) in "the wise few." There are no wise few. Every aristocracy that has ever existed has behaved, in all essential points, exactly like a small mob. Every oligarchy is merely a knot of men in the street—that is to say, it is very jolly, but not infallible. And no oligarchies in the world's history have ever come off so badly in practical affairs as the very proud oligarchies—the oligarchy of Poland, the oligarchy of Venice. And the armies that have most swiftly and suddenly broken their enemies in pieces have been the religious armies—the Moslem Armies, for instance, or the Puritan Armies. And a religious army may, by its nature, be defined as an army in which every man is taught not to exalt but to abase himself. Many modern Englishmen talk of themselves as the sturdy descendants of their sturdy Puritan fathers. As a fact, they would run away from a cow. If you asked one of their Puritan fathers, if you asked Bunyan, for instance, whether he was sturdy, he would have answered, with tears, that he was as weak as water. And because of this he would have borne tortures. And this virtue of humility, while being practical enough to win battles, will always be paradoxical enough to puzzle pedants. It is at one with the virtue of charity in this respect. Every generous person will admit that the one kind of sin which charity should cover is the sin which is inexcusable. And every generous person will equally agree that the one kind of pride which is wholly damnable is the pride of the man who has something to be proud of. The pride which, proportionally speaking, does not hurt the character, is the pride in things which reflect no credit on the person at all. Thus it does a man no harm to be proud of his country, and comparatively little harm to be proud of his remote ancestors. It does him more harm to be proud of having made money, because in that he has a little more reason for pride. It does him more harm still to be proud of what is nobler than money—intellect. And it does him most harm of all to value himself for the most valuable thing on earth—goodness. The man who is proud of what is really creditable to him is the Pharisee, the man whom Christ Himself could not forbear to strike.

My objection to Mr. Lowes Dickinson and the reassertors of the pagan ideal is, then, this. I accuse them of ignoring definite human discoveries in the moral world, discoveries as definite, though not as material, as the discovery of the circulation of the blood. We cannot go back to an ideal of reason and sanity. For mankind has discovered that reason does not lead to sanity. We cannot go back to an ideal of pride and enjoyment. For mankind has discovered that pride does not lead to enjoyment. I do not know by what extraordinary mental accident modern writers so constantly connect the idea of progress with the idea of independent thinking. Progress is obviously the antithesis of independent thinking. For under independent or individualistic thinking, every man starts at the beginning, and goes, in all probability, just as far as his father before him. But if there really be anything of the nature of progress, it must mean, above all things, the careful study and assumption of the whole of the past. I accuse Mr. Lowes Dickinson and his school of reaction in the only real sense. If he likes, let him ignore these great historic mysteries—the mystery of charity, the mystery of chivalry, the mystery of faith. If he likes, let him ignore the plough or the printing-press. But if we do revive and pursue the pagan ideal of a simple and rational self-completion we shall end—where Paganism ended. I do not mean that we shall end in destruction. I mean that we shall end in Christianity.

CELTS AND CELTOPHILES

Science in the modern world has many uses; its chief use, however, is to provide long words to cover the errors of the rich. The word "kleptomania" is a vulgar example of what I mean. It is on a par with that strange theory, always advanced when a wealthy or prominent person is in the dock, that exposure is more of a punishment for the rich than for the poor. Of course, the very reverse is the truth. Exposure is more of a punishment for the poor than for the rich. The richer a man is the easier it is for him to be a tramp. The richer a man is the easier it is for him to be popular and generally respected in the Cannibal Islands. But the poorer a man is the more likely it is that he will have to use his past life whenever he wants to get a bed for the night. Honour is a luxury for aristocrats, but it is a necessity for hall-porters. This is a secondary matter, but it is an example of the general proposition I offer—the proposition that an enormous amount of modern ingenuity is expended on finding defences for the indefensible conduct of the powerful. As I have said above, these defences generally exhibit themselves most emphatically in the form of appeals to physical science. And of all the forms in which science, or pseudo-science, has come to the rescue of the rich and stupid, there is none so singular as the singular invention of the theory of races.

When a wealthy nation like the English discovers the perfectly patent fact that it is making a ludicrous mess of the government of a poorer nation like the Irish, it pauses for a moment in consternation, and then begins to talk about Celts and Teutons. As far as I can understand the theory, the Irish are Celts and the English are Teutons. Of course, the Irish are not Celts any more than the English are Teutons. I have not followed the ethnological discussion with much energy, but the last scientific conclusion which I read inclined on the whole to the summary that the English were mainly Celtic and the Irish mainly Teutonic. But no man alive, with even the glimmering of a real scientific sense, would ever dream of applying the terms "Celtic" or "Teutonic" to either of them in any positive or useful sense.

That sort of thing must be left to people who talk about the Anglo-Saxon race, and extend the expression to America. How much of the blood of the Angles and Saxons (whoever they were) there remains in our mixed British, Roman, German, Dane, Norman, and Picard stock is a matter only interesting to wild antiquaries. And how much of that diluted blood can possibly remain in that roaring whirlpool of America into which a cataract of Swedes, Jews, Germans, Irishmen, and Italians is perpetually pouring, is a matter only interesting to lunatics. It would have been wiser for the English governing class to have called upon some other god. All other gods, however weak and warring, at least boast of being constant. But science boasts of being in a flux for ever; boasts of being unstable as water.

And England and the English governing class never did call on this absurd deity of race until it seemed, for an instant, that they had no other god to call on. All the most genuine Englishmen in history would have yawned or laughed in your face if you had begun to talk about Anglo-Saxons. If you had attempted to substitute the ideal of race for the ideal of nationality, I really do not like to think what they would have said. I certainly should not like to have been the officer of Nelson who suddenly discovered his French blood on the eve of Trafalgar. I should not like to have been the Norfolk or Suffolk gentleman who had to expound to Admiral Blake by what demonstrable ties of genealogy he was irrevocably bound to the Dutch. The truth of the whole matter is very simple. Nationality exists, and has nothing in the world to do with race. Nationality is a thing like a church or a secret society; it is a product of the human soul and will; it is a spiritual product. And there are men in the modern world who would think anything and do anything rather than admit that anything could be a spiritual product.

A nation, however, as it confronts the modern world, is a purely spiritual product. Sometimes it has been born in independence, like Scotland. Sometimes it has been born in dependence, in subjugation, like Ireland. Sometimes it is a large thing cohering out of many smaller things, like Italy. Sometimes it is a small thing breaking away from larger things, like Poland. But in each and every case its quality is purely spiritual, or, if you will, purely psychological. It is a moment when five men become a sixth man. Every one knows it who has ever founded a club. It is a moment when five places become one place. Every one must know it who has ever had to repel an invasion. Mr. Timothy Healy, the most serious intellect in the present House of Commons, summed up nationality to perfection when he simply called it something for which people will die, As he excellently said in reply to Lord Hugh Cecil, "No one, not even the noble lord, would die for the meridian of Greenwich." And that is the great tribute to its purely psychological character. It is idle to ask why Greenwich should not cohere in this spiritual manner while Athens or Sparta did. It is like asking why a man falls in love with one woman and not with another.

Now, of this great spiritual coherence, independent of external circumstances, or of race, or of any obvious physical thing, Ireland is the most remarkable example. Rome conquered nations, but Ireland has conquered races. The Norman has gone there and become Irish, the Scotchman has gone there and become Irish, the Spaniard has gone there and become Irish, even the bitter soldier of Cromwell has gone there and become Irish. Ireland, which did not exist even politically, has been stronger than all the races that existed scientifically. The purest Germanic blood, the purest Norman blood, the purest blood of the passionate Scotch patriot, has not been so attractive as a nation without a flag. Ireland, unrecognized and oppressed, has easily absorbed races, as such trifles are easily absorbed. She has easily disposed of physical science, as such superstitions are easily disposed of. Nationality in its weakness has been stronger than ethnology in its strength. Five triumphant races have been absorbed, have been defeated by a defeated nationality.

This being the true and strange glory of Ireland, it is impossible to hear without impatience of the attempt so constantly made among her modern sympathizers to talk about Celts and Celticism. Who were the Celts? I defy anybody to say. Who are the Irish? I defy any one to be indifferent, or to pretend not to know. Mr. W. B. Yeats, the great Irish genius who has appeared in our time, shows his own admirable penetration in discarding altogether the argument from a Celtic race. But he does not wholly escape, and his followers hardly ever escape, the general objection to the Celtic argument. The tendency of that argument is to represent the Irish or the Celts as a strange and separate race, as a tribe of eccentrics in the modern world immersed in dim legends and fruitless dreams. Its tendency is to exhibit the Irish as odd, because they see the fairies. Its trend is to make the Irish seem weird and wild because they sing old songs and join in strange dances. But this is quite an error; indeed, it is the opposite of the truth. It is the English who are odd because they do not see the fairies. It is the inhabitants of Kensington who are weird and wild because they do not sing old songs and join in strange dances. In all this the Irish are not in the least strange and separate, are not in the least Celtic, as the word is commonly and popularly used. In all this the Irish are simply an ordinary sensible nation, living the life of any other ordinary and sensible nation which has not been either sodden with smoke or oppressed by money-lenders, or otherwise corrupted with wealth and science. There is nothing Celtic about having legends. It is merely human. The Germans, who are (I suppose) Teutonic, have hundreds of legends, wherever it happens that the Germans are human. There is nothing Celtic about loving poetry; the English loved poetry more, perhaps, than any other people before they came under the shadow of the chimney-pot and the shadow of the chimney-pot hat. It is not Ireland which is mad and mystic; it is Manchester which is mad and mystic, which is incredible, which is a wild exception among human things. Ireland has no need to play the silly game of the science of races; Ireland has no need to pretend to be a tribe of visionaries apart. In the matter of visions, Ireland is more than a nation, it is a model nation.

ON CERTAIN MODERN WRITERS AND THE INSTITUTION OF THE FAMILY

The family may fairly be considered, one would think, an ultimate human institution. Every one would admit that it has been the main cell and central unit of almost all societies hitherto, except, indeed, such societies as that of Lacedaemon, which went in for "efficiency," and has, therefore, perished, and left not a trace behind. Christianity, even enormous as was its revolution, did not alter this ancient and savage sanctity; it merely reversed it. It did not deny the trinity of father, mother, and child. It merely read it backwards, making it run child, mother, father. This it called, not the family, but the Holy Family, for many things are made holy by being turned upside down. But some sages of our own decadence have made a serious attack on the family. They have impugned it, as I think wrongly; and its defenders have defended it, and defended it wrongly. The common defence of the family is that, amid the stress and fickleness of life, it is peaceful, pleasant, and at one. But there is another defence of the family which is possible, and to me evident; this defence is that the family is not peaceful and not pleasant and not at one.

It is not fashionable to say much nowadays of the advantages of the small community. We are told that we must go in for large empires and large ideas. There is one advantage, however, in the small state, the city, or the village, which only the wilfully blind can overlook. The man who lives in a small community lives in a much larger world. He knows much more of the fierce varieties and uncompromising divergences of men. The reason is obvious. In a large community we can choose our companions. In a small community our companions are chosen for us. Thus in all extensive and highly civilized societies groups come into existence founded upon what is called sympathy, and shut out the real world more sharply than the gates of a monastery. There is nothing really narrow about the clan; the thing which is really narrow is the clique. The men of the clan live together because they all wear the same tartan or are all descended from the same sacred cow; but in their souls, by the divine luck of things, there will always be more colours than in any tartan. But the men of the clique live together because they have the same kind of soul, and their narrowness is a narrowness of spiritual coherence and contentment, like that which exists in hell. A big society exists in order to form cliques. A big society is a society for the promotion of narrowness. It is a machinery for the purpose of guarding the solitary and sensitive individual from all experience of the bitter and bracing human compromises. It is, in the most literal sense of the words, a society for the

75

prevention of Christian knowledge.

We can see this change, for instance, in the modern transformation of the thing called a club. When London was smaller, and the parts of London more self-contained and parochial, the club was what it still is in villages, the opposite of what it is now in great cities. Then the club was valued as a place where a man could be sociable. Now the club is valued as a place where a man can be unsociable. The more the enlargement and elaboration of our civilization goes on the more the club ceases to be a place where a man can have a noisy argument, and becomes more and more a place where a man can have what is somewhat fantastically called a quiet chop. Its aim is to make a man comfortable, and to make a man comfortable is to make him the opposite of sociable. Sociability, like all good things, is full of discomforts, dangers, and renunciations. The club tends to produce the most degraded of all combinations—the luxurious anchorite, the man who combines the self-indulgence of Lucullus with the insane loneliness of St. Simeon Stylites.

If we were to-morrow morning snowed up in the street in which we live, we should step suddenly into a much larger and much wilder world than we have ever known. And it is the whole effort of the typically modern person to escape from the street in which he lives. First he invents modern hygiene and goes to Margate. Then he invents modern culture and goes to Florence. Then he invents modern imperialism and goes to Timbuctoo. He goes to the fantastic borders of the earth. He pretends to shoot tigers. He almost rides on a camel. And in all this he is still essentially fleeing from the street in which he was born; and of this flight he is always ready with his own explanation. He says he is fleeing from his street because it is dull; he is lying. He is really fleeing from his street because it is a great deal too exciting. It is exciting because it is exacting; it is exacting because it is alive. He can visit Venice because to him the Venetians are only Venetians; the people in his own street are men. He can stare at the Chinese because for him the Chinese are a passive thing to be stared at; if he stares at the old lady in the next garden, she becomes active. He is forced to flee, in short, from the too stimulating society of his equals—of free men, perverse, personal, deliberately different from himself. The street in Brixton is too glowing and overpowering. He has to soothe and quiet himself among tigers and vultures, camels and crocodiles. These creatures are indeed very different from himself. But they do not put their shape or colour or custom into a decisive intellectual competition with his own. They do not seek to destroy his principles and assert their own; the stranger monsters of the suburban street do seek to do this. The camel does not contort his features into a fine sneer because Mr. Robinson has not got a hump; the cultured gentleman at No. 5 does exhibit a sneer because Robinson has not got a dado. The vulture will not roar with laughter because a man does not fly;

but the major at No. 9 will roar with laughter because a man does not smoke. The complaint we commonly have to make of our neighbours is that they will not, as we express it, mind their own business. We do not really mean that they will not mind their own business. If our neighbours did not mind their own business they would be asked abruptly for their rent, and would rapidly cease to be our neighbours. What we really mean when we say that they cannot mind their own business is something much deeper. We do not dislike them because they have so little force and fire that they cannot be interested in themselves. We dislike them because they have so much force and fire that they can be interested in us as well. What we dread about our neighbours, in short, is not the narrowness of their horizon, but their superb tendency to broaden it. And all aversions to ordinary humanity have this general character. They are not aversions to its feebleness (as is pretended), but to its energy. The misanthropes pretend that they despise humanity for its weakness. As a matter of fact, they hate it for its strength.

Of course, this shrinking from the brutal vivacity and brutal variety of common men is a perfectly reasonable and excusable thing as long as it does not pretend to any point of superiority. It is when it calls itself aristocracy or aestheticism or a superiority to the bourgeoisie that its inherent weakness has in justice to be pointed out. Fastidiousness is the most pardonable of vices; but it is the most unpardonable of virtues. Nietzsche, who represents most prominently this pretentious claim of the fastidious, has a description somewhere—a very powerful description in the purely literary sense—of the disgust and disdain which consume him at the sight of the common people with their common faces, their common voices, and their common minds. As I have said, this attitude is almost beautiful if we may regard it as pathetic. Nietzsche's aristocracy has about it all the sacredness that belongs to the weak. When he makes us feel that he cannot endure the innumerable faces, the incessant voices, the overpowering omnipresence which belongs to the mob, he will have the sympathy of anybody who has ever been sick on a steamer or tired in a crowded omnibus. Every man has hated mankind when he was less than a man. Every man has had humanity in his eyes like a blinding fog, humanity in his nostrils like a suffocating smell. But when Nietzsche has the incredible lack of humour and lack of imagination to ask us to believe that his aristocracy is an aristocracy of strong muscles or an aristocracy of strong wills, it is necessary to point out the truth. It is an aristocracy of weak nerves.

We make our friends; we make our enemies; but God makes our next-door neighbour. Hence he comes to us clad in all the careless terrors of nature; he is as strange as the stars, as reckless and indifferent as the rain. He is Man, the most terrible of the beasts. That is why the old religions and the old scriptural language showed so sharp a wisdom when they spoke, not of one's duty towards humanity, but one's duty towards one's neighbour. The duty towards humanity may often take the form of some choice which is personal or even pleasurable. That duty may be a hobby; it may even be a dissipation. We may work in the East End because we are peculiarly fitted to work in the East End, or because we think we are; we may fight for the cause of international peace because we are very fond of fighting. The most monstrous martyrdom, the most repulsive experience, may be the result of choice or a kind of taste. We may be so made as to be particularly fond of lunatics or specially interested in leprosy. We may love negroes because they are black or German Socialists because they are pedantic. But we have to love our neighbour because he is there—a much more alarming reason for a much more serious operation. He is the sample of humanity which is actually given us. Precisely because he may be anybody he is everybody. He is a symbol because he is an accident.

Doubtless men flee from small environments into lands that are very deadly. But this is natural enough; for they are not fleeing from death. They are fleeing from life. And this principle applies to ring within ring of the social system of humanity. It is perfectly reasonable that men should seek for some particular variety of the human type, so long as they are seeking for that variety of the human type, and not for mere human variety. It is quite proper that a British diplomatist should seek the society of Japanese generals, if what he wants is Japanese generals. But if what he wants is people different from himself, he had much better stop at home and discuss religion with the housemaid. It is quite reasonable that the village genius should come up to conquer London if what he wants is to conquer London. But if he wants to conquer something fundamentally and symbolically hostile and also very strong, he had much better remain where he is and have a row with the rector. The man in the suburban street is quite right if he goes to Ramsgate for the sake of Ramsgate—a difficult thing to imagine. But if, as he expresses it, he goes to Ramsgate "for a change," then he would have a much more romantic and even melodramatic change if he jumped over the wall into his neighbours garden. The consequences would be bracing in a sense far beyond the possibilities of Ramsgate hygiene.

Now, exactly as this principle applies to the empire, to the nation within the empire, to the city within the nation, to the street within the city, so it applies to the home within the street. The institution of the family is to be commended for precisely the same reasons that the institution of the nation, or the institution of the city, are in this matter to be commended. It is a good thing for a man to live in a family for the same reason that it is a good thing for a man to be besieged in a city. It is a good thing for a man to live in a family in the same sense that it is a beautiful and delightful thing for a man to be snowed up in a street. They all force him to realize that life is not a thing from outside, but a thing from inside. Above all, they all insist upon the fact that life, if it be a truly stimulating and fascinating life, is a thing which, of its nature, exists in spite of ourselves. The modern writers who have suggested, in a more or less open manner, that the family is a bad institution, have generally confined themselves to suggesting, with much sharpness, bitterness, or pathos, that perhaps the family is not always very congenial. Of course the family is a good institution because it is uncongenial. It is wholesome precisely because it contains so many divergencies and varieties. It is, as the sentimentalists say, like a little kingdom, and, like most other little kingdoms, is generally in a state of something resembling anarchy. It is exactly because our brother George is not interested in our religious difficulties, but is interested in the Trocadero Restaurant, that the family has some of the bracing qualities of the commonwealth. It is precisely because our uncle Henry does not approve of the theatrical ambitions of our sister Sarah that the family is like humanity. The men and women who, for good reasons and bad, revolt against the family, are, for good reasons and bad, simply revolting against mankind. Aunt Elizabeth is unreasonable, like mankind. Papa is excitable, like mankind Our youngest brother is mischievous, like mankind. Grandpapa is stupid, like the world; he is old, like the world.

Those who wish, rightly or wrongly, to step out of all this, do definitely wish to step into a narrower world. They are dismayed and terrified by the largeness and variety of the family. Sarah wishes to find a world wholly consisting of private theatricals; George wishes to think the Trocadero a cosmos. I do not say, for a moment, that the flight to this narrower life may not be the right thing for the individual, any more than I say the same thing about flight into a monastery. But I do say that anything is bad and artificial which tends to make these people succumb to the strange delusion that they are stepping into a world which is actually larger and more varied than their own. The best way that a man could test his readiness to encounter the common variety of mankind would be to climb down a chimney into any house at random, and get on as well as possible with the people inside. And that is essentially what each one of us did on the day that he was born.

This is, indeed, the sublime and special romance of the family. It is romantic because it is a toss-up. It is romantic because it is everything that its enemies call it. It is romantic because it is arbitrary. It is romantic because it is there. So long as you have groups of men chosen rationally, you have some special or sectarian atmosphere. It is when you have groups of men chosen irrationally that you have men. The element of adventure begins to exist; for an adventure is, by its nature, a thing that comes to us. It is a thing that chooses us, not a thing that we choose. Falling in love has been often regarded as the supreme adventure, the supreme romantic accident. In so much as there is in it something outside ourselves, something of a sort of merry fatalism, this is very true. Love does take us and transfigure and torture us. It does break our hearts with an unbearable beauty, like the unbearable beauty of music. But in so far as we have certainly something to do with the matter; in so far as we are in some sense prepared to fall in love and in some sense jump into it; in so far as we do to some extent choose and to some extent even judge—in all this falling in love is not truly romantic, is not truly adventurous at all. In this degree the supreme adventure is not falling in love. The supreme adventure is being born. There we do walk suddenly into a splendid and startling trap. There we do see something of which we have not dreamed before. Our father and mother do lie in wait for us and leap out on us, like brigands from a bush. Our uncle is a surprise. Our aunt is, in the beautiful common expression, a bolt from the blue. When we step into the family, by the act of being born, we do step into a world which is incalculable, into a world which has its own strange laws, into a world which could do without us, into a world that we have not made. In other words, when we step into the family we step into a fairy-tale.

This colour as of a fantastic narrative ought to cling to the family and to our relations with it throughout life. Romance is the deepest thing in life; romance is deeper even than reality. For even if reality could be proved to be misleading, it still could not be proved to be unimportant or unimpressive. Even if the facts are false, they are still very strange. And this strangeness of life, this unexpected and even perverse element of things as they fall out, remains incurably interesting. The circumstances we can regulate may become tame or pessimistic; but the "circumstances over which we have no control" remain god-like to those who, like Mr. Micawber, can call on them and renew their strength. People wonder why the novel is the most popular form of literature; people wonder why it is read more than books of science or books of metaphysics. The reason is very simple; it is merely that the novel is more true than they are. Life may sometimes legitimately appear as a book of science. Life may sometimes appear, and with a much greater legitimacy, as a book of metaphysics. But life is always a novel. Our existence may cease to be a song; it may cease even to be a beautiful lament. Our existence may not be an intelligible justice, or even a recognizable wrong. But our existence is still a story. In the fiery alphabet of every sunset is written, "to be continued in our next." If we have sufficient intellect, we can finish a philosophical and exact deduction, and be certain that we are finishing it right. With the adequate brain-power we could finish any scientific discovery, and be certain that we were finishing it right. But not with the most gigantic intellect could we finish the simplest or silliest story, and be certain that we were finishing it right. That is because a story has behind it, not merely intellect which is partly mechanical, but will, which is in its essence divine. The narrative writer can send his hero to the gallows if he likes in the last chapter but one. He can do it by the same divine caprice whereby he, the author, can go to the gallows himself, and to hell afterwards if he chooses. And the same civilization, the chivalric European civilization which asserted freewill in the thirteenth century, produced the thing called "fiction" in the eighteenth. When Thomas Aquinas asserted the spiritual liberty of man, he created all the bad novels in the circulating libraries.

But in order that life should be a story or romance to us, it is necessary that a great part of it, at any rate, should be settled for us without our permission. If we wish life to be a system, this may be a nuisance; but if we wish it to be a drama, it is an essential. It may often happen, no doubt, that a drama may be written by somebody else which we like very little. But we should like it still less if the author came before the curtain every hour or so, and forced on us the whole trouble of inventing the next act. A man has control over many things in his life; he has control over enough things to be the hero of a novel. But if he had control over everything, there would be so much hero that there would be no novel. And the reason why the lives of the rich are at bottom so tame and uneventful is simply that they can choose the events. They are dull because they are omnipotent. They fail to feel adventures because they can make the adventures. The thing which keeps life romantic and full of fiery possibilities is the existence of these great plain limitations which force all of us to meet the things we do not like or do not expect. It is vain for the supercilious moderns to talk of being in uncongenial surroundings. To be in a romance is to be in uncongenial surroundings. To be born into this earth is to be born into uncongenial surroundings, hence to be born into a romance. Of all these great limitations and frameworks which fashion and create the poetry and variety of life, the family is the most definite and important. Hence it is misunderstood by the moderns, who imagine that romance would exist most perfectly in a complete state of what they call liberty. They think that if a man makes a gesture it would be a startling and romantic matter that the sun should fall from the sky. But the startling and romantic thing about the sun is that it does not fall from the sky. They are seeking under every shape and form a world where there are no limitations—that is, a world where there are no outlines; that is, a world where there are no shapes. There is nothing baser than that infinity. They say they wish to be, as strong as the universe, but they really wish the whole universe as weak as themselves.

ON SMART NOVELISTS AND THE SMART SET

In one sense, at any rate, it is more valuable to read bad literature than good literature. Good literature may tell us the mind of one man; but bad literature may tell us the mind of many men. A good novel tells us the truth about its hero; but a bad novel tells us the truth about its author. It does much more than that, it tells us the truth about its readers; and, oddly enough, it tells us this all the more the more cynical and immoral be the motive of its manufacture. The more dishonest a book is as a book the more honest it is as a public document. A sincere novel exhibits the simplicity of one particular man; an insincere novel exhibits the simplicity of mankind. The pedantic decisions and definable readjustments of man may be found in scrolls and statute books and scriptures; but men's basic assumptions and everlasting energies are to be found in penny dreadfuls and halfpenny novelettes. Thus a man, like many men of real culture in our day, might learn from good literature nothing except the power to appreciate good literature. But from bad literature he might learn to govern empires and look over the map of mankind.

There is one rather interesting example of this state of things in which the weaker literature is really the stronger and the stronger the weaker. It is the case of what may be called, for the sake of an approximate description, the literature of aristocracy; or, if you prefer the description, the literature of snobbishness. Now if any one wishes to find a really effective and comprehensible and permanent case for aristocracy well and sincerely stated, let him read, not the modern philosophical conservatives, not even Nietzsche, let him read the Bow Bells Novelettes. Of the case of Nietzsche I am confessedly more doubtful. Nietzsche and the Bow Bells Novelettes have both obviously the same fundamental character; they both worship the tall man with curling moustaches and herculean bodily power, and they both worship him in a manner which is somewhat feminine and hysterical. Even here, however, the Novelette easily maintains its philosophical superiority, because it does attribute to the strong man those virtues which do commonly belong to him, such virtues as laziness and kindliness and a rather reckless benevolence, and a great dislike of hurting the weak. Nietzsche, on the other hand, attributes to the strong man that scorn against weakness which only exists among invalids. It is not, however, of the secondary merits of the great German philosopher, but of the primary merits of the Bow Bells Novelettes, that it is my present affair to speak. The picture of aristocracy in the popular sentimental novelette seems to me very satisfactory as a permanent political and philosophical guide. It may be inaccurate about details such as the title by which a baronet is addressed or the width of a mountain chasm which a baronet can conveniently leap, but it is not a bad description of the general idea and intention of aristocracy as they exist in human affairs. The essential dream of aristocracy is magnificence and valour; and if the Family Herald Supplement sometimes distorts or exaggerates these things, at least, it does not fall short in them. It never errs by making the mountain chasm too narrow or the title of the baronet insufficiently impressive. But above this sane reliable old literature of snobbishness there has arisen in our time another kind of literature of snobbishness which, with its much higher pretensions, seems to me worthy of very much less respect. Incidentally (if that matters), it is much better literature. But it is immeasurably worse philosophy, immeasurably worse ethics and politics, immeasurably worse vital rendering of aristocracy and humanity as they really are. From such books as those of which I wish now to speak we can discover what a clever man can do with the idea of aristocracy. But from the Family Herald Supplement literature we can learn what the idea of aristocracy can do with a man who is not clever. And when we know that we know English history.

This new aristocratic fiction must have caught the attention of everybody who has read the best fiction for the last fifteen years. It is that genuine or alleged literature of the Smart Set which represents that set as distinguished, not only by smart dresses, but by smart sayings. To the bad baronet, to the good baronet, to the romantic and misunderstood baronet who is supposed to be a bad baronet, but is a good baronet, this school has added a conception undreamed of in the former years—the conception of an amusing baronet. The aristocrat is not merely to be taller than mortal men and stronger and handsomer, he is also to be more witty. He is the long man with the short epigram. Many eminent, and deservedly eminent, modern novelists must accept some responsibility for having supported this worst form of snobbishness—an intellectual snobbishness. The talented author of "Dodo" is responsible for having in some sense created the fashion as a fashion. Mr. Hichens, in the "Green Carnation," reaffirmed the strange idea that young noblemen talk well; though his case had some vague biographical foundation, and in consequence an excuse. Mrs. Craigie is considerably guilty in the matter, although, or rather because, she has combined the aristocratic note with a note of some moral and even religious sincerity. When you are saving a man's soul, even in a novel, it is indecent to mention that he is a gentleman. Nor can blame in this matter be altogether removed from a man of much greater ability, and a man who has proved his possession of the highest of human instinct, the romantic instinct—I mean Mr. Anthony Hope. In a galloping, impossible melodrama like "The Prisoner of Zenda," the blood of kings fanned an excellent fantastic thread or theme. But the blood of kings is not a thing that can be taken seriously. And when, for example, Mr. Hope devotes so much serious and sympathetic study to the man called Tristram of Blent, a man who throughout burning boyhood thought of nothing but a silly old estate, we feel even in Mr. Hope the hint of this excessive concern about the oligarchic idea. It is hard for any ordinary person to feel so much interest in a young man whose whole aim is to own the house of Blent at the time when every other young man is owning the stars.

Mr. Hope, however, is a very mild case, and in him there is not only an element of romance, but also a fine element of irony which warns us against taking all this elegance too seriously. Above all, he shows his sense in not making his noblemen so incredibly equipped with impromptu repartee. This habit of insisting on the wit of the wealthier classes is the last and most servile of all the servilities. It is, as I have said, immeasurably more contemptible than the snobbishness of the novelette which describes the nobleman as smiling like an Apollo or riding a mad elephant. These may be exaggerations of beauty and courage, but beauty and courage are the unconscious ideals of aristocrats, even of stupid aristocrats.

The nobleman of the novelette may not be sketched with any very close or conscientious attention to the daily habits of noblemen. But he is something more important than a reality; he is a practical ideal. The gentleman of fiction may not copy the gentleman of real life; but the gentleman of real life is copying the gentleman of fiction. He may not be particularly good-looking, but he would rather be good-looking than anything else; he may not have ridden on a mad elephant, but he rides a pony as far as possible with an air as if he had. And, upon the whole, the upper class not only especially desire these qualities of beauty and courage, but in some degree, at any rate, especially possess them. Thus there is nothing really mean or sycophantic about the popular literature which makes all its marquises seven feet high. It is snobbish, but it is not servile. Its exaggeration is based on an exuberant and honest admiration; its honest admiration is based upon something which is in some degree, at any rate, really there. The English lower classes do not fear the English upper classes in the least; nobody could. They simply and freely and sentimentally worship them. The strength of the aristocracy is not in the aristocracy at all; it is in the slums. It is not in the House of Lords; it is not in the Civil Service; it is not in the Government offices; it is not even in the huge and disproportionate monopoly of the English land. It is in a certain spirit. It is in the fact that when a navvy wishes to praise a man, it comes readily to his tongue to say that he has behaved like a gentleman. From a democratic point of view he might as well say that he had behaved like a viscount. The oligarchic character of the modern English commonwealth does not rest, like many oligarchies, on the cruelty of the rich to the poor. It does not even rest on the kindness of the rich to the poor. It rests on the perennial and unfailing kindness of the poor to the rich.

The snobbishness of bad literature, then, is not servile; but the snobbishness of good literature is servile. The old-fashioned halfpenny romance where the duchesses sparkled with diamonds was not servile; but the new romance where they sparkle with epigrams is servile. For in thus attributing a special and startling degree of intellect and conversational or controversial power to the upper classes, we are attributing something which is not especially their virtue or even especially their aim. We are, in the words of Disraeli (who, being a genius and not a gentleman, has perhaps primarily to answer for the introduction of this method of flattering the gentry), we are performing the essential function of flattery which is flattering the people for the qualities they have not got. Praise may be gigantic and insane without having any quality of flattery so long as it is praise of something that is noticeably in existence. A man may say that a giraffe's head strikes the stars, or that a whale fills the German Ocean, and still be only in a rather excited state about a favourite animal. But when he begins to congratulate the giraffe on his feathers, and the whale on the elegance of his legs, we find ourselves confronted with that social element which we call flattery. The middle and lower orders of London can sincerely, though not perhaps safely, admire the health and grace of the English aristocracy. And this for the very simple reason that the aristocrats are, upon the whole, more healthy and graceful than the poor. But they cannot honestly admire the wit of the aristocrats. And this for the simple reason that the aristocrats are not more witty than the poor, but a very great deal less so. A man does not hear, as in the smart novels, these gems of verbal felicity dropped between diplomatists at dinner. Where he really does hear them is between two omnibus conductors in a block in Holborn. The witty peer whose impromptus fill the books of Mrs. Craigie or Miss Fowler, would, as a matter of fact, be torn to shreds in the art of conversation by the first boot-black he had the misfortune to fall foul of. The poor are merely sentimental, and very excusably sentimental, if they praise the gentleman for having a ready hand and ready money. But they are strictly slaves and sycophants if they praise him for having a ready tongue. For that they have far more themselves.

The element of oligarchical sentiment in these novels, however, has, I think, another and subtler aspect, an aspect more difficult to understand and more worth understanding. The modern gentleman, particularly the modern English gentleman, has become so central and important in these books, and through them in the whole of our current literature and our current mode of thought, that certain qualities of his, whether original or recent, essential or accidental, have altered the quality of our English comedy. In particular, that stoical ideal, absurdly supposed to be the English ideal, has stiffened and chilled us. It is not the English ideal; but it is to some extent the aristocratic ideal; or it may be only the ideal of

85

aristocracy in its autumn or decay. The gentleman is a Stoic because he is a sort of savage, because he is filled with a great elemental fear that some stranger will speak to him. That is why a third-class carriage is a community, while a first-class carriage is a place of wild hermits. But this matter, which is difficult, I may be permitted to approach in a more circuitous way.

The haunting element of ineffectualness which runs through so much of the witty and epigrammatic fiction fashionable during the last eight or ten years, which runs through such works of a real though varying ingenuity as "Dodo," or "Concerning Isabel Carnaby," or even "Some Emotions and a Moral," may be expressed in various ways, but to most of us I think it will ultimately amount to the same thing. This new frivolity is inadequate because there is in it no strong sense of an unuttered joy. The men and women who exchange the repartees may not only be hating each other, but hating even themselves. Any one of them might be bankrupt that day, or sentenced to be shot the next. They are joking, not because they are merry, but because they are not; out of the emptiness of the heart the mouth speaketh. Even when they talk pure nonsense it is a careful nonsense—a nonsense of which they are economical, or, to use the perfect expression of Mr. W. S. Gilbert in "Patience," it is such "precious nonsense." Even when they become light-headed they do not become light-hearted. All those who have read anything of the rationalism of the moderns know that their Reason is a sad thing. But even their unreason is sad.

The causes of this incapacity are also not very difficult to indicate. The chief of all, of course, is that miserable fear of being sentimental, which is the meanest of all the modern terrors—meaner even than the terror which produces hygiene. Everywhere the robust and uproarious humour has come from the men who were capable not merely of sentimentalism, but a very silly sentimentalism. There has been no humour so robust or uproarious as that of the sentimentalist Steele or the sentimentalist Sterne or the sentimentalist Dickens. These creatures who wept like women were the creatures who laughed like men. It is true that the humour of Micawber is good literature and that the pathos of little Nell is bad. But the kind of man who had the courage to write so badly in the one case is the kind of man who would have the courage to write so well in the other. The same unconsciousness, the same violent innocence, the same gigantesque scale of action which brought the Napoleon of Comedy his Jena brought him also his Moscow. And herein is especially shown the frigid and feeble limitations of our modern wits. They make violent efforts, they make heroic and almost pathetic efforts, but they cannot really write badly. There are moments when we almost think that they are achieving the effect, but our hope shrivels to nothing the moment we compare their little failures with the enormous imbecilities of Byron or Shakespeare.

For a hearty laugh it is necessary to have touched the heart. I do not know why touching the heart should always be connected only with the idea of touching it to compassion or a sense of distress. The heart can be touched to joy and triumph; the heart can be touched to amusement. But all our comedians are tragic comedians. These later fashionable writers are so pessimistic in bone and marrow that they never seem able to imagine the heart having any concern with mirth. When they speak of the heart, they always mean the pangs and disappointments of the emotional life. When they say that a man's heart is in the right place, they mean, apparently, that it is in his boots. Our ethical societies understand fellowship, but they do not understand good fellowship. Similarly, our wits understand talk, but not what Dr. Johnson called a good talk. In order to have, like Dr. Johnson, a good talk, it is emphatically necessary to be, like Dr. Johnson, a good man—to have friendship and honour and an abysmal tenderness. Above all, it is necessary to be openly and indecently humane, to confess with fulness all the primary pities and fears of Adam. Johnson was a clear-headed humorous man, and therefore he did not mind talking seriously about religion. Johnson was a brave man, one of the bravest that ever walked, and therefore he did not mind avowing to any one his consuming fear of death.

The idea that there is something English in the repression of one's feelings is one of those ideas which no Englishman ever heard of until England began to be governed exclusively by Scotchmen, Americans, and Jews. At the best, the idea is a generalization from the Duke of Wellington—who was an Irishman. At the worst, it is a part of that silly Teutonism which knows as little about England as it does about anthropology, but which is always talking about Vikings. As a matter of fact, the Vikings did not repress their feelings in the least. They cried like babies and kissed each other like girls; in short, they acted in that respect like Achilles and all strong heroes the children of the gods. And though the English nationality has probably not much more to do with the Vikings than the French nationality or the Irish nationality, the English have certainly been the children of the Vikings in the matter of tears and kisses. It is not merely true that all the most typically English men of letters, like Shakespeare and Dickens, Richardson and Thackeray, were sentimentalists. It is also true that all the most typically English men of action were sentimentalists, if possible, more sentimental. In the great Elizabethan age, when the English nation was finally hammered out, in the great eighteenth century when the British Empire was being built up everywhere, where in all these times, where was this symbolic stoical Englishman who dresses in drab and black and represses his feelings? Were all the Elizabethan palladins and pirates like that? Were any of them like that? Was Grenville concealing his emotions when he broke wine-glasses to pieces with his teeth and bit them till the blood poured down? Was Essex restraining his excitement when he threw his hat into the sea? Did Raleigh think it sensible to answer the Spanish guns only, as Stevenson says, with a flourish of insulting trumpets? Did Sydney ever miss an opportunity of making a theatrical remark in the whole course of his life and death? Were even the Puritans Stoics? The English Puritans repressed a good deal, but even they were too English to repress their feelings. It was by a great miracle of genius assuredly that Carlyle contrived to admire simultaneously two things so irreconcilably opposed as silence and Oliver Cromwell. Cromwell was the very reverse of a strong, silent man. Cromwell was always talking, when he was not crying. Nobody, I suppose, will accuse the author of "Grace Abounding" of being ashamed of his feelings. Milton, indeed, it might be possible to represent as a Stoic; in some sense he was a Stoic, just as he was a prig and a polygamist and several other unpleasant and heathen things. But when we have passed that great and desolate name, which may really be counted an exception, we find the tradition of English emotionalism immediately resumed and unbrokenly continuous. Whatever may have been the moral beauty of the passions of Etheridge and Dorset, Sedley and Buckingham, they cannot be accused of the fault of fastidiously concealing them. Charles the Second was very popular with the English because, like all the jolly English kings, he displayed his passions. William the Dutchman was very unpopular with the English because, not being an Englishman, he did hide his emotions. He was, in fact, precisely the ideal Englishman of our modern theory; and precisely for that reason all the real Englishmen loathed him like leprosy. With the rise of the great England of the eighteenth century, we find this open and emotional tone still maintained in letters and politics, in arts and in arms. Perhaps the only quality which was possessed in common by the great Fielding, and the great Richardson was that neither of them hid their feelings. Swift, indeed, was hard and logical, because Swift was Irish. And when we pass to the soldiers and the rulers, the patriots and the empire-builders of the eighteenth century, we find, as I have said, that they were, If possible, more romantic than the romancers, more poetical than the poets. Chatham, who showed the world all his strength, showed the House of Commons all his weakness. Wolfe walked about the room with a drawn sword calling himself Caesar and Hannibal, and went to death with poetry in his mouth. Clive was a man of the same type as Cromwell or Bunyan, or, for the matter of that, Johnson—that is, he was a strong, sensible man with a kind of running spring of hysteria and melancholy in him. Like Johnson, he was all the more healthy because he was morbid. The tales of all the admirals and adventurers of that England are full of braggadocio, of sentimentality, of splendid affectation. But it is scarcely necessary to multiply examples of the essentially romantic Englishman when one example towers above them all. Mr. Rudyard Kipling has said complacently of the English, "We do not fall on the neck and kiss when we come together." It is true that this ancient and universal custom has vanished with the modern weakening of England. Sydney would have thought nothing of kissing Spenser. But I willingly concede that Mr. Broderick would not be likely to kiss Mr. Arnold-Foster, if that be any proof of the increased manliness and military greatness of England. But the Englishman who does not show his feelings has not altogether given up the power of seeing something English in the great sea-hero of the Napoleonic war. You cannot break the legend of Nelson. And across the sunset of that glory is written in flaming letters for ever the great English sentiment, "Kiss me, Hardy."

This ideal of self-repression, then, is, whatever else it is, not English. It is, perhaps, somewhat Oriental, it is slightly Prussian, but in the main it does not come, I think, from any racial or national source. It is, as I have said, in some sense aristocratic; it comes not from a people, but from a class. Even aristocracy, I think, was not quite so stoical in the days when it was really strong. But whether this unemotional ideal be the genuine tradition of the gentleman, or only one of the inventions of the modern gentleman (who may be called the decayed gentleman), it certainly has something to do with the unemotional quality in these society novels. From representing aristocrats as people who suppressed their feelings, it has been an easy step to representing aristocrats as people who had no feelings to suppress. Thus the modern oligarchist has made a virtue for the oligarchy of the hardness as well as the brightness of the diamond. Like a sonneteer addressing his lady in the seventeenth century, he seems to use the word "cold" almost as a eulogium, and the word "heartless" as a kind of compliment. Of course, in people so incurably kind-hearted and babyish as are the English gentry, it would be impossible to create anything that can be called positive cruelty; so in these books they exhibit a sort of negative cruelty. They cannot be cruel in acts, but they can be so in words. All this means one thing, and one thing only. It means that the living and invigorating ideal of England must be looked for in the masses; it must be looked for where Dickens found it—Dickens among whose glories it was to be a humorist, to be a sentimentalist, to be an optimist, to be a poor man, to be an Englishman, but the greatest of whose glories was that he saw all mankind in its amazing and tropical luxuriance, and did not even notice the aristocracy; Dickens, the greatest of whose glories was that he could not describe a gentleman.

ON MR. MCCABE AND A DIVINE FRIVOLITY

A critic once remonstrated with me saying, with an air of indignant reasonableness, "If you must make jokes, at least you need not make them on such serious subjects." I replied with a natural simplicity and wonder, "About what other subjects can one make jokes except serious subjects?" It is quite useless to talk about profane jesting. All jesting is in its nature profane, in the sense that it must be the sudden realization that something which thinks itself solemn is not so very solemn after all. If a joke is not a joke about religion or morals, it is a joke about police-magistrates or scientific professors or undergraduates dressed up as Queen Victoria. And people joke about the police-magistrate more than they joke about the Pope, not because the police-magistrate is a more frivolous subject, but, on the contrary, because the police-magistrate is a more serious subject than the Pope. The Bishop of Rome has no jurisdiction in this realm of England; whereas the police-magistrate may bring his solemnity to bear quite suddenly upon us. Men make jokes about old scientific professors, even more than they make them about bishops—not because science is lighter than religion, but because science is always by its nature more solemn and austere than religion. It is not I; it is not even a particular class of journalists or jesters who make jokes about the matters which are of most awful import; it is the whole human race. If there is one thing more than another which any one will admit who has the smallest knowledge of the world, it is that men are always speaking gravely and earnestly and with the utmost possible care about the things that are not important, but always talking frivolously about the things that are. Men talk for hours with the faces of a college of cardinals about things like golf, or tobacco, or waistcoats, or party politics. But all the most grave and dreadful things in the world are the oldest jokes in the world—being married; being hanged.

One gentleman, however, Mr. McCabe, has in this matter made to me something that almost amounts to a personal appeal; and as he happens to be a man for whose sincerity and intellectual virtue I have a high respect, I do not feel inclined to let it pass without some attempt to satisfy my critic in the matter. Mr. McCabe devotes a considerable part of the last essay in the collection called "Christianity and Rationalism on Trial" to an objection, not to my thesis, but to my method, and a very friendly and dignified appeal to me to alter it. I am much inclined to defend myself in this matter out of mere respect for Mr. McCabe, and still more so out of mere respect for the truth which is, I think, in danger by his error, not only in this question, but in others. In order that there may be no injustice done in the matter, I will quote Mr. McCabe himself. "But before I follow Mr. Chesterton in some detail I would make a general observation on his method. He is as serious as I am in his ultimate purpose, and I respect him for that. He knows, as I do, that humanity stands at a solemn parting of the ways. Towards some unknown goal it presses through the ages, impelled by an overmastering desire of happiness. To-day it hesitates, lightheartedly enough, but every serious thinker knows how momentous the decision may be. It is, apparently, deserting the path of religion and entering upon the path of secularism. Will it lose itself in quagmires of sensuality down this new path, and pant and toil through years of civic and industrial anarchy, only to learn it had lost the road, and must return to religion? Or will it find that at last it is leaving the mists and the quagmires behind it; that it is ascending the slope of the hill so long dimly discerned ahead, and making straight for the long-sought Utopia? This is the drama of our time, and every man and every woman should understand it.

"Mr. Chesterton understands it. Further, he gives us credit for understanding it. He has nothing of that paltry meanness or strange density of so many of his colleagues, who put us down as aimless iconoclasts or moral anarchists. He admits that we are waging a thankless war for what we take to be Truth and Progress. He is doing the same. But why, in the name of all that is reasonable, should we, when we are agreed on the momentousness of the issue either way, forthwith desert serious methods of conducting the controversy? Why, when the vital need of our time is to induce men and women to collect their thoughts occasionally, and be men and women—nay, to remember that they are really gods that hold the destinies of humanity on their knees—why should we think that this kaleidoscopic play of phrases is inopportune? The ballets of the Alhambra, and the fireworks of the Crystal Palace, and Mr. Chesterton's Daily News articles, have their place in life. But how a serious social student can think of curing the thoughtlessness of our generation by strained paradoxes; of giving people a sane grasp of social problems by literary sleight-of-hand; of settling important questions by a reckless shower of rocket-metaphors and inaccurate 'facts,' and the substitution of imagination for judgment, I cannot see."

I quote this passage with a particular pleasure, because Mr. McCabe certainly cannot put too strongly the degree to which I give him and his school credit for their complete sincerity and responsibility of philosophical attitude. I am quite certain that they mean every word they say. I also mean every word I say. But why is it that Mr. McCabe has some sort of mysterious hesitation about admitting that I mean every word I say; why is it that he is not quite as certain of my mental responsibility as I am of his mental responsibility? If we attempt to answer the question directly and well, we shall, I think, have come to the root of the matter by the shortest cut.

Mr. McCabe thinks that I am not serious but only funny, because Mr. McCabe thinks that funny is the opposite of serious. Funny is the opposite of not funny, and of nothing else. The question of whether a man expresses himself in a grotesque or laughable phraseology, or in a stately and restrained phraseology, is not a question of motive or of moral state, it is a question of instinctive language and self-expression. Whether a man chooses to tell the truth in long sentences or short jokes is a problem analogous to whether he chooses to tell the truth in French or German. Whether a man preaches his gospel grotesquely or gravely is merely like the question of whether he preaches it in prose or verse. The question of whether Swift was funny in his irony is quite another sort of question to the question of whether Swift was serious in his pessimism. Surely even Mr. McCabe would not maintain that the more funny "Gulliver" is in its method the less it can be sincere in its object. The truth is, as I have said, that in this sense the two qualities of fun and seriousness have nothing whatever to do with each other, they are no more comparable than black and triangular. Mr. Bernard Shaw is funny and sincere. Mr. George Robey is funny and not sincere. Mr. McCabe is sincere and not funny. The average Cabinet Minister is not sincere and not funny.

In short, Mr. McCabe is under the influence of a primary fallacy which I have found very common in men of the clerical type. Numbers of clergymen have from time to time reproached me for making jokes about religion; and they have almost always invoked the authority of that very sensible commandment which says, "Thou shalt not take the name of the Lord thy God in vain." Of course, I pointed out that I was not in any conceivable sense taking the name in vain. To take a thing and make a joke out of it is not to take it in vain. It is, on the contrary, to take it and use it for an uncommonly good object. To use a thing in vain means to use it without use. But a joke may be exceedingly useful; it may contain the whole earthly sense, not to mention the whole heavenly sense, of a situation. And those who find in the Bible the commandment can find in the Bible any number of the jokes. In the same book in which God's name is fenced from being taken in vain, God himself overwhelms Job with a torrent of terrible levities. The same book which says that God's name must not be taken vainly, talks easily and carelessly about God laughing and God winking. Evidently it is not here that we have to look for genuine examples of what is meant by a vain use of the name. And it is not very difficult to see where we have really to look for it. The people (as I tactfully pointed out to them) who really take the name of the Lord in vain are the clergymen themselves. The thing which is fundamentally and really frivolous is not a careless joke. The thing which is fundamentally and really frivolous is a careless solemnity. If Mr. McCabe really wishes to know what sort of guarantee of reality and solidity is afforded by the mere act of what is called talking seriously, let him spend a happy Sunday in going the round of the pulpits. Or, better still, let him drop in at the House of Commons or the House of Lords. Even Mr. McCabe would admit that these men are solemn—more solemn than I am. And even Mr. McCabe, I think, would admit that these men are frivolous—more frivolous than I am. Why should Mr. McCabe be so eloquent about the danger arising from fantastic and paradoxical writers? Why should he be so ardent in desiring grave and verbose writers? There are not so very many fantastic and paradoxical writers. But there are a gigantic number of grave and verbose writers; and it is by the efforts of the grave and verbose writers that everything that Mr. McCabe detests (and everything that I detest, for that matter) is kept in existence and energy. How can it have come about that a man as intelligent as Mr. McCabe can think that paradox and jesting stop the way? It is solemnity that is stopping the way in every department of modern effort. It is his own favourite "serious methods;" it is his own favourite "momentousness;" it is his own favourite "judgment" which stops the way everywhere. Every man who has ever headed a deputation to a minister knows this. Every man who has ever written a letter to the Times knows it. Every rich man who wishes to stop the mouths of the poor talks about "momentousness." Every Cabinet minister who has not got an answer suddenly develops a "judgment." Every sweater who uses vile methods recommends "serious methods." I said a moment ago that sincerity had nothing to do with solemnity, but I confess that I am not so certain that I was right. In the modern world, at any rate, I am not so sure that I was right. In the modern world solemnity is the direct enemy of sincerity. In the modern world sincerity is almost always on one side, and solemnity almost always on the other. The only answer possible to the fierce and glad attack of sincerity is the miserable answer of solemnity. Let Mr. McCabe, or any one else who is much concerned that we should be grave in order to be sincere, simply imagine the scene in some government office in which Mr. Bernard Shaw should head a Socialist deputation to Mr. Austen Chamberlain. On which side would be the solemnity? And on which the sincerity?

I am, indeed, delighted to discover that Mr. McCabe reckons Mr. Shaw along with me in his system of condemnation of frivolity. He said once, I believe, that he always wanted Mr. Shaw to label his paragraphs serious or comic. I do not know which paragraphs of Mr. Shaw are paragraphs to be labelled serious; but surely there can be no doubt that this paragraph of Mr. McCabe's is one to be labelled comic. He also says, in the article I am now discussing, that Mr. Shaw has the reputation of deliberately saying everything which his hearers do not expect him to say. I need not labour the inconclusiveness and weakness of this, because it has already been dealt with in my remarks on Mr. Bernard Shaw. Suffice it to say here that the only serious reason which I can imagine inducing any one person to listen to any other is, that the first person looks to the second person with an ardent faith and a fixed attention, expecting him to say what he does not expect him to say. It may be a paradox, but that is because paradoxes are true. It may not be rational, but that is because rationalism is wrong. But clearly it is quite true that whenever we go to hear a prophet or teacher we may or may not expect wit, we may or may not expect eloquence, but we do expect what we do not expect. We may not expect the true, we may not even expect the wise, but we do expect the unexpected. If we do not expect the unexpected, why do we go there at all? If we expect the expected, why do we not sit at home and expect it by ourselves? If Mr. McCabe means merely this about Mr. Shaw, that he always has some unexpected application of his doctrine to give to those who listen to him, what he says is quite true, and to say it is only to say that Mr. Shaw is an original man. But if he means that Mr. Shaw has ever professed or preached any doctrine but one, and that his own, then what he says is not true. It is not my business to defend Mr. Shaw; as has been seen already, I disagree with him altogether. But I do not mind, on his behalf offering in this matter a flat defiance to all his ordinary opponents, such as Mr. McCabe. I defy Mr. McCabe, or anybody else, to mention one single instance in which Mr. Shaw has, for the sake of wit or novelty, taken up any position which was not directly deducible from the body of his doctrine as elsewhere expressed. I have been, I am happy to say, a tolerably close student of Mr. Shaw's utterances, and I request Mr. McCabe, if he will not believe that I mean anything else, to believe that I mean this challenge.

All this, however, is a parenthesis. The thing with which I am here immediately concerned is Mr. McCabe's appeal to me not to be so frivolous. Let me return to the actual text of that appeal. There are, of course, a great many things that I might say about it in detail. But I may start with saying that Mr. McCabe is in error in supposing that the danger which I anticipate from the disappearance of religion is the increase of sensuality. On the contrary, I should be inclined to anticipate a decrease in sensuality, because I anticipate a decrease in life. I do not think that under modern Western materialism we should have anarchy. I doubt whether we should have enough individual valour and spirit even to have liberty. It is quite an old-fashioned fallacy to suppose that our objection to scepticism is that it removes the discipline from life. Our objection to scepticism is that it removes the motive power. Materialism is not a thing which destroys mere restraint. Materialism itself is the great restraint. The McCabe school advocates a political liberty, but it denies spiritual liberty. That is, it abolishes the laws which could be broken, and substitutes laws that cannot. And that is the real slavery.

The truth is that the scientific civilization in which Mr. McCabe believes has one rather particular defect; it is perpetually tending to destroy that democracy or power of the ordinary man in which Mr. McCabe also believes. Science means specialism, and specialism means oligarchy. If you once establish the habit of trusting particular men to produce particular results in physics or astronomy, you leave the door open for the equally natural demand that you should trust particular men to do particular things in government and the coercing of men. If, you feel it to be reasonable that one beetle should be the only study of one man, and that one man the only student of that one beetle, it is surely a very harmless consequence to go on to say that politics should be the only study of one man, and that one man the only student of politics. As I have pointed out elsewhere in this book, the expert is more aristocratic than the aristocrat, because the aristocrat is only the man who lives well, while the expert is the man who knows better. But if we look at the progress of our scientific civilization we see a gradual increase everywhere of the specialist over the popular function. Once men sang together round a table in chorus; now one man sings alone, for the absurd reason that he can sing better. If scientific civilization goes on (which is most improbable) only one man will laugh, because he can laugh better than the rest.

I do not know that I can express this more shortly than by taking as a text the single sentence of Mr. McCabe, which runs as follows: "The ballets of the Alhambra and the fireworks of the Crystal Palace and Mr. Chesterton's Daily News articles have their places in life." I wish that my articles had as noble a place as either of the other two things mentioned. But let us ask ourselves (in a spirit of love, as Mr. Chadband would say), what are the ballets of the Alhambra? The ballets of the Alhambra are institutions in which a particular selected row of persons in pink go through an operation known as dancing. Now, in all commonwealths dominated by a religion—in the Christian commonwealths of the Middle Ages and in many rude societies—this habit of dancing was a common habit with everybody, and was not necessarily confined to a professional class. A person could dance without being a dancer; a person could dance without being a specialist; a person could dance without being pink. And, in proportion as Mr. McCabe's scientific civilization advances—that is, in proportion as religious civilization (or real civilization) decays—the more and more "well trained," the more and more pink, become the people who do dance, and the more and more numerous become the people who don't. Mr. McCabe may recognize an example of what I mean in the gradual discrediting in society of the ancient European waltz or dance with partners, and the substitution of that horrible and degrading oriental interlude which is known as skirt-dancing. That is the whole essence of decadence, the effacement of five people who do a thing for fun by one person who does it for money. Now it follows, therefore, that when Mr. McCabe says that the ballets of the Alhambra and my articles "have their place in life," it ought to be pointed out to him that he is doing his best to create a world in which dancing, properly speaking, will have no place in life at all. He is, indeed, trying to create a world in which there will be no life for dancing to have a place in. The very fact that Mr. McCabe thinks of dancing as a thing belonging to some hired women at the Alhambra is an illustration of the same principle by which he is able to think of religion as a thing belonging to some hired men in white neckties. Both these things are things which should not be done for us, but by us. If Mr. McCabe were really religious he would be happy. If he were really happy he would dance.

Briefly, we may put the matter in this way. The main point of modern life is not that the Alhambra ballet has its place in life. The main point, the main enormous tragedy of modern life, is that Mr. McCabe has not his place in the Alhambra ballet. The joy of changing and graceful posture, the joy of suiting the swing of music to the swing of limbs, the joy of whirling drapery, the joy of standing on one leg,—all these should belong by rights to Mr. McCabe and to me; in short, to the ordinary healthy citizen. Probably we should not consent to go through these evolutions. But that is because we are miserable moderns and rationalists. We do not merely love ourselves more than we love duty; we actually love ourselves more than we love joy.

When, therefore, Mr. McCabe says that he gives the Alhambra dances (and my articles) their place in life, I think we are justified in pointing out that by the very nature of the case of his philosophy and of his favourite civilization he gives them a very inadequate place. For (if I may pursue the too flattering parallel) Mr. McCabe thinks of the Alhambra and of my articles as two very odd and absurd things, which some special people do (probably for money) in order to amuse him. But if he had ever felt himself the ancient, sublime, elemental, human instinct to dance, he would have discovered that dancing is not a frivolous thing at all, but a very serious thing. He would have discovered that it is the one grave and chaste and decent method of expressing a certain class of emotions. And similarly, if he had ever had, as Mr. Shaw and I have had, the impulse to what he calls paradox, he would have discovered that paradox again is not a frivolous thing, but a very serious thing. He would have found that paradox simply means a certain defiant joy which belongs to belief. I should regard any civilization which was without a universal habit of uproarious dancing as being, from the full human point of view, a defective civilization. And I should regard any mind which had not got the habit in one form or another of uproarious thinking as being, from the full human point of view, a defective mind. It is vain for Mr. McCabe to say that a ballet is a part of him. He should be part of a ballet, or else he is only part of a man. It is in vain for him to say that he is "not quarrelling with the importation of humour into the controversy." He ought himself to be importing humour into every controversy; for unless a man is in part a humorist, he is only in part a man. To sum up the whole matter very simply, if Mr. McCabe asks me why I import frivolity into a discussion of the nature of man, I answer, because frivolity is a part of the nature of man. If he asks me why I introduce what he calls paradoxes into a philosophical problem, I answer, because all philosophical problems tend to become paradoxical. If he objects to my treating of life riotously, I reply that life is a riot. And I say that the Universe as I see it, at any rate, is very much more like the fireworks at the Crystal Palace than it is like his own philosophy. About the whole cosmos there is a tense and secret festivity—like preparations for Guy Fawkes' day. Eternity is the eve of something. I never look up at the stars without feeling that they are the fires of a schoolboy's rocket, fixed in their everlasting fall.

ON THE WIT OF WHISTLER

That capable and ingenious writer, Mr. Arthur Symons, has included in a book of essays recently published, I believe, an apologia for "London Nights," in which he says that morality should be wholly subordinated to art in criticism, and he uses the somewhat singular argument that art or the worship of beauty is the same in all ages, while morality differs in every period and in every respect. He appears to defy his critics or his readers to mention any permanent feature or quality in ethics. This is surely a very curious example of that extravagant bias against morality which makes so many ultra-modern aesthetes as morbid and fanatical as any Eastern hermit. Unquestionably it is a very common phrase of modern intellectualism to say that the morality of one age can be entirely different to the morality of another. And like a great many other phrases of modern intellectualism, it means literally nothing at all. If the two moralities are entirely different, why do you call them both moralities? It is as if a man said, "Camels in various places are totally diverse; some have six legs, some have none, some have scales, some have feathers, some have horns, some have wings, some are green, some are triangular. There is no point which they have in common." The ordinary man of sense would reply, "Then what makes you call them all camels? What do you mean by a camel? How do you know a camel when you see one?" Of course, there is a permanent substance of morality, as much as there is a permanent substance of art; to say that is only to say that morality is morality, and that art is art. An ideal art critic would, no doubt, see the enduring beauty under every school; equally an ideal moralist would see the enduring ethic under every code. But practically some of the best Englishmen that ever lived could see nothing but filth and idolatry in the starry piety of the Brahmin. And it is equally true that practically the greatest group of artists that the world has ever seen, the giants of the Renaissance, could see nothing but barbarism in the ethereal energy of Gothic.

This bias against morality among the modern aesthetes is nothing very much paraded. And yet it is not really a bias against morality; it is a bias against other people's morality. It is generally founded on a very definite moral preference for a certain sort of life, pagan, plausible, humane. The modern aesthete, wishing us to believe that he values beauty more than conduct, reads Mallarme, and drinks absinthe in a tavern. But this is not only his favourite kind of beauty; it is also his favourite kind of conduct. If he really wished us to believe that he cared for beauty only, he ought to go to nothing but Wesleyan school treats, and paint the sunlight in the hair of the Wesleyan babies. He ought to read nothing but very eloquent theological sermons by old-fashioned Presbyterian divines. Here the lack of all possible moral sympathy would prove that his interest was purely verbal or pictorial, as it is; in all the books he reads and writes he clings to the skirts of his own morality and his own immorality. The champion of l'art pour l'art is always denouncing Ruskin for his moralizing. If he were really a champion of l'art pour l'art, he would be always insisting on Ruskin for his style.

The doctrine of the distinction between art and morality owes a great part of its success to art and morality being hopelessly mixed up in the persons and performances of its greatest exponents. Of this lucky contradiction the very incarnation was Whistler. No man ever preached the impersonality of art so well; no man ever preached the impersonality of art so personally. For him pictures had nothing to do with the problems of character; but for all his fiercest admirers his character was, as a matter of fact far more interesting than his pictures. He gloried in standing as an artist apart from right and wrong. But he succeeded by talking from morning till night about his rights and about his wrongs. His talents were many, his virtues, it must be confessed, not many, beyond that kindness to tried friends, on which many of his biographers insist, but which surely is a quality of all sane men, of pirates and pickpockets; beyond this, his outstanding virtues limit themselves chiefly to two admirable ones—courage and an abstract love of good work. Yet I fancy he won at last more by those two virtues than by all his talents. A man must be something of a moralist if he is to preach, even if he is to preach unmorality. Professor Walter Raleigh, in his "In Memoriam: James McNeill Whistler," insists, truly enough, on the strong streak of an eccentric honesty in matters strictly pictorial, which ran through his complex and slightly confused character. "He would destroy any of his works rather than leave a careless or inexpressive touch within the limits of the frame. He would begin again a hundred times over rather than attempt by patching to make his work seem better than it was."

No one will blame Professor Raleigh, who had to read a sort of funeral oration over Whistler at the opening of the Memorial Exhibition, if, finding himself in that position, he confined himself mostly to the merits and the stronger qualities of his subject. We should naturally go to some other type of composition for a proper consideration of the weaknesses of Whistler. But these must never be omitted from our view of him. Indeed, the truth is that it was not so much a question of the weaknesses of Whistler as of the intrinsic and primary weakness of Whistler. He was one of those people who live up to their emotional incomes, who are always taut and tingling with vanity. Hence he had no strength to spare; hence he had no kindness, no geniality; for geniality is almost definable as strength to spare. He had no god-like carelessness; he never forgot himself; his whole life was, to use his own expression, an arrangement. He went in for "the art of living"—a miserable trick. In a word, he was a great artist; but emphatically not a great man. In this connection I must differ strongly with Professor Raleigh upon what is, from a superficial literary point of view, one of his most effective points. He compares Whistler's laughter to the laughter of another man who was a great man as well as a great artist. "His attitude to the public was exactly the attitude taken up by Robert Browning, who suffered as long a period of neglect and mistake, in those lines of 'The Ring and the Book'—

> "'Well, British Public, ye who like me not,
> (God love you!) and will have your proper laugh
> At the dark question; laugh it! I'd laugh first.'

"Mr. Whistler," adds Professor Raleigh, "always laughed first." The truth is, I believe, that Whistler never laughed at all. There was no laughter in his nature; because there was no thoughtlessness and self-abandonment, no humility. I cannot understand anybody reading "The Gentle Art of Making Enemies" and thinking that there is any laughter in the wit. His wit is a torture to him. He twists himself into arabesques of verbal felicity; he is full of a fierce carefulness; he is inspired with the complete seriousness of sincere malice. He hurts himself to hurt his opponent. Browning did laugh, because Browning did not care; Browning did not care, because Browning was a great man. And when Browning said in brackets to the simple, sensible people who did not like his books, "God love you!" he was not sneering in the least. He was laughing—that is to say, he meant exactly what he said.

There are three distinct classes of great satirists who arc also great men—that is to say, three classes of men who can laugh at something without losing their souls. The satirist of the first type is the man who, first of all enjoys himself, and then enjoys his enemies. In this sense he loves his enemy, and by a kind of exaggeration of Christianity he loves his enemy the more the more he becomes an enemy. He has a sort of overwhelming and aggressive happiness in his assertion of anger; his curse is as human as a benediction. Of this type of satire the great example is Rabelais. This is the first typical example of satire, the satire which is voluble, which is violent, which is indecent, but which is not malicious. The satire of Whistler was not this. He was never in any of his controversies simply happy; the proof of it is that he never talked absolute nonsense. There is a second type of mind which produces satire with the quality of greatness. That is embodied in the satirist whose passions are released and let go by some intolerable sense of wrong. He is maddened by the sense of men being maddened; his tongue becomes an unruly member, and testifies against all mankind. Such a man was Swift, in whom the saeva indignatio was a bitterness to others, because it was a bitterness to himself. Such a satirist Whistler was not. He did not laugh because he was happy, like Rabelais. But neither did he laugh because he was unhappy, like Swift.

The third type of great satire is that in which he satirist is enabled to rise superior to his victim in the only serious sense which superiority can bear, in that of pitying the sinner and respecting the man even while he satirises both. Such an achievement can be found in a thing like Pope's "Atticus" a poem in which the satirist feels that he is satirising the weaknesses which belong specially to literary genius. Consequently he takes a pleasure in pointing out his enemy's strength before he points out his weakness. That is, perhaps, the highest and most honourable form of satire. That is not the satire of Whistler. He is not full of a great sorrow for the wrong done to human nature; for him the wrong is altogether done to himself.

He was not a great personality, because he thought so much about himself. And the case is stronger even than that. He was sometimes not even a great artist, because he thought so much about art. Any man with a vital knowledge of the human psychology ought to have the most profound suspicion of anybody who claims to be an artist, and talks a great deal about art. Art is a right and human thing, like walking or saying one's prayers; but the moment it begins to be talked about very solemnly, a man may be fairly certain that the thing has come into a congestion and a kind of difficulty.

The artistic temperament is a disease that afflicts amateurs. It is a disease which arises from men not having sufficient power of expression to utter and get rid of the element of art in their being. It is healthful to every sane man to utter the art within him; it is essential to every sane man to get rid of the art within him at all costs. Artists of a large and wholesome vitality get rid of their art easily, as they breathe easily, or perspire easily. But in artists of less force, the thing becomes a pressure, and produces a definite pain, which is called the artistic temperament. Thus, very great artists are able to be ordinary men—men like Shakespeare or Browning. There are many real tragedies of the artistic temperament, tragedies of vanity or violence or fear. But the great tragedy of the artistic temperament is that it cannot produce any art.

Whistler could produce art; and in so far he was a great man. But he could not forget art; and in so far he was only a man with the artistic temperament. There can be no stronger manifestation of the man who is a really great artist than the fact that he can dismiss the subject of art; that he can, upon due occasion, wish art at the bottom of the sea. Similarly, we should always be much more inclined to trust a solicitor who did not talk about conveyancing over the nuts and wine. What we really desire of any man conducting any business is that the full force of an ordinary man should be put into that particular study. We do not desire that the full force of that study should be put into an ordinary man. We do not in the least wish that our particular law-suit should pour its energy into our barrister's games with his children, or rides on his bicycle, or meditations on the morning star. But we do, as a matter of fact, desire that his games with his children, and his rides on his bicycle, and his meditations on the morning star should pour something of their energy into our law-suit. We do desire that if he has gained any especial lung development from the bicycle, or any bright and pleasing metaphors from the morning star, that the should be placed at our disposal in that particular forensic controversy. In a word, we are very glad that he is an ordinary man, since that may help him to be an exceptional lawyer.

Whistler never ceased to be an artist. As Mr. Max Beerbohm pointed out in one of his extraordinarily sensible and sincere critiques, Whistler really regarded Whistler as his greatest work of art. The white lock, the single eyeglass, the remarkable hat—these were much dearer to him than any nocturnes or arrangements that he ever threw off. He could throw off the nocturnes; for some mysterious reason he could not throw off the hat. He never threw off from himself that disproportionate accumulation of aestheticism which is the burden of the amateur.

It need hardly be said that this is the real explanation of the thing which has puzzled so many dilettante critics, the problem of the extreme ordinariness of the behaviour of so many great geniuses in history. Their behaviour was so ordinary that it was not recorded; hence it was so ordinary that it seemed mysterious. Hence people say that Bacon wrote Shakespeare. The modern artistic temperament cannot understand how a man who could write such lyrics as Shakespeare wrote, could be as keen as Shakespeare was on business transactions in a little town in Warwickshire. The explanation is simple enough; it is that Shakespeare had a real lyrical impulse, wrote a real lyric, and so got rid of the impulse and went about his business. Being an artist did not prevent him from being an ordinary man, any more than being a sleeper at night or being a diner at dinner prevented him from being an ordinary man.

All very great teachers and leaders have had this habit of assuming their point of view to be one which was human and casual, one which would readily appeal to every passing man. If a man is genuinely superior to his fellows the first thing that he believes in is the equality of man. We can see this, for instance, in that strange and innocent rationality with which Christ addressed any motley crowd that happened to stand about Him. "What man of you having a hundred sheep, and losing one, would not leave the ninety and nine in the wilderness, and go after that which was lost?" Or, again, "What man of you if his son ask for bread will he give him a stone, or if he ask for a fish will he give him a serpent?" This plainness, this almost prosaic camaraderie, is the note of all very great minds.

To very great minds the things on which men agree are so immeasurably more important than the things on which they differ, that the latter, for all practical purposes, disappear. They have too much in them of an ancient laughter even to endure to discuss the difference between the hats of two men who were both born of a woman, or between the subtly varied cultures of two men who have both to die. The first-rate great man is equal with other men, like Shakespeare. The second-rate great man is on his knees to other men, like Whitman. The third-rate great man is superior to other men, like Whistler.

THE FALLACY OF THE YOUNG NATION

To say that a man is an idealist is merely to say that he is a man; but, nevertheless, it might be possible to effect some valid distinction between one kind of idealist and another. One possible distinction, for instance, could be effected by saying that humanity is divided into conscious idealists and unconscious idealists. In a similar way, humanity is divided into conscious ritualists and unconscious ritualists. The curious thing is, in that example as in others, that it is the conscious ritualism which is comparatively simple, the unconscious ritual which is really heavy and complicated. The ritual which is comparatively rude and straightforward is the ritual which people call "ritualistic." It consists of plain things like bread and wine and fire, and men falling on their faces. But the ritual which is really complex, and many coloured, and elaborate, and needlessly formal, is the ritual which people enact without knowing it. It consists not of plain things like wine and fire, but of really peculiar, and local, and exceptional, and ingenious things—things like door-mats, and door-knockers, and electric bells, and silk hats, and white ties, and shiny cards, and confetti. The truth is that the modern man scarcely ever gets back to very old and simple things except when he is performing some religious mummery. The modern man can hardly get away from ritual except by entering a ritualistic church. In the case of these old and mystical formalities we can at least say that the ritual is not mere ritual; that the symbols employed are in most cases symbols which belong to a primary human poetry. The most ferocious opponent of the Christian ceremonials must admit that if Catholicism had not instituted the bread and wine, somebody else would most probably have done so. Any one with a poetical instinct will admit that to the ordinary human instinct bread symbolizes something which cannot very easily be symbolized otherwise; that wine, to the ordinary human instinct, symbolizes something which cannot very easily be symbolized otherwise. But white ties in the evening are ritual, and nothing else but ritual. No one would pretend that white ties in the evening are primary and poetical. Nobody would maintain that the ordinary human instinct would in any age or country tend to symbolize the idea of evening by a white necktie. Rather, the ordinary human instinct would, I imagine, tend to symbolize evening by cravats with some of the colours of the sunset, not white neckties, but tawny or crimson neckties—neckties of purple or olive, or some darkened gold. Mr. J. A. Kensit, for example, is under the impression that he is not a ritualist. But the daily life of Mr. J. A. Kensit, like that of any ordinary modern man, is, as a matter of fact, one continual and compressed catalogue of mystical mummery and flummery.

To take one instance out of an inevitable hundred: I imagine that Mr. Kensit takes off his hat to a lady; and what can be more solemn and absurd, considered in the abstract, than, symbolizing the existence of the other sex by taking off a portion of your clothing and waving it in the air? This, I repeat, is not a natural and primitive symbol, like fire or food. A man might just as well have to take off his waistcoat to a lady; and if a man, by the social ritual of his civilization, had to take off his waistcoat to a lady, every chivalrous and sensible man would take off his waistcoat to a lady. In short, Mr. Kensit, and those who agree with him, may think, and quite sincerely think, that men give too much incense and ceremonial to their adoration of the other world. But nobody thinks that he can give too much incense and ceremonial to the adoration of this world. All men, then, are ritualists, but are either conscious or unconscious ritualists. The conscious ritualists are generally satisfied with a few very simple and elementary signs; the unconscious ritualists are not satisfied with anything short of the whole of human life, being almost insanely ritualistic. The first is called a ritualist because he invents and remembers one rite; the other is called an anti-ritualist because he obeys and forgets a thousand. And a somewhat similar distinction to this which I have drawn with some unavoidable length, between the conscious ritualist and the unconscious ritualist, exists between the conscious idealist and the unconscious idealist. It is idle to inveigh against cynics and materialists—there are no cynics, there are no materialists. Every man is idealistic; only it so often happens that he has the wrong ideal. Every man is incurably sentimental; but, unfortunately, it is so often a false sentiment. When we talk, for instance, of some unscrupulous commercial figure, and say that he would do anything for money, we use quite an inaccurate expression, and we slander him very much. He would not do anything for money. He would do some things for money; he would sell his soul for money, for instance; and, as Mirabeau humorously said, he would be quite wise "to take money for muck." He would oppress humanity for money; but then it happens that humanity and the soul are not things that he believes in; they are not his ideals. But he has his own dim and delicate ideals; and he would not violate these for money. He would not drink out of the soup-tureen, for money. He would not wear his coat-tails in front, for money. He would not spread a report that he had softening of the brain, for money. In the actual practice of life we find, in the matter of ideals, exactly what we have already found in the matter of ritual. We find that while there is a perfectly genuine danger of fanaticism from the men who have unworldly ideals, the permanent and urgent danger of fanaticism is from the men who have worldly ideals.

People who say that an ideal is a dangerous thing, that it deludes and intoxicates, are perfectly right. But the ideal which intoxicates most is the least idealistic kind of ideal. The ideal which intoxicates least is the very ideal ideal; that sobers us suddenly, as all heights and precipices and great distances do. Granted that it is a great evil to mistake a cloud for a cape; still, the cloud, which can be most easily mistaken for a cape, is the cloud that is nearest the earth. Similarly, we may grant that it may be dangerous to mistake an ideal for something practical. But we shall still point out that, in this respect, the most dangerous ideal of all is the ideal which looks a little practical. It is difficult to attain a high ideal; consequently, it is almost impossible to persuade ourselves that we have attained it. But it is easy to attain a low ideal; consequently, it is easier still to persuade ourselves that we have attained it when we have done nothing of the kind. To take a random example. It might be called a high ambition to wish to be an archangel; the man who entertained such an ideal would very possibly exhibit asceticism, or even frenzy, but not, I think, delusion. He would not think he was an archangel, and go about flapping his hands under the impression that they were wings. But suppose that a sane man had a low ideal; suppose he wished to be a gentleman. Any one who knows the world knows that in nine weeks he would have persuaded himself that he was a gentleman; and this being manifestly not the case, the result will be very real and practical dislocations and calamities in social life. It is not the wild ideals which wreck the practical world; it is the tame ideals.

The matter may, perhaps, be illustrated by a parallel from our modern politics. When men tell us that the old Liberal politicians of the type of Gladstone cared only for ideals, of course, they are talking nonsense—they cared for a great many other things, including votes. And when men tell us that modern politicians of the type of Mr. Chamberlain or, in another way, Lord Rosebery, care only for votes or for material interest, then again they are talking nonsense—these men care for ideals like all other men. But the real distinction which may be drawn is this, that to the older politician the ideal was an ideal, and nothing else. To the new politician his dream is not only a good dream, it is a reality. The old politician would have said, "It would be a good thing if there were a Republican Federation dominating the world." But the modern politician does not say, "It would be a good thing if there were a British Imperialism dominating the world." He says, "It is a good thing that there is a British Imperialism dominating the world;" whereas clearly there is nothing of the kind. The old Liberal would say "There ought to be a good Irish government in Ireland." But the ordinary modern Unionist does not say, "There ought to be a good English government in Ireland." He says, "There is a good English government in Ireland;" which is absurd. In short, the modern politicians seem to think that a man becomes practical merely by making assertions entirely about practical things. Apparently, a delusion does not matter as long as it is a materialistic delusion. Instinctively most of us feel that, as a practical matter, even the contrary is true. I certainly would much rather share my apartments with a gentleman who thought he was God than with a gentleman who thought he was a grasshopper. To be continually haunted by practical images and practical problems, to be constantly thinking of things as actual, as urgent, as in process of completion—these things do not prove a man to be practical; these things, indeed, are among the most ordinary signs of a lunatic. That our modern statesmen are materialistic is nothing against their being also morbid. Seeing angels in a vision may make a man a supernaturalist to excess. But merely seeing snakes in delirium tremens does not make him a naturalist.

And when we come actually to examine the main stock notions of our modern practical politicians, we find that those main stock notions are mainly delusions. A great many instances might be given of the fact. We might take, for example, the case of that strange class of notions which underlie the word "union," and all the eulogies heaped upon it. Of course, union is no more a good thing in itself than separation is a good thing in itself. To have a party in favour of union and a party in favour of separation is as absurd as to have a party in favour of going upstairs and a party in favour of going downstairs. The question is not whether we go up or down stairs, but where we are going to, and what we are going, for? Union is strength; union is also weakness. It is a good thing to harness two horses to a cart; but it is not a good thing to try and turn two hansom cabs into one four-wheeler. Turning ten nations into one empire may happen to be as feasible as turning ten shillings into one half-sovereign. Also it may happen to be as preposterous as turning ten terriers into one mastiff. The question in all cases is not a question of union or absence of union, but of identity or absence of identity. Owing to certain historical and moral causes, two nations may be so united as upon the whole to help each other. Thus England and Scotland pass their time in paying each other compliments; but their energies and atmospheres run distinct and parallel, and consequently do not clash. Scotland continues to be educated and Calvinistic; England continues to be uneducated and happy. But owing to certain other Moral and certain other political causes, two nations may be so united as only to hamper each other; their lines do clash and do not run parallel. Thus, for instance, England and Ireland are so united that the Irish can sometimes rule England, but can never rule Ireland. The educational systems, including the last Education Act, are here, as in the case of Scotland, a very good test of the matter. The overwhelming majority of Irishmen believe in a strict Catholicism; the overwhelming majority of Englishmen believe in a vague Protestantism. The Irish party in the Parliament of Union is just large enough to prevent the English education being indefinitely Protestant, and just small enough to prevent the Irish education being definitely Catholic. Here we have a state of things which no man in his senses would ever dream of wishing to continue if he had not been bewitched by the sentimentalism of the mere word "union."

This example of union, however, is not the example which I propose to take of the ingrained futility and deception underlying all the assumptions of the modern practical politician. I wish to speak especially of another and much more general delusion. It pervades the minds and speeches of all the practical men of all parties; and it is a childish blunder built upon a single false metaphor. I refer to the universal modern talk about young nations and new nations; about America being young, about New Zealand being new. The whole thing is a trick of words. America is not young, New Zealand is not new. It is a very discussable question whether they are not both much older than England or Ireland.

Of course we may use the metaphor of youth about America or the colonies, if we use it strictly as implying only a recent origin. But if we use it (as we do use it) as implying vigour, or vivacity, or crudity, or inexperience, or hope, or a long life before them or any of the romantic attributes of youth, then it is surely as clear as daylight that we are duped by a stale figure of speech. We can easily see the matter clearly by applying it to any other institution parallel to the institution of an independent nationality. If a club called "The Milk and Soda League" (let us say) was set up yesterday, as I have no doubt it was, then, of course, "The Milk and Soda League" is a young club in the sense that it was set up yesterday, but in no other sense. It may consist entirely of moribund old gentlemen. It may be moribund itself. We may call it a young club, in the light of the fact that it was founded yesterday. We may also call it a very old club in the light of the fact that it will most probably go bankrupt to-morrow. All this appears very obvious when we put it in this form. Any one who adopted the young-community delusion with regard to a bank or a butcher's shop would be sent to an asylum. But the whole modern political notion that America and the colonies must be very vigorous because they are very new, rests upon no better foundation. That America was founded long after England does not make it even in the faintest degree more probable that America will not perish a long time before England. That England existed before her colonies does not make it any the less likely that she will exist after her colonies. And when we look at the actual history of the world, we find that great European nations almost invariably have survived the vitality of their colonies. When we look at the actual history of the world, we find, that if there is a thing that is born old and dies young, it is a colony. The Greek colonies went to pieces long before the Greek civilization. The Spanish colonies have gone to pieces long before the nation of Spain—nor does there seem to be any reason to doubt the possibility or even the probability of the conclusion that the colonial civilization, which owes its origin to England, will be much briefer and much less vigorous than the civilization of England itself. The English nation will still be going the way of all

European nations when the Anglo-Saxon race has gone the way of all fads. Now, of course, the interesting question is, have we, in the case of America and the colonies, any real evidence of a moral and intellectual youth as opposed to the indisputable triviality of a merely chronological youth? Consciously or unconsciously, we know that we have no such evidence, and consciously or unconsciously, therefore, we proceed to make it up. Of this pure and placid invention, a good example, for instance, can be found in a recent poem of Mr. Rudyard Kipling's. Speaking of the English people and the South African War Mr. Kipling says that "we fawned on the younger nations for the men that could shoot and ride." Some people considered this sentence insulting. All that I am concerned with at present is the evident fact that it is not true. The colonies provided very useful volunteer troops, but they did not provide the best troops, nor achieve the most successful exploits. The best work in the war on the English side was done, as might have been expected, by the best English regiments. The men who could shoot and ride were not the enthusiastic corn merchants from Melbourne, any more than they were the enthusiastic clerks from Cheapside. The men who could shoot and ride were the men who had been taught to shoot and ride in the discipline of the standing army of a great European power. Of course, the colonials are as brave and athletic as any other average white men. Of course, they acquitted themselves with reasonable credit. All I have here to indicate is that, for the purposes of this theory of the new nation, it is necessary to maintain that the colonial forces were more useful or more heroic than the gunners at Colenso or the Fighting Fifth. And of this contention there is not, and never has been, one stick or straw of evidence.

A similar attempt is made, and with even less success, to represent the literature of the colonies as something fresh and vigorous and important. The imperialist magazines are constantly springing upon us some genius from Queensland or Canada, through whom we are expected to smell the odours of the bush or the prairie. As a matter of fact, any one who is even slightly interested in literature as such (and I, for one, confess that I am only slightly interested in literature as such), will freely admit that the stories of these geniuses smell of nothing but printer's ink, and that not of first-rate quality. By a great effort of Imperial imagination the generous English people reads into these works a force and a novelty. But the force and the novelty are not in the new writers; the force and the novelty are in the ancient heart of the English. Anybody who studies them impartially will know that the first-rate writers of the colonies are not even particularly novel in their note and atmosphere, are not only not producing a new kind of good literature, but are not even in any particular sense producing a new kind of bad literature. The first-rate writers of the new countries are really almost exactly like the second-rate writers of the old countries. Of course they do feel the mystery of the wilderness, the mystery of the bush, for all simple and honest men feel this in Melbourne, or Margate, or South St. Pancras. But when they write most sincerely and most successfully, it is not with a background of the mystery of the bush, but with a background, expressed or assumed, of our own romantic cockney civilization. What really moves their souls with a kindly terror is not the mystery of the wilderness, but the Mystery of a Hansom Cab.

Of course there are some exceptions to this generalization. The one really arresting exception is Olive Schreiner, and she is quite as certainly an exception that proves the rule. Olive Schreiner is a fierce, brilliant, and realistic novelist; but she is all this precisely because she is not English at all. Her tribal kinship is with the country of Teniers and Maarten Maartens— that is, with a country of realists. Her literary kinship is with the pessimistic fiction of the continent; with the novelists whose very pity is cruel. Olive Schreiner is the one English colonial who is not conventional, for the simple reason that South Africa is the one English colony which is not English, and probably never will be. And, of course, there are individual exceptions in a minor way. I remember in particular some Australian tales by Mr. McIlwain which were really able and effective, and which, for that reason, I suppose, are not presented to the public with blasts of a trumpet. But my general contention if put before any one with a love of letters, will not be disputed if it is understood. It is not the truth that the colonial civilization as a whole is giving us, or shows any signs of giving us, a literature which will startle and renovate our own. It may be a very good thing for us to have an affectionate illusion in the matter; that is quite another affair. The colonies may have given England a new emotion; I only say that they have not given the world a new book.

Touching these English colonies, I do not wish to be misunderstood. I do not say of them or of America that they have not a future, or that they will not be great nations. I merely deny the whole established modern expression about them. I deny that they are "destined" to a future. I deny that they are "destined" to be great nations. I deny (of course) that any human thing is destined to be anything. All the absurd physical metaphors, such as youth and age, living and dying, are, when applied to nations, but pseudo-scientific attempts to conceal from men the awful liberty of their lonely souls.

In the case of America, indeed, a warning to this effect is instant and essential. America, of course, like every other human thing, can in spiritual sense live or die as much as it chooses. But at the present moment the matter which America has very seriously to consider is not how near it is to its birth and beginning, but how near it may be to its end. It is only a verbal question whether the American civilization is young; it may become a very practical and urgent question whether it is dying. When once we have cast aside, as we inevitably have after a moment's thought, the fanciful physical metaphor involved in the word "youth," what serious evidence have we that America is a fresh force and not a stale one? It has a great many people, like China; it has a great deal of money, like defeated Carthage or dying Venice. It is full of bustle and excitability, like Athens after its ruin, and all the Greek cities in their decline. It is fond of new things; but the old are always fond of new things. Young men read chronicles, but old men read newspapers. It admires strength and good looks; it admires a big and barbaric beauty in its women, for instance; but so did Rome when the Goth was at the gates. All these are things quite compatible with fundamental tedium and decay. There are three main shapes or symbols in which a nation can show itself essentially glad and great—by the heroic in government, by the heroic in arms, and by the heroic in art. Beyond government, which is, as it were, the very shape and body of a nation, the most significant thing about any citizen is his artistic attitude towards a holiday and his moral attitude towards a fight—that is, his way of accepting life and his way of accepting death.

Subjected to these eternal tests, America does not appear by any means as particularly fresh or untouched. She appears with all the weakness and weariness of modern England or of any other Western power. In her politics she has broken up exactly as England has broken up, into a bewildering opportunism and insincerity. In the matter of war and the national attitude towards war, her resemblance to England is even more manifest and melancholy. It may be said with rough accuracy that there are three stages in the life of a strong people. First, it is a small power, and fights small powers. Then it is a great power, and fights great powers. Then it is a great power, and fights small powers, but pretends that they are great powers, in order to rekindle the ashes of its ancient emotion and vanity. After that, the next step is to become a small power itself. England exhibited this symptom of decadence very badly in the war with the Transvaal; but America exhibited it worse in the war with Spain. There was exhibited more sharply and absurdly than anywhere else the ironic contrast between the very careless choice of a strong line and the very careful choice of a weak enemy. America added to all her other late Roman or Byzantine elements the element of the Caracallan triumph, the triumph over nobody.

But when we come to the last test of nationality, the test of art and letters, the case is almost terrible. The English colonies have produced no great artists; and that fact may prove that they are still full of silent possibilities and reserve force. But America has produced great artists. And that fact most certainly proves that she is full of a fine futility and the end of all things. Whatever the American men of genius are, they are not young gods making a young world. Is the art of Whistler a brave, barbaric art, happy and headlong? Does Mr. Henry James infect us with the spirit of a schoolboy? No; the colonies have not spoken, and they are safe. Their silence may be the silence of the unborn. But out of America has come a sweet and startling cry, as unmistakable as the cry of a dying man.

SLUM NOVELISTS AND THE SLUMS

Odd ideas are entertained in our time about the real nature of the doctrine of human fraternity. The real doctrine is something which we do not, with all our modern humanitarianism, very clearly understand, much less very closely practise. There is nothing, for instance, particularly undemocratic about kicking your butler downstairs. It may be wrong, but it is not unfraternal. In a certain sense, the blow or kick may be considered as a confession of equality: you are meeting your butler body to body; you are almost according him the privilege of the duel. There is nothing, undemocratic, though there may be something unreasonable, in expecting a great deal from the butler, and being filled with a kind of frenzy of surprise when he falls short of the divine stature. The thing which is really undemocratic and unfraternal is not to expect the butler to be more or less divine. The thing which is really undemocratic and unfraternal is to say, as so many modern humanitarians say, "Of course one must make allowances for those on a lower plane." All things considered indeed, it may be said, without undue exaggeration, that the really undemocratic and unfraternal thing is the common practice of not kicking the butler downstairs.

It is only because such a vast section of the modern world is out of sympathy with the serious democratic sentiment that this statement will seem to many to be lacking in seriousness. Democracy is not philanthropy; it is not even altruism or social reform. Democracy is not founded on pity for the common man; democracy is founded on reverence for the common man, or, if you will, even on fear of him. It does not champion man because man is so miserable, but because man is so sublime. It does not object so much to the ordinary man being a slave as to his not being a king, for its dream is always the dream of the first Roman republic, a nation of kings.

Next to a genuine republic, the most democratic thing in the world is a hereditary despotism. I mean a despotism in which there is absolutely no trace whatever of any nonsense about intellect or special fitness for the post. Rational despotism—that is, selective despotism—is always a curse to mankind, because with that you have the ordinary man misunderstood and misgoverned by some prig who has no brotherly respect for him at all. But irrational despotism is always democratic, because it is the ordinary man enthroned. The worst form of slavery is that which is called Caesarism, or the choice of some bold or brilliant man as despot because he is suitable. For that means that men choose a representative, not because he represents them, but because he does not. Men trust an ordinary man like George III or William IV. because they are themselves ordinary men and understand him. Men trust an ordinary man because they trust themselves. But men

113

trust a great man because they do not trust themselves. And hence the worship of great men always appears in times of weakness and cowardice; we never hear of great men until the time when all other men are small.

Hereditary despotism is, then, in essence and sentiment democratic because it chooses from mankind at random. If it does not declare that every man may rule, it declares the next most democratic thing; it declares that any man may rule. Hereditary aristocracy is a far worse and more dangerous thing, because the numbers and multiplicity of an aristocracy make it sometimes possible for it to figure as an aristocracy of intellect. Some of its members will presumably have brains, and thus they, at any rate, will be an intellectual aristocracy within the social one. They will rule the aristocracy by virtue of their intellect, and they will rule the country by virtue of their aristocracy. Thus a double falsity will be set up, and millions of the images of God, who, fortunately for their wives and families, are neither gentlemen nor clever men, will be represented by a man like Mr. Balfour or Mr. Wyndham, because he is too gentlemanly to be called merely clever, and just too clever to be called merely a gentleman. But even an hereditary aristocracy may exhibit, by a sort of accident, from time to time some of the basically democratic quality which belongs to a hereditary despotism. It is amusing to think how much conservative ingenuity has been wasted in the defence of the House of Lords by men who were desperately endeavouring to prove that the House of Lords consisted of clever men. There is one really good defence of the House of Lords, though admirers of the peerage are strangely coy about using it; and that is, that the House of Lords, in its full and proper strength, consists of stupid men. It really would be a plausible defence of that otherwise indefensible body to point out that the clever men in the Commons, who owed their power to cleverness, ought in the last resort to be checked by the average man in the Lords, who owed their power to accident. Of course, there would be many answers to such a contention, as, for instance, that the House of Lords is largely no longer a House of Lords, but a House of tradesmen and financiers, or that the bulk of the commonplace nobility do not vote, and so leave the chamber to the prigs and the specialists and the mad old gentlemen with hobbies. But on some occasions the House of Lords, even under all these disadvantages, is in some sense representative. When all the peers flocked together to vote against Mr. Gladstone's second Home Rule Bill, for instance, those who said that the peers represented the English people, were perfectly right. All those dear old men who happened to be born peers were at that moment, and upon that question, the precise counterpart of all the dear old men who happened to be born paupers or middle-class gentlemen. That mob of peers did really represent the English people—that is to say, it was honest, ignorant, vaguely excited, almost unanimous, and obviously wrong. Of course, rational democracy is better as an expression of the public will than the haphazard hereditary method. While we are about having any kind of democracy, let it be rational democracy. But if we are to have any kind of oligarchy, let it be irrational oligarchy. Then at least we shall be ruled by men.

But the thing which is really required for the proper working of democracy is not merely the democratic system, or even the democratic philosophy, but the democratic emotion. The democratic emotion, like most elementary and indispensable things, is a thing difficult to describe at any time. But it is peculiarly difficult to describe it in our enlightened age, for the simple reason that it is peculiarly difficult to find it. It is a certain instinctive attitude which feels the things in which all men agree to be unspeakably important, and all the things in which they differ (such as mere brains) to be almost unspeakably unimportant. The nearest approach to it in our ordinary life would be the promptitude with which we should consider mere humanity in any circumstance of shock or death. We should say, after a somewhat disturbing discovery, "There is a dead man under the sofa." We should not be likely to say, "There is a dead man of considerable personal refinement under the sofa." We should say, "A woman has fallen into the water." We should not say, "A highly educated woman has fallen into the water." Nobody would say, "There are the remains of a clear thinker in your back garden." Nobody would say, "Unless you hurry up and stop him, a man with a very fine ear for music will have jumped off that cliff." But this emotion, which all of us have in connection with such things as birth and death, is to some people native and constant at all ordinary times and in all ordinary places. It was native to St. Francis of Assisi. It was native to Walt Whitman. In this strange and splendid degree it cannot be expected, perhaps, to pervade a whole commonwealth or a whole civilization; but one commonwealth may have it much more than another commonwealth, one civilization much more than another civilization. No community, perhaps, ever had it so much as the early Franciscans. No community, perhaps, ever had it so little as ours.

Everything in our age has, when carefully examined, this fundamentally undemocratic quality. In religion and morals we should admit, in the abstract, that the sins of the educated classes were as great as, or perhaps greater than, the sins of the poor and ignorant. But in practice the great difference between the mediaeval ethics and ours is that ours concentrate attention on the sins which are the sins of the ignorant, and practically deny that the sins which are the sins of the educated are sins at all. We are always talking about the sin of intemperate drinking, because it is quite obvious that the poor have it more than the rich. But we are always denying that there is any such thing as the sin of pride, because it would be quite obvious that the rich have it more than the poor. We are always ready to make a saint or prophet of the educated man who goes into cottages to give a little kindly advice to the uneducated. But the medieval idea of a saint or prophet was something quite different. The mediaeval saint or prophet was an uneducated man who walked into grand houses to give a little kindly advice to the educated. The old tyrants had enough insolence to despoil the poor, but they had not enough insolence to preach to them. It was the gentleman who oppressed the slums; but it was the slums that admonished the gentleman. And just as we are undemocratic in faith and morals, so we are, by the very nature of our attitude in such matters, undemocratic in the tone of our practical politics. It is a sufficient proof that we are not an essentially democratic state that we are always wondering what we shall do with the poor. If we were democrats, we should be wondering what the poor will do with us. With us the governing class is always saying to itself, "What laws shall we make?" In a purely democratic state it would be always saying, "What laws can we obey?" A purely democratic state perhaps there has never been. But even the feudal ages were in practice thus far democratic, that every feudal potentate knew that any laws which he made would in all probability return upon himself. His feathers might be cut off for breaking a sumptuary law. His head might be cut off for high treason. But the modern laws are almost always laws made to affect the governed class, but not the governing. We have public-house licensing laws, but not sumptuary laws. That is to say, we have laws against the festivity and hospitality of the poor, but no laws against the festivity and hospitality of the rich. We have laws against blasphemy—that is, against a kind of coarse and offensive speaking in which nobody but a rough and obscure man would be likely to indulge. But we have no laws against heresy—that is, against the intellectual poisoning of the whole people, in which only a prosperous and prominent man would be likely to be successful. The evil of aristocracy is not that it necessarily leads to the infliction of bad things or the suffering of sad ones; the evil of aristocracy is that it places everything in the hands of a class of people who can always inflict what they can never suffer. Whether what they inflict is, in their intention, good or bad, they become equally frivolous. The case against the governing class of modern England is not in the least that it is selfish; if you like, you may call the English oligarchs too fantastically unselfish. The case against them simply is that when they legislate for all men, they always omit themselves.

We are undemocratic, then, in our religion, as is proved by our efforts to "raise" the poor. We are undemocratic in our government, as is proved by our innocent attempt to govern them well. But above all we are undemocratic in our literature, as is proved by the torrent of novels about the poor and serious studies of the poor which pour from our publishers every month. And the more "modern" the book is the more certain it is to be devoid of democratic sentiment.

A poor man is a man who has not got much money. This may seem a simple and unnecessary description, but in the face of a great mass of modern fact and fiction, it seems very necessary indeed; most of our realists and sociologists talk about a poor man as if he were an octopus or an alligator. There is no more need to study the psychology of poverty than to study the psychology of bad temper, or the psychology of vanity, or the psychology of animal spirits. A man ought to know something of the emotions of an insulted man, not by being insulted, but simply by being a man. And he ought to know something of the emotions of a poor man, not by being poor, but simply by being a man. Therefore, in any writer who is describing poverty, my first objection to him will be that he has studied his subject. A democrat would have imagined it.

A great many hard things have been said about religious slumming and political or social slumming, but surely the most despicable of all is artistic slumming. The religious teacher is at least supposed to be interested in the costermonger because he is a man; the politician is in some dim and perverted sense interested in the costermonger because he is a citizen; it is only the wretched writer who is interested in the costermonger merely because he is a costermonger. Nevertheless, so long as he is merely seeking impressions, or in other words copy, his trade, though dull, is honest. But when he endeavours to represent that he is describing the spiritual core of a costermonger, his dim vices and his delicate virtues, then we must object that his claim is preposterous; we must remind him that he is a journalist and nothing else. He has far less psychological authority even than the foolish missionary. For he is in the literal and derivative sense a journalist, while the missionary is an eternalist. The missionary at least pretends to have a version of the man's lot for all time; the journalist only pretends to have a version of it from day to day. The missionary comes to tell the poor man that he is in the same condition with all men. The journalist comes to tell other people how different the poor man is from everybody else.

If the modern novels about the slums, such as novels of Mr. Arthur Morrison, or the exceedingly able novels of Mr. Somerset Maugham, are intended to be sensational, I can only say that that is a noble and reasonable object, and that they attain it. A sensation, a shock to the imagination, like the contact with cold water, is always a good and exhilarating thing; and, undoubtedly, men will always seek this sensation (among other forms) in the form of the study of the strange antics of remote or alien peoples. In the twelfth century men obtained this sensation by reading about dog-headed men in Africa. In the twentieth century they obtained it by reading about pig-headed Boers in Africa. The men of the twentieth century were certainly, it must be admitted, somewhat the more credulous of the two. For it is not recorded of the men in the twelfth century that they organized a sanguinary crusade solely for the purpose of altering the singular formation of the heads of the Africans. But it may be, and it may even legitimately be, that since all these monsters have faded from the popular mythology, it is necessary to have in our fiction the image of the horrible and hairy East-ender, merely to keep alive in us a fearful and childlike wonder at external peculiarities. But the Middle Ages (with a great deal more common sense than it would now be fashionable to admit) regarded natural history at bottom rather as a kind of joke; they regarded the soul as very important. Hence, while they had a natural history of dog-headed men, they did not profess to have a psychology of dog-headed men. They did not profess to mirror the mind of a dog-headed man, to share his tenderest secrets, or mount with his most celestial musings. They did not write novels about the semi-canine creature, attributing to him all the oldest morbidities and all the newest fads. It is permissible to present men as monsters if we wish to make the reader jump; and to make anybody jump is always a Christian act. But it is not permissible to present men as regarding themselves as monsters, or as making themselves jump. To summarize, our slum fiction is quite defensible as aesthetic fiction; it is not defensible as spiritual fact.

One enormous obstacle stands in the way of its actuality. The men who write it, and the men who read it, are men of the middle classes or the upper classes; at least, of those who are loosely termed the educated classes. Hence, the fact that it is the life as the refined man sees it proves that it cannot be the life as the unrefined man lives it. Rich men write stories about poor men, and describe them as speaking with a coarse, or heavy, or husky enunciation. But if poor men wrote novels about you or me they would describe us as speaking with some absurd shrill and affected voice, such as we only hear from a duchess in a three-act farce. The slum novelist gains his whole effect by the fact that some detail is strange to the reader; but that detail by the nature of the case cannot be strange in itself. It cannot be strange to the soul which he is professing to study. The slum novelist gains his effects by describing the same grey mist as draping the dingy factory and the dingy tavern. But to the man he is supposed to be studying there must be exactly the same difference between the factory and the tavern that there is to a middle-class man between a late night at the office and a supper at Pagani's. The slum novelist is content with pointing out that to the eye of his particular class a pickaxe looks dirty and a pewter pot looks dirty. But the man he is supposed to be studying sees the difference between them exactly as a clerk sees the difference between a ledger and an edition de luxe. The chiaroscuro of the life is inevitably lost; for to us the high lights and the shadows are a light grey. But the high lights and the shadows are not a light grey in that life any more than in any other. The kind of man who could really express the pleasures of the poor would be also the kind of man who could share them. In short, these books are not a record of the psychology of poverty. They are a record of the psychology of wealth and culture when brought in contact with poverty. They are not a description of the state of the slums. They are only a very dark and dreadful description of the state of the slummers. One might give innumerable examples of the essentially unsympathetic and unpopular quality of these realistic writers. But perhaps the simplest and most obvious example with which we could conclude is the mere fact that these writers are realistic. The poor have many other vices, but, at least, they are never realistic. The poor are melodramatic and romantic in grain; the poor all believe in high moral platitudes and copy-book maxims; probably this is the ultimate meaning of the great saying, "Blessed are the poor." Blessed are the poor, for they are always making life, or trying to make life like an Adelphi play. Some innocent educationalists and philanthropists (for even philanthropists can be innocent) have expressed a grave astonishment that the masses prefer shilling shockers to scientific treatises and melodramas to problem plays. The reason is very simple. The realistic story is certainly more artistic than the melodramatic story. If what you desire is deft handling, delicate proportions, a unit of artistic atmosphere, the realistic story has a full advantage over the melodrama. In everything that is light and bright and ornamental the realistic story has a full advantage over the melodrama. But, at least, the melodrama has one indisputable advantage over the realistic story. The melodrama is much more like life. It is much more like man, and especially the poor man. It is very banal and very inartistic when a poor woman at the Adelphi says, "Do you think I will sell my own child?" But poor women in the Battersea High Road do say, "Do you think I will sell my own child?" They say it on every available occasion; you can hear a sort of murmur or babble of it all the way down the street. It is very stale and weak dramatic art (if that is all) when the workman confronts his master and says, "I'm a man." But a workman does say "I'm a man" two or three times every day. In fact, it is tedious, possibly, to hear poor men being melodramatic behind the footlights; but that is because one can always hear them being melodramatic in the street outside. In short, melodrama, if it is dull, is dull because it is too accurate. Somewhat the same problem exists in the case of stories about schoolboys. Mr. Kipling's "Stalky and Co." is much more amusing (if you are talking about amusement) than the late Dean Farrar's "Eric; or, Little by Little." But "Eric" is immeasurably more like real school-life. For real school-life, real boyhood, is full of the things of which Eric is full—priggishness, a crude piety, a silly sin, a weak but continual attempt at the heroic, in a word, melodrama. And if we wish to lay a firm basis for any efforts to help the poor, we must not become realistic and see them from the outside. We must become melodramatic, and see them from the inside. The novelist must not take out his notebook and say, "I am an expert." No; he must imitate the workman in the Adelphi play. He must slap himself on the chest and say, "I am a man."

CONCLUDING REMARKS ON THE IMPORTANCE OF ORTHODOXY

Whether the human mind can advance or not, is a question too little discussed, for nothing can be more dangerous than to found our social philosophy on any theory which is debatable but has not been debated. But if we assume, for the sake of argument, that there has been in the past, or will be in the future, such a thing as a growth or improvement of the human mind itself, there still remains a very sharp objection to be raised against the modern version of that improvement. The vice of the modern notion of mental progress is that it is always something concerned with the breaking of bonds, the effacing of boundaries, the casting away of dogmas. But if there be such a thing as mental growth, it must mean the growth into more and more definite convictions, into more and more dogmas. The human brain is a machine for coming to conclusions; if it cannot come to conclusions it is rusty. When we hear of a man too clever to believe, we are hearing of something having almost the character of a contradiction in terms. It is like hearing of a nail that was too good to hold down a carpet; or a bolt that was too strong to keep a door shut. Man can hardly be defined, after the fashion of Carlyle, as an animal who makes tools; ants and beavers and many other animals make tools, in the sense that they make an apparatus. Man can be defined as an animal that makes dogmas. As he piles doctrine on doctrine and conclusion on conclusion in the formation of some tremendous scheme of philosophy and religion, he is, in the only legitimate sense of which the expression is capable, becoming more and more human. When he drops one doctrine after another in a refined scepticism, when he declines to tie himself to a system, when he says that he has outgrown definitions, when he says that he disbelieves in finality, when, in his own imagination, he sits as God, holding no form of creed but contemplating all, then he is by that very process sinking slowly backwards into the vagueness of the vagrant animals and the unconsciousness of the grass. Trees have no dogmas. Turnips are singularly broad-minded.

If then, I repeat, there is to be mental advance, it must be mental advance in the construction of a definite philosophy of life. And that philosophy of life must be right and the other philosophies wrong. Now of all, or nearly all, the able modern writers whom I have briefly studied in this book, this is especially and pleasingly true, that they do each of them have a constructive and affirmative view, and that they do take it seriously and ask us to take it seriously. There is nothing merely sceptically progressive about Mr. Rudyard Kipling. There is nothing in the least broad minded about Mr.

Bernard Shaw. The paganism of Mr. Lowes Dickinson is more grave than any Christianity. Even the opportunism of Mr. H. G. Wells is more dogmatic than the idealism of anybody else. Somebody complained, I think, to Matthew Arnold that he was getting as dogmatic as Carlyle. He replied, "That may be true; but you overlook an obvious difference. I am dogmatic and right, and Carlyle is dogmatic and wrong." The strong humour of the remark ought not to disguise from us its everlasting seriousness and common sense; no man ought to write at all, or even to speak at all, unless he thinks that he is in truth and the other man in error. In similar style, I hold that I am dogmatic and right, while Mr. Shaw is dogmatic and wrong. But my main point, at present, is to notice that the chief among these writers I have discussed do most sanely and courageously offer themselves as dogmatists, as founders of a system. It may be true that the thing in Mr. Shaw most interesting to me, is the fact that Mr. Shaw is wrong. But it is equally true that the thing in Mr. Shaw most interesting to himself, is the fact that Mr. Shaw is right. Mr. Shaw may have none with him but himself; but it is not for himself he cares. It is for the vast and universal church, of which he is the only member.

The two typical men of genius whom I have mentioned here, and with whose names I have begun this book, are very symbolic, if only because they have shown that the fiercest dogmatists can make the best artists. In the fin de siecle atmosphere every one was crying out that literature should be free from all causes and all ethical creeds. Art was to produce only exquisite workmanship, and it was especially the note of those days to demand brilliant plays and brilliant short stories. And when they got them, they got them from a couple of moralists. The best short stories were written by a man trying to preach Imperialism. The best plays were written by a man trying to preach Socialism. All the art of all the artists looked tiny and tedious beside the art which was a byproduct of propaganda.

The reason, indeed, is very simple. A man cannot be wise enough to be a great artist without being wise enough to wish to be a philosopher. A man cannot have the energy to produce good art without having the energy to wish to pass beyond it. A small artist is content with art; a great artist is content with nothing except everything. So we find that when real forces, good or bad, like Kipling and G. B. S., enter our arena, they bring with them not only startling and arresting art, but very startling and arresting dogmas. And they care even more, and desire us to care even more, about their startling and arresting dogmas than about their startling and arresting art. Mr. Shaw is a good dramatist, but what he desires more than anything else to be is a good politician. Mr. Rudyard Kipling is by divine caprice and natural genius an unconventional poet; but what he desires more than anything else to be is a conventional poet. He desires to be the poet of his people, bone of their bone, and flesh of their flesh, understanding their origins, celebrating their destiny. He desires to be Poet Laureate, a most sensible and honourable and public-spirited desire. Having been given by the gods originality—that is, disagreement with others—he desires divinely to agree with them. But the most striking instance of all, more striking, I think, even than either of these, is the instance of Mr. H. G. Wells. He began in a sort of insane infancy of pure art. He began by making a new heaven and a new earth, with the same irresponsible instinct by which men buy a new necktie or button-hole. He began by trifling with the stars and systems in order to make ephemeral anecdotes; he killed the universe for a joke. He has since become more and more serious, and has become, as men inevitably do when they become more and more serious, more and more parochial. He was frivolous about the twilight of the gods; but he is serious about the London omnibus. He was careless in "The Time Machine," for that dealt only with the destiny of all things; but he is careful, and even cautious, in "Mankind in the Making," for that deals with the day after to-morrow. He began with the end of the world, and that was easy. Now he has gone on to the beginning of the world, and that is difficult. But the main result of all this is the same as in the other cases. The men who have really been the bold artists, the realistic artists, the uncompromising artists, are the men who have turned out, after all, to be writing "with a purpose." Suppose that any cool and cynical art-critic, any art-critic fully impressed with the conviction that artists were greatest when they were most purely artistic, suppose that a man who professed ably a humane aestheticism, as did Mr. Max Beerbohm, or a cruel aestheticism, as did Mr. W. E. Henley, had cast his eye over the whole fictional literature which was recent in the year 1895, and had been asked to select the three most vigorous and promising and original artists and artistic works, he would, I think, most certainly have said that for a fine artistic audacity, for a real artistic delicacy, or for a whiff of true novelty in art, the things that stood first were "Soldiers Three," by a Mr. Rudyard Kipling; "Arms and the Man," by a Mr. Bernard Shaw; and "The Time Machine," by a man called Wells. And all these men have shown themselves ingrainedly didactic. You may express the matter if you will by saying that if we want doctrines we go to the great artists. But it is clear from the psychology of the matter that this is not the true statement; the true statement is that when we want any art tolerably brisk and bold we have to go to the doctrinaires.

In concluding this book, therefore, I would ask, first and foremost, that men such as these of whom I have spoken should not be insulted by being taken for artists. No man has any right whatever merely to enjoy the work of Mr. Bernard Shaw; he might as well enjoy the invasion of his country by the French. Mr. Shaw writes either to convince or to enrage us. No man has any business to be a Kiplingite without being a politician, and an Imperialist politician. If a man is first with us, it should be because of what is first with him. If a man convinces us at all, it should be by his convictions. If we hate a poem of Kipling's from political passion, we are hating it for the same reason that the poet loved it; if we dislike him because of his opinions, we are disliking him for the best of all possible reasons. If a man comes into Hyde Park to preach it is permissible to hoot him; but it is discourteous to applaud him as a performing bear. And an artist is only a performing bear compared with the meanest man who fancies he has anything to say.

There is, indeed, one class of modern writers and thinkers who cannot altogether be overlooked in this question, though there is no space here for a lengthy account of them, which, indeed, to confess the truth, would consist chiefly of abuse. I mean those who get over all these abysses and reconcile all these wars by talking about "aspects of truth," by saying that the art of Kipling represents one aspect of the truth, and the art of William Watson another; the art of Mr. Bernard Shaw one aspect of the truth, and the art of Mr. Cunningham Grahame another; the art of Mr. H. G. Wells one aspect, and the art of Mr. Coventry Patmore (say) another. I will only say here that this seems to me an evasion which has not even had the sense to disguise itself ingeniously in words. If we talk of a certain thing being an aspect of truth, it is evident that we claim to know what is truth; just as, if we talk of the hind leg of a dog, we claim to know what is a dog. Unfortunately, the philosopher who talks about aspects of truth generally also asks, "What is truth?" Frequently even he denies the existence of truth, or says it is inconceivable by the human intelligence. How, then, can he recognize its aspects? I should not like to be an artist who brought an architectural sketch to a builder, saying, "This is the south aspect of Sea-View Cottage. Sea-View Cottage, of course, does not exist." I should not even like very much to have to explain, under such circumstances, that Sea-View Cottage might exist, but was unthinkable by the human mind. Nor should I like any better to be the bungling and absurd metaphysician who professed to be able to see everywhere the aspects of a truth that is not there. Of course, it is perfectly obvious that there are truths in Kipling, that there are truths in Shaw or Wells. But the degree to which we can perceive them depends strictly upon how far we have a definite conception inside us of what is truth. It is ludicrous to suppose that the more sceptical we are the more we see good in everything. It is clear that the more we are certain what good is, the more we shall see good in everything.

I plead, then, that we should agree or disagree with these men. I plead that we should agree with them at least in having an abstract belief. But I know that there are current in the modern world many vague objections to having an abstract belief, and I feel that we shall not get any further until we have dealt with some of them. The first objection is easily stated.

A common hesitation in our day touching the use of extreme

convictions is a sort of notion that extreme convictions specially upon cosmic matters, have been responsible in the past for the thing which is called bigotry. But a very small amount of direct experience will dissipate this view. In real life the people who are most bigoted are the people who have no convictions at all. The economists of the Manchester school who disagree with Socialism take Socialism seriously. It is the young man in Bond Street, who does not know what socialism means much less whether he agrees with it, who is quite certain that these socialist fellows are making a fuss about nothing. The man who understands the Calvinist philosophy enough to agree with it must understand the Catholic philosophy in order to disagree with it. It is the vague modern who is not at all certain what is right who is most certain that Dante was wrong. The serious opponent of the Latin Church in history, even in the act of showing that it produced great infamies, must know that it produced great saints. It is the hard-headed stockbroker, who knows no history and believes no religion, who is, nevertheless, perfectly convinced that all these priests are knaves. The Salvationist at the Marble Arch may be bigoted, but he is not too bigoted to yearn from a common human kinship after the dandy on church parade. But the dandy on church parade is so bigoted that he does not in the least yearn after the Salvationist at the Marble Arch. Bigotry may be roughly defined as the anger of men who have no opinions. It is the resistance offered to definite ideas by that vague bulk of people whose ideas are indefinite to excess. Bigotry may be called the appalling frenzy of the indifferent. This frenzy of the indifferent is in truth a terrible thing; it has made all monstrous and widely pervading persecutions. In this degree it was not the people who cared who ever persecuted; the people who cared were not sufficiently numerous. It was the people who did not care who filled the world with fire and oppression. It was the hands of the indifferent that lit the faggots; it was the hands of the indifferent that turned the rack. There have come some persecutions out of the pain of a passionate certainty; but these produced, not bigotry, but fanaticism—a very different and a somewhat admirable thing. Bigotry in the main has always been the pervading omnipotence of those who do not care crushing out those who care in darkness and blood.

There are people, however, who dig somewhat deeper than this into the possible evils of dogma. It is felt by many that strong philosophical conviction, while it does not (as they perceive) produce that sluggish and fundamentally frivolous condition which we call bigotry, does produce a certain concentration, exaggeration, and moral impatience, which we may agree to call fanaticism. They say, in brief, that ideas are dangerous things. In politics, for example, it is commonly urged against a man like Mr. Balfour, or against a man like Mr. John Morley, that a wealth of ideas is dangerous. The true doctrine on this point, again, is surely not very difficult to state. Ideas are dangerous, but the man to whom they are least dangerous is the man of ideas. He is acquainted with ideas, and moves among them like a lion-tamer. Ideas are dangerous, but the man to whom they are most dangerous is the man of no ideas. The man of no ideas will find the first idea fly to his head like wine to the head of a teetotaller. It is a common error, I think, among the Radical idealists of my own party and period to suggest that financiers and business men are a danger to the empire because they are so sordid or so materialistic. The truth is that financiers and business men are a danger to the empire because they can be sentimental about any sentiment, and idealistic about any ideal, any ideal that they find lying about. just as a boy who has not known much of women is apt too easily to take a woman for the woman, so these practical men, unaccustomed to causes, are always inclined to think that if a thing is proved to be an ideal it is proved to be the ideal. Many, for example, avowedly followed Cecil Rhodes because he had a vision. They might as well have followed him because he had a nose; a man without some kind of dream of perfection is quite as much of a monstrosity as a noseless man. People say of such a figure, in almost feverish whispers, "He knows his own mind," which is exactly like saying in equally feverish whispers, "He blows his own nose." Human nature simply cannot subsist without a hope and aim of some kind; as the sanity of the Old Testament truly said, where there is no vision the people perisheth. But it is precisely because an ideal is necessary to man that the man without ideals is in permanent danger of fanaticism. There is nothing which is so likely to leave a man open to the sudden and irresistible inroad of an unbalanced vision as the cultivation of business habits. All of us know angular business men who think that the earth is flat, or that Mr. Kruger was at the head of a great military despotism, or that men are graminivorous, or that Bacon wrote Shakespeare. Religious and philosophical beliefs are, indeed, as dangerous as fire, and nothing can take from them that beauty of danger. But there is only one way of really guarding ourselves against the excessive danger of them, and that is to be steeped in philosophy and soaked in religion.

Briefly, then, we dismiss the two opposite dangers of bigotry and fanaticism, bigotry which is a too great vagueness and fanaticism which is a too great concentration. We say that the cure for the bigot is belief; we say that the cure for the idealist is ideas. To know the best theories of existence and to choose the best from them (that is, to the best of our own strong conviction) appears to us the proper way to be neither bigot nor fanatic, but something more firm than a bigot and more terrible than a fanatic, a man with a definite opinion. But that definite opinion must in this view begin with the basic matters of human thought, and these must not be dismissed as irrelevant, as religion, for instance, is too often in our days dismissed as irrelevant. Even if we think religion insoluble, we cannot think it irrelevant.

Even if we ourselves have no view of the ultimate verities, we must feel that wherever such a view exists in a man it must be more important than anything else in him. The instant that the thing ceases to be the unknowable, it becomes the indispensable. There can be no doubt, I think, that the idea does exist in our time that there is something narrow or irrelevant or even mean about attacking a man's religion, or arguing from it in matters of politics or ethics. There can be quite as little doubt that such an accusation of narrowness is itself almost grotesquely narrow. To take an example from comparatively current events: we all know that it was not uncommon for a man to be considered a scarecrow of bigotry and obscurantism because he distrusted the Japanese, or lamented the rise of the Japanese, on the ground that the Japanese were Pagans. Nobody would think that there was anything antiquated or fanatical about distrusting a people because of some difference between them and us in practice or political machinery. Nobody would think it bigoted to say of a people, "I distrust their influence because they are Protectionists." No one would think it narrow to say, "I lament their rise because they are Socialists, or Manchester Individualists, or strong believers in militarism and conscription." A difference of opinion about the nature of Parliaments matters very much; but a difference of opinion about the nature of sin does not matter at all. A difference of opinion about the object of taxation matters very much; but a difference of opinion about the object of human existence does not matter at all. We have a right to distrust a man who is in a different kind of municipality; but we have no right to mistrust a man who is in a different kind of cosmos. This sort of enlightenment is surely about the most unenlightened that it is possible to imagine. To recur to the phrase which I employed earlier, this is tantamount to saying that everything is important with the exception of everything. Religion is exactly the thing which cannot be left out—because it includes everything. The most absent-minded person cannot well pack his Gladstone-bag and leave out the bag. We have a general view of existence, whether we like it or not; it alters or, to speak more accurately, it creates and involves everything we say or do, whether we like it or not. If we regard the Cosmos as a dream, we regard the Fiscal Question as a dream. If we regard the Cosmos as a joke, we regard St. Paul's Cathedral as a joke. If everything is bad, then we must believe (if it be possible) that beer is bad; if everything be good, we are forced to the rather fantastic conclusion that scientific philanthropy is good. Every man in the street must hold a metaphysical system, and hold it firmly. The possibility is that he may have held it so firmly and so long as to have forgotten all about its existence.

This latter situation is certainly possible; in fact, it is the situation of the whole modern world. The modern world is filled with men who hold dogmas so strongly that they do not even know that they are dogmas. It may be said even that the modern world, as a corporate body, holds certain dogmas so strongly that it does not know that they are dogmas. It may be thought "dogmatic," for instance, in some circles accounted progressive, to assume the perfection or improvement of man in another world. But it is not thought "dogmatic" to assume the perfection or improvement of man in this world; though that idea of progress is quite as unproved as the idea of immortality, and from a rationalistic point of view quite as improbable. Progress happens to be one of our dogmas, and a dogma means a thing which is not thought dogmatic. Or, again, we see nothing "dogmatic" in the inspiring, but certainly most startling, theory of physical science, that we should collect facts for the sake of facts, even though they seem as useless as sticks and straws. This is a great and suggestive idea, and its utility may, if you will, be proving itself, but its utility is, in the abstract, quite as disputable as the utility of that calling on oracles or consulting shrines which is also said to prove itself. Thus, because we are not in a civilization which believes strongly in oracles or sacred places, we see the full frenzy of those who killed themselves to find the sepulchre of Christ. But being in a civilization which does believe in this dogma of fact for facts' sake, we do not see the full frenzy of those who kill themselves to find the North Pole. I am not speaking of a tenable ultimate utility which is true both of the Crusades and the polar explorations. I mean merely that we do see the superficial and aesthetic singularity, the startling quality, about the idea of men crossing a continent with armies to conquer the place where a man died. But we do not see the aesthetic singularity and startling quality of men dying in agonies to find a place where no man can live—a place only interesting because it is supposed to be the meeting-place of some lines that do not exist.

Let us, then, go upon a long journey and enter on a dreadful search. Let us, at least, dig and seek till we have discovered our own opinions. The dogmas we really hold are far more fantastic, and, perhaps, far more beautiful than we think. In the course of these essays I fear that I have spoken from time to time of rationalists and rationalism, and that in a disparaging sense. Being full of that kindliness which should come at the end of everything, even of a book, I apologize to the rationalists even for calling them rationalists. There are no rationalists. We all believe fairy-tales, and live in them. Some, with a sumptuous literary turn, believe in the existence of the lady clothed with the sun. Some, with a more rustic, elvish instinct, like Mr. McCabe, believe merely in the impossible sun itself. Some hold the undemonstrable dogma of the existence of God; some the equally undemonstrable dogma of the existence of the man next door.

Truths turn into dogmas the instant that they are disputed. Thus every man who utters a doubt defines a religion. And the scepticism of our time does not really destroy the beliefs, rather it creates them; gives them their limits and their plain and defiant shape. We who are Liberals once held Liberalism lightly as a truism. Now it has been disputed, and we hold it fiercely as a faith. We who believe in patriotism once thought patriotism to be reasonable, and thought little more about it. Now we know it to be unreasonable, and know it to be right. We who are Christians never knew the great philosophic common sense which inheres in that mystery until the anti-Christian writers pointed it out to us. The great march of mental destruction will go on. Everything will be denied. Everything will become a creed. It is a reasonable position to deny the stones in the street; it will be a religious dogma to assert them. It is a rational thesis that we are all in a dream; it will be a mystical sanity to say that we are all awake. Fires will be kindled to testify that two and two make four. Swords will be drawn to prove that leaves are green in summer. We shall be left defending, not only the incredible virtues and sanities of human life, but something more incredible still, this huge impossible universe which stares us in the face. We shall fight for visible prodigies as if they were invisible. We shall look on the impossible grass and the skies with a strange courage. We shall be of those who have seen and yet have believed.

THE END

ORTHODOXY

G. K. Chesterton

[1908]

PREFACE

This book is meant to be a companion to "Heretics," and to put the positive side in addition to the negative. Many critics complained of the book called "Heretics" because it merely criticised current philosophies without offering any alternative philosophy. This book is an attempt to answer the challenge. It is unavoidably affirmative and therefore unavoidably autobiographical. The writer has been driven back upon somewhat the same difficulty as that which beset Newman in writing his Apologia; he has been forced to be egotistical only in order to be sincere. While everything else may be different the motive in both cases is the same. It is the purpose of the writer to attempt an explanation, not of whether the Christian Faith can be believed, but of how he personally has come to believe it. The book is therefore arranged upon the positive principle of a riddle and its answer. It deals first with all the writer's own solitary and sincere speculations and then with all the startling style in which they were all suddenly satisfied by the Christian Theology. The writer regards it as amounting to a convincing creed. But if it is not that it is at least a repeated and surprising coincidence.

Gilbert K. Chesterton.

Introduction in Defence of Everything Else

The only possible excuse for this book is that it is an answer to a challenge. Even a bad shot is dignified when he accepts a duel. When some time ago I published a series of hasty but sincere papers, under the name of "Heretics," several critics for whose intellect I have a warm respect (I may mention specially Mr. G.S. Street) said that it was all very well for me to tell everybody to affirm his cosmic theory, but that I had carefully avoided supporting my precepts with example. "I will begin to worry about my philosophy," said Mr. Street, "when Mr. Chesterton has given us his." It was perhaps an incautious suggestion to make to a person only too ready to write books upon the feeblest provocation. But after all, though Mr. Street has inspired and created this book, he need not read it. If he does read it, he will find that in its pages I have attempted in a vague and personal way, in a set of mental pictures rather than in a series of deductions, to state the philosophy in which I have come to believe. I will not call it my philosophy; for I did not make it. God and humanity made it; and it made me.

I have often had a fancy for writing a romance about an English yachtsman who slightly miscalculated his course and discovered England under the impression that it was a new island in the South Seas. I always find, however, that I am either too busy or too lazy to write this fine work, so I may as well give it away for the purposes of philosophical illustration. There will probably be a general impression that the man who landed (armed to the teeth and talking by signs) to plant the British flag on that barbaric temple which turned out to be the Pavilion at Brighton, felt rather a fool. I am not here concerned to deny that he looked a fool. But if you imagine that he felt a fool, or at any rate that the sense of folly was his sole or his dominant emotion, then you have not studied with sufficient delicacy the rich romantic nature of the hero of this tale. His mistake was really a most enviable mistake; and he knew it, if he was the man I take him for. What could be more delightful than to have in the same few minutes all the fascinating terrors of going abroad combined with all the humane security of coming home again? What could be better than to have all the fun of discovering South Africa without the disgusting necessity of landing there? What could be more glorious than to brace one's self up to discover New South Wales and then realize, with a gush of happy tears, that it was really old South Wales. This at least seems to me the main problem for philosophers, and is in a manner the main problem of this book. How can we contrive to be at once astonished at the world and yet at home in it? How can this queer cosmic town, with its many-legged citizens, with its monstrous and ancient lamps, how can this world give us at once the fascination of a strange town and the comfort and honour of being our own town?

To show that a faith or a philosophy is true from every standpoint would be too big an undertaking even for a much bigger book than this; it is necessary to follow one path of argument; and this is the path that I here propose to follow. I wish to set forth my faith as particularly answering this double spiritual need, the need for that mixture of the familiar and the unfamiliar which Christendom has rightly named romance. For the very word "romance" has in it the mystery and ancient meaning of Rome. Any one setting out to dispute anything ought always to begin by saying what he does not dispute. Beyond stating what he proposes to prove he should always state what he does not propose to prove. The thing I do not propose to prove, the thing I propose to take as common ground between myself and any average reader, is this desirability of an active and imaginative life, picturesque and full of a poetical curiosity, a life such as western man at any rate always seems to have desired. If a man says that extinction is better than existence or blank existence better than variety and adventure, then he is not one of the ordinary people to whom I am talking. If a man prefers nothing I can give him nothing. But nearly all people I have ever met in this western society in which I live would agree to the general proposition that we need this life of practical romance; the combination of something that is strange with something that is secure. We need so to view the world as to combine an idea of wonder and an idea of welcome. We need to be happy in this wonderland without once being merely comfortable. It is THIS achievement of my creed that I shall chiefly pursue in these pages.

But I have a peculiar reason for mentioning the man in a yacht, who discovered England. For I am that man in a yacht. I discovered England. I do not see how this book can avoid being egotistical; and I do not quite see (to tell the truth) how it can avoid being dull. Dulness will, however, free me from the charge which I most lament; the charge of being flippant. Mere light sophistry is the thing that I happen to despise most of all things, and it is perhaps a wholesome fact that this is the thing of which I am generally accused. I know nothing so contemptible as a mere paradox; a mere ingenious defence of the indefensible. If it were true (as has been said) that Mr. Bernard Shaw lived upon paradox, then he ought to be a mere common millionaire; for a man of his mental activity could invent a sophistry every six minutes. It is as easy as lying; because it is lying. The truth is, of course, that Mr. Shaw is cruelly hampered by the fact that he cannot tell any lie unless he thinks it is the truth. I find myself under the same intolerable bondage. I never in my life said anything merely because I thought it funny; though of course, I have had ordinary human vainglory, and may have thought it funny because I had said it. It is one thing to describe an interview with a gorgon or a griffin, a creature who does not exist. It is another thing to discover that the rhinoceros does exist and then take pleasure in the fact that he looks as if he didn't. One searches for truth, but it may be that one pursues instinctively the more extraordinary truths. And I offer this book with the heartiest sentiments to all the jolly people who hate what I write, and regard it (very justly, for all I know), as a piece of poor clowning or a single tiresome joke.

For if this book is a joke it is a joke against me. I am the man who with the utmost daring discovered what had been discovered before. If there is an element of farce in what follows, the farce is at my own expense; for this book explains how I fancied I was the first to set foot in Brighton and then found I was the last. It recounts my elephantine adventures in pursuit of the obvious. No one can think my case more ludicrous than I think it myself; no reader can accuse me here of trying to make a fool of him: I am the fool of this story, and no rebel shall hurl me from my throne. I freely confess all the idiotic ambitions of the end of the nineteenth century. I did, like all other solemn little boys, try to be in advance of the age. Like them I tried to be some ten minutes in advance of the truth. And I found that I was eighteen hundred years behind it. I did strain my voice with a painfully juvenile exaggeration in uttering my truths. And I was punished in the fittest and funniest way, for I have kept my truths: but I have discovered, not that they were not truths, but simply that they were not mine. When I fancied that I stood alone I was really in the ridiculous position of being backed up by all Christendom. It may be, Heaven forgive me, that I did try to be original; but I only succeeded in inventing all by myself an inferior copy of the existing traditions of civilized religion. The man from the yacht thought he was the first to find England; I thought I was the first to find Europe. I did try to found a heresy of my own; and when I had put the last touches to it, I discovered that it was orthodoxy.

It may be that somebody will be entertained by the account of this happy fiasco. It might amuse a friend or an enemy to read how I gradually learnt from the truth of some stray legend or from the falsehood of some dominant philosophy, things that I might have learnt from my catechism— if I had ever learnt it. There may or may not be some entertainment in reading how I found at last in an anarchist club or a Babylonian temple what I might have found in the nearest parish church. If any one is entertained by learning how the flowers of the field or the phrases in an omnibus, the accidents of politics or the pains of youth came together in a certain order to produce a certain conviction of Christian orthodoxy, he may possibly read this book. But there is in everything a reasonable division of labour. I have written the book, and nothing on earth would induce me to read it.

I add one purely pedantic note which comes, as a note naturally should, at the beginning of the book. These essays are concerned only to discuss the actual fact that the central Christian theology (sufficiently summarized in the Apostles' Creed) is the best root of energy and sound ethics. They are not intended to discuss the very fascinating but quite different question of what is the present seat of authority for the proclamation of that creed. When the word "orthodoxy" is used here it means the Apostles' Creed, as understood by everybody calling himself Christian until a very short time ago and the general historic conduct of those who held such a creed. I have been forced by mere space to confine myself to what I have got from this creed; I do not touch the matter much disputed among modern Christians, of where we ourselves got it. This is not an ecclesiastical treatise but a sort of slovenly autobiography. But if any one wants my opinions about the actual nature of the authority, Mr. G.S. Street has only to throw me another challenge, and I will write him another book.

THE MANIAC

Thoroughly worldly people never understand even the world; they rely altogether on a few cynical maxims which are not true. Once I remember walking with a prosperous publisher, who made a remark which I had often heard before; it is, indeed, almost a motto of the modern world. Yet I had heard it once too often, and I saw suddenly that there was nothing in it. The publisher said of somebody, "That man will get on; he believes in himself." And I remember that as I lifted my head to listen, my eye caught an omnibus on which was written "Hanwell." I said to him, "Shall I tell you where the men are who believe most in themselves? For I can tell you. I know of men who believe in themselves more colossally than Napoleon or Caesar. I know where flames the fixed star of certainty and success. I can guide you to the thrones of the Super-men. The men who really believe in themselves are all in lunatic asylums." He said mildly that there were a good many men after all who believed in themselves and who were not in lunatic asylums. "Yes, there are," I retorted, "and you of all men ought to know them. That drunken poet from whom you would not take a dreary tragedy, he believed in himself. That elderly minister with an epic from whom you were hiding in a back room, he believed in himself. If you consulted your business experience instead of your ugly individualistic philosophy, you would know that believing in himself is one of the commonest signs of a rotter. Actors who can't act believe in themselves; and debtors who won't pay. It would be much truer to say that a man will certainly fail, because he believes in himself. Complete self-confidence is not merely a sin; complete self-confidence is a weakness. Believing utterly in one's self is a hysterical and superstitious belief like believing in Joanna Southcote: the man who has it has 'Hanwell' written on his face as plain as it is written on that omnibus." And to all this my friend the publisher made this very deep and effective reply, "Well, if a man is not to believe in himself, in what is he to believe?" After a long pause I replied, "I will go home and write a book in answer to that question." This is the book that I have written in answer to it.

But I think this book may well start where our argument started— in the neighbourhood of the mad-house. Modern masters of science are much impressed with the need of beginning all inquiry with a fact. The ancient masters of religion were quite equally impressed with that necessity. They began with the fact of sin—a fact as practical as potatoes. Whether or no man could be washed in miraculous waters, there was no doubt at any rate that he wanted washing. But certain religious leaders in London, not mere materialists, have begun in our day not to deny the highly disputable water, but to deny the indisputable dirt. Certain new theologians dispute original sin, which is the only part of Christian theology which can really be proved. Some followers of the Reverend R.J. Campbell, in their almost too fastidious spirituality, admit divine sinlessness, which they cannot see even in their dreams. But they essentially deny human sin, which they can see in the street. The strongest saints and the strongest sceptics alike took positive evil as the starting-point of their argument. If it be true (as it certainly is) that a man can feel exquisite happiness in skinning a cat, then the religious philosopher can only draw one of two deductions. He must either deny the existence of God, as all atheists do; or he must deny the present union between God and man, as all Christians do. The new theologians seem to think it a highly rationalistic solution to deny the cat.

In this remarkable situation it is plainly not now possible (with any hope of a universal appeal) to start, as our fathers did, with the fact of sin. This very fact which was to them (and is to me) as plain as a pikestaff, is the very fact that has been specially diluted or denied. But though moderns deny the existence of sin, I do not think that they have yet denied the existence of a lunatic asylum. We all agree still that there is a collapse of the intellect as unmistakable as a falling house. Men deny hell, but not, as yet, Hanwell. For the purpose of our primary argument the one may very well stand where the other stood. I mean that as all thoughts and theories were once judged by whether they tended to make a man lose his soul, so for our present purpose all modern thoughts and theories may be judged by whether they tend to make a man lose his wits.

It is true that some speak lightly and loosely of insanity as in itself attractive. But a moment's thought will show that if disease is beautiful, it is generally some one else's disease. A blind man may be picturesque; but it requires two eyes to see the picture. And similarly even the wildest poetry of insanity can only be enjoyed by the sane. To the insane man his insanity is quite prosaic, because it is quite true. A man who thinks himself a chicken is to himself as ordinary as a chicken. A man who thinks he is a bit of glass is to himself as dull as a bit of glass. It is the homogeneity of his mind which makes him dull, and which makes him mad. It is only because we see the irony of his idea that we think him even amusing; it is only because he does not see the irony of his idea that he is put in Hanwell at all. In short, oddities only strike ordinary people. Oddities do not strike odd people. This is why ordinary people have a much more exciting time; while odd people are always complaining of the dulness of life. This is also why the new novels die so quickly, and why the old fairy tales endure for ever. The old fairy tale makes the hero a normal human boy; it is his adventures that are startling; they startle him because he is normal. But in the modern psychological novel the hero is abnormal; the centre is not central. Hence the fiercest adventures fail to affect him adequately, and the book is monotonous. You can make a story out of a hero among dragons; but not out of a dragon among dragons. The fairy tale discusses what a sane man will do in a mad world. The sober realistic novel of to-day discusses what an essential lunatic will do in a dull world.

Let us begin, then, with the mad-house; from this evil and fantastic inn let us set forth on our intellectual journey. Now, if we are to glance at the philosophy of sanity, the first thing to do in the matter is to blot out one big and common mistake. There is a notion adrift everywhere that imagination, especially mystical imagination, is dangerous to man's mental balance. Poets are commonly spoken of as psychologically unreliable; and generally there is a vague association between wreathing laurels in your hair and sticking straws in it. Facts and history utterly contradict this view. Most of the very great poets have been not only sane, but extremely business-like; and if Shakespeare ever really held horses, it was because he was much the safest man to hold them. Imagination does not breed insanity. Exactly what does breed insanity is reason. Poets do not go mad; but chess-players do. Mathematicians go mad, and cashiers; but creative artists very seldom. I am not, as will be seen, in any sense attacking logic: I only say that this danger does lie in logic, not in imagination. Artistic paternity is as wholesome as physical paternity. Moreover, it is worthy of remark that when a poet really was morbid it was commonly because he had some weak spot of rationality on his brain. Poe, for instance, really was morbid; not because he was poetical, but because he was specially analytical. Even chess was too poetical for him; he disliked chess because it was full of knights and castles, like a poem. He avowedly preferred the black discs of draughts, because they were more like the mere black dots on a diagram. Perhaps the strongest case of all is this: that only one great English poet went mad, Cowper. And he was definitely driven mad by logic, by the ugly and alien logic of predestination. Poetry was not the disease, but the medicine; poetry partly kept him in health. He could sometimes forget the red and thirsty hell to which his hideous necessitarianism dragged him among the wide waters and the white flat lilies of the Ouse. He was damned by John Calvin; he was almost saved by John Gilpin. Everywhere we see that men do not go mad by dreaming. Critics are much madder than poets. Homer is complete and calm enough; it is his critics who tear him into extravagant tatters. Shakespeare is quite himself; it is only some of his critics who have discovered that he was somebody else. And though St. John the Evangelist saw many strange monsters in his vision, he saw no creature so wild as one of his own commentators. The general fact is simple. Poetry is sane because it floats easily in an infinite sea; reason seeks to cross the infinite sea, and so make it finite. The result is mental exhaustion, like the physical exhaustion of Mr. Holbein. To accept everything is an exercise, to understand everything a strain. The poet only desires exaltation and expansion, a world to stretch himself in. The poet only asks to get his head into the heavens. It is the logician who seeks to get the heavens into his head. And it is his head that splits.

It is a small matter, but not irrelevant, that this striking mistake is commonly supported by a striking misquotation. We have all heard people cite the celebrated line of Dryden as "Great genius is to madness near allied." But Dryden did not say that great genius was to madness near allied. Dryden was a great genius himself, and knew better. It would have been hard to find a man more romantic than he, or more sensible. What Dryden said was this, "Great wits are oft to madness near allied"; and that is true. It is the pure promptitude of the intellect that is in peril of a breakdown. Also people might remember of what sort of man Dryden was talking. He was not talking of any unworldly visionary like Vaughan or George Herbert. He was talking of a cynical man of the world, a sceptic, a diplomatist, a great practical politician. Such men are indeed to madness near allied. Their incessant calculation of their own brains and other people's brains is a dangerous trade. It is always perilous to the mind to reckon up the mind. A flippant person has asked why we say, "As mad as a hatter." A more flippant person might answer that a hatter is mad because he has to measure the human head.

And if great reasoners are often maniacal, it is equally true that maniacs are commonly great reasoners. When I was engaged in a controversy with the CLARION on the matter of free will, that able writer Mr. R.B. Suthers said that free will was lunacy, because it meant causeless actions, and the actions of a lunatic would be causeless. I do not dwell here upon the disastrous lapse in determinist logic. Obviously if any actions, even a lunatic's, can be causeless, determinism is done for. If the chain of causation can be broken for a madman, it can be broken for a man. But my purpose is to point out something more practical. It was natural, perhaps, that a modern Marxian Socialist should not know anything about free will. But it was certainly remarkable that a modern Marxian Socialist should not know anything about lunatics. Mr. Suthers evidently did not know anything about lunatics. The last thing that can be said of a lunatic is that his actions are causeless. If any human acts may loosely be called causeless, they are the minor acts of a healthy man; whistling as he walks; slashing the grass with a stick; kicking his heels or rubbing his hands. It is the happy man who does the useless things; the sick man is not strong enough to be idle. It is exactly such careless and causeless actions that the madman could never understand; for the madman (like the determinist) generally sees too much cause in everything. The madman would read a conspiratorial significance into those empty activities. He would think that the lopping of the grass was an attack on private property. He would think that the kicking of the heels was a signal to an accomplice. If the madman could for an instant

138

become careless, he would become sane. Every one who has had the misfortune to talk with people in the heart or on the edge of mental disorder, knows that their most sinister quality is a horrible clarity of detail; a connecting of one thing with another in a map more elaborate than a maze. If you argue with a madman, it is extremely probable that you will get the worst of it; for in many ways his mind moves all the quicker for not being delayed by the things that go with good judgment. He is not hampered by a sense of humour or by charity, or by the dumb certainties of experience. He is the more logical for losing certain sane affections. Indeed, the common phrase for insanity is in this respect a misleading one. The madman is not the man who has lost his reason. The madman is the man who has lost everything except his reason.

The madman's explanation of a thing is always complete, and often in a purely rational sense satisfactory. Or, to speak more strictly, the insane explanation, if not conclusive, is at least unanswerable; this may be observed specially in the two or three commonest kinds of madness. If a man says (for instance) that men have a conspiracy against him, you cannot dispute it except by saying that all the men deny that they are conspirators; which is exactly what conspirators would do. His explanation covers the facts as much as yours. Or if a man says that he is the rightful King of England, it is no complete answer to say that the existing authorities call him mad; for if he were King of England that might be the wisest thing for the existing authorities to do. Or if a man says that he is Jesus Christ, it is no answer to tell him that the world denies his divinity; for the world denied Christ's.

Nevertheless he is wrong. But if we attempt to trace his error in exact terms, we shall not find it quite so easy as we had supposed. Perhaps the nearest we can get to expressing it is to say this: that his mind moves in a perfect but narrow circle. A small circle is quite as infinite as a large circle; but, though it is quite as infinite, it is not so large. In the same way the insane explanation is quite as complete as the sane one, but it is not so large. A bullet is quite as round as the world, but it is not the world. There is such a thing as a narrow universality; there is such a thing as a small and cramped eternity; you may see it in many modern religions. Now, speaking quite externally and empirically, we may say that the strongest and most unmistakable MARK of madness is this combination between a logical completeness and a spiritual contraction. The lunatic's theory explains a large number of things, but it does not explain them in a large way. I mean that if you or I were dealing with a mind that was growing morbid, we should be chiefly concerned not so much to give it arguments as to give it air, to convince it that there was something cleaner and cooler outside the suffocation of a single argument. Suppose, for instance, it were the first case that I took as typical; suppose it were the case of a man who accused everybody of conspiring against him. If we could express our deepest feelings of protest and appeal against this obsession, I suppose we should say something like this: "Oh, I admit that you have your case and have it by heart, and that many things do fit into other things as you say. I admit that your explanation explains a great deal; but what a great deal it leaves out! Are there no other stories in the world except yours; and are all men busy with your business? Suppose we grant the details; perhaps when the man in the street did not seem to see you it was only his cunning; perhaps when the policeman asked you your name it was only because he knew it already. But how much happier you would be if you only knew that these people cared nothing about you! How much larger your life would be if your self could become smaller in it; if you could really look at other men with common curiosity and pleasure; if you could see them walking as they are in their sunny selfishness and their virile indifference! You would begin to be interested in them, because they were not interested in you. You would break out of this tiny and tawdry theatre in which your own little plot is always being played, and you would find yourself under a freer sky, in a street full of splendid strangers." Or suppose it were the second case of madness, that of a man who claims the crown, your impulse would be to answer, "All right! Perhaps you know that you are the King of England; but why do you care? Make one magnificent effort and you will be a human being and look down on all the kings of the earth." Or it might be the third case, of the madman who called himself Christ. If we said what we felt, we should say, "So you are the Creator and Redeemer of the world: but what a small world it must be! What a little heaven you must inhabit, with angels no bigger than butterflies! How sad it must be to be God; and an inadequate God! Is there really no life fuller and no love more marvellous than yours; and is it really in your small and painful pity that all flesh must put its faith? How much happier you would be, how much more of you there would be, if the hammer of a higher God could smash your small cosmos, scattering the stars like spangles, and leave you in the open, free like other men to look up as well as down!"

And it must be remembered that the most purely practical science does take this view of mental evil; it does not seek to argue with it like a heresy but simply to snap it like a spell. Neither modern science nor ancient religion believes in complete free thought. Theology rebukes certain thoughts by calling them blasphemous. Science rebukes certain thoughts by calling them morbid. For example, some religious societies discouraged men more or less from thinking about sex. The new scientific society definitely discourages men from thinking about death; it is a fact, but it is considered a morbid fact. And in dealing with those whose morbidity has a touch of mania, modern science cares far less for pure logic than a dancing Dervish. In these cases it is not enough that the unhappy man should desire truth; he must desire health. Nothing can save him but a blind hunger for normality, like that of a beast. A man cannot think himself out of mental evil; for it is actually the organ of thought that has become diseased, ungovernable, and, as it were, independent. He can only be saved by will or faith. The moment his mere reason moves, it moves in the old circular rut; he will go round and round his logical circle, just as a man in a third-class carriage on the Inner Circle will go round and round the Inner Circle unless he performs the voluntary, vigorous, and mystical act of getting out at Gower Street. Decision is the whole business here; a door must be shut for ever. Every remedy is a desperate remedy. Every cure is a miraculous cure. Curing a madman is not arguing with a philosopher; it is casting out a devil. And however quietly doctors and psychologists may go to work in the matter, their attitude is profoundly intolerant— as intolerant as Bloody Mary. Their attitude is really this: that the man must stop thinking, if he is to go on living. Their counsel is one of intellectual amputation. If thy HEAD offend thee, cut it off; for it is better, not merely to enter the Kingdom of Heaven as a child, but to enter it as an imbecile, rather than with your whole intellect to be cast into hell— or into Hanwell.

Such is the madman of experience; he is commonly a reasoner, frequently a successful reasoner. Doubtless he could be vanquished in mere reason, and the case against him put logically. But it can be put much more precisely in more general and even aesthetic terms. He is in the clean and well-lit prison of one idea: he is sharpened to one painful point. He is without healthy hesitation and healthy complexity. Now, as I explain in the introduction, I have determined in these early chapters to give not so much a diagram of a doctrine as some pictures of a point of view. And I have described at length my vision of the maniac for this reason: that just as I am affected by the maniac, so I am affected by most modern thinkers. That unmistakable mood or note that I hear from Hanwell, I hear also from half the chairs of science and seats of learning to-day; and most of the mad doctors are mad doctors in more senses than one. They all have exactly that combination we have noted: the combination of an expansive and exhaustive reason with a contracted common sense. They are universal only in the sense that they take one thin explanation and carry it very far. But a pattern can stretch for ever and still be a small pattern. They see a chess-board white on black, and if the universe is paved with it, it is still white on black. Like the lunatic, they cannot alter their standpoint; they cannot make a mental effort and suddenly see it black on white.

Take first the more obvious case of materialism. As an explanation of the world, materialism has a sort of insane simplicity. It has just the quality of the madman's argument; we have at once the sense of it covering everything and the sense of it leaving everything out. Contemplate some able and sincere materialist, as, for instance, Mr. McCabe, and you will have exactly this unique sensation. He understands everything, and everything does not seem worth understanding. His cosmos may be complete in every rivet and cog-wheel, but still his cosmos is smaller than our world. Somehow his scheme, like the lucid scheme of the madman, seems unconscious of the alien energies and the large indifference of the earth; it is not thinking of the real things of the earth, of fighting peoples or proud mothers, or first love or fear upon the sea. The earth is so very large, and the cosmos is so very small. The cosmos is about the smallest hole that a man can hide his head in.

It must be understood that I am not now discussing the relation of these creeds to truth; but, for the present, solely their relation to health. Later in the argument I hope to attack the question of objective verity; here I speak only of a phenomenon of psychology. I do not for the present attempt to prove to Haeckel that materialism is untrue, any more than I attempted to prove to the man who thought he was Christ that he was labouring under an error. I merely remark here on the fact that both cases have the same kind of completeness and the same kind of incompleteness. You can explain a man's detention at Hanwell by an indifferent public by saying that it is the crucifixion of a god of whom the world is not worthy. The explanation does explain. Similarly you may explain the order in the universe by saying that all things, even the souls of men, are leaves inevitably unfolding on an utterly unconscious tree— the blind destiny of matter. The explanation does explain, though not, of course, so completely as the madman's. But the point here is that the normal human mind not only objects to both, but feels to both the same objection. Its approximate statement is that if the man in Hanwell is the real God, he is not much of a god. And, similarly, if the cosmos of the materialist is the real cosmos, it is not much of a cosmos. The thing has shrunk. The deity is less divine than many men; and (according to Haeckel) the whole of life is something much more grey, narrow, and trivial than many separate aspects of it. The parts seem greater than the whole.

For we must remember that the materialist philosophy (whether true or not) is certainly much more limiting than any religion. In one sense, of course, all intelligent ideas are narrow. They cannot be broader than themselves. A Christian is only restricted in the same sense that an atheist is restricted. He cannot think Christianity false and continue to be a Christian; and the atheist cannot think atheism false and continue to be an atheist. But as it happens, there is a very special sense in which materialism has more restrictions than spiritualism. Mr. McCabe thinks me a slave because I am not allowed to believe in determinism. I think Mr. McCabe a slave because he is not allowed to believe in fairies. But if we examine the two vetoes we shall see that his is really much more of a pure veto than mine. The Christian is quite free to believe that there is a considerable amount of settled order and inevitable development in the universe. But the materialist is not allowed to admit into his spotless machine the slightest speck of spiritualism or miracle. Poor Mr. McCabe is not allowed to retain even the tiniest imp, though it might be hiding in a pimpernel. The Christian admits that the universe is manifold and even miscellaneous, just as a sane man knows that he is complex. The sane man knows that he has a touch of the beast, a touch of the devil, a touch of the saint, a touch of the citizen. Nay, the really sane man knows that he has a touch of the madman. But the materialist's world is quite simple and solid, just as the madman is quite sure he is sane. The materialist is sure that history has been simply and solely a chain of causation, just as the interesting person before mentioned is quite sure that he is simply and solely a chicken. Materialists and madmen never have doubts.

Spiritual doctrines do not actually limit the mind as do materialistic denials. Even if I believe in immortality I need not think about it. But if I disbelieve in immortality I must not think about it. In the first case the road is open and I can go as far as I like; in the second the road is shut. But the case is even stronger, and the parallel with madness is yet more strange. For it was our case against the exhaustive and logical theory of the lunatic that, right or wrong, it gradually destroyed his humanity. Now it is the charge against the main deductions of the materialist that, right or wrong, they gradually destroy his humanity; I do not mean only kindness, I mean hope, courage, poetry, initiative, all that is human. For instance, when materialism leads men to complete fatalism (as it generally does), it is quite idle to pretend that it is in any sense a liberating force. It is absurd to say that you are especially advancing freedom when you only use free thought to destroy free will. The determinists come to bind, not to loose. They may well call their law the "chain" of causation. It is the worst chain that ever fettered a human being. You may use the language of liberty, if you like, about materialistic teaching, but it is obvious that this is just as inapplicable to it as a whole as the same language when applied to a man locked up in a madhouse. You may say, if you like, that the man is free to think himself a poached egg. But it is surely a more massive and important fact that if he is a poached egg he is not free to eat, drink, sleep, walk, or smoke a cigarette. Similarly you may say, if you like, that the bold determinist speculator is free to disbelieve in the reality of the will. But it is a much more massive and important fact that he is not free to raise, to curse, to thank, to justify, to urge, to punish, to resist temptations, to incite mobs, to make New Year resolutions, to pardon sinners, to rebuke tyrants, or even to say "thank you" for the mustard.

In passing from this subject I may note that there is a queer fallacy to the effect that materialistic fatalism is in some way favourable to mercy, to the abolition of cruel punishments or punishments of any kind. This is startlingly the reverse of the truth. It is quite tenable that the doctrine of necessity makes no difference at all; that it leaves the flogger flogging and the kind friend exhorting as before. But obviously if it stops either of them it stops the kind exhortation. That the sins are inevitable does not prevent punishment; if it prevents anything it prevents persuasion. Determinism is quite as likely to lead to cruelty as it is certain to lead to cowardice. Determinism is not inconsistent with the cruel treatment of criminals. What it is (perhaps) inconsistent with is the generous treatment of criminals; with any appeal to their better feelings or encouragement in their moral struggle. The determinist does not believe in appealing to the will, but he does believe in changing the environment. He must not say to the sinner, "Go and sin no more," because the sinner cannot help it. But he can put him in boiling oil; for boiling oil is an environment. Considered as a figure, therefore, the materialist has the fantastic outline of the figure of the madman. Both take up a position at once unanswerable and intolerable.

Of course it is not only of the materialist that all this is true. The same would apply to the other extreme of speculative logic. There is a sceptic far more terrible than he who believes that everything began in matter. It is possible to meet the sceptic who believes that everything began in himself. He doubts not the existence of angels or devils, but the existence of men and cows. For him his own friends are a mythology made up by himself. He created his own father and his own mother. This horrible fancy has in it something decidedly attractive to the somewhat mystical egoism of our day. That publisher who thought that men would get on if they believed in themselves, those seekers after the Superman who are always looking for him in the looking-glass, those writers who talk about impressing their personalities instead of creating life for the world, all these people have really only an inch between them and this awful emptiness. Then when this kindly world all round the man has been blackened out like a lie; when friends fade into ghosts, and the foundations of the world fail; then when the man, believing in nothing and in no man, is alone in his own nightmare, then the great individualistic motto shall be written over him in avenging irony. The stars will be only dots in the blackness of his own brain; his mother's face will be only a sketch from his own insane pencil on the walls of his cell. But over his cell shall be written, with dreadful truth, "He believes in himself."

All that concerns us here, however, is to note that this panegoistic extreme of thought exhibits the same paradox as the other extreme of materialism. It is equally complete in theory and equally crippling in practice. For the sake of simplicity, it is easier to state the notion by saying that a man can believe that he is always in a dream. Now, obviously there can be no positive proof given to him that he is not in a dream, for the simple reason that no proof can be offered that might not be offered in a dream. But if the man began to burn down London and say that his housekeeper would soon call him to breakfast, we should take him and put him with other logicians in a place which has often been alluded to in the course of this chapter. The man who cannot believe his senses, and the man who cannot believe anything else, are both insane, but their insanity is proved not by any error in their argument, but by the manifest mistake of their whole lives. They have both locked themselves up in two boxes, painted inside with the sun and stars; they are both unable to get out, the one into the health and happiness of heaven, the other even into the health and happiness of the earth. Their position is quite reasonable; nay, in a sense it is infinitely reasonable, just as a threepenny bit is infinitely circular. But there is such a thing as a mean infinity, a base and slavish eternity. It is amusing to notice that many of the moderns, whether sceptics or mystics, have taken as their sign a certain eastern symbol, which is the very symbol of this ultimate nullity. When they wish to represent eternity, they represent it by a serpent with his tail in his mouth. There is a startling sarcasm in the image of that very unsatisfactory meal. The eternity of the material fatalists, the eternity of the eastern pessimists, the eternity of the supercilious theosophists and higher scientists of to-day is, indeed, very well presented by a serpent eating his tail, a degraded animal who destroys even himself.

This chapter is purely practical and is concerned with what actually is the chief mark and element of insanity; we may say in summary that it is reason used without root, reason in the void. The man who begins to think without the proper first principles goes mad; he begins to think at the wrong end. And for the rest of these pages we have to try and discover what is the right end. But we may ask in conclusion, if this be what drives men mad, what is it that keeps them sane? By the end of this book I hope to give a definite, some will think a far too definite, answer. But for the moment it is possible in the same solely practical manner to give a general answer touching what in actual human history keeps men sane. Mysticism keeps men sane. As long as you have mystery you have health; when you destroy mystery you create morbidity. The ordinary man has always been sane because the ordinary man has always been a mystic. He has permitted the twilight. He has always had one foot in earth and the other in fairyland. He has always left himself free to doubt his gods; but (unlike the agnostic of to-day) free also to believe in them. He has always cared more for truth than for consistency. If he saw two truths that seemed to contradict each other, he would take the two truths and the contradiction along with them. His spiritual sight is stereoscopic, like his physical sight: he sees two different pictures at once and yet sees all the better for that. Thus he has always believed that there was such a thing as fate, but such a thing as free will also. Thus he believed that children were indeed the kingdom of heaven, but nevertheless ought to be obedient to the kingdom of earth. He admired youth because it was young and age because it was not. It is exactly this balance of apparent contradictions that has been the whole buoyancy of the healthy man. The whole secret of mysticism is this: that man can understand everything by the help of what he does not understand. The morbid logician seeks to make everything lucid, and succeeds in making everything mysterious. The mystic allows one thing to be mysterious, and everything else becomes lucid. The determinist makes the theory of causation quite clear, and then finds that he cannot say "if you please" to the housemaid. The Christian permits free will to remain a sacred mystery; but because of this his relations with the housemaid become of a sparkling and crystal clearness. He puts the seed of dogma in a central darkness; but it branches forth in all directions with abounding natural health. As we have taken the circle as the symbol of reason and madness, we may very well take the cross as the symbol at once of mystery and of health. Buddhism is centripetal, but Christianity is centrifugal: it breaks out. For the circle is perfect and infinite in its nature; but it is fixed for ever in its size; it can never be larger or smaller. But the cross, though it has at its heart a collision and a contradiction, can extend its four arms for ever without altering its shape. Because it has a paradox in its centre it can grow without changing. The circle returns upon itself and is bound. The cross opens its arms to the four winds; it is a signpost for free travellers.

Symbols alone are of even a cloudy value in speaking of this deep matter; and another symbol from physical nature will express sufficiently well the real place of mysticism before mankind. The one created thing which we cannot look at is the one thing in the light of which we look at everything. Like the sun at noonday, mysticism explains everything else by the blaze of its own victorious invisibility. Detached intellectualism is (in the exact sense of a popular phrase) all moonshine; for it is light without heat, and it is secondary light, reflected from a dead world. But the Greeks were right when they made Apollo the god both of imagination and of sanity; for he was both the patron of poetry and the patron of healing. Of necessary dogmas and a special creed I shall speak later. But that transcendentalism by which all men live has primarily much the position of the sun in the sky. We are conscious of it as of a kind of splendid confusion; it is something both shining and shapeless, at once a blaze and a blur. But the circle of the moon is as clear and unmistakable, as recurrent and inevitable, as the circle of Euclid on a blackboard. For the moon is utterly reasonable; and the moon is the mother of lunatics and has given to them all her name.

146

THE SUICIDE OF THOUGHT

The phrases of the street are not only forcible but subtle: for a figure of speech can often get into a crack too small for a definition. Phrases like "put out" or "off colour" might have been coined by Mr. Henry James in an agony of verbal precision. And there is no more subtle truth than that of the everyday phrase about a man having "his heart in the right place." It involves the idea of normal proportion; not only does a certain function exist, but it is rightly related to other functions. Indeed, the negation of this phrase would describe with peculiar accuracy the somewhat morbid mercy and perverse tenderness of the most representative moderns. If, for instance, I had to describe with fairness the character of Mr. Bernard Shaw, I could not express myself more exactly than by saying that he has a heroically large and generous heart; but not a heart in the right place. And this is so of the typical society of our time.

The modern world is not evil; in some ways the modern world is far too good. It is full of wild and wasted virtues. When a religious scheme is shattered (as Christianity was shattered at the Reformation), it is not merely the vices that are let loose. The vices are, indeed, let loose, and they wander and do damage. But the virtues are let loose also; and the virtues wander more wildly, and the virtues do more terrible damage. The modern world is full of the old Christian virtues gone mad. The virtues have gone mad because they have been isolated from each other and are wandering alone. Thus some scientists care for truth; and their truth is pitiless. Thus some humanitarians only care for pity; and their pity (I am sorry to say) is often untruthful. For example, Mr. Blatchford attacks Christianity because he is mad on one Christian virtue: the merely mystical and almost irrational virtue of charity. He has a strange idea that he will make it easier to forgive sins by saying that there are no sins to forgive. Mr. Blatchford is not only an early Christian, he is the only early Christian who ought really to have been eaten by lions. For in his case the pagan accusation is really true: his mercy would mean mere anarchy. He really is the enemy of the human race—because he is so human. As the other extreme, we may take the acrid realist, who has deliberately killed in himself all human pleasure in happy tales or in the healing of the heart. Torquemada tortured people physically for the sake of moral truth. Zola tortured people morally for the sake of physical truth. But in Torquemada's time there was at least a system that could to some extent make righteousness and peace kiss each other. Now they do not even bow. But a much stronger case than these two of truth and pity can be found in the remarkable case of the dislocation of humility.

It is only with one aspect of humility that we are here concerned.

Humility was largely meant as a restraint upon the arrogance and infinity of the appetite of man. He was always outstripping his mercies with his own newly invented needs. His very power of enjoyment destroyed half his joys. By asking for pleasure, he lost the chief pleasure; for the chief pleasure is surprise. Hence it became evident that if a man would make his world large, he must be always making himself small. Even the haughty visions, the tall cities, and the toppling pinnacles are the creations of humility. Giants that tread down forests like grass are the creations of humility. Towers that vanish upwards above the loneliest star are the creations of humility. For towers are not tall unless we look up at them; and giants are not giants unless they are larger than we. All this gigantesque imagination, which is, perhaps, the mightiest of the pleasures of man, is at bottom entirely humble. It is impossible without humility to enjoy anything— even pride.

But what we suffer from to-day is humility in the wrong place. Modesty has moved from the organ of ambition. Modesty has settled upon the organ of conviction; where it was never meant to be. A man was meant to be doubtful about himself, but undoubting about the truth; this has been exactly reversed. Nowadays the part of a man that a man does assert is exactly the part he ought not to assert—himself. The part he doubts is exactly the part he ought not to doubt—the Divine Reason. Huxley preached a humility content to learn from Nature. But the new sceptic is so humble that he doubts if he can even learn. Thus we should be wrong if we had said hastily that there is no humility typical of our time. The truth is that there is a real humility typical of our time; but it so happens that it is practically a more poisonous humility than the wildest prostrations of the ascetic. The old humility was a spur that prevented a man from stopping; not a nail in his boot that prevented him from going on. For the old humility made a man doubtful about his efforts, which might make him work harder. But the new humility makes a man doubtful about his aims, which will make him stop working altogether.

At any street corner we may meet a man who utters the frantic and blasphemous statement that he may be wrong. Every day one comes across somebody who says that of course his view may not be the right one. Of course his view must be the right one, or it is not his view. We are on the road to producing a race of men too mentally modest to believe in the multiplication table. We are in danger of seeing philosophers who doubt the law of gravity as being a mere fancy of their own. Scoffers of old time were too proud to be convinced; but these are too humble to be convinced. The meek do inherit the earth; but the modern sceptics are too meek even to claim their inheritance. It is exactly this intellectual helplessness which is our second problem.

The last chapter has been concerned only with a fact of observation: that what peril of morbidity there is for man comes rather from his reason than his imagination. It was not meant to attack the authority of reason; rather it is the ultimate purpose to defend it. For it needs defence. The whole modern world is at war with reason; and the tower already reels.

The sages, it is often said, can see no answer to the riddle of religion. But the trouble with our sages is not that they cannot see the answer; it is that they cannot even see the riddle. They are like children so stupid as to notice nothing paradoxical in the playful assertion that a door is not a door. The modern latitudinarians speak, for instance, about authority in religion not only as if there were no reason in it, but as if there had never been any reason for it. Apart from seeing its philosophical basis, they cannot even see its historical cause. Religious authority has often, doubtless, been oppressive or unreasonable; just as every legal system (and especially our present one) has been callous and full of a cruel apathy. It is rational to attack the police; nay, it is glorious. But the modern critics of religious authority are like men who should attack the police without ever having heard of burglars. For there is a great and possible peril to the human mind: a peril as practical as burglary. Against it religious authority was reared, rightly or wrongly, as a barrier. And against it something certainly must be reared as a barrier, if our race is to avoid ruin.

That peril is that the human intellect is free to destroy itself. Just as one generation could prevent the very existence of the next generation, by all entering a monastery or jumping into the sea, so one set of thinkers can in some degree prevent further thinking by teaching the next generation that there is no validity in any human thought. It is idle to talk always of the alternative of reason and faith. Reason is itself a matter of faith. It is an act of faith to assert that our thoughts have any relation to reality at all. If you are merely a sceptic, you must sooner or later ask yourself the question, "Why should ANYTHING go right; even observation and deduction? Why should not good logic be as misleading as bad logic? They are both movements in the brain of a bewildered ape?" The young sceptic says, "I have a right to think for myself." But the old sceptic, the complete sceptic, says, "I have no right to think for myself. I have no right to think at all."

There is a thought that stops thought. That is the only thought that ought to be stopped. That is the ultimate evil against which all religious authority was aimed. It only appears at the end of decadent ages like our own: and already Mr. H.G. Wells has raised its ruinous banner; he has written a delicate piece of scepticism called "Doubts of the Instrument." In this he questions the brain itself, and endeavours to remove all reality from all his own assertions, past, present, and to come. But it was against this remote ruin that all the military systems in religion were originally ranked and ruled. The creeds and the crusades, the hierarchies and the horrible persecutions were not organized, as is ignorantly said, for the suppression of reason. They were organized for the difficult defence of reason. Man, by a blind instinct, knew that if once things were wildly questioned, reason could be questioned first. The authority of priests to absolve, the authority of popes to define the authority, even of inquisitors to terrify: these were all only dark defences erected round one central authority, more undemonstrable, more supernatural than all—the authority of a man to think. We know now that this is so; we have no excuse for not knowing it. For we can hear scepticism crashing through the old ring of authorities, and at the same moment we can see reason swaying upon her throne. In so far as religion is gone, reason is going. For they are both of the same primary and authoritative kind. They are both methods of proof which cannot themselves be proved. And in the act of destroying the idea of Divine authority we have largely destroyed the idea of that human authority by which we do a long-division sum. With a long and sustained tug we have attempted to pull the mitre off pontifical man; and his head has come off with it.

Lest this should be called loose assertion, it is perhaps desirable, though dull, to run rapidly through the chief modern fashions of thought which have this effect of stopping thought itself. Materialism and the view of everything as a personal illusion have some such effect; for if the mind is mechanical, thought cannot be very exciting, and if the cosmos is unreal, there is nothing to think about. But in these cases the effect is indirect and doubtful. In some cases it is direct and clear; notably in the case of what is generally called evolution.

Evolution is a good example of that modern intelligence which, if it destroys anything, destroys itself. Evolution is either an innocent scientific description of how certain earthly things came about; or, if it is anything more than this, it is an attack upon thought itself. If evolution destroys anything, it does not destroy religion but rationalism. If evolution simply means that a positive thing called an ape turned very slowly into a positive thing called a man, then it is stingless for the most orthodox; for a personal God might just as well do things slowly as quickly, especially if, like the Christian God, he were outside time. But if it means anything more, it means that there is no such thing as an ape to change, and no such thing as a man for him to change into. It means that there is no such thing as a thing. At best, there is only one thing, and that is a flux of everything and anything. This is an attack not upon the faith, but upon the mind; you cannot think if there are no things to think about. You cannot think if you are not separate from the subject of thought. Descartes said, "I think; therefore I am." The philosophic evolutionist reverses and negatives the epigram. He says, "I am not; therefore I cannot think."

Then there is the opposite attack on thought: that urged by Mr. H.G. Wells when he insists that every separate thing is "unique," and there are no categories at all. This also is merely destructive. Thinking means connecting things, and stops if they cannot be connected. It need hardly be said that this scepticism forbidding thought necessarily forbids speech; a man cannot open his mouth without contradicting it. Thus when Mr. Wells says (as he did somewhere), "All chairs are quite different," he utters not merely a misstatement, but a contradiction in terms. If all chairs were quite different, you could not call them "all chairs."

Akin to these is the false theory of progress, which maintains that we alter the test instead of trying to pass the test. We often hear it said, for instance, "What is right in one age is wrong in another." This is quite reasonable, if it means that there is a fixed aim, and that certain methods attain at certain times and not at other times. If women, say, desire to be elegant, it may be that they are improved at one time by growing fatter and at another time by growing thinner. But you cannot say that they are improved by ceasing to wish to be elegant and beginning to wish to be oblong. If the standard changes, how can there be improvement, which implies a standard? Nietzsche started a nonsensical idea that men had once sought as good what we now call evil; if it were so, we could not talk of surpassing or even falling short of them. How can you overtake Jones if you walk in the other direction? You cannot discuss whether one people has succeeded more in being miserable than another succeeded in being happy. It would be like discussing whether Milton was more puritanical than a pig is fat.

It is true that a man (a silly man) might make change itself his object or ideal. But as an ideal, change itself becomes unchangeable. If the change-worshipper wishes to estimate his own progress, he must be sternly loyal to the ideal of change; he must not begin to flirt gaily with the ideal of monotony. Progress itself cannot progress. It is worth remark, in passing, that when Tennyson, in a wild and rather weak manner, welcomed the idea of infinite alteration in society, he instinctively took a metaphor which suggests an imprisoned tedium. He wrote—

> "Let the great world spin for ever down the ringing
> grooves of change."

He thought of change itself as an unchangeable groove; and so it is. Change is about the narrowest and hardest groove that a man can get into.

The main point here, however, is that this idea of a fundamental alteration in the standard is one of the things that make thought about the past or future simply impossible. The theory of a complete change of standards in human history does not merely deprive us of the pleasure of honouring our fathers; it deprives us even of the more modern and aristocratic pleasure of despising them.

151

This bald summary of the thought-destroying forces of our time would not be complete without some reference to pragmatism; for though I have here used and should everywhere defend the pragmatist method as a preliminary guide to truth, there is an extreme application of it which involves the absence of all truth whatever. My meaning can be put shortly thus. I agree with the pragmatists that apparent objective truth is not the whole matter; that there is an authoritative need to believe the things that are necessary to the human mind. But I say that one of those necessities precisely is a belief in objective truth. The pragmatist tells a man to think what he must think and never mind the Absolute. But precisely one of the things that he must think is the Absolute. This philosophy, indeed, is a kind of verbal paradox. Pragmatism is a matter of human needs; and one of the first of human needs is to be something more than a pragmatist. Extreme pragmatism is just as inhuman as the determinism it so powerfully attacks. The determinist (who, to do him justice, does not pretend to be a human being) makes nonsense of the human sense of actual choice. The pragmatist, who professes to be specially human, makes nonsense of the human sense of actual fact.

To sum up our contention so far, we may say that the most characteristic current philosophies have not only a touch of mania, but a touch of suicidal mania. The mere questioner has knocked his head against the limits of human thought; and cracked it. This is what makes so futile the warnings of the orthodox and the boasts of the advanced about the dangerous boyhood of free thought. What we are looking at is not the boyhood of free thought; it is the old age and ultimate dissolution of free thought. It is vain for bishops and pious bigwigs to discuss what dreadful things will happen if wild scepticism runs its course. It has run its course. It is vain for eloquent atheists to talk of the great truths that will be revealed if once we see free thought begin. We have seen it end. It has no more questions to ask; it has questioned itself. You cannot call up any wilder vision than a city in which men ask themselves if they have any selves. You cannot fancy a more sceptical world than that in which men doubt if there is a world. It might certainly have reached its bankruptcy more quickly and cleanly if it had not been feebly hampered by the application of indefensible laws of blasphemy or by the absurd pretence that modern England is Christian. But it would have reached the bankruptcy anyhow. Militant atheists are still unjustly persecuted; but rather because they are an old minority than because they are a new one. Free thought has exhausted its own freedom. It is weary of its own success. If any eager freethinker now hails philosophic freedom as the dawn, he is only like the man in Mark Twain who came out wrapped in blankets to see the sun rise and was just in time to see it set. If any frightened curate still says that it will be awful if the darkness of free thought should spread, we can only answer him in the high and powerful words of Mr. Belloc, "Do not, I beseech you, be troubled about the increase of forces already in dissolution. You have mistaken the hour of the night: it is already morning." We have no more questions left to ask. We have looked for questions in the darkest corners and on the wildest peaks. We have found all the questions that can be found. It is time we gave up looking for questions and began looking for answers.

But one more word must be added. At the beginning of this preliminary negative sketch I said that our mental ruin has been wrought by wild reason, not by wild imagination. A man does not go mad because he makes a statue a mile high, but he may go mad by thinking it out in square inches. Now, one school of thinkers has seen this and jumped at it as a way of renewing the pagan health of the world. They see that reason destroys; but Will, they say, creates. The ultimate authority, they say, is in will, not in reason. The supreme point is not why a man demands a thing, but the fact that he does demand it. I have no space to trace or expound this philosophy of Will. It came, I suppose, through Nietzsche, who preached something that is called egoism. That, indeed, was simpleminded enough; for Nietzsche denied egoism simply by preaching it. To preach anything is to give it away. First, the egoist calls life a war without mercy, and then he takes the greatest possible trouble to drill his enemies in war. To preach egoism is to practise altruism. But however it began, the view is common enough in current literature. The main defence of these thinkers is that they are not thinkers; they are makers. They say that choice is itself the divine thing. Thus Mr. Bernard Shaw has attacked the old idea that men's acts are to be judged by the standard of the desire of happiness. He says that a man does not act for his happiness, but from his will. He does not say, "Jam will make me happy," but "I want jam." And in all this others follow him with yet greater enthusiasm. Mr. John Davidson, a remarkable poet, is so passionately excited about it that he is obliged to write prose. He publishes a short play with several long prefaces. This is natural enough in Mr. Shaw, for all his plays are prefaces: Mr. Shaw is (I suspect) the only man on earth who has never written any poetry. But that Mr. Davidson (who can write excellent poetry) should write instead laborious metaphysics in defence of this doctrine of will, does show that the doctrine of will has taken hold of men. Even Mr. H.G. Wells has half spoken in its language; saying that one should test acts not like a thinker, but like an artist, saying, "I FEEL this curve is right," or "that line SHALL go thus." They are all excited; and well they may be. For by this doctrine of the divine authority of will, they think they can break out of the doomed fortress of rationalism. They think they can escape.

But they cannot escape. This pure praise of volition ends in the same break up and blank as the mere pursuit of logic. Exactly as complete free thought involves the doubting of thought itself, so the acceptance of mere "willing" really paralyzes the will. Mr. Bernard Shaw has not perceived the real difference between the old utilitarian test of pleasure (clumsy, of course, and easily misstated) and that which he propounds. The real difference between the test of happiness and the test of will is simply that the test of happiness is a test and the other isn't. You can discuss whether a man's act in jumping over a cliff was directed towards happiness; you cannot discuss whether it was derived from will. Of course it was. You can praise an action by saying that it is calculated to bring pleasure or pain to discover truth or to save the soul. But you cannot praise an action because it shows will; for to say that is merely to say that it is an action. By this praise of will you cannot really choose one course as better than another. And yet choosing one course as better than another is the very definition of the will you are praising.

The worship of will is the negation of will. To admire mere choice is to refuse to choose. If Mr. Bernard Shaw comes up to me and says, "Will something," that is tantamount to saying, "I do not mind what you will," and that is tantamount to saying, "I have no will in the matter." You cannot admire will in general, because the essence of will is that it is particular. A brilliant anarchist like Mr. John Davidson feels an irritation against ordinary morality, and therefore he invokes will—will to anything. He only wants humanity to want something. But humanity does want something. It wants ordinary morality. He rebels against the law and tells us to will something or anything. But we have willed something. We have willed the law against which he rebels.

All the will-worshippers, from Nietzsche to Mr. Davidson, are really quite empty of volition. They cannot will, they can hardly wish. And if any one wants a proof of this, it can be found quite easily. It can be found in this fact: that they always talk of will as something that expands and breaks out. But it is quite the opposite. Every act of will is an act of self-limitation. To desire action is to desire limitation. In that sense every act is an act of self-sacrifice. When you choose anything, you reject everything else. That objection, which men of this school used to make to the act of marriage, is really an objection to every act. Every act is an irrevocable selection and exclusion. Just as when you marry one woman you give up all the others, so when you take one course of action you give up all the other courses. If you become King of England, you give up the post of Beadle in Brompton. If you go to Rome, you sacrifice a rich suggestive life in Wimbledon. It is the existence of this negative or limiting side of will that makes most of the talk of the anarchic will-worshippers little better than nonsense. For instance, Mr. John Davidson tells us to have nothing to do with "Thou shalt not"; but it is surely obvious that "Thou shalt not" is only one of the necessary corollaries of "I will." "I will go to the Lord Mayor's Show, and thou shalt not stop me." Anarchism adjures us to be bold creative artists, and care for no laws or limits. But it is impossible to be an artist and not care for laws and limits. Art is limitation; the essence of every picture is the frame. If you draw a giraffe, you must draw him with a long neck. If, in your bold creative way, you hold yourself free to draw a giraffe with a short neck, you will really find that you are not free to draw a giraffe. The moment you step into the world of facts, you step into a world of limits. You can free things from alien or accidental laws, but not from the laws of their own nature. You may, if you like, free a tiger from his bars; but do not free him from his stripes. Do not free a camel of the burden of his hump: you may be freeing him from being a camel. Do not go about as a demagogue, encouraging triangles to break out of the prison of their three sides. If a triangle breaks out of its three sides, its life comes to a lamentable end. Somebody wrote a work called "The Loves of the Triangles"; I never read it, but I am sure that if triangles ever were loved, they were loved for being triangular. This is certainly the case with all artistic creation, which is in some ways the most decisive example of pure will. The artist loves his limitations: they constitute the THING he is doing. The painter is glad that the canvas is flat. The sculptor is glad that the clay is colourless.

In case the point is not clear, an historic example may illustrate it. The French Revolution was really an heroic and decisive thing, because the Jacobins willed something definite and limited. They desired the freedoms of democracy, but also all the vetoes of democracy. They wished to have votes and NOT to have titles. Republicanism had an ascetic side in Franklin or Robespierre as well as an expansive side in Danton or Wilkes. Therefore they have created something with a solid substance and shape, the square social equality and peasant wealth of France. But since then the revolutionary or speculative mind of Europe has been weakened by shrinking from any proposal because of the limits of that proposal. Liberalism has been degraded into liberality. Men have tried to turn "revolutionise" from a transitive to an intransitive verb. The Jacobin could tell you not only the system he would rebel against, but (what was more important) the system he would NOT rebel against, the system he would trust. But the new rebel is a Sceptic, and will not entirely trust anything. He has no loyalty; therefore he can never be really a revolutionist. And the fact that he doubts everything really gets in his way when he wants to denounce anything. For all denunciation implies a moral doctrine of some kind; and the modern revolutionist doubts not only the institution he denounces, but the doctrine by which he denounces it. Thus he writes one book complaining that imperial oppression insults the purity of women, and then he writes another book (about the sex problem) in which he insults it himself. He curses the Sultan because Christian girls lose their virginity, and then curses Mrs. Grundy because they keep it. As a politician, he will cry out that war is a waste of life, and then, as a philosopher, that all life is waste of time. A Russian pessimist will denounce a policeman for killing a peasant, and then prove by the highest philosophical principles that the peasant ought to have killed himself. A man denounces marriage as a lie, and then denounces aristocratic profligates for treating it as a lie. He calls a flag a bauble, and then blames the oppressors of Poland or Ireland because they take away that bauble. The man of this school goes first to a political meeting, where he complains that savages are treated as if they were beasts; then he takes his hat and umbrella and goes on to a scientific meeting, where he proves that they practically are beasts. In short, the modern revolutionist, being an infinite sceptic, is always engaged in undermining his own mines. In his book on politics he attacks men for trampling on morality; in his book on ethics he attacks morality for trampling on men. Therefore the modern man in revolt has become practically useless for all purposes of revolt. By rebelling against everything he has lost his right to rebel against anything.

It may be added that the same blank and bankruptcy can be observed in all fierce and terrible types of literature, especially in satire. Satire may be mad and anarchic, but it presupposes an admitted superiority in certain things over others; it presupposes a standard. When little boys in the street laugh at the fatness of some distinguished journalist, they are unconsciously assuming a standard of Greek sculpture. They are appealing to the marble Apollo. And the curious disappearance of satire from our literature is an instance of the fierce things fading for want of any principle to be fierce about. Nietzsche had some natural talent for sarcasm: he could sneer, though he could not laugh; but there is always something bodiless and without weight in his satire, simply because it has not any mass of common morality behind it. He is himself more preposterous than anything he denounces. But, indeed, Nietzsche will stand very well as the type of the whole of this failure of abstract violence. The softening of the brain which ultimately overtook him was not a physical accident. If Nietzsche had not ended in imbecility, Nietzscheism would end in imbecility. Thinking in isolation and with pride ends in being an idiot. Every man who will not have softening of the heart must at last have softening of the brain.

This last attempt to evade intellectualism ends in intellectualism, and therefore in death. The sortie has failed. The wild worship of lawlessness and the materialist worship of law end in the same void. Nietzsche scales staggering mountains, but he turns up ultimately in Tibet. He sits down beside Tolstoy in the land of nothing and Nirvana. They are both helpless—one because he must not grasp anything, and the other because he must not let go of anything. The Tolstoyan's will is frozen by a Buddhist instinct that all special actions are evil. But the Nietzscheite's will is quite equally frozen by his view that all special actions are good; for if all special actions are good, none of them are special. They stand at the crossroads, and one hates all the roads and the other likes all the roads. The result is—well, some things are not hard to calculate. They stand at the cross-roads.

Here I end (thank God) the first and dullest business of this book—the rough review of recent thought. After this I begin to sketch a view of life which may not interest my reader, but which, at any rate, interests me. In front of me, as I close this page, is a pile of modern books that I have been turning over for the purpose—a pile of ingenuity, a pile of futility. By the accident of my present detachment, I can see the inevitable smash of the philosophies of Schopenhauer and Tolstoy, Nietzsche and Shaw, as clearly as an inevitable railway smash could be seen from a balloon. They are all on the road to the emptiness of the asylum. For madness may be defined as using mental activity so as to reach mental helplessness; and they have nearly reached it. He who thinks he is made of glass, thinks to the destruction of thought; for glass cannot think. So he who wills to reject nothing, wills the destruction of will; for will is not only the choice of something, but the rejection of almost everything. And as I turn and tumble over the clever, wonderful, tiresome, and useless modern books, the title of one of them rivets my eye. It is called "Jeanne d'Arc," by Anatole France. I have only glanced at it, but a glance was enough to remind me of Renan's "Vie de Jesus." It has the same strange method of the reverent sceptic. It discredits supernatural stories that have some foundation, simply by telling natural stories that have no foundation. Because we cannot believe in what a saint did, we are to pretend that we know exactly what he felt. But I do not mention either book in order to criticise it, but because the accidental combination of the names called up two startling images of Sanity which blasted all the books before me. Joan of Arc was not stuck at the cross-roads, either by rejecting all the paths like Tolstoy, or by accepting them all like Nietzsche. She chose a path, and went down it like a thunderbolt. Yet Joan, when I came to think of her, had in her all that was true either in Tolstoy or Nietzsche, all that was even tolerable in either of them. I thought of all that is noble in Tolstoy, the pleasure in plain things, especially in plain pity, the actualities of the earth, the reverence for the poor, the dignity of the bowed back. Joan of Arc had all that and with this great addition, that she endured poverty as well as admiring it; whereas Tolstoy is only a typical aristocrat trying to find out its secret. And then I thought of all that was brave and proud and pathetic in poor Nietzsche, and his mutiny against the emptiness and timidity of our time. I thought of his cry for the ecstatic equilibrium of danger, his hunger for the rush of great horses, his cry to arms. Well, Joan of Arc had all that, and again with this difference, that she did not praise fighting, but fought. We KNOW that she was not afraid of an army, while Nietzsche, for all we know, was afraid of a cow. Tolstoy only praised the peasant; she was the peasant. Nietzsche only praised the warrior; she was the warrior. She beat them both at their own antagonistic ideals;

she was more gentle than the one, more violent than the other. Yet she was a perfectly practical person who did something, while they are wild speculators who do nothing. It was impossible that the thought should not cross my mind that she and her faith had perhaps some secret of moral unity and utility that has been lost. And with that thought came a larger one, and the colossal figure of her Master had also crossed the theatre of my thoughts. The same modern difficulty which darkened the subject-matter of Anatole France also darkened that of Ernest Renan. Renan also divided his hero's pity from his hero's pugnacity. Renan even represented the righteous anger at Jerusalem as a mere nervous breakdown after the idyllic expectations of Galilee. As if there were any inconsistency between having a love for humanity and having a hatred for inhumanity! Altruists, with thin, weak voices, denounce Christ as an egoist. Egoists (with even thinner and weaker voices) denounce Him as an altruist. In our present atmosphere such cavils are comprehensible enough. The love of a hero is more terrible than the hatred of a tyrant. The hatred of a hero is more generous than the love of a philanthropist. There is a huge and heroic sanity of which moderns can only collect the fragments. There is a giant of whom we see only the lopped arms and legs walking about. They have torn the soul of Christ into silly strips, labelled egoism and altruism, and they are equally puzzled by His insane magnificence and His insane meekness. They have parted His garments among them, and for His vesture they have cast lots; though the coat was without seam woven from the top throughout.

THE ETHICS OF ELFLAND

When the business man rebukes the idealism of his office-boy, it is commonly in some such speech as this: "Ah, yes, when one is young, one has these ideals in the abstract and these castles in the air; but in middle age they all break up like clouds, and one comes down to a belief in practical politics, to using the machinery one has and getting on with the world as it is." Thus, at least, venerable and philanthropic old men now in their honoured graves used to talk to me when I was a boy. But since then I have grown up and have discovered that these philanthropic old men were telling lies. What has really happened is exactly the opposite of what they said would happen. They said that I should lose my ideals and begin to believe in the methods of practical politicians. Now, I have not lost my ideals in the least; my faith in fundamentals is exactly what it always was. What I have lost is my old childlike faith in practical politics. I am still as much concerned as ever about the Battle of Armageddon; but I am not so much concerned about the General Election. As a babe I leapt up on my mother's knee at the mere mention of it. No; the vision is always solid and reliable. The vision is always a fact. It is the reality that is often a fraud. As much as I ever did, more than I ever did, I believe in Liberalism. But there was a rosy time of innocence when I believed in Liberals.

I take this instance of one of the enduring faiths because, having now to trace the roots of my personal speculation, this may be counted, I think, as the only positive bias. I was brought up a Liberal, and have always believed in democracy, in the elementary liberal doctrine of a self-governing humanity. If any one finds the phrase vague or threadbare, I can only pause for a moment to explain that the principle of democracy, as I mean it, can be stated in two propositions. The first is this: that the things common to all men are more important than the things peculiar to any men. Ordinary things are more valuable than extraordinary things; nay, they are more extraordinary. Man is something more awful than men; something more strange. The sense of the miracle of humanity itself should be always more vivid to us than any marvels of power, intellect, art, or civilization. The mere man on two legs, as such, should be felt as something more heartbreaking than any music and more startling than any caricature. Death is more tragic even than death by starvation. Having a nose is more comic even than having a Norman nose.

This is the first principle of democracy: that the essential things in men are the things they hold in common, not the things they hold separately. And the second principle is merely this: that the political instinct or desire is one of these things which they hold in common. Falling in love is more poetical than dropping into poetry. The democratic contention is that government (helping to rule the tribe) is a thing like falling in love, and not a thing like dropping into poetry. It is not something analogous to playing the church organ, painting on vellum, discovering the North Pole (that insidious habit), looping the loop, being Astronomer Royal, and so on. For these things we do not wish a man to do at all unless he does them well. It is, on the contrary, a thing analogous to writing one's own love-letters or blowing one's own nose. These things we want a man to do for himself, even if he does them badly. I am not here arguing the truth of any of these conceptions; I know that some moderns are asking to have their wives chosen by scientists, and they may soon be asking, for all I know, to have their noses blown by nurses. I merely say that mankind does recognize these universal human functions, and that democracy classes government among them. In short, the democratic faith is this: that the most terribly important things must be left to ordinary men themselves—the mating of the sexes, the rearing of the young, the laws of the state. This is democracy; and in this I have always believed.

But there is one thing that I have never from my youth up been able to understand. I have never been able to understand where people got the idea that democracy was in some way opposed to tradition. It is obvious that tradition is only democracy extended through time. It is trusting to a consensus of common human voices rather than to some isolated or arbitrary record. The man who quotes some German historian against the tradition of the Catholic Church, for instance, is strictly appealing to aristocracy. He is appealing to the superiority of one expert against the awful authority of a mob. It is quite easy to see why a legend is treated, and ought to be treated, more respectfully than a book of history. The legend is generally made by the majority of people in the village, who are sane. The book is generally written by the one man in the village who is mad. Those who urge against tradition that men in the past were ignorant may go and urge it at the Carlton Club, along with the statement that voters in the slums are ignorant. It will not do for us. If we attach great importance to the opinion of ordinary men in great unanimity when we are dealing with daily matters, there is no reason why we should disregard it when we are dealing with history or fable. Tradition may be defined as an extension of the franchise. Tradition means giving votes to the most obscure of all classes, our ancestors. It is the democracy of the dead. Tradition refuses to submit to the small and arrogant oligarchy of those who merely happen to be walking about. All democrats object to men being disqualified by the accident of birth; tradition objects to their being disqualified by the accident of death. Democracy tells us not to neglect a good man's opinion, even if he is our groom; tradition asks us not to neglect a good man's opinion, even if he is our father. I, at any rate, cannot separate the two ideas of democracy and tradition; it seems evident to me that they are the same idea. We will have the dead at our councils. The ancient Greeks voted by stones; these shall vote by tombstones. It is all quite regular and official, for most tombstones, like most ballot papers, are marked with a cross.

I have first to say, therefore, that if I have had a bias, it was always a bias in favour of democracy, and therefore of tradition. Before we come to any theoretic or logical beginnings I am content to allow for that personal equation; I have always been more inclined to believe the ruck of hard-working people than to believe that special and troublesome literary class to which I belong. I prefer even the fancies and prejudices of the people who see life from the inside to the clearest demonstrations of the people who see life from the outside. I would always trust the old wives' fables against the old maids' facts. As long as wit is mother wit it can be as wild as it pleases.

Now, I have to put together a general position, and I pretend to no training in such things. I propose to do it, therefore, by writing down one after another the three or four fundamental ideas which I have found for myself, pretty much in the way that I found them. Then I shall roughly synthesise them, summing up my personal philosophy or natural religion; then I shall describe my startling discovery that the whole thing had been discovered before. It had been discovered by Christianity. But of these profound persuasions which I have to recount in order, the earliest was concerned with this element of popular tradition. And without the foregoing explanation touching tradition and democracy I could hardly make my mental experience clear. As it is, I do not know whether I can make it clear, but I now propose to try.

My first and last philosophy, that which I believe in with unbroken certainty, I learnt in the nursery. I generally learnt it from a nurse; that is, from the solemn and star-appointed priestess at once of democracy and tradition. The things I believed most then, the things I believe most now, are the things called fairy tales. They seem to me to be the entirely reasonable things. They are not fantasies: compared with them other things are fantastic. Compared with them religion and rationalism are both abnormal, though religion is abnormally right and rationalism abnormally wrong. Fairyland is nothing but the sunny country of common sense. It is not earth that judges heaven, but heaven that judges earth; so for me at least it was not earth that criticised elfland, but elfland that criticised the earth. I knew the magic beanstalk before I had tasted beans; I was sure of the Man in the Moon before I was certain of the moon. This was at one with all popular tradition. Modern minor poets are naturalists, and talk about the bush or the brook; but the singers of the old epics and fables were supernaturalists, and talked about the gods of brook and bush. That is what the moderns mean when they say that the ancients did not "appreciate Nature," because they said that Nature was divine. Old nurses do not tell children about the grass, but about the fairies that dance on the grass; and the old Greeks could not see the trees for the dryads.

But I deal here with what ethic and philosophy come from being fed on fairy tales. If I were describing them in detail I could note many noble and healthy principles that arise from them. There is the chivalrous lesson of "Jack the Giant Killer"; that giants should be killed because they are gigantic. It is a manly mutiny against pride as such. For the rebel is older than all the kingdoms, and the Jacobin has more tradition than the Jacobite. There is the lesson of "Cinderella," which is the same as that of the Magnificat— EXALTAVIT HUMILES. There is the great lesson of "Beauty and the Beast"; that a thing must be loved BEFORE it is loveable. There is the terrible allegory of the "Sleeping Beauty," which tells how the human creature was blessed with all birthday gifts, yet cursed with death; and how death also may perhaps be softened to a sleep. But I am not concerned with any of the separate statutes of elfland, but with the whole spirit of its law, which I learnt before I could speak, and shall retain when I cannot write. I am concerned with a certain way of looking at life, which was created in me by the fairy tales, but has since been meekly ratified by the mere facts.

It might be stated this way. There are certain sequences or developments (cases of one thing following another), which are, in the true sense of the word, reasonable. They are, in the true sense of the word, necessary. Such are mathematical and merely logical sequences. We in fairyland (who are the most reasonable of all creatures) admit that reason and that necessity. For instance, if the Ugly Sisters are older than Cinderella, it is (in an iron and awful sense) NECESSARY that Cinderella is younger than the Ugly Sisters. There is no getting out of it. Haeckel may talk as much fatalism about that fact as he pleases: it really must be. If Jack is the son of a miller, a miller is the father of Jack. Cold reason decrees it from her awful throne: and we in fairyland submit. If the three brothers all ride horses, there are six animals and eighteen legs involved: that is true rationalism, and fairyland is full of it. But as I put my head over the hedge of the elves and began to take notice of the natural world, I observed an extraordinary thing. I observed that learned men in spectacles were talking of the actual things that happened— dawn and death and so on—as if THEY were rational and inevitable. They talked as if the fact that trees bear fruit were just as NECESSARY as the fact that two and one trees make three. But it is not. There is an enormous difference by the test of fairyland; which is the test of the imagination. You cannot IMAGINE two and one not making three. But you can easily imagine trees not growing fruit; you can imagine them growing golden candlesticks or tigers hanging on by the tail. These men in spectacles spoke much of a man named Newton, who was hit by an apple, and who discovered a law. But they could not be got to see the distinction between a true law, a law of reason, and the mere fact of apples falling. If the apple hit Newton's nose, Newton's nose hit the apple. That is a true necessity: because we cannot conceive the one occurring without the other. But we can quite well conceive the apple not falling on his nose; we can fancy it flying ardently through the air to hit some other nose, of which it had a more definite dislike. We have always in our fairy tales kept this sharp distinction between the science of mental relations, in which there really are laws, and the science of physical facts, in which there are no laws, but only weird repetitions. We believe in bodily miracles, but not in mental impossibilities. We believe that a Bean-stalk climbed up to Heaven; but that does not at all confuse our convictions on the philosophical question of how many beans make five.

Here is the peculiar perfection of tone and truth in the nursery tales. The man of science says, "Cut the stalk, and the apple will fall"; but he says it calmly, as if the one idea really led up to the other. The witch in the fairy tale says, "Blow the horn, and the ogre's castle will fall"; but she does not say it as if it were something in which the effect obviously arose out of the cause. Doubtless she has given the advice to many champions, and has seen many castles fall, but she does not lose either her wonder or her reason. She does not muddle her head until it imagines a necessary mental connection between a horn and a falling tower. But the scientific men do muddle their heads, until they imagine a necessary mental connection between an apple leaving the tree and an apple reaching the ground. They do really talk as if they had found not only a set of marvellous facts, but a truth connecting those facts. They do talk as if the connection of two strange things physically connected them philosophically. They feel that because one incomprehensible thing constantly follows another incomprehensible thing the two together somehow make up a comprehensible thing. Two black riddles make a white answer.

In fairyland we avoid the word "law"; but in the land of science they are singularly fond of it. Thus they will call some interesting conjecture about how forgotten folks pronounced the alphabet, Grimm's Law. But Grimm's Law is far less intellectual than Grimm's Fairy Tales. The tales are, at any rate, certainly tales; while the law is not a law. A law implies that we know the nature of the generalisation and enactment; not merely that we have noticed some of the effects. If there is a law that pick-pockets shall go to prison, it implies that there is an imaginable mental connection between the idea of prison and the idea of picking pockets. And we know what the idea is. We can say why we take liberty from a man who takes liberties. But we cannot say why an egg can turn into a chicken any more than we can say why a bear could turn into a fairy prince. As IDEAS, the egg and the chicken are further off from each other than the bear and the prince; for no egg in itself suggests a chicken, whereas some princes do suggest bears.

Granted, then, that certain transformations do happen, it is essential that we should regard them in the philosophic manner of fairy tales, not in the unphilosophic manner of science and the "Laws of Nature." When we are asked why eggs turn to birds or fruits fall in autumn, we must answer exactly as the fairy godmother would answer if Cinderella asked her why mice turned to horses or her clothes fell from her at twelve o'clock. We must answer that it is MAGIC. It is not a "law," for we do not understand its general formula. It is not a necessity, for though we can count on it happening practically, we have no right to say that it must always happen. It is no argument for unalterable law (as Huxley fancied) that we count on the ordinary course of things. We do not count on it; we bet on it. We risk the remote possibility of a miracle as we do that of a poisoned pancake or a world-destroying comet. We leave it out of account, not because it is a miracle, and therefore an impossibility, but because it is a miracle, and therefore an exception. All the terms used in the science books, "law," "necessity," "order," "tendency," and so on, are really unintellectual, because they assume an inner synthesis, which we do not possess. The only words that ever satisfied me as describing Nature are the terms used in the fairy books, "charm," "spell," "enchantment." They express the arbitrariness of the fact and its mystery. A tree grows fruit because it is a MAGIC tree. Water runs downhill because it is bewitched. The sun shines because it is bewitched.

I deny altogether that this is fantastic or even mystical. We may have some mysticism later on; but this fairy-tale language about things is simply rational and agnostic. It is the only way I can express in words my clear and definite perception that one thing is quite distinct from another; that there is no logical connection between flying and laying eggs. It is the man who talks about "a law" that he has never seen who is the mystic. Nay, the ordinary scientific man is strictly a sentimentalist. He is a sentimentalist in this essential sense, that he is soaked and swept away by mere associations. He has so often seen birds fly and lay eggs that he feels as if there must be some dreamy, tender connection between the two ideas, whereas there is none. A forlorn lover might be unable to dissociate the moon from lost love; so the materialist is unable to dissociate the moon from the tide. In both cases there is no connection, except that one has seen them together. A sentimentalist might shed tears at the smell of apple-blossom, because, by a dark association of his own, it reminded him of his boyhood. So the materialist professor (though he conceals his tears) is yet a sentimentalist, because, by a dark association of his own, apple-blossoms remind him of apples. But the cool rationalist from fairyland does not see why, in the abstract, the apple tree should not grow crimson tulips; it sometimes does in his country.

This elementary wonder, however, is not a mere fancy derived from the fairy tales; on the contrary, all the fire of the fairy tales is derived from this. Just as we all like love tales because there is an instinct of sex, we all like astonishing tales because they touch the nerve of the ancient instinct of astonishment. This is proved by the fact that when we are very young children we do not need fairy tales: we only need tales. Mere life is interesting enough. A child of seven is excited by being told that Tommy opened a door and saw a dragon. But a child of three is excited by being told that Tommy opened a door. Boys like romantic tales; but babies like realistic tales—because they find them romantic. In fact, a baby is about the only person, I should think, to whom a modern realistic novel could be read without boring him. This proves that even nursery tales only echo an almost pre-natal leap of interest and amazement. These tales say that apples were golden only to refresh the forgotten moment when we found that they were green. They make rivers run with wine only to make us remember, for one wild moment, that they run with water. I have said that this is wholly reasonable and even agnostic. And, indeed, on this point I am all for the higher agnosticism; its better name is Ignorance. We have all read in scientific books, and, indeed, in all romances, the story of the man who has forgotten his name. This man walks about the streets and can see and appreciate everything; only he cannot remember who he is. Well, every man is that man in the story. Every man has forgotten who he is. One may understand the cosmos, but never the ego; the self is more distant than any star. Thou shalt love the Lord thy God; but thou shalt not know thyself. We are all under the same mental calamity; we have all forgotten our names. We have all forgotten what we really are. All that we call common sense and rationality and practicality and positivism only means that for certain dead levels of our life we forget that we have forgotten. All that we call spirit and art and ecstasy only means that for one awful instant we remember that we forget.

But though (like the man without memory in the novel) we walk the streets with a sort of half-witted admiration, still it is admiration. It is admiration in English and not only admiration in Latin. The wonder has a positive element of praise. This is the next milestone to be definitely marked on our road through fairyland. I shall speak in the next chapter about optimists and pessimists in their intellectual aspect, so far as they have one. Here I am only trying to describe the enormous emotions which cannot be described. And the strongest emotion was that life was as precious as it was puzzling. It was an ecstasy because it was an adventure; it was an adventure because it was an opportunity. The goodness of the fairy tale was not affected by the fact that there might be more dragons than princesses; it was good to be in a fairy tale. The test of all happiness is gratitude; and I felt grateful, though I hardly knew to whom. Children are grateful when Santa Claus puts in their stockings gifts of toys or sweets.

Could I not be grateful to Santa Claus when he put in my stockings the gift of two miraculous legs? We thank people for birthday presents of cigars and slippers. Can I thank no one for the birthday present of birth?

There were, then, these two first feelings, indefensible and indisputable. The world was a shock, but it was not merely shocking; existence was a surprise, but it was a pleasant surprise. In fact, all my first views were exactly uttered in a riddle that stuck in my brain from boyhood. The question was, "What did the first frog say?" And the answer was, "Lord, how you made me jump!" That says succinctly all that I am saying. God made the frog jump; but the frog prefers jumping. But when these things are settled there enters the second great principle of the fairy philosophy.

Any one can see it who will simply read "Grimm's Fairy Tales" or the fine collections of Mr. Andrew Lang. For the pleasure of pedantry I will call it the Doctrine of Conditional Joy. Touchstone talked of much virtue in an "if"; according to elfin ethics all virtue is in an "if." The note of the fairy utterance always is, "You may live in a palace of gold and sapphire, if you do not say the word `cow'"; or "You may live happily with the King's daughter, if you do not show her an onion." The vision always hangs upon a veto. All the dizzy and colossal things conceded depend upon one small thing withheld. All the wild and whirling things that are let loose depend upon one thing that is forbidden. Mr. W.B. Yeats, in his exquisite and piercing elfin poetry, describes the elves as lawless; they plunge in innocent anarchy on the unbridled horses of the air—

"Ride on the crest of the dishevelled tide, And dance
upon the mountains like a flame."

It is a dreadful thing to say that Mr. W.B. Yeats does not understand fairyland. But I do say it. He is an ironical Irishman, full of intellectual reactions. He is not stupid enough to understand fairyland. Fairies prefer people of the yokel type like myself; people who gape and grin and do as they are told. Mr. Yeats reads into elfland all the righteous insurrection of his own race. But the lawlessness of Ireland is a Christian lawlessness, founded on reason and justice. The Fenian is rebelling against something he understands only too well; but the true citizen of fairyland is obeying something that he does not understand at all. In the fairy tale an incomprehensible happiness rests upon an incomprehensible condition. A box is opened, and all evils fly out. A word is forgotten, and cities perish. A lamp is lit, and love flies away. A flower is plucked, and human lives are forfeited. An apple is eaten, and the hope of God is gone.

This is the tone of fairy tales, and it is certainly not lawlessness or even liberty, though men under a mean modern tyranny may think it liberty by comparison. People out of Portland Gaol might think Fleet Street free; but closer study will prove that both fairies and journalists are the slaves of duty. Fairy godmothers seem at least as strict as other godmothers. Cinderella received a coach out of Wonderland and a coachman out of nowhere, but she received a command—which might have come out of Brixton—that she should be back by twelve. Also, she had a glass slipper; and it cannot be a coincidence that glass is so common a substance in folklore. This princess lives in a glass castle, that princess on a glass hill; this one sees all things in a mirror; they may all live in glass houses if they will not throw stones. For this thin glitter of glass everywhere is the expression of the fact that the happiness is bright but brittle, like the substance most easily smashed by a housemaid or a cat. And this fairy-tale sentiment also sank into me and became my sentiment towards the whole world. I felt and feel that life itself is as bright as the diamond, but as brittle as the window-pane; and when the heavens were compared to the terrible crystal I can remember a shudder. I was afraid that God would drop the cosmos with a crash.

Remember, however, that to be breakable is not the same as to be perishable. Strike a glass, and it will not endure an instant; simply do not strike it, and it will endure a thousand years. Such, it seemed, was the joy of man, either in elfland or on earth; the happiness depended on NOT DOING SOMETHING which you could at any moment do and which, very often, it was not obvious why you should not do. Now, the point here is that to ME this did not seem unjust. If the miller's third son said to the fairy, "Explain why I must not stand on my head in the fairy palace," the other might fairly reply, "Well, if it comes to that, explain the fairy palace." If Cinderella says, "How is it that I must leave the ball at twelve?" her godmother might answer, "How is it that you are going there till twelve?" If I leave a man in my will ten talking elephants and a hundred winged horses, he cannot complain if the conditions partake of the slight eccentricity of the gift. He must not look a winged horse in the mouth. And it seemed to me that existence was itself so very eccentric a legacy that I could not complain of not understanding the limitations of the vision when I did not understand the vision they limited. The frame was no stranger than the picture. The veto might well be as wild as the vision; it might be as startling as the sun, as elusive as the waters, as fantastic and terrible as the towering trees.

For this reason (we may call it the fairy godmother philosophy) I never could join the young men of my time in feeling what they called the general sentiment of REVOLT. I should have resisted, let us hope, any rules that were evil, and with these and their definition I shall deal in another chapter. But I did not feel disposed to resist any rule merely because it was mysterious. Estates are sometimes held by foolish forms, the breaking of a stick or the payment of a peppercorn: I was willing to hold the huge estate

167

of earth and heaven by any such feudal fantasy. It could not well be wilder than the fact that I was allowed to hold it at all. At this stage I give only one ethical instance to show my meaning. I could never mix in the common murmur of that rising generation against monogamy, because no restriction on sex seemed so odd and unexpected as sex itself. To be allowed, like Endymion, to make love to the moon and then to complain that Jupiter kept his own moons in a harem seemed to me (bred on fairy tales like Endymion's) a vulgar anti-climax. Keeping to one woman is a small price for so much as seeing one woman. To complain that I could only be married once was like complaining that I had only been born once. It was incommensurate with the terrible excitement of which one was talking. It showed, not an exaggerated sensibility to sex, but a curious insensibility to it. A man is a fool who complains that he cannot enter Eden by five gates at once. Polygamy is a lack of the realization of sex; it is like a man plucking five pears in mere absence of mind. The aesthetes touched the last insane limits of language in their eulogy on lovely things. The thistledown made them weep; a burnished beetle brought them to their knees. Yet their emotion never impressed me for an instant, for this reason, that it never occurred to them to pay for their pleasure in any sort of symbolic sacrifice. Men (I felt) might fast forty days for the sake of hearing a blackbird sing. Men might go through fire to find a cowslip. Yet these lovers of beauty could not even keep sober for the blackbird. They would not go through common Christian marriage by way of recompense to the cowslip. Surely one might pay for extraordinary joy in ordinary morals. Oscar Wilde said that sunsets were not valued because we could not pay for sunsets. But Oscar Wilde was wrong; we can pay for sunsets. We can pay for them by not being Oscar Wilde.

Well, I left the fairy tales lying on the floor of the nursery, and I have not found any books so sensible since. I left the nurse guardian of tradition and democracy, and I have not found any modern type so sanely radical or so sanely conservative. But the matter for important comment was here: that when I first went out into the mental atmosphere of the modern world, I found that the modern world was positively opposed on two points to my nurse and to the nursery tales. It has taken me a long time to find out that the modern world is wrong and my nurse was right. The really curious thing was this: that modern thought contradicted this basic creed of my boyhood on its two most essential doctrines. I have explained that the fairy tales founded in me two convictions; first, that this world is a wild and startling place, which might have been quite different, but which is quite delightful; second, that before this wildness and delight one may well be modest and submit to the queerest limitations of so queer a kindness. But I found the whole modern world running like a high tide against both my tendernesses; and the shock of that collision created two sudden and spontaneous sentiments, which I have had ever since and which, crude as they were, have since hardened into convictions.

First, I found the whole modern world talking scientific fatalism; saying that everything is as it must always have been, being unfolded without fault from the beginning. The leaf on the tree is green because it could never have been anything else. Now, the fairy-tale philosopher is glad that the leaf is green precisely because it might have been scarlet. He feels as if it had turned green an instant before he looked at it. He is pleased that snow is white on the strictly reasonable ground that it might have been black. Every colour has in it a bold quality as of choice; the red of garden roses is not only decisive but dramatic, like suddenly spilt blood. He feels that something has been DONE. But the great determinists of the nineteenth century were strongly against this native feeling that something had happened an instant before. In fact, according to them, nothing ever really had happened since the beginning of the world. Nothing ever had happened since existence had happened; and even about the date of that they were not very sure.

The modern world as I found it was solid for modern Calvinism, for the necessity of things being as they are. But when I came to ask them I found they had really no proof of this unavoidable repetition in things except the fact that the things were repeated. Now, the mere repetition made the things to me rather more weird than more rational. It was as if, having seen a curiously shaped nose in the street and dismissed it as an accident, I had then seen six other noses of the same astonishing shape. I should have fancied for a moment that it must be some local secret society. So one elephant having a trunk was odd; but all elephants having trunks looked like a plot. I speak here only of an emotion, and of an emotion at once stubborn and subtle. But the repetition in Nature seemed sometimes to be an excited repetition, like that of an angry schoolmaster saying the same thing over and over again. The grass seemed signalling to me with all its fingers at once; the crowded stars seemed bent upon being understood. The sun would make me see him if he rose a thousand times. The recurrences of the universe rose to the maddening rhythm of an incantation, and I began to see an idea.

All the towering materialism which dominates the modern mind rests ultimately upon one assumption; a false assumption. It is supposed that if a thing goes on repeating itself it is probably dead; a piece of clockwork. People feel that if the universe was personal it would vary; if the sun were alive it would dance. This is a fallacy even in relation to known fact. For the variation in human affairs is generally brought into them, not by life, but by death; by the dying down or breaking off of their strength or desire. A man varies his movements because of some slight element of failure or fatigue. He gets into an omnibus because he is tired of walking; or he walks because

169

he is tired of sitting still. But if his life and joy were so gigantic that he never tired of going to Islington, he might go to Islington as regularly as the Thames goes to Sheerness. The very speed and ecstasy of his life would have the stillness of death. The sun rises every morning. I do not rise every morning; but the variation is due not to my activity, but to my inaction. Now, to put the matter in a popular phrase, it might be true that the sun rises regularly because he never gets tired of rising. His routine might be due, not to a lifelessness, but to a rush of life. The thing I mean can be seen, for instance, in children, when they find some game or joke that they specially enjoy. A child kicks his legs rhythmically through excess, not absence, of life. Because children have abounding vitality, because they are in spirit fierce and free, therefore they want things repeated and unchanged. They always say, "Do it again"; and the grown-up person does it again until he is nearly dead. For grown-up people are not strong enough to exult in monotony. But perhaps God is strong enough to exult in monotony. It is possible that God says every morning, "Do it again" to the sun; and every evening, "Do it again" to the moon. It may not be automatic necessity that makes all daisies alike; it may be that God makes every daisy separately, but has never got tired of making them. It may be that He has the eternal appetite of infancy; for we have sinned and grown old, and our Father is younger than we. The repetition in Nature may not be a mere recurrence; it may be a theatrical ENCORE. Heaven may ENCORE the bird who laid an egg. If the human being conceives and brings forth a human child instead of bringing forth a fish, or a bat, or a griffin, the reason may not be that we are fixed in an animal fate without life or purpose. It may be that our little tragedy has touched the gods, that they admire it from their starry galleries, and that at the end of every human drama man is called again and again before the curtain. Repetition may go on for millions of years, by mere choice, and at any instant it may stop. Man may stand on the earth generation after generation, and yet each birth be his positively last appearance.

This was my first conviction; made by the shock of my childish emotions meeting the modern creed in mid-career. I had always vaguely felt facts to be miracles in the sense that they are wonderful: now I began to think them miracles in the stricter sense that they were WILFUL. I mean that they were, or might be, repeated exercises of some will. In short, I had always believed that the world involved magic: now I thought that perhaps it involved a magician. And this pointed a profound emotion always present and sub-conscious; that this world of ours has some purpose; and if there is a purpose, there is a person. I had always felt life first as a story: and if there is a story there is a story-teller.

But modern thought also hit my second human tradition. It went against the fairy feeling about strict limits and conditions. The one thing it loved to talk about was expansion and largeness. Herbert Spencer would have been greatly annoyed if any one had called him an imperialist, and therefore it is highly regrettable that nobody did. But he was an imperialist of the lowest type. He popularized this contemptible notion that the size of the solar system ought to over-awe the spiritual dogma of man. Why should a man surrender his dignity to the solar system any more than to a whale? If mere size proves that man is not the image of God, then a whale may be the image of God; a somewhat formless image; what one might call an impressionist portrait. It is quite futile to argue that man is small compared to the cosmos; for man was always small compared to the nearest tree. But Herbert Spencer, in his headlong imperialism, would insist that we had in some way been conquered and annexed by the astronomical universe. He spoke about men and their ideals exactly as the most insolent Unionist talks about the Irish and their ideals. He turned mankind into a small nationality. And his evil influence can be seen even in the most spirited and honourable of later scientific authors; notably in the early romances of Mr. H.G. Wells. Many moralists have in an exaggerated way represented the earth as wicked. But Mr. Wells and his school made the heavens wicked. We should lift up our eyes to the stars from whence would come our ruin.

But the expansion of which I speak was much more evil than all this. I have remarked that the materialist, like the madman, is in prison; in the prison of one thought. These people seemed to think it singularly inspiring to keep on saying that the prison was very large. The size of this scientific universe gave one no novelty, no relief. The cosmos went on for ever, but not in its wildest constellation could there be anything really interesting; anything, for instance, such as forgiveness or free will. The grandeur or infinity of the secret of its cosmos added nothing to it. It was like telling a prisoner in Reading gaol that he would be glad to hear that the gaol now covered half the county. The warder would have nothing to show the man except more and more long corridors of stone lit by ghastly lights and empty of all that is human. So these expanders of the universe had nothing to show us except more and more infinite corridors of space lit by ghastly suns and empty of all that is divine.

In fairyland there had been a real law; a law that could be broken, for the definition of a law is something that can be broken. But the machinery of this cosmic prison was something that could not be broken; for we ourselves were only a part of its machinery. We were either unable to do things or we were destined to do them. The idea of the mystical condition quite disappeared; one can neither have the firmness of keeping laws nor the fun of breaking them. The largeness of this universe had nothing of that freshness and airy outbreak which we have praised in the universe of the poet. This modern universe is literally an empire; that is, it was vast, but it is not free. One went into larger and larger windowless rooms, rooms big with

Babylonian perspective; but one never found the smallest window or a whisper of outer air.

Their infernal parallels seemed to expand with distance; but for me all good things come to a point, swords for instance. So finding the boast of the big cosmos so unsatisfactory to my emotions I began to argue about it a little; and I soon found that the whole attitude was even shallower than could have been expected. According to these people the cosmos was one thing since it had one unbroken rule. Only (they would say) while it is one thing, it is also the only thing there is. Why, then, should one worry particularly to call it large? There is nothing to compare it with. It would be just as sensible to call it small. A man may say, "I like this vast cosmos, with its throng of stars and its crowd of varied creatures." But if it comes to that why should not a man say, "I like this cosy little cosmos, with its decent number of stars and as neat a provision of live stock as I wish to see"? One is as good as the other; they are both mere sentiments. It is mere sentiment to rejoice that the sun is larger than the earth; it is quite as sane a sentiment to rejoice that the sun is no larger than it is. A man chooses to have an emotion about the largeness of the world; why should he not choose to have an emotion about its smallness?

It happened that I had that emotion. When one is fond of anything one addresses it by diminutives, even if it is an elephant or a life-guardsman. The reason is, that anything, however huge, that can be conceived of as complete, can be conceived of as small. If military moustaches did not suggest a sword or tusks a tail, then the object would be vast because it would be immeasurable. But the moment you can imagine a guardsman you can imagine a small guardsman. The moment you really see an elephant you can call it "Tiny." If you can make a statue of a thing you can make a statuette of it. These people professed that the universe was one coherent thing; but they were not fond of the universe. But I was frightfully fond of the universe and wanted to address it by a diminutive. I often did so; and it never seemed to mind. Actually and in truth I did feel that these dim dogmas of vitality were better expressed by calling the world small than by calling it large. For about infinity there was a sort of carelessness which was the reverse of the fierce and pious care which I felt touching the pricelessness and the peril of life. They showed only a dreary waste; but I felt a sort of sacred thrift. For economy is far more romantic than extravagance. To them stars were an unending income of halfpence; but I felt about the golden sun and the silver moon as a schoolboy feels if he has one sovereign and one shilling.

These subconscious convictions are best hit off by the colour and tone of certain tales. Thus I have said that stories of magic alone can express my sense that life is not only a pleasure but a kind of eccentric privilege. I may express this other feeling of cosmic cosiness by allusion to another book always read in boyhood, "Robinson Crusoe," which I read about this time, and which owes its eternal vivacity to the fact that it celebrates the poetry of limits, nay, even the wild romance of prudence. Crusoe is a man on a small rock with a few comforts just snatched from the sea: the best thing in the book is simply the list of things saved from the wreck. The greatest of poems is an inventory. Every kitchen tool becomes ideal because Crusoe might have dropped it in the sea. It is a good exercise, in empty or ugly hours of the day, to look at anything, the coal-scuttle or the book-case, and think how happy one could be to have brought it out of the sinking ship on to the solitary island. But it is a better exercise still to remember how all things have had this hair-breadth escape: everything has been saved from a wreck. Every man has had one horrible adventure: as a hidden untimely birth he had not been, as infants that never see the light. Men spoke much in my boyhood of restricted or ruined men of genius: and it was common to say that many a man was a Great Might-Have-Been. To me it is a more solid and startling fact that any man in the street is a Great Might-Not-Have-Been.

But I really felt (the fancy may seem foolish) as if all the order and number of things were the romantic remnant of Crusoe's ship. That there are two sexes and one sun, was like the fact that there were two guns and one axe. It was poignantly urgent that none should be lost; but somehow, it was rather fun that none could be added. The trees and the planets seemed like things saved from the wreck: and when I saw the Matterhorn I was glad that it had not been overlooked in the confusion. I felt economical about the stars as if they were sapphires (they are called so in Milton's Eden): I hoarded the hills. For the universe is a single jewel, and while it is a natural cant to talk of a jewel as peerless and priceless, of this jewel it is literally true. This cosmos is indeed without peer and without price: for there cannot be another one.

Thus ends, in unavoidable inadequacy, the attempt to utter the unutterable things. These are my ultimate attitudes towards life; the soils for the seeds of doctrine. These in some dark way I thought before I could write, and felt before I could think: that we may proceed more easily afterwards, I will roughly recapitulate them now. I felt in my bones; first, that this world does not explain itself. It may be a miracle with a supernatural explanation; it may be a conjuring trick, with a natural explanation. But the explanation of the conjuring trick, if it is to satisfy me, will have to be better than the natural explanations I have heard. The thing is magic, true or false. Second, I came to feel as if magic must have a meaning, and meaning must have some one to mean it. There was something personal in the world, as in a work of art; whatever it meant it meant violently. Third, I thought this purpose beautiful in its old design, in spite of its defects, such as dragons. Fourth, that the proper form of thanks to it is some form of humility and restraint: we should thank God for beer and Burgundy by not drinking too much of them. We owed, also, an obedience to whatever made us. And last, and strangest, there had come into my mind a vague and vast impression that in some way all good was a remnant to be stored and held sacred out of some primordial ruin. Man had saved his good as Crusoe saved his goods: he had saved them from a wreck. All this I felt and the age gave me no encouragement to feel it. And all this time I had not even thought of Christian theology.

THE FLAG OF THE WORLD

When I was a boy there were two curious men running about who were called the optimist and the pessimist. I constantly used the words myself, but I cheerfully confess that I never had any very special idea of what they meant. The only thing which might be considered evident was that they could not mean what they said; for the ordinary verbal explanation was that the optimist thought this world as good as it could be, while the pessimist thought it as bad as it could be. Both these statements being obviously raving nonsense, one had to cast about for other explanations. An optimist could not mean a man who thought everything right and nothing wrong. For that is meaningless; it is like calling everything right and nothing left. Upon the whole, I came to the conclusion that the optimist thought everything good except the pessimist, and that the pessimist thought everything bad, except himself. It would be unfair to omit altogether from the list the mysterious but suggestive definition said to have been given by a little girl, "An optimist is a man who looks after your eyes, and a pessimist is a man who looks after your feet." I am not sure that this is not the best definition of all. There is even a sort of allegorical truth in it. For there might, perhaps, be a profitable distinction drawn between that more dreary thinker who thinks merely of our contact with the earth from moment to moment, and that happier thinker who considers rather our primary power of vision and of choice of road.

But this is a deep mistake in this alternative of the optimist and the pessimist. The assumption of it is that a man criticises this world as if he were house-hunting, as if he were being shown over a new suite of apartments. If a man came to this world from some other world in full possession of his powers he might discuss whether the advantage of midsummer woods made up for the disadvantage of mad dogs, just as a man looking for lodgings might balance the presence of a telephone against the absence of a sea view. But no man is in that position. A man belongs to this world before he begins to ask if it is nice to belong to it. He has fought for the flag, and often won heroic victories for the flag long before he has ever enlisted. To put shortly what seems the essential matter, he has a loyalty long before he has any admiration.

In the last chapter it has been said that the primary feeling that this world is strange and yet attractive is best expressed in fairy tales. The reader may, if he likes, put down the next stage to that bellicose and even jingo literature which commonly comes next in the history of a boy. We all owe much sound morality to the penny dreadfuls. Whatever the reason, it seemed and still seems to me that our attitude towards life can be better expressed in terms of a kind of military loyalty than in terms of criticism and approval. My acceptance of the universe is not optimism, it is more like patriotism. It is a matter of primary loyalty. The world is not a lodging-house at Brighton, which we are to leave because it is miserable. It is the fortress of our family, with the flag flying on the turret, and the more miserable it is the less we should leave it. The point is not that this world is too sad to love or too glad not to love; the point is that when you do love a thing, its gladness is a reason for loving it, and its sadness a reason for loving it more. All optimistic thoughts about England and all pessimistic thoughts about her are alike reasons for the English patriot. Similarly, optimism and pessimism are alike arguments for the cosmic patriot.

Let us suppose we are confronted with a desperate thing—say Pimlico. If we think what is really best for Pimlico we shall find the thread of thought leads to the throne or the mystic and the arbitrary. It is not enough for a man to disapprove of Pimlico: in that case he will merely cut his throat or move to Chelsea. Nor, certainly, is it enough for a man to approve of Pimlico: for then it will remain Pimlico, which would be awful. The only way out of it seems to be for somebody to love Pimlico: to love it with a transcendental tie and without any earthly reason. If there arose a man who loved Pimlico, then Pimlico would rise into ivory towers and golden pinnacles; Pimlico would attire herself as a woman does when she is loved. For decoration is not given to hide horrible things: but to decorate things already adorable. A mother does not give her child a blue bow because he is so ugly without it. A lover does not give a girl a necklace to hide her neck. If men loved Pimlico as mothers love children, arbitrarily, because it is THEIRS, Pimlico in a year or two might be fairer than Florence. Some readers will say that this is a mere fantasy. I answer that this is the actual history of mankind. This, as a fact, is how cities did grow great. Go back to the darkest roots of civilization and you will find them knotted round some sacred stone or encircling some sacred well. People first paid honour to a spot and afterwards gained glory for it. Men did not love Rome because she was great. She was great because they had loved her.

The eighteenth-century theories of the social contract have been exposed to much clumsy criticism in our time; in so far as they meant that there is at the back of all historic government an idea of content and co-operation, they were demonstrably right. But they really were wrong, in so far as they suggested that men had ever aimed at order or ethics directly by a conscious exchange of interests. Morality did not begin by one man saying to another, "I will not hit you if you do not hit me"; there is no trace of such a transaction. There IS a trace of both men having said, "We must not hit each other in the holy place." They gained their morality by guarding their religion. They did not cultivate courage. They fought for the shrine, and found they had become courageous. They did not cultivate cleanliness. They purified themselves for the altar, and found that they were clean. The history of the Jews is the only early document known to most Englishmen, and the facts can be judged sufficiently from that. The Ten Commandments which have been found substantially common to mankind were merely military commands; a code of regimental orders, issued to protect a certain ark across a certain desert. Anarchy was evil because it endangered the sanctity. And only when they made a holy day for God did they find they had made a holiday for men.

If it be granted that this primary devotion to a place or thing is a source of creative energy, we can pass on to a very peculiar fact. Let us reiterate for an instant that the only right optimism is a sort of universal patriotism. What is the matter with the pessimist? I think it can be stated by saying that he is the cosmic anti-patriot. And what is the matter with the anti-patriot? I think it can be stated, without undue bitterness, by saying that he is the candid friend. And what is the matter with the candid friend? There we strike the rock of real life and immutable human nature.

I venture to say that what is bad in the candid friend is simply that he is not candid. He is keeping something back— his own gloomy pleasure in saying unpleasant things. He has a secret desire to hurt, not merely to help. This is certainly, I think, what makes a certain sort of anti-patriot irritating to healthy citizens. I do not speak (of course) of the anti-patriotism which only irritates feverish stockbrokers and gushing actresses; that is only patriotism speaking plainly. A man who says that no patriot should attack the Boer War until it is over is not worth answering intelligently; he is saying that no good son should warn his mother off a cliff until she has fallen over it. But there is an anti-patriot who honestly angers honest men, and the explanation of him is, I think, what I have suggested: he is the uncandid candid friend; the man who says, "I am sorry to say we are ruined," and is not sorry at all. And he may be said, without rhetoric, to be a traitor; for he is using that ugly knowledge which was allowed him to strengthen the army, to discourage people from joining it. Because he is allowed to be pessimistic as a military adviser he is being pessimistic as a recruiting sergeant. Just in the same way the pessimist (who is the cosmic anti-patriot) uses the freedom that life allows to her counsellors to lure away the people from her flag. Granted that he states only facts, it is still essential to know what are his emotions, what is his motive. It may be that twelve hundred men in Tottenham are down with smallpox; but we want to know whether this is stated by some great philosopher who wants to curse the gods, or only by some common clergyman who wants to help the men.

The evil of the pessimist is, then, not that he chastises gods and men, but that he does not love what he chastises—he has not this primary and supernatural loyalty to things. What is the evil of the man commonly called an optimist? Obviously, it is felt that the optimist, wishing to defend the honour of this world, will defend the indefensible. He is the jingo of the universe; he will say, "My cosmos, right or wrong." He will be less inclined to the reform of things; more inclined to a sort of front-bench official answer to all attacks, soothing every one with assurances. He will not wash the world, but whitewash the world. All this (which is true of a type of optimist) leads us to the one really interesting point of psychology, which could not be explained without it.

We say there must be a primal loyalty to life: the only question is, shall it be a natural or a supernatural loyalty? If you like to put it so, shall it be a reasonable or an unreasonable loyalty? Now, the extraordinary thing is that the bad optimism (the whitewashing, the weak defence of everything) comes in with the reasonable optimism. Rational optimism leads to stagnation: it is irrational optimism that leads to reform. Let me explain by using once more the parallel of patriotism. The man who is most likely to ruin the place he loves is exactly the man who loves it with a reason. The man who will improve the place is the man who loves it without a reason. If a man loves some feature of Pimlico (which seems unlikely), he may find himself defending that feature against Pimlico itself. But if he simply loves Pimlico itself, he may lay it waste and turn it into the New Jerusalem. I do not deny that reform may be excessive; I only say that it is the mystic patriot who reforms. Mere jingo self-contentment is commonest among those who have some pedantic reason for their patriotism. The worst jingoes do not love England, but a theory of England. If we love England for being an empire, we may overrate the success with which we rule the Hindoos. But if we love it only for being a nation, we can face all events: for it would be a nation even if the Hindoos ruled us. Thus also only those will permit their patriotism to falsify history whose patriotism depends on history. A man who loves England for being English will not mind how she arose. But a man who loves England for being Anglo-Saxon may go against all facts for his fancy. He may end (like Carlyle and Freeman) by maintaining that the Norman Conquest was a Saxon Conquest. He may end in utter unreason—because he has a reason. A man who loves France for being military will palliate the army of 1870. But a man who loves France for being France will improve the army of 1870. This is exactly what the French have done, and France is a good instance of the working paradox. Nowhere else is patriotism more purely abstract and arbitrary; and nowhere else is reform more drastic and sweeping. The more transcendental is your patriotism, the more practical are your politics.

Perhaps the most everyday instance of this point is in the case of women; and their strange and strong loyalty. Some stupid people started the idea that because women obviously back up their own people through everything, therefore women are blind and do not see anything. They can hardly have known any women. The same women who are ready to defend their men through thick and thin are (in their personal intercourse with the man) almost morbidly lucid about the thinness of his excuses or the thickness of his head. A man's friend likes him but leaves him as he is: his wife loves him and is always trying to turn him into somebody else. Women who are utter mystics in their creed are utter cynics in their criticism. Thackeray expressed this well when he made Pendennis' mother, who worshipped her son as a god, yet assume that he would go wrong as a man. She underrated his virtue, though she overrated his value. The devotee is entirely free to criticise; the fanatic can safely be a sceptic. Love is not blind; that is the last thing that it is. Love is bound; and the more it is bound the less it is blind.

This at least had come to be my position about all that was called optimism, pessimism, and improvement. Before any cosmic act of reform we must have a cosmic oath of allegiance. A man must be interested in life, then he could be disinterested in his views of it. "My son give me thy heart"; the heart must be fixed on the right thing: the moment we have a fixed heart we have a free hand. I must pause to anticipate an obvious criticism. It will be said that a rational person accepts the world as mixed of good and evil with a decent satisfaction and a decent endurance. But this is exactly the attitude which I maintain to be defective. It is, I know, very common in this age; it was perfectly put in those quiet lines of Matthew Arnold which are more piercingly blasphemous than the shrieks of Schopenhauer—

> "Enough we live:—and if a life, With large results so little rife, Though bearable, seem hardly worth This pomp of worlds, this pain of birth."

I know this feeling fills our epoch, and I think it freezes our epoch. For our Titanic purposes of faith and revolution, what we need is not the cold acceptance of the world as a compromise, but some way in which we can heartily hate and heartily love it. We do not want joy and anger to neutralize each other and produce a surly contentment; we want a fiercer delight and a fiercer discontent. We have to feel the universe at once as an ogre's castle, to be stormed, and yet as our own cottage, to which we can return at evening.

No one doubts that an ordinary man can get on with this world: but we demand not strength enough to get on with it, but strength enough to get it on. Can he hate it enough to change it, and yet love it enough to think it worth changing? Can he look up at its colossal good without once feeling acquiescence? Can he look up at its colossal evil without once feeling despair? Can he, in short, be at once not only a pessimist and an optimist, but a fanatical pessimist and a fanatical optimist? Is he enough of a pagan to die for the world, and enough of a Christian to die to it? In this combination, I maintain, it is the rational optimist who fails, the irrational optimist who succeeds. He is ready to smash the whole universe for the sake of itself.

I put these things not in their mature logical sequence, but as they came: and this view was cleared and sharpened by an accident of the time. Under the lengthening shadow of Ibsen, an argument arose whether it was not a very nice thing to murder one's self. Grave moderns told us that we must not even say "poor fellow," of a man who had blown his brains out, since he was an enviable person, and had only blown them out because of their exceptional excellence. Mr. William Archer even suggested that in the golden age there would be penny-in-the-slot machines, by which a man could kill himself for a penny. In all this I found myself utterly hostile to many who called themselves liberal and humane. Not only is suicide a sin, it is the sin. It is the ultimate and absolute evil, the refusal to take an interest in existence; the refusal to take the oath of loyalty to life. The man who kills a man, kills a man. The man who kills himself, kills all men; as far as he is concerned he wipes out the world. His act is worse (symbolically considered) than any rape or dynamite outrage. For it destroys all buildings: it insults all women. The thief is satisfied with diamonds; but the suicide is not: that is his crime. He cannot be bribed, even by the blazing stones of the Celestial City. The thief compliments the things he steals, if not the owner of them. But the suicide insults everything on earth by not stealing it. He defiles every flower by refusing to live for its sake. There is not a tiny creature in the cosmos at whom his death is not a sneer. When a man hangs himself on a tree, the leaves might fall off in anger and the birds fly away in fury: for each has received a personal affront. Of course there may be pathetic emotional excuses for the act. There often are for rape, and there almost always are for dynamite. But if it comes to clear ideas and the intelligent meaning of things, then there is much more rational and philosophic truth in the burial at the cross-roads and the stake driven through the body, than in Mr. Archer's suicidal automatic machines. There is a meaning in burying the suicide apart. The man's crime is different from other crimes—for it makes even crimes impossible.

About the same time I read a solemn flippancy by some free thinker: he said that a suicide was only the same as a martyr. The open fallacy of this helped to clear the question. Obviously a suicide is the opposite of a martyr. A martyr is a man who cares so much for something outside him, that he forgets his own personal life. A suicide is a man who cares so little for anything outside him, that he wants to see the last of everything. One wants something to begin: the other wants everything to end. In other words, the martyr is noble, exactly because (however he renounces the world or execrates all humanity) he confesses this ultimate link with life; he sets his heart outside himself: he dies that something may live. The suicide is ignoble because he has not this link with being: he is a mere destroyer; spiritually, he destroys the universe. And then I remembered the stake and the cross-roads, and the queer fact that Christianity had shown this weird harshness to the suicide. For Christianity had shown a wild encouragement of the martyr. Historic Christianity was accused, not entirely without reason, of carrying martyrdom and asceticism to a point, desolate and pessimistic. The early Christian martyrs talked of death with a horrible happiness. They blasphemed the beautiful duties of the body: they smelt the grave afar off like a field of flowers. All this has seemed to many the very poetry of pessimism. Yet there is the stake at the crossroads to show what Christianity thought of the pessimist.

This was the first of the long train of enigmas with which Christianity entered the discussion. And there went with it a peculiarity of which I shall have to speak more markedly, as a note of all Christian notions, but which distinctly began in this one. The Christian attitude to the martyr and the suicide was not what is so often affirmed in modern morals. It was not a matter of degree. It was not that a line must be drawn somewhere, and that the self-slayer in exaltation fell within the line, the self-slayer in sadness just beyond it. The Christian feeling evidently was not merely that the suicide was carrying martyrdom too far. The Christian feeling was furiously for one and furiously against the other: these two things that looked so much alike were at opposite ends of heaven and hell. One man flung away his life; he was so good that his dry bones could heal cities in pestilence. Another man flung away life; he was so bad that his bones would pollute his brethren's. I am not saying this fierceness was right; but why was it so fierce?

Here it was that I first found that my wandering feet were in some beaten track. Christianity had also felt this opposition of the martyr to the suicide: had it perhaps felt it for the same reason? Had Christianity felt what I felt, but could not (and cannot) express—this need for a first loyalty to things, and then for a ruinous reform of things? Then I remembered that it was actually the charge against Christianity that it combined these two things which I was wildly trying to combine. Christianity was accused, at one and the same time, of being too optimistic about the universe and of being too pessimistic about the world. The coincidence made me suddenly stand still.

An imbecile habit has arisen in modern controversy of saying that such and such a creed can be held in one age but cannot be held in another. Some dogma, we are told, was credible in the twelfth century, but is not credible in the twentieth. You might as well say that a certain philosophy can be believed on Mondays, but cannot be believed on Tuesdays. You might as well say of a view of the cosmos that it was suitable to half-past three, but not suitable to half-past four. What a man can believe depends upon his philosophy, not upon the clock or the century. If a man believes in unalterable natural law, he cannot believe in any miracle in any age. If a man believes in a will behind law, he can believe in any miracle in any age. Suppose, for the sake of argument, we are concerned with a case of thaumaturgic healing. A materialist of the twelfth century could not believe it any more than a materialist of the twentieth century. But a Christian Scientist of the twentieth century can believe it as much as a Christian of the twelfth century. It is simply a matter of a man's theory of things. Therefore in dealing with any historical answer, the point is not whether it was given in our time, but whether it was given in answer to our question. And the more I thought about when and how Christianity had come into the world, the more I felt that it had actually come to answer this question.

It is commonly the loose and latitudinarian Christians who pay quite indefensible compliments to Christianity. They talk as if there had never been any piety or pity until Christianity came, a point on which any mediaeval would have been eager to correct them. They represent that the remarkable thing about Christianity was that it was the first to preach simplicity or self-restraint, or inwardness and sincerity. They will think me very narrow (whatever that means) if I say that the remarkable thing about Christianity was that it was the first to preach Christianity. Its peculiarity was that it was peculiar, and simplicity and sincerity are not peculiar, but obvious ideals for all mankind. Christianity was the answer to a riddle, not the last truism uttered after a long talk. Only the other day I saw in an excellent weekly paper of Puritan tone this remark, that Christianity when stripped of its armour of dogma (as who should speak of a man stripped of his armour of bones), turned out to be nothing but the Quaker doctrine of the Inner Light. Now, if I were to say that Christianity came into the world specially to destroy the doctrine of the Inner Light, that would be an exaggeration. But it would be very much nearer to the truth. The last Stoics, like Marcus Aurelius, were exactly the people who did believe in the Inner Light. Their dignity, their weariness, their sad external care for others, their incurable internal care for themselves, were all due to the Inner Light, and existed only by that dismal illumination. Notice that Marcus Aurelius insists, as such introspective moralists always do, upon small things done or undone; it is because he has not hate or love enough to make a moral revolution. He gets up early in the morning, just as our own aristocrats living the Simple Life get up early in the morning; because such altruism is much easier than stopping the games of the amphitheatre or giving the English people back their land. Marcus Aurelius is the most intolerable of human types. He is an unselfish egoist. An unselfish egoist is a man who has pride without the excuse of passion. Of all conceivable forms of enlightenment the worst is what these people call the Inner Light. Of all horrible religions the most horrible is the worship of the god within. Any one who knows any body knows how it would work; any one who knows any one from the Higher Thought Centre knows how it does work. That Jones shall worship the god within him turns out ultimately to mean that Jones shall worship Jones. Let Jones worship the sun or moon, anything rather than the Inner Light; let Jones worship cats or crocodiles, if he can find any in his street, but not the god within. Christianity came into the world firstly in order to assert with violence that a man had not only to look inwards, but to look outwards, to behold with astonishment and enthusiasm a divine company and a divine captain. The only fun of being a Christian was that a man was not left alone with the Inner Light, but definitely recognized an outer light, fair as the sun, clear as the moon, terrible as an army with banners.

All the same, it will be as well if Jones does not worship the sun and moon. If he does, there is a tendency for him to imitate them; to say, that because the sun burns insects alive, he may burn insects alive. He thinks that because the sun gives people sun-stroke, he may give his neighbour measles. He thinks that because the moon is said to drive men mad, he may drive his wife mad. This ugly side of mere external optimism had also shown itself in the ancient world. About the time when the Stoic idealism had begun to show the weaknesses of pessimism, the old nature worship of the ancients had begun to show the enormous weaknesses of optimism. Nature worship is natural enough while the society is young, or, in other words, Pantheism is all right as long as it is the worship of Pan. But Nature has another side which experience and sin are not slow in finding out, and it is no flippancy to say of the god Pan that he soon showed the cloven hoof. The only objection to Natural Religion is that somehow it always becomes unnatural. A man loves Nature in the morning for her innocence and amiability, and at nightfall, if he is loving her still, it is for her darkness and her cruelty. He washes at dawn in clear water as did the Wise Man of the Stoics, yet, somehow at the dark end of the day, he is bathing in hot bull's blood, as did Julian the Apostate. The mere pursuit of health always leads to something unhealthy. Physical nature must not be made the direct object of obedience; it must be enjoyed, not worshipped. Stars and mountains must not be taken seriously. If they are, we end where the pagan nature worship ended. Because the earth is kind, we can imitate all her cruelties. Because sexuality is sane, we can all go mad about sexuality. Mere optimism had reached its insane and appropriate termination. The theory that everything was good had become an orgy of everything that was bad.

On the other side our idealist pessimists were represented by the old remnant of the Stoics. Marcus Aurelius and his friends had really given up the idea of any god in the universe and looked only to the god within. They had no hope of any virtue in nature, and hardly any hope of any virtue in society. They had not enough interest in the outer world really to wreck or revolutionise it. They did not love the city enough to set fire to it. Thus the ancient world was exactly in our own desolate dilemma. The only people who really enjoyed this world were busy breaking it up; and the virtuous people did not care enough about them to knock them down. In this dilemma (the same as ours) Christianity suddenly stepped in and offered a singular answer, which the world eventually accepted as THE answer. It was the answer then, and I think it is the answer now.

This answer was like the slash of a sword; it sundered; it did not in any sense sentimentally unite. Briefly, it divided God from the cosmos. That transcendence and distinctness of the deity which some Christians now want to remove from Christianity, was really the only reason why any one wanted to be a Christian. It was the whole point of the Christian answer to the unhappy pessimist and the still more unhappy optimist. As I am here only concerned with their particular problem, I shall indicate only briefly this great metaphysical suggestion. All descriptions of the creating or sustaining principle in things must be metaphorical, because they must be verbal. Thus the pantheist is forced to speak of God in all things as if he were in a box. Thus the evolutionist has, in his very name, the idea of being unrolled like a carpet. All terms, religious and irreligious, are open to this charge. The only question is whether all terms are useless, or whether one can, with such a phrase, cover a distinct IDEA about the origin of things. I think one can, and so evidently does the evolutionist, or he would not talk about evolution. And the root phrase for all Christian theism was this, that God was a creator, as an artist is a creator. A poet is so separate from his poem that he himself speaks of it as a little thing he has "thrown off." Even in giving it forth he has flung it away. This principle that all creation and procreation is a breaking off is at least as consistent through the cosmos as the evolutionary principle that all growth is a branching out. A woman loses a child even in having a child. All creation is separation. Birth is as solemn a parting as death.

It was the prime philosophic principle of Christianity that this divorce in the divine act of making (such as severs the poet from the poem or the mother from the new-born child) was the true description of the act whereby the absolute energy made the world. According to most philosophers, God in making the world enslaved it. According to Christianity, in making it, He set it free. God had written, not so much a poem, but rather a play; a play he had planned as perfect, but which had necessarily been left to human actors and stage-managers, who had since made a great mess of it. I will discuss the truth of this theorem later. Here I have only to point out with what a startling smoothness it passed the dilemma we have discussed in this chapter. In this way at least one could be both happy and indignant without degrading one's self to be either a pessimist or an optimist. On this system one could fight all the forces of existence without deserting the flag of existence. One could be at peace with the universe and yet be at war with the world. St. George could still fight the dragon, however big the monster bulked in the cosmos, though he were bigger than the mighty cities or bigger than the everlasting hills. If he were as big as the world he could yet be killed in the name of the world. St. George had not to consider any obvious odds or proportions in the scale of things, but only the original secret of their design. He can shake his sword at the dragon, even if it is everything; even if the empty heavens over his head are only the huge arch of its open jaws.

And then followed an experience impossible to describe. It was as if I had been blundering about since my birth with two huge and unmanageable machines, of different shapes and without apparent connection—the world and the Christian tradition. I had found this hole in the world: the fact that one must somehow find a way of loving the world without trusting it; somehow one must love the world without being worldly. I found this projecting feature of Christian theology, like a sort of hard spike, the dogmatic insistence that God was personal, and had made a world separate from Himself. The spike of dogma fitted exactly into the hole in the world—it had evidently been meant to go there— and then the strange thing began to happen. When once these two parts of the two machines had come together, one after another, all the other parts fitted and fell in with an eerie exactitude. I could hear bolt after bolt over all the machinery falling into its place with a kind of click of relief. Having got one part right, all the other parts were repeating that rectitude, as clock after clock strikes noon. Instinct after instinct was answered by doctrine after doctrine. Or, to vary the metaphor, I was like one who had advanced into a hostile country to take one high fortress. And when that fort had fallen the whole country surrendered and turned solid behind me. The whole land was lit up, as it were, back to the first fields of my childhood. All those blind fancies of boyhood which in the fourth chapter I have tried in vain to trace on the darkness, became suddenly transparent and sane. I was right when I felt that roses were red by some sort of choice: it was the divine choice. I was right when I felt that I would almost rather say that grass was the wrong colour than say it must by necessity have been that colour: it might verily have been any other. My sense that happiness hung on the crazy thread of a condition did mean something when all was said: it meant the whole doctrine of the Fall. Even those dim and shapeless monsters of notions which I have not been able to describe, much less defend, stepped quietly into their places like colossal caryatides of the creed. The fancy that the cosmos was not vast and void, but small and cosy, had a fulfilled significance now, for anything that is a work of art must be small in the sight of the artist; to God the stars might be only small and dear, like diamonds. And my haunting instinct that somehow good was not merely a tool to be used, but a relic to be guarded, like the goods from Crusoe's ship— even that had been the wild whisper of something originally wise, for, according to Christianity, we were indeed the survivors of a wreck, the crew of a golden ship that had gone down before the beginning of the world.

But the important matter was this, that it entirely reversed the reason for optimism. And the instant the reversal was made it felt like the abrupt ease when a bone is put back in the socket. I had often called myself an optimist, to avoid the too evident blasphemy of pessimism. But all the optimism of the age had been false and disheartening for this reason, that it had always been trying to prove that we fit in to the world. The Christian optimism is based on the fact that we do NOT fit in to the world. I had tried to be happy by telling myself that man is an animal, like any other which sought its meat from God. But now I really was happy, for I had learnt that man is a monstrosity. I had been right in feeling all things as odd, for I myself was at once worse and better than all things. The optimist's pleasure was prosaic, for it dwelt on the naturalness of everything; the Christian pleasure was poetic, for it dwelt on the unnaturalness of everything in the light of the supernatural. The modern philosopher had told me again and again that I was in the right place, and I had still felt depressed even in acquiescence. But I had heard that I was in the WRONG place, and my soul sang for joy, like a bird in spring. The knowledge found out and illuminated forgotten chambers in the dark house of infancy. I knew now why grass had always seemed to me as queer as the green beard of a giant, and why I could feel homesick at home.

THE PARADOXES OF CHRISTIANITY

The real trouble with this world of ours is not that it is an unreasonable world, nor even that it is a reasonable one. The commonest kind of trouble is that it is nearly reasonable, but not quite. Life is not an illogicality; yet it is a trap for logicians. It looks just a little more mathematical and regular than it is; its exactitude is obvious, but its inexactitude is hidden; its wildness lies in wait. I give one coarse instance of what I mean. Suppose some mathematical creature from the moon were to reckon up the human body; he would at once see that the essential thing about it was that it was duplicate. A man is two men, he on the right exactly resembling him on the left. Having noted that there was an arm on the right and one on the left, a leg on the right and one on the left, he might go further and still find on each side the same number of fingers, the same number of toes, twin eyes, twin ears, twin nostrils, and even twin lobes of the brain. At last he would take it as a law; and then, where he found a heart on one side, would deduce that there was another heart on the other. And just then, where he most felt he was right, he would be wrong.

It is this silent swerving from accuracy by an inch that is the uncanny element in everything. It seems a sort of secret treason in the universe. An apple or an orange is round enough to get itself called round, and yet is not round after all. The earth itself is shaped like an orange in order to lure some simple astronomer into calling it a globe. A blade of grass is called after the blade of a sword, because it comes to a point; but it doesn't. Everywhere in things there is this element of the quiet and incalculable. It escapes the rationalists, but it never escapes till the last moment. From the grand curve of our earth it could easily be inferred that every inch of it was thus curved. It would seem rational that as a man has a brain on both sides, he should have a heart on both sides. Yet scientific men are still organizing expeditions to find the North Pole, because they are so fond of flat country. Scientific men are also still organizing expeditions to find a man's heart; and when they try to find it, they generally get on the wrong side of him.

Now, actual insight or inspiration is best tested by whether it guesses these hidden malformations or surprises. If our mathematician from the moon saw the two arms and the two ears, he might deduce the two shoulder-blades and the two halves of the brain. But if he guessed that the man's heart was in the right place, then I should call him something more than a mathematician. Now, this is exactly the claim which I have since come to propound for Christianity. Not merely that it deduces logical truths, but that when it suddenly becomes illogical, it has found, so to speak, an illogical truth. It not only goes right about things, but it goes wrong (if one may say so) exactly where the things go wrong. Its plan suits the secret irregularities, and expects the unexpected. It is simple about the simple truth; but it is stubborn about the subtle truth. It will admit that a man has two hands, it will not admit (though all the Modernists wail to it) the obvious deduction that he has two hearts. It is my only purpose in this chapter to point this out; to show that whenever we feel there is something odd in Christian theology, we shall generally find that there is something odd in the truth.

I have alluded to an unmeaning phrase to the effect that such and such a creed cannot be believed in our age. Of course, anything can be believed in any age. But, oddly enough, there really is a sense in which a creed, if it is believed at all, can be believed more fixedly in a complex society than in a simple one. If a man finds Christianity true in Birmingham, he has actually clearer reasons for faith than if he had found it true in Mercia. For the more complicated seems the coincidence, the less it can be a coincidence. If snowflakes fell in the shape, say, of the heart of Midlothian, it might be an accident. But if snowflakes fell in the exact shape of the maze at Hampton Court, I think one might call it a miracle. It is exactly as of such a miracle that I have since come to feel of the philosophy of Christianity. The complication of our modern world proves the truth of the creed more perfectly than any of the plain problems of the ages of faith. It was in Notting Hill and Battersea that I began to see that Christianity was true. This is why the faith has that elaboration of doctrines and details which so much distresses those who admire Christianity without believing in it. When once one believes in a creed, one is proud of its complexity, as scientists are proud of the complexity of science. It shows how rich it is in discoveries. If it is right at all, it is a compliment to say that it's elaborately right. A stick might fit a hole or a stone a hollow by accident. But a key and a lock are both complex. And if a key fits a lock, you know it is the right key.

But this involved accuracy of the thing makes it very difficult to do what I now have to do, to describe this accumulation of truth. It is very hard for a man to defend anything of which he is entirely convinced. It is comparatively easy when he is only partially convinced. He is partially convinced because he has found this or that proof of the thing, and he can expound it. But a man is not really convinced of a philosophic theory when he finds that something proves it. He is only really convinced when he finds that everything proves it. And the more converging reasons he finds pointing to this conviction, the more bewildered he is if asked suddenly to sum them up. Thus, if one asked an ordinary intelligent man, on the spur of the moment, "Why do you prefer civilization to savagery?" he would look wildly round at object after object, and would only be able to answer vaguely, "Why, there is that bookcase . . . and the coals in the coal-scuttle . . . and pianos . . . and policemen." The whole case for civilization is that the case for it is complex. It has done so many things. But that very multiplicity of proof which ought to make reply overwhelming makes reply impossible.

There is, therefore, about all complete conviction a kind of huge helplessness. The belief is so big that it takes a long time to get it into action. And this hesitation chiefly arises, oddly enough, from an indifference about where one should begin. All roads lead to Rome; which is one reason why many people never get there. In the case of this defence of the Christian conviction I confess that I would as soon begin the argument with one thing as another; I would begin it with a turnip or a taximeter cab. But if I am to be at all careful about making my meaning clear, it will, I think, be wiser to continue the current arguments of the last chapter, which was concerned to urge the first of these mystical coincidences, or rather ratifications. All I had hitherto heard of Christian theology had alienated me from it. I was a pagan at the age of twelve, and a complete agnostic by the age of sixteen; and I cannot understand any one passing the age of seventeen without having asked himself so simple a question. I did, indeed, retain a cloudy reverence for a cosmic deity and a great historical interest in the Founder of Christianity. But I certainly regarded Him as a man; though perhaps I thought that, even in that point, He had an advantage over some of His modern critics. I read the scientific and sceptical literature of my time—all of it, at least, that I could find written in English and lying about; and I read nothing else; I mean I read nothing else on any other note of philosophy. The penny dreadfuls which I also read were indeed in a healthy and heroic tradition of Christianity; but I did not know this at the time. I never read a line of Christian apologetics. I read as little as I can of them now. It was Huxley and Herbert Spencer and Bradlaugh who brought me back to orthodox theology. They sowed in my mind my first wild doubts of doubt. Our grandmothers were quite right when they said that Tom Paine and the free-thinkers unsettled the mind. They do. They unsettled mine horribly. The rationalist made me question whether reason was of any use whatever; and when I had finished Herbert Spencer I had got as far as doubting (for the first time) whether evolution had occurred at all. As I laid down the last of Colonel Ingersoll's atheistic lectures the dreadful thought broke across my mind, "Almost thou persuadest me to be a Christian." I was in a desperate way.

This odd effect of the great agnostics in arousing doubts deeper than their own might be illustrated in many ways. I take only one. As I read and re-read all the non-Christian or anti-Christian accounts of the faith, from Huxley to Bradlaugh, a slow and awful impression grew gradually but graphically upon my mind—the impression that Christianity must be a most extraordinary thing. For not only (as I understood) had Christianity the most flaming vices, but it had apparently a mystical talent for combining vices which seemed inconsistent with each other. It was attacked on all sides and for all contradictory reasons. No sooner had one rationalist demonstrated that it was too far to the east than another demonstrated with equal clearness that it was much too far to the west. No sooner had my indignation died down at its angular and aggressive squareness than I was called up again to notice and condemn its enervating and sensual roundness. In case any reader has not come across the thing I mean, I will give such instances as I remember at random of this self-contradiction in the sceptical attack. I give four or five of them; there are fifty more.

Thus, for instance, I was much moved by the eloquent attack on Christianity as a thing of inhuman gloom; for I thought (and still think) sincere pessimism the unpardonable sin. Insincere pessimism is a social accomplishment, rather agreeable than otherwise; and fortunately nearly all pessimism is insincere. But if Christianity was, as these people said, a thing purely pessimistic and opposed to life, then I was quite prepared to blow up St. Paul's Cathedral. But the extraordinary thing is this. They did prove to me in Chapter I. (to my complete satisfaction) that Christianity was too pessimistic; and then, in Chapter II., they began to prove to me that it was a great deal too optimistic. One accusation against Christianity was that it prevented men, by morbid tears and terrors, from seeking joy and liberty in the bosom of Nature. But another accusation was that it comforted men with a fictitious providence, and put them in a pink-and-white nursery. One great agnostic asked why Nature was not beautiful enough, and why it was hard to be free. Another great agnostic objected that Christian optimism, "the garment of make-believe woven by pious hands," hid from us the fact that Nature was ugly, and that it was impossible to be free. One rationalist had hardly done calling Christianity a nightmare before another began to call it a fool's paradise. This puzzled me; the charges seemed inconsistent. Christianity could not at once be the black mask on a white world, and also the white mask on a black world. The state of the Christian could not be at once so comfortable that he was a coward to cling to it, and so uncomfortable that he was a fool to stand it. If it falsified human vision it must falsify it one way or another; it could not wear both green and rose-coloured spectacles. I rolled on my tongue with a terrible joy, as did all young men of that time, the taunts which Swinburne hurled at the dreariness of the creed—

"Thou hast conquered, O pale Galilaean, the world has grown gray with Thy breath."

But when I read the same poet's accounts of paganism (as in "Atalanta"), I gathered that the world was, if possible, more gray before the Galilean breathed on it than afterwards. The poet maintained, indeed, in the abstract, that life itself was pitch dark. And yet, somehow, Christianity had darkened it. The very man who denounced Christianity for pessimism was himself a pessimist. I thought there must be something wrong. And it did for one wild moment cross my mind that, perhaps, those might not be the very best judges of the relation of religion to happiness who, by their own account, had neither one nor the other.

It must be understood that I did not conclude hastily that the accusations were false or the accusers fools. I simply deduced that Christianity must be something even weirder and wickeder than they made out. A thing might have these two opposite vices; but it must be a rather queer thing if it did. A man might be too fat in one place and too thin in another; but he would be an odd shape. At this point my thoughts were only of the odd shape of the Christian religion; I did not allege any odd shape in the rationalistic mind.

Here is another case of the same kind. I felt that a strong case against Christianity lay in the charge that there is something timid, monkish, and unmanly about all that is called "Christian," especially in its attitude towards resistance and fighting. The great sceptics of the nineteenth century were largely virile. Bradlaugh in an expansive way, Huxley, in a reticent way, were decidedly men. In comparison, it did seem tenable that there was something weak and over patient about Christian counsels. The Gospel paradox about the other cheek, the fact that priests never fought, a hundred things made plausible the accusation that Christianity was an attempt to make a man too like a sheep. I read it and believed it, and if I had read nothing different, I should have gone on believing it. But I read something very different. I turned the next page in my agnostic manual, and my brain turned up-side down. Now I found that I was to hate Christianity not for fighting too little, but for fighting too much. Christianity, it seemed, was the mother of wars. Christianity had deluged the world with blood. I had got thoroughly angry with the Christian, because he never was angry. And now I was told to be angry with him because his anger had been the most huge and horrible thing in human history; because his anger had soaked the earth and smoked to the sun. The very people who reproached Christianity with the meekness and non-resistance of the monasteries were the very people who reproached it also with the violence and valour of the Crusades. It was the fault of poor old Christianity (somehow or other) both that Edward the Confessor did not fight and that Richard Coeur de Leon did. The Quakers (we were told) were the only characteristic Christians; and yet the massacres of Cromwell and Alva were characteristic Christian crimes. What could it all mean? What was this Christianity which always forbade war and always produced wars? What could be the nature of the thing which one could abuse first because it would not fight, and second because it was always fighting? In what world of riddles was born this monstrous murder and this monstrous meekness? The shape of Christianity grew a queerer shape every instant.

I take a third case; the strangest of all, because it involves the one real objection to the faith. The one real objection to the Christian religion is simply that it is one religion. The world is a big place, full of very different kinds of people. Christianity (it may reasonably be said) is one thing confined to one kind of people; it began in Palestine, it has practically stopped with Europe. I was duly impressed with this argument in my youth, and I was much drawn towards the doctrine often preached in Ethical Societies— I mean the doctrine that there is one great unconscious church of all humanity founded on the omnipresence of the human conscience. Creeds, it was said, divided men; but at least morals united them. The soul might seek the strangest and most remote lands and ages and still find essential ethical common sense. It might find Confucius under Eastern trees, and he would be writing "Thou shalt not steal." It might decipher the darkest hieroglyphic on the most primeval desert, and the meaning when deciphered would be "Little boys should tell the truth." I believed this doctrine of the brotherhood of all men in the possession of a moral sense, and I believe it still—with other things. And I was thoroughly annoyed with Christianity for suggesting (as I supposed) that whole ages and empires of men had utterly escaped this light of justice and reason. But then I found an astonishing thing. I found that the very people who said that mankind was one church from Plato to Emerson were the very people who said that morality had changed altogether, and that what was right in one age was wrong in another. If I asked, say, for an altar, I was told that we needed none, for men our brothers gave us clear oracles and one creed in their universal customs and ideals. But if I mildly pointed out that one of men's universal customs was to have an altar, then my agnostic teachers turned clean round and told me that men had always been in darkness and the superstitions of savages. I found it was their daily taunt against Christianity that it was the light of one people and had left all others to die in the dark. But I also found that it was their special boast for themselves that science and progress were the discovery of one people, and that all other peoples had died in the dark. Their chief insult to Christianity was actually their chief compliment to themselves, and there seemed to be a strange unfairness about all their relative insistence on the two things. When considering some pagan or agnostic, we were to remember that all men had one religion; when considering some mystic or spiritualist, we were only to consider what absurd religions some men had. We could trust the ethics of Epictetus, because ethics had never changed. We must not trust the ethics of Bossuet, because ethics had changed. They changed in two hundred years, but not in two thousand.

This began to be alarming. It looked not so much as if Christianity was bad enough to include any vices, but rather as if any stick was good enough to beat Christianity with. What again could this astonishing thing be like which people were so anxious to contradict, that in doing so they did not mind contradicting themselves? I saw the same thing on every side. I can give no further space to this discussion of it in detail; but lest any one supposes that I have unfairly selected three accidental cases I will run briefly through a few others. Thus, certain sceptics wrote that the great crime of Christianity had been its attack on the family; it had dragged women to the loneliness and contemplation of the cloister, away from their homes and their children. But, then, other sceptics (slightly more advanced) said that the great crime of Christianity was forcing the family and marriage upon us; that it doomed women to the drudgery of their homes and children, and forbade them loneliness and contemplation. The charge was actually reversed. Or, again, certain phrases in the Epistles or the marriage service, were said by the anti-Christians to show contempt for woman's intellect. But I found that the anti-Christians themselves had a contempt for woman's intellect; for it was their great sneer at the Church on the Continent that "only women" went to it. Or again, Christianity was reproached with its naked and hungry habits; with its sackcloth and dried peas. But the next minute Christianity was being reproached with its pomp and its ritualism; its shrines of porphyry and its robes of gold. It was abused for being too plain and for being too coloured. Again Christianity had always been accused of restraining sexuality too much, when Bradlaugh the Malthusian discovered that it restrained it too little. It is often accused in the same breath of prim respectability and of religious extravagance. Between the covers of the same atheistic pamphlet I have found the faith rebuked for its disunion, "One thinks one thing, and one another," and rebuked also for its union, "It is difference of opinion that prevents the world from going to the dogs." In the same conversation a free-thinker, a friend of mine, blamed Christianity for despising Jews, and then despised it himself for being Jewish.

I wished to be quite fair then, and I wish to be quite fair now; and I did not conclude that the attack on Christianity was all wrong. I only concluded that if Christianity was wrong, it was very wrong indeed. Such hostile horrors might be combined in one thing, but that thing must be very strange and solitary. There are men who are misers, and also spendthrifts; but they are rare. There are men sensual and also ascetic; but they are rare. But if this mass of mad contradictions really existed, quakerish and bloodthirsty, too gorgeous and too thread-bare, austere, yet pandering preposterously to the lust of the eye, the enemy of women and their foolish refuge, a solemn pessimist and a silly optimist, if this evil existed, then there was in this evil something quite supreme and unique. For I found in my rationalist teachers no explanation of such exceptional corruption. Christianity (theoretically speaking) was in their eyes only one of the ordinary myths and errors of mortals. THEY gave me no key to this twisted and unnatural badness. Such a paradox of evil rose to the stature of the supernatural. It was, indeed, almost as supernatural as the infallibility of the Pope. An historic institution, which never went right, is really quite as much of a miracle as an institution that cannot go wrong. The only explanation which immediately occurred to my mind was that Christianity did not come from heaven, but from hell. Really, if Jesus of Nazareth was not Christ, He must have been Antichrist.

And then in a quiet hour a strange thought struck me like a still thunderbolt. There had suddenly come into my mind another explanation. Suppose we heard an unknown man spoken of by many men. Suppose we were puzzled to hear that some men said he was too tall and some too short; some objected to his fatness, some lamented his leanness; some thought him too dark, and some too fair. One explanation (as has been already admitted) would be that he might be an odd shape. But there is another explanation. He might be the right shape. Outrageously tall men might feel him to be short. Very short men might feel him to be tall. Old bucks who are growing stout might consider him insufficiently filled out; old beaux who were growing thin might feel that he expanded beyond the narrow lines of elegance. Perhaps Swedes (who have pale hair like tow) called him a dark man, while negroes considered him distinctly blonde. Perhaps (in short) this extraordinary thing is really the ordinary thing; at least the normal thing, the centre. Perhaps, after all, it is Christianity that is sane and all its critics that are mad—in various ways. I tested this idea by asking myself whether there was about any of the accusers anything morbid that might explain the accusation. I was startled to find that this key fitted a lock. For instance, it was certainly odd that the modern world charged Christianity at once with bodily austerity and with artistic pomp. But then it was also odd, very odd, that the modern world itself combined extreme bodily luxury with an extreme absence of artistic pomp. The modern man thought Becket's robes too rich and his meals too poor. But then the modern man was really exceptional in history; no man before ever ate such elaborate dinners in such ugly clothes. The modern man found the church too simple exactly where modern life is too complex; he found the church too gorgeous exactly where modern life is too dingy. The man who disliked the plain fasts and feasts was mad on entrees. The man who disliked vestments wore a pair of preposterous trousers. And surely if there was any insanity involved in the matter at all it was in the trousers, not in the simply falling robe. If there was any insanity at all, it was in the extravagant entrees, not in the bread and wine.

I went over all the cases, and I found the key fitted so far. The fact that Swinburne was irritated at the unhappiness of Christians and yet more irritated at their happiness was easily explained. It was no longer a complication of diseases in Christianity, but a complication of diseases in Swinburne. The restraints of Christians saddened him simply because he was more hedonist than a healthy man should be. The faith of Christians angered him because he was more pessimist than a healthy man should be. In the same way the Malthusians by instinct attacked Christianity; not because there is anything especially anti-Malthusian about Christianity, but because there is something a little anti-human about Malthusianism.

Nevertheless it could not, I felt, be quite true that Christianity was merely sensible and stood in the middle. There was really an element in it of emphasis and even frenzy which had justified the secularists in their superficial criticism. It might be wise, I began more and more to think that it was wise, but it was not merely worldly wise; it was not merely temperate and respectable. Its fierce crusaders and meek saints might balance each other; still, the crusaders were very fierce and the saints were very meek, meek beyond all decency. Now, it was just at this point of the speculation that I remembered my thoughts about the martyr and the suicide. In that matter there had been this combination between two almost insane positions which yet somehow amounted to sanity. This was just such another contradiction; and this I had already found to be true. This was exactly one of the paradoxes in which sceptics found the creed wrong; and in this I had found it right. Madly as Christians might love the martyr or hate the suicide, they never felt these passions more madly than I had felt them long before I dreamed of Christianity. Then the most difficult and interesting part of the mental process opened, and I began to trace this idea darkly through all the enormous thoughts of our theology. The idea was that which I had outlined touching the optimist and the pessimist; that we want not an amalgam or compromise, but both things at the top of their energy; love and wrath both burning. Here I shall only trace it in relation to ethics. But I need not remind the reader that the idea of this combination is indeed central in orthodox theology. For orthodox theology has specially insisted that Christ was not a being apart from God and man, like an elf, nor yet a being half human and half not, like a centaur, but both things at once and both things thoroughly, very man and very God. Now let me trace this notion as I found it.

All sane men can see that sanity is some kind of equilibrium; that one may be mad and eat too much, or mad and eat too little. Some moderns have indeed appeared with vague versions of progress and evolution which seeks to destroy the MESON or balance of Aristotle. They seem to suggest that we are meant to starve progressively, or to go on eating larger and larger breakfasts every morning for ever. But the great truism of the

MESON remains for all thinking men, and these people have not upset any balance except their own. But granted that we have all to keep a balance, the real interest comes in with the question of how that balance can be kept. That was the problem which Paganism tried to solve: that was the problem which I think Christianity solved and solved in a very strange way.

Paganism declared that virtue was in a balance; Christianity declared it was in a conflict: the collision of two passions apparently opposite. Of course they were not really inconsistent; but they were such that it was hard to hold simultaneously. Let us follow for a moment the clue of the martyr and the suicide; and take the case of courage. No quality has ever so much addled the brains and tangled the definitions of merely rational sages. Courage is almost a contradiction in terms. It means a strong desire to live taking the form of a readiness to die. "He that will lose his life, the same shall save it," is not a piece of mysticism for saints and heroes. It is a piece of everyday advice for sailors or mountaineers. It might be printed in an Alpine guide or a drill book. This paradox is the whole principle of courage; even of quite earthly or quite brutal courage. A man cut off by the sea may save his life if he will risk it on the precipice.

He can only get away from death by continually stepping within an inch of it. A soldier surrounded by enemies, if he is to cut his way out, needs to combine a strong desire for living with a strange carelessness about dying. He must not merely cling to life, for then he will be a coward, and will not escape. He must not merely wait for death, for then he will be a suicide, and will not escape. He must seek his life in a spirit of furious indifference to it; he must desire life like water and yet drink death like wine. No philosopher, I fancy, has ever expressed this romantic riddle with adequate lucidity, and I certainly have not done so. But Christianity has done more: it has marked the limits of it in the awful graves of the suicide and the hero, showing the distance between him who dies for the sake of living and him who dies for the sake of dying. And it has held up ever since above the European lances the banner of the mystery of chivalry: the Christian courage, which is a disdain of death; not the Chinese courage, which is a disdain of life.

And now I began to find that this duplex passion was the Christian key to ethics everywhere. Everywhere the creed made a moderation out of the still crash of two impetuous emotions. Take, for instance, the matter of modesty, of the balance between mere pride and mere prostration. The average pagan, like the average agnostic, would merely say that he was content with himself, but not insolently self-satisfied, that there were many better and many worse, that his deserts were limited, but he would see that he got them. In short, he would walk with his head in the air; but not necessarily with his nose in the air. This is a manly and rational position, but it is open to the objection we noted against the compromise between optimism and pessimism—the "resignation" of Matthew Arnold. Being a mixture of two things, it is a dilution of two things; neither is present in its full strength or contributes its full colour. This proper pride does not lift the heart like the tongue of trumpets; you cannot go clad in crimson and gold for this. On the other hand, this mild rationalist modesty does not cleanse the soul with fire and make it clear like crystal; it does not (like a strict and searching humility) make a man as a little child, who can sit at the feet of the grass. It does not make him look up and see marvels; for Alice must grow small if she is to be Alice in Wonderland. Thus it loses both the poetry of being proud and the poetry of being humble. Christianity sought by this same strange expedient to save both of them.

It separated the two ideas and then exaggerated them both. In one way Man was to be haughtier than he had ever been before; in another way he was to be humbler than he had ever been before. In so far as I am Man I am the chief of creatures. In so far as I am a man I am the chief of sinners. All humility that had meant pessimism, that had meant man taking a vague or mean view of his whole destiny—all that was to go. We were to hear no more the wail of Ecclesiastes that humanity had no pre-eminence over the brute, or the awful cry of Homer that man was only the saddest of all the beasts of the field. Man was a statue of God walking about the garden. Man had pre-eminence over all the brutes; man was only sad because he was not a beast, but a broken god. The Greek had spoken of men creeping on the earth, as if clinging to it. Now Man was to tread on the earth as if to subdue it. Christianity thus held a thought of the dignity of man that could only be expressed in crowns rayed like the sun and fans of peacock plumage. Yet at the same time it could hold a thought about the abject smallness of man that could only be expressed in fasting and fantastic submission, in the gray ashes of St. Dominic and the white snows of St. Bernard. When one came to think of ONE'S SELF, there was vista and void enough for any amount of bleak abnegation and bitter truth. There the realistic gentleman could let himself go—as long as he let himself go at himself. There was an open playground for the happy pessimist. Let him say anything against himself short of blaspheming the original aim of his being; let him call himself a fool and even a damned fool (though that is Calvinistic); but he must not say that fools are not worth saving. He must not say that a man, QUA man, can be valueless. Here, again in short, Christianity got over the difficulty of combining furious opposites, by keeping them both, and keeping them both furious. The Church was positive on both points. One can hardly think too little of one's self. One can hardly think too much of one's soul.

Take another case: the complicated question of charity, which some highly uncharitable idealists seem to think quite easy. Charity is a paradox, like modesty and courage. Stated baldly, charity certainly means one of two things—pardoning unpardonable acts, or loving unlovable people. But if we ask ourselves (as we did in the case of pride) what a sensible pagan would feel about such a subject, we shall probably be beginning at the bottom of it. A sensible pagan would say that there were some people one could forgive, and some one couldn't: a slave who stole wine could be laughed at; a slave who betrayed his benefactor could be killed, and cursed even after he was killed. In so far as the act was pardonable, the man was pardonable. That again is rational, and even refreshing; but it is a dilution. It leaves no place for a pure horror of injustice, such as that which is a great beauty in the innocent. And it leaves no place for a mere tenderness for men as men, such as is the whole fascination of the charitable. Christianity came in here as before. It came in startlingly with a sword, and clove one thing from another. It divided the crime from the criminal. The criminal we must forgive unto seventy times seven. The crime we must not forgive at all. It was not enough that slaves who stole wine inspired partly anger and partly kindness. We must be much more angry with theft than before, and yet much kinder to thieves than before. There was room for wrath and love to run wild. And the more I considered Christianity, the more I found that while it had established a rule and order, the chief aim of that order was to give room for good things to run wild.

Mental and emotional liberty are not so simple as they look. Really they require almost as careful a balance of laws and conditions as do social and political liberty. The ordinary aesthetic anarchist who sets out to feel everything freely gets knotted at last in a paradox that prevents him feeling at all. He breaks away from home limits to follow poetry. But in ceasing to feel home limits he has ceased to feel the "Odyssey." He is free from national prejudices and outside patriotism. But being outside patriotism he is outside "Henry V." Such a literary man is simply outside all literature: he is more of a prisoner than any bigot. For if there is a wall between you and the world, it makes little difference whether you describe yourself as locked in or as locked out. What we want is not the universality that is outside all normal sentiments; we want the universality that is inside all normal sentiments. It is all the difference between being free from them, as a man is free from a prison, and being free of them as a man is free of a city. I am free from Windsor Castle (that is, I am not forcibly detained there), but I am by no means free of that building. How can man be approximately free of fine emotions, able to swing them in a clear space without breakage or wrong? THIS was the achievement of this Christian paradox of the parallel passions. Granted the primary dogma of the war between divine and diabolic, the revolt and ruin of the world, their optimism and pessimism, as pure poetry, could be loosened like cataracts.

St. Francis, in praising all good, could be a more shouting optimist than Walt Whitman. St. Jerome, in denouncing all evil, could paint the world blacker than Schopenhauer. Both passions were free because both were kept in their place. The optimist could pour out all the praise he liked on the gay music of the march, the golden trumpets, and the purple banners going into battle. But he must not call the fight needless. The pessimist might draw as darkly as he chose the sickening marches or the sanguine wounds. But he must not call the fight hopeless. So it was with all the other moral problems, with pride, with protest, and with compassion. By defining its main doctrine, the Church not only kept seemingly inconsistent things side by side, but, what was more, allowed them to break out in a sort of artistic violence otherwise possible only to anarchists. Meekness grew more dramatic than madness. Historic Christianity rose into a high and strange COUP DE THEATRE of morality—things that are to virtue what the crimes of Nero are to vice. The spirits of indignation and of charity took terrible and attractive forms, ranging from that monkish fierceness that scourged like a dog the first and greatest of the Plantagenets, to the sublime pity of St. Catherine, who, in the official shambles, kissed the bloody head of the criminal. Poetry could be acted as well as composed. This heroic and monumental manner in ethics has entirely vanished with supernatural religion. They, being humble, could parade themselves: but we are too proud to be prominent. Our ethical teachers write reasonably for prison reform; but we are not likely to see Mr. Cadbury, or any eminent philanthropist, go into Reading Gaol and embrace the strangled corpse before it is cast into the quicklime. Our ethical teachers write mildly against the power of millionaires; but we are not likely to see Mr. Rockefeller, or any modern tyrant, publicly whipped in Westminster Abbey.

Thus, the double charges of the secularists, though throwing nothing but darkness and confusion on themselves, throw a real light on the faith. It is true that the historic Church has at once emphasised celibacy and emphasised the family; has at once (if one may put it so) been fiercely for having children and fiercely for not having children. It has kept them side by side like two strong colours, red and white, like the red and white upon the shield of St. George. It has always had a healthy hatred of pink. It hates that combination of two colours which is the feeble expedient of the philosophers. It hates that evolution of black into white which is tantamount to a dirty gray. In fact, the whole theory of the Church on virginity might be symbolized in the statement that white is a colour: not merely the absence of a colour. All that I am urging here can be expressed by saying that Christianity sought in most of these cases to keep two colours coexistent but pure. It is not a mixture like russet or purple; it is rather like a shot silk, for a shot silk is always at right angles, and is in the pattern of the cross.

So it is also, of course, with the contradictory charges of the anti-Christians about submission and slaughter. It IS true that the Church told some men to fight and others not to fight; and it IS true that those who fought were like thunderbolts and those who did not fight were like statues.

All this simply means that the Church preferred to use its Supermen and to use its Tolstoyans. There must be SOME good in the life of battle, for so many good men have enjoyed being soldiers. There must be SOME good in the idea of non-resistance, for so many good men seem to enjoy being Quakers. All that the Church did (so far as that goes) was to prevent either of these good things from ousting the other. They existed side by side. The Tolstoyans, having all the scruples of monks, simply became monks. The Quakers became a club instead of becoming a sect. Monks said all that Tolstoy says; they poured out lucid lamentations about the cruelty of battles and the vanity of revenge. But the Tolstoyans are not quite right enough to run the whole world; and in the ages of faith they were not allowed to run it. The world did not lose the last charge of Sir James Douglas or the banner of Joan the Maid. And sometimes this pure gentleness and this pure fierceness met and justified their juncture; the paradox of all the prophets was fulfilled, and, in the soul of St. Louis, the lion lay down with the lamb. But remember that this text is too lightly interpreted. It is constantly assured, especially in our Tolstoyan tendencies, that when the lion lies down with the lamb the lion becomes lamb-like. But that is brutal annexation and imperialism on the part of the lamb. That is simply the lamb absorbing the lion instead of the lion eating the lamb. The real problem is—Can the lion lie down with the lamb and still retain his royal ferocity? THAT is the problem the Church attempted; THAT is the miracle she achieved.

This is what I have called guessing the hidden eccentricities of life. This is knowing that a man's heart is to the left and not in the middle. This is knowing not only that the earth is round, but knowing exactly where it is flat. Christian doctrine detected the oddities of life. It not only discovered the law, but it foresaw the exceptions. Those underrate Christianity who say that it discovered mercy; any one might discover mercy. In fact every one did. But to discover a plan for being merciful and also severe— THAT was to anticipate a strange need of human nature. For no one wants to be forgiven for a big sin as if it were a little one. Any one might say that we should be neither quite miserable nor quite happy. But to find out how far one MAY be quite miserable without making it impossible to be quite happy—that was a discovery in psychology. Any one might say, "Neither swagger nor grovel"; and it would have been a limit. But to say, "Here you can swagger and there you can grovel"—that was an emancipation.

This was the big fact about Christian ethics; the discovery of the new balance. Paganism had been like a pillar of marble, upright because proportioned with symmetry. Christianity was like a huge and ragged and romantic rock, which, though it sways on its pedestal at a touch, yet, because its exaggerated excrescences exactly balance each other, is enthroned there for a thousand years. In a Gothic cathedral the columns were all different, but they were all necessary. Every support seemed an accidental and fantastic support; every buttress was a flying buttress. So in Christendom apparent accidents balanced. Becket wore a hair shirt under his gold and crimson, and there is much to be said for the combination; for Becket got the benefit of the hair shirt while the people in the street got the benefit of the crimson and gold. It is at least better than the manner of the modern millionaire, who has the black and the drab outwardly for others, and the gold next his heart. But the balance was not always in one man's body as in Becket's; the balance was often distributed over the whole body of Christendom. Because a man prayed and fasted on the Northern snows, flowers could be flung at his festival in the Southern cities; and because fanatics drank water on the sands of Syria, men could still drink cider in the orchards of England. This is what makes Christendom at once so much more perplexing and so much more interesting than the Pagan empire; just as Amiens Cathedral is not better but more interesting than the Parthenon. If any one wants a modern proof of all this, let him consider the curious fact that, under Christianity, Europe (while remaining a unity) has broken up into individual nations. Patriotism is a perfect example of this deliberate balancing of one emphasis against another emphasis. The instinct of the Pagan empire would have said, "You shall all be Roman citizens, and grow alike; let the German grow less slow and reverent; the Frenchmen less experimental and swift." But the instinct of Christian Europe says, "Let the German remain slow and reverent, that the Frenchman may the more safely be swift and experimental. We will make an equipoise out of these excesses. The absurdity called Germany shall correct the insanity called France."

Last and most important, it is exactly this which explains what is so inexplicable to all the modern critics of the history of Christianity. I mean the monstrous wars about small points of theology, the earthquakes of emotion about a gesture or a word. It was only a matter of an inch; but an inch is everything when you are balancing. The Church could not afford to swerve a hair's breadth on some things if she was to continue her great and daring experiment of the irregular equilibrium. Once let one idea become less powerful and some other idea would become too powerful. It was no flock of sheep the Christian shepherd was leading, but a herd of bulls and tigers, of terrible ideals and devouring doctrines, each one of them strong enough to turn to a false religion and lay waste the world. Remember that the Church went in specifically for dangerous ideas; she was a lion tamer. The idea of birth through a Holy Spirit, of the death of a divine being, of the forgiveness of sins, or the fulfilment of prophecies, are ideas which, any one can see, need but a touch to turn them into something blasphemous or ferocious. The smallest link was let drop by the artificers of the Mediterranean, and the lion of ancestral pessimism burst his chain in the forgotten forests of the north. Of these theological equalisations I have to speak afterwards. Here it is enough to notice that if some small mistake were made in doctrine, huge blunders might be made in human happiness. A sentence phrased wrong about the nature of symbolism would have broken all the best statues in Europe. A slip in the definitions might stop all the dances; might wither all the Christmas trees or break all the Easter eggs. Doctrines had to be defined within strict limits, even in order that man might enjoy general human liberties. The Church had to be careful, if only that the world might be careless.

This is the thrilling romance of Orthodoxy. People have fallen into a foolish habit of speaking of orthodoxy as something heavy, humdrum, and safe. There never was anything so perilous or so exciting as orthodoxy. It was sanity: and to be sane is more dramatic than to be mad. It was the equilibrium of a man behind madly rushing horses, seeming to stoop this way and to sway that, yet in every attitude having the grace of statuary and the accuracy of arithmetic. The Church in its early days went fierce and fast with any warhorse; yet it is utterly unhistoric to say that she merely went mad along one idea, like a vulgar fanaticism. She swerved to left and right, so exactly as to avoid enormous obstacles. She left on one hand the huge bulk of Arianism, buttressed by all the worldly powers to make Christianity too worldly. The next instant she was swerving to avoid an orientalism, which would have made it too unworldly. The orthodox Church never took the tame course or accepted the conventions; the orthodox Church was never respectable. It would have been easier to have accepted the earthly power of the Arians. It would have been easy, in the Calvinistic seventeenth century, to fall into the bottomless pit of predestination. It is easy to be a madman: it is easy to be a heretic. It is always easy to let the age have its head; the difficult thing is to keep one's own. It is always easy to be a modernist; as it is easy to be a snob. To have fallen into any of those open traps of error and exaggeration which fashion after fashion and sect after sect set along the historic path of Christendom—that would indeed have been simple. It is always simple to fall; there are an infinity of angles at which one falls, only one at which one stands. To have fallen into any one of the fads from Gnosticism to Christian Science would indeed have been obvious and tame. But to have avoided them all has been one whirling adventure; and in my vision the heavenly chariot flies thundering through the ages, the dull heresies sprawling and prostrate, the wild truth reeling but erect.

THE ETERNAL REVOLUTION

The following propositions have been urged: First, that some faith in our life is required even to improve it; second, that some dissatisfaction with things as they are is necessary even in order to be satisfied; third, that to have this necessary content and necessary discontent it is not sufficient to have the obvious equilibrium of the Stoic. For mere resignation has neither the gigantic levity of pleasure nor the superb intolerance of pain. There is a vital objection to the advice merely to grin and bear it. The objection is that if you merely bear it, you do not grin. Greek heroes do not grin: but gargoyles do—because they are Christian. And when a Christian is pleased, he is (in the most exact sense) frightfully pleased; his pleasure is frightful. Christ prophesied the whole of Gothic architecture in that hour when nervous and respectable people (such people as now object to barrel organs) objected to the shouting of the gutter-snipes of Jerusalem. He said, "If these were silent, the very stones would cry out." Under the impulse of His spirit arose like a clamorous chorus the facades of the mediaeval cathedrals, thronged with shouting faces and open mouths. The prophecy has fulfilled itself: the very stones cry out.

If these things be conceded, though only for argument, we may take up where we left it the thread of the thought of the natural man, called by the Scotch (with regrettable familiarity), "The Old Man." We can ask the next question so obviously in front of us. Some satisfaction is needed even to make things better. But what do we mean by making things better? Most modern talk on this matter is a mere argument in a circle—that circle which we have already made the symbol of madness and of mere rationalism. Evolution is only good if it produces good; good is only good if it helps evolution. The elephant stands on the tortoise, and the tortoise on the elephant.

Obviously, it will not do to take our ideal from the principle in nature; for the simple reason that (except for some human or divine theory), there is no principle in nature. For instance, the cheap anti-democrat of to-day will tell you solemnly that there is no equality in nature. He is right, but he does not see the logical addendum. There is no equality in nature; also there is no inequality in nature. Inequality, as much as equality, implies a standard of value. To read aristocracy into the anarchy of animals is just as sentimental as to read democracy into it. Both aristocracy and democracy are human ideals: the one saying that all men are valuable, the other that some men are more valuable. But nature does not say that cats are more valuable than mice; nature makes no remark on the subject. She does not even say that the cat is enviable or the mouse pitiable. We think the cat superior because we have (or most of us have) a particular philosophy to the effect that life is better than death. But if the mouse were a German pessimist mouse, he might not think that the cat had beaten him at all. He might think he had beaten the cat by getting to the grave first. Or he might feel that he had actually inflicted frightful punishment on the cat by keeping him alive. Just as a microbe might feel proud of spreading a pestilence, so the pessimistic mouse might exult to think that he was renewing in the cat the torture of conscious existence. It all depends on the philosophy of the mouse. You cannot even say that there is victory or superiority in nature unless you have some doctrine about what things are superior. You cannot even say that the cat scores unless there is a system of scoring. You cannot even say that the cat gets the best of it unless there is some best to be got.

We cannot, then, get the ideal itself from nature, and as we follow here the first and natural speculation, we will leave out (for the present) the idea of getting it from God. We must have our own vision. But the attempts of most moderns to express it are highly vague.

Some fall back simply on the clock: they talk as if mere passage through time brought some superiority; so that even a man of the first mental calibre carelessly uses the phrase that human morality is never up to date. How can anything be up to date?— a date has no character. How can one say that Christmas celebrations are not suitable to the twenty-fifth of a month? What the writer meant, of course, was that the majority is behind his favourite minority—or in front of it. Other vague modern people take refuge in material metaphors; in fact, this is the chief mark of vague modern people. Not daring to define their doctrine of what is good, they use physical figures of speech without stint or shame, and, what is worst of all, seem to think these cheap analogies are exquisitely spiritual and superior to the old morality. Thus they think it intellectual to talk about things being "high." It is at least the reverse of intellectual; it is a mere phrase from a steeple or a weathercock. "Tommy was a good boy" is a pure philosophical statement, worthy of Plato or Aquinas. "Tommy lived the higher life" is a gross metaphor from a ten-foot rule.

This, incidentally, is almost the whole weakness of Nietzsche, whom some are representing as a bold and strong thinker. No one will deny that he was a poetical and suggestive thinker; but he was quite the reverse of strong. He was not at all bold. He never put his own meaning before himself in bald abstract words: as did Aristotle and Calvin, and even Karl Marx, the hard, fearless men of thought. Nietzsche always escaped a question by a physical metaphor, like a cheery minor poet. He said, "beyond good and evil," because he had not the courage to say, "more good than good and evil," or, "more evil than good and evil." Had he faced his thought without metaphors, he would have seen that it was nonsense. So, when he describes his hero, he does not dare to say, "the purer man," or "the happier man," or "the sadder man," for all these are ideas; and ideas are alarming. He says "the upper man," or "over man," a physical metaphor from acrobats or alpine climbers. Nietzsche is truly a very timid thinker. He does not really know in the least what sort of man he wants evolution to produce. And if he does not know, certainly the ordinary evolutionists, who talk about things being "higher," do not know either.

Then again, some people fall back on sheer submission and sitting still. Nature is going to do something some day; nobody knows what, and nobody knows when. We have no reason for acting, and no reason for not acting. If anything happens it is right: if anything is prevented it was wrong. Again, some people try to anticipate nature by doing something, by doing anything. Because we may possibly grow wings they cut off their legs. Yet nature may be trying to make them centipedes for all they know.

Lastly, there is a fourth class of people who take whatever it is that they happen to want, and say that that is the ultimate aim of evolution. And these are the only sensible people. This is the only really healthy way with the word evolution, to work for what you want, and to call THAT evolution. The only intelligible sense that progress or advance can have among men, is that we have a definite vision, and that we wish to make the whole world like that vision. If you like to put it so, the essence of the doctrine is that what we have around us is the mere method and preparation for something that we have to create. This is not a world, but rather the material for a world. God has given us not so much the colours of a picture as the colours of a palette. But he has also given us a subject, a model, a fixed vision. We must be clear about what we want to paint. This adds a further principle to our previous list of principles. We have said we must be fond of this world, even in order to change it. We now add that we must be fond of another world (real or imaginary) in order to have something to change it to.

We need not debate about the mere words evolution or progress: personally I prefer to call it reform. For reform implies form. It implies that we are trying to shape the world in a particular image; to make it something that we see already in our minds. Evolution is a metaphor from mere automatic unrolling. Progress is a metaphor from merely walking along a road—very likely the wrong road. But reform is a metaphor for reasonable and determined men: it means that we see a certain thing out of shape and we mean to put it into shape. And we know what shape.

Now here comes in the whole collapse and huge blunder of our age. We have mixed up two different things, two opposite things. Progress should mean that we are always changing the world to suit the vision. Progress does mean (just now) that we are always changing the vision. It should mean that we are slow but sure in bringing justice and mercy among men: it does mean that we are very swift in doubting the desirability of justice and mercy: a wild page from any Prussian sophist makes men doubt it. Progress should mean that we are always walking towards the New Jerusalem. It does mean that the New Jerusalem is always walking away from us. We are not altering the real to suit the ideal. We are altering the ideal: it is easier.

Silly examples are always simpler; let us suppose a man wanted a particular kind of world; say, a blue world. He would have no cause to complain of the slightness or swiftness of his task; he might toil for a long time at the transformation; he could work away (in every sense) until all was blue. He could have heroic adventures; the putting of the last touches to a blue tiger. He could have fairy dreams; the dawn of a blue moon. But if he worked hard, that high-minded reformer would certainly (from his own point of view) leave the world better and bluer than he found it. If he altered a blade of grass to his favourite colour every day, he would get on slowly. But if he altered his favourite colour every day, he would not get on at all. If, after reading a fresh philosopher, he started to paint everything red or yellow, his work would be thrown away: there would be nothing to show except a few blue tigers walking about, specimens of his early bad manner. This is exactly the position of the average modern thinker. It will be said that this is avowedly a preposterous example. But it is literally the fact of recent history. The great and grave changes in our political civilization all belonged to the early nineteenth century, not to the later. They belonged to the black and white epoch when men believed fixedly in Toryism, in Protestantism, in Calvinism, in Reform, and not unfrequently in Revolution. And whatever each man believed in he hammered at steadily, without scepticism: and there was a time when the Established Church might have fallen, and the House of Lords nearly fell. It was because Radicals were wise enough to be constant and consistent; it was because Radicals were wise enough to be Conservative. But in the existing atmosphere there is not enough time and tradition in Radicalism to pull anything down. There is a great deal of truth in Lord Hugh Cecil's suggestion (made in a fine speech) that the era of change is over, and that ours is an era of conservation and repose. But probably it would pain Lord Hugh Cecil if he realized (what is certainly the case) that ours is only an age of conservation because it is an age of complete unbelief. Let beliefs fade fast and frequently, if you wish institutions to remain the same. The more the life of the mind is unhinged, the more the machinery of matter will be left to itself. The net result of all our political suggestions, Collectivism, Tolstoyanism, Neo-Feudalism, Communism, Anarchy, Scientific Bureaucracy—the plain fruit of all of them is that the Monarchy and the House of Lords will remain. The net result of all the new religions will be that the Church of England will not (for heaven knows how long) be disestablished. It was Karl Marx, Nietzsche, Tolstoy, Cunninghame Grahame, Bernard Shaw and Auberon Herbert, who between them, with bowed gigantic backs, bore up the throne of the Archbishop of Canterbury.

We may say broadly that free thought is the best of all the safeguards against freedom. Managed in a modern style the emancipation of the slave's mind is the best way of preventing the emancipation of the slave. Teach him to worry about whether he wants to be free, and he will not free himself. Again, it may be said that this instance is remote or extreme. But, again, it is exactly true of the men in the streets around us. It is true that the negro slave, being a debased barbarian, will probably have either a human affection of loyalty, or a human affection for liberty. But the man we see every day—the worker in Mr. Gradgrind's factory, the little clerk in Mr. Gradgrind's office—he is too mentally worried to believe in freedom. He is kept quiet with revolutionary literature. He is calmed and kept in his place by a constant succession of wild philosophies. He is a Marxian one day, a Nietzscheite the next day, a Superman (probably) the next day; and a slave every day. The only thing that remains after all the philosophies is the factory. The only man who gains by all the philosophies is Gradgrind. It would be worth his while to keep his commercial helotry supplied with sceptical literature. And now I come to think of it, of course, Gradgrind is famous for giving libraries. He shows his sense. All modern books are on his side. As long as the vision of heaven is always changing, the vision of earth will be exactly the same. No ideal will remain long enough to be realized, or even partly realized. The modern young man will never change his environment; for he will always change his mind.

This, therefore, is our first requirement about the ideal towards which progress is directed; it must be fixed. Whistler used to make many rapid studies of a sitter; it did not matter if he tore up twenty portraits. But it would matter if he looked up twenty times, and each time saw a new person sitting placidly for his portrait. So it does not matter (comparatively speaking) how often humanity fails to imitate its ideal; for then all its old failures are fruitful. But it does frightfully matter how often humanity changes its ideal; for then all its old failures are fruitless. The question therefore becomes this: How can we keep the artist discontented with his pictures while preventing him from being vitally discontented with his art? How can we make a man always dissatisfied with his work, yet always satisfied with working? How can we make sure that the portrait painter will throw the portrait out of window instead of taking the natural and more human course of throwing the sitter out of window?

A strict rule is not only necessary for ruling; it is also necessary for rebelling. This fixed and familiar ideal is necessary to any sort of revolution. Man will sometimes act slowly upon new ideas; but he will only act swiftly upon old ideas. If I am merely to float or fade or evolve, it may be towards something anarchic; but if I am to riot, it must be for something respectable. This is the whole weakness of certain schools of progress and moral evolution. They suggest that there has been a slow movement towards morality, with an imperceptible ethical change in every year or at every instant. There is only one great disadvantage in this theory. It talks of a slow movement towards justice; but it does not permit a swift movement. A man is not allowed to leap up and declare a certain state of things to be intrinsically intolerable. To make the matter clear, it is better to take a specific example. Certain of the idealistic vegetarians, such as Mr. Salt, say that the time has now come for eating no meat; by implication they assume that at one time it was right to eat meat, and they suggest (in words that could be quoted) that some day it may be wrong to eat milk and eggs. I do not discuss here the question of what is justice to animals. I only say that whatever is justice ought, under given conditions, to be prompt justice. If an animal is wronged, we ought to be able to rush to his rescue. But how can we rush if we are, perhaps, in advance of our time? How can we rush to catch a train which may not arrive for a few centuries? How can I denounce a man for skinning cats, if he is only now what I may possibly become in drinking a glass of milk? A splendid and insane Russian sect ran about taking all the cattle out of all the carts. How can I pluck up courage to take the horse out of my hansom-cab, when I do not know whether my evolutionary watch is only a little fast or the cabman's a little slow? Suppose I say to a sweater, "Slavery suited one stage of evolution." And suppose he answers, "And sweating suits this stage of evolution." How can I answer if there is no eternal test? If sweaters can be behind the current morality, why should not philanthropists be in front of it? What on earth is the current morality, except in its literal sense—the morality that is always running away?

Thus we may say that a permanent ideal is as necessary to the innovator as to the conservative; it is necessary whether we wish the king's orders to be promptly executed or whether we only wish the king to be promptly executed. The guillotine has many sins, but to do it justice there is nothing evolutionary about it. The favourite evolutionary argument finds its best answer in the axe. The Evolutionist says, "Where do you draw the line?" the Revolutionist answers, "I draw it HERE: exactly between your head and body." There must at any given moment be an abstract right and wrong if any blow is to be struck; there must be something eternal if there is to be anything sudden. Therefore for all intelligible human purposes, for altering things or for keeping things as they are, for founding a system for ever, as in China, or for altering it every month as in the early French Revolution, it is equally necessary that the vision should be a fixed vision. This is our first requirement.

When I had written this down, I felt once again the presence of something else in the discussion: as a man hears a church bell above the sound of the street. Something seemed to be saying, "My ideal at least is fixed; for it was fixed before the foundations of the world. My vision of perfection assuredly cannot be altered; for it is called Eden. You may alter the place to which you are going; but you cannot alter the place from which you have come. To the orthodox there must always be a case for revolution; for in the hearts of men God has been put under the feet of Satan. In the upper world hell once rebelled against heaven. But in this world heaven is rebelling against hell. For the orthodox there can always be a revolution; for a revolution is a restoration. At any instant you may strike a blow for the perfection which no man has seen since Adam. No unchanging custom, no changing evolution can make the original good any thing but good. Man may have had concubines as long as cows have had horns: still they are not a part of him if they are sinful. Men may have been under oppression ever since fish were under water; still they ought not to be, if oppression is sinful. The chain may seem as natural to the slave, or the paint to the harlot, as does the plume to the bird or the burrow to the fox; still they are not, if they are sinful. I lift my prehistoric legend to defy all your history. Your vision is not merely a fixture: it is a fact." I paused to note the new coincidence of Christianity: but I passed on.

I passed on to the next necessity of any ideal of progress. Some people (as we have said) seem to believe in an automatic and impersonal progress in the nature of things. But it is clear that no political activity can be encouraged by saying that progress is natural and inevitable; that is not a reason for being active, but rather a reason for being lazy. If we are bound to improve, we need not trouble to improve. The pure doctrine of progress is the best of all reasons for not being a progressive. But it is to none of these obvious comments that I wish primarily to call attention.

The only arresting point is this: that if we suppose improvement to be natural, it must be fairly simple. The world might conceivably be working towards one consummation, but hardly towards any particular arrangement of many qualities. To take our original simile: Nature by herself may be growing more blue; that is, a process so simple that it might be impersonal. But Nature cannot be making a careful picture made of many picked colours, unless Nature is personal. If the end of the world were mere darkness or mere light it might come as slowly and inevitably as dusk or dawn. But if the end of the world is to be a piece of elaborate and artistic chiaroscuro, then there must be design in it, either human or divine. The world, through mere time, might grow black like an old picture, or white like an old coat; but if it is turned into a particular piece of black and white art— then there is an artist.

If the distinction be not evident, I give an ordinary instance. We constantly hear a particularly cosmic creed from the modern humanitarians; I use the word humanitarian in the ordinary sense, as meaning one who upholds the claims of all creatures against those of humanity. They suggest that through the ages we have been growing more and more humane, that is to say, that one after another, groups or sections of beings, slaves, children, women, cows, or what not, have been gradually admitted to mercy or to justice. They say that we once thought it right to eat men (we didn't); but I am not here concerned with their history, which is highly unhistorical. As a fact, anthropophagy is certainly a decadent thing, not a primitive one. It is much more likely that modern men will eat human flesh out of affectation than that primitive man ever ate it out of ignorance. I am here only following the outlines of their argument, which consists in maintaining that man has been progressively more lenient, first to citizens, then to slaves, then to animals, and then (presumably) to plants. I think it wrong to sit on a man. Soon, I shall think it wrong to sit on a horse. Eventually (I suppose) I shall think it wrong to sit on a chair. That is the drive of the argument. And for this argument it can be said that it is possible to talk of it in terms of evolution or inevitable progress. A perpetual tendency to touch fewer and fewer things might—one feels, be a mere brute unconscious tendency, like that of a species to produce fewer and fewer children. This drift may be really evolutionary, because it is stupid.

Darwinism can be used to back up two mad moralities, but it cannot be used to back up a single sane one. The kinship and competition of all living creatures can be used as a reason for being insanely cruel or insanely sentimental; but not for a healthy love of animals. On the evolutionary basis you may be inhumane, or you may be absurdly humane; but you cannot be human. That you and a tiger are one may be a reason for being tender to a tiger. Or it may be a reason for being as cruel as the tiger. It is one way to train the tiger to imitate you, it is a shorter way to imitate the tiger. But in neither case does evolution tell you how to treat a tiger reasonably, that is, to admire his stripes while avoiding his claws.

If you want to treat a tiger reasonably, you must go back to the garden of Eden. For the obstinate reminder continued to recur: only the supernatural has taken a sane view of Nature. The essence of all pantheism, evolutionism, and modern cosmic religion is really in this proposition: that Nature is our mother. Unfortunately, if you regard Nature as a mother, you discover that she is a step-mother. The main point of Christianity was this: that Nature is not our mother: Nature is our sister. We can be proud of her beauty, since we have the same father; but she has no authority over us; we have to admire, but not to imitate. This gives to the typically Christian pleasure in this earth a strange touch of lightness that is almost frivolity. Nature was a solemn mother to the worshippers of Isis and Cybele. Nature was a solemn mother to Wordsworth or to Emerson. But Nature is not solemn to Francis of Assisi or to George Herbert. To St. Francis, Nature is a sister, and even a younger sister: a little, dancing sister, to be laughed at as well as loved.

This, however, is hardly our main point at present; I have admitted it only in order to show how constantly, and as it were accidentally, the key would fit the smallest doors. Our main point is here, that if there be a mere trend of impersonal improvement in Nature, it must presumably be a simple trend towards some simple triumph. One can imagine that some automatic tendency in biology might work for giving us longer and longer noses. But the question is, do we want to have longer and longer noses? I fancy not; I believe that we most of us want to say to our noses, "thus far, and no farther; and here shall thy proud point be stayed:" we require a nose of such length as may ensure an interesting face. But we cannot imagine a mere biological trend towards producing interesting faces; because an interesting face is one particular arrangement of eyes, nose, and mouth, in a most complex relation to each other. Proportion cannot be a drift: it is either an accident or a design. So with the ideal of human morality and its relation to the humanitarians and the anti-humanitarians. It is conceivable that we are going more and more to keep our hands off things: not to drive horses; not to pick flowers. We may eventually be bound not to disturb a man's mind even by argument; not to disturb the sleep of birds even by coughing. The ultimate apotheosis would appear to be that of a man sitting quite still, nor daring to stir for fear of disturbing a fly, nor to eat for fear of incommoding a microbe. To so crude a consummation as that we might perhaps unconsciously drift. But do we want so crude a consummation? Similarly, we might unconsciously evolve along the opposite or Nietzschian line of development—superman crushing superman in one tower of tyrants until the universe is smashed up for fun. But do we want the universe smashed up for fun? Is it not quite clear that what we really hope for is one particular management and proposition of these two things; a certain amount of restraint and respect, a certain amount of energy and mastery? If our life is ever really as beautiful as a fairy-tale, we shall have to remember that all the beauty of a fairy-tale lies in this: that the prince has a wonder which just stops short of being fear. If he is afraid of the giant, there is an end of him; but also if he is not astonished at the giant, there is an end of the fairy-tale. The whole point depends upon his being at once humble enough to wonder, and haughty enough to defy. So our attitude to the giant of the world must not merely be increasing delicacy or increasing contempt: it must be one particular proportion of the two—which is exactly right. We must have in us enough reverence for all things outside us to make us tread fearfully on the grass. We must also have enough disdain for all things outside us, to make us, on due occasion, spit at the stars. Yet these two things (if we are to be good or happy) must be combined, not in any combination, but in one particular combination. The perfect happiness of men on the earth (if it ever comes) will not be a flat and solid thing, like the satisfaction of animals. It will be an exact and perilous balance; like that of a desperate romance. Man must have just enough faith in himself to have adventures, and just enough doubt of himself to enjoy them.

This, then, is our second requirement for the ideal of progress. First, it must be fixed; second, it must be composite. It must not (if it is to satisfy our souls) be the mere victory of some one thing swallowing up everything else, love or pride or peace or adventure; it must be a definite picture composed of these elements in their best proportion and relation. I am not concerned at this moment to deny that some such good culmination may be, by the constitution of things, reserved for the human race. I only point out that if this composite happiness is fixed for us it must be fixed by some mind; for only a mind can place the exact proportions of a composite happiness. If the beatification of the world is a mere work of nature, then it must be as simple as the freezing of the world, or the burning up of the world. But if the beatification of the world is not a work of nature but a work of art, then it involves an artist. And here again my contemplation was cloven by the ancient voice which said, "I could have told you all this a long time ago. If there is any certain progress it can only be my kind of progress, the progress towards a complete city of virtues and dominations where righteousness and peace contrive to kiss each other. An impersonal force might be leading you to a wilderness of perfect flatness or a peak of perfect height. But only a personal God can possibly be leading you (if, indeed, you are being led) to a city with just streets and architectural proportions, a city in which each of you can contribute exactly the right amount of your own colour to the many coloured coat of Joseph."

Twice again, therefore, Christianity had come in with the exact answer that I required. I had said, "The ideal must be fixed," and the Church had answered, "Mine is literally fixed, for it existed before anything else." I said secondly, "It must be artistically combined, like a picture"; and the Church answered, "Mine is quite literally a picture, for I know who painted it." Then I went on to the third thing, which, as it seemed to me, was needed for an Utopia or goal of progress. And of all the three it is infinitely the hardest to express. Perhaps it might be put thus: that we need watchfulness even in Utopia, lest we fall from Utopia as we fell from Eden.

We have remarked that one reason offered for being a progressive is that things naturally tend to grow better. But the only real reason for being a progressive is that things naturally tend to grow worse. The corruption in things is not only the best argument for being progressive; it is also the only argument against being conservative. The conservative theory would really be quite sweeping and unanswerable if it were not for this one fact. But all conservatism is based upon the idea that if you leave things alone you leave them as they are. But you do not. If you leave a thing alone you leave it to a torrent of change. If you leave a white post alone it will soon be a black post. If you particularly want it to be white you must be always painting it again; that is, you must be always having a revolution. Briefly, if you want the old white post you must have a new white post. But this which is true even of inanimate things is in a quite special and terrible sense true of all human things. An almost unnatural vigilance is really required of the citizen because of the horrible rapidity with which human institutions grow old. It is the custom in passing romance and journalism to talk of men suffering under old tyrannies. But, as a fact, men have almost always suffered under new tyrannies; under tyrannies that had been public liberties hardly twenty years before. Thus England went mad with joy over the patriotic monarchy of Elizabeth; and then (almost immediately afterwards) went mad with rage in the trap of the tyranny of Charles the First. So, again, in France the monarchy became intolerable, not just after it had been tolerated, but just after it had been adored. The son of Louis the well-beloved was Louis the guillotined. So in the same way in England in the nineteenth century the Radical manufacturer was entirely trusted as a mere tribune of the people, until suddenly we heard the cry of the Socialist that he was a tyrant eating the people like bread. So again, we have almost up to the last instant trusted the newspapers as organs of public opinion. Just recently some of us have seen (not slowly, but with a start) that they are obviously nothing of the kind. They are, by the nature of the case, the hobbies of a few rich men. We have not any need to rebel against antiquity; we have to rebel against novelty. It is the new rulers, the capitalist or the editor, who really hold up the modern world. There is no fear that a modern king will attempt to override the constitution; it is more likely that he will ignore the constitution and work behind its back; he will take no advantage of his kingly power; it is more likely that he will take advantage of his kingly powerlessness, of the fact that he is free from criticism and publicity. For the king is the most private person of our time. It will not be necessary for any one to fight again against the proposal of a censorship of the press. We do not need a censorship of the press. We have a censorship by the press.

This startling swiftness with which popular systems turn oppressive is the third fact for which we shall ask our perfect theory of progress to allow. It must always be on the look out for every privilege being abused, for every working right becoming a wrong. In this matter I am entirely on the side of the revolutionists. They are really right to be always suspecting human institutions; they are right not to put their trust in princes nor in any child of man. The chieftain chosen to be the friend of the people becomes the enemy of the people; the newspaper started to tell the truth now exists to prevent the truth being told. Here, I say, I felt that I was really at last on the side of the revolutionary. And then I caught my breath again: for I remembered that I was once again on the side of the orthodox.

Christianity spoke again and said: "I have always maintained that men were naturally backsliders; that human virtue tended of its own nature to rust or to rot; I have always said that human beings as such go wrong, especially happy human beings, especially proud and prosperous human beings. This eternal revolution, this suspicion sustained through centuries, you (being a vague modern) call the doctrine of progress. If you were a philosopher you would call it, as I do, the doctrine of original sin. You may call it the cosmic advance as much as you like; I call it what it is—the Fall."

I have spoken of orthodoxy coming in like a sword; here I confess it came in like a battle-axe. For really (when I came to think of it) Christianity is the only thing left that has any real right to question the power of the well-nurtured or the well-bred. I have listened often enough to Socialists, or even to democrats, saying that the physical conditions of the poor must of necessity make them mentally and morally degraded. I have listened to scientific men (and there are still scientific men not opposed to democracy) saying that if we give the poor healthier conditions vice and wrong will disappear. I have listened to them with a horrible attention, with a hideous fascination. For it was like watching a man energetically sawing from the tree the branch he is sitting on. If these happy democrats could prove their case, they would strike democracy dead. If the poor are thus utterly demoralized, it may or may not be practical to raise them. But it is certainly quite practical to disfranchise them. If the man with a bad bedroom cannot give a good vote, then the first and swiftest deduction is that he shall give no vote. The governing class may not unreasonably say: "It may take us some time to reform his bedroom. But if he is the brute you say, it will take him very little time to ruin our country. Therefore we will take your hint and not give him the chance." It fills me with horrible amusement to observe the way in which the earnest Socialist industriously lays the foundation of all aristocracy, expatiating blandly upon the evident unfitness of the poor to rule. It is like listening to somebody at an evening party apologising for entering without evening dress, and explaining that he had recently been intoxicated, had a personal habit of taking off his clothes in the street, and had, moreover, only just changed from prison uniform. At any moment, one feels, the host might say that really, if it was as bad as that, he need not come in at all. So it is when the ordinary Socialist, with a beaming face, proves that the poor, after their smashing experiences, cannot be really trustworthy. At any moment the rich may say, "Very well, then, we won't trust them," and bang the door in his face. On the basis of Mr. Blatchford's view of heredity and environment, the case for the aristocracy is quite overwhelming. If clean homes and clean air make clean souls, why not give the power (for the present at any rate) to those who undoubtedly have the clean air? If better conditions will make the poor more fit to govern themselves, why should not better conditions already make the rich more fit to govern them? On the ordinary environment argument the matter is fairly manifest. The comfortable class must be merely our vanguard in Utopia.

Is there any answer to the proposition that those who have had the best opportunities will probably be our best guides? Is there any answer to the argument that those who have breathed clean air had better decide for those who have breathed foul? As far as I know, there is only one answer, and that answer is Christianity. Only the Christian Church can offer any rational objection to a complete confidence in the rich. For she has maintained from the beginning that the danger was not in man's environment, but in man. Further, she has maintained that if we come to talk of a dangerous environment, the most dangerous environment of all is the commodious environment. I know that the most modern manufacture has been really occupied in trying to produce an abnormally large needle. I know that the most recent biologists have been chiefly anxious to discover a very small camel. But if we diminish the camel to his smallest, or open the eye of the needle to its largest—if, in short, we assume the words of Christ to have meant the very least that they could mean, His words must at the very least mean this— that rich men are not very likely to be morally trustworthy. Christianity even when watered down is hot enough to boil all modern society to rags. The mere minimum of the Church would be a deadly ultimatum to the world. For the whole modern world is absolutely based on the assumption, not that the rich are necessary (which is tenable), but that the rich are trustworthy, which (for a Christian) is not tenable. You will hear everlastingly, in all discussions about newspapers, companies, aristocracies, or party politics, this argument that the rich man cannot be bribed. The fact is, of course, that the rich man is bribed; he has been bribed already. That is why he is a rich man. The whole case for Christianity is that a man who is dependent upon the luxuries of this life is a corrupt man, spiritually corrupt, politically corrupt, financially corrupt. There is one thing that Christ and all the Christian saints have said with a sort of savage monotony. They have said simply that to be rich is to be in peculiar danger of moral wreck. It is not demonstrably un-Christian to kill the rich as violators of definable justice. It is not demonstrably un-Christian to crown the rich as convenient rulers of society. It is not certainly un-Christian to rebel against the rich or to submit to the rich. But it is quite certainly un-Christian to trust the rich, to regard the rich as more morally safe than the poor. A Christian may consistently say, "I respect that man's rank, although he takes bribes." But a Christian cannot say, as all modern men are saying at lunch and breakfast, "a man of that rank would not take bribes." For it is a part of Christian dogma that any man in any rank may take bribes. It is a part of Christian dogma; it also happens by a curious coincidence that it is a part of obvious human history. When people say that a man "in that position" would be incorruptible, there is no need to bring Christianity into the discussion. Was Lord Bacon a bootblack? Was the Duke of Marlborough a crossing sweeper? In the best Utopia, I must be prepared for the moral fall of any man in any position at any moment; especially for my fall from my position at this moment.

Much vague and sentimental journalism has been poured out to the effect that Christianity is akin to democracy, and most of it is scarcely strong or clear enough to refute the fact that the two things have often quarrelled. The real ground upon which Christianity and democracy are one is very much deeper. The one specially and peculiarly un-Christian idea is the idea of Carlyle— the idea that the man should rule who feels that he can rule. Whatever else is Christian, this is heathen. If our faith comments on government at all, its comment must be this—that the man should rule who does NOT think that he can rule. Carlyle's hero may say, "I will be king"; but the Christian saint must say "Nolo episcopari." If the great paradox of Christianity means anything, it means this— that we must take the crown in our hands, and go hunting in dry places and dark corners of the earth until we find the one man who feels himself unfit to wear it. Carlyle was quite wrong; we have not got to crown the exceptional man who knows he can rule. Rather we must crown the much more exceptional man who knows he can't.

Now, this is one of the two or three vital defences of working democracy. The mere machinery of voting is not democracy, though at present it is not easy to effect any simpler democratic method. But even the machinery of voting is profoundly Christian in this practical sense—that it is an attempt to get at the opinion of those who would be too modest to offer it. It is a mystical adventure; it is specially trusting those who do not trust themselves. That enigma is strictly peculiar to Christendom. There is nothing really humble about the abnegation of the Buddhist; the mild Hindoo is mild, but he is not meek. But there is something psychologically Christian about the idea of seeking for the opinion of the obscure rather than taking the obvious course of accepting the opinion of the prominent. To say that voting is particularly Christian may seem somewhat curious. To say that canvassing is Christian may seem quite crazy. But canvassing is very Christian in its primary idea. It is encouraging the humble; it is saying to the modest man, "Friend, go up higher." Or if there is some slight defect in canvassing, that is in its perfect and rounded piety, it is only because it may possibly neglect to encourage the modesty of the canvasser.

Aristocracy is not an institution: aristocracy is a sin; generally a very venial one. It is merely the drift or slide of men into a sort of natural pomposity and praise of the powerful, which is the most easy and obvious affair in the world.

It is one of the hundred answers to the fugitive perversion of modern "force" that the promptest and boldest agencies are also the most fragile or full of sensibility. The swiftest things are the softest things. A bird is active, because a bird is soft. A stone is helpless, because a stone is hard. The stone must by its own nature go downwards, because hardness is weakness. The bird can of its nature go upwards, because fragility is force. In perfect force there is a kind of frivolity, an airiness that can maintain itself in the air. Modern investigators of miraculous history have solemnly admitted that a characteristic of the great saints is their power of "levitation." They might go further; a characteristic of the great saints is their power of levity. Angels can fly because they can take themselves lightly. This has been always the instinct of Christendom, and especially the instinct of Christian art. Remember how Fra Angelico represented all his angels, not only as birds, but almost as butterflies. Remember how the most earnest mediaeval art was full of light and fluttering draperies, of quick and capering feet. It was the one thing that the modern Pre-raphaelites could not imitate in the real Pre-raphaelites. Burne-Jones could never recover the deep levity of the Middle Ages. In the old Christian pictures the sky over every figure is like a blue or gold parachute. Every figure seems ready to fly up and float about in the heavens. The tattered cloak of the beggar will bear him up like the rayed plumes of the angels. But the kings in their heavy gold and the proud in their robes of purple will all of their nature sink downwards, for pride cannot rise to levity or levitation. Pride is the downward drag of all things into an easy solemnity. One "settles down" into a sort of selfish seriousness; but one has to rise to a gay self-forgetfulness. A man "falls" into a brown study; he reaches up at a blue sky. Seriousness is not a virtue. It would be a heresy, but a much more sensible heresy, to say that seriousness is a vice. It is really a natural trend or lapse into taking one's self gravely, because it is the easiest thing to do. It is much easier to write a good TIMES leading article than a good joke in PUNCH. For solemnity flows out of men naturally; but laughter is a leap. It is easy to be heavy: hard to be light. Satan fell by the force of gravity.

Now, it is the peculiar honour of Europe since it has been Christian that while it has had aristocracy it has always at the back of its heart treated aristocracy as a weakness—generally as a weakness that must be allowed for. If any one wishes to appreciate this point, let him go outside Christianity into some other philosophical atmosphere. Let him, for instance, compare the classes of Europe with the castes of India. There aristocracy is far more awful, because it is far more intellectual. It is seriously felt that the scale of classes is a scale of spiritual values; that the baker is better than the butcher in an invisible and sacred sense. But no Christianity, not even the most ignorant or perverse, ever suggested that a baronet was better than a butcher in that sacred sense. No Christianity, however ignorant or extravagant, ever suggested that a duke would not be damned. In pagan society there may have been (I do not know) some such serious division between the free man and the slave. But in Christian society we have always thought the gentleman a sort of joke, though I admit that in some great crusades and councils he earned the right to be called a practical joke. But we in Europe never really and at the root of our souls took aristocracy seriously. It is only an occasional non-European alien (such as Dr. Oscar Levy, the only intelligent Nietzscheite) who can even manage for a moment to take aristocracy seriously. It may be a mere patriotic bias, though I do not think so, but it seems to me that the English aristocracy is not only the type, but is the crown and flower of all actual aristocracies; it has all the oligarchical virtues as well as all the defects. It is casual, it is kind, it is courageous in obvious matters; but it has one great merit that overlaps even these. The great and very obvious merit of the English aristocracy is that nobody could possibly take it seriously.

In short, I had spelled out slowly, as usual, the need for an equal law in Utopia; and, as usual, I found that Christianity had been there before me. The whole history of my Utopia has the same amusing sadness. I was always rushing out of my architectural study with plans for a new turret only to find it sitting up there in the sunlight, shining, and a thousand years old. For me, in the ancient and partly in the modern sense, God answered the prayer, "Prevent us, O Lord, in all our doings." Without vanity, I really think there was a moment when I could have invented the marriage vow (as an institution) out of my own head; but I discovered, with a sigh, that it had been invented already. But, since it would be too long a business to show how, fact by fact and inch by inch, my own conception of Utopia was only answered in the New Jerusalem, I will take this one case of the matter of marriage as indicating the converging drift, I may say the converging crash of all the rest.

When the ordinary opponents of Socialism talk about impossibilities and alterations in human nature they always miss an important distinction. In modern ideal conceptions of society there are some desires that are possibly not attainable: but there are some desires that are not desirable. That all men should live in equally beautiful houses is a dream that may or may not be attained. But that all men should live in the same beautiful house is not a dream at all; it is a nightmare. That a man should love all old women is an ideal that may not be attainable. But that a man should regard all old women exactly as he regards his mother is not only an unattainable ideal, but an ideal which ought not to be attained. I do not know if the reader agrees with me in these examples; but I will add the example which has always affected me most. I could never conceive or tolerate any Utopia which did not leave to me the liberty for which I chiefly care, the liberty to bind myself. Complete anarchy would not merely make it impossible to have any discipline or fidelity; it would also make it impossible to have any fun. To take an obvious instance, it would not be worth while to bet if a bet were not binding. The dissolution of all contracts would not only ruin morality but spoil sport. Now betting and such sports are only the stunted and twisted shapes of the original instinct of man for adventure and romance, of which much has been said in these pages. And the perils, rewards, punishments, and fulfilments of an adventure must be real, or the adventure is only a shifting and heartless nightmare. If I bet I must be made to pay, or there is no poetry in betting. If I challenge I must be made to fight, or there is no poetry in challenging. If I vow to be faithful I must be cursed when I am unfaithful, or there is no fun in vowing. You could not even make a fairy tale from the experiences of a man who, when he was swallowed by a whale, might find himself at the top of the Eiffel Tower, or when he was turned into a frog might begin to behave like a flamingo. For the purpose even of the wildest romance results must be real; results must be irrevocable. Christian marriage is the great example of a real and irrevocable result; and that is why it is the chief subject and centre of all our romantic writing. And this is my last instance of the things that I should ask, and ask imperatively, of any social paradise; I should ask to be kept to my bargain, to have my oaths and engagements taken seriously; I should ask Utopia to avenge my honour on myself.

All my modern Utopian friends look at each other rather doubtfully, for their ultimate hope is the dissolution of all special ties. But again I seem to hear, like a kind of echo, an answer from beyond the world. "You will have real obligations, and therefore real adventures when you get to my Utopia. But the hardest obligation and the steepest adventure is to get there."

THE ROMANCE OF ORTHODOXY

It is customary to complain of the bustle and strenuousness of our epoch. But in truth the chief mark of our epoch is a profound laziness and fatigue; and the fact is that the real laziness is the cause of the apparent bustle. Take one quite external case; the streets are noisy with taxicabs and motorcars; but this is not due to human activity but to human repose. There would be less bustle if there were more activity, if people were simply walking about. Our world would be more silent if it were more strenuous. And this which is true of the apparent physical bustle is true also of the apparent bustle of the intellect. Most of the machinery of modern language is labour-saving machinery; and it saves mental labour very much more than it ought. Scientific phrases are used like scientific wheels and piston-rods to make swifter and smoother yet the path of the comfortable. Long words go rattling by us like long railway trains. We know they are carrying thousands who are too tired or too indolent to walk and think for themselves. It is a good exercise to try for once in a way to express any opinion one holds in words of one syllable. If you say "The social utility of the indeterminate sentence is recognized by all criminologists as a part of our sociological evolution towards a more humane and scientific view of punishment," you can go on talking like that for hours with hardly a movement of the gray matter inside your skull. But if you begin "I wish Jones to go to gaol and Brown to say when Jones shall come out," you will discover, with a thrill of horror, that you are obliged to think. The long words are not the hard words, it is the short words that are hard. There is much more metaphysical subtlety in the word "damn" than in the word "degeneration."

But these long comfortable words that save modern people the toil of reasoning have one particular aspect in which they are especially ruinous and confusing. This difficulty occurs when the same long word is used in different connections to mean quite different things. Thus, to take a well-known instance, the word "idealist" has one meaning as a piece of philosophy and quite another as a piece of moral rhetoric. In the same way the scientific materialists have had just reason to complain of people mixing up "materialist" as a term of cosmology with "materialist" as a moral taunt. So, to take a cheaper instance, the man who hates "progressives" in London always calls himself a "progressive" in South Africa.

A confusion quite as unmeaning as this has arisen in connection with the word "liberal" as applied to religion and as applied to politics and society. It is often suggested that all Liberals ought to be freethinkers, because they ought to love everything that is free. You might just as well say that all idealists ought to be High Churchmen, because they ought to love everything that is high. You might as well say that Low Churchmen ought

220

to like Low Mass, or that Broad Churchmen ought to like broad jokes. The thing is a mere accident of words. In actual modern Europe a freethinker does not mean a man who thinks for himself. It means a man who, having thought for himself, has come to one particular class of conclusions, the material origin of phenomena, the impossibility of miracles, the improbability of personal immortality and so on. And none of these ideas are particularly liberal. Nay, indeed almost all these ideas are definitely illiberal, as it is the purpose of this chapter to show.

In the few following pages I propose to point out as rapidly as possible that on every single one of the matters most strongly insisted on by liberalisers of theology their effect upon social practice would be definitely illiberal. Almost every contemporary proposal to bring freedom into the church is simply a proposal to bring tyranny into the world. For freeing the church now does not even mean freeing it in all directions. It means freeing that peculiar set of dogmas loosely called scientific, dogmas of monism, of pantheism, or of Arianism, or of necessity. And every one of these (and we will take them one by one) can be shown to be the natural ally of oppression. In fact, it is a remarkable circumstance (indeed not so very remarkable when one comes to think of it) that most things are the allies of oppression. There is only one thing that can never go past a certain point in its alliance with oppression—and that is orthodoxy. I may, it is true, twist orthodoxy so as partly to justify a tyrant. But I can easily make up a German philosophy to justify him entirely.

Now let us take in order the innovations that are the notes of the new theology or the modernist church. We concluded the last chapter with the discovery of one of them. The very doctrine which is called the most old-fashioned was found to be the only safeguard of the new democracies of the earth. The doctrine seemingly most unpopular was found to be the only strength of the people. In short, we found that the only logical negation of oligarchy was in the affirmation of original sin. So it is, I maintain, in all the other cases.

I take the most obvious instance first, the case of miracles. For some extraordinary reason, there is a fixed notion that it is more liberal to disbelieve in miracles than to believe in them. Why, I cannot imagine, nor can anybody tell me. For some inconceivable cause a "broad" or "liberal" clergyman always means a man who wishes at least to diminish the number of miracles; it never means a man who wishes to increase that number. It always means a man who is free to disbelieve that Christ came out of His grave; it never means a man who is free to believe that his own aunt came out of her grave. It is common to find trouble in a parish because the parish priest cannot admit that St. Peter walked on water; yet how rarely do we find trouble in a parish because the clergyman says that his father walked on the Serpentine? And this is not because (as the swift secularist debater would immediately retort) miracles cannot be believed in our experience. It is not because "miracles do not happen," as in the dogma which Matthew Arnold recited with simple faith. More supernatural things are ALLEGED to have happened in our time than would have been possible eighty years ago. Men of science believe in such marvels much more than they did: the most perplexing, and even horrible, prodigies of mind and spirit are always being unveiled in modern psychology. Things that the old science at least would frankly have rejected as miracles are hourly being asserted by the new science. The only thing which is still old-fashioned enough to reject miracles is the New Theology. But in truth this notion that it is "free" to deny miracles has nothing to do with the evidence for or against them. It is a lifeless verbal prejudice of which the original life and beginning was not in the freedom of thought, but simply in the dogma of materialism. The man of the nineteenth century did not disbelieve in the Resurrection because his liberal Christianity allowed him to doubt it. He disbelieved in it because his very strict materialism did not allow him to believe it. Tennyson, a very typical nineteenth century man, uttered one of the instinctive truisms of his contemporaries when he said that there was faith in their honest doubt. There was indeed. Those words have a profound and even a horrible truth. In their doubt of miracles there was a faith in a fixed and godless fate; a deep and sincere faith in the incurable routine of the cosmos. The doubts of the agnostic were only the dogmas of the monist.

Of the fact and evidence of the supernatural I will speak afterwards. Here we are only concerned with this clear point; that in so far as the liberal idea of freedom can be said to be on either side in the discussion about miracles, it is obviously on the side of miracles. Reform or (in the only tolerable sense) progress means simply the gradual control of matter by mind. A miracle simply means the swift control of matter by mind. If you wish to feed the people, you may think that feeding them miraculously in the wilderness is impossible—but you cannot think it illiberal. If you really want poor children to go to the seaside, you cannot think it illiberal that they should go there on flying dragons; you can only think it unlikely. A holiday, like Liberalism, only means the liberty of man. A miracle only means the liberty of God. You may conscientiously deny either of them, but you cannot call your denial a triumph of the liberal idea. The Catholic Church believed that man and God both had a sort of spiritual freedom. Calvinism took away the freedom from man, but left it to God. Scientific materialism binds the Creator Himself; it chains up God as the Apocalypse chained the devil. It leaves nothing free in the universe. And those who assist this process are called the "liberal theologians."

This, as I say, is the lightest and most evident case. The assumption that there is something in the doubt of miracles akin to liberality or reform is literally the opposite of the truth. If a man cannot believe in miracles there is an end of the matter; he is not particularly liberal, but he is perfectly honourable and logical, which are much better things. But if he can believe in miracles, he is certainly the more liberal for doing so; because they mean first, the freedom of the soul, and secondly, its control over the tyranny of circumstance. Sometimes this truth is ignored in a singularly naive way, even by the ablest men. For instance, Mr. Bernard Shaw speaks with hearty old-fashioned contempt for the idea of miracles, as if they were a sort of breach of faith on the part of nature: he seems strangely unconscious that miracles are only the final flowers of his own favourite tree, the doctrine of the omnipotence of will. Just in the same way he calls the desire for immortality a paltry selfishness, forgetting that he has just called the desire for life a healthy and heroic selfishness. How can it be noble to wish to make one's life infinite and yet mean to wish to make it immortal? No, if it is desirable that man should triumph over the cruelty of nature or custom, then miracles are certainly desirable; we will discuss afterwards whether they are possible.

But I must pass on to the larger cases of this curious error; the notion that the "liberalising" of religion in some way helps the liberation of the world. The second example of it can be found in the question of pantheism—or rather of a certain modern attitude which is often called immanentism, and which often is Buddhism. But this is so much more difficult a matter that I must approach it with rather more preparation.

The things said most confidently by advanced persons to crowded audiences are generally those quite opposite to the fact; it is actually our truisms that are untrue. Here is a case. There is a phrase of facile liberality uttered again and again at ethical societies and parliaments of religion: "the religions of the earth differ in rites and forms, but they are the same in what they teach." It is false; it is the opposite of the fact. The religions of the earth do not greatly differ in rites and forms; they do greatly differ in what they teach. It is as if a man were to say, "Do not be misled by the fact that the CHURCH TIMES and the FREETHINKER look utterly different, that one is painted on vellum and the other carved on marble, that one is triangular and the other hectagonal; read them and you will see that they say the same thing." The truth is, of course, that they are alike in everything except in the fact that they don't say the same thing. An atheist stockbroker in Surbiton looks exactly like a Swedenborgian stockbroker in Wimbledon. You may walk round and round them and subject them to the most personal and offensive study without seeing anything Swedenborgian in the hat or anything particularly godless in the umbrella. It is exactly in their souls that they are divided. So the truth is that the difficulty of all the creeds of the earth is not as alleged in this cheap maxim: that they agree in meaning, but differ in machinery. It is exactly the opposite. They agree in machinery; almost every great religion on earth works with the same external methods, with priests, scriptures, altars, sworn brotherhoods, special feasts. They agree in the mode of teaching; what they differ about is the thing to be taught. Pagan optimists and Eastern pessimists would both have temples, just as Liberals and Tories would both have newspapers. Creeds that exist to destroy each other both have scriptures, just as armies that exist to destroy each other both have guns.

The great example of this alleged identity of all human religions is the alleged spiritual identity of Buddhism and Christianity. Those who adopt this theory generally avoid the ethics of most other creeds, except, indeed, Confucianism, which they like because it is not a creed. But they are cautious in their praises of Mahommedanism, generally confining themselves to imposing its morality only upon the refreshment of the lower classes. They seldom suggest the Mahommedan view of marriage (for which there is a great deal to be said), and towards Thugs and fetish worshippers their attitude may even be called cold. But in the case of the great religion of Gautama they feel sincerely a similarity.

Students of popular science, like Mr. Blatchford, are always insisting that Christianity and Buddhism are very much alike, especially Buddhism. This is generally believed, and I believed it myself until I read a book giving the reasons for it. The reasons were of two kinds: resemblances that meant nothing because they were common to all humanity, and resemblances which were not resemblances at all. The author solemnly explained that the two creeds were alike in things in which all creeds are alike, or else he described them as alike in some point in which they are quite obviously different. Thus, as a case of the first class, he said that both Christ and Buddha were called by the divine voice coming out of the sky, as if you would expect the divine voice to come out of the coal-cellar. Or, again, it was gravely urged that these two Eastern teachers, by a singular coincidence, both had to do with the washing of feet. You might as well say that it was a remarkable coincidence that they both had feet to wash. And the other class of similarities were those which simply were not similar. Thus this reconciler of the two religions draws earnest attention to the fact that at certain religious feasts the robe of the Lama is rent in pieces out of respect, and the remnants highly valued. But this is the reverse of a resemblance, for the garments of Christ were not rent in pieces out of respect, but out of derision; and the remnants were not highly valued except for what they would fetch in the rag shops. It is rather like alluding to the obvious connection between the two ceremonies of the sword: when it taps a man's shoulder, and when it cuts off his head. It is not at all similar for the man. These scraps of puerile pedantry would indeed matter little if it were not also true that the alleged philosophical resemblances are also of these two kinds, either proving too much or not proving anything. That Buddhism approves of mercy or of self-restraint is not to say that it is specially like Christianity; it is only to say that it is not utterly unlike all human existence. Buddhists disapprove in theory of cruelty or excess because all sane human beings disapprove in theory of cruelty or excess. But to say that Buddhism and Christianity give the same philosophy of these things is simply false. All humanity does agree that we are in a net of sin. Most of humanity agrees that there is some way out. But as to what is the way out, I do not think that there are two institutions in the universe which contradict each other so flatly as Buddhism and Christianity.

Even when I thought, with most other well-informed, though unscholarly, people, that Buddhism and Christianity were alike, there was one thing about them that always perplexed me; I mean the startling difference in their type of religious art. I do not mean in its technical style of representation, but in the things that it was manifestly meant to represent. No two ideals could be more opposite than a Christian saint in a Gothic cathedral and a Buddhist saint in a Chinese temple. The opposition exists at every point; but perhaps the shortest statement of it is that the Buddhist saint always has his eyes shut, while the Christian saint always has them very wide open. The Buddhist saint has a sleek and harmonious body, but his eyes are heavy and sealed with sleep. The mediaeval saint's body is wasted to its crazy bones, but his eyes are frightfully alive. There cannot be any real community of spirit between forces that produced symbols so different as that. Granted that both images are extravagances, are perversions of the pure creed, it must be a real divergence which could produce such opposite extravagances. The Buddhist is looking with a peculiar intentness inwards. The Christian is staring with a frantic intentness outwards. If we follow that clue steadily we shall find some interesting things.

A short time ago Mrs. Besant, in an interesting essay, announced that there was only one religion in the world, that all faiths were only versions or perversions of it, and that she was quite prepared to say what it was. According to Mrs. Besant this universal Church is simply the universal self. It is the doctrine that we are really all one person; that there are no real walls of individuality between man and man. If I may put it so, she does not tell us to love our neighbours; she tells us to be our neighbours. That is Mrs. Besant's thoughtful and suggestive description of the religion in which all men must find themselves in agreement. And I never heard of any suggestion in my life with which I more violently disagree. I want to love my neighbour not because he is I, but precisely because he is not I. I want to adore the world, not as one likes a looking-glass, because it is one's self, but as one loves a woman, because she is entirely different. If souls are separate love is possible. If souls are united love is obviously impossible. A man may be said loosely to love himself, but he can hardly fall in love with himself, or, if he does, it must be a monotonous courtship. If the world is full of real selves, they can be really unselfish selves. But upon Mrs. Besant's principle the whole cosmos is only one enormously selfish person.

It is just here that Buddhism is on the side of modern pantheism and immanence. And it is just here that Christianity is on the side of humanity and liberty and love. Love desires personality; therefore love desires division. It is the instinct of Christianity to be glad that God has broken the universe into little pieces, because they are living pieces. It is her instinct to say "little children love one another" rather than to tell one large person to love himself. This is the intellectual abyss between Buddhism and Christianity; that for the Buddhist or Theosophist personality is the fall of man, for the Christian it is the purpose of God, the whole point of his cosmic idea. The world-soul of the Theosophists asks man to love it only in order that man may throw himself into it. But the divine centre of Christianity actually threw man out of it in order that he might love it. The oriental deity is like a giant who should have lost his leg or hand and be always seeking to find it; but the Christian power is like some giant who in a strange generosity should cut off his right hand, so that it might of its own accord shake hands with him. We come back to the same tireless note touching the nature of Christianity; all modern philosophies are chains which connect and fetter; Christianity is a sword which separates and sets free. No other philosophy makes God actually rejoice in the separation of the universe into living souls. But according to orthodox Christianity this separation between God and man is sacred, because this is eternal. That a man may love God it is necessary that there should be not only a God to be loved, but a man to love him. All those vague theosophical minds for whom the universe is an immense melting-pot are exactly the minds which shrink instinctively from that earthquake saying of our Gospels, which declare that the Son of God came not with peace but with a sundering sword. The saying rings entirely true even considered as what it obviously is; the statement that any man who preaches real love is bound to beget hate. It is as true of democratic fraternity as a divine love; sham love ends in compromise and common philosophy; but real love has always ended in bloodshed. Yet there is another and yet more awful truth behind the obvious meaning of this utterance of our Lord. According to Himself the Son was a sword separating brother and brother that they should for an aeon hate each other. But the Father also was a sword, which in the black beginning separated brother and brother, so that they should love each other at last.

This is the meaning of that almost insane happiness in the eyes of the mediaeval saint in the picture. This is the meaning of the sealed eyes of the superb Buddhist image. The Christian saint is happy because he has verily been cut off from the world; he is separate from things and is staring at them in astonishment. But why should the Buddhist saint be astonished at things?— since there is really only one thing, and that being impersonal can hardly be astonished at itself. There have been many pantheist poems suggesting wonder, but no really successful ones. The pantheist cannot wonder, for he cannot praise God or praise anything as really distinct from himself. Our immediate business here, however, is with the effect of this Christian admiration (which strikes outwards, towards a deity distinct from the worshipper) upon the general need for ethical activity and social reform. And surely its effect is sufficiently obvious. There is no real possibility of getting out of pantheism, any special impulse to moral action. For pantheism implies in its nature that one thing is as good as another; whereas action implies in its nature that one thing is greatly preferable to another. Swinburne in the high summer of his scepticism tried in vain to wrestle with this difficulty. In "Songs before Sunrise," written under the inspiration of Garibaldi and the revolt of Italy he proclaimed the newer religion and the purer God which should wither up all the priests of the world:

> "What doest thou now Looking Godward to cry I am I,
> thou art thou, I am low, thou art high, I am thou that thou
> seekest to find him, find thou but thyself, thou art I."

Of which the immediate and evident deduction is that tyrants are as much the sons of God as Garibaldis; and that King Bomba of Naples having, with the utmost success, "found himself" is identical with the ultimate good in all things. The truth is that the western energy that dethrones tyrants has been directly due to the western theology that says "I am I, thou art thou." The same spiritual separation which looked up and saw a good king in the universe looked up and saw a bad king in Naples. The worshippers of Bomba's god dethroned Bomba. The worshippers of Swinburne's god have covered Asia for centuries and have never dethroned a tyrant. The Indian saint may reasonably shut his eyes because he is looking at that which is I and Thou and We and They and It. It is a rational occupation: but it is not true in theory and not true in fact that it helps the Indian to keep an eye on Lord Curzon. That external vigilance which has always been the mark of Christianity (the command that we should WATCH and pray) has expressed itself both in typical western orthodoxy and in typical western politics: but both depend on the idea of a divinity transcendent, different from ourselves, a deity that disappears. Certainly the most sagacious creeds may suggest that we should pursue God into deeper and deeper rings of the labyrinth of our own ego. But only we of Christendom have said that we should hunt God like an eagle upon the mountains: and we have killed all monsters in the chase.

Here again, therefore, we find that in so far as we value democracy and the self-renewing energies of the west, we are much more likely to find them in the old theology than the new. If we want reform, we must adhere to orthodoxy: especially in this matter (so much disputed in the counsels of Mr. R.J. Campbell), the matter of insisting on the immanent or the transcendent deity. By insisting specially on the immanence of God we get introspection, self-isolation, quietism, social indifference—Tibet. By insisting specially on the transcendence of God we get wonder, curiosity, moral and political adventure, righteous indignation—Christendom. Insisting that God is inside man, man is always inside himself. By insisting that God transcends man, man has transcended himself.

If we take any other doctrine that has been called old-fashioned we shall find the case the same. It is the same, for instance, in the deep matter of the Trinity. Unitarians (a sect never to be mentioned without a special respect for their distinguished intellectual dignity and high intellectual honour) are often reformers by the accident that throws so many small sects into such an attitude. But there is nothing in the least liberal or akin to reform in the substitution of pure monotheism for the Trinity. The complex God of the Athanasian Creed may be an enigma for the intellect; but He is far less likely to gather the mystery and cruelty of a Sultan than the lonely god of Omar or Mahomet. The god who is a mere awful unity is not only a king but an Eastern king. The HEART of humanity, especially of European humanity, is certainly much more satisfied by the strange hints and symbols that gather round the Trinitarian idea, the image of a council at which mercy pleads as well as justice, the conception of a sort of liberty and variety existing even in the inmost chamber of the world. For Western religion has always felt keenly the idea "it is not well for man to be alone." The social instinct asserted itself everywhere as when the Eastern idea of hermits was practically expelled by the Western idea of monks. So even asceticism became brotherly; and the Trappists were sociable even when they were silent. If this love of a living complexity be our test, it is certainly healthier to have the Trinitarian religion than the Unitarian. For to us Trinitarians (if I may say it with reverence)—to us God Himself is a society. It is indeed a fathomless mystery of theology, and even if I were theologian enough to deal with it directly, it would not be relevant to do so here. Suffice it to say here that this triple enigma is as comforting as wine and open as an English fireside; that this thing that bewilders the intellect utterly quiets the heart: but out of the desert, from the dry places and the dreadful suns, come the cruel children of the lonely God; the real Unitarians who with scimitar in hand have laid waste the world. For it is not well for God to be alone.

Again, the same is true of that difficult matter of the danger of the soul, which has unsettled so many just minds. To hope for all souls is imperative; and it is quite tenable that their salvation is inevitable. It is tenable, but it is not specially favourable to activity or progress. Our fighting and creative society ought rather to insist on the danger of everybody, on the fact that every man is hanging by a thread or clinging to a precipice. To say that all will be well anyhow is a comprehensible remark: but it cannot be called the blast of a trumpet. Europe ought rather to emphasize possible perdition; and Europe always has emphasized it. Here its highest religion is at one with all its cheapest romances. To the Buddhist or the eastern fatalist existence is a science or a plan, which must end up in a certain way. But to a Christian existence is a STORY, which may end up in any way. In a thrilling novel (that purely Christian product) the hero is not eaten by cannibals; but it is essential to the existence of the thrill that he MIGHT be eaten by cannibals. The hero must (so to speak) be an eatable hero. So Christian morals have always said to the man, not that he would lose his soul, but that he must take care that he didn't. In Christian morals, in short, it is wicked to call a man "damned": but it is strictly religious and philosophic to call him damnable.

All Christianity concentrates on the man at the cross-roads. The vast and shallow philosophies, the huge syntheses of humbug, all talk about ages and evolution and ultimate developments. The true philosophy is concerned with the instant. Will a man take this road or that?—that is the only thing to think about, if you enjoy thinking. The aeons are easy enough to think about, any one can think about them. The instant is really awful: and it is because our religion has intensely felt the instant, that it has in literature dealt much with battle and in theology dealt much with hell. It is full of DANGER, like a boy's book: it is at an immortal crisis. There is a great deal of real similarity between popular fiction and the religion of the western people. If you say that popular fiction is vulgar and tawdry, you only say what the dreary and well-informed say also about the images in the Catholic churches. Life (according to the faith) is very like a serial story in a magazine: life ends with the promise (or menace) "to be continued in our next." Also, with a noble vulgarity, life imitates the serial and leaves off at the exciting moment. For death is distinctly an exciting moment.

But the point is that a story is exciting because it has in it so strong an element of will, of what theology calls free-will. You cannot finish a sum how you like. But you can finish a story how you like. When somebody discovered the Differential Calculus there was only one Differential Calculus he could discover. But when Shakespeare killed Romeo he might have married him to Juliet's old nurse if he had felt inclined. And Christendom has excelled in the narrative romance exactly because it has insisted on the theological free-will. It is a large matter and too much to one side of the road to be discussed adequately here; but this is the real objection to that torrent of modern talk about treating crime as disease, about making a prison merely a hygienic environment like a hospital, of healing sin by slow scientific methods. The fallacy of the whole thing is that evil is a matter of active choice whereas disease is not. If you say that you are going to cure a profligate as you cure an asthmatic, my cheap and obvious answer is, "Produce the people who want to be asthmatics as many people want to be profligates." A man may lie still and be cured of a malady. But he must not lie still if he wants to be cured of a sin; on the contrary, he must get up and jump about violently. The whole point indeed is perfectly expressed in the very word which we use for a man in hospital; "patient" is in the passive mood; "sinner" is in the active. If a man is to be saved from influenza, he may be a patient. But if he is to be saved from forging, he must be not a patient but an IMPATIENT. He must be personally impatient with forgery. All moral reform must start in the active not the passive will.

Here again we reach the same substantial conclusion. In so far as we desire the definite reconstructions and the dangerous revolutions which have distinguished European civilization, we shall not discourage the thought of possible ruin; we shall rather encourage it. If we want, like the Eastern saints, merely to contemplate how right things are, of course we shall only say that they must go right. But if we particularly want to MAKE them go right, we must insist that they may go wrong.

Lastly, this truth is yet again true in the case of the common modern attempts to diminish or to explain away the divinity of Christ. The thing may be true or not; that I shall deal with before I end. But if the divinity is true it is certainly terribly revolutionary. That a good man may have his back to the wall is no more than we knew already; but that God could have his back to the wall is a boast for all insurgents for ever. Christianity is the only religion on earth that has felt that omnipotence made God incomplete. Christianity alone has felt that God, to be wholly God, must have been a rebel as well as a king. Alone of all creeds, Christianity has added courage to the virtues of the Creator. For the only courage worth calling courage must necessarily mean that the soul passes a breaking point—and does not break. In this indeed I approach a matter more dark and awful than it is easy to discuss; and I apologise in advance if any of my phrases fall wrong or seem irreverent touching a matter which the greatest saints and thinkers have justly feared to approach. But in that terrific tale of the Passion there is a distinct emotional suggestion that the author of all things (in some unthinkable way) went not only through agony, but through doubt. It is written, "Thou shalt not tempt the Lord thy God." No; but the Lord thy God may tempt Himself; and it seems as if this was what happened in Gethsemane. In a garden Satan tempted man: and in a garden God tempted God. He passed in some superhuman manner through our human horror of pessimism. When the world shook and the sun was wiped out of heaven, it was not at the crucifixion, but at the cry from the cross: the cry which confessed that God was forsaken of God. And now let the revolutionists choose a creed from all the creeds and a god from all the gods of the world, carefully weighing all the gods of inevitable recurrence and of unalterable power. They will not find another god who has himself been in revolt. Nay, (the matter grows too difficult for human speech,) but let the atheists themselves choose a god. They will find only one divinity who ever uttered their isolation; only one religion in which God seemed for an instant to be an atheist.

These can be called the essentials of the old orthodoxy, of which the chief merit is that it is the natural fountain of revolution and reform; and of which the chief defect is that it is obviously only an abstract assertion. Its main advantage is that it is the most adventurous and manly of all theologies. Its chief disadvantage is simply that it is a theology. It can always be urged against it that it is in its nature arbitrary and in the air. But it is not so high in the air but that great archers spend their whole lives in shooting arrows at it—yes, and their last arrows; there are men who will ruin themselves and ruin their civilization if they may ruin also this old fantastic tale. This is the last and most astounding fact about this faith; that its enemies will use any weapon against it, the swords that cut their own fingers, and the firebrands that burn their own homes. Men who begin to fight the Church for the sake of freedom and humanity end by flinging away freedom and humanity if only they may fight the Church. This is no exaggeration; I could fill a book with the instances of it. Mr. Blatchford set out, as an ordinary Bible-smasher, to prove that Adam was guiltless of sin against God; in manoeuvring so as to maintain this he admitted, as a mere side issue, that all the tyrants, from Nero to King Leopold, were guiltless of any sin against humanity. I know a man who has such a passion for proving that he will have no personal existence after death that he falls back on the position that he has no personal existence now. He invokes Buddhism and says that all souls fade into each other; in order to prove that he cannot go to heaven he proves that he cannot go to Hartlepool. I have known people who protested against religious education with arguments against any education, saying that the child's mind must grow freely or that the old must not teach the young. I have known people who showed that there could be no divine judgment by showing that there can be no human judgment, even for practical purposes. They burned their own corn to set fire to the church; they smashed their own tools to smash it; any stick was good enough to beat it with, though it were the last stick of their own dismembered furniture. We do not admire, we hardly excuse, the fanatic who wrecks this world for love of the other. But what are we to say of the fanatic who wrecks this world out of hatred of the other? He sacrifices the very existence of humanity to the non-existence of God. He offers his victims not to the altar, but merely to assert the idleness of the altar and the emptiness of the throne. He is ready to ruin even that primary ethic by

231

which all things live, for his strange and eternal vengeance upon some one who never lived at all.

And yet the thing hangs in the heavens unhurt. Its opponents only succeed in destroying all that they themselves justly hold dear. They do not destroy orthodoxy; they only destroy political and common courage sense. They do not prove that Adam was not responsible to God; how could they prove it? They only prove (from their premises) that the Czar is not responsible to Russia. They do not prove that Adam should not have been punished by God; they only prove that the nearest sweater should not be punished by men. With their oriental doubts about personality they do not make certain that we shall have no personal life hereafter; they only make certain that we shall not have a very jolly or complete one here. With their paralysing hints of all conclusions coming out wrong they do not tear the book of the Recording Angel; they only make it a little harder to keep the books of Marshall & Snelgrove. Not only is the faith the mother of all worldly energies, but its foes are the fathers of all worldly confusion. The secularists have not wrecked divine things; but the secularists have wrecked secular things, if that is any comfort to them. The Titans did not scale heaven; but they laid waste the world.

AUTHORITY AND THE ADVENTURER

The last chapter has been concerned with the contention that orthodoxy is not only (as is often urged) the only safe guardian of morality or order, but is also the only logical guardian of liberty, innovation and advance. If we wish to pull down the prosperous oppressor we cannot do it with the new doctrine of human perfectibility; we can do it with the old doctrine of Original Sin. If we want to uproot inherent cruelties or lift up lost populations we cannot do it with the scientific theory that matter precedes mind; we can do it with the supernatural theory that mind precedes matter. If we wish specially to awaken people to social vigilance and tireless pursuit of practise, we cannot help it much by insisting on the Immanent God and the Inner Light: for these are at best reasons for contentment; we can help it much by insisting on the transcendent God and the flying and escaping gleam; for that means divine discontent. If we wish particularly to assert the idea of a generous balance against that of a dreadful autocracy we shall instinctively be Trinitarian rather than Unitarian. If we desire European civilization to be a raid and a rescue, we shall insist rather that souls are in real peril than that their peril is ultimately unreal. And if we wish to exalt the outcast and the crucified, we shall rather wish to think that a veritable God was crucified, rather than a mere sage or hero. Above all, if we wish to protect the poor we shall be in favour of fixed rules and clear dogmas. The RULES of a club are occasionally in favour of the poor member. The drift of a club is always in favour of the rich one.

And now we come to the crucial question which truly concludes the whole matter. A reasonable agnostic, if he has happened to agree with me so far, may justly turn round and say, "You have found a practical philosophy in the doctrine of the Fall; very well. You have found a side of democracy now dangerously neglected wisely asserted in Original Sin; all right. You have found a truth in the doctrine of hell; I congratulate you. You are convinced that worshippers of a personal God look outwards and are progressive; I congratulate them. But even supposing that those doctrines do include those truths, why cannot you take the truths and leave the doctrines? Granted that all modern society is trusting the rich too much because it does not allow for human weakness; granted that orthodox ages have had a great advantage because (believing in the Fall) they did allow for human weakness, why cannot you simply allow for human weakness without believing in the Fall? If you have discovered that the idea of damnation represents a healthy idea of danger, why can you not simply take the idea of danger and leave the idea of damnation? If you see clearly the kernel of common-sense in the nut of Christian orthodoxy, why cannot you simply take the kernel and leave the nut? Why cannot you (to use that cant phrase of the newspapers which I, as a highly scholarly agnostic, am a little ashamed of using) why cannot you simply take what is good in Christianity, what you can define as valuable, what you can comprehend, and leave all the rest, all the absolute dogmas that are in their nature incomprehensible?" This is the real question; this is the last question; and it is a pleasure to try to answer it.

The first answer is simply to say that I am a rationalist. I like to have some intellectual justification for my intuitions. If I am treating man as a fallen being it is an intellectual convenience to me to believe that he fell; and I find, for some odd psychological reason, that I can deal better with a man's exercise of freewill if I believe that he has got it. But I am in this matter yet more definitely a rationalist. I do not propose to turn this book into one of ordinary Christian apologetics; I should be glad to meet at any other time the enemies of Christianity in that more obvious arena. Here I am only giving an account of my own growth in spiritual certainty. But I may pause to remark that the more I saw of the merely abstract arguments against the Christian cosmology the less I thought of them. I mean that having found the moral atmosphere of the Incarnation to be common sense, I then looked at the established intellectual arguments against the Incarnation and found them to be common nonsense. In case the argument should be thought to suffer from the absence of the ordinary apologetic I will here very briefly summarise my own arguments and conclusions on the purely objective or scientific truth of the matter.

If I am asked, as a purely intellectual question, why I believe in Christianity, I can only answer, "For the same reason that an intelligent agnostic disbelieves in Christianity." I believe in it quite rationally upon the evidence. But the evidence in my case, as in that of the intelligent agnostic, is not really in this or that alleged demonstration; it is in an enormous accumulation of small but unanimous facts. The secularist is not to be blamed because his objections to Christianity are miscellaneous and even scrappy; it is precisely such scrappy evidence that does convince the mind. I mean that a man may well be less convinced of a philosophy from four books, than from one book, one battle, one landscape, and one old friend. The very fact that the things are of different kinds increases the importance of the fact that they all point to one conclusion. Now, the non-Christianity of the average educated man to-day is almost always, to do him justice, made up of these loose but living experiences. I can only say that my evidences for Christianity are of the same vivid but varied kind as his evidences against it. For when I look at these various anti-Christian truths, I simply discover that none of them are true. I discover that the true tide and force of all the facts flows the other way. Let us take cases. Many a sensible modern man must have abandoned Christianity under the pressure of three such converging convictions as these: first, that men, with their shape, structure, and sexuality, are, after all, very much like beasts, a mere variety of the animal kingdom; second, that primeval religion arose in ignorance and fear; third, that priests have blighted societies with bitterness and gloom. Those three anti-Christian arguments are very different; but they are all quite logical and legitimate; and they all converge. The only objection to them (I discover) is that they are all untrue. If you leave off looking at books about beasts and men, if you begin to look at beasts and men then (if you have any humour or imagination, any sense of the frantic or the farcical) you will observe that the startling thing is not how like man is to the brutes, but how unlike he is. It is the monstrous scale of his divergence that requires an explanation. That man and brute are like is, in a sense, a truism; but that being so like they should then be so insanely unlike, that is the shock and the enigma. That an ape has hands is far less interesting to the philosopher than the fact that having hands he does next to nothing with them; does not play knuckle-bones or the violin; does not carve marble or carve mutton. People talk of barbaric architecture and debased art. But elephants do not build colossal temples of ivory even in a roccoco style; camels do not paint even bad pictures, though equipped with the material of many camel's-hair brushes. Certain modern dreamers say that ants and bees have a society superior to ours. They have, indeed, a civilization; but that very truth only reminds us that it is an inferior civilization. Who ever found an ant-hill decorated with the statues of celebrated ants? Who has seen a bee-hive carved with the images of gorgeous queens of old? No; the chasm between man and other creatures may have a natural explanation, but it is a chasm. We talk of wild animals; but man is the only wild animal. It is man that has broken out. All other animals are tame animals; following the rugged respectability of the tribe or type. All other animals are domestic animals; man alone is ever undomestic, either as a profligate or a monk. So that this first superficial reason for materialism is, if anything, a reason for its opposite; it is exactly where biology leaves off that all religion begins.

It would be the same if I examined the second of the three chance rationalist arguments; the argument that all that we call divine began in some darkness and terror. When I did attempt to examine the foundations of this modern idea I simply found that there were none. Science knows nothing whatever about pre-historic man; for the excellent reason that he is pre-historic. A few professors choose to conjecture that such things as human sacrifice were once innocent and general and that they gradually dwindled; but there is no direct evidence of it, and the small amount of indirect evidence is very much the other way. In the earliest legends we have, such as the tales of Isaac and of Iphigenia, human sacrifice is not introduced as something old, but rather as something new; as a strange and frightful exception darkly demanded by the gods. History says nothing; and legends all say that the earth was kinder in its earliest time. There is no tradition of progress; but the whole human race has a tradition of the Fall. Amusingly enough, indeed, the very dissemination of this idea is used against its authenticity. Learned men literally say that this pre-historic calamity cannot be true because every race of mankind remembers it. I cannot keep pace with these paradoxes.

And if we took the third chance instance, it would be the same; the view that priests darken and embitter the world. I look at the world and simply discover that they don't. Those countries in Europe which are still influenced by priests, are exactly the countries where there is still singing and dancing and coloured dresses and art in the open-air. Catholic doctrine and discipline may be walls; but they are the walls of a playground. Christianity is the only frame which has preserved the pleasure of Paganism. We might fancy some children playing on the flat grassy top of some tall island in the sea. So long as there was a wall round the cliff's edge they could fling themselves into every frantic game and make the place the noisiest of nurseries. But the walls were knocked down, leaving the naked peril of the precipice. They did not fall over; but when their friends returned to them they were all huddled in terror in the centre of the island; and their song had ceased.

Thus these three facts of experience, such facts as go to make an agnostic, are, in this view, turned totally round. I am left saying, "Give me an explanation, first, of the towering eccentricity of man among the brutes; second, of the vast human tradition of some ancient happiness; third, of the partial perpetuation of such pagan joy in the countries of the Catholic Church." One explanation, at any rate, covers all three: the theory that twice was the natural order interrupted by some explosion or revelation such as people now call "psychic." Once Heaven came upon the earth with a power or seal called the image of God, whereby man took command of Nature; and once again (when in empire after empire men had been found wanting) Heaven came to save mankind in the awful shape of a man. This would explain why the mass of men always look backwards; and why the only corner where they in any sense look forwards is the little continent where Christ has His Church. I know it will be said that Japan has become progressive. But how can this be an answer when even in saying "Japan has become progressive," we really only mean, "Japan has become European"? But I wish here not so much to insist on my own explanation as to insist on my original remark. I agree with the ordinary unbelieving man in the street in being guided by three or four odd facts all pointing to something; only when I came to look at the facts I always found they pointed to something else.

I have given an imaginary triad of such ordinary anti-Christian arguments; if that be too narrow a basis I will give on the spur of the moment another. These are the kind of thoughts which in combination create the impression that Christianity is something weak and diseased. First, for instance, that Jesus was a gentle creature, sheepish and unworldly, a mere ineffectual appeal to the world; second, that Christianity arose and flourished in the dark ages of ignorance, and that to these the Church would drag us back; third, that the people still strongly religious or (if you will) superstitious—such people as the Irish—are weak, unpractical, and behind the times. I only mention these ideas to affirm the same thing: that when I looked into them independently I found, not that the conclusions were unphilosophical, but simply that the facts were not facts. Instead of looking at books and pictures about the New Testament I looked at the New Testament. There I found an account, not in the least of a person with his hair parted in the middle or his hands clasped in appeal, but of an extraordinary being with lips of thunder and acts of lurid decision, flinging down tables, casting out devils, passing with the wild secrecy of the wind from mountain isolation to a sort of dreadful demagogy; a being who often acted like an angry god— and always like a god. Christ had even a literary style of his own, not to be found, I think, elsewhere; it consists of an almost furious use of the A FORTIORI. His "how much more" is piled one upon another like castle upon castle in the clouds. The diction used ABOUT Christ has been, and perhaps wisely, sweet and submissive. But the diction used by Christ is quite curiously gigantesque; it is full of camels leaping through needles and mountains hurled into the sea. Morally it is equally terrific; he called himself a sword of slaughter, and told men to buy swords if they sold their coats for them. That he used other even wilder words on the side of non-resistance greatly increases the mystery; but it also, if anything, rather increases the violence. We cannot even explain it by calling such a being insane; for insanity is usually along one consistent channel. The maniac is generally a monomaniac. Here we must remember the difficult definition of Christianity already given; Christianity is a superhuman paradox whereby two opposite passions may blaze beside each other. The one explanation of the Gospel language that does explain it, is that it is the survey of one who from some supernatural height beholds some more startling synthesis.

I take in order the next instance offered: the idea that Christianity belongs to the Dark Ages. Here I did not satisfy myself with reading modern generalisations; I read a little history. And in history I found that Christianity, so far from belonging to the Dark Ages, was the one path across the Dark Ages that was not dark. It was a shining bridge connecting two shining civilizations. If any one says that the faith arose in ignorance and savagery the answer is simple: it didn't. It arose in the Mediterranean civilization in the full summer of the Roman Empire. The world was swarming with sceptics, and pantheism was as plain as the sun, when

Constantine nailed the cross to the mast. It is perfectly true that afterwards the ship sank; but it is far more extraordinary that the ship came up again: repainted and glittering, with the cross still at the top. This is the amazing thing the religion did: it turned a sunken ship into a submarine. The ark lived under the load of waters; after being buried under the debris of dynasties and clans, we arose and remembered Rome. If our faith had been a mere fad of the fading empire, fad would have followed fad in the twilight, and if the civilization ever re-emerged (and many such have never re-emerged) it would have been under some new barbaric flag. But the Christian Church was the last life of the old society and was also the first life of the new. She took the people who were forgetting how to make an arch and she taught them to invent the Gothic arch. In a word, the most absurd thing that could be said of the Church is the thing we have all heard said of it. How can we say that the Church wishes to bring us back into the Dark Ages? The Church was the only thing that ever brought us out of them.

I added in this second trinity of objections an idle instance taken from those who feel such people as the Irish to be weakened or made stagnant by superstition. I only added it because this is a peculiar case of a statement of fact that turns out to be a statement of falsehood. It is constantly said of the Irish that they are impractical. But if we refrain for a moment from looking at what is said about them and look at what is DONE about them, we shall see that the Irish are not only practical, but quite painfully successful. The poverty of their country, the minority of their members are simply the conditions under which they were asked to work; but no other group in the British Empire has done so much with such conditions. The Nationalists were the only minority that ever succeeded in twisting the whole British Parliament sharply out of its path. The Irish peasants are the only poor men in these islands who have forced their masters to disgorge. These people, whom we call priest-ridden, are the only Britons who will not be squire-ridden. And when I came to look at the actual Irish character, the case was the same. Irishmen are best at the specially HARD professions—the trades of iron, the lawyer, and the soldier. In all these cases, therefore, I came back to the same conclusion: the sceptic was quite right to go by the facts, only he had not looked at the facts. The sceptic is too credulous; he believes in newspapers or even in encyclopedias. Again the three questions left me with three very antagonistic questions. The average sceptic wanted to know how I explained the namby-pamby note in the Gospel, the connection of the creed with mediaeval darkness and the political impracticability of the Celtic Christians. But I wanted to ask, and to ask with an earnestness amounting to urgency, "What is this incomparable energy which appears first in one walking the earth like a living judgment and this energy which can die with a dying civilization and yet force it to a resurrection from the dead; this energy which last of all can inflame a bankrupt peasantry with so fixed a faith in justice that they get what they ask, while others go empty away; so that the most helpless island of the Empire can actually help itself?"

There is an answer: it is an answer to say that the energy is truly from outside the world; that it is psychic, or at least one of the results of a real psychical disturbance. The highest gratitude and respect are due to the great human civilizations such as the old Egyptian or the existing Chinese. Nevertheless it is no injustice for them to say that only modern Europe has exhibited incessantly a power of self-renewal recurring often at the shortest intervals and descending to the smallest facts of building or costume. All other societies die finally and with dignity. We die daily. We are always being born again with almost indecent obstetrics. It is hardly an exaggeration to say that there is in historic Christendom a sort of unnatural life: it could be explained as a supernatural life. It could be explained as an awful galvanic life working in what would have been a corpse. For our civilization OUGHT to have died, by all parallels, by all sociological probability, in the Ragnorak of the end of Rome. That is the weird inspiration of our estate: you and I have no business to be here at all. We are all REVENANTS; all living Christians are dead pagans walking about. Just as Europe was about to be gathered in silence to Assyria and Babylon, something entered into its body. And Europe has had a strange life—it is not too much to say that it has had the JUMPS— ever since.

I have dealt at length with such typical triads of doubt in order to convey the main contention—that my own case for Christianity is rational; but it is not simple. It is an accumulation of varied facts, like the attitude of the ordinary agnostic. But the ordinary agnostic has got his facts all wrong. He is a non-believer for a multitude of reasons; but they are untrue reasons. He doubts because the Middle Ages were barbaric, but they weren't; because Darwinism is demonstrated, but it isn't; because miracles do not happen, but they do; because monks were lazy, but they were very industrious; because nuns are unhappy, but they are particularly cheerful; because Christian art was sad and pale, but it was picked out in peculiarly bright colours and gay with gold; because modern science is moving away from the supernatural, but it isn't, it is moving towards the supernatural with the rapidity of a railway train.

But among these million facts all flowing one way there is, of course, one question sufficiently solid and separate to be treated briefly, but by itself; I mean the objective occurrence of the supernatural. In another chapter I have indicated the fallacy of the ordinary supposition that the world must be impersonal because it is orderly. A person is just as likely to desire an orderly thing as a disorderly thing. But my own positive conviction that personal creation is more conceivable than material fate, is,

I admit, in a sense, undiscussable. I will not call it a faith or an intuition, for those words are mixed up with mere emotion, it is strictly an intellectual conviction; but it is a PRIMARY intellectual conviction like the certainty of self of the good of living. Any one who likes, therefore, may call my belief in God merely mystical; the phrase is not worth fighting about. But my belief that miracles have happened in human history is not a mystical belief at all; I believe in them upon human evidences as I do in the discovery of America. Upon this point there is a simple logical fact that only requires to be stated and cleared up. Somehow or other an extraordinary idea has arisen that the disbelievers in miracles consider them coldly and fairly, while believers in miracles accept them only in connection with some dogma. The fact is quite the other way. The believers in miracles accept them (rightly or wrongly) because they have evidence for them. The disbelievers in miracles deny them (rightly or wrongly) because they have a doctrine against them. The open, obvious, democratic thing is to believe an old apple-woman when she bears testimony to a miracle, just as you believe an old apple-woman when she bears testimony to a murder. The plain, popular course is to trust the peasant's word about the ghost exactly as far as you trust the peasant's word about the landlord. Being a peasant he will probably have a great deal of healthy agnosticism about both. Still you could fill the British Museum with evidence uttered by the peasant, and given in favour of the ghost. If it comes to human testimony there is a choking cataract of human testimony in favour of the supernatural. If you reject it, you can only mean one of two things. You reject the peasant's story about the ghost either because the man is a peasant or because the story is a ghost story. That is, you either deny the main principle of democracy, or you affirm the main principle of materialism— the abstract impossibility of miracle. You have a perfect right to do so; but in that case you are the dogmatist. It is we Christians who accept all actual evidence—it is you rationalists who refuse actual evidence being constrained to do so by your creed. But I am not constrained by any creed in the matter, and looking impartially into certain miracles of mediaeval and modern times, I have come to the conclusion that they occurred. All argument against these plain facts is always argument in a circle. If I say, "Mediaeval documents attest certain miracles as much as they attest certain battles," they answer, "But mediaevals were superstitious"; if I want to know in what they were superstitious, the only ultimate answer is that they believed in the miracles. If I say "a peasant saw a ghost," I am told, "But peasants are so credulous." If I ask, "Why credulous?" the only answer is—that they see ghosts. Iceland is impossible because only stupid sailors have seen it; and the sailors are only stupid because they say they have seen Iceland. It is only fair to add that there is another argument that the unbeliever may rationally use against miracles, though he himself generally forgets to use it.

He may say that there has been in many miraculous stories a notion of spiritual preparation and acceptance: in short, that the miracle could only come to him who believed in it. It may be so, and if it is so how are we to test it? If we are inquiring whether certain results follow faith, it is useless to repeat wearily that (if they happen) they do follow faith. If faith is one of the conditions, those without faith have a most healthy right to laugh. But they have no right to judge. Being a believer may be, if you like, as bad as being drunk; still if we were extracting psychological facts from drunkards, it would be absurd to be always taunting them with having been drunk. Suppose we were investigating whether angry men really saw a red mist before their eyes. Suppose sixty excellent householders swore that when angry they had seen this crimson cloud: surely it would be absurd to answer "Oh, but you admit you were angry at the time." They might reasonably rejoin (in a stentorian chorus), "How the blazes could we discover, without being angry, whether angry people see red?" So the saints and ascetics might rationally reply, "Suppose that the question is whether believers can see visions—even then, if you are interested in visions it is no point to object to believers." You are still arguing in a circle—in that old mad circle with which this book began.

The question of whether miracles ever occur is a question of common sense and of ordinary historical imagination: not of any final physical experiment. One may here surely dismiss that quite brainless piece of pedantry which talks about the need for "scientific conditions" in connection with alleged spiritual phenomena. If we are asking whether a dead soul can communicate with a living it is ludicrous to insist that it shall be under conditions in which no two living souls in their senses would seriously communicate with each other. The fact that ghosts prefer darkness no more disproves the existence of ghosts than the fact that lovers prefer darkness disproves the existence of love. If you choose to say, "I will believe that Miss Brown called her fiancé a periwinkle or, any other endearing term, if she will repeat the word before seventeen psychologists," then I shall reply, "Very well, if those are your conditions, you will never get the truth, for she certainly will not say it." It is just as unscientific as it is unphilosophical to be surprised that in an unsympathetic atmosphere certain extraordinary sympathies do not arise. It is as if I said that I could not tell if there was a fog because the air was not clear enough; or as if I insisted on perfect sunlight in order to see a solar eclipse.

As a common-sense conclusion, such as those to which we come about sex or about midnight (well knowing that many details must in their own nature be concealed) I conclude that miracles do happen. I am forced to it by a conspiracy of facts: the fact that the men who encounter elves or angels are not the mystics and the morbid dreamers, but fishermen, farmers, and all men at once coarse and cautious; the fact that we all know men who testify to spiritualistic incidents but are not spiritualists, the fact that science itself admits such things more and more every day. Science will even admit the Ascension if you call it Levitation, and will very likely admit the Resurrection when it has thought of another word for it. I suggest the Regalvanisation. But the strongest of all is the dilemma above mentioned, that these supernatural things are never denied except on the basis either of anti-democracy or of materialist dogmatism—I may say materialist mysticism. The sceptic always takes one of the two positions; either an ordinary man need not be believed, or an extraordinary event must not be believed. For I hope we may dismiss the argument against wonders attempted in the mere recapitulation of frauds, of swindling mediums or trick miracles. That is not an argument at all, good or bad. A false ghost disproves the reality of ghosts exactly as much as a forged banknote disproves the existence of the Bank of England— if anything, it proves its existence.

Given this conviction that the spiritual phenomena do occur (my evidence for which is complex but rational), we then collide with one of the worst mental evils of the age. The greatest disaster of the nineteenth century was this: that men began to use the word "spiritual" as the same as the word "good." They thought that to grow in refinement and uncorporeality was to grow in virtue. When scientific evolution was announced, some feared that it would encourage mere animality. It did worse: it encouraged mere spirituality. It taught men to think that so long as they were passing from the ape they were going to the angel. But you can pass from the ape and go to the devil. A man of genius, very typical of that time of bewilderment, expressed it perfectly. Benjamin Disraeli was right when he said he was on the side of the angels. He was indeed; he was on the side of the fallen angels. He was not on the side of any mere appetite or animal brutality; but he was on the side of all the imperialism of the princes of the abyss; he was on the side of arrogance and mystery, and contempt of all obvious good. Between this sunken pride and the towering humilities of heaven there are, one must suppose, spirits of shapes and sizes. Man, in encountering them, must make much the same mistakes that he makes in encountering any other varied types in any other distant continent. It must be hard at first to know who is supreme and who is subordinate. If a shade arose from the under world, and stared at Piccadilly, that shade would not quite understand the idea of an ordinary closed carriage. He would suppose that the coachman on the box was a triumphant conqueror, dragging behind him a kicking and imprisoned captive. So, if we see spiritual facts for the first time, we may mistake who is uppermost. It is not enough to find the gods; they are obvious; we must find God, the real chief of the gods. We must have a long historic experience in supernatural phenomena— in order to discover which are really natural. In this light I find the history of

Christianity, and even of its Hebrew origins, quite practical and clear. It does not trouble me to be told that the Hebrew god was one among many. I know he was, without any research to tell me so. Jehovah and Baal looked equally important, just as the sun and the moon looked the same size. It is only slowly that we learn that the sun is immeasurably our master, and the small moon only our satellite. Believing that there is a world of spirits, I shall walk in it as I do in the world of men, looking for the thing that I like and think good. Just as I should seek in a desert for clean water, or toil at the North Pole to make a comfortable fire, so I shall search the land of void and vision until I find something fresh like water, and comforting like fire; until I find some place in eternity, where I am literally at home. And there is only one such place to be found.

I have now said enough to show (to any one to whom such an explanation is essential) that I have in the ordinary arena of apologetics, a ground of belief. In pure records of experiment (if these be taken democratically without contempt or favour) there is evidence first, that miracles happen, and second that the nobler miracles belong to our tradition. But I will not pretend that this curt discussion is my real reason for accepting Christianity instead of taking the moral good of Christianity as I should take it out of Confucianism.

I have another far more solid and central ground for submitting to it as a faith, instead of merely picking up hints from it as a scheme. And that is this: that the Christian Church in its practical relation to my soul is a living teacher, not a dead one. It not only certainly taught me yesterday, but will almost certainly teach me to-morrow. Once I saw suddenly the meaning of the shape of the cross; some day I may see suddenly the meaning of the shape of the mitre. One fine morning I saw why windows were pointed; some fine morning I may see why priests were shaven. Plato has told you a truth; but Plato is dead. Shakespeare has startled you with an image; but Shakespeare will not startle you with any more. But imagine what it would be to live with such men still living, to know that Plato might break out with an original lecture to-morrow, or that at any moment Shakespeare might shatter everything with a single song. The man who lives in contact with what he believes to be a living Church is a man always expecting to meet Plato and Shakespeare to-morrow at breakfast. He is always expecting to see some truth that he has never seen before. There is one only other parallel to this position; and that is the parallel of the life in which we all began. When your father told you, walking about the garden, that bees stung or that roses smelt sweet, you did not talk of taking the best out of his philosophy. When the bees stung you, you did not call it an entertaining coincidence. When the rose smelt sweet you did not say "My father is a rude, barbaric symbol, enshrining (perhaps unconsciously) the deep delicate truths that flowers smell." No: you believed your father, because you had found him to be a living fountain of facts, a thing that really knew more than you; a thing that would tell you truth to-morrow, as well as to-day. And if this was true of your father, it was even truer of your mother; at least it was true of mine, to whom this book is dedicated. Now, when society is in a rather futile fuss about the subjection of women, will no one say how much every man owes to the tyranny and privilege of women, to the fact that they alone rule education until education becomes futile: for a boy is only sent to be taught at school when it is too late to teach him anything. The real thing has been done already, and thank God it is nearly always done by women. Every man is womanised, merely by being born. They talk of the masculine woman; but every man is a feminised man. And if ever men walk to Westminster to protest against this female privilege, I shall not join their procession.

For I remember with certainty this fixed psychological fact; that the very time when I was most under a woman's authority, I was most full of flame and adventure. Exactly because when my mother said that ants bit they did bite, and because snow did come in winter (as she said); therefore the whole world was to me a fairyland of wonderful fulfilments, and it was like living in some Hebraic age, when prophecy after prophecy came true. I went out as a child into the garden, and it was a terrible place to me, precisely because I had a clue to it: if I had held no clue it would not have been terrible, but tame. A mere unmeaning wilderness is not even impressive. But the garden of childhood was fascinating, exactly because everything had a fixed meaning which could be found out in its turn. Inch by inch I might discover what was the object of the ugly shape called a rake; or form some shadowy conjecture as to why my parents kept a cat.

So, since I have accepted Christendom as a mother and not merely as a chance example, I have found Europe and the world once more like the little garden where I stared at the symbolic shapes of cat and rake; I look at everything with the old elvish ignorance and expectancy. This or that rite or doctrine may look as ugly and extraordinary as a rake; but I have found by experience that such things end somehow in grass and flowers. A clergyman may be apparently as useless as a cat, but he is also as fascinating, for there must be some strange reason for his existence. I give one instance out of a hundred; I have not myself any instinctive kinship with that enthusiasm for physical virginity, which has certainly been a note of historic Christianity. But when I look not at myself but at the world, I perceive that this enthusiasm is not only a note of Christianity, but a note of Paganism, a note of high human nature in many spheres. The Greeks felt virginity when they carved Artemis, the Romans when they robed the vestals, the worst and wildest of the great Elizabethan playwrights clung to the literal purity of a woman as to the central pillar of the world. Above all, the modern world (even while mocking sexual innocence) has flung itself into a generous idolatry of sexual innocence— the great modern worship of children. For any man who loves children will agree that their peculiar beauty is hurt by a hint of physical sex. With all this human experience, allied with the Christian authority, I simply conclude that I am wrong, and the church right; or rather that I am defective, while the church is universal. It takes all sorts to make a church; she does not ask me to be celibate. But the fact that I have no appreciation of the celibates, I accept like the fact that I have no ear for music. The best human experience is against me, as it is on the subject of Bach. Celibacy is one flower in my father's garden, of which I have not been told the sweet or terrible name. But I may be told it any day.

This, therefore, is, in conclusion, my reason for accepting the religion and not merely the scattered and secular truths out of the religion. I do it because the thing has not merely told this truth or that truth, but has revealed itself as a truth-telling thing. All other philosophies say the things that plainly seem to be true; only this philosophy has again and again said the thing that does not seem to be true, but is true. Alone of all creeds it is convincing where it is not attractive; it turns out to be right, like my father in the garden. Theosophists for instance will preach an obviously attractive idea like re-incarnation; but if we wait for its logical results, they are spiritual superciliousness and the cruelty of caste. For if a man is a beggar by his own pre-natal sins, people will tend to despise the beggar. But Christianity preaches an obviously unattractive idea, such as original sin; but when we wait for its results, they are pathos and brotherhood, and a thunder of laughter and pity; for only with original sin we can at once pity the beggar and distrust the king. Men of science offer us health, an obvious benefit; it is only afterwards that we discover that by health, they mean bodily slavery and spiritual tedium. Orthodoxy makes us jump by the sudden brink of hell; it is only afterwards that we realise that jumping was an athletic exercise highly beneficial to our health. It is only afterwards that we realise that this danger is the root of all drama and romance. The strongest argument for the divine grace is simply its ungraciousness. The unpopular parts of Christianity turn out when examined to be the very props of the people. The outer ring of Christianity is a rigid guard of ethical abnegations and professional priests; but inside that inhuman guard you will find the old human life dancing like children, and drinking wine like men; for Christianity is the only frame for pagan freedom. But in the modern philosophy the case is opposite; it is its outer ring that is obviously artistic and emancipated; its despair is within.

And its despair is this, that it does not really believe that there is any meaning in the universe; therefore it cannot hope to find any romance; its romances will have no plots. A man cannot expect any adventures in the land of anarchy. But a man can expect any number of adventures if he goes travelling in the land of authority. One can find no meanings in a jungle of scepticism; but the man will find more and more meanings who walks through a forest of doctrine and design. Here everything has a story tied to its tail, like the tools or pictures in my father's house; for it is my father's house. I end where I began—at the right end. I have entered at last the gate of all good philosophy. I have come into my second childhood.

But this larger and more adventurous Christian universe has one final mark difficult to express; yet as a conclusion of the whole matter I will attempt to express it. All the real argument about religion turns on the question of whether a man who was born upside down can tell when he comes right way up. The primary paradox of Christianity is that the ordinary condition of man is not his sane or sensible condition; that the normal itself is an abnormality. That is the inmost philosophy of the Fall. In Sir Oliver Lodge's interesting new Catechism, the first two questions were: "What are you?" and "What, then, is the meaning of the Fall of Man?" I remember amusing myself by writing my own answers to the questions; but I soon found that they were very broken and agnostic answers. To the question, "What are you?" I could only answer, "God knows." And to the question, "What is meant by the Fall?" I could answer with complete sincerity, "That whatever I am, I am not myself." This is the prime paradox of our religion; something that we have never in any full sense known, is not only better than ourselves, but even more natural to us than ourselves. And there is really no test of this except the merely experimental one with which these pages began, the test of the padded cell and the open door. It is only since I have known orthodoxy that I have known mental emancipation. But, in conclusion, it has one special application to the ultimate idea of joy.

It is said that Paganism is a religion of joy and Christianity of sorrow; it would be just as easy to prove that Paganism is pure sorrow and Christianity pure joy. Such conflicts mean nothing and lead nowhere. Everything human must have in it both joy and sorrow; the only matter of interest is the manner in which the two things are balanced or divided. And the really interesting thing is this, that the pagan was (in the main) happier and happier as he approached the earth, but sadder and sadder as he approached the heavens. The gaiety of the best Paganism, as in the playfulness of Catullus or Theocritus, is, indeed, an eternal gaiety never to be forgotten by a grateful humanity. But it is all a gaiety about the facts of life, not about its origin. To the pagan the small things are as sweet as the small brooks breaking out of the mountain; but the broad things are as bitter as the sea. When the pagan looks at the very core of the cosmos he is struck cold. Behind the gods, who are merely despotic, sit the fates, who are deadly. Nay, the fates are worse than deadly; they are dead. And when rationalists say that the ancient world was more enlightened than the Christian, from their point of view they are right. For when they say "enlightened" they mean darkened with incurable despair. It is profoundly true that the ancient world was more modern than the Christian. The common bond is in the fact that ancients and moderns have both been miserable about existence, about everything, while mediaevals were happy about that at least. I freely grant that the pagans, like the moderns, were only miserable about everything—they were quite jolly about everything else. I concede that the Christians of the Middle Ages were only at peace about everything—they were at war about everything else. But if the question turn on the primary pivot of the cosmos, then there was more cosmic contentment in the narrow and bloody streets of Florence than in the theatre of Athens or the open garden of Epicurus. Giotto lived in a gloomier town than Euripides, but he lived in a gayer universe.

The mass of men have been forced to be gay about the little things, but sad about the big ones. Nevertheless (I offer my last dogma defiantly) it is not native to man to be so. Man is more himself, man is more manlike, when joy is the fundamental thing in him, and grief the superficial. Melancholy should be an innocent interlude, a tender and fugitive frame of mind; praise should be the permanent pulsation of the soul. Pessimism is at best an emotional half-holiday; joy is the uproarious labour by which all things live. Yet, according to the apparent estate of man as seen by the pagan or the agnostic, this primary need of human nature can never be fulfilled. Joy ought to be expansive; but for the agnostic it must be contracted, it must cling to one corner of the world. Grief ought to be a concentration; but for the agnostic its desolation is spread through an unthinkable eternity. This is what I call being born upside down. The sceptic may truly be said to be topsy-turvy; for his feet are dancing upwards in idle ecstasies, while his brain is in the abyss. To the modern man the heavens are actually below the earth. The explanation is simple; he is standing on his head; which is a very weak pedestal to stand on. But when he has found his feet again he knows it. Christianity satisfies suddenly and perfectly man's ancestral instinct for being the right way up; satisfies it supremely in this; that by its creed joy becomes something gigantic and sadness something special and small. The vault above us is not deaf because the universe is an idiot; the silence is not the heartless silence of an endless and aimless world. Rather the silence around us is a small and pitiful stillness like the prompt stillness in a sick-room. We are perhaps permitted tragedy as a sort of merciful comedy: because the frantic energy of divine things would knock us down like a drunken farce. We can take our own tears more lightly than we could take the tremendous levities of the angels. So we sit perhaps in a starry chamber of silence, while the laughter of the heavens is too loud for us to hear.

Joy, which was the small publicity of the pagan, is the gigantic secret of the Christian. And as I close this chaotic volume I open again the strange small book from which all Christianity came; and I am again haunted by a kind of confirmation. The tremendous figure which fills the Gospels towers in this respect, as in every other, above all the thinkers who ever thought themselves tall. His pathos was natural, almost casual. The Stoics, ancient and modern, were proud of concealing their tears. He never concealed His tears; He showed them plainly on His open face at any daily sight, such as the far sight of His native city. Yet He concealed something. Solemn supermen and imperial diplomatists are proud of restraining their anger. He never restrained His anger. He flung furniture down the front steps of the Temple, and asked men how they expected to escape the damnation of Hell. Yet He restrained something. I say it with reverence; there was in that shattering personality a thread that must be called shyness. There was something that He hid from all men when He went up a mountain to pray. There was something that He covered constantly by abrupt silence or impetuous isolation. There was some one thing that was too great for God to show us when He walked upon our earth; and I have sometimes fancied that it was His mirth.

THE END

THE EVERLASTING MAN

G. K. Chesterton

[1925]

Preparatory Note

This book needs a preliminary note that its scope be not misunderstood. The view suggested is historical rather than theological, and does not deal directly with a religious change which has been the chief event of my own life; and about which I am already writing a more purely controversial volume. It is impossible, I hope, for any Catholic to write any book on any subject, above all this subject, without showing that he is a Catholic; but this study is not specially concerned with the differences between a Catholic and a Protestant. Much of it is devoted to many sorts of Pagans rather than any sort of Christians; and its thesis is that those who say that Christ stands side by side with similar myths, and his religion side by side with similar religions, are only repeating a very stale formula contradicted by a very striking fact. To suggest this I have not needed to go much beyond matters known to us all; I make no claim to learning; and have to depend for some things, as has rather become the fashion, on those who are more learned.

As I have more than once differed from Mr. H. G. Wells in his view of history, it is the more right that I should here congratulate him on the courage and constructive imagination which carried through his vast and varied and intensely interesting work; but still more on having asserted the reasonable right of the amateur to do what he can with the facts which the specialists provide.

250

INTRODUCTION: THE PLAN OF THIS BOOK

There are two ways of getting home; and one of them is to stay there. The other is to walk round the whole world till we come back to the same place; and I tried to trace such a journey in a story I once wrote. It is, however, a relief to turn from that topic to another story that I never wrote. Like every book I never wrote, it is by far the best book I have ever written. It is only too probable that I shall never write it, so I will use it symbolically here; for it was a symbol of the same truth. I conceived it as a romance of those vast valleys with sloping sides, like those along which the ancient White Horses of Wessex are scrawled along the flanks of the hills. It concerned some boy whose farm or cottage stood on such a slope, and who went on his travels to find something, such as the effigy and grave of some giant; and when he was far enough from home he looked back and saw that his own farm and kitchen-garden, shining flat on the hill-side like the colours and quarterings of a shield, were but parts of some such gigantic figure, on which he had always lived, but which was too large and too close to be seen. That, I think, is a true picture of the progress of any really independent intelligence today; and that is the point of this book.

The point of this book, in other words, is that the next best thing to being really inside Christendom is to be really outside it. And a particular point of it is that the popular critics of Christianity are not really outside it. They are on a debatable ground, in every sense of the term. They are doubtful in their very doubts. Their criticism has taken on a curious tone; as of a random and illiterate heckling. Thus they make current and anti-clerical cant as a sort of small-talk. They will complain of parsons dressing like parsons; as if we should be any more free if all the police who shadowed or collared us were plain clothes detectives. Or they will complain that a sermon cannot be interrupted, and call a pulpit a coward's castle; though they do not call an editor's office a coward's castle. It would be unjust both to journalists and priests; but it would be much truer of journalist. The clergyman appears in person and could easily be kicked as he came out of church; the journalist conceals even his name so that nobody can kick him. They write wild and pointless articles and letters in the press about why the churches are empty, without even going there to find out if they are empty, or which of them are empty. Their suggestions are more vapid and vacant than the most insipid curate in a three-act farce, and move us to comfort him after the manner of the curate in the Bab Ballads; 'Your mind is not so blank as that of Hopley Porter.' So we may truly say to the very feeblest cleric: 'Your mind is not so blank as that of Indignant Layman or Plain Man or Man in the Street, or any of your critics in the newspapers; for they have not the most shadowy notion of what they want themselves. Let alone of what you ought to give them.' They will suddenly turn round and revile the Church for not having prevented the War, which they themselves did not want to prevent; and which nobody had ever professed to be able to prevent, except some of that very school of progressive and cosmopolitan sceptics who are the chief enemies of the Church. It was the anti-clerical and agnostic world that was always prophesying the advent of universal peace; it is that world that was, or should have been, abashed and confounded by the advent of universal war. As for the general view that the Church was discredited by the War--they might as well say that the Ark was discredited by the Flood. When the world goes wrong, it proves rather that the Church is right. The Church is justified, not because her children do not sin, but because they do. But that marks their mood about the whole religious tradition they are in a state of reaction against it. It is well with the boy when he lives on his father's land; and well with him again when he is far enough from it to look back on it and see it as a whole. But these people have got into an intermediate state, have fallen into an intervening valley from which they can see neither the heights beyond them nor the heights behind. They cannot get out of the penumbra of Christian controversy. They cannot be Christians and they can not leave off being Anti-Christians. Their whole atmosphere is the atmosphere of a reaction: sulks, perversity, petty criticism. They still live in the shadow of the faith and have lost the light of the faith.

Now the best relation to our spiritual home is to be near enough to love it. But the next best is to be far enough away not to hate it. It is the contention of these pages that while the best judge of Christianity is a Christian, the next best judge would be something more like a Confucian. The worst judge of all is the man now most ready with his judgements; the ill-educated Christian turning gradually into the ill-tempered agnostic, entangled in the end of a feud of which he never understood the beginning, blighted with a sort of hereditary boredom with he knows not what, and already weary of hearing what he has never heard. He does not judge Christianity calmly as a Confucian would; he does not judge it as he would judge Confucianism. He cannot by an effort of fancy set the Catholic Church thousands of miles away in strange skies of morning and judge it as impartially as a Chinese pagoda. It is said that the great St. Francis Xavier, who very nearly succeeded in setting up the Church there as a tower overtopping all pagodas, failed partly because his followers were accused by their fellow missionaries of representing the Twelve Apostles with the garb or attributes of Chinamen. But it would be far better to see them as Chinamen, and judge them fairly as Chinamen, than to see them as featureless idols merely made to be battered by iconoclasts; or rather as cockshies to be pelted by empty-handed cockneys. It would be better to see the whole thing as a remote Asiatic cult; the mitres of its bishops as the towering head dresses of mysterious bonzes; its pastoral staffs as the sticks twisted like serpents carried in some Asiatic procession; to see the prayer book as fantastic as the prayer-wheel and the Cross as crooked as the Swastika. Then at least we should not lose our temper as some of the skeptical critics seem to lose their temper, not to mention their wits. Their anti-clericalism has become an atmosphere, an atmosphere of negation and hostility from which they cannot escape. Compared with that, it would be better to see the whole thing as something belonging to another continent, or to another planet. It would be more philosophical to stare indifferently at bonzes than to be perpetually and pointlessly grumbling at bishops. It would be better to walk past a church as if it were a pagoda than to stand permanently in the porch, impotent either to go inside and help or to go outside and forget. For those in whom a mere reaction has thus become an obsession, I do seriously recommend the imaginative effort of conceiving the Twelve Apostles as Chinamen. In other words, I recommend these critics to try to do as much justice to Christian saints as if they were Pagan sages.

But with this we come to the final and vital point I shall try to show in these pages that when we do make this imaginative effort to see the whole thing from the outside, we find that it really looks like what is traditionally said about it inside. It is exactly when the boy gets far enough off to see the giant that he sees that he really is a giant. It is exactly when we do at last see the Christian Church afar under those clear and level eastern skies that we see that it is really the Church of Christ. To put it shortly, the moment we are really impartial about it, we know why people are partial to it. But this second proposition requires more serious discussion; and I shall here set myself to discuss it.

As soon as I had clearly in my mind this conception of something solid in the solitary and unique character of the divine story, it struck me that there was exactly the same strange and yet solid character in the human story that had led up to it; because that human story also had a root that was divine. I mean that just as the Church seems to grow more remarkable when it is fairly compared with the common religious life of mankind, so mankind itself seems to grow more remarkable when we compare it with the common life of nature. And I have noticed that most modern history is driven to something like sophistry, first to soften the sharp transition from animals to men, and then to soften the sharp transition from heathens to Christians. Now the more we really read in a realistic spirit of those two transitions the sharper we shall find them to be. It is because the critics are not detached that they do not see this detachment; it is because they are not looking at things in a dry light that they cannot see the difference between black and white. It is because they are in a particular mood of reaction and revolt that they have a motive for making out that all the white is dirty grey and the black not so black as it is painted. I do not say there are not human excuses for their revolt; I do not say it is not in some ways sympathetic; what I say is that it is not in any way scientific. An iconoclast may be indignant; an iconoclast may be justly indignant; but an iconoclast is not impartial. And it is stark hypocrisy to pretend that nine-tenths of the higher critics and scientific evolutionists and professors of comparative religion are in the least impartial. Why should they be impartial, what is being impartial, when the whole world is at war about whether one thing is a devouring superstition or a divine hope? I do not pretend to be impartial in the sense that the final act of faith fixes a man's mind because it satisfies his mind. But I do profess to be a great deal more impartial than they are; in the sense that I can tell the story fairly, with some sort of imaginative justice to all sides; and they cannot. I do profess to be impartial in the sense that I should be ashamed to talk such nonsense about the Lama of Thibet as they do about the Pope of Rome, or to have as little sympathy with Julian the Apostate as they have with the Society of Jesus. They are not impartial; they never by any chance hold the historical scales even; and above all they are never impartial upon this point of evolution and transition. They suggest everywhere the grey gradations of twilight, because they believe it is the twilight of the gods. I propose to maintain that whether or not it is the twilight of gods, it is not the daylight of men.

I maintain that when brought out into the daylight these two things look altogether strange and unique; and that it is only in the false twilight of an imaginary period of transition that they can be made to look in the least like anything else. The first of these is the creature called man and the second is the man called Christ. I have therefore divided this book into two parts: the former being a sketch of the main adventure of the human race in so far as it remained heathen; and the second a summary of the real difference that was made by it becoming Christian. Both motives necessitate a certain method, a method which is not very easy to manage, and perhaps even less easy to define or defend.

In order to strike, in the only sane or possible sense, the note of impartiality, it is necessary to touch the nerve of novelty. I mean that in one sense we see things fairly when we see them first. That, I may remark in passing, is why children generally have very little difficulty about the dogmas of the Church. But the Church, being a highly practical thing for working and fighting, is necessarily a thing for men and not merely for children. There must be in it for working purposes a great deal of tradition, of familiarity, and even of routine. So long as its fundamentals are sincerely felt, this may even be the saner condition. But when its fundamentals are doubted, as at present, we must try to recover the candour and wonder of the child; the unspoilt realism and objectivity of innocence. Or if we cannot do that, we must try at least to shake off the cloud of mere custom and see the thing as new, if only by seeing it as unnatural. Things that may well be familiar so long as familiarity breeds affection had much better become unfamiliar when familiarity breeds contempt. For in connection with things so great as are here considered, whatever our view of them, contempt must be a mistake. Indeed contempt must be an illusion. We must invoke the most wild and soaring sort of imagination; the imagination that can see what is there.

The only way to suggest the point is by an example of something, indeed of almost anything, that has been considered beautiful or wonderful. George Wyndham once told me that he had seen one of the first aeroplanes rise for the first time and it was very wonderful but not so wonderful as a horse allowing a man to ride on him. Somebody else has said that a fine man on a fine horse is the noblest bodily object in the world. Now, so long as people feel this in the right way, all is well. The first and best way of appreciating it is to come of people with a tradition of treating animals properly; of men in the right relation to horses. A boy who remembers his father who rode a horse, who rode it well and treated it well, will know that the relation can be satisfactory and will be satisfied. He will be all the more indignant at the ill-treatment of horses because he knows how they ought to be treated; but he will see nothing but what is normal in a man riding on a horse. He will not listen to the great modern philosopher who explains to him that the horse ought to be riding on the man. He will not pursue the pessimist fancy of Swift and say that men must be despised as monkeys and horses worshipped as gods. And horse and man together making an image that is to him human and civilised, it will be easy, as it were, to lift horse and man together into something heroic or symbolical; like a vision of St. George in the clouds. The fable of the winged horse will not be wholly unnatural to him: and he will know why Ariosto set many a Christian hero in such an airy saddle, and made him the rider of the sky. For the horse has really been lifted up along with the man in the wildest fashion in the very word we use when we speak 'chivalry.' The very name of the horse has been given to the highest mood and moment of the man; so that we might almost say that the handsomest compliment to a man is to call him a horse.

But if a man has got into a mood in which he is not able to feel this sort of wonder, then his cure must begin right at the other end. We must now suppose that he has drifted into a dull mood, in which somebody sitting on a horse means no more than somebody sitting on a chair. The wonder of which Wyndham spoke, the beauty that made the thing seem an equestrian statue, the meaning of the more chivalric horseman, may have become to him merely a convention and a bore. Perhaps they have been merely a fashion; perhaps they have gone out of fashion; perhaps they have been talked about too much. For talked about in the wrong way; perhaps it was then difficult to care for horses without the horrible risk of being horsy. Anyhow, he has got into a condition when he cares no more for a horse than for a towel-horse. His grandfather's charge at Balaclava seems to him as dull and dusty as the album containing such family portraits. Such a person has not really become enlightened about the album; on the contrary, he has only become blind with the dust. But when he has reached that degree of blindness, he will not be able to look at a horse or a horseman at all until he has seen the whole thing as a thing entirely unfamiliar and almost unearthly.

Out of some dark forest under some ancient dawn there must come towards us, with lumbering yet dancing motions, one of the very queerest of the prehistoric creatures. We must see for the first time the strangely small head set on a neck not only longer but thicker than itself, as the face of a gargoyle is thrust out upon a gutter-spout, the one disproportionate crest of hair running along the ridge of that heavy neck like a beard in the wrong place; the feet, each like a solid club of horn, alone amid the feet of so many cattle; so that the true fear is to be found in showing, not the cloven, but the uncloven hoof. Nor is it mere verbal fancy to see him thus as a unique monster; for in a sense a monster means what is unique, and he is really unique. But the point is that when we thus see him as the first man saw him, we begin once more to have some imaginative sense of what it meant when the first man rode him. In such a dream he may seem ugly, but he does not seem unimpressive; and certainly that two-legged dwarf who could get on top of him will not seem unimpressive. By a longer and more erratic road we shall come back to the same marvel of the man and the horse; and the marvel will be, if possible, even more marvellous. We shall have again a glimpse of St. George; the more glorious because St. George is not riding on the horse, but rather riding on the dragon.

In this example, which I have taken merely because it is an example, it will be noted that I do not say that the nightmare seen by the first man of the forest is either more true or more wonderful than the normal mare of the stable seen by the civilised person who can appreciate what is normal. Of the two extremes, I think on the whole that the traditional grasp of truth is the better. But I say that the truth is found at one or other of these two extremes, and is lost in the intermediate condition of mere fatigue and forgetfulness of tradition. In other words, I say it is better to see a horse as a monster than to see it only as a slow substitute for a motor-car. If we have got into that state of mind about a horse as something stale, it is far better to be frightened of a horse because it is a good deal too fresh.

Now, as it is with the monster that is called a horse, so it is with the monster that is called a man. Of course the best condition of all, in my opinion, is always to have regarded man as he is regarded in my philosophy. He who holds the Christian and Catholic view of human nature will feel certain that it is a universal and therefore a sane view, and will be satisfied. But if he has lost the pose to strike wherever possible this note of what is new and strange, and for that reason the style even on so serious a subject may sometimes be deliberately grotesque and fanciful. I do desire to help the reader to see Christendom from the outside in the sense of seeing it as a whole, against the background of other historic things; just as I desire him to see humanity as a whole against the background of natural things. And I say that in both cases, when seen thus, they stand out from their background like supernatural things. They do not fade into the rest with the colours of impressionism; they stand out from the rest with the colours of heraldry; as vivid as a red cross on a white shield or a black lion on a ground of gold. So stands the Red Clay against the green field of nature, or the White Christ against the red clay of his race.

But in order to see them clearly we have to see them as a whole. We have to see how they developed as well as how they began; for the most incredible part of the story is that things which began thus should have developed thus. Anyone who chooses to indulge in mere imagination can imagine that other things might have happened or other entities evolved. Anyone thinking of what might have happened may conceive a sort of evolutionary equality; but anyone facing what did happen must face an exception and a prodigy. If there was ever a moment when man was only an animal, we can if we choose make a fancy picture of his career transferred to some other animal. An entertaining fantasia might be made in which elephants built in elephantine architecture, with towers and turrets like tusks and trunks, cities beyond the scale of any colossus. A pleasant fable might be conceived in which a cow had developed a costume, and put on four boots and two pairs of trousers. We could imagine a Supermonkey more marvellous than any Superman, a quadrumanous creature carving and painting with his hands and cooking and carpentering with his feet. But if we are considering what did happen, we shall certainly decide that man has distanced everything else with a distance like that of the astronomical spaces and a speed like that of the still thunderbolt of the light. And in the same fashion, while we can if we choose see the Church amid a mob of Mithraic or Manichean superstitions squabbling and killing each other at the end of the Empire, while we can if we choose imagine the Church killed in the struggle and some other chance cult taking its place, we shall be the more surprised (and possibly puzzled) if we meet it two thousand years afterwards rushing through the ages as the winged thunderbolt of thought and everlasting enthusiasm; a thing without rival or resemblance; and still as new as it is old.

PART I

ON THE CREATURE CALLED MAN

THE MAN IN THE CAVE

Far away in some strange constellation in skies infinitely remote, there is a small star, which astronomers may some day discover. At least I could never observe in the faces or demeanour of most astronomers or men of science any evidence that they have discovered it; though as a matter of fact they were walking about on it all the time. It is a star that brings forth out of itself very strange plants and very strange animals; and none stranger than the men of science. That at least is the way in which I should begin a history of the world, if I had to follow the scientific custom of beginning with an account of the astronomical universe. I should try to see even this earth from the outside, not by the hackneyed insistence of its relative position to the sun, but by some imaginative effort to conceive its remote position for the dehumanised spectator. Only I do not believe in being dehumanised in order to study humanity. I do not believe in dwelling upon the distances that are supposed to dwarf the world; I think there is even something a trifle vulgar about this idea of trying to rebuke spirit by size. And as the first idea is not feasible, that of making the earth a strange planet so as to make it significant, I will not stoop to the other trick of making it a small planet in order to make it insignificant. I would rather insist that we do not even know that it is a planet at all, in the sense in which we know that it is a place; and a very extraordinary place too. That is the note which I wish to strike from the first, if not in the astronomical, then in some more familiar fashion.

One of my first journalistic adventures, or misadventures, concerned a comment on Grant Allen, who had written a book about the Evolution of the Idea of God. I happened to remark that it would be much more interesting if God wrote a book about the evolution of the idea of Grant Allen. And I remember that the editor objected to my remark on the ground that it was blasphemous; which naturally amused me not a little. For the joke of it was, of course, that it never occurred to him to notice the title of the book itself, which really was blasphemous; for it was, when translated into English, 'I will show you how this nonsensical notion that there is God grew up among men.' My remark was strictly pious and proper confessing the divine purpose even in its most seemingly dark or meaningless manifestations. In that hour I learned many things, including the fact that there is something purely acoustic in much of that agnostic sort of reverence. The editor had not seen the point, because in the title of the book the long word came at the beginning and the short word at the end; whereas in my comments the short word came at the beginning and gave him a sort of shock. I have noticed that if you put a word like God into the same sentence with a word like dog, these abrupt and angular words affect people like pistol-shots. Whether you say that God made the dog or the dog made God does not seem to matter; that is only one of the sterile disputations of the too subtle theologians. But so long as you begin with a long word like evolution the rest will roll harmlessly past; very probably the editor had not read the whole of the title, for it is rather a long title and he was rather a busy man.

But this little incident has always lingered in my mind as a sort of parable. Most modern histories of mankind begin with the word evolution, and with a rather wordy exposition of evolution, for much the same reason that operated in this case. There is something slow and soothing and gradual about the word and even about the idea. As a matter of fact, it is not, touching these primary things, a very practical word or a very profitable idea. Nobody can imagine how nothing could turn into something. Nobody can get an inch nearer to it by explaining how something could turn into something else. It is really far more logical to start by saying 'In the beginning God created heaven and earth' even if you only mean 'In the beginning some unthinkable power began some unthinkable process.' For God is by its nature a name of mystery, and nobody ever supposed that man could imagine how a world was created any more than he could create one. But evolution really is mistaken for explanation. It has the fatal quality of leaving on many minds the impression that they do understand it and everything else; just as many of them live under a sort of illusion that they have read the Origin of Species.

But this notion of something smooth and slow, like the ascent of a slope, is a great part of the illusion. It is an illogicality as well as an illusion; for slowness has really nothing to do with the question. An event is not any more intrinsically intelligible or unintelligible because of the pace at which it moves. For a man who does not believe in a miracle, a slow miracle would be just as incredible as a swift one. The Greek witch may have turned sailors to swine with a stroke of the wand. But to see a naval gentleman of our acquaintance looking a little more like a pig every day, till he ended with four trotters and a curly tail, would not be any more soothing. It might be rather more creepy and uncanny. The medieval wizard may have flown through the air from the top of a tower; but to see an old gentleman walking through the air, in a leisurely and lounging manner, would still seem to call for some explanation. Yet there runs through all the rationalistic treatment of history this curious and confused idea that difficulty is avoided, or even mystery eliminated, by dwelling on mere delay or on something dilatory in the processes of things. There will be something to be said upon particular examples elsewhere; the question here is the false atmosphere of facility and ease given by the mere suggestion of going slow;

the sort of comfort that might be given to a nervous old woman travelling for the first time in a motor-car.

Mr. H. G. Wells has confessed to being a prophet; and in this matter he was a prophet at his own expense. It is curious that his first fairy-tale was a complete answer to his last book of history. The Time Machine destroyed in advance all comfortable conclusions founded on the mere relativity of time. In that sublime nightmare the hero saw trees shoot up like green rockets, and vegetation spread visibly like a green conflagration, or the sun shoot across the sky from east to west with the swiftness of a meteor. Yet in his sense these things were quite as natural when they went swiftly; and in our sense they are quite as supernatural when they go slowly. The ultimate question is why they go at all; and anybody who really understands that question will know that it always has been and always will be a religious question; or at any rate a philosophical or metaphysical question. And most certainly he will not think the question answered by some substitution of gradual for abrupt change; or, in other words by a merely relative question of the same story being spun out or rattled rapidly through, as can be done with any story at a cinema by turning a handle.

Now what is needed for these problems of primitive existence is something more like a primitive spirit. In calling up this vision of the first things, I would ask the reader to make with me a sort of experiment in simplicity. And by simplicity I do not mean stupidity, but rather the sort of clarity that sees things like life rather than words like evolution. For this purpose it would really be better to turn the handle of the Time Machine a little more quickly and see the grass growing and the trees springing up into the sky, if that experiment could contract and concentrate and make vivid the upshot of the whole affair. What we know, in a sense in which we know nothing else, is that the trees and the grass did grow and that number of other extraordinary things do in fact happen; that queer creatures support themselves in the empty air by beating it with fans of various fantastic shapes; that other queer creatures steer themselves about alive under a load of mighty waters; that other queer creatures walk about on four legs, and that the queerest creature of all walks about on two. These are things and not theories; and compared with them evolution and the atom and even the solar system are merely theories. The matter here is one of history and not of philosophy so that it need only be noted that no philosopher denies that a mystery still attaches to the two great transitions: the origin of the universe itself and the origin of the principle of life itself. Most philosophers have the enlightenment to add that a third mystery attaches to the origin of man himself. In other words, a third bridge was built across a third abyss of the unthinkable when there came into the world what we call reason and what we call will. Man is not merely an evolution but rather a revolution. That he has a backbone or other parts upon a similar pattern to birds and fishes is an obvious fact, whatever be the meaning of the fact. But if we attempt to regard him, as it were, as a quadruped standing on his hind legs, we shall find what follows far more fantastic and subversive than if he were standing on his head.

I will take one example to serve for an introduction to the story of man. It illustrates what I mean by saying that a certain childish directness is needed to see the truth about the childhood of the world. It illustrates what I mean by saying that a mixture of popular science and journalistic jargon have confused the facts about the first things, so that we cannot see which of them really comes first. It illustrates, though only in one convenient illustration, all that I mean by the necessity of seeing the sharp differences that give its shape to history, instead of being submerged in all these generalisations about slowness and sameness. For we do indeed require, in Mr. Wells's phrase, an outline of history. But we may venture to say, in Mr. Mantalini's phrase, that this evolutionary history has no outline or is a dead outline. But, above all, it illustrates what I mean by saying that the more we really look at man as an animal, the less he will look like one.

To-day all our novels and newspapers will be found swarming with numberless allusions to a popular character called a Cave-Man. He seems to be quite familiar to us, not only as a public character but as a private character. His psychology is seriously taken into account in psychological fiction and psychological medicine. So far as I can understand, his chief occupation in life was knocking his wife about, or treating women in general with what is, I believe, known in the world of the film as 'rough stuff.' I have never happened to come upon the evidence for this idea; and I do not know on what primitive diaries or prehistoric divorce-reports it is founded. Nor, as I have explained elsewhere, have I ever been able to see the probability of it, even considered a priori. We are always told without any explanation or authority that primitive man waved a club and knocked the woman down before he carried her off. But on every animal analogy, it would seem an almost morbid modesty and reluctance, on the part of the lady, always to insist on being knocked down before consenting to be carried off. And I repeat that I can never comprehend why, when the male was so very rude, the female should have been so very refined. The cave man may have been a brute, but there is no reason why he should have been more brutal than the brutes. And the loves of the giraffes and the river romance of the hippopotami are effected without any of this preliminary fracas or shindy. The cave-man may have been no better that the cave-bear; but the child she-bear, so famous in hymnology, is not trained with any such bias for spinsterhood. In short these details of the domestic life of the cave puzzle me upon either the revolutionary or the static hypothesis; and in any case I should like to look into the evidence for them, but unfortunately I have never been able to find it. But the curious thing is this:

that while ten thousand tongues of more or less scientific or literary gossip seemed to be talking at once about this unfortunate fellow, under the title of the cave-man, the one connection in which it is really relevant and sensible to talk about him as the cave-man has been comparatively neglected. People have used this loose term in twenty loose ways, but they have never even looked at their own term for what could really be learned from it.

In fact, people have been interested in everything about the cave-man except what he did in the cave. Now there does happen to be some real evidence of what he did in the cave. It is little enough, like all the prehistoric evidence, but it is concerned with the real cave-man and his cave and not the literary cave-man and his club. And it will be valuable to our sense of reality to consider quite simply what that real evidence is, and not to go beyond it. What was found in the cave was not the club, the horrible gory club notched with the number of women it had knocked on the head. The cave was not a Bluebeard's Chamber filled with the skeletons of slaughtered wives; it was not filled with female skulls all arranged in rows and all cracked like eggs. It was something quite unconnected, one way or the other, with all the modern phrases and philosophical implications and literary rumours which confuse the whole question for us. And if we wish to see as it really is this authentic glimpse of the morning of the world, it will be far better to conceive even the story of its discovery as some such legend of the land of morning. It would be far better to tell the tale of what was really found as simply as the tale of heroes finding the Golden Fleece or the Gardens of the Hesperides, if we could so escape from a fog of controversial theories into the clear colours and clean-cut outlines of such a dawn. The old epic poets at least knew how to tell a story, possibly a tall story but never a twisted story, never a story tortured out of its own shape to fit theories and philosophies invented centuries afterwards. It would be well if modern investigators could describe their discoveries in the bald narrative style of the earliest travellers, and without any of these long allusive words that are full of irrelevant implication and suggestion. Then we might realise exactly what we do know about the cave-man, or at any rate about the cave.

A priest and a boy entered sometime ago a hollow in the hills and passed into a sort of subterranean tunnel that led into a labyrinth of such sealed and secret corridors of rock. They crawled through cracks that seemed almost impassable, they crept through tunnels that might have been made for moles, they dropped into holes as hopeless as wells, they seemed to be burying themselves alive seven times over beyond the hope of resurrection. This is but the commonplace of all such courageous exploration; but what is needed here is some one who shall put such stories in the primary light, in which they are not commonplace. There is, for instance, something strangely symbolic in the accident that the first intruders into that sunken world were a priest and a boy, the types of the antiquity and of youth of the world. But here I am even more concerned with the symbolism of the boy than with that of the priest. Nobody who remembers boyhood needs to be told what it might be to a boy to enter like Peter Pan under a roof of the roots of all the trees and go deeper and deeper, till he reach what William Morris called the very roots of the mountains. Suppose somebody, with that simple and unspoilt realism that is a part of innocence, to pursue that journey to its end, not for the sake of what he could deduce or demonstrate in some dusty magazine controversy, but simply for the sake of what he could see. What he did see at last was a cavern so far from the light of day that it might have been the legendary Domdaniel cavern, that was under the floor of the sea. This secret chamber of rock, when illuminated after its long night of unnumbered ages, revealed on its walls large and sprawling outlines diversified with coloured earths; and when they followed the lines of them they recognised, across that vast and void of ages, the movement and the gesture of a man's hand. They were drawings or paintings of animals; and they were drawn or painted not only by a man but by an artist. Under whatever archaic limitations, they showed that love of the long sweeping or the long wavering line which any man who has ever drawn or tried to draw will recognise; and about which no artist will allow himself to be contradicted by any scientist. They showed the experimental and adventurous spirit of the artist, the spirit that does not avoid but attempt difficult things; as where the draughtsman had represented the action of the stag when he swings his head clean round and noses towards his tail, an action familiar enough in the horse. But there are many modern animal-painters who would set themselves something of a task in rendering it truly. In this and twenty other details it is clear that the artist had watched animals with a certain interest and presumably a certain pleasure. In that sense it would seem that he was not only an artist but a naturalist; the sort of naturalist who is really natural.

Now it is needless to note, except in passing, that there is nothing whatever in the atmosphere of that cave to suggest the bleak and pessimistic atmosphere of that journalistic cave of the winds, that blows and bellows about us with countless echoes concerning the cave-man. So far as any human character can be hinted at by such traces of the past, that human character is quite human and even humane. It is certainly not the ideal of an inhuman character, like the abstraction invoked in popular science. When novelists and educationists and psychologists of all sorts talk about the cave-man, they never conceive him in connection with anything that is really in the cave. When the realist of the sex novel writes, 'Red sparks danced in Dagmar Doubledick's brain; he felt the spirit of the cave-man rising within him,' the novelist's readers would be very much disappointed if Dagmar only went off and drew large pictures of cows on the drawing-room wall. When the psycho-analyst writes to a patient, 'The submerged instincts of the cave-man are doubtless prompting you to gratify a violent impulse,' he does not refer to the impulse to paint in water-colours; or to make conscientious studies of how cattle swing their heads when they graze. Yet we do know for a fact that the cave man did these mild and innocent things; and we have not the most minute speck of evidence that he did any of the violent and ferocious things. In other words the cave-man as commonly presented to us is simply a myth or rather a muddle; for a myth has at least an imaginative outline of truth. The whole of the current way of talking is simply a confusion and a misunderstanding, founded on no sort of scientific evidence and valued only as an excuse for a very modern mood of anarchy. If any gentleman wants to knock a woman about, he can surely be a cad without taking away the character of the cave-man, about whom we know next to nothing except what we can gather from a few harmless and pleasing pictures on a wall.

But this is not the point about the pictures or the particular moral here to be drawn from them. That moral is something much larger and simpler, so large and simple that when it is first stated it will sound childish. And indeed it is in the highest sense childish; and that is why I have in this apologue in some sense seen it through the eyes of a child. It is the biggest of all the facts really facing the boy in the cavern; and is perhaps too big to be seen. If the boy was one of the flock of the priest, it may be presumed that he had been trained in a certain quality of common sense; that common sense that often comes to us in the form of tradition. In that case he would simply recognise the primitive man's work as the work of a man, interesting but in no way incredible in being primitive. He would see what was there to see; and he would not be tempted into seeing what was not there, by any evolutionary excitement or fashionable speculation. If he had heard of such things he would admit, of course, that the speculations might be true and were not incompatible with the facts that were true. The artist may have had another side to his character besides that which he has alone left on record in his works of art. The primitive man may have taken a pleasure in beating women as well as in drawing animals; all we can say is that the drawings record the one but not the other. It may be true that when the cave-man's finished jumping on his mother, or his wife as the case may be, he loves to hear the little brook a-gurgling, and also to watch the deer as they come down to drink at the brook. These things are not impossible, but they are irrelevant. The common sense of the child could confine itself to learning from the facts what the facts have to teach; and the pictures in the cave are very nearly all the facts there are. So far as that evidence goes, the child would be justified in assuming that a man had represented animals with rock and red ochre for the same reason as he himself was in the habit of trying to represent animals with charcoal and red chalk. The man had drawn a stag just as the child had drawn a horse; because it was fun. The man had drawn a stag with his head turned as the child had drawn a pig with his eyes shut; because it was difficult. The child and the man, being both human, would be united by the brotherhood of men; and the brotherhood of men is even nobler when it bridges the abyss of ages than when it bridges only the chasm of class. But anyhow he would see no evidence of the cave man of crude evolutionism; because there is none to be seen. If somebody told him that the pictures had all been drawn by St. Francis of Assisi out of pure and saintly love of animals, there would be nothing in the cave to contradict it.

Indeed I once knew a lady who half-humorously suggested that the cave was a creche, in which the babies were put to be specially safe, and that coloured animals were drawn on the walls to amuse them; very much as diagrams of elephants and giraffes adorn a modern infant school. And though this was but a jest, it does draw attention to some of the other assumptions that we make only too readily. The pictures do not prove even that the cave-men lived in caves, any more than the discovery of a wine cellar in Balham (long after that suburb had been destroyed by human or divine wrath) would prove that the Victorian middle classes lived entirely underground. The cave might have had a special purpose like the cellar; it might have been a religious shrine or a refuge in war or the meeting place of a secret society or all sorts of things. But it is quite true that its artistic decoration has much more of the atmosphere of a nursery than of any of these nightmares of anarchical fury and fear. I have conceived a child as standing in the cave; and it is easy to conceive any child, modern or immeasurably remote, as making a living gesture as if to pat the painted beasts upon the wall. In that gesture there is a foreshadowing, as we shall see later, of another cavern and another child.

But suppose the boy had not been taught by a priest but by a professor, by one of the professors who simplify the relation of men and beasts to a mere evolutionary variation. Suppose the boy saw himself, with the same simplicity and sincerity, as a mere Mowgli running with the pack of nature and roughly indistinguishable from the rest save by a relative and recent variation. What would be for him the simplest lesson of that strange stone picture-book? After all, it would come back to this; that he had dug very deep and found the place where a man had drawn the picture of a reindeer. But he would dig a good deal deeper before he found a place where a reindeer had drawn a picture of a man. That sounds like a truism, but in this connection it is really a very tremendous truth. He might descend to depths unthinkable, he might sink into sunken continents as strange as remote stars, he might find himself in the inside of the world as far from men as the other side of the moon; he might see in those cold chasms or colossal terraces of stone, traced in the faint hieroglyphic of the fossil, the ruins of lost dynasties of biological life, rather like the ruins of successive creations and separate universes than the stages in the story of one. He would find the trail of monsters blindly developing in directions outside all our common imagery of fish and bird; groping and grasping and touching life with every extravagant elongation of horn and tongue and tentacle; growing a forest of fantastic caricatures of the claw and the fin and the finger. But nowhere would he find one finger that had traced one significant line upon the sand; nowhere one claw that had even begun to scratch the faint suggestion of a form. To all appearance, the thing would be as unthinkable in all those countless cosmic variations of forgotten aeons as it would be in the beasts and birds before our eyes. The child would no more expect to see it than to see the cat scratch on the wall a vindictive caricature of the dog. The childish common sense would keep the most evolutionary child from expecting to see anything like that; yet in the traces of the rude and recently evolved ancestors of humanity he would have seen exactly that. It must surely strike him as strange that men so remote from him should be so near, and that beasts so near to him should be so remote. To his simplicity it must seem at least odd that he could not find any trace of the beginning of any arts among any animals. That is the simplest lesson to learn in the cavern of the coloured pictures; only it is too simple to be learnt. It is the simple truth that man does differ from the brutes in kind and not in degree; and the proof of it is here; that it sounds like a truism to say that the most primitive man drew a picture of a monkey and that it sounds like a joke to say that the most intelligent monkey drew a picture of a man. Something of division and disproportion has appeared; and it is unique. Art is the signature of man.

That is the sort of simple truth with which a story of the beginnings ought really to begin. The evolutionist stands staring in the painted cavern at the things that are too large to be seen and too simple to be understood. He tries to deduce all sorts of other indirect and doubtful things from the details of the pictures, because he can not see the primary significance of the whole; thin and theoretical deductions about the absence of religion or the presence of superstition; about tribal government and hunting and human sacrifice and heaven knows what. In the next chapter I shall try to trace in a little more detail the much disputed question about these prehistoric origins of human ideas and especially of the religious idea. Here I am only taking this one case of the cave as a sort of symbol of the simpler sort of truth with which the story ought to start. When all is said, the main fact that the record of the reindeer men attests, along with all other records, is that the reindeer man could draw and the reindeer could not. If the reindeer man was as much an animal as the reindeer, it was all the more extraordinary that he could do what all other animals could not. If he was an ordinary product of biological growth, like any other beast or bird, then it is all the more extraordinary that he was not in the least like any other beast or bird. He seems rather more supernatural as a natural product than as a supernatural one.

But I have begun this story in the cave, like the cave of the speculations of Plato, because it is a sort of model of the mistake of merely evolutionary introductions and prefaces. It is useless to begin by saying that everything was slow and smooth and a mere matter of development and degree. For in the plain matter like the pictures there is in fact not a trace of any such development or degree. Monkeys did not begin pictures and men finish them; Pithecanthropus did not draw a reindeer badly and Homo Sapiens draw it well. The higher animals did not draw better and better portraits; the dog did not paint better in his best period than in his early bad manner as a jackal; the wild horse was not an Impressionist and the race-horse a Post-Impressionist. All we can say of this notion of reproducing things in shadow or representative shape is that it exists nowhere in nature except in man; and that we cannot even talk about it without treating man as something separate from nature. In other words, every sane sort of history must begin with man as man, a thing standing absolute and alone. How he came there, or indeed how anything else came there, is a thing for theologians and philosophers and scientists and not for historians. But an excellent test case of this isolation and mystery is the matter of the impulse of art. This creature was truly different from all other creatures; because he was a creator as well as a creature. Nothing in that sense could be made in any other image but the image of man. But the truth is so true that, even in the absence of any religious belief, it must be assumed in the form of some moral or metaphysical principle. In the next chapter we shall see how this principle applies to all the historical hypotheses and evolutionary ethics now in fashion; to the origins of tribal government or mythological belief. But the clearest and most convenient example to start with is this popular one of what the cave-man really did in his cave. It means that somehow or other a new thing had appeared in the cavernous night of nature, a mind that is like a mirror. It is like a mirror because it is truly a thing of reflection. It is like a mirror because in it alone all the other shapes can be seen like shining shadows in a vision. Above all, it is like a mirror because it is the only thing of its kind. Other things may resemble it or resemble each other in various ways; other things may excel it or excel each other in various ways; just as in the furniture of a room a table may be round like a mirror or a cupboard may be larger than a mirror. But the mirror is the only thing that can contain them all. Man is the microcosm; man is the measure of all things; man is the image of God These are the only real lessons to be learnt in the cave, and it is time to leave it for the open road.

It will be well in this place, however, to sum up once and for all what is meant by saying that man is at once the exception to everything and the mirror and the measure of all things. But to see man as he is, it is necessary once more to keep close to that simplicity that can clear itself of accumulated clouds of sophistry. The simplest truth about man is that he is a very strange being; almost in the sense of being a stranger on the earth. In all sobriety, he has much more of the external appearance of one bringing alien habits from another land than of a mere growth of this one. He has an unfair advantage and an unfair disadvantage. He cannot sleep in his own skin; he cannot trust his own instincts. He is at once a creator moving miraculous hands and fingers and a kind of cripple. He is wrapped in artificial bandages called clothes; he is propped on artificial crutches called furniture. His mind has the same doubtful liberties and the same wild limitations. Alone among the animals, he is shaken with the beautiful madness called laughter; as if he had caught sight of some secret in the very shape of the universe hidden from the universe itself. Alone among the animals he feels the need of averting his thought from the root realities of his own bodily being; of hiding them as in the presence of some higher possibility which creates the mystery of shame. Whether we praise these things as natural to man or abuse them as artificial in nature, they remain in the same sense unique. This is realised by the whole popular instinct called religion, until disturbed by pedants, especially the laborious pedants of the Simple Life. The most sophistical of all sophists are gymnosophists.

It is not natural to see man as a natural product. It is not common sense to call man a common object of the country or the seashore. It is not seeing straight to see him as an animal. It is not sane. It sins against the light; against that broad daylight of proportion which is the principle of all reality. It is reached by stretching a point, by making out a case, by artificially selecting a certain light and shade, by bringing into prominence the lesser or lower things which may happen to be similar. The solid thing standing in the sunlight, the thing we can walk round and see from all sides, is quite different. It is also quite extraordinary, and the more sides we see of it the more extraordinary it seems. It is emphatically not a thing that follows or flows naturally from anything else. If we imagine that an inhuman or impersonal intelligence could have felt from the first the general nature of the non-human world sufficiently to see that things would evolve in whatever way they did evolve, there would have been nothing whatever in all that natural world to prepare such a mind for such an unnatural novelty. To such a mind, man would most certainly not have seemed something like one herd out of a hundred herds finding richer pasture, or one swallow out of a hundred swallows making a summer under a strange sky. It would not be in the same scale and scarcely in the same dimension. We might as truly say that it would not be in the same universe. It would be more like seeing one cow out of a hundred cows suddenly jump over the moon or one pig out of a hundred pigs grow wings in a flash and fly. It would not be a question of the cattle finding their own grazing ground but of their building their own cattle-sheds, not a question of one swallow making a summer but of his making a summer house. For the very fact that birds do build nests is one of those similarities that sharpen the startling difference. The very fact that a bird can get as far as building a nest, and cannot get any farther, proves that he has not a mind as man has a mind; it proves it more completely than if he built nothing at all. If he built nothing at all, he might possibly be a philosopher of the Quietist or Buddhistic school, indifferent to all but the mind within. But when he builds as he does build and is satisfied and sings aloud with satisfaction, then we know there is really an invisible veil like a pane of glass between him and us, like the window on which a bird will beat in vain. But suppose our abstract onlooker saw one of the birds begin to build as men build. Suppose in an incredibly short space of time there were seven styles of architecture for one style of nest. Suppose the bird carefully selected forked twigs and pointed leaves to express the piercing piety of Gothic, but turned to broad foliage and black mud when he sought in a darker mood to call up the heavy columns of Bel and Ashtaroth; making his nest indeed one of the hanging gardens of Babylon. Suppose the bird made little clay statues of birds celebrated in letters or politics and stuck them up in front of the nest. Suppose that one bird out of a thousand birds began to do one of the thousand things that man had already done even in the morning of the world; and we can be quite certain that the onlooker would not regard such a bird as a mere evolutionary variety of the other birds; he would regard it as a very fearful wild-fowl indeed; possibly as a bird of ill-omen, certainly as an omen. That bird would tell the augurs, not of something that would happen, but of some thing that had happened. That something would be the appearance of a mind with a new dimension of depth; a mind like that of man. If there be no God, no other mind could conceivably have foreseen it.

Now, as a matter of fact, there is not a shadow of evidence that this thing was evolved at all. There is not a particle of roof that this transition came slowly, or even that it came naturally. In a strictly scientific sense, we simply know nothing whatever about how it grew, or whether it grew, or what it is. There may be a broken trail of stone and bone faintly suggesting the development of the human body. There is nothing even faintly suggesting such a development of this human mind. It was not and it was; we know not in what instant or in what infinity of years. Something happened; and it has all the appearance of a transaction outside of time. It has therefore nothing to do with history in the ordinary sense. The historian must take it or something like it for granted; it is not his business as a historian to explain it. But if he cannot explain it as a historian, he will not explain it as a biologist. In neither case is there any disgrace to him in accepting it without explaining it; for it is a reality, and history and biology deal with realities. He is quite justified in calmly confronting the pig with wings and the cow that jumped over the moon, merely because they have happened. He can reasonably accept man as a freak, because he accepts man as a fact. He can be perfectly comfortable in a crazy and disconnected world, or in a world that can produce such a crazy and disconnected thing. For reality is a thing in which we can all repose, even if it hardly seems related to anything else. The thing is there; and that is enough for most of us. But if we do indeed want to know how it can conceivably have come there, if we do indeed wish to see it related realistically to other things, if we do insist on seeing it evolved before our very eyes from an environment nearer to its own nature, then assuredly it is to very different things that we must go. We must stir very strange memories and return to very simple dreams, if we desire some origin that can make man other than a monster. We shall have discovered very different causes before he becomes a creature of causation; and invoked other authority to turn him into something reasonable, or even into anything probable. That way lies all that is at once awful and familiar and forgotten, with dreadful faces thronged and fiery arms. We can accept man as a fact, if we are content with an unexplained fact. We can accept him as an animal, if we can live with a fabulous animal. But if we must needs have sequence and necessity, then indeed we must provide a prelude and crescendo of mounting miracles, that ushered in with unthinkable thunders in all the seven heavens of another order, a man may be an ordinary thing.

PROFESSORS AND PREHISTORIC MEN

Science is weak about these prehistoric things in a way that has hardly been noticed. The science whose modern marvels we all admire succeeds by incessantly adding to its data. In all practical inventions, in most natural discoveries, it can always increase evidence by experiment. But it cannot experiment in making men; or even in watching to see what the first men make. An inventor can advance step by step in the construction of an aeroplane, even if he is only experimenting with sticks and scraps of metal in his own back-yard. But he cannot watch the Missing Link evolving in his own back-yard. If he has made a mistake in his calculations, the aeroplane will correct it by crashing to the ground. But if he has made a mistake about the arboreal habitat of his ancestor, he cannot see his arboreal ancestor falling off the tree. He cannot keep a cave-man like a cat in the back-yard and watch him to see whether he does really practice cannibalism or carry off his mate on the principles of marriage by capture. He cannot keep a tribe of primitive men like a pack of hounds and notice how far they are influenced by the herd instinct. If he sees a particular bird behave in a particular way, he can get other birds and see if they behave in that way; but if he finds a skull, or the scrap of a skull, in the hollow of a hill, he cannot multiply it into a vision of the valley of dry bones. In dealing with a past that has almost entirely perished, he can only go by evidence and not by experiment. And there is hardly enough evidence to be even evidential. Thus while most science moves in a sort of curve, being constantly corrected by new evidence, this science flies off into space in a straight line uncorrected by anything. But the habit of forming conclusions, as they can really be formed in more fruitful fields, is so fixed in the scientific mind that it cannot resist talking like this. It talks about the idea suggested by one scrap of bone as if it were something like the aeroplane which is constructed at last out of whole scrapheaps of scraps of metal. The trouble with the professor of the prehistoric is that he cannot scrap his scrap. The marvellous and triumphant aeroplane is made out of a hundred mistakes. The student of origins can only make one mistake and stick to it.

We talk very truly of the patience of science; but in this department it would be truer to talk of the impatience of science. Owing to the difficulty above described, the theorist is in far too much of a hurry. We have a series of hypotheses so hasty that they may well be called fancies, and cannot in any case be further corrected by facts. The most empirical anthropologist is here as limited as an antiquary. He can only cling to a fragment of the past and has no way of increasing it for the future He can only clutch his fragment of fact, almost as the primitive man clutched his fragment of flint. And indeed he does deal with it in much the same way and for much the same reason. It is his tool and his only tool. It is his weapon and his only weapon. He often wields it with a fanaticism far in excess of anything shown by men of science when they can collect more facts from experience and even add new facts by experiment. Sometimes the professor with his bone becomes almost as dangerous as a dog with his bone. And the dog at least does not deduce a theory from it, proving that mankind is going to the dogs--or that it came from them.

For instance, I have pointed out the difficulty of keeping a monkey and watching it evolve into a man. Experimental evidence of such an evolution being impossible, the professor is not content to say (as most of us would be ready to say) that such an evolution is likely enough anyhow. He produces his little bone, or little collection of bones, and deduces the most marvellous things from it. He found in Java a piece of a skull, seeming by its contour to be smaller than the human. Somewhere near it he found an upright thigh-bone and in the same scattered fashion some teeth that were not human. If they all form part of one creature, which is doubtful, our conception of the creature would be almost equally doubtful. But the effect on popular science was to produce a complete and even complex figure, finished down to the last details of hair and habits. He was given a name as if he were an ordinary historical character. People talked of Pithecanthropus as of Pitt or Fox or Napoleon. Popular histories published portraits of him like the portraits of Charles the First and George the Fourth. A detailed drawing was reproduced, carefully shaded, to show that the very hairs of his head were all numbered No uninformed person looking at its carefully lined face and wistful eyes would imagine for a moment that this was the portrait of a thigh-bone; or of a few teeth and a fragment of a cranium. In the same way people talked about him as if he were an individual whose influence and character were familiar to us all. I have just read a story in a magazine about Java, and how modern white inhabitants of that island are prevailed on to misbehave themselves by the personal influence of poor old Pithecanthropus. That the modern inhabitants of Java misbehave themselves I can very readily believe; but I do not imagine that they need any encouragement from the discovery of a few highly doubtful bones. Anyhow, those bones are far too few and fragmentary and dubious to fill up the whole of the vast void that does in reason and in reality lie between man and his bestial ancestors, if they were his ancestors. On the assumption of that evolutionary connection (a connection which I am not in the least concerned to deny), the really arresting and remarkable fact is the comparative absence of any such remains recording that connection at that point. The sincerity of Darwin really admitted this; and that is how we came to use such a term as the Missing Link. But the dogmatism of Darwinians has been too strong for the agnosticism of Darwin; and men have insensibly fallen into turning this entirely negative term into a positive image. They talk of searching for the habits and habitat of the Missing Link; as if one were to talk of being on friendly terms with the gap in a narrative or the hole in an argument, of taking a walk with a non-sequitur or dining with an undistributed middle.

In this sketch, therefore, of man in his relation to certain religious and historical problems, I shall waste no further space on these speculations on the nature of man before he became man. His body may have been evolved from the brutes; but we know nothing of any such transition that throws the smallest light upon his soul as it has shown itself in history. Unfortunately the same school of writers pursue the same style of reasoning when they come to the first real evidence about the first real men. Strictly speaking of course we know nothing about prehistoric man, for the simple reason that he was prehistoric. The history of prehistoric man is a very obvious contradiction in terms. It is the sort of unreason in which only rationalists are allowed to indulge. If a parson had casually observed that the Flood was ante-diluvian, it is possible that he might be a little chaffed about his logic. If a bishop were to say that Adam was Preadamite, we might think it a little odd. But we are not supposed to notice such verbal trifles when sceptical historians talk of the part of history that is prehistoric. The truth is that they are using the terms historic and prehistoric without any clear test or definition in their minds. What they mean is that there are traces of human lives before the beginning of human stories; and in that sense we do at least know that humanity was before history.

Human civilisation is older than human records. That is the sane way of stating our relations to these remote things. Humanity has left examples of its other arts earlier than the art of writing; or at least of any writing that we can read. But it is certain that the primitive arts were arts; and it is in every way probable that the primitive civilisations were civilisations. The man left a picture of the reindeer, but he did not leave a narrative of how he hunted the reindeer; and therefore what we say of him is hypothesis and not history. But the art he did practise was quite artistic; his drawing was quite intelligent and there is no reason to doubt that his story of the hunt would be quite intelligent, only if it exists it is not intelligible. In short, the prehistoric period need not mean the primitive period, in the sense of the barbaric or bestial period. It does not mean the time before civilisation or the time before arts and crafts. It simply means the time before any connected narratives that we can read. This does indeed make all the practical difference between remembrance and forgetfulness; but it is perfectly possible that there were all sorts of forgotten forms of civilisation, as well as all sorts of forgotten forms of barbarism. And in any case everything indicated that many of these forgotten or half-forgotten social stages were much more civilised and much less barbaric than is vulgarly imagined today. But even about these unwritten histories of humanity, when humanity was quite certainly human, we can only conjecture with the greatest doubt and caution. And unfortunately doubt and caution are the last things commonly encouraged by the loose evolutionism of current culture. For that culture is full of curiosity; and the one thing that it cannot endure is the agony of agnosticism. It was in the Darwinian age that the word first became known and the thing first became impossible.

It is necessary to say plainly that all this ignorance is simply covered by impudence. Statements are made so plainly and positively that men have hardly the moral courage to pause upon them and find that they are without support. The other day a scientific summary of the state of a prehistoric tribe began confidently with the words 'They wore no clothes.' Not one reader in a hundred probably stopped to ask himself how we should come to know whether clothes had once been worn by people of whom everything has perished except a few chips of bone and stone. It was doubtless hoped that we should find a stone hat as well as a stone hatchet. It was evidently anticipated that we might discover an everlasting pair of trousers of the same substance as the everlasting rock. But to persons of a less sanguine temperament it will be immediately apparent that people might wear simple garments, or even highly ornamental garments, without leaving any more traces of them than these people have left. The plaiting of rushes and grasses, for instance, might have become more and more elaborate without in the least becoming more eternal. One civilisation might specialise in things that happened to be perishable, like weaving and embroidery, and not in things that happen to be more permanent, like architecture and sculpture. There have been plenty of examples of such specialist societies. A man of the future finding the ruins of our factory machinery might as fairly say that we were acquainted with iron and with no other substance; and announce the discovery that the proprietor and manager of the factory undoubtedly walked about naked--or possibly wore iron hats and trousers.

It is not contended here that these primitive men did wear clothes any more than they did weave rushes; but merely that we have not enough evidence to know whether they did or not. But it may be worthwhile to look back for a moment at some of the very few things that we do know and that they did do. If we consider them, we shall certainly not find them inconsistent with such ideas as dress and decoration. We do not know whether they decorated other things. We do not know whether they had embroideries, and if they had the embroideries could not be expected to have remained. But we do know that they did have pictures; and the pictures have remained. And there remains with them, as already suggested, the testimony to something that is absolute and unique; that belongs to man and to nothing else except man; that is a difference of kind and not a difference of degree. A monkey does not draw clumsily and a man cleverly;

a monkey does not begin the art of representation and a man carry it to perfection. A monkey does not do it at all; he does not begin to do it at all; he does not begin to begin to do it at all. A line of some kind is crossed before the first faint line can begin.

Another distinguished writer, again, in commenting on the cave drawings attributed to the neolithic men of the reindeer period, said that none of their pictures appeared to have any religious purpose; and he seemed almost to infer that they had no religion. I can hardly imagine a thinner thread of argument than this which reconstructs the very inmost moods of the pre-historic mind from the fact that somebody who has scrawled a few sketches on a rock, from what motive we do not know, for what purpose we do not know, acting under what customs or conventions we do not know, may possibly have found it easier to draw reindeer than to draw religion. He may have drawn it because it was his religious symbol. He may have drawn it because it was not his religious symbol. He may have drawn anything except his religious symbol. He may have drawn his real religious symbol somewhere else; or it may have been deliberately destroyed when it was drawn. He may have done or not done half a million things; but in any case it is an amazing leap of logic to infer that he had no religious symbol, or even to infer from his having no religious symbol that he had no religion. Now this particular case happens to illustrate the insecurity of these guesses very clearly. For a little while afterwards, people discovered not only paintings but sculptures of animals in the caves. Some of these were said to be damaged with dints or holes supposed to be the marks of arrows; and the damaged images were conjectured to be the remains of some magic rite of killing the beasts in effigy; while the undamaged images were explained in connection with another magic rite invoking fertility upon the herds. Here again there is something faintly humorous about the scientific habit of having it both ways. If the image is damaged it proves one superstition and if it is undamaged it proves another. Here again there is a rather reckless jumping to conclusions; it has hardly occurred to the speculators that a crowd of hunters imprisoned in winter in a cave might conceivably have aimed at a mark for fun, as a sort of primitive parlour game. But in any case, if it was done out of superstition, what has become of the thesis that it had nothing to do with religion? The truth is that all this guess work has nothing to do with anything. It is not half such a good parlour game as shooting arrows at a carved reindeer, for it is shooting them into the air.

Such speculators rather tend to forget, for instance, that men in the modern world also sometimes make marks in caves. When a crowd of trippers is conducted through the labyrinth of the Marvelous Grotto or the Magic Stalactite Cavern, it has been observed that hieroglyphics spring into sight where they have passed; initials and inscriptions which the learned refuse to refer to any remote date. But the time will come when these inscriptions will really be of remote date. And if the professors of the future are anything like the professors of the present, they will be able to deduce a vast number of very vivid and interesting things from these cave-writings of the twentieth century. If I know anything about the breed, and if they have not fallen away from the full-blooded confidence of their fathers, they will be able to discover the most fascinating facts about us from the initials left in the Magic Grotto by 'Arry and 'Arriet, possibly in the form of two intertwined A's. From this alone they will know (1) That as the letters are rudely chipped with a blunt pocket knife, the twentieth century possessed no delicate graving-tools and was unacquainted with the art of sculpture. (2) That as the letters are capital letters, our civilization never evolved any small letters or anything like a running hand. (3) That because initial consonants stand together in an unpronounceable fashion, our language was possibly akin to Welsh or more probably of the early Semitic type that ignored vowels. (4) That as the initials of 'Arry and 'Arriet do not in any special fashion profess to be religious symbols, our civilisation possessed no religion. Perhaps the last is about the nearest to the truth; for a civilisation that had religion would have a little more reason.

It is commonly affirmed, again, that religion grew in a very slow and evolutionary manner; and even that it grew not from one cause; but from a combination that might be called a coincidence. Generally speaking, the three chief elements in the combination are, first, the fear of the chief of the tribe (whom Mr. Wells insists on calling, with regrettable familiarity, the Old Man), second, the phenomena of dreams, and third, the sacrificial associations of the harvest and the resurrection symbolised in the growing corn. I may remark in passing that it seems to me very doubtful psychology to refer one living and single spirit to three dead and disconnected causes, if they were merely dead and disconnected causes. Suppose Mr. Wells, in one of his fascinating novels of the future, were to tell us that there would arise among men a new and as yet nameless passion, of which men will dream as they dream of first love, for which they will die as they die for a flag and a fatherland. I think we should be a little puzzled if he told us that this singular sentiment would be a combination of the habit of smoking Woodbines, the increase of the income tax and the pleasure of a motorist in exceeding the speed limit. We could not easily imagine this, because we could not imagine any connection between the three or any common feeling that could include them all. Nor could anyone imagine any connection between corn and dreams and an old chief with a spear, unless there was already a common feeling to include them all. But if there was such a common feeling it could only be the religious feeling; and these things could not be the beginnings of a religious feeling that existed already. I think anybody's common sense will tell him that it is far more likely that this sort of mystical sentiment did exist already; and that in the light of it dreams and kings and corn-fields could appear mystical then, as they can appear mystical now.

For the plain truth is that all this is a trick of making things seem distant and dehumanised, merely by pretending not to understand things that we do understand. It is like saying that prehistoric men had an ugly and uncouth habit of opening their mouths wide at intervals and stuffing strange substances into them, as if we had never heard of eating. It is like saying that the terrible Troglodytes of the Stone Age lifted alternate legs in rotation, as if we never heard of walking. If it were meant to touch the mystical nerve and awaken us to the wonder of walking and eating, it might be a legitimate fancy. As it is here intended to kill the mystical nerve and deaden us to the wonder of religion, it is irrational rubbish. It pretends to find some thing incomprehensible in the feelings that we all comprehend. Who does not find dreams mysterious, and feel that they lie on the dark borderland of being? Who does not feel the death and resurrection of the growing things of the earth as something near to the secret of the universe? Who does not understand that there must always be the savour of something sacred about authority and the solidarity that is the soul of the tribe? If there be any anthropologist who really finds these things remote and impossible to realise, we can say nothing of that scientific gentleman except that he has not got so large and enlightened a mind as a primitive man. To me it seems obvious that nothing but a spiritual sentiment already active could have clothed these separate and diverse things with sanctity. To say that religion came from reverencing a chief or sacrificing at a harvest is to put a highly elaborate cart before a really primitive horse. It is like saying that the impulse to draw pictures came from the contemplation of the pictures of reindeers in the cave. In other words, it is explaining painting by saying that it arose out of the work of painters; or accounting for art by saying that it arose out of art. It is even more like saying that the thing we call poetry arose as the result of certain customs; such as that of an ode being officially composed to celebrate the advent of spring; or that of a young man rising at a regular hour to listen to the skylark and then writing his report on a piece of paper. It is quite true that young men often become poets in the spring; and it is quite true that when once there are poets, no mortal power can restrain them from writing about the skylark. But the poems did not exist before the poets. The poetry did not arise out of the poetic forms. In other words, it is hardly an adequate explanation of how a thing appeared for the first time to say it existed already. Similarly, we cannot say that religion arose out of the religious forms, because that is only another way of saying that it only arose when it existed already. It needed a certain sort of mind to see that there was anything mystical about the dreams or the dead, as it needed a particular sort of mind to see that there was any thing poetical about the skylark or the spring. That mind was presumably what we call the human mind, very much as it exists to this day; for mystics still meditate upon death and dreams as poets still write about spring and skylarks. But there is not the faintest hint to suggest that anything short of the human mind we know feels any of these mystical associations at all. A cow in a field seems to derive no lyrical impulse or instruction from her unrivalled opportunities for listening to the skylark. And similarly there is no reason to suppose that live sheep will ever begin to use dead sheep as the basis of a system of elaborate ancestor-worship. It is true that in the spring a young quadruped's fancy may lightly turn to thoughts of love, but no succession of springs has ever led it to turn however lightly to thoughts of literature. And in the same way, while it is true that a dog has dreams, while most other quadrupeds do not seem even to have that, we have waited a long time for the dog to develop his dreams into an elaborate system or religious ceremonial. We have waited so long that we have really ceased to expect it; and we no more look to see a dog apply his dreams to ecclesiastical construction than to see him examine his dreams by the rules of psycho-analysis. It is obvious, in short, that for some reason or other these natural experiences, and even natural excitements, never do pass the line that separates them from creative expression like art and religion, in any creature except man. They never do, they never have, and it is now to all appearance very improbable that they ever will. It is not impossible, in the sense of self-contradictory, that we should see cows fasting from grass every Friday or going on their knees as in the old legend about Christmas Eve. It is not in that sense impossible that cows should contemplate death until they can lift up a sublime psalm of lamentation to the tune the old cow died of. It is not in that sense impossible that they should express their hopes of a heavenly career in a symbolic dance, in honour of the cow that jumped over the moon. It may be that the dog will at last have laid in a sufficient store of dreams to enable him to build a temple to Cerberus as a sort of canine trinity. It may be that his dreams have already begun to turn into visions capable of verbal expression, in some revelation about the Dog Star as the spiritual home for lost dogs. These things are logically possible, in the sense that it is logically difficult to prove the universal negative which we call an impossibility. But all that instinct for the probable, which we call common sense, must long ago have told us that the animals are not to all appearance evolving in that sense; and that, to say the least, we are not likely to have any personal evidence of their passing from the animal experience to the human experiments. But spring and death and even dreams, considered merely as experiences, are their experiences as much as ours. The only possible conclusion is that these experiences, considered as experiences, do not generate anything like a religious sense in any mind except a mind like ours. We come back to the fact of a certain kind of mind that was already alive and alone. It was unique and it could make creeds as it could make cave-drawings. The materials for religion had lain there for countless ages like the materials for everything else; but the power of religion was in the mind. Man could already see in these things the riddles and hints and hopes that he still sees in them. He could not only dream but dream about dreams. He could not only see the dead but see the shadow of death; and was possessed with that mysterious mystification that forever finds death incredible.

It is quite true that we have even these hints chiefly about man when he unmistakably appears as man. We cannot affirm this or anything else about the alleged animal originally connecting man and the brutes. But that is only because he is not an animal but an allegation. We cannot be certain the Pithecanthropus ever worshipped, because we cannot be certain that he ever lived. He is only a vision called up to fill the void that does in fact yawn between the first creatures who were certainly men and any other creatures that are certainly apes or other animals. A few very doubtful fragments are scraped together to suggest such an intermediate creature because it is required by a certain philosophy; but nobody supposes that these are sufficient to establish anything philosophical even in support of that philosophy. A scrap of skull found in Java cannot establish anything about religion or about the absence of religion. If there ever was any such ape-man, he may have exhibited as much ritual in religion as a man or as much simplicity in religion as an ape. He may have been a mythologist or he may have been a myth. It might be interesting to inquire whether this mystical quality appeared in a transition from the ape to the man, if there were really any types of the transition to inquire about. In other words, the missing link might or might not be mystical if he were not missing. But compared with the evidence we have of real human beings, we have no evidence that he was a human being or a half-human being or a being at all. Even the most extreme evolutionists do not attempt to deduce any evolutionary views about the origin of religion from him. Even in trying to prove that religion grew slowly from rude or irrational sources, they begin their proof with the first men who were men. But their own proof only proves that the men who were already men were already mystics. They used the rude and irrational elements as only men and mystics can use them. We come back once more to the simple truth; that at sometime too early for these critics to trace, a transition had occurred to which bones and stones cannot in their nature bear witness; and man became a living soul.

Touching this matter of the origin of religion, the truth is that those who are thus trying to explain it are trying to explain it away. Subconsciously they feel that it looks less formidable when thus lengthened out into a gradual and almost invisible process. But in fact this perspective entirely falsifies the reality of experience. They bring together two things that are totally different, the stray hints of evolutionary origins and the solid and self-evident block of humanity, and try to shift their standpoint till they see them in a single foreshortened line. But it is an optical illusion. Men do not in fact stand related to monkeys or missing links in any such chain as that in which men stand related to men. There may have been intermediate creatures whose faint traces can be found here and there in the huge gap. Of these beings, if they ever existed, it may be true that they were things very unlike men or men very unlike ourselves. But of prehistoric men, such as those called the cave-men or the reindeer men, it is not true in any sense whatever. Prehistoric men of that sort were things exactly like men and men exceedingly like our selves. They only happened to be men about whom we do not know much, for the simple reason that they have left no records or chronicles; but all that we do know about them makes them just as human and ordinary as men in a medieval manor or a Greek city.

Looking from our human standpoint up the long perspective of humanity, we simply recognise this thing as human. If we had to recognise it as animal we should have had to recognise it as abnormal. If we chose to look through the other end of the telescope, as I have done more than once in these speculations, if we chose to project the human figure forward out of an unhuman world, we could only say that one of the animals had obviously gone mad. But seeing the thing from the right end, or rather from the inside, we know it is sanity; and we know that these primitive men were sane. We hail a certain human freemasonry wherever we see it, in savages, in foreigners or in historical characters. For instance, all we can infer from primitive legend, and all we know of barbaric life, supports a certain moral and even mystical idea of which the commonest symbol is clothes. For clothes are very literally vestments and man wears them because he is a priest. It is true that even as an animal he is here different from the animals. Nakedness is not nature to him; it is not his life but rather his death; even in the vulgar sense of his death of cold. But clothes are worn for dignity or decency or decoration where they are not in any way wanted for warmth. It would sometimes appear that they are valued for ornament before they are valued for use. It would almost always appear that they are felt to have some connection with decorum. Conventions of this sort vary a great deal with various times and places; and there are some who cannot get over this reflection, and for whom it seems a sufficient argument for letting all conventions slide. They never tire of repeating, with simple wonder, that dress is different in the Cannibal Islands and in Camden Town; they cannot get any further and throw up the whole idea of decency in despair. They might as well say that because there have been hats of a good many different shapes, and some rather eccentric shapes, therefore hats do not matter or do not exist. They would probably add that there is no such thing as sunstroke or going bald. Men have felt everywhere that certain norms were necessary to fence off and protect certain private things from contempt or coarse misunderstanding; and the keeping of those forms, whatever they were, made for dignity and mutual respect. The fact that they mostly refer, more or less remotely, to the relations of the sexes illustrates the two facts that must be put at the very beginning of the record of the race. The first is the fact that original sin is really original. Not merely in theology but in history it is a thing rooted in the origins. Whatever else men have believed, they have all believed that there is something the matter with mankind. This sense of sin has made it impossible to be natural and have no clothes, just as it has made it impossible to be natural and have no laws. But above all it is to be found in that other fact, which is the father and mother of all laws as it is itself founded on a father and mother; the thing that is before all thrones and even all commonwealths.

That fact is the family. Here again we must keep the enormous proportions of a normal thing clear of various modifications and degrees and doubts more or less reasonable, like clouds clinging about a mountain. It may be that what we call the family had to fight its way from or through various anarchies and aberrations; but it certainly survived them and is quite as likely as not to have also preceded them. As we shall see in the case of communism and nomadism, more formless things could and did lie on the flank of societies that had taken a fixed form; but there is nothing to show that the form did not exist before the formlessness. What is vital is that form is more important than formlessness; and that the material called mankind has taken this form. For instance, of the rules revolving round sex, which were recently mentioned, none is more curious than the savage custom commonly called the couvade. That seems like a law out of topsyturvydom; by which the father is treated as if he were the mother. In any case it clearly involves the mystical sense of sex; but many have maintained that it is really a symbolic act by which the father accepts the responsibility of fatherhood. In that case that grotesque antic is really a very solemn act; for it is the foundation of all we call the family and all we know as human society. Some groping in these dark beginnings have said that mankind was once under a matriarchy; I suppose that under a matriarchy it would not be called mankind but womankind. But others have conjectured that what is called matriarchy was simply moral anarchy, in which the mother alone remained fixed because all the fathers were fugitive and irresponsible. Then came the moment when the man decided to guard and guide what he had created. So he became the head of the family, not as a bully with a big club to beat women with, but rather as a respectable person trying to be a responsible person. Now all that might be perfectly true, and might even have been the first family act, and it would still be true that man then for the first time acted like a man, and therefore for the first time became fully a man. But it might quite as well be true that the matriarchy or moral anarchy, or whatever we call it, was only one of the hundred social dissolutions or barbaric backslidings which may have occurred at intervals in prehistoric as they certainly did in historic times. A symbol like the couvade, if it was really such a symbol, may have commemorated the suppression of a heresy rather than the first rise of a religion. We cannot conclude with any certainty about these things, except in their big results in the building of mankind, but we can say in what style the bulk of it and the best of it is built. We can say that the family is the unit of the state; that it is the cell that makes up the formation. Round the family do indeed gather the sanctities that separate men from ants and bees. Decency is the curtain of that tent; liberty is the wall of that city; property is but the family farm; honour is but the family flag. In the practical proportions of human history, we come back to that fundamental of the father and the mother and the child. It has been said already that if this story cannot start with religious assumptions, it must none the less start with some moral or metaphysical assumptions, or no sense can be made of the story of man. And this is a very good instance of that alternative necessity. If we are not of those who begin by invoking a divine Trinity, we must none the less invoke a human Trinity; and see that triangle repeated everywhere in the pattern of the world. For the highest event in history, to which all history looks forward and leads up, is only something that is at once the reversal and the renewal of that triangle. Or rather it is the one triangle superimposed so as to intersect the other, making a sacred pentacle of which, in a mightier sense than that of the magicians, the fiends are afraid. The old Trinity was of father and mother and child and is called the human family. The new is of child and mother and father and has the name of the Holy Family. It is in no way altered except in being entirely reversed; just as the world which is transformed was not in the least different, except in being turned upside-down.

THE ANTIQUITY OF CIVILISATION

The modern man looking at the most ancient origins has been like a man watching for daybreak in a strange land; and expecting to see that dawn breaking behind bare uplands or solitary peaks. But that dawn is breaking behind the black bulk of great cities long builded and lost for us in the original night; colossal cities like the houses of giants, in which even the carved ornamental animals are taller than the palm-trees; in which the painted portrait can be twelve times the size of the man; with tombs like mountains of man set four-square and pointing to the stars; with winged and bearded bulls standing and staring enormous at the gates of temples; standing still eternally as if a stamp would shake the world. The dawn of history reveals a humanity already civilized. Perhaps it reveals a civilisation already old. And among other more important things, it reveals the folly of most of the generalisations about the previous and unknown period when it was really young. The two first human societies of which we have any reliable and detailed record are Babylon and Egypt. It so happens that these two vast and splendid achievements of the genius of the ancients bear witness against two of the commonest and crudest assumptions of the culture of the moderns. If we want to get rid of half the nonsense about nomads and cave-men and the old man of the forest, we need only look steadily at the two solid and stupendous facts called Egypt and Babylon.

Of course most of these speculators who are talking about primitive men are thinking about modern savages. They prove their progressive evolution by assuming that a great part of the human race has not progressed or evolved; or even changed in any way at all. I do not agree with their theory of change; nor do I agree with their dogma of things unchangeable. I may not believe that civilised man has had so rapid and recent a progress; but I cannot quite understand why uncivilised man should be so mystically immortal and immutable. A somewhat simpler mode of thought and speech seems to me to be needed throughout this inquiry. Modern savages cannot be exactly like primitive man, because they are not primitive. Modern savages are not ancient because they are modern. Something has happened to their race as much as to ours, during the thousands of years of our existence and endurance on the earth. They have had some experiences, and have presumably acted on them if not profited by them. Like the rest of us. They have had some environment, and even some change of environment, and have presumably adapted themselves to it in a proper and decorous evolutionary manner. This would be true even if the experiences were mild or the environment dreary; for there is an effect in mere time when it takes the moral form of monotony. But it has appeared to a good many intelligent and well-informed people quite as probable that the experience of the savages has been that of a decline from civilisation. Most of those who criticise this view do not seem to have any very clear notion of what a decline from civilisation would be like. Heaven help them, it is likely enough that they will soon find out. They seem to be content if cave-men and cannibal islanders have some things in common, such as certain particular implements. But it is obvious on the face of it that any peoples reduced for any reason to a ruder life would have some things in common. If we lost all our firearms we should make bows and arrows; but we should not necessarily resemble in every way the first men who made bows and arrows. It is said that the Russians in their great retreat were so short of armament that they fought with clubs cut in the wood. But a professor of the future would err in supposing that the Russian army of 1916 was a naked Scythian tribe that had never been out of the wood. It is like saying that a man in his second childhood must exactly copy his first. A baby is bald like an old man; but it would be an error for one ignorant of infancy to infer that the baby had a long white beard. Both a baby and an old man walk with difficulty; but he who shall expect the old gentleman to lie on his back, and kick joyfully instead, will be disappointed.

It is therefore absurd to argue that the first pioneers of humanity must have been identical with some of the last and most stagnant leavings of it. There were almost certainly some things, there were probably many things, in which the two were widely different or flatly contrary. An example of the way in which this distinction works, and an example essential to our argument here, is that of the nature and origin of government I have already alluded to Mr. H. G. Wells and the Old Man, with whom he appears to be on such intimate terms. If we considered the cold facts of prehistoric evidence for this portrait of the prehistoric chief of the tribe, we could only excuse it by saying that its brilliant and versatile author simply forgot for a moment that he was supposed to be writing a history, and dreamed he was writing one of his own very wonderful and imaginative romances. At least I cannot imagine how he can possibly know that the prehistoric ruler was called the Old Man or that court etiquette requires it to be spelt with capital letters. He says of the same potentate, 'No one was allowed to touch his spear or to sit in his seat.' I have difficulty in believing that anybody has dug up a prehistoric spear with a prehistoric label, 'Visitors are Requested not to Touch,' or a complete throne with the inscription, 'Reserved for the Old Man.' But it may be presumed that the writer, who can hardly be supposed to be merely making up things out of his own head, was merely taking for granted this very dubious parallel between the prehistoric and the decivilised man. It may be that in certain savage tribes the chief is called the Old Man and nobody is allowed to touch his spear or sit on his seat. It may be that in those cases he is surrounded with superstitious and traditional terrors; and it may be that in those cases, for all I know, he is despotic and tyrannical. But there is not a grain of evidence that primitive government was despotic and tyrannical. It may have been, of course, for it may have been anything or even nothing; it may not have existed at all. But the despotism in certain dingy and decayed tribes in the twentieth century does not prove that the first men were ruled despotically. It does not even suggest it; it does not even begin to hint at it. If there is one fact we really can prove, from the history that we really do know, it is that despotism can be a development, often a late development and very often indeed the end of societies that have been highly democratic. A despotism may almost be defined as a tired democracy. As fatigue falls on a community, the citizens are less inclined for that eternal vigilance which has truly been called the price of liberty; and they prefer to arm only one single sentinel to watch the city while they sleep. It is also true that they sometimes needed him for some sudden and militant act of reform; it is equally true that he often took advantage of being the strong man armed to be a tyrant like some of the Sultans of the East. But I cannot see why the Sultan should have appeared any earlier in history than many other human figures. On the contrary, the strong man armed obviously depends upon the superiority of his armour, and armament of that sort comes with more complex civilisation. One man may kill twenty with a machine-gun; it is obviously less likely that he could do it with a piece of flint. As for the current cant about the strongest man ruling by force and fear, it is simply a nursery fairy-tale about a giant with a hundred hands. Twenty men could hold down the strongest strong man in any society, ancient or modern. Undoubtedly they might admire, in a romantic and poetical sense, the man who was really the strongest; but that is quite a different thing, and is as purely moral and even mystical as the admiration for the purest or the wisest. But the spirit that endures the mere cruelties and caprices of an established despot is the spirit of an ancient and settled and probably stiffened society, not the spirit of a new one. As his name implies, the Old Man is the ruler of an old humanity.

It is far more probable that a primitive society was something like a pure democracy. To this day the comparatively simple agricultural communities are by far the purest democracies. Democracy is a thing which is always breaking down through the complexity of civilisation. Anyone who likes may state it by saying that democracy is the foe of civilisation. But he must remember that some of us really prefer democracy to civilisation, in the sense of preferring democracy to complexity. Anyhow, peasants tilling patches of their own land in a rough equality, and meeting to vote directly under a village tree, are the most truly self-governing of men. It is surely as likely as not that such a simple idea was found in the first condition of even simpler men. Indeed the despotic vision is exaggerated, even if we do not regard the men as men. Even on an evolutionary assumption of the most materialistic sort, there is really no reason why men should not have had at least as much camaraderie as rats or rooks. Leadership of some sort they doubtless had, as have the gregarious animals; but leadership implies no such irrational servility as that attributed to the superstitious subjects of the Old Man. There was doubtless some body corresponding, to use Tennyson's expression, to the many-wintered crow that leads the clanging rookery home. But I fancy that if that venerable fowl began to act after the fashion of some Sultans in ancient and decayed Asia, it would become a very clanging rookery and the many-wintered crow would not see many more winters. It may be remarked, in this connection, but even among animals it would seem that something else is respected more than bestial violence, if it be only the familiarity which in men is called tradition or the experience which in men is called wisdom. I do not know if crows really follow the oldest crow, but if they do they are certainly not following the strongest crow. And I do know, in the human case, that if some ritual of seniority keeps savages reverencing somebody called Old Man, then at least they have not our own servile sentimental weakness for worshipping the Strong Man.

It may be said then that primitive government, like primitive art and religion and everything else, is very imperfectly known or rather guessed at; but that it is at least as good a guess to suggest that it was as popular as a Balkan or Pyrenean village as that it was as capricious and secret as a Turkish divan. Both the mountain democracy and the oriental palace are modern in the sense that they are still there, or are some sort of growth of history; but of the two the palace has much more the look of being an accumulation and a corruption, the village much more the look of being a really unchanged and primitive thing. But my suggestions at this point do not go beyond expressing a wholesome doubt about the current assumption. I think it interesting, for instance, that liberal institutions have been traced even by moderns back to barbarians or undeveloped states, when it happened to be convenient for the support of some race or nation or philosophy. So the Socialists profess that their ideal of communal property existed in very early times. So the Jews are proud of the Jubilees or juster redistributions under their ancient law. So the Teutonists boasted of tracing parliaments and juries and various popular things among the Germanic tribes of the north. So the Celtophiles and those testifying to the wrongs of Ireland have pleaded the more equal justice of the clan system, to which the Irish chiefs bore witness before Strongbow. The strength of the case varies in the different cases; but as there is some case for all of them, I suspect there is some case for the general proposition that popular institutions of some sort were by no means uncommon in early and simple societies. Each of these separate schools were making the admission to prove a particular modern thesis; but taken together they suggest a more ancient and general truth, that there was something more in prehistoric councils than ferocity and fear. Each of these separate theorists had his own axe to grind, but he was willing to use a stone axe; and he manages to suggest that the stone axe might have been as republican as the guillotine.

But the truth is that the curtain rises upon the play already in progress. In one sense it is a true paradox that there was history before history. But it is not the irrational paradox implied in prehistoric history; for it is a history we do not know. Very probably it was exceedingly like the history we do know, except in the one detail that we do not know it. It is thus the very opposite of the pretentious prehistoric history, which professes to trace everything in a consistent course from the amoeba to the anthropoid and from the anthropoid to the agnostic. So far from being a question of our knowing all about queer creatures very different from ourselves, they were very probably people very like ourselves, except that we know nothing about them. In other words, our most ancient records only reach back to a time when humanity had long been human, and even long been civilised. The most ancient records we have not only mention but take for granted things like kings and priests and princes and assemblies of the people; they describe communities that are roughly recognisable as communities in our own sense. Some of them are despotic; but we cannot tell that they have always been despotic. Some of them may be already decadent and nearly all are mentioned as if they were old. We do not know what really happened in the world before those records; but the little we do know would leave us anything but astonished if we learnt that it was very much like what happens in this world now. There would be nothing inconsistent or confounding about the discovery that those unknown ages were full of republics collapsing under monarchies and rising again as republics, empires expanding and finding colonies and then losing colonies. Kingdoms combining again into world states and breaking up again into small nationalities, classes selling themselves into slavery and marching out once more into liberty; all that procession of humanity which may or may not be a progress but most assuredly a romance. But the first chapters of the romance have been torn out of the book; and we shall never read them.

It is so also with the more special fancy about evolution and social stability. According to the real records available, barbarism and civilisation were not successive states in the progress of the world. They were conditions that existed side by side, as they still exist side by side. There were civilisations then as there are civilisations now; there are savages now as there were savages then. It is suggested that all men passed through a nomadic stage; but it is certain that there are some who have never passed out of it, and it seems not unlikely that there were some who never passed into it. It is probable that from very primitive times the static tiller of the soil and the wandering shepherd were two distinct types of men; and the chronological rearrangement of them is but a mark of that mania for progressive stages that has largely falsified history. It is suggested that there was a communist stage, in which private property was everywhere unknown, a whole humanity living on the negation of property; but the evidences of this negation are themselves rather negative. Redistributions of property, jubilees, and agrarian laws, occur at various intervals and in various forms; but that humanity inevitably passed through a communist stage seems as doubtful as the parallel proposition that humanity will inevitably return to it. It is chiefly interesting as evidence that the boldest plans for the future invoke the authority of the past; and that even a revolutionary seeks to satisfy himself that he is also a reactionary. There is an amusing parallel example in the case of what is called feminism. In spite of all the pseudo-scientific gossip about marriage by capture and the cave-man beating the cave-woman with a club, it may be noted that as soon as feminism became a fashionable cry, it was insisted that human civilisation in its first stage had been a matriarchy. Apparently it was the cave-woman who carried the club. Anyhow all these ideas are little better than guesses; they have a curious way of following the fortune of modern theories and fads. In any case they are not history in the sense of record; and we may repeat that when it comes to record, the broad truth is that barbarism and civilisation have always dwelt side by side in the world, the civilisation sometimes spreading to absorb the barbarians, sometimes decaying into relative barbarism, and in almost all cases possessing in a more finished form certain ideas and institutions which the barbarians possess in a ruder form; such as government or social authority, the arts and especially the decorative arts, mysteries and taboos of various kinds especially surrounding the matter of sex, and some form of that fundamental thing which is the chief concern of this enquiry; the thing that we call religion.

Now Egypt and Babylon, those two primeval monsters, might in this matter have been specially provided as models. They might almost be called working models to show how these modern theories do not work. The two great truths we know about these two great cultures happen to contradict flatly the two current fallacies which have just been considered. The story of Egypt might have been invented to point the moral that man does not necessarily begin with despotism because he is barbarous, but very often finds his way to despotism because he is civilised. He finds it because he is experienced; or, what is often much the same thing, because he is exhausted And the story of Babylon might have been invented to point the moral that man need not be a nomad or a communist before he becomes a peasant or a citizen, and that such cultures are not always in successive stages but often in contemporary states. Even touching these great civilisations with which our written history begins there is a temptation of course to be too ingenious or too cocksure. We can read the bricks of Babylon in a very different sense from that in which we guess about the Cup and Ring stones; and we do definitely know what is meant by the animals in the Egyptian hieroglyphic as we know nothing of the animal in the neolithic cave. But even here the admirable archeologists who have deciphered line after line of miles of hieroglyphics may be tempted to read too much between the lines; even the real authority on Babylon may forget how fragmentary is his hard-won knowledge; may forget that Babylon has only heaved half a brick at him, though half a brick is better than no cuneiform. But some truths, historic and not prehistoric, dogmatic and not evolutionary, facts and not fancies, do indeed emerge from Egypt and Babylon; and these two truths are among them.

Egypt is a green ribbon along the river edging the dark red desolation of the desert. It is a proverb, and one of vast antiquity, that it is created by the mysterious bounty and almost sinister benevolence of the Nile. When we first hear of Egyptians they are living as in a string of river-side villages, in small and separate but co-operative communities along the bank of the Nile. Where the river branched into the broad Delta there was traditionally the beginning of a somewhat different district or people; but this need not complicate the main truth. These more or less independent though interdependent peoples were considerably civilised already. They had a sort of heraldry; that is, decorative art used for symbolic and social purposes; each sailing the Nile under its own ensign representing some bird or animal. Heraldry involves two things of enormous importance to normal humanity; the combination of the two making that noble thing called co-operation; on which rest all peasantries and peoples that are free. The art of heraldry means independence; an image chosen by the imagination to express the individuality. The science of heraldry means interdependence; an agreement between different bodies to recognise different images; a science of imagery. We have here therefore exactly that compromise of co-operation between free families or groups which is the most normal mode of life for humanity and is particularly apparent wherever men own their own land and live on it. With the very mention of the image of bird and beast the student of mythology will murmur the word 'totem' almost in his sleep. But to my mind much of the trouble arises from his habit of saying such words as if in his sleep. Throughout this rough outline I have made a necessarily inadequate attempt to keep on the inside rather than the outside of such things; to consider them where possible in terms of thought and not merely in terms of terminology. There is very little value in talking about totems unless we have some feeling of what it really felt like to have a totem. Granted that they had totems and we have no totems; was it because they had more fear of animals or more familiarity with animals? Did a man whose totem was a wolf feel like a were-wolf or like a man running away from a were-wolf? Did he feel like Uncle Remus about Brer Wolf or like St.

Francis about his brother the wolf, or like Mowgli about his brothers the wolves? Was a totem a thing like the British lion or a thing like the British bull-dog? Was the worship of a totem like the feeling of niggers about Mumbo Jumbo, or of children about Jumbo? I have never read any book of folk-lore, however learned, that gave me any light upon this question, which I think by far the most important one. I will confine myself to repeating that the earliest Egyptian communities had a common understanding about the images that stood for their individual states; and that this amount of communication is prehistoric in the sense that it is already there at the beginning of history. But as history unfolds itself, this question of communication is clearly the main question of these riverside communities. With the need of communication comes the need of a common government and the growing greatness and spreading shadow of the king. The other binding force besides the king, and perhaps older than the king, is the priesthood; and the priesthood has presumably even more to do with these ritual symbols and signals by which men can communicate. And here in Egypt arose probably the primary and certainly the typical invention to which we owe all history, and the whole difference between the historic and the prehistoric: the archetypal script, the art of writing.

The popular pictures of these primeval empires are not half so popular as they might be. There is shed over them the shadow of an exaggerated gloom, more than the normal and even healthy sadness of heathen men. It is part of the same sort of secret pessimism that loves to make primitive man a crawling creature, whose body is filth and whose soul is fear. It comes of course from the fact that men are moved most by their religion; especially when it is irreligion. For them anything primary and elemental must be evil. But it is the curious consequence that while we have been deluged with the wildest experiments in primitive romance, they have all missed the real romance of being primitive. They have described scenes that are wholly imaginary, in which the men of the Stone Age are men of stone like walking statues; in which the Assyrians or Egyptians are as stiff or as painted as their own most archaic art. But none of these makers of imaginary scenes have tried to imagine what it must really have been like to see those things as fresh which we see as familiar. They have not seen a man discovering fire like a child discovering fireworks. They have not seen a man playing with the wonderful invention called the wheel, like a boy playing at putting up a wireless station. They have never put the spirit of youth into their descriptions of the youth of the world. It follows that amid all their primitive or prehistoric fancies there are no jokes. There are not even practical jokes, in connection with the practical inventions. And this is very sharply defined in the particular case of hieroglyphics; for there seems to be serious indication that the whole high human art of scripture or writing began with a joke.

There are some who will learn with regret that it seems to have begun with a pun. The king or the priests or some responsible persons, wishing to send a message up the river in that inconveniently long and narrow territory, hit on the idea of sending it in picture writing, like that of the Red Indian. Like most people who have written picture-writing for fun, he found the words did not always fit. But when the word for taxes sounded rather like the word for pig, he boldly put down a pig as a bad pun and chanced it. So a modern hieroglyphist might represent 'at once' by unscrupulously drawing a hat followed by a series of upright numerals. It was good enough for the Pharaohs and ought to be good enough for him. But it must have been great fun to write or even to read these messages, when writing and reading were really a new thing. And if people must write romances about ancient Egypt (and it seems that neither prayers nor tears nor curses can withhold them from the habit), I suggest that scenes like this would really remind us that the ancient Egyptians were human beings. I suggest that somebody should describe the scene of the great monarch sitting among his priests, and all of them roaring with laughter and bubbling over with suggestions as the royal puns grew more and more wild and indefensible. There might be another scene of almost equal excitement about the decoding of this cipher; the guesses and clues and discoveries having all the popular thrill of a detective story. That is how primitive romance and primitive history really ought to be written. For whatever was the quality of the religious or moral life of remote times, and it was probably much more human than is conventionally supposed, the scientific interest of such a time must have been intense. Words must have been more wonderful than wireless telegraphy; and experiments with common things a series of electric shocks. We are still waiting for somebody to write a lively story of primitive life. The point is in some sense a parenthesis here; but it is connected with the general matter of political development, by the institution which was most active in these first and most fascinating of all the fairy-tales of science.

It is admitted that we owe most of this science to the priests. Modern writers like Mr. Wells cannot be accused of any weakness of sympathy with a pontifical hierarchy; but they agree at least in recognising what pagan priesthoods did for the arts and sciences. Among the more ignorant of the enlightened there was indeed a convention of saying that priests had obstructed progress in all ages; and a politician once told me in a debate that I was resisting modern reforms exactly as some ancient priest probably resisted the discovery of wheels. I pointed out, in reply, that it was far more likely that the ancient priest made the discovery of the wheels. It is overwhelmingly probable that the ancient priest had a great deal to do with the discovery of the art of writing. It is obvious enough in the fact that the very word hieroglyphic is akin to the word hierarchy. The religion of these priests was apparently a more or less tangled polytheism of a type that is more particularly described elsewhere. It passed through a period when it cooperated with the king, another period when it was temporarily destroyed by the king, who happened to be a prince with a private theism of his own, and a third period when it practically destroyed the king and ruled in his stead. But the world has to thank it for many things which it considers common and necessary: and the creators of those common things ought really to have a place among the heroes of humanity. If we were at rest in a real paganism, instead of being restless in a rather irrational reaction from Christianity, we might pay some sort of pagan honour to these nameless makers of mankind. We might have veiled statues of the man who first found fire or the man who first made a boat or the man who first tamed a horse. And if we brought them garlands or sacrifices, there would be more sense in it than in disfiguring our cities with cockney statues of stale politicians and philanthropists. But one of the strange marks of the strength of Christianity is that, since it came, no pagan in our civilisation has been able to be really human.

The point is here, however, that the Egyptian government, whether pontifical or royal, found it more and more necessary to establish communication; and there always went with communication a certain element of coercion. It is not necessarily an indefensible thing that the state grew more despotic as it grew more civilised; it is arguable that it had to grow more despotic in order to grow more civilised. That is the argument for autocracy in every age; and the interest lies in seeing it illustrated in the earliest age. But it is emphatically not true that it was most despotic in the earliest age and grew more liberal in a later age; the practical process of history is exactly the reverse. It is not true that the tribe began in the extreme of terror of the Old Man and his seat and spear; it is probable, at least in Egypt, that the Old Man was rather a New Man armed to attack new conditions. His spear grew longer and longer and his throne rose higher and higher, as Egypt rose into a complex and complete civilisation. That is what I mean by saying that the history of the Egyptian territory is in this the history of the earth; and directly denies the vulgar assumption that terrorism can only come at the beginning and cannot come at the end. We do not know what was the very first condition of the more or less feudal amalgam of land owners, peasants and slaves in the little commonwealths beside the Nile; but it may have been a peasantry of an even more popular sort. What we do know is that it was by experience and education that little commonwealths lose their liberty; that absolute sovereignty is something not merely ancient but rather relatively modern; and it is at the end of the path called progress that men return to the king.

Egypt exhibits, in that brief record of its remotest beginnings, the primary problem of liberty and civilisation. It is the fact that men actually lose variety by complexity. We have not solved the problem properly any more than they did; but it vulgarises the human dignity of the problem itself to suggest that even tyranny has no motive save in tribal terror. And just as the Egyptian example refutes the fallacy about despotism and civilisation, so does the Babylonian example refute the fallacy about civilisation and barbarism. Babylon also we first hear of when it is already civilised; for the simple reason that we cannot hear of anything until it is educated enough to talk. It talks to us in what is called cuneiform; that strange and stiff triangular symbolism that contrasts with the picturesque alphabet of Egypt. However relatively rigid Egyptian art may be, there is always something different from the Babylonian spirit which was too rigid to have any art. There is always a living grace in the lines of the lotus and something of rapidity as well as rigidity in the movement of the arrows and the birds. Perhaps there is something of the restrained but living curve of the river, which makes us in talking of the serpent of old Nile almost think of the Nile as a serpent. Babylon was a civilisation of diagrams rather than of drawings. Mr. W.B. Yeats who has a historical imagination to match his mythological imagination (and indeed the former is impossible without the latter) wrote truly of the men who watched the stars 'from their pedantic Babylon.' The cuneiform was cut upon bricks, of which all their architecture was built up; the bricks were of baked mud and perhaps the material had something in it forbidding the sense of form to develop in sculpture or relief. Theirs was a static but a scientific civilisation, far advanced in the machinery of life and in some ways highly modern. It is said that they had much of the modern cult of the higher spinsterhood and recognised an official class of independent working women. There is perhaps something in that mighty stronghold of hardened mud that suggests the utilitarian activity of a huge hive. But though it was huge it was human; we see many of the same social problems as in ancient Egypt or modern England; and whatever its evils this also was one of the earliest masterpieces of man. It stood, of course, in the triangle formed by the almost legendary rivers of Tigris and Euphrates, and the vast agriculture of its empire, on which its towns depended, was perfected by a highly scientific system of canals. It had by tradition a high intellectual life, though rather philosophic than artistic; and there preside over its primal foundation those figures who have come to stand for the star-gazing wisdom of antiquity; the teachers of Abraham; the Chaldees.

Against this solid society, as against some vast bare wall of brick, there surged age after age the nameless armies of the Nomads. They came out of the deserts where the nomadic life had been lived from the beginning and where it is still lived to-day. It is needless to dwell on the nature of that life; it was obvious enough and even easy enough to follow a herd or a flock which generally found its own grazing-ground and to live on the milk or meat it provided. Nor is there any reason to doubt that this habit of life could give almost every human thing except a home. Many such shepherds or herds men may have talked in the earliest time of all the truths and enigmas of the Book of Job; and of these were Abraham and his children, who have given to the modern world for an endless enigma the almost mono-maniac monotheism of the Jews. But they were a wild people without comprehension of complex social organisation; and a spirit like the wind within them made them wage war on it again and again. The history of Babylonia is largely the history of its defence against the desert hordes; who came on at intervals of a century or two and generally retreated as they came. Some say that an admixture of nomad invasion built at Nineveh the arrogant kingdom of the Assyrians, who carved great monsters upon their temples, bearded bulls with wings like cherubim, and who sent forth many military conquerors who stamped the world as if with such colossal hooves. Assyria was an imperial interlude; but it was an interlude. The main story of all that land is the war between the wandering peoples and the state that was truly static. Presumably in prehistoric times, and certainly in historic times, those wanderers went westward to waste whatever they could find. The last time they came they found Babylon vanished; but that was in historic times and the name of their leader was Mahomet.

Now it is worth while to pause upon that story because, as has been suggested, it directly contradicts the impression still current that nomadism is merely a prehistoric thing and social settlement a comparatively recent thing. There is nothing to show that the Babylonians had ever wandered; there is very little to show that the tribes of the desert ever settled down. Indeed it is probable that this notion of a nomadic stage followed by a static stage has already been abandoned by the sincere and genuine scholars to whose researches we all owe so much. But I am not at issue in this book with sincere and genuine scholars, but with a vast and vague public opinion which has been prematurely spread from certain imperfect investigations, and which has made fashionable a false notion of the whole history of humanity. It is the whole vague notion that a monkey evolved into a man and in the same way a barbarian evolved into a civilised man and therefore at every stage we have to look back to barbarism and forward to civilisation. Unfortunately this notion is in a double sense entirely in the air. It is an atmosphere in which men live rather than a thesis which they defend. Men in that mood are more easily answered by objects than by theories; and it will be well if anyone tempted to make that assumption, in some trivial turn of talk or writing, can be checked for a moment by shutting his eyes and seeing for an instant, vast and vaguely crowded, like a populous precipice, the wonder of the Babylonian wall.

One fact does certainly fall across us like its shadow. Our glimpses of both these early empires show that the first domestic relation had been complicated by something which was less human, but was often regarded as equally domestic. The dark giant called Slavery had been called up like a genius and was labouring on gigantic works of brick and stone. Here again we must not too easily assume that what was backward was barbaric; in the matter of manumission the earlier servitude seems in some ways more liberal than the later; perhaps more liberal than the servitude of the future. To insure food for humanity by forcing part of it to work was after all a very human expedient; which is why it will probably be tried again. But in one sense there is a significance in the old slavery. It stands for one fundamental fact about all antiquity before Christ; something to be assumed from first to last. It is the insignificance of the individual before the State. It was as true of the most democratic City State in Hellas as of any despotism in Babylon. It is one of the signs of this spirit that a whole class of individuals could be insignificant or even invisible. It must be normal because it was needed for what would now be called 'social service.' Somebody said, 'The Man is nothing and the Work is all,' meaning it for a breezy Carlylean commonplace. It was the sinister motto of the heathen Servile State. In that sense there is truth in the traditional vision of vast pillars and pyramids going up under those everlasting skies for ever by the labour of numberless and nameless men, toiling like ants and dying like flies, wiped out by the work of their own hands.

But there are two other reasons for beginning with the two fixed points of Egypt and Babylon. For one thing they are fixed in tradition as the types of antiquity; and history without tradition is dead. Babylon is still the burden of a nursery rhyme, and Egypt (with its enormous population of princesses awaiting reincarnation) is still the topic of an unnecessary number of novels. But a tradition is generally a truth; so long as the tradition is sufficiently popular; even if it is almost vulgar. And there is a significance in this Babylonian and Egyptian element in nursery rhymes and novels; even the news papers, normally so much behind the times, have already got as far as the reign of Tutankhamen. The first reason is full of the common sense of popular legend; it is the simple fact that we do know more of these traditional things than of other contemporary things; and that we always did. All travellers from Herodotus to Lord Carnarvon follow this route. Scientific speculations of to-day do indeed spread out a map of the whole primitive world, with streams of racial emigration or admixture marked in dotted lines everywhere; over spaces which the unscientific medieval map-maker would have been content to call 'Terra incognita,' if he did not fill the inviting blank with a picture of a dragon, to indicate the probable reception given to pilgrims. But these speculations are only speculations at the best; and at the worst the dotted lines can be far more fabulous than the dragon.

There is unfortunately one fallacy here into which it is very easy for men to fall, even those who are most intelligent and perhaps especially those who are most imaginative. It is the fallacy of suppositing that because an idea is greater in the sense of larger, therefore it is greater in the sense of more fundamental and fixed and certain. If a man lives alone in a straw hut in the middle of Thibet, he may be told that he is living in the Chinese Empire; and the Chinese Empire is certainly a splendid and spacious and impressive thing. Or alternatively he may be told that he is living in the British Empire, and be duly impressed. But the curious thing is that in certain mental states he can feel much more certain about the Chinese Empire that he can not see than about the straw hut that he can see. He has some strange magical juggle in his mind, by which his argument begins with the empire though his experience begins with the hut. Sometimes he goes mad and appears to be proving that a straw hut cannot exist in the domains of the Dragon Throne; that it is impossible for such a civilisation as he enjoys to contain such a hovel as he inhabits. But his insanity arises from the intellectual slip of supposing that because China is a large and all-embracing hypothesis, therefore it is something more than a hypothesis. Now modern people are perpetually arguing in this way; and they extend it to things much less real and certain than the Chinese Empire. They seem to forget, for instance, that a man is not even certain of the Solar System as he is certain of the South Downs. The Solar System is a deduction, and doubtless a true deduction; but the point is that it is a very vast and far-reaching deduction and therefore he forgets that it is a deduction at all and treats it as a first principle. He might discover that the whole calculation is a mis-calculation; and the sun and stars and street-lamps would look exactly the same. But he has forgotten that it is a calculation, and is almost ready to contradict the sun if it does not fit into the solar system. If this is a fallacy even in the case of facts pretty well ascertained, such as the Solar System and the Chinese Empire, it is an even more devastating fallacy in connection with theories and other things that are not really ascertained at all. Thus history, especially prehistoric history, has a horrible habit of beginning with certain generalisations about races. I will not describe the disorder and misery this inversion has produced in modern politics. Because the race is vaguely supposed to have produced the nation, men talk as if the nation were something vaguer than the race. Because they have themselves invented a reason to explain a result, they almost deny the result in order to justify the reason. They first treat a Celt as an axiom and then treat an Irishman as an inference. And then they are surprised that a great fighting, roaring Irishman is angry at being treated as an inference. They cannot see that the Irish are Irish whether or no they are Celtic, whether or no there ever were any Celts. And what misleads them once more is the size of the theory; the sense that the fancy is bigger than the fact. A great scattered Celtic race is supposed to contain the Irish, so of course the Irish must depend for their very existence upon it. The same confusion, of course, has eliminated the English and the Germans by swamping them in the Teutonic race; and some tried to prove from the races being at one that the nations could not be at war. But I only give these vulgar and hackneyed examples in passing, as more familiar examples of the fallacy; the matter at issue here is not its application to these modern things but rather to the most ancient things. But the more remote and unrecorded was the racial problem, the more fixed was this curious inverted certainty in the Victorian man of science. To this day it gives a man of those scientific traditions the same sort of shock to question these things, which were only the last inferences when he turned them into first principles. He is still more certain that he is an Aryan even than that he is an Anglo-Saxon, just as he is more certain that he is an Anglo-Saxon than that he is an Englishman. He has never really discovered that he is a European. But he has never doubted that he is an Indo-European. These Victorian theories have shifted a great deal in their shape and scope; but this habit of a rapid hardening of a hypothesis into a theory, and of a theory into an assumption, has hardly yet gone out of fashion. People cannot easily get rid of the mental confusion of feeling that the foundations of history must surely be secure; that the first steps must be safe; that the biggest generalisation must be obvious. But though the contradiction may seem to them a paradox, this is the very contrary of the truth. It is the large thing that is secret and invisible; it is the small thing that is evident and enormous.

Every race on the face of the earth has been the subject of these speculations, and it is impossible even to suggest an outline of the subject. But if we take the European race alone, its history, or rather its prehistory, has undergone many retrospective revolutions in the short period of my own lifetime. It used to be called the Caucasian race; and I read in childhood an account of its collision with the Mongolian race; it was written by Bret Harte and opened with the query 'Or is the Caucasian played out?' Apparently the Caucasian was played out, for in a very short time he had been turned into the Indo-European man; sometimes, I regret to say, proudly presented as the Indo-Germanic man. It seems that the Hindu and the German have similar words for mother or father; there were other similarities between Sanskrit and various Western tongues; and with that all superficial differences between a Hindu and a German seemed suddenly to disappear. Generally this composite person was more conveniently described as the Aryan, and the really important point was that he had marched westward out of those high lands of India where fragments of his language could still be found. When I read this as a child, I had the fancy that after all the Aryan need not have marched westward and left his language behind him; he might also have marched eastward and taken his language with him. If I were to read it now, I should content myself with confessing my ignorance of the whole matter. But as a matter of fact I have great difficulty in reading it now, because it is not being written now. It looks as if the Aryan is also played out. Anyhow he has not merely changed his name but changed his address; his starting-place and his route of travel. One new theory maintains that our race did not come to its present home from the East but from the South. Some say the Europeans did not come from Asia but from Africa. Some have even had the wild idea that the Europeans came from Europe; or rather that they never left it.

Then there is a certain amount of evidence of a more or less prehistoric pressure from the North, such as that which seems to have brought the Greeks to inherit the Cretan culture and so often brought the Gauls over the hills into the fields in Italy. But I merely mention this example of European ethnology to point out that the learned have pretty well boxed the compass by this time; and that I, who am not one of the learned, cannot pretend for a moment to decide where such doctors disagree. But I can use my own common sense, and I sometimes fancy that theirs is a little rusty from want of use. The first act of common sense is to recognise the difference between a cloud and a mountain. And I will affirm that nobody knows any of these things, in the sense that we all know of the existence of the Pyramids of Egypt.

The truth, it may be repeated, is that what we really see, as distinct from what we may reasonably guess, in this earliest phase of history is darkness covering the earth and great darkness the peoples, with a light or two gleaming here and there on chance patches of humanity; and that two of these flames do burn upon two of these tall primeval towns; upon the high terraces of Babylon and the huge pyramids of the Nile. There are indeed other ancient lights, or lights that may be conjectured to be very ancient, in very remote parts of that vast wilderness of night. Far away to the east there is a high civilisation of vast antiquity in China; there are the remains of civilisations in Mexico and South America and other places, some of them apparently so high in civilisation as to have reached the most refined forms of devil-worship. But the difference lies in the element old tradition; the tradition of these lost cultures has been broken off, and though the tradition of China still lives, it is doubtful whether we know anything about it. Moreover, a man trying to measure the Chinese antiquity has to use Chinese traditions of measurement; and he has a strange sensation of having passed into another world under other laws of time and space. Time is telescoped outwards and centuries assume the slow and stiff movement of aeons; the white man trying to see it as the yellow man sees, feels as if his head were turning round and wonders wildly whether it is growing a pigtail. Any how he cannot take in a scientific sense that queer perspective that leads up to the primeval pagoda of the first of the Sons of Heaven. He is the real antipodes; the only true alternative world to Christendom; and he is after a fashion walking upside down. I have spoken of the medieval map-maker and his dragon; but what medieval traveller, however much interested in monsters, would expect to find a country where a dragon is a benevolent and amiable being? Of the more serious side of Chinese tradition something will be said in another connection; but I am only talking of tradition and the test of antiquity. And I only mention China as an antiquity that is not for us reached by a bridge old tradition; and Babylon and Egypt as antiquities that are. Herodotus is a human being, in a sense in which a Chinaman in a billy-cock hat, sitting opposite to us in a London tea shop, is hardly human. We feel as if we knew what David and Isaiah felt like, in a way in which we never were quite certain what Li Hung Chang felt like. The very sins that snatched away Helen or Bathsheba have passed into a proverb of private human weakness, of pathos and even of pardon. The very virtues of the Chinaman have about them something terrifying. This is the difference made by the destruction or preservation of a continuous historical inheritance; as from ancient Egypt to modern Europe. But when we ask what was that world that we inherit, and why those particular people and places seem to belong to it, we are led to the central fact of civilised history.

That centre was the Mediterranean; which was not so much a piece of water as a world. But it was a world with something of the character of such a water; for it became more and more a place of unification in which the streams of strange and very diverse cultures met. The Nile and the Tiber alike flow into the Mediterranean; so did the Egyptian and the Etrurian alike contribute to a Mediterranean civilisation. The glamour of the great sea spread indeed very far in land and the unity was felt among the Arabs alone in the deserts and the Gauls beyond the northern hills. But the gradual building up of a common culture running round all the coasts of this inner sea is the main business of antiquity. As will be seen, it was sometimes a bad business as well as a good business. In that orbis terrarum or circle of lands there were the extremes of evil and of piety, there were contrasted races and still more contrasted religions. It was the scene of an endless struggle between Asia and Europe from the night of the Persian ships at Salamis to the flight of the Turkish ships at Lepanto. It was the scene, as will be more especially suggested later, of a supreme spiritual struggle between the two types of paganism, confronting each other in the Latin and the Phoenician cities; in the Roman forum and the Punic mart. It was the world of war and peace, the world of good and evil, the world of all that matters most, with all respect to the Aztecs and the Mongols of the Far East, they did not matter as the Mediterranean tradition mattered and still matters. Between it and the Far East there were, of course, interesting cults and conquests of various kinds, more or less in touch with it, and in proportion as they were so intelligible also to us. The Persians came riding in to make an end of Babylon; and we are told in a Greek story how these barbarians learned to draw the bow and tell the truth. Alexander the great Greek marched with his Macedonians into the sunrise and brought back strange birds coloured like the sunrise clouds and strange flowers and jewels from the gardens and treasuries of nameless kings. Islam went eastward into that world and made it partly imaginable to us; precisely because Islam itself was born in that circle of lands that fringed our own ancient and ancestral sea. In the Middle Ages the empire of the Moguls increased its majesty without losing its mystery; the Tartars conquered China and the Chinese apparently took very little notice of them. All these things are interesting in themselves; but it is impossible to shift the centre of gravity to the inland spaces of Asia from the inland sea of Europe. When all is said, if there were nothing in the world but what was said and done and written and built in the lands lying round the Mediterranean, it would still be in all the most vital and valuable things the world in which we live. When that southern culture spread to the north-west it produced many very wonderful things; of which doubtless we ourselves are the most wonderful. When it spread thence to colonies and new countries, it was still the same culture so long as it was culture at all. But round that little sea like a lake were the things themselves, apart from all extensions and echoes and commentaries on the things, the Republic and the Church; the Bible and the heroic epics; Islam and Israel and the memories of the lost empires, Aristotle and the measure of all things. It is because the first light upon this world is really light, the daylight in which we are still walking to-day, and not merely the doubtful visitation of strange stars, that I have begun here with noting where that light first falls on the towered cities of the eastern Mediterranean.

But though Babylon and Egypt have thus a sort of first claim, in the very fact of being familiar and traditional, fascinating riddles to us but also fascinating riddles to our fathers, we must not imagine that they were the only old civilisations on the southern sea; or that all the civilisation was merely Sumerian or Semitic or Coptic, still less merely Asiatic or African. Real research is more and more exalting the ancient civilisation of Europe and especially of what we may still vaguely call the Greeks. It must be understood in the sense that there were Greeks before the Greeks, as in so many of their mythologies there were gods before the gods. The island of Crete was the centre of the civilisation now called Minoan, after the Minos who lingered in ancient legend and whose labyrinth was actually discovered by modern archeology. This elaborate European society, with its harbours and its drainage and its domestic machinery, seems to have gone down before some invasion of its northern neighbours, who made or inherited the Hellas we know in history. But that earlier period did not pass till it had given to the world gifts so great that the world has ever since been striving in vain to repay them, if only by plagiarism.

Somewhere along the Ionian coast opposite Crete and the islands was a town of some sort, probably of the sort that we should call a village or hamlet with a wall. It was called Ilion but it came to be called Troy, and the name will never perish from the earth. A poet who may have been a beggar and a ballad-monger, who may have been unable to read and write, and was described by tradition as a blind, composed a poem about the Greeks going to war with this town to recover the most beautiful woman in the world. That the most beautiful woman in the world lived in that one little town sounds like a legend; that the most beautiful poem in the world was written by somebody who knew of nothing larger than such little towns is a historical fact. It is said that the poem came at the end of the period; that the primitive culture brought it forth in its decay; in which case one would like to have seen that culture in its prime. But anyhow it is true that this, which is our first poem, might very well be our last poem too. It might well be the last word as well as the first word spoken by man about his mortal lot, as seen by merely mortal vision. If the world becomes pagan and perishes, the last man left alive would do well to quote the Iliad and die.

But in this one great human revelation of antiquity there is another element of great historical importance; which has hardly I think been given its proper place in history. The poet has so conceived the poem that his sympathies apparently, and those of his reader certainly, are on the side of the vanquished rather than of the victor. And this is a sentiment which increases in the poetical tradition even as the poetical origin itself recedes. Achilles had some status as a sort of demigod in pagan times; but he disappears altogether in late times. But Hector grows greater as the ages pass, and it is his name that is the name of a Knight of the Round Table and his sword that legend puts into the hand of Roland, laying about him with the weapon of the defeated Hector in the last ruin and splendour of his own defeat. The name anticipates all the defeats through which our race and religion were to pass; that survival of a hundred defeats that is its triumph.

The tale of the end of Troy shall have no ending, for it is lifted up forever into living echoes, immortal as our hopelessness and our hope. Troy standing was a small thing that may have stood nameless for ages. But Troy falling has been caught up in a flame and suspended in an immortal instant of annihilation; and because it was destroyed with fire the fire shall never be destroyed. And as with the city so with the hero; traced in archaic lines in that primeval twilight is found the first figure of the Knight. There is a prophetic coincidence in his title; we have spoken of the word chivalry and how it seems to mingle the horseman with the horse. It is almost anticipated ages before in the thunder of the Homeric hexameter, and that long leaping word with which the Iliad ends. It is that very unity for which we can find no name but the holy centaur of chivalry. But there are other reasons for giving in this glimpse of antiquity the name upon the sacred town. The sanctity of such towns ran like a fire round the coasts and islands of the northern Mediterranean, the high-fenced hamlet for which heroes died. From the smallness of the city came the greatness of the citizen. Hellas with her hundred statues produced nothing statelier than that walking statue; the ideal of the self-commanding man. Hellas of the hundred statues was one legend and literature; and all that labyrinth of little walled nations resounding with the lament of Troy.

A later legend, an afterthought but not an accident, said that stragglers from Troy founded a republic on the Italian shore. It was true in spirit that republican virtue had such a root. A mystery of honour, that was not born of Babylon or the Egyptian pride, there shone like the shield of Hector, defying Asia and Africa; till the light of a new day was loosened, with the rushing of the eagles and the coming of the name; the name that came like a thunderclap when the world woke to Rome.

GOD AND COMPARATIVE RELIGION

I was once escorted over the Roman foundations of an ancient British city by a professor, who said something that seems to me a satire on a good many other professors. Possibly the professor saw the joke, though he maintained an iron gravity, and may or may not have realised that it was a joke against a great deal of what is called comparative religion. I pointed out a sculpture of the head of the sun with the usual halo of rays, but with the difference that the face in the disc, instead of being boyish like Apollo, was bearded like Neptune or Jupiter. 'Yes,' he said with a certain delicate exactitude, 'that is supposed to represent the local god Sul. The best authorities identify Sul with Minerva, but this has been held to show that the identification is not complete.'

That is what we call a powerful understatement. The modern world is madder than any satires on it; long ago Mr. Belloc made his burlesque don say that a bust of Ariadne had been proved by modern research to be a Silenus. But that is not better than the real appearance of Minerva as the Bearded Woman of Mr. Barnum. Only both of them are very like many identifications by 'the best authorities' on comparative religion; and when Catholic creeds are identified with various wild myths, I do not laugh or curse or misbehave myself; I confine myself decorously to saying that the identification is not complete.

In the days of my youth the Religion of Humanity was a term commonly applied to Comtism, the theory of certain rationalists who worshipped corporate mankind as a Supreme Being. Even in the days of my youth, I remarked that there was something slightly odd about despising and dismissing the doctrine of the Trinity as a mystical and even maniacal contradiction; and then asking us to adore a deity who is a hundred million persons in one God, neither confounding the persons nor dividing the substance.

But there is another entity, more or less definable and much more imaginable than the many-headed and monstrous idol of mankind. And it has a much better light to be called, in a reasonable sense, the religion of humanity. Man is not indeed the idol; but man is almost everywhere the idolator. And these multitudinous idolatries of man kind have something about them in many ways more human and sympathetic than modern metaphysical abstractions. If an Asiatic god has three heads and seven arms, there is at least in it an idea of material incarnation bringing an unknown power nearer to us and not farther away. But if our friends Brown, Jones, and Robinson, when out for a Sunday walk, were transformed and amalgamated into an Asiatic idol before our eyes, they would surely seem farther away. If the arms of Brown and the legs of Robinson waved from the same composite body, they would seem to be waving something of a sad farewell. If the heads of an three gentlemen appeared smiling on the same neck, we should hesitate even by what name to address our new and somewhat abnormal friend. In the many-headed and many-handed Oriental idol there is a certain sense of mysteries be coming at least partly intelligible; of formless forces of nature taking some dark but material form, but though this may be true of the multiform god it is not so of the multiform man The human beings be come less human by becoming less separate; we might say less human in being less lonely. The human beings become less intelligible as they become less isolated; we might say with strict truth that the closer they are to us the farther they are away. An Ethical Hymn-book of this humanitarian sort of religion was carefully selected and expurgated on the principle of preserving anything human and eliminating anything divine. One consequence was that a hymn appeared in the amended form of 'Nearer Mankind to Thee, nearer to Thee.' It always suggested to me the sensations of a strap-hanged during a crush on the Tube. But it is strange and wonderful how far away the souls of men can seem, when their bodies are so near as all that.

The human unity with which I deal here is not to be confounded with this modern industrial monotony and herding, which is rather a congestion than a communion. It is a thing to which human groups left to themselves, and even human individuals left to themselves, have everywhere tended by an instinct that may truly be called human. Like all healthy human things, it has varied very much within the limits of a general character; for that is characteristic of everything belonging to that ancient land of liberty that lies before and around the servile industrial town. Industrialism actually boasts that its products are all of one pattern; that men in Jamaica or Japan can break the same seal and drink the same bad whiskey, that a man at the North Pole and another at the South might recognise the same optimistic level on the same dubious tinned salmon. But wine, the gift of gods to men, can vary with every valley and every vineyard, can turn into a hundred wines without any wine once reminding us of whiskey; and cheeses can change from county to county without forgetting the difference between chalk and cheese. When I am speaking of this thing therefore, I am speaking of something that doubtless includes very wide differences; nevertheless I will here maintain that it is one thing. I will maintain that most of the modern botheration comes from not realising that it is really one thing. I will advance the thesis that before all talk about comparative religion and the separate religious founders of the world, the first essential is to recognise this thing as a whole, as a thing almost native and normal to the great fellowship that we call mankind. This thing is Paganism, and I propose to show in these pages that it is the one real rival to the Church of Christ.

Comparative religion is very comparative indeed. That is, it is so much a matter of degree and distance and difference that it is only comparatively successful when it tries to compare. When we come to look at it closely we find it comparing things that are really quite incomparable. We are accustomed to see a table or catalogue of the world's great religions in parallel columns, until we fancy they are really parallel. We are accustomed to see the names of the great religious founders all in a row: Christ; Mahomet; Buddha; Confucius. But in truth this is only a trick, another of these optical illusions by which any objects may be put into a particular relation by shifting to a particular point of sight. Those religions and religious founders, or rather those whom we choose to lump together as religions and religious founders, do not really show any common character. The illusion is partly produced by Islam coming immediately after Christianity in the list; as Islam did come after Christianity and was largely an imitation of Christianity. But the other eastern religions, or what we call religions, not only do not resemble the Church but do not resemble each other. When we come to Confucianism at the end of the list, we come to something in a totally different world of thought. To compare the Christian and Confucian religions is like comparing a theist with an English squire or asking whether a man is a believer in immortality or a hundred-per-cent American. Confucianism may be a civilisation but it is not a religion.

In truth the Church is too unique to prove herself unique. For most popular and easy proof is by parallel; and here there is no parallel. It is not easy, therefore, to expose the fallacy by which a false classification is created to swamp a unique thing, when it really is a unique thing. As there is nowhere else exactly the same fact, so there is nowhere else exactly the same fallacy. But I will take the nearest thing I can find to such a solitary social phenomenon, in order to show how it is thus swamped and assimilated. I imagine most of us would agree that there is something unusual and unique about the position of the Jews. There is nothing that is quite in the same sense an international nation; an ancient culture scattered in different countries but still distinct and indestructible. Now this business is like an attempt to make a list of Nomadic Nations in order to soften the strange solitude of the Jew. It would be easy enough to do it, by the same process of putting a plausible approximation first, and then tailing off into totally different things thrown in somehow to make up the list. Thus in the new list of nomadic nations the Jews would be followed by the Gypsies; who at least are really nomadic if they are not really national. Then the professor of the new science of Comparative Nomadics could pass easily on to something different; even if it was very different. He could remark on the wandering adventure of the English who had scattered their colonies over so many seas; and call them nomads. It is quite true that a great many Englishmen seem to be strangely restless in England. It is quite true that not all of them have left their country for their country's good. The moment we mention the wandering empire of the English, we must add the strange exiled empire of the Irish. For it is a curious fact, to be noted in our imperial literature, that the same ubiquity and unrest which is a proof of English enterprise and triumph is a proof of Irish futility and failure. Then the professor of Nomadism would look round thoughtfully and remember that there was great talk recently of German waiters, German barbers, German clerks, Germans naturalising themselves in England and the United States and the South American republics. The Germans would go down as the fifth nomadic race; the words Wanderlust and Folk-Wandering would come in very useful here. For there really have been historians who explained the Crusades by suggesting that the Germans were found wandering (as the police say) in what happened to be the neighbourhood of Palestine. Then the professor, feeling he was now near the end, would make a last leap in desperation. He would recall the fact that the French army has captured nearly every capital in Europe, that it marched across countless conquered lands under Charlemagne or Napoleon; and that would be wanderlust and that would be the note of a nomadic race. Thus he would have his six nomadic nations all compact and complete, and would feel that the Jew was no longer a sort of mysterious and even mystical exception. But people with more common sense would probably realise that he had only extended nomadism by extending the meaning of nomadism, and that he had extended that until it really had no meaning at all. It is quite true that the French soldier has made some of the finest marches in all military history. But it is equally true, and far more self-evident, that if the French peasant is not a rooted reality there is no such thing as a rooted reality in the world; or in other words, if he is a nomad there is nobody who is not a nomad.

Now that is the sort of trick that has been tried in the case of comparative religion and the world's religious founders all standing respectably in a row. It seeks to classify Jesus as the other would classify Jews, by inventing a new class for the purpose and filling up the rest of it with stop-gaps and second-rate copies. I do not mean that these other things are not often great things in their own real character and class. Confucianism and Buddhism are great things, but it is not true to call them Churches; just as the French and English are great peoples, but it is nonsense to call them nomads. There are some points of resemblance between Christendom and its imitation in Islam; for that matter there are some points of resemblance between Jews and Gypsies. But after that the lists are made up of anything that comes to hand; of anything that can be put in the same catalogue without being in the same category.

In this sketch of religious history, with all decent deference to men much more learned than myself, I propose to cut across and disregard this modern method of classification, which I feel sure has falsified the facts of history. I shall here submit an alternative classification of religion or religions, which I believe would be found to cover all the facts and, what is quite as important here, all the fancies. Instead of dividing religion geographically and as it were vertically, into Christian, Moslem, Brahmin, Buddhist, and so on, I would divide it psychologically and in some sense horizontally; into the strata of spiritual elements and influences that could sometimes exist in the same country, or even in the same man. Putting the Church apart for the moment, I should be disposed to divide the natural religion of the mass of mankind under such headings as these: God; the Gods; the Demons; the Philosophers. I believe some such classification will help us to sort out the spiritual experiences of men much more successfully than the conventional business of comparing religions; and that many famous figures will naturally fall into their place in this way who are only forced into their place in the other. As I shall make use of these titles or terms more than once in narrative and allusion, it will be well to define at this stage for what I mean them to stand. And I will begin with the first, the simplest and the most sublime, in this chapter.

In considering the elements of pagan humanity, we must begin by an attempt to describe the indescribable. Many get over the difficulty of describing it by the expedient of denying it, or at least ignoring it; but the whole point of it is that it was something that was never quite eliminated even when it was ignored. They are obsessed by their evolutionary monomania that every great thing grows from a seed, or something smaller than itself. They seem to forget that every seed comes from a tree, or something larger than itself. Now there is very good ground for guessing that religion did not originally come from some detail that was forgotten, because it was too small to be traced. Much more probably it was an idea that was abandoned because it was too large to be managed. There is very good reason to suppose that many people did begin with the simple but overwhelming idea of one God who governs all; and afterwards fell away into such things as demon-worship almost as a sort of secret dissipation. Even the test of savage beliefs, of which the folk-lore students are so fond, is admittedly often found to support such a view. Some of the very rudest savages, primitive in every sense in which anthropologists use the word, the Australian aborigines for instance, are found to have a pure monotheism with a high moral tone. A missionary was preaching to a very wild tribe of polytheists, who had told him all their polytheistic tales, and telling them in return of the existence of the one good God who is a spirit and judges men by spiritual standards. And there was a sudden buzz of excitement among these stolid barbarians, as at somebody who was letting out a secret, and they cried to each other, 'Atahocan! He is speaking of Atahocan!'

309

Probably it was a point of politeness and even decency among those polytheists not to speak of Atahocan. The name is not perhaps so much adapted as some of our own to direct and solemn religious exhortation but many other social forces are always covering up and confusing such simple ideas. Possibly the old god stood for an old morality found irksome in more expansive moments; possibly intercourse with demons was more fashionable among the best people, as in the modern fashion of Spiritualism. Anyhow, there are any number of similar examples. They all testify to the unmistakable psychology of a thing taken for granted, as distinct from a thing talked about. There is a striking example in a tale taken down word for word from a Red Indian in California which starts out with hearty legendary and literary relish: 'The sun is the father and ruler of the heavens. He is the big chief. The moon is his wife and the stars are their children'; and so on through a most ingenious and complicated story, in the middle of which is a sudden parenthesis saying that the sun and moon have to do something because 'It is ordered that way by the Great Spirit Who lives above the place of all.' That is exactly the attitude of most paganism towards God. He is something assumed and forgotten and remembered by accident; a habit possibly not peculiar to pagans. Sometimes the higher deity is remembered in the higher moral grades and is a sort of mystery. But always, it has been truly said, the savage is talkative about his mythology and taciturn about his religion. The Australian savages, indeed, exhibit a topsyturveydom such as the ancients might have thought truly worthy of the antipodes. The savage who thinks nothing of tossing off such a trifle as a tale of the sun and moon being the halves of a baby chopped in two, or dropping into small-talk about a colossal cosmic cow milked to make the rain, merely in order to be sociable, will then retire to secret caverns sealed against women and white men, temples of terrible initiation where to the thunder of the bull-roarer and the dripping of sacrificial blood, the priest whispers the final secrets, known only to the initiate: that honesty is the best policy, that a little kindness does nobody any harm, that all men are brothers and that there is but one God, the Father Almighty, maker of all things visible and invisible.

In other words, we have here the curiosity of religious history that the savage seems to be parading all the most repulsive and impossible parts of his belief and concealing all the most sensible and creditable parts. But the explanation is that they are not in that sense parts of his belief, or at least not parts of the same sort of belief. The myths are merely tall stories, though as tall as the sky, the water spout, or the tropic rain. The mysteries are true stories, and are taken secretly that they may be taken seriously. Indeed it is only too easy to forget that there is a thrill in theism. A novel in which a number of separate characters all turned out to be the same character would certainly be a sensational novel. It is so with the idea that sun and tree and river are the disguises of one god and not of many. Alas, we also find it only too easy to take Atahocan for granted. But whether he is allowed to fade into a truism or preserved as a sensation by being preserved as a secret, it is clear that he is always either an old truism or an old tradition. There is nothing to show that he is an improved product of the mere mythology and everything to show that he preceded it. He is worshipped by the simplest tribes with no trace of ghosts or grave-offerings, or any of the complications in which Herbert Spencer and Grant Allen sought the origin of the simplest of all ideas. Whatever else there was, there was never as such thing as the Evolution of the Idea of God. The idea was concealed, was avoided, was almost forgotten, was even explained away; but it was never evolved.

There are not a few indications of this change in other places It is implied, for instance, in the fact that even polytheism seems often the combination of several monotheisms. A god will gain only a minor seat on Mount Olympus, when he had owned earth and heaven and all the stars while he lived in his own little valley. Like many a small nation melting in a great empire, he gives up local universality only to come under universal limitation. The very name of Pan suggests that he became a god of the wood when he had been a god of the world. The very name of Jupiter is almost a pagan translation of the words 'Our Father which art in heaven.' As with the Great Father symbolised by the sky, so with the Great Mother whom we still call Mother Earth. Demeter and Ceres and Cybele often seem to be almost capable of taking over the whole business of godhood, so that men should need no other gods. It seems reasonably probable that a good many men did have no other gods but one of these, worshipped as the author of all.

Over some of the most immense and populous tracts of the world such as China, it would seem that the simpler idea of the Great Father has never been very much complicated with rival cults, though it may have in some sense ceased to be a cult itself. The best authorities seem to think that though Confucianism is in one sense agnosticism, it does not directly contradict the old theism, precisely because it has become a rather vague theism. It is one in which God is called Heaven, as in the case of polite persons tempted to swear in drawing-rooms. But Heaven is still overhead, even if it is very far overhead. We have all the impression of a simple truth that has receded, until it was remote without ceasing to be true. And this phrase alone would bring us back to the same idea even in the pagan mythology of the West. There is surely something of this very notion of the withdrawal of some higher power, in all those mysterious and very imaginative myths about the separation of earth and sky. In a hundred forms we are told that heaven and earth were once lovers, or were once at one, when some upstart thing, often some undutiful child, thrust them apart; and the world was built on an abyss; upon a division and a parting. One of its grossest versions was given by Greek civilisation in the myth of Uranus and Saturn. One of its most charming versions was that of some savage niggers, who say that a little pepper-plant grew taller and taller and lifted the whole sky like a lid; a beautiful barbaric vision of daybreak for some of our painters who love that tropical twilight. Of myths, and the highly mythical explanations which the moderns offer of myths, something will be said in another section; for I cannot but think that most mythology is on another and more superficial plane. But in this primeval vision of the rending of one world into two there is surely something more of ultimate ideas. As to what it means, a man will learn far more about it by lying on his back in a field, and merely looking at the sky, than by reading all the libraries even of the most learned and valuable folklore. He will know what is meant by saying that the sky ought to be nearer to us than it is, that perhaps it was once nearer than it is, that it is not a thing merely alien and abysmal but in some fashion sundered from us and saying farewell. There will creep across his mind the curious suggestion that after all, perhaps, the myth-maker was not merely a moon-calf or village idiot thinking he could cut up the clouds like a cake, but had in him something more than it is fashionable to attribute to the Troglodyte; that it is just possible that Thomas Hood was not talking like a Troglodyte when he said that, as time went on, the tree-tops only told him he was further off from heaven than when he was a boy. But anyhow the legend of Uranus the Lord of Heaven dethroned by Saturn the Time Spirit would mean something to the author of that poem. And it would mean, among other things, this banishment of the first fatherhood. There is the idea of God in the very notion that there were gods before the gods. There is an idea of greater simplicity in all the allusions to that more ancient order. The suggestion is supported by the process of propagation we see in historic times. Gods and demigods and heroes breed like herrings before our very eyes and suggest of themselves that the family may have had one founder; mythology grows more and more complicated, and the very complication suggests that at the beginning it was more simple. Even on the external evidence, of the sort called scientific, there is therefore a very good case for the suggestion that man began with monotheism before it developed or degenerated into polytheism. But I am concerned rather with an internal than an external truth; and, as I have already said, the internal truth is almost indescribable. We have to speak of something of which it is the whole point that people did not speak of it; we have not merely to translate from a strange tongue or speech, but from a strange silence.

I suspect an immense implication behind all polytheism and paganism. I suspect we have only a hint of it here and there in these savage creeds or Greek origins. It is not exactly what we mean by the presence of God; in a sense it might more truly be called the absence of God. But absence does not mean non-existence; and a man drinking the toast of absent friends does not mean that from his life all friendship is absent. It is a void but it is not a negation; it is some thing as positive as an empty chair. It would be an exaggeration to say that the pagan saw higher than Olympus an empty throne. It would be nearer the truth to take the gigantic imagery of the Old Testament, in which the prophet saw God from behind; it was as if some immeasurable presence had turned its back on the world. Yet the meaning will again be missed, if it is supposed to be anything so conscious and vivid as the monotheism of Moses and his people. I do not mean that the pagan peoples were in the least overpowered by this idea merely because it is overpowering. On the contrary, it was so large that they all carried it lightly, as we all carry the load of the sky. Gazing at some detail like a bird or a cloud, we can all ignore its awful blue background; we can neglect the sky; and precisely because it bears down upon us with an annihilating force it is felt as nothing. A thing of this kind can only be an impressing and a rather subtle impression; but to me it is a very strong impression made by pagan literature and religion. I repeat that in our special sacramental sense there is, of course, the absence of the presence of God. But there is in a very real sense the presence of the absence of God. We feel it in the unfathomable sadness of pagan poetry; for I doubt if there was ever in all the marvellous manhood of antiquity a man who was happy as St. Francis was happy. We feel it in the legend of a Golden Age and again in the vague implication that the gods themselves are ultimately related to something else, even when that Unknown God has faded into a Fate. Above all we feel it in those immortal moments when the pagan literature seems to return to a more innocent antiquity and speak with a more direct voice, so that no word is worthy of it except our own monotheistic monosyllable. We cannot say anything but 'God' in a sentence like that of Socrates bidding farewell to his judges: 'I go to die and you remain to live; and God alone knows which of us goes the better way.' We can use no other word even for the best moments of Marcus Aurelius: 'Can they say dear city of Cecrops, and canst thou not say dear city of God?' We can use no other word in that mighty line in which Virgil spoke to all who suffer with the veritable cry of a Christian before Christ: 'O you that have borne things more terrible, to this also God shall give an end.'

In short, there is a feeling that there is something higher than the gods; but because it is higher it is also further away. Not yet could even Virgil have read the riddle and the paradox of that other divinity, who is both higher and nearer. For them what was truly divine was very distant, so distant that they dismissed it more and more from their minds. It had less and less to do with the mere mythology of which I shall write later. Yet even in this there was a sort of tacit admission of its intangible purity, when we consider what most of the mythologies like. As the Jews would not degrade it by images, so the Greeks did not degrade it even by imaginations. When the gods were more and more remembered only by pranks and profligacies, it was relatively a movement of reverence. It was an act of piety to forget God. In other words, there is something in the whole tone of the time suggesting that men had accepted a lower level, and still were half conscious that it was a lower level. It is hard to find words for these things; yet the one really just word stands ready. These men were conscious of the Fall if they were conscious of nothing else; and the same is true of an heathen humanity. Those who have fallen may remember the fall, even when they forget the height. Some such tantalising blank or break in memory is at the back of all pagan sentiment. There is such a thing as the momentary power to remember that we forget. And the most ignorant of humanity know by the very look of earth that they have forgotten heaven. But it remains true that even for these men there were moments, like the memories of childhood, when they heard themselves talking with a simpler language; there were moments when the Roman, like Virgil in the line already quoted, cut his way with a sword-stroke of song out of the tangle of the mythologies, the motley mob of gods and goddesses sank suddenly out of sight and the Sky-Father was alone in the sky.

This latter example is very relevant to the next step in the process. A white light as of a lost morning still lingers on the figure of Jupiter, of Pan or of the elder Apollo; and it may well be, as already noted, that each was once a divinity as solitary as Jehovah or Allah. They lost this lonely universality by a process it is here very necessary to note; a process of amalgamation very like what was afterwards called syncretism. The whole pagan world set itself to build a Pantheon. They admitted more and more gods, gods not only of the Greeks but of the barbarians; gods not only of Europe but of Asia and Africa. The more the merrier, though some of the Asian and African ones were not very merry. They admitted them to equal thrones with their own, sometimes they identified them with their own. They may have regarded it as an enrichment of their religious life; but it meant the final loss of all that we now call religion. It meant that ancient light of simplicity, that had a single source like the sun, finally fades away in a dazzle of conflicting Lights and colours. God is really sacrificed to the Gods; in a very literal sense of the flippant phrase, they have been too many for him.

Polytheism, therefore, was really a sort of pool; in the sense of the pagans having consented to the pooling of their pagan religions. And this point is very important in many controversies ancient and modern. It is regarded as a liberal and enlightened thing to say that the god of the stranger may be as good as our own; and doubtless the pagans thought themselves very liberal and enlightened when they agreed to add to the gods of the city or the hearth some wild and fantastic Dionysus coming down from the mountains or some shaggy and rustic Pan creeping out of the woods. But exactly what it lost by these larger ideas is the largest idea of all. It is the idea of the fatherhood that makes the whole world one. And the converse is also true. Doubtless those more antiquated men of antiquity who clung to their solitary statues and their single sacred names were regarded as superstitious savages benighted and left behind. But these superstitious savages were preserving something that is much more like the cosmic power as conceived by philosophy, or even as conceived by science. This paradox by which the rude reactionary was a sort of prophetic progressive has one consequence very much to the point. In a purely historical sense, and apart from any other controversies in the same connection, it throws a light, a single and a steady light, that shines from the beginning on a little and lonely people. In this paradox, as in some riddle of religion of which the answer was sealed up for centuries, lies the mission and the meaning of the Jews.

It is true in this sense, humanly speaking, that the world owes God to the Jews. It owes that truth to much that is blamed on the Jews, possibly to much that is blameable in the Jews. We have already noted the nomadic position of the Jews amid the other pastoral peoples upon the fringe of the Babylonian Empire, and something of that strange erratic course of theirs blazed across the dark territory of extreme antiquity, as they passed from the seat of Abraham and the shepherd princes into Egypt and doubled back into the Palestinian hills and held them against the Philistines from Crete and fell into captivity in Babylon; and yet again returned to their mountain city by the Zionist policy of the Persian conquerors; and so continued that amazing romance of restlessness of which we have not yet seen the end. But through all their wanderings, and especially through all their early wanderings, they did indeed carry the fate of the world in that wooden tabernacle, that held perhaps a featureless symbol and certainly an invisible god. We may say that one most essential feature was that it was featureless. Much as we may prefer that creative liberty which the Christian culture has declared and by which it has eclipsed even the arts of antiquity, we must not underrate the determining importance at the time of the Hebrew inhibition of images. It is a typical example of one of those limitations that did in fact preserve and perpetuate enlargement, like a wall built round a wide open space. The God who could not have a statue remained a spirit. Nor would his statue in any case have had the disarming dignity and grace of the Greek statues then or the Christian statues afterwards. He was living in a land of monsters. We shall have occasion to consider more fully what those monsters were, Moloch and Dagon and Tanit the terrible goddess. If the deity of Israel had ever had an image, he would have had a phallic image. By merely giving him a body they would have brought in all the worst elements of mythology; all the polygamy of polytheism; the vision of the harem in heaven. This point about the refusal of art is the first example of the limitations which are often adversely criticised, only because the critics themselves are limited. But an even stronger case can be found in the other criticism offered by the same critics. It is often said with a sneer that the God of Israel was only a God of battles, 'a mere barbaric Lord of Hosts' pitted in rivalry against other gods only as their envious foe. Well it is for the world that he was a God of Battles. Well it is for us that he was to all the rest only a rival and a foe. In the ordinary way, it would have been only too easy for them to have achieved the desolate disaster of conceiving him as a friend. It would have been only too easy for them to have seen him stretching out his hands in love and reconciliation, embracing Baal and kissing the painted face of Astarte, feasting in fellowship with the gods; the last god to sell his crown of stars for the Soma of the Indian pantheon or the nectar of Olympus or the mead of Valhalla. It would have been easy enough for his worshippers to follow the enlightened course of Syncretism and the pooling of all the pagan traditions. It is obvious indeed that his followers were always sliding down this easy slope; and it required the almost demoniac energy of certain inspired demagogues, who testified to the divine unity in words that are still like winds of inspiration and ruin. The more we really understand of the ancient conditions that contributed to the final culture of the Faith, the more we shall have a real and even a realistic reverence for the greatness of the Prophets of Israel. As it was, while the whole world melted into this mass of confused mythology, this Deity who is called tribal and narrow, precisely because he was what is called tribal and narrow, preserved the primary religion of all mankind. He was tribal enough to be universal. He was as narrow as the universe. In a word, there was a popular pagan god called Jupiter-Ammon. There was never a god called Jehovah-Ammon. There was never a god called Jehovah-Jupiter. If there had been, there would certainly have been another called Jehovah-Moloch. Long before the liberal and enlightened amalgamators had got so far afield as Jupiter, the image of the Lord of Hosts would have been deformed out of all suggestion of a monotheistic maker and ruler and would have become an idol far worse than any savage fetish; for he might have been as civilised as the gods of Tyre and Carthage. What that civilisation meant we shall consider more fully in the chapter that follows; when we note how the power of demons nearly destroyed Europe and even the heathen health of the world. But the world's destiny would have been distorted still more fatally if monotheism had failed in the Mosaic tradition. I hope in a subsequent section to show that I am not without sympathy with all that health in the heathen world that made its fairy-tales and its fanciful romances of religion. But I hope also to show that these were bound to fail in the long run; and the world would have been lost if it had been unable to return to that great original simplicity of a single authority in all things. That we do preserve something of that primary simplicity that poets and philosophers can still indeed in some sense say an Universal Prayer, that we live in a large and serene world under a sky that stretches paternally over all the peoples of the earth, that philosophy and philanthropy are truisms in a religion of reasonable men, all that we do most truly owe, under heaven, to a secretive and restless nomadic people; who bestowed on men the supreme and serene blessing of a jealous God.

The unique possession was not available or accessible to the pagan world, because it was also the possession of a jealous people. The Jews were unpopular, partly because of this narrowness already noted in the Roman world, partly perhaps because they had already fallen into that habit of merely handling things for exchange instead of working to make them with their hands. It was partly also because polytheism had become a sort of jungle in which solitary monotheism could be lost; but it is strange to realise how completely it really was lost. Apart from more disputed matters, there were things in the tradition of Israel which belong to all humanity now, and might have belonged to all humanity then. They had one of the colossal corner-stones of the world: the Book of Job. It obviously stands over against the Iliad and the Greek tragedies; and even more than they it was an early meeting and parting of poetry and philosophy in the mornings of the world. It is a solemn and uplifting sight to see those two eternal fools, the optimist and the pessimist, destroyed in the dawn of time. And the philosophy really perfects the pagan tragic irony, precisely because it is more monotheistic and therefore more mystical. Indeed the Book of Job avowedly only answers mystery with mystery. Job is comforted with riddles; but he is comforted. Herein is indeed a type, in the sense of a prophecy, of things speaking with authority. For when he who doubts can only say 'I do not understand,' it is true that he who knows can only reply or repeat 'You do not understand.' And under that rebuke there is always a sudden hope in the heart; and the sense of something that would be worth understanding. But this mighty monotheistic poem remained unremarked by the whole world of antiquity, which was thronged with polytheistic poetry. It is a sign of the way in which the Jews stood apart and kept their tradition unshaken and unshared, that they should have kept a thing like the Book of Job out of the whole intellectual world of antiquity. It is as if the Egyptians had modestly concealed the Great Pyramid. But there were other reasons for a cross-purpose and an impasse, characteristic of the whole of the end of paganism. After all, the tradition of Israel had only got hold of one-half of the truth, even if we use the popular paradox and call it the bigger half. I shall try to sketch in the next chapter that love of locality and personality that ran through mythology; here it need only be said that there was a truth in it that could not be let out though it were a lighter and less essential truth. The sorrow of Job had to be joined with the sorrow of Hector; and while the former was the sorrow of the universe the latter was the sorrow of the city; for Hector could only stand pointing to heaven as the pillar of holy Troy. When God speaks out of the whirlwind he may well speak in the wilderness. But the monotheism of the nomad was not enough for all that varied civilisation of fields and fences and walled cities and temples and towns; and the turn of these things also was to come, when the two could be combined in a more definite and domestic religion. Here and there in all that pagan crowd could be found a philosopher whose thought ran of pure theism; but he never had, or supposed that he had, the power to change the customs of the whole populace. Nor is it easy even in such philosophies to find a true definition of this deep business of the relation of polytheism and theism. Perhaps the nearest we can come to striking the note, or giving the thing a name, is in something far away from all that civilization and more remote from Rome than the isolation of Israel. It is in a saying I once heard from some Hindu tradition; that gods as well as men are only the dreams of Brahma; and will perish when Brahma wakes. There is indeed in such an image something of the soul of Asia which is less sane than the soul of Christendom. We should call it despair, even if they would call it peace. This note of nihilism can be considered later in a fuller comparison between Asia and Europe. It is enough to say here that there is more of disillusion in that idea of a divine awakening than is implied for us in the passage from mythology to religion. But the symbol is very subtle and exact in one respect; that it does suggest the disproportion and even disruption between the very ideas of mythology and religion, the chasm between the two categories. It is really the collapse of comparative religion that there is no comparison between God and the gods. There is no more comparison than there is between a man and the men who walked about in his dreams. Under the next heading some attempt will be made to indicate the twilight of that dream in which the gods walk about like men. But if anyone fancies the contrast of monotheism and polytheism is only a matter of some people having one god and others a few more, for him it will be far nearer the truth to plunge into the elephantine extravagance of Brahmin cosmology; that he may feel a shudder going through the veil of things, the many-handed creators, and the throned and haloed animals and all the network of entangled stars and rulers of the night, as the eyes of Brahma open like dawn upon the death of all.

MAN AND MYTHOLOGIES

What are here called the Gods might almost alternatively be called the day-dreams. To compare them to dreams is not to deny that dreams can come true. To compare them to travellers' tales is not to deny that they may be true tales, or at least truthful tales. In truth they are the sort of tales the traveller tells to himself. All this mythological business belongs to the poetical part of men. It seems strangely forgotten nowadays that a myth is a work of imagination and therefore a work of art. It needs a poet to make it. It needs a poet to criticize it. There are more poets than non-poets in the world, as is proved by the popular origin of such legends. But for some reason I have never heard explained, it is only the minority of unpoetical people who are allowed to write critical studies of these popular poems. We do not submit a sonnet to a mathematician or a song to a calculating boy; but we do indulge the equally fantastic idea that folk-lore can be treated as a science. Unless these things are appreciated artistically they are not appreciated at all. When the professor is told by the Polynesian that once there was nothing except a great feathered serpent, unless the learned man feels a thrill and a half temptation to wish it were true, he is no judge of such things at all. When he is assured, on the best Red Indian authority, that a primitive hero carried the sun and moon and stars in a box, unless he clasps his hands and almost kicks his legs as a child would at such a charming fancy, he knows nothing about the matter. This test is not nonsensical; primitive children and barbaric children do laugh and kick like other children; and we must have a certain simplicity to repicture the childhood of the world. When Hiawatha was told by his nurse that a warrior threw his grandmother up to the moon, he laughed like any English child told by his nurse that a cow jumped over the moon. The child sees the joke as well as most men, and better than some scientific men. But the ultimate test even of the fantastic is the appropriateness of the inappropriate. And the test must appear merely arbitrary because it is merely artistic. If any student tells me that the infant Hiawatha only laughed out of respect for tribal custom of sacrificing the aged to economical housekeeping, I say he did not. If any scholar tells me that the cow jumped over the moon only because a heifer was sacrificed to Diana, I answer that it did not. It happened because it is obviously the right thing for a cow to jump over the moon. Mythology is a lost art, one of the few arts that really are lost; but it is an art. The horned moon and the horned mooncalf make a harmonious and almost a quiet pattern. And throwing your grandmother into the sky is not good behaviour; but it is perfectly good taste.

Thus scientists seldom understand, as artists understand, that one branch of the beautiful is the ugly. They seldom allow for the legitimate liberty of the grotesque. And they will dismiss a savage myth as merely coarse and clumsy and an evidence of degradation, because it has not all the beauty of the herald Mercury new lighted on a heaven-kissing hill; when it really has the beauty of the Mock Turtle or the Mad Hatter. It is the supreme proof of a man being prosaic that he always insists on poetry being poetical. Sometimes the humour is in the very subject as well as the style of the fable. The Australian aborigines, regarded as the rudest of savages, have a story about a giant frog who had swallowed the sea and all the waters of the world; and who was only forced to spill them by being made to laugh. All the animals with all their antics passed before him and, like Queen Victoria, he was not amused. He collapsed at last before an eel who stood delicately balanced on the tip of its tail, doubtless with a rather desperate dignity. Any amount of fine fantastic literature might be made out of that fable. There is philosophy in that vision of the dry world before the beatific Deluge of laughter. There is imagination in the mountainous monster erupting like an aqueous volcano; there is plenty of fun in the thought of his goggling visage as the pelican or the penguin passed by. Anyhow the frog laughed; but the folk-lore student remains grave.

Moreover, even where the fables are inferior as art, they cannot be properly judged by science; still less properly judged as science. Some myths are very crude and queer like the early drawings of children; but the child is trying to draw. It is none the less an error to treat his drawing as if it were a diagram, or intended to be a diagram. The student cannot make a scientific statement about the savage, because the savage is not making a scientific statement about the world. He is saying something quite different; what might be called the gossip of the gods. We may say, if we like, that it is believed before there is time to examine it. It would be truer to say it is accepted before there is time to believe it.

I confess I doubt the whole theory of the dissemination of myths or (as it commonly is) of one myth. It is true that something in our nature and conditions makes many stories similar; but each of them may be original. One man does not borrow the story from the other man, though he may tell it from the same motive as the other man. It would be easy to apply the whole argument about legend to literature; and turn it into a vulgar monomania of plagiarism. I would undertake to trace a notion like that of the Golden Bough through individual modern novels as easily as through communal and antiquated myths. I would undertake to find something like a bunch of flowers figuring again and again from the fatal bouquet of Becky Sharpe to the spray of roses sent by the Princess of Ruritania. But though these flowers may spring from the same soil, it is not the same faded flower that is flung from hand to hand. Those flowers are always fresh.

The true origin of all the myths has been discovered much too often. There are too many keys to mythology, as there are too many cryptograms in Shakespeare. Everything is phallic; everything is totemistic; everything is seed-time and harvest; everything is ghosts and grave-offerings; everything is the golden bough of sacrifice; everything is the sun and moon; everything is everything. Every folk-lore student who knew a little more than his own monomania, every man of wider reading and critical culture like Andrew Lang, has practically confessed that the bewilderment of these things left his brain spinning. Yet the whole trouble comes from a man trying to look at these stories from the outside, as if they were scientific objects. He has only to look at them from the inside, and ask himself how he would begin a story. A story may start with anything and go anywhere. It may start with a bird without the bird being a totem; it may start with the sun without being a solar myth. It is said there are only ten plots in the world; and there will certainly be common and recurrent elements. Set ten thousand children talking at once, and telling tarradiddles about what they did in the wood, and it will not be hard to find parallels suggesting sun-worship or animal worship. Some of the stories may be pretty and some silly and some perhaps dirty; but they can only be judged as stories. In the modern dialect, they can only be judged aesthetically. It is strange that aesthetics, or mere feeling, which is now allowed to usurp where it has no rights at all, to wreck reason with pragmatism and morals with anarchy, is apparently not allowed to give a purely aesthetic judgement on what is obviously a purely aesthetic question. We may be fanciful about everything except fairy-tales.

Now the first fact is that the most simple people have the most subtle ideas. Everybody ought to know that, for everybody has been a child. Ignorant as a child is, he knows more than he can say and feels not only atmospheres but fine shades. And in this matter there are several fine shades. Nobody understands it who has not had what can only be called the ache of the artist to find some sense and some story in the beautiful things he sees; his hunger for secrets and his anger at any tower or tree escaping with its tale untold. He feels that nothing is perfect unless it is personal. Without that the blind unconscious beauty of the world stands in its garden like a headless statue. One need only be a very minor poet to have wrestled with the tower or the tree until it spoke like a titan or a dryad. It is often said that pagan mythology was a personification of the powers of nature. The phrase is true in a sense, but it is very unsatisfactory; because it implies that the forces are abstractions and the personification is artificial. Myths are not allegories. Natural powers are not in this case abstractions. It is not as if there were a God of Gravitation. There may be a genius of the waterfall; but not of mere falling, even less than of mere water. The impersonation is not of something impersonal. The point is that the personality perfects the water with significance. Father Christmas is not an allegory of snow and holly; he is not merely the stuff called snow afterwards artificially given a human form, like a snow man. He is something that gives a new meaning to the white world and the evergreens, so that snow itself seems to be warm rather than cold. The test therefore is purely imaginative. But imaginative does not mean imaginary. It does not follow that it is all what the moderns call subjective, when they mean false. Every true artist does feel, consciously or unconsciously, that he is touching transcendental truths; that his images are shadows of things seen through the veil. In other words, the natural mystic does know that there is something there; something behind the clouds or within the trees; but he believes that the pursuit of beauty is the way to find it; that imagination is a sort of incantation that can call it up.

Now we do not comprehend this process in ourselves, far less in our most remote fellow-creatures And the danger of these things being classified is that they may seem to be comprehended. A really fine work of folklore, like The Golden Bough, will leave too many readers with the idea, for instance, that this or that story of a giant's or wizard's heart in a casket or a cave only 'means' some stupid and static superstition called 'the external soul.' But we do not know what these things mean, simply because we do not know what we ourselves mean when we are moved by them. Suppose somebody in a story says 'Pluck this flower and a princess will die in a castle beyond the sea,' we do not know why something stirs in the subconsciousness, or why what is impossible seems almost inevitable. Suppose we read 'And in the hour when the king extinguished the candle his ships were wrecked far away on the coast of Hebrides.' We do not know why the imagination has accepted that image before the reason can reject it; or why such correspondences seem really to correspond to something in the soul. Very deep things in our nature, some dim sense of the dependence of great things upon small, some dark suggestion that the things nearest to us stretch far beyond our power, some sacramental feeling of the magic in material substances, and many more emotions past fading out, are in an idea like that of the external soul. The power even in the myths of savages is like the power in the metaphors of poets. The soul of such a metaphor is often very emphatically an external soul. The best critics have remarked that in the best poets the simile is often a picture that seems quite separate from the text. It is as irrelevant as the remote castle to the flower or the Hebridean coast to the candle. Shelley compares the skylark to a young woman on a turret, to a rose embedded in thick foliage, to a series of things that seem to be about as unlike a skylark in the sky as anything we can imagine. I suppose the most potent piece of pure magic in English literature is the much-quoted passage in Keats's Nightingale about the casements opening on the perilous foam. And nobody notices that the image seems to come from nowhere; that it appears abruptly after some almost equally irrelevant remarks about Ruth; and that it has nothing in the world to do with the subject of the poem. If there is one place in the world where nobody could reasonably expect to find a nightingale, it is on a window-sill at the seaside. But it is only in the same sense that nobody would expect to find a giant's heart in a casket under the sea. Now, it would be very dangerous to classify the metaphors of the poets. When Shelley says that the cloud will rise 'like a child from the womb, like a ghost from the tomb,' it would be quite possible to call the first a case of the coarse primitive birth-myth and the second a survival of the ghost-worship which became ancestor-worship. But it is the wrong way of dealing with a cloud; and is liable to leave the learned in the condition of Polonius, only too ready to think it like a weasel, or very like a whale.

Two facts follow from this psychology of day-dreams, which must be kept in mind throughout their development in mythologies and even religions. First, these imaginative impressions are often strictly local. So far from being abstractions turned into allegories, they are often images almost concentrated into idols. The poet feels the mystery of a particular forest; not of the science of afforestation or the department of woods and forests. He worships the peak of a particular mountain, not the abstract idea of altitude. So we find the god is not merely water but often one special river; he may be the sea because the sea is single like a stream; the river that runs round the world. Ultimately doubtless many deities are enlarged into elements; but they are something more than omnipresent. Apollo does not merely dwell wherever the sun shines; his home is on the rock of Delphi. Diana is great enough to be in three places at once, earth and heaven and hell, but greater is Diana of the Ephesians. This localised feeling has its lowest form in the mere fetish or talisman, such as millionaires put on their motor-cars. But it can also harden into something like a high and serious religion, where it is connected with high and serious duties; into the gods of the city or even the gods of the hearth.

The second consequence is this; that in these pagan cults there is every shade of sincerity--and insincerity. In what sense exactly did an Athenian really think he had to sacrifice to Pallas Athena? What scholar is really certain of the answer? In what sense did Dr. Johnson really think that he had to touch all the posts in the street or that he had to collect orange-peel? In what sense does a child really think that he ought to step on every alternate paving-stone? Two things are at least fairly clear. First, in simpler and less self-conscious times these forms could become more solid without really becoming more serious. Day-dreams could be acted in broad daylight, with more liberty of artistic expression; but still perhaps with something of the light step of the somnambulist. Wrap Dr. Johnson in an antique mantle, crown him (by his kind permission) with a garland, and he will move in state under those ancient skies of morning; touching a series of sacred posts carved with the heads of the strange terminal gods, that stand at the limits of the land and of the life of man. Make the child free of the marbles and mosaics of some classic temples to play on a whole floor inlaid with squares of black and white; and he will willingly make this fulfilment of his idle and drifting daydream the clear field for a grave and graceful dance. But the posts and the paving-stones are little more and little less real than they are under modern limits. They are not really much more serious for being taken seriously. They have the sort of sincerity that they always had; the sincerity of art as a symbol that expresses very real spiritualities under the surface of life. But they are only sincere in the same sense as art; not sincere in the same sense as morality. The eccentric's collection of orange-peel may turn to oranges in a Mediterranean festival or to golden apples in a Mediterranean myth. But they are never on the same plane with the difference between giving the orange to a blind beggar and carefully placing the orange-peel so that the beggar may fall and break his leg. Between these two things there is a difference of kind and not of degree. The child does not think it wrong to step on the paving-stone as he thinks it wrong to step on the dog's tail. And it is very certain that whatever jest or sentiment or fancy first set Johnson touching the wooden posts, he never touched wood with any of the feeling with which he stretched out his hands to the timber of that terrible tree, which was the death of God and the life of man.

As already noted, this does not mean that there was no reality or even no religious sentiment in such a mood. As a matter of fact the Catholic Church has taken over with uproarious success the whole of this popular business of giving people local legends and lighter ceremonial movements. In so far as all this sort of paganism was innocent and in touch with nature, there is no reason why it should not be patronised by patron saints as much as by pagan gods. And in any case there are degrees of seriousness in the most natural make-believe. There is all the difference between fancying there are fairies in the wood, which often only means fancying a certain wood as fit for fairies, and really frightening ourselves until we walk a mile rather than pass a house we have told ourselves is haunted. Behind all these things is the fact that beauty and terror are very real things and related to a real spiritual world; and to touch them at all, even in doubt or fancy, is to stir the deep things of the soul. We all understand that and the pagans understood it. The point is that paganism did not really stir the soul except with these doubts and fancies, with the consequence that we to-day can have little beyond doubts and fancies about paganism. All the best critics agree that all the greatest poets, in pagan Hellas for example, had an attitude towards their gods which is quite queer and puzzling to men in the Christian era. There seems to be an admitted conflict between the god and the man; but everybody seems to be doubtful about which is the hero and which is the villain. This doubt does not merely apply to a doubter like

Euripides in the Bacchae; it applies to a moderate conservative like Sophocles in the Antigone; or even to a regular Tory and reactionary like Aristophanes in the Frogs. Sometimes it would seem that the Greeks believed above all things in reverence, only they had nobody to revere. But the point of the puzzle is this, that all this vagueness and variation arise from the fact that the whole thing began in fancy and in dreaming; and that there are no rules of architecture for a castle in the clouds.

This is the mighty and branching tree called mythology which ramifies round the whole world, whose remote branches under separate skies bear like coloured birds the costly idols of Asia and the half-baked fetishes of Africa and the fairy kings and princesses of the folk-tales of the forest, and buried amid vines and olives the Lares of the Latins, and carried on the clouds of Olympus the buoyant supremacy of the gods of Greece. These are the myths: and he who has no sympathy with myths has no sympathy with men. But he who has most sympathy with myths will most fully realise that they are not and never were a religion, in the sense that Christianity or even Islam is a religion. They satisfy some of the needs satisfied by a religion; and notably the need for doing certain things at certain dates; the need of the twin ideas of festivity and formality. But though they provide a man with a calendar they do not provide him with a creed. A man did not stand up and say 'I believe in Jupiter and Juno and Neptune,' etc., as he stands up and says 'I believe in God the Father Almighty,' and the rest of the Apostles Creed. Many believed in some and not in others, or more in some and less in others, or only in a very vague poetical sense in any. There was no moment when they were all collected into an orthodox order which men would fight and be tortured to keep intact. Still less did anybody ever say in that fashion: 'I believe in Odin and Thor and Freya,' for outside Olympus even the Olympian order grows cloudy and chaotic. It seems clear to me that Thor was not a god at all but a hero. Nothing resembling a religion would picture anybody resembling a god as groping like a pigmy in a great cavern, that turned out to be the glove of a giant. That is the glorious ignorance called adventure Thor may have been a great adventurer; but to call him a god is like trying to compare Jehovah with Jack and the Beanstalk. Odin seems to have been a real barbarian chief, possibly of the Dark Ages after Christianity. Polytheism fades away at its fringes into fairytales or barbaric memories; it is not a thing like monotheism as held by serious monotheists. Again it does satisfy the need to cry out on some uplifted name or some noble memory in moments that are themselves noble and uplifted; such as the birth of a child or the saving of a city. But the name was so used by many to whom it was only a name. Finally it did satisfy, or rather it partially satisfied, a thing very deep in humanity indeed; the idea of surrendering something as the portion of the unknown powers; of pouring of wine upon the ground, of throwing a ring into the sea; in a word, of sacrifice. It is the wise and worthy idea of not taking our advantage to the full; of putting something in the other balance to ballast our dubious pride, of paying tithes to nature for our land. This deep truth of the danger of insolence, or being too big for our boots, runs through all the great Greek tragedies and makes them great. But it runs side by side with an almost cryptic agnosticism about the real nature of the gods to be propitiated. Where that gesture of surrender is most magnificent, as among the great Greeks, there is really much more idea that the man will be the better for losing the ox than that the god will be the better for getting it. It is said that in its grosser forms there are often actions grotesquely suggestive of the god really eating the sacrifice. But this fact is falsified by the error that I put first in this note on mythology. It is misunderstanding the psychology of day-dreams. A child pretending there is a goblin in a hollow tree will do a crude and material thing, like leaving a piece of cake for him. A poet might do a more dignified and elegant thing, like bringing to the god fruits as well as flowers. But the degree of seriousness in both acts may be the same or it may vary in almost any degree. The crude fancy is no more a creed than the ideal fancy is a creed. Certainly the pagan does not disbelieve like an atheist, any more than he believes like a Christian. He feels the presence of powers about which he guesses and invents. St. Paul said that the Greeks had one altar to an unknown god. But in truth all their gods were unknown gods. And the real break in history did come when St. Paul declared to them whom they had ignorantly worshipped.

The substance of all such paganism may be summarised thus. It is an attempt to reach the divine reality through the imagination alone; in its own field reason does not restrain it at all. It is vital to view of all history that reason is something separate from religion even in the most rational of these civilisations. It is only as an afterthought, when such cults are decadent or on the defensive, that a few Neo-Platonists or a few Brahmins are found trying to rationalise them, and even then only by trying to allegorise them. But in reality the rivers of mythology and philosophy run parallel and do not mingle till they meet in the sea of Christendom. Simple secularists still talk as if the Church had introduced a sort of schism between reason and religion. The truth is that the Church was actually the first thing that ever tried to combine reason and religion. There had never before been any such union of the priests and the philosophers. Mythology, then, sought god through the imagination; or sought truth by means of beauty, in the sense in which beauty includes much of the most grotesque ugliness. But the imagination has its own laws and therefore its own triumphs, which neither logicians nor men of science can understand It remained true to that imaginative instinct through a thousand extravagances, through every crude cosmic pantomime of a pig eating the moon or the world being cut out of a cow, through all the dizzy convolutions and mystic malformations of Asiatic art, through all the stark and staring rigidity of Egyptian and Assyrian portraiture, through every kind of cracked mirror of mad art that seemed to deform the world and displace the sky, it remained true to something about which there can be no argument; something that makes it possible for some artist of some school to stand suddenly still before that particular deformity and say, 'My dream has come true.' Therefore do we all in fact feel that pagan or primitive myths are infinitely suggestive, so long as we are wise enough not to inquire what they suggest. Therefore we all feel what is meant by Prometheus stealing fire from heaven, until some prig of a pessimist or progressive person explains what it means. Therefore we all know the meaning of Jack and the Beanstalk, until we are told. In this sense it is true that it is the ignorant who accept myths, but only because it is the ignorant who appreciate poems. Imagination has its own laws and triumphs; and a tremendous power began to clothe its images, whether images in the mind or in the mud, whether in the bamboo of the South Sea Islands or the marble of the mountains of Hellas. But there was always a trouble in the triumph, which in these pages I have tried to analyse in vain; but perhaps I might in conclusion state it thus.

The crux and crisis is that man found it natural to worship; even natural to worship unnatural things. The posture of the idol might be stiff and strange; but the gesture of the worshipper was generous and beautiful. He not only felt freer when he bent; he actually felt taller when he bowed. Henceforth anything that took away the gesture of worship would stunt and even maim him for ever. Henceforth being merely secular would be a servitude and an inhibition. If man cannot pray he is gagged; if he cannot kneel he is in irons. We therefore feel throughout the whole of paganism a curious double feeling of trust and distrust. When the man makes the gesture of salutation and of sacrifice, when he pours out the libation or lifts up the sword, he knows he is doing a worthy and a virile thing. He knows he is doing one of the things for which a man was made. His imaginative experiment is therefore justified. But precisely because it began with imagination, there is to the end something of mockery in it, and especially in the object of it. This mockery, in the more in tense moments of the intellect, becomes the almost intolerable irony of Greek tragedy. There seems a disproportion between the priest and the altar or between the altar and the god. The priest seems more solemn and almost more sacred than the god. All the order of the temple is solid and sane and satisfactory to certain parts of our nature; except the very centre of it, which seems strangely mutable and dubious, like a dancing flame. It is the first thought round which the whole has been built; and the first thought is still a fancy and almost a frivolity. In that strange place of meeting, the man seems more statuesque than the statue. He himself can stand for ever in the noble and natural attitude of the statue of the Praying Boy. But whatever name be written on the pedestal, whether Zeus or Ammon or Apollo, the god whom he worships is Proteus.

The Praying Boy may be said to express a need rather than to satisfy a need. It is by a normal and necessary action that his hands are lifted; but it is no less a parable that his hands are empty. About the nature of that need there will be more to say; but at this point it may be said that perhaps after all this true instinct, that player and sacrifice are a liberty and an enlargement, refers back to that vast and half-forgotten conception of universal fatherhood, which we have already seen everywhere fading from the morning sky. This is true; and yet it is not all the truth. There remains an indestructible instinct, in the poet as represented by the pagan, that he is not entirely wrong in localizing his God. It is something in the soul of poetry if not of piety. And the greatest of poets, when he defined the poet, did not say that he gave us the universe or the absolute or the infinite; but, in his own larger language, a local habitation and a name. No poet is merely a pantheist; those who are counted most pantheistic, like Shelley, start with some local and particular image as the pagans did. After all, Shelley wrote of the skylark because it was a skylark. You could not issue an imperial or international translation of it for use in South America, in which it was changed to an ostrich. So the mythological imagination moves as it were in circles, hovering either to find a place or to return to it. In a word, mythology is a search; it is something that combines a recurrent desire with a recurrent doubt, mixing a most hungry sincerity in the idea of seeking for a place with a most dark and deep and mysterious levity about all the places found. So far could the lonely imagination lead, and we must turn later to the lonely reason. Nowhere along this road did the two ever travel together.

That is where all these things differed from religion or the reality in which these different dimensions met in a sort of solid. They differed from the reality not in what they looked like but in what they were. A picture may look like a landscape; it may look in every detail exactly like a landscape. The only detail in which it differs is that it is not a landscape. The difference is only that which divides a portrait of Queen Elizabeth from Queen Elizabeth. Only in this mythical and mystical world the portrait could exist before the person; and the portrait was therefore more vague and doubtful. But anybody who has felt and fed on the atmosphere of these myths will know what I mean, when I say that in one sense they did not really profess to be realities. The pagans had dreams about realities; and they would have been the first to admit, in their own words, that some came through the gate of ivory and others through the gate of horn. The dreams do indeed tend to be very vivid dreams when they touch on those tender or tragic things, which can really make a sleeper awaken with the sense that his heart has been broken in his sleep. They tend continually to hover over certain passionate themes of meeting and parting, of a life that ends in death or a death that is the beginning of life. Demeter wanders over a stricken world looking for a stolen child; Isis stretches out her arms over the earth in vain to gather the limbs of Osiris; and there is lamentation upon the hills for Atys and through the woods for Adonis. There mingles with all such mourning the mystical and profound sense that death can be a deliverer and an appeasement; that such death gives us a divine blood for a renovating river and that all good is found in gathering the broken body of the god. We may truly call these foreshadowing; so long as we remember that foreshadowings are shadows. And the metaphor of a shadow happens to hit very exactly the truth that is very vital here. For a shadow is a shape; a thing which reproduces shape but not texture. These things were something like the real thing; and to say that they were like is to say that they were different. Saying something is like a dog is another way of saying it is not a dog; and it is in this sense of identity that a myth is not a man. Nobody really thought of Isis as a human being, nobody really thought of Demeter as a historical character, nobody thought of Adonis as the founder of a Church. There was no idea that any one of them had changed the world; but rather that their recurrent death and life bore the sad and beautiful burden of the changelessness of the world. Not one of them was a revolution, save in the sense of the revolution of the sun and moon. Their whole meaning is missed if we do not see that they mean the shadows that we are and the shadows that we pursue. In certain sacrificial and communal aspects they naturally suggest what sort of a god might satisfy them; but they do not profess to be satisfied. Anyone who says they do is a bad judge of poetry.

Those who talk about Pagan Christs have less sympathy with Paganism than with Christianity. Those who call these cults 'religions,' and 'compare' them with the certitude and challenge of the Church have much less appreciation than we have of what made heathenism human, or of why classic literature is still something that hangs in the air like a song. It is no very human tenderness for the hungry to prove that hunger is the same as food. It is no very genial understanding of youth to argue that hope destroys the need for happiness. And it is utterly unreal to argue that these images in the mind, admired entirely in the abstract, were even in the same world with a living man and a living polity that were worshipped because they were concrete. We might as well say that a boy playing at robbers is the same as a man in his first day in the trenches; or that boy's first fancies about 'the not impossible she' are the same as the sacrament of marriage. They are fundamentally different exactly where they are superficially similar; we might almost say they are not the same even when they are the same. They are only different because one is real and the other is not. I do not mean merely that I myself believe that one is true and the other is not. I mean that one was never meant to be true in the same sense as the other. The sense in which it was meant to be true I have tried to suggest vaguely here, but it is undoubtedly very subtle and almost indescribable. It is so subtle that the students who profess to put it up as a rival to our religion miss the whole meaning and purport of their own study. We know better than the scholars, even those of us who are no scholars, what was in that hollow cry that went forth over the dead Adonis and why the Great Mother had a daughter wedded to death. We have entered more deeply than they into the Eleusinian Mysteries and have passed a higher grade, where gate within gate guarded the wisdom of Orpheus. We know the meaning of all the myths. We know the last secret revealed to the perfect initiate. And it is not the voice of a priest or a prophet saying 'These things are.' It is the voice of a dreamer and an idealist crying, 'Why cannot these things be?

THE DEMONS AND THE PHILOSOPHERS

I have dwelt at some little length on this imaginative sort of paganism, which has crowded the world with temples and is everywhere the parent of popular festivity. For the central history of civilisation, as I see it, consists of two further stages before the final stage of Christendom. The first was the struggle between this paganism and something less worthy than itself, and the second the process by which it grew in itself less worthy. In this very varied and often very vague polytheism there was a weakness of original sin. Pagan gods were depicted as tossing men like dice; and indeed they are loaded dice. About sex especially men are born unbalanced; we might almost say men are born mad. They scarcely reach sanity till they reach sanctity. This disproportion dragged down the winged fancies; and filled the end of paganism with a mere filth and litter of spawning gods. But the first point to realise is that this sort of paganism had an early collision with another sort of paganism; and that the issue of that essentially spiritual struggle really determined the history of the world. In order to understand it we must pass to a review of the other kind of paganism. It can be considered much more briefly; indeed there is a very real sense in which the less that is said about it the better. If we have called the first sort of mythology the day-dream, we might very well call the second sort of mythology the nightmare.

Superstition recurs in all ages, and especially in rationalistic ages. I remember defending the religious tradition against a whole luncheon table of distinguished agnostics; and before the end of our conversation every one of them had procured from his pocket, or exhibited on his watch-chain, some charm or talisman from which he admitted that he was never separated. I was the only person present who had neglected to provide himself with a fetish. Superstition recurs in a rationalist age because it rests on something which, if not identical with rationalism, is not unconnected with scepticism. It is at least very closely connected with agnosticism. It rests on something that is really a very human and intelligible sentiment, like the local invocations of the numen in popular paganism. But it is an agnostic sentiment, for it rests on two feelings: first that we do not really know the laws of the universe; and second that they may be very different to all we call reason. Such men realise the real truth that enormous things do often turn upon tiny things. When a whisper comes, from tradition or what not, that one particular tiny thing is the key or clue, something deep and not altogether senseless in human nature tells them that it is not unlikely. This feeling exists in both the forms of paganism here under consideration. But when we come to the second form of it, we find it transformed and filled with another and more terrible spirit.

In dealing with the lighter thing called mythology, I have said little about the most disputable aspect of it; the extent to which such invocation of the spirits of the sea or the elements can indeed call spirits from the vasty deep; or rather, (as the Shakespearean scoffer put it) whether the spirits come when they are called. I believe that I am right in thinking that this problem, practical as it sounds, did not play a dominant part in the poetical business of mythology. But I think it even more obvious, on the evidence, that things of that sort have sometimes appeared, even if they were only appearances. But when we come to the world of superstition, in a more subtle sense, there is a shade of difference; a deepening and a darkening shade. Doubtless most popular superstition is as frivolous as any popular mythology. Men do not believe as a dogma that God would throw a thunderbolt at them for walking under a ladder; more often they amuse themselves with the not very laborious exercise of walking round it. There is no more in it than what I have already adumbrated; a sort of airy agnosticism about the possibilities of so strange a world. But there is another sort of superstition that does definitely look for results; what might be called a realistic superstition. And with that the question of whether spirits do answer or do appear becomes much more serious. As I have said, it seems to me pretty certain that they sometimes do; but about that there is a distinction that has been the beginning of much evil in the world. Whether it be because the Fall has really brought men nearer to less desirable neighbours in the spiritual world, or whether it is merely that the mood of men eager or greedy finds it easier to imagine evil, I believe that the black magic of witchcraft has been much more practical and much less poetical than the white magic of mythology. I fancy the garden of the witch has been kept much more carefully than the woodland of the nymph. I fancy the evil field has even been more fruitful than the good. To start with, some impulse, perhaps a sort of desperate impulse, drove men to the darker powers when dealing with practical problems. There was a sort of secret and perverse feeling that the darker powers would really do things; that they had no nonsense about them. And indeed that popular phase exactly expresses the point. The gods of mere mythology had a great deal of nonsense about them. They had a great deal of good nonsense about them; in the happy and hilarious sense in which we talk of the nonsense of Jabberwocky or the Land where Jumblies live. But the man consulting a demon felt as many a man has felt in consulting a detective, especially a private detective; that it was dirty work but the work would really be done. A man did not exactly go into the wood to meet a nymph; he rather went with the hope of meeting a nymph. It was an adventure rather than an assignation. But the devil really kept his appointments and even in one sense kept his promises; even if a man sometimes wished afterwards, like Macbeth, that he had broken them.

In the accounts given us of many rude or savage races we gather that the cult of demons often came after the cult of deities, and even after the cult of one single and supreme deity. It may be suspected that in almost all such places the higher deity is felt to be too far off for appeal in certain petty matters, and men invoke the spirits because they are in a more literal sense familiar spirits. But with the idea of employing the demons who get things done, a new idea appears more worthy of the demons. It may indeed be truly described as the idea of being worthy of the demons; of making oneself fit for their fastidious and exacting society. Superstition of the lighter sort toys with the idea that some trifle, some small gesture such as throwing the salt, may touch the hidden spring that works the mysterious machinery of the world. And there is after all something in the idea of such an Open Sesame. But with the appeal to lower spirits comes the horrible notion that the gesture must not only be very small but very low; that it must be a monkey trick of an utterly ugly and unworthy sort. Sooner or later a man deliberately sets himself to do the most disgusting thing he can think of. It is felt that the extreme of evil will extort a sort of attention or answer from the evil powers under the surface of the world. This is the meaning of most of the cannibalism in the world. For most cannibalism is not a primitive or even a bestial habit. It is artificial and even artistic, a sort of art for art's sake. Men do not do it because they do not think it horrible; but, on the contrary, because they do think it horrible. They wish, in the most literal sense, to sup on horrors. That is why it is often found that rude races like the Australian natives are not cannibals; while much more refined and intelligent races, like the New Zealand Maories, occasionally are. They are refined and intelligent enough to indulge sometimes in a self-conscious diabolism. But if we could understand their minds, or even really understand their language, we should probably find that they were not acting as ignorant, that is as innocent cannibals. They are not doing it because they do not think it wrong, but precisely because they do think it wrong. They are acting like a Parisian decadent at a Black Mass. But the Black Mass has to hide underground from the presence of the real Mass. In other words, the demons have really been in hiding since the coming of Christ on earth. The cannibalism of the higher barbarians is in hiding from the civilisation of the white man. But before Christendom, and especially outside Europe, this was not always so. In the ancient world the demons often wandered abroad like dragons. They could be positively and publicly enthroned as gods. Their enormous images could be set up in public temples in the centre of populous cities. And all over the world the traces can be found of this striking and solid fact, so curiously overlooked by the moderns who speak of all such evil as primitive and early in evolution, that as a matter of fact some of the very highest civilisations of the world were the very places where the horns of Satan were exalted, not only to the stars but in the face of the sun. Take for example the Aztecs and American Indians of the ancient empires of Mexico and Peru. They were at least as elaborate as Egypt or China and only less lively than that central civilisation which is our own. But those who criticise that central civilisation (which is always their own civilisation) have a curious habit of not merely doing their legitimate duty in condemning its crimes, but of going out of their way to idealise its victims. They always assume that before the advent of Europe there was nothing anywhere but Eden. And Swinburne, in that spirited chorus of the nations in 'Songs before Sunrise,' used an expression about Spain in her South American conquests which always struck me as very strange. He said something about 'her sins and sons through sinless lands dispersed,' and how they 'made accursed the name of man and thrice accursed the name of God.' It may be reasonable enough that he should say the Spaniards were sinful, but why in the world should he say that the South Americans were sinless? Why should he have supposed that continent to be exclusively populated by archangels or saints perfect in heaven? It would be a strong thing to say of the most respectable neighbourhood; but when we come to think of what we really do know of that society the remark is rather funny. We know that the sinless priests of this sinless people worshipped sinless gods, who accepted as the nectar and ambrosia of their sunny paradise nothing but incessant human sacrifice accompanied by horrible torments. We may note also in the mythology of this American civilisation that element of reversal or violence against instinct of which Dante wrote; which runs backwards everywhere through the unnatural religion of the demons. It is notable not only in ethics but in aesthetics. A South American idol was made as ugly as possible, as a Greek image was made as beautiful as possible. They were seeking the secret of power, by working backwards against their own nature and the nature of things. There was always a sort of yearning to carve at last, in gold or granite or the dark red timber of the forests, a face at which the sky itself would break like a cracked mirror.

In any case it is clear enough that the painted and gilded civilization of tropical America systematically indulged in human sacrifice. It is by no means clear, so far as I know, that the Eskimos ever indulged in human sacrifice. They were not civilised enough. They were too closely imprisoned by the white winter and the endless dark. Chill penury repressed their noble rage and froze the genial current of the soul. It was in brighter days and broader daylight that the noble rage is found unmistakably raging. It was in richer and more instructed lands that the genial current flowed on the altars, to be drunk by great gods wearing goggling and grinning masks and called on in terror or torment by long cacophonous names that sound like laughter in hell. A warmer climate and a more scientific cultivation were needed to bring forth these blooms; to draw up towards the sun the large leaves and flamboyant blossoms that gave their gold and crimson and purple to that garden, which Swinburne compares to the Hesperides. There was at least no doubt about the dragon.

I do not raise in this connection the special controversy about Spain and Mexico; but I may remark in passing that it resembles exactly the question that must in some sense be raised afterwards about Rome and Carthage. In both cases there has been a queer habit among the English of always siding against the Europeans, and representing the rival civilisation, in Swinburne's phrase, as sinless; when its sins were obviously crying or rather screaming to heaven. For Carthage also was a high civilisation, indeed a much more highly civilised civilisation. And Carthage also founded that civilisation on a religion of fear, sending up everywhere the smoke of human sacrifice. Now it is very right to rebuke our own race or religion for falling short of our own standards and ideals. But it is absurd to pretend that they fell lower than the other races and religions that professed the very opposite standards and ideals. There is a very real sense in which the Christian is worse than the heathen, the Spaniard worse than the Red Indian, or even the Roman potentially worse than the Carthaginian. But there is only one sense in which he is worse; and that is not in being positively worse. The Christian is only worse because it is his business to be better.

This inverted imagination produces things of which it is better not to speak. Some of them indeed might almost be named without being known; for they are of that extreme evil which seems innocent to the innocent. They are too inhuman even to be indecent. But without dwelling much longer in these dark corners, it may be noted as not irrelevant here that certain anti-human antagonisms seem to recur in this tradition of black magic. There may be suspected as running through it everywhere, for instance, a mystical hatred of the idea of childhood. People would understand better the popular fury against the witches, if they remembered that the malice most commonly attributed to them was preventing the birth of children. The Hebrew prophets were perpetually protesting against the Hebrew race relapsing into an idolatry that involved such a war upon children; and it is probable enough that this abominable apostasy from the God of Israel has occasionally appeared in Israel since, in the form of what is called ritual murder; not of course by any representative of the religion of Judaism, but by individual and irresponsible diabolists who did happen to be Jews. This sense that the forces of evil especially threaten childhood is found again in the enormous popularity of the Child Martyr of the Middle Ages. Chaucer did but give another version of a very national English legend, when he conceived the wickedest of all possible witches as the dark alien woman watching behind her high lattice and heading, like the babble of a brook down the stony street, the singing of little St. Hugh.

Anyhow the part of such speculations that concerns this story centered especially round that eastern end of the Mediterranean, where the nomads had turned gradually into traders and had begun to trade with the whole world. Indeed in the sense of trade and travel and colonial extension, it already had something like an empire of the whole world. Its purple dye, the emblem of its rich pomp and luxury, had steeped the wares which were sold far away amid the last crags of Cornwall and the sails that entered the silence of tropic seas amid all the mystery of Africa. It might be said truly to have painted the map purple. It was already a world-wide success, when the princes of Tyre would hardly have troubled to notice that one of their princesses had condescended to marry the chief of some tribe called Judah; when the merchants of its African outpost would only have curled their bearded and Semitic lips with a slight smile at the mention of a village called Rome. And indeed no two things could have seemed more distant from each other, not only in space but in Spirit, than the monotheism of the Palestinian tribe and the very virtues of the small Italian republic. There was but one thing between them; and the thing which divided them has united them. Very various and incompatible were the things that could be loved by the consuls of Rome and the prophets of Israel; but they were at one in what they hated. It is very easy in both cases to represent that hatred as something merely hateful. It is easy enough to make a merely harsh and inhuman figure either of Elijah raving above the slaughter of Carmel or Cato thundering against the amnesty of Africa. These men had their limitations and their local passions; but this criticism of them is unimaginative and therefore unreal. It leaves out something, something immense and intermediate, facing east and west and calling up this passion in its eastern and western enemies; and that something is the first subject of this chapter.

The civilisation that centered in Tyre and Sidon was above all things practical. It has left little in the way of art and nothing in the way of poetry. But it prided itself upon being very efficient; and it followed in its philosophy and religion that strange and sometimes secret train of thought which we have already noted in those who look for immediate effects. There is always in such a mentality an idea that there is a short cut to the secret of all success; something that would shock the world by this sort of shameless thoroughness. They believed, in the appropriate modern phrase, in people who delivered the goods. In their dealings with their god Moloch, they themselves were always careful to deliver the goods. It was an interesting transaction, upon which we shall have to touch more than once in the rest of the narrative; it is enough to say here that it involved the theory I have suggested, about a certain attitude towards children. This was what called up against it in simultaneous fury the servant of one God in Palestine and the guardians of all the household gods in Rome This is what challenged two things naturally so much divided by every sort of distance and disunion, whose union was to save the world.

I have called the fourth and final division of the spiritual elements into which I should divide heathen humanity by the name of The Philosophers. I confess that it covers in my mind much that would generally be classified otherwise; and that what are here called philosophies are very often called religions. I believe however that my own description will be found to be much the more realistic and not the less respectful. But we must first take philosophy in its purest and clearest form that we may trace its normal outline; and that is to be found in the world of the purest and clearest outlines, that culture of the Mediterranean of which we have been considering the mythologies and idolatries in the last two chapters.

Polytheism, or that aspect of paganism, was never to the pagan what Catholicism is to the Catholic. It was never a view of the universe satisfying all sides of life; a complete and complex truth with something to say about everything. It was only a satisfaction of one side of the soul of man, even if we call it the religious side; and I think it is truer to call it the imaginative side. But this it did satisfy; in the end it satisfied it to satiety. All that world was a tissue of interwoven tales and cults, and there ran in and out of it, as we have already seen, that black thread among its more blameless colours; the darker paganism that was really diabolism. But we all know that this did not mean that all pagan men thought of nothing but pagan gods. Precisely because mythology only satisfied one mood, they turned in other moods to something totally different. But it is very important to realise that it was totally different. It was too different to be inconsistent. It was so alien that it did not clash. While a mob of people were pouring on a public holiday to the feast of Adonis or the games in honour of Apollo, this or that man would prefer to stop at home and think out a little theory about the nature of things. Sometimes his hobby would even take the form of thinking about the nature of God; or even in that sense about the nature of the gods. But he very seldom thought of pitting his nature of the gods against the gods of nature.

It is necessary to insist on this abstraction in the first student of abstractions. He was not so much antagonistic as absent-minded. His hobby might be the universe; but at first the hobby was as private as if it had been numismatics or playing draughts. And even when his wisdom came to be a public possession, and almost a political situation, it was very seldom on the same plane as the popular and religious institutions. Aristotle, with his colossal common sense, was perhaps the greatest of all philosophers; certainly the most practical of all philosophies But Aristotle would no more have set up the Absolute side by side with the Apollo of

Delphi, as a similar or rival religion, than Archimedes would have thought of setting up the lever as a sort of idol or fetish to be substituted for the Palladium of the city. Or we might as well imagine Euclid building an altar to an isosceles triangle, or offering sacrifices to the square of the hypotenuse. The one man meditated on metaphysics as the other man did on mathematics; for the love of truth or for curiosity or for the fun of the thing. But that sort of fun never seems to have interfered very much with the other sort of fun; the fun of dancing or singing to celebrate some rascally romance about Zeus becoming a bull or a swan. It is perhaps the proof of a certain superficiality and even insincerity about the popular polytheism, that men could be philosophers and even sceptics without disturbing it. These thinkers could move the foundations of the world without altering even the outline of that coloured cloud that hung above it in the air.

For the thinkers did move the foundations of the world, even when a curious compromise seemed to prevent them from moving the foundations of the city. The two great philosophers of antiquity do indeed appear to us as defenders of sane and even of sacred ideas; their maxims often read like the answers to sceptical questions too completely answered to be always recorded. Aristotle annihilated a hundred anarchists and nature worshipping cranks by the fundamental statement that man is a political animal. Plato in some sense anticipated the Catholic realism, as attacked by the heretical nominalism, by insisting on the equally fundamental fact that ideas are realities; that ideas exist just as men exist. Plato however seemed sometimes almost to fancy that ideas exist as men do not exist; or that the men need hardly be considered where they conflict with the ideas. He had something of the social sentiment that we call Fabian in his ideal of fitting the citizen to the city. Like an imaginary head to an ideal hat; and great and glorious as he remains, he has been the Father of all faddists. Aristotle anticipated more fully the sacramental sanity that was to combine the body and the soul of things; for he considered the nature of men as well as the nature of morals, and looked to the eyes as well as to the light. But though these great men were in that sense constructive and conservative, they belonged to a world where thought was free to the point of being fanciful. Many other great intellects did indeed follow them, some exalting an abstract vision of virtue, others following more rationalistically the necessity of the human pursuit of happiness. The former had the name of Stoics; and their name has passed into a proverb for what is indeed one of the main moral ideals of mankind: that of strengthening the mind itself until it is of a texture to resist calamity or even pain. But it is admitted that a great number of the philosophers degenerated into what we still call sophists. They became a sort of professional sceptics who went about asking uncomfortable questions, and were handsomely paid for making themselves a nuisance to normal people.

It was perhaps an accidental resemblance to such questioning quacks that was responsible for the unpopularity of the great Socrates; whose death might seem to contradict the suggestion of the permanent truce between the philosophers and the gods. But Socrates did not die as a monotheist who denounced polytheism; certainly not as a prophet who denounced idols. It is clear to anyone reading between the lines that there was some notion, right or wrong, of a purely personal influence affecting morals and perhaps politics The general compromise remained, whether it was that the Greeks thought their myths a joke or that they thought their theories a joke. There was never any collision in which one really destroyed the other, and there was never any combination in which one was really reconciled with the other. They certainly did not work together; if anything the philosopher was a rival of the priest. But both seemed to have accepted a sort of separation of functions and remained parts of the same social system. Another important tradition descends from Pythagoras; who is significant because he stands nearest to the Oriental mystics who must be considered in their turn. He taught a sort of mysticism of mathematics, that number is the ultimate reality; but he also seems to have taught the transmigration of souls like the Brahmins; and to have left to his followers certain traditional tricks of vegetarianism and water-drinking very common among the eastern sages, especially those who figure in fashionable drawing-rooms, like those of the later Roman Empire. But in passing to eastern sages, and the somewhat different atmosphere of the east, we may approach a rather important truth by other path.

One of the great philosophers said that it would be well if philosophers were kings, or kings were philosophers. He spoke as of something too good to be true; but, as a matter of fact, it not unfrequently was true. A certain type, perhaps too little noticed in history, may really be called the royal philosopher. To begin with, apart from actual royalty, it did occasionally become possible for the sage, though he was not what we call a religious founder, to be something like a political founder. And the great example of this, one of the very greatest in the world, will with the very thought of it carry us thousands of miles across the vast spaces of Asia to that very wonderful and in some ways that very wise world of ideas and institutions, which we dismiss somewhat cheaply when we talk of China. Men have served many very strange gods; and trusted themselves loyally to many ideals and even idols. China is a society that has really chosen to believe in intellect. It has taken intellect seriously; and it may be that it stands alone in the world. From a very early age it faced the dilemma of the king and the philosopher by actually appointing a philosopher to advise the king. It made a public institution out of a private individual, who had nothing in the world to do but to be intellectual. It had and has, of course, many other things on the same pattern. It creates all ranks and privileges by public examination; it has nothing that we call an aristocracy; it is a democracy dominated by an intelligensia. But the point here is that it had philosophers to advise kings; and one of those philosophers must have been a great philosopher and a great statesman.

Confucius was not a religious founder or even a religious teacher; possibly not even a religious man. He was not an atheist; he was apparently what we call an agnostic. But the really vital point is that it is utterly irrelevant to talk about his religion at all. It is like talking of theology as the first thing in the story of how Rowland Hill established the postal system or Baden Powell organised the Boy Scouts. Confucius was not there to bring a message from heaven to humanity, but to organise China; and he must have organised it exceedingly well. It follows that he dealt much with morals; but he bound them up strictly with manners. The peculiarity of his scheme and of his country, in which it contrasts with its great pendant the system of Christendom, is that he insisted on perpetuating an external life with all its forms, that outward continuity might preserve internal peace. Anyone who knows how much habit has to do with health, of mind as well as body, will see the truth in his idea. But he will also see that the ancestor-worship and the reverence for the Sacred Emperor were habits and not creeds. It is unfair to the great Confucius to say he was a religious founder. It is even unfair to him to say he was not a religious founder. It is as unfair as going out of one's way to say that Jeremy Bentham was not a Christian martyr.

But there is a class of most interesting cases in which philosophers were kings, and not merely the friends of kings. The combination is not accidental. It has a great deal to do with this rather elusive question of the function of the philosopher. It contains in it some hint of why philosophy and mythology seldom came to an open rupture. It was not only because there was something a little frivolous about the mythology. It was also because there was something a little supercilious about the philosopher. He despised the myths, but he also despised the mob; and thought they suited each other. The pagan philosopher was seldom a man of the people, at any rate in spirit; he was seldom a democrat and often a bitter critic of democracy. He had about him an air of aristocratic and humane leisure; and his part was most easily played by men who happened to be in such a position. It was very easy and natural for a prince or a prominent person to play at being as philosophical as Hamlet or Theseus in the Midsummer Night's Dream. And from very early ages we find ourselves in the presence of these princely intellectuals. In fact, we find one of them in the very first recorded ages of the world; sitting on the primeval throne that looked over ancient Egypt.

The most intense interest of the incident of Akenahten, commonly called the Heretic Pharaoh, lies in the fact that he was the one example, at any rate before Christian times, of one of these royal philosophers who set himself to fight popular mythology in the name of private philosophy. Most of them assumed the attitude of Marcus Aurelius, who is in many ways the model of this sort of monarch and sage. Marcus Aurelius has been blamed for tolerating the pagan amphitheatre or the Christian martyrdoms. But it was characteristic; for this sort of man really thought of popular religion just as he thought of popular circuses. Of him Professor Phillimore has profoundly said 'a great and good man—and he knew it.' The heretic Pharaoh had a philosophy more earnest and perhaps more humble. For there is a corollary to the conception of being too proud to fight. It is that the humble have to do most of the fighting. Anyhow, the Egyptian prince was simple enough to take his own philosophy seriously, and alone among such intellectual princes he affected a sort of coup d'etat; hurling down the high gods of Egypt with one imperial gesture and lifting up for all men, like a blazing mirror of monotheistic truth, the disc of the universal sun. He had other interesting ideas often to be found in such idealists. In the sense in which we speak of a Little Englander he was a Little Egypter. In art he was a realist because he was an idealist; for realism is more impossible than any other ideal. But after all there falls on him something of the shadow of Marcus Aurelius, stalked by the shadow of Professor Phillimore. That is the matter with this noble sort of prince is that he has nowhere quite escaped being something of a prig. Priggishness is so pungent a smell that it clings amid the faded spices even to an Egyptian mummy. That was the matter with the heretic Pharaoh, as with a good many other heretics, was that he probably never paused to ask himself whether there was anything in the popular beliefs and tales of people less educated than himself. And, as already suggested, there was something in them. There was a real human hunger in all that element of feature and locality, that procession of deities like enormous pet animals, in that unwearied watching at certain haunted spots, in all the many wanderings of mythology. Nature may not have the name of Isis; Isis may not be really looking for Osiris. But it is true that Nature is really looking for something; Nature is always looking for the supernatural. Something much more definite was to satisfy that need; but a dignified monarch with a disc of the sun did not satisfy it. The royal experiment failed amid a roaring reaction of popular superstitions, in which the priests rose on the shoulders of the people and ascended the throne of the kings.

The next great example I shall take of the princely sage is Gautama, the great Lord Buddha. I know he is not generally classed merely with the philosophers; but I am more and more convinced from all information that reaches me, that this is the real interpretation of his immense importance. He was by far the greatest and the best of these intellectuals born in the purple. His reaction was perhaps the noblest and most sincere of all the resultant actions of that combination of thinkers and of thrones. For his reaction was renunciation. Marcus Aurelius was content to say, with a refined irony, that even in a palace life could be lived well. The fierier Egyptian king concluded that it could be lived even better after a palace revolution. But the great Gautama was the only one of them who proved he could really do without his palace. One fell back on toleration and the other on revolution. But after all there is something more absolute about abdication. Abdication is perhaps the one really absolute action of an absolute monarch. The Indian prince, reared in Oriental luxury and pomp, deliberately went out and lived the life of a beggar. That is magnificent, but it is not war; that is, it is not necessarily a Crusade in the Christian sense. It does not decide the question of whether the life of a beggar was the life of a saint or the life of a philosopher. It does not decide whether this great man is really to go into the tub of Diogenes or the cave of St. Jerome. Now those who seem to be nearest to the study of Buddha, and certainly those who write most clearly and intelligently about him, convince me for one that he was simply a philosopher who founded a successful school of philosophy, and was turned into a sort of divus or sacred being merely by the more mysterious and unscientific atmosphere of all such traditions in Asia. So that it is necessary to say at this point a word about that invisible yet vivid border-line that we cross in passing from the Mediterranean into the mystery of the East.

Perhaps there are no things out of which we get so little of the truth as the truisms; especially when they are really true. We are all in the habit of saying certain things about Asia, which are true enough but which hardly help us because we do not understand their truth; as that Asia is old or looks to the past or is not progressive. Now it is true that Christendom is more progressive, in a sense that has very little to do with the rather provincial notion of an endless fuss of political improvement. Christendom does believe, for Christianity does believe, that man can eventually get somewhere, here or hereafter, or in various ways according to various doctrines. The world's desire can somehow be satisfied as desires are satisfied, whether by a new life or an old love or some form of positive possession and fulfilment. For the rest, we all know there is a rhythm and not a mere progress in things, that things rise and fall; only with us the rhythm is a fairly free and incalculable rhythm. For most of Asia the rhythm has hardened into a recurrence. It is no longer merely a rather topsy-turvy sort of world; it is a wheel. What has happened to all those highly intelligent and highly civilized peoples is that they have been caught up in a sort of cosmic rotation, of which the hollow hub is really nothing. In that sense the worst part of existence is that it may just as well go on like that forever. That is what we really mean when we say that Asia is old or unprogressive or looking backwards. That is why we see even her curved swords as arcs broken from that blinding wheel; why we see her serpentine ornament as returning everywhere, like a snake that is never slain. It has very little to do with the political varnish of progress; all Asiatics might have top-hats on their heads but if they had this spirit still in their hearts, they would only think the hats would vanish and come round again like the planets; not that running after a hat could lead them to heaven or even to home.

Now when the genius of Buddha arose to deal with the matter, this sort of cosmic sentiment was already common to almost everything in the east. There was indeed the jungle of an extraordinarily extravagant and almost asphyxiating mythology. Nevertheless it is possible to have more sympathy with this popular fruitfulness in folk-lore than with some of the higher pessimism that might have withered it. It must always be remembered, however, when all fair allowances are made, that a great deal of spontaneous eastern imagery really is idolatry; the local and literal worship of an idol. This is probably not true of the ancient Brahminical system, at least as seen by Brahmins. But that phrase alone will remind us of a reality of much greater moment. This great reality is the Caste System of ancient India. It may have had some of the practical advantages of the Guild System of Medieval Europe. But it contrasts not only with that Christian democracy, but with every extreme type of Christian aristocracy, in the fact that it does really conceive the social superiority as a spiritual superiority. This not only divides it fundamentally from the fraternity of Christendom, but leaves it standing like a mighty and terraced mountain of pride between the relatively egalitarian levels both of Islam and of China. But the fixity of this formation through thousands of years is another illustration of that spirit of repetition that has marked time from time immemorial. Now we may also presume the prevalence of another idea which we associate with the Buddhists as interpreted by the Theosophists. As a fact, some of the strictest Buddhists repudiate the idea and still more scornfully repudiate the Theosophists. But whether the idea is in Buddhism, or only in the birthplace of Buddhism, or only in a tradition or a travesty of Buddhism, it is an idea entirely proper to this principle of recurrence. I mean of course the idea of Reincarnation.

But Reincarnation is not really a mystical idea. It is not really a transcendental idea, or in that sense a religious idea. Mysticism conceives something transcending experience; religion seeks glimpses of a better good or a worse evil than experience can give. Reincarnation need only extend experiences in the sense of repeating them. It is no more transcendental for a man to remember what he did in Babylon before he was born than to remember what he did in Brixton before he had a knock on the head. His successive lives need not be any more than human lives, under whatever limitations burden human life. It has nothing to do with seeing God or even conjuring up the devil. In other words, reincarnation as such does not necessarily escape from the wheel of destiny, in some sense it is the wheel of destiny And whether it was something that Buddha founded, or something that Buddha found, or something that Buddha entirely renounced when he found, it is certainly something having the general character of that Asiatic atmosphere in which he had to play his part. And the part he played was that of an intellectual philosopher, with a particular theory about the right intellectual attitude towards it.

I can understand that Buddhists might resent the view that Buddhism is merely a philosophy, if we understand by a philosophy merely an intellectual game such as Greek sophists played, tossing up worlds and catching them like balls. Perhaps a more exact statement would be that Buddha was a man who made a metaphysical discipline; which might even be called a psychological discipline. He proposed a way of escaping from all this recurrent sorrow; and that was simply by getting rid of the delusion that is called desire. It was emphatically not that we should get what we want better by restraining our impatience for part of it, or that we should get it in a better way or in a better world. It was emphatically that we should leave off wanting it. If once a man realized that there is really no reality, that everything, including his soul, is in dissolution at every instant, he would anticipate disappointment and be intangible to change, existing (in so far as he could be said to exist) in a sort of ecstasy of indifference. The Buddhists call this beatitude and we will not stop our story to argue the point; certainly to us it is indistinguishable from despair. I do not see, for instance, why the disappointment of desire should not apply as much to the most benevolent desires as to the most selfish ones. Indeed the Lord of Compassion seems to pity people for living rather than for dying. For the rest, an intelligent Buddhist wrote 'the explanation of popular Chinese and Japanese Buddhism is that it is not Buddhism.' That has doubtless ceased to be a mere philosophy, but only by becoming a mere mythology. One thing is certain; it has never become anything remotely resembling what we call a Church.

It will appear only a jest to say that all religious history has really been a pattern of noughts and crosses. But I do not by noughts mean nothings, but only things that are negative compared with the positive shape or pattern of the other. And though the symbol is of course only a coincidence, it is a coincidence that really does coincide. The mind of Asia can really be represented by a round 0, if not in the sense of a cypher at least of a circle. The great Asiatic symbol of a serpent with its tail in its mouth is really a very perfect image of a certain idea of unity and recurrence that does indeed belong to the Eastern philosophies and religions. It really is a curve that in one sense includes everything, and in another sense comes to nothing. In that sense it does confess, or rather boast, that all argument is an argument in a circle. And though the figure is but a symbol, we can see how sound is the symbolic sense that produces it, the parallel symbol of the

Wheel of Buddha generally called the Swastika. The cross is a thing at right angles pointing boldly in opposite directions; but the Swastika is the same thing in the very act of returning to the recurrent curve. That crooked cross is in fact a cross turning into a wheel. Before we dismiss even these symbols as if they were arbitrary symbols, we must remember how intense was the imaginative instinct that produced them or selected them both in the east and the west. The cross has become something more than a historical memory; it does convey, almost as by a mathematical diagram, the truth about the real point at issue; the idea of a conflict stretching outwards into eternity. It is true, and even tautological, to say that the cross is the crux of the whole matter.

In other words the cross, in fact as well as figure, does really stand for the idea of breaking out of the circle that is everything and nothing. It does escape from the circular argument by which everything begins and ends in the mind. Since we are still dealing in symbols, it might be put in a parable in the form of that story about St. Francis, which says that the birds departing with his benediction could wing their way into the infinites of the four winds of heaven, their tracks making a vast cross upon the sky; for compared with the freedom of that flight of birds, the very shape of the Swastika is like a kitten chasing its tail. In a more popular allegory, we might say that when St. George thrust his spear into the monster's jaws, he broke in upon the solitude of the self-devouring serpent and gave it something to bite besides its own tail. But while many fancies might be used as figures of the truth, the truth itself is abstract and absolute; though it is not very easy to sum up except by such figures. Christianity does appeal to a solid truth outside itself; to something which is in that sense external as well as eternal. It does declare that things are really there; or in other words that things are really things--In this Christianity is at one with common sense; but all religious history shows that this common sense perishes except where there is Christianity to preserve it.

It cannot otherwise exist, or at least endure, because mere thought does not remain sane. In a sense it becomes too simple to be sane. The temptation of the philosophers is simplicity rather than subtlety. They are always attracted by insane simplifications, as men poised above abysses are fascinated by death and nothingness and the empty air. It needed another kind of philosopher to stand poised upon the pinnacle of the Temple and keep his balance without casting himself down. One of these obvious, these too obvious explanations is that everything is a dream and a delusion and there is nothing outside the ego. Another is that all things recur; another, which is said to be Buddhist and is certainly Oriental, is the idea that what is the matter with us is our creation, in the sense of our coloured differentiation and personality, and that nothing will be well till we are again melted into one unity. By this theory, in short, the Creation was the Fall. It is important historically because it was stored up in the dark heart of Asia and went forth at various times in various forms over the dim borders of Europe. Here we can place the mysterious figure of Manes or Manichaeus, the mystic of inversion, whom we should call a pessimist, parent of many sects and heresies; here, in a higher place, the figure of Zoroaster. He has been popularly identified with another of these too simple explanations; the equality of evil and good, balanced and battling in every atom. He also is of the school of sages that may be called mystics; and from the same mysterious Persian garden came upon ponderous wings Mithras, the unknown god, to trouble the last twilight of Rome.

That circle or disc of the sun set up in the morning of the world by the remote Egyptian has been a mirror and a model for all the philosophers. They have made many things out of it, and sometimes gone mad about it, especially when as in these eastern sages the circle became a wheel going round and round in their heads. But the point about them is that they all think that existence can be represented by a diagram instead of a drawing; and the rude drawings of the childish myth-makers are a sort of crude and spirited protest against that view. They cannot believe that religion is really not a pattern but a picture. Still less can they believe that it is a picture of something that really exists outside our minds. Sometimes the philosophy paints the disc all black and calls himself a pessimist; sometimes he paints it all white and calls himself an optimist; sometimes he divides it exactly into halves of black and white and calls himself a dualist, like those Persian mystics to whom I wish there were space to do justice. None of them could understand a thing that began to draw the proportions just as if they were real proportions, disposed in the living fashion which the mathematical draughtsman would call disproportionate. Like the first artist in the cave, it revealed to incredulous eyes the suggestion of a new purpose in what looked like a wildly crooked pattern; he seemed only to be distorting his diagram, when he began for the first time in all the ages to trace the lines of a form--and of a Face.

THE WAR OF THE GODS AND DEMONS

The materialist theory of history, that all politics and ethics are the expression of economics, is a very simple fallacy indeed. It consists simply of confusing the necessary conditions of life with the normal preoccupations of life, that are quite a different thing. It is like saying that because a man can only walk about on two legs, therefore he never walks about except to buy shoes and stockings. Man cannot live without the two props of food and drink, which support him like two legs; but to suggest that they have been the motives of all his movements in history is like saying that the goal of all his military marches or religious pilgrimages must have been the Golden Leg of Miss Kilmansegg or the ideal and perfect leg of Sir Willoughby Patterne. But it is such movements that make up the story of mankind and without them there would practically be no story at all. Cows may be purely economic, in the sense that we cannot see that they do much beyond grazing and seeking better grazing grounds; and that is why a history of cows in twelve volumes would not be very lively reading. Sheep and goats may be pure economists in their external action at least; but that is why the sheep has hardly been a hero of epic wars and empires thought worthy of detailed narration; and even the more active quadruped has not inspired a book for boys called Golden Deeds of Gallant Goats or any similar title. But so far from the movements that make up the story of man being economic, we may say that the story only begins where the motive of the cows and sheep leaves off. It will be hard to maintain that the Crusaders went from their homes into a howling wilderness because cows go from a wilderness to a more comfortable grazing-grounds. It will be hard to maintain that the Arctic explorers went north with the same material motive that made the swallows go south. And if you leave things like all the religious wars and all the merely adventurous explorations out of the human story, it will not only cease to be human at all but cease to be a story at all. The outline of history is made of these decisive curves and angles determined by the will of man. Economic history would not even be history.

But there is a deeper fallacy besides this obvious fact; that men need not live for food merely because they cannot live without food The truth is that the thing most present to the mind of man is not the economic machinery necessary to his existence; but rather that existence itself; the world which he sees when he wakes every morning and the nature of his general position in it. There is something that is nearer to him than livelihood, and that is life. For once that he remembers exactly what work produces his wages and exactly what wages produce his meals, he reflects ten times that it is a fine day or it is a queer world, or wonders whether life is worth living, or wonders whether marriage is a failure, or is pleased and puzzled with his own children, or remembers his own youth, or in any such fashion vaguely reviews the mysterious lot of man. This is true of the majority even of the wage-slaves of our morbid modern industrialism, which by its hideousness and in-humanity has really forced the economic issue to the front. It is immeasurably more true of the multitude of peasants or hunters or fishers who make up the real mass of mankind. Even those dry pedants who think that ethics depend on economics must admit that economics depend on existence. And any number of normal doubts and day-dreams are about existence; not about how we can live, but about why we do. And the proof of it is simple; as simple as suicide. Turn the universe upside down in the mind and you turn all the political economists upside down with it. Suppose that a man wishes to die, and the professor of political economy becomes rather a bore with his elaborate explanations of how he is to live. And all the departures and decisions that make our human past into a story have this character of diverting the direct course of pure economics. As the economist may be excused from calculating the future salary of a suicide, so he may be excused from providing an old age pension for a martyr. As he need not provide for the future of a martyr so he need not provide for the family of a monk. His plan is modified in lesser and varying degrees by a man being a soldier and dying for his own country, by a man being a peasant and specially loving his own land, by a man being more or less affected by any religion that forbids or allows him to do this or that. But all these come back not to an economic calculation about livelihood but to an elemental outlook upon life. They all come back to what a man fundamentally feels, when he looks forth from those strange windows which we call the eyes, upon that strange vision that we call the world.

No wise man will wish to bring more long words into the world. But it may be allowable to say that we need a new thing; which may be called psychological history. I mean the consideration of what things meant in the mind of a man, especially an ordinary man; as distinct from what is defined or deduced merely from official forms or political pronouncements. I have already touched on it in such a case as the totem or indeed any other popular myth. It is not enough to be told that a tom-cat was called a totem; especially when it was not called a totem. We want to know what it felt like. Was it like Whittington's cat or like a witch's cat? Was its real name Pashtl or Puss-in-Boots? That is the sort of thing we need touching the nature of political and social relations. We want to know the real sentiment that was the social bond of many common men, as sane and as selfish as we are. What did soldiers feel when they saw splendid in the sky that strange totem that we call the Golden Eagle of the Legions? What did vassals feel about those other totems the lions or the leopards upon the shield of their lord?

So long as we neglect this subjective side of history, which may more simply be called the inside of history, there will always be a certain limitation on that science which can be better transcended by art. So long as the historian cannot do that, fiction will be truer than fact. There will be more reality in a novel; yes, even in a historical novel.

In nothing is this new history needed so much as in the psychology of war. Our history is stiff with official documents, public or private, which tell us nothing of the thing itself. At the worst we only have the official posters, which could not have been spontaneous precisely because they were official. At the best we have only the secret diplomacy, which could not have been popular precisely because it was secret. Upon one or other of these is based the historical judgement about the real reasons that sustained the struggle. Governments fight for colonies or commercial rights; governments fight about harbours or high tariffs; governments fight for a gold mine or a pearl fishery. It seems sufficient to answer that governments do not fight at all. Why do the fighters fight? What is the psychology that sustains the terrible and wonderful thing called a war? Nobody who knows anything of soldiers believes the silly notion of the dons, that millions of men can be ruled by force. If they were all to slack, it would be impossible to punish all the slackers And the least little touch of slacking would lose a whole campaign in half a day. What did men really feel about the policy? If it be said that they accepted the policy from the politician, what did they feel about the politician? If the vassals warred blindly for their prince what did those blind men see in their prince?

There is something we all know which can only be rendered, in an appropriate language, as realpolitik. As a matter of fact, it is an almost insanely unreal politik. It is always stubbornly and stupidly repeating that men fight for material ends, without reflecting for a moment that the material ends are hardly ever material to the men who fight. In any case no man will die for practical politics, just as no man will die for pay. Nero could not hire a hundred Christians to be eaten by lions at a shilling an hour; for men will not be martyred for money. But the vision called up by real politik, or realistic politics, is beyond example crazy and incredible. Does anybody in the world believe that d soldier says, 'My leg is nearly dropping off, but I shall go on till it drops; for after all I shall enjoy all the advantages of my government obtaining a warm-water port in the Gulf of Finland.' Can anybody suppose that a clerk turned conscript says, 'If I am gassed I shall probably die in torments, but it is a comfort to reflect that should I ever decide to become a pearl-diver in the South Seas, that career is now open to me and my countrymen.' Materialist history is the most madly incredible of all histories, or even of all romances. Whatever starts wars, the thing that sustains wars is something in the soul; that is something akin to religion. It is what men feel about life and about death. A man near to death is dealing directly with an absolute; it is nonsense to say he is concerned only with relative and remote complications that death in any case will end. If he is sustained by certain loyalties, they must be loyalties as simple as death. They are generally two ideas, which are only two sides of one idea. The first is the love of something said to be threatened, if it be only vaguely known as home; the second is dislike and defiance of some strange thing that threatens it. The first is far more philosophical than it sounds, though we need not discuss it here. A man does not want his national home destroyed or even changed, because he cannot even remember all the good things that go with it; just as he does not want his house burnt down, because he can hardly count all the things he would miss. Therefore he fights for what sounds like a hazy abstraction, but is really a house. But the negative side of it is quite as noble as well as quite as strong. Men fight hardest when they feel that the foe is at once an old enemy and an eternal stranger, that his atmosphere is alien and antagonistic, as the French feel about the Prussian or the Eastern Christians about the Turk. If we say it is a difference of religion, people will drift into dreary bickerings about sects and dogmas. We will pity them and say it is a difference about death and daylight; a difference that does really come like a dark shadow between our eyes and the day. Men can think of this difference even at the point of death; for it is a difference about the meaning of life.

Men are moved in these things by something far higher and holier than policy; by hatred. When men hung on in the darkest days of the Great War, suffering either in their bodies or in their souls for those they loved, they were long past caring about details of diplomatic objects as motives for their refusal to surrender. Of myself and those I knew best I can answer for the vision that made surrender impossible. It was the vision of the German Emperor's face as he rode into Paris. This is not the sentiment which some of my idealistic friends describe as Love. I am quite content to call it hatred; the hatred of hell and all its works, and to agree that as they do not believe in hell they need not believe in hatred. But in the face of this prevalent prejudice, this long introduction has been unfortunately necessary, to ensure an understanding of what is meant by a religious war. There is a religious war when two worlds meet; that is when two visions of the world meet; or in more modern language when two moral atmospheres meet. What is the one man's breath is the other man's poison; and it is vain to talk of giving a pestilence a place in the sun. And this is what we must understand, even at the expense of digression, if we would see what really happened in the Mediterranean; when right athwart the rising of the Republic on the Tiber, a thing overtopping and disdaining it, dark with all the riddles of Asia and trailing all the tribes and dependencies of imperialism, came Carthage riding on the sea.

The ancient religion of Italy was on the whole that mixture which we have considered under the head of mythology; save that where the Greeks had a natural turn for the mythology, the Latins seem to have had a real turn for religion. Both multiplied gods, yet they sometimes seem to have multiplied them for almost opposite reasons. It would seem sometimes as if the Greek polytheism branched and blossomed upwards like the boughs of a tree, while the Italian polytheism ramified downward like the roots. Perhaps it would be truer to say that the former branches lifted themselves lightly, bearing flowers; while the latter hung down, being heavy with fruit. I mean that the Latins seem to multiply gods to bring them nearer to men, while the Greek gods rose and radiated outwards into the morning sky. What strikes us in the Italian cults is their local and especially their domestic character. We gain the impression of divinities swarming about the house like flies; of deities clustering and clinging like bats about the pillars or building like birds under the eaves. We have a vision of a god of roofs and a god of gate-posts, of a god of doors and even a god of drains. It has been suggested that all mythology was a sort of fairy-tale; but this was a particular sort of fairy-tale which may truly be called a fireside tale, or a nursery-tale; because it was a tale of the interior of the home; like those which make chairs and tables talk like elves. The old household gods of the Italian peasants seem to have been great, clumsy, wooden images, more featureless than the figure-head which Quilp battered with the poker. This religion of the home was very homely. Of course there were other less human elements in the tangle of Italian mythology. There were Greek deities superimposed on the Roman; there were here and there uglier things underneath, experiments in the cruel kind of paganism, like the Arician rite of the priest slaying the slayer. But these things were always potential in paganism; they are certainly not the peculiar character of Latin paganism. The peculiarity of that may be roughly covered by saying that if mythology personified the forces of nature, this mythology personified nature as transformed by the forces of man. It was the god of the corn and not of the grass, of the cattle and not the wild things of the forest; in short the cult was literally a culture; as when we speak of it as agriculture.

With this there was a paradox which is still for many the puzzle or riddle of the Latins. With religion running through every domestic detail like a climbing plant, there went what seems to many the very opposite spirit; the spirit of revolt. Imperialists and reactionaries often involve Rome as the very model of order and obedience; but Rome was the very reverse. The real history of ancient Rome is much more like the history of modern Paris. It might be called in modern language a city built out of barricades. It is said that the gate of Janus was never closed because there was an eternal war without; it is almost as true that there was an eternal revolution within. From the first Plebeian riots to the last Servile Wars, the state that imposed peace on the world was never really at peace. The rulers were themselves rebels.

There is a real relation between this religion in private and this revolution in public life. Stories none the less heroic for being hackneyed remind us that the Republic was founded on a tyrannicide that avenged an insult to a wife; that the Tribunes of the people were re-established after another which avenged an insult to a daughter. The truth is that only men to whom the family is sacred will ever have a standard or a status by which to criticise the state. They alone can appeal to something more holy than the gods of the city; the gods of the hearth. That is why men are mystified in seeing that the same nations that are thought rigid in domesticity are also thought restless in politics, for instance the Irish and the French. It is worth while to dwell on this domestic point because it is an exact example of what is meant here by the inside of history, like the inside of houses. Merely political histories of Rome may be right enough in saying that this or that was a cynical or cruel act of the Roman politicians; but the spirit that lifted Rome from beneath was the spirit of all the Romans; and it is not a cant to call it the ideal of Cincinnatus passing from the senate to the plough. Men of that sort had strengthened their village on every side, had extended its victories already over Italians and even over Greeks, when they found themselves confronted with a war that changed the world. I have called it here the war of the gods and demons.

There was established on the opposite coast of the inland sea a city that bore the name of the New Town. It was already much older, more powerful, and more prosperous than the Italian town; but there still remained about it an atmosphere that made the name not inappropriate. It had been called new because it was a colony like New York or New Zealand. It was an outpost or settlement of the energy and expansion of the great commercial cities of Tyre and Sidon. There was a note of the new countries and colonies about it, a confident and commercial outlook. It was fond of saying things that rang with a certain metallic assurance; as that nobody could wash his hands in the sea without the leave of the New Town. For it depended almost entirely on the greatness of its ships, as did the two great ports and markets from which its people came. It brought from Tyre and Sidon a prodigious talent for trade and considerable experience of travel. It brought other things as well.

In a previous chapter I have hinted at something of the psychology that lies behind a certain type of religion. There was a tendency in those hungry for practical results, apart from poetical results, to call upon spirits of terror and compulsion; to move Acheron in despair of bending the Gods. There is always a sort of dim idea that these darker powers will really do things, with no nonsense about it. In the interior psychology of the Punic peoples this strange sort of pessimistic practicality had grown to great proportions. In the New Town, which the Romans called Carthage, as in the parent cities of Phoenicia, the god who got things done bore the name of Moloch, who was perhaps identical with the other deity whom we know as Baal, the Lord. The Romans did not at first quite know what to call him or what to make of him; they had to go back to the grossest myth of Greek or Roman origins and compare him to Saturn devouring his children. But the worshippers of Moloch were not gross or primitive. They were members of a mature and polished civilisation, abounding in refinements and luxuries; they were probably far more civilised than the Romans. And Moloch was not a myth; or at any rate his meal was not a myth. These highly civilised people really met together to invoke the blessing of heaven on their empire by throwing hundreds of their infants into a large furnace. We can only realise the combination by imagining a number of Manchester merchants with chimney-pot hats and mutton-chop whiskers, going to church every Sunday at eleven o'clock to see a baby roasted alive.

The first stages of the political or commercial quarrel can be followed in far too much detail, precisely because it is merely political or commercial. The Punic Wars looked at one time as if they would never end; and it is not easy to say when they ever began. The Greeks and the Sicilians had already been fighting vaguely on the European side against the African city. Carthage had defeated Greece and conquered Sicily. Carthage had also planted herself firmly in Spain; and between Spain and Sicily the Latin city was contained and would have been crushed; if the Romans had been of the sort to be easily crushed. Yet the interest of the story really consists in the fact that Rome was crushed. If there had not been certain moral elements as well as the material elements, the story would have ended where Carthage certainly thought it had ended. It is common enough to blame Rome for not making peace. But it was a true popular instinct that there could be no peace with that sort of people It is common enough to blame the Roman for his Delenda est Carthago; Carthage must be destroyed. It is commoner to forget that, to all appearance, Rome itself was destroyed. The sacred savour that hung round Rome for ever, it is too often forgotten, clung to her partly because she had risen suddenly from the dead. Carthage was an aristocracy, as are most of such mercantile states. The pressure of the rich on the poor was impersonal as well as irresistible. For such aristocracies never permit personal government, which is perhaps why this one was jealous of personal talent. But genius can turn up anywhere, even in a governing class. As if to make the world's supreme test as terrible as possible, it was ordained that one of the great houses of Carthage should produce a man who came out of those gilded palaces with all the energy and originality of Napoleon coming from nowhere. At the worst crisis of the war Rome learned that Italy itself, by a military miracle, was invaded from the north. Hannibal, the Grace of Baal as his name ran in his own tongue, had dragged a ponderous chain of armaments over the starry solitudes of the Alps; and pointed southward to the city which he had been pledged by all his dreadful gods to destroy.

Hannibal marched down the road to Rome, and the Romans who rushed to war with him felt as if they were fighting with a magician. Two great armies sank to right and left of him into the swamps of the Trebia; more and more were sucked into the horrible whirlpool of Cannae; more and more went forth only to fall in ruin at his touch. The supreme sign of all disasters, which is treason, turned tribe after tribe against the falling cause of Rome, and still the unconquerable enemy rolled nearer and nearer to the city; and following their great leader the swelling cosmopolitan army of Carthage passed like a pageant of the whole world; the elephants shaking the earth like marching mountains and the gigantic Gauls with their barbaric panoply and the dark Spaniards girt in gold and the brown Numidians on their unbridled desert horses wheeling and darting like hawks, and whole mobs of deserters and mercenaries and miscellaneous peoples; and the grace of Baal went before them.

The Roman augurs and scribes who said in that hour that it brought forth unearthly prodigies, that a child was born with the head of an elephant or that stars fell down like hailstones, had a far more philosophical grasp of what had really happened than the modern historian who can see nothing in it but a success of strategy concluding a rivalry in commerce. Something far different was felt at the time and on the spot, as it is always felt by those who experience a foreign atmosphere entering their own like a fog or a foul savour. It was no mere military defeat, it was certainly no mere mercantile rivalry, that filled the Roman imagination with such hideous omens of nature herself becoming unnatural. It was Moloch upon the mountain of the Latins, looking with his appalling face across the plain; it was Baal who trampled the vineyards with his feet of stone; it was the voice of Tanit the invisible, behind her trailing veils, whispering of the love that is more horrible than hate. The burning of the Italian cornfields, the ruin of the Italian vines, were some thing more than actual; they were allegorical. They were the destruction of domestic and fruitful things, the withering of what was human before that inhumanity that is far beyond the human thing called cruelty. The household gods bowed low in darkness under their lowly roofs; and above them went the demons upon a wind from beyond all walls, blowing the trumpet of the Tramontane. The door of the Alps was broken down; and in no vulgar but a very solemn sense, it was Hell let loose. The war of the gods and demons seemed already to have ended; and the gods were dead. The eagles were lost, the legions were broken; and in Rome nothing remained but honour and the cold courage of despair.

In the whole world one thing still threatened Carthage, and that was Carthage. There still remained the inner working of an element strong in all successful commercial states, and the presence of a spirit that we know. There was still the solid sense and shrewdness of the men who manage big enterprises; there was still the advice of the best financial experts; there was still business government; there was still the broad and sane outlook of practical men of affairs, and in these things could the Romans hope. As the war trailed on to what seemed its tragic end, there grew gradually a faint and strange possibility that even now they might not hope in vain. The plain business men of Carthage, thinking as such men do in terms of living and dying races, saw clearly that Rome was not only dying but dead The war was over; it was obviously hopeless for the Italian city to resist any longer, and inconceivable that anybody should resist when it was hopeless. Under these circumstances, another set of broad, sound business principles remained to be considered. Wars were waged with money, and consequently cost money; perhaps they felt in their hearts, as do so many of their kind, that after all war must be a little wicked because it costs money. The time had now come for peace; and still more for economy. The messages sent by Hannibal from time to time asking for reinforcements were a ridiculous anachronism; there were much more important things to attend to now. It might be true that some consul or other had made a last dash to the Metaurus, had killed Hannibal's brother and flung his head, with Latin fury, into Hannibal's camp; and mad actions of that sort showed how utterly hopeless the Latins felt about their cause. But even excitable Latins could not be so mad as to cling to a lost cause for ever. So argued the best financial experts; and tossed aside more and more letters, full of rather queer alarmist reports. So argued and acted the great Carthaginian Empire. That meaningless prejudice, the curse of commercial states, that stupidity is in some way practical and that genius is in some way futile, led them to starve and abandon that great artist in the school of arms, whom the gods had given them in vain.

Why do men entertain this queer idea that what is sordid must always overthrow what is magnanimous; that there is some dim connection between brains and brutality, or that it does not matter if a man is dull so long as he is also mean? Why do they vaguely think of all chivalry as sentiment and all sentiment as weakness? They do it because they are, like all men, primarily inspired by religion. For them, as for all men, the first fact is their notion of the nature of things; their idea about what world they are living in. And it is their faith that the only ultimate thing is fear and therefore that the very heart of the world is evil. They believe that death is stronger than life, and therefore dead things must be stronger than living things; whether those dead things are gold and iron and machinery or rocks and rivers and forces of nature. It may sound fanciful to say that men we meet at tea-tables or talk to at garden-parties are secretly worshippers of Baal or Moloch. But this sort of commercial mind has its own cosmic vision and it is the vision of Carthage. It has in it the brutal blunder that was the ruin of Carthage. The Punic power fell because there is in this materialism a mad indifference to real thought. By disbelieving in the soul, it comes to disbelieving in the mind. Being too practical to be moral, it denies what every practical soldier calls the moral of an army. It fancies that money will fight when men will no longer fight. So it was with the Punic merchant princes. Their religion was a religion of despair, even when their practical fortunes were hopeful. How could they understand that the Romans could hope even when their fortunes were hopeless? Their religion was a religion of force and fear; how could they understand that men can still despise fear even when they submit to force? Their philosophy of the world had weariness in its very heart; above all they were weary of warfare; how should they understand those who still wage war even when they are weary of it? In a word, how should they understand the mind of Man, who had so long bowed down before mindless things, money and brute force and gods who had the hearts of beasts? They awoke suddenly to the news that the embers they had disdained too much even to tread out were again breaking everywhere into flames; that Hasdrubal was defeated, that Hannibal was outnumbered, that Scipio had carried the war into Spain; that he had carried it into Africa. Before the very gates of the golden city Hannibal fought his last fight for it and lost; and Carthage fell as nothing has fallen since Satan. The name of the New City remains only as a name. There is no stone of it left upon the sand. Another war was indeed waged before the final destruction: but the destruction was final. Only men digging in its deep foundation centuries after found a heap of hundreds of little skeletons, the holy relics of that religion. For Carthage fell because she was faithful to her own philosophy and had followed out to its logical conclusion her own vision of the universe. Moloch had eaten his children.

The gods had risen again, and the demons had been defeated after all. But they had been defeated by the defeated, and almost defeated by the dead. Nobody understands the romance of Rome, and why she rose afterwards to a representative leadership that seemed almost fated and fundamentally natural. Who does not keep in mind the agony of horror and humiliation through which she had continued to testify to the sanity that is the soul of Europe? She came to stand alone in the midst of an empire because she had once stood alone in the midst of a ruin and a waste. After that all men knew in their hearts that she had been representative of mankind, even when she was rejected of men. And there fell on her the shadow from a shining and as yet invisible light and the burden of things to be. It is not for us to guess in what manner or moment the mercy of God might in any case have rescued the world; but it is certain that the struggle which established Christendom would have been very different if there had been an empire of Carthage instead of an empire of Rome. We have to thank the patience of the Punic wars if, in after ages, divine things descended at least upon human things and not inhuman. Europe evolved into its own vices and its own impotence, as will be suggested on another page; but the worst into which it evolved was not like what it had escaped. Can any man in his senses compare the great wooden doll, whom the children expected to eat a little bit of the dinner, with the great idol who would have been expected to eat the children? That is the measure of how far the world went astray, compared with how far it might have gone astray. If the Romans were ruthless, it was in a true sense to an enemy, and certainly not merely a rival. They remembered not trade routes and regulations, but the faces of sneering men; and hated the hateful soul of Carthage. And we owe them something if we never needed to cut down the groves of Venus exactly as men cut down the groves of Baal. We owe it partly to their harshness that our thoughts of our human past are not wholly harsh. If the passage from heathenry to Christianity was a bridge as well as a breach, we owe it to those who kept that heathenry human. If, after all these ages, we are in some sense at peace with paganism, and can think more kindly of our fathers, it is well to remember the things that were and the things that might have been. For this reason alone we can take lightly the load of antiquity and need not shudder at a nymph on a fountain or a cupid on a valentine. Laughter and sadness link us with things long past away and remembered without dishonour; and we can see not altogether without tenderness the twilight sinking around the Sabine farm and hear the household gods rejoice when Catullus comes home to Sirmio. Deleta est Carthago.

THE END OF THE WORLD

I was once sitting on a summer day in a meadow in Kent under the shadow of a little village church, with a rather curious companion with whom I had just been walking through the woods. He was one of a group of eccentrics I had come across in my wanderings who had a new religion called Higher Thought; in which I had been so far initiated as to realise a general atmosphere of loftiness or height, and was hoping at some later and more esoteric stage to discover the beginnings of thought. My companion was the most amusing of them, for however he may have stood towards thought, he was at least very much their superior in experience, having travelled beyond the tropics while they were meditating in the suburbs; though he had been charged with excess in telling travellers' tales. In spite of anything said against him, I preferred him to his companions and willingly went with him through the wood; where I could not but feel that his sunburnt face and fierce tufted eyebrows and pointed beard gave him something of the look of Pan. Then we sat down in the meadow and gazed idly at the tree-tops and the spire of the village church; while the warm afternoon began to mellow into early evening and the song of a speck of a bird was faint far up in the sky and no more than a whisper of breeze soothed rather than stirred the ancient orchards of the garden of England. Then my companion said to me: 'Do you know why the spire of that church goes up like that, I expressed a respectable agnosticism, and he answered in an off-hand way, 'Oh, the same as the obelisks; the Phallic Worship of antiquity.' Then I looked across at him suddenly as he lay there leering above his goatlike beard; and for the moment I thought he was not Pan but the Devil. No mortal words can express the immense, the insane incongruity and unnatural perversion of thought involved in saying such a thing at such a moment and in such a place. For one moment I was in the mood in which men burned witches; and then a sense of absurdity equally enormous seemed to open about me like a dawn. 'Why, of course,' I said after a moment's reflection, 'if it hadn't been for phallic worship, they would have built the spire pointing downwards and standing on its own apex.' I could have sat in that field and laughed for an hour. My friend did not seem offended, for indeed he was never thin-skinned about his scientific discoveries. I had only met him by chance and I never met him again, and I believe he is now dead; but though it has nothing to do with the argument, it may be worth while to mention the name of this adherent of Higher Thought and interpreter of primitive religious origins; or at any rate the name by which he was known. It was Louis de Rougemont.

That insane image of the Kentish church standing on the point of its spire, as in some old rustic, topsy-turvy tale, always comes back into my imagination when I hear these things said about pagan origins; and calls to my aid the laughter of the giants. Then I feel as genially and charitably to all other scientific investigators, higher critics, and authorities on ancient and modern religion, as I do to poor Louis de Rougemont. But the memory of that immense absurdity remains as a sort of measure and check by which to keep sane, not only on the subject of Christian churches, but also on the subject of heathen temples. Now a great many people have talked about heathen origins as the distinguished traveller talked about Christian origins. Indeed a great many modern heathens have been very hard on heathenism. A great many modern humanitarians have been very hard on the real religion of humanity. They have represented it as being everywhere and from the first rooted only in these repulsive arcana; and carrying the character of something utterly shameless and anarchical. Now I do not believe this for a moment. I should never dream of thinking about the whole worship of Apollo what De Rougemont could think about the worship of Christ. I would never admit that there was such an atmosphere in a Greek city as that madman was able to smell in a Kentish village. On the contrary, it is the whole point, even of this final chapter upon the final decay of paganism, to insist once more that the worst sort of paganism had already been defeated by the best sort. It was the best sort of paganism that conquered the gold of Carthage. It was the best sort of paganism that wore the laurels of Rome. It was the best thing the world had yet seen, all things considered and on any large scale, that ruled from the wall of the Grampians to the garden of the Euphrates. It was the best that conquered; it was the best that ruled; and it was the best that began to decay.

Unless this broad truth be grasped, the whole story is seen askew. Pessimism is not in being tired of evil but in being tired of good. Despair does not lie in being weary of suffering, but in being weary of joy. It is when for some reason or other the good things in a society no longer work that the society begins to decline; when its food does not feed, when its cures do not cure, when its blessings refuse to bless. We might almost say that in a society without such good things we should hardly have any test by which to register a decline; that is why some of the static commercial oligarchies like Carthage have rather an air in history of standing and staring like mummies, so dried up and swathed and embalmed that no man knows when they are new or old. But Carthage at any rate was dead, and the worst assault ever made by the demons on mortal society had been defeated. But how much would it matter that the worst was dead if the best was dying?

To begin with, it must be noted that the relation of Rome to Carthage was partially repeated and extended in her relation to nations more normal and more nearly akin to her than Carthage. I am not here concerned to controvert the merely political view that Roman statesmen acted unscrupulously towards Corinth or the Greek cities. But I am concerned to contradict the notion that there was nothing but a hypocritical excuse in the ordinary Roman dislike of Greek cities. I am not presenting these pagans as paladins of chivalry, with a sentiment about nationalism never known until Christian times. But I am presenting them as men with the feelings of men; and those feelings were not a pretence. The truth is that one of the weaknesses in nature-worship and mere mythology had already produced a perversion among the Greeks due to the worst sophistry; the sophistry of simplicity. Just as they became unnatural by worshipping nature, so they actually became unmanly by worshipping man. If Greece led her conqueror, she might have misled her conqueror; but these were things he did originally wish to conquer—ever in himself. It is true that in one sense there was less inhumanity even in Sodom and Gomorrah than in Tyre and Sidon. When we consider the war of the demons on the children, we cannot compare even Greek decadence to Punic devil-worship. But it is not true that the sincere revulsion from either need be merely pharisaical. It is not true to human nature or to common sense. Let any lad who has had the luck to grow up sane and simple in his day-dreams of love hear for the first time of the cult of Ganymede; he will not be merely shocked but sickened. And that first impression, as has been said here so often about first impressions, will be right. Our cynical indifference is an illusion; it is the greatest of all illusions; the illusion of familiarity. It is right to conceive the more or less rustic virtues of the ruck of the original Romans as reacting against the very rumour of it, with complete spontaneity and sincerity. It is right to regard them as reacting, if in a lesser degree, exactly as they did against the cruelty of Carthage. Because it was in a less degree they did not destroy Corinth as they destroyed Carthage. But if their attitude and action was rather destructive, in neither case need their indignation have been mere self-righteousness covering mere selfishness. And if anybody insists that nothing could have operated in either case but reasons of state and commercial conspiracies, we can only tell him that there is something which he does not understand; something which possibly he will never understand; something which, until he does understand, he will never understand the Latins. That something is called democracy. He has probably heard the word a good many times and even used it himself; but he has no notion of what it means. All through the revolutionary history of Rome there was an incessant drive towards democracy; the state and the statesman could do nothing without a considerable backing of democracy; the sort of democracy that never has anything to do with diplomacy. It is precisely because of the presence of Roman democracy that we hear so much about Roman oligarchy. For instance, recent historians have tried to explain the valour and victory of Rome in terms of that detestable and detested usury which was practised by some of the Patricians; as if Curius had conquered the men of the Macedonian phalanx by lending them money; or the consul Nero had negotiated the victory of Metaurus at five per cent. But we realise the usury of the Patricians because of the perpetual revolt of the Plebeians. The rule of the Punic merchant princes had the very soul of usury. But there was never a Punic mob that dared to call them usurers.

Burdened like all mortal things with all mortal sin and weakness, the rise of Rome had really been the rise of normal and especially of popular things; and in nothing more than in the thoroughly normal and profoundly popular hatred of perversion. Now among the Greeks a perversion had become a convention. It is true that it had become so much of a convention, especially a literary convention, that it was sometimes conventionally copied by Roman literary men. But this is one of those complications that always arise out of conventions. It must not obscure our sense of the difference of tone in the two societies as a whole. It is true that Virgil would once in a way take over a theme of Theocritus; but nobody can get the impression that Virgil was particularly fond of that theme. The themes of Virgil were specially and notably the normal themes and nowhere more than in morals; piety and patriotism and the honour of the countryside. And we may well pause upon the name of the poet as we pass into the autumn of antiquity; upon his name who was in so supreme a sense the very voice of autumn of its maturity and its melancholy; of its fruits of fulfilment and its prospect of decay. Nobody who reads even a few lines of Virgil can doubt that he understood what moral sanity means to mankind. Nobody can doubt his feelings when the demons were driven in flight before the household gods. But there are two particular points about him and his work which are particularly important to the main thesis here. The first is that the whole of his great patriotic epic is in a very peculiar sense founded upon the fall of Troy; that is upon an avowed pride in Troy although she had fallen. In tracing to Trojans the foundation of his beloved race and republic, he began what may be called the great Trojan tradition which runs through medieval and modern history. We have already seen the first hint of it in the pathos of Homer about Hector. But Virgil turned it not merely into a literature but into a legend. And it was a legend of the almost divine dignity that belongs to the defeated. This was one of the traditions that did truly prepare the world for the coming of Christianity and especially of Christian chivalry. This is what did help to sustain civilisation through the incessant defeats of the Dark Ages and the barbarian wars; out of which what we call chivalry was born. It is the moral attitude of the man with his back to the wall; and it was the wall of Troy. All through medieval and modern times this version of the virtues in the Homeric conflict can be traced in a hundred ways co-operating with all that was akin to it in Christian sentiment. Our own countrymen, and the men of other countries, loved to claim like Virgil that their own nation was descended from the heroic Trojans. All sorts of people thought it the most superb sort of heraldry to claim to be descended from Hector. Nobody seems to have wanted to be descended from Achilles. The very fact that the Trojan name has become a Christian name, and been scattered to the last limits of Christendom, to Ireland or the Gaelic Highlands, while the Greek name has remained relatively rare and pedantic, is a tribute to the same truth. Indeed it involves a curiosity of language almost in the nature of a joke. The name has been turned into a verb; and the very phrase about hectoring, in the sense of swaggering, suggests the myriads of soldiers who have taken the fallen Trojan for a model. As a matter of fact, nobody in antiquity was less given to hectoring than Hector. But even the bully pretending to be a conqueror took his title from the conquered. That is why the popularisation of the Trojan origin by Virgil has a vital relation to all those elements that have made men say that Virgil was almost a Christian. It is almost as if two great tools or toys of the same timber, the divine and the human, had been in the hands of Providence; and the only thing comparable to the Wooden Cross of Calvary was the Wooden Horse of Troy. So, in some wild allegory, pious in purpose if almost profane in form, the Holy Child might have fought the dragon with a wooden sword and a wooden horse.

The other element in Virgil which is essential to the argument is the particular nature of his relation to mythology; or what may here in a special sense be called folklore, the faiths and fancies of the populace. Everybody knows that his poetry at its most perfect is less concerned with the pomposity of Olympus than with the numina of natural and agricultural life. Everyone knows where Virgil looked for the causes of things. He speaks of finding them not so much in cosmic allegories of Uranus and Chronos; but rather in Pan and the sisterhood of the nymphs and Sylvanus the old man of the forest. He is perhaps most himself in some passages of the Eclogues, in which he has perpetuated for ever the great legend of Arcadia and the shepherds. Here again it is easy enough to miss the point with petty criticism about all the things that happen to separate his literary convention from ours. There is nothing more artificial than the cry of artificiality as directed against the old pastoral poetry. We have entirely missed all that our fathers meant by looking at the externals of what they wrote. People have been so much amused with the mere fact that the china shepherdess was made of china that they have not even asked why she was made at all. They have been so content to consider the Merry Peasant as a figure in an opera that they have not asked even how he came to go to the opera, or how he strayed on to the stage.

In short, one have only to ask why there is a china shepherdess and not a china shopkeeper. Why were not mantelpieces adorned with figures of city merchants in elegant attitudes; of ironmasters wrought in iron or gold speculators in gold? Why did the opera exhibit a Merry Peasant and not a Merry Politician? Why was there not a ballet of bankers, pirouetting upon pointed toes? Because the ancient instinct and humour of humanity have always told them, under whatever conventions, that the conventions of complex cities were less really healthy and happy than the customs of the countryside. So it is with the eternity of the Eclogues. A modern poet did indeed write things called Fleet Street Eclogues, in which poets took the place of the shepherds. But nobody has yet written anything called Wall Street Eclogues, in which millionaires should take the place of the poets. And the reason is that there is a real if only a recurrent yearning for that sort of simplicity; and there is never that sort of yearning for that sort of complexity. The key to the mystery of the Merry Peasant is that the peasant often is merry. Those who do not believe it are simply those who do not know anything about him, and therefore do not know which are his times for merriment. Those who do not believe in the shepherd's feast or song are merely ignorant of the shepherd's calendar. The real shepherd is indeed very different from the ideal shepherd, but that is no reason for forgetting the reality at the root of the ideal. It needs a truth to make a tradition. It needs a tradition to make a convention. Pastoral poetry is certainly often a convention, especially in a social decline. It was in a social decline that Watteau shepherds and shepherdesses lounged about the gardens of Versailles. It was also in a social decline that shepherds and shepherdesses continued to pipe and dance through the most faded imitations of Virgil. But that is no reason for dismissing the dying paganism without ever understanding its life. It is no reason for forgetting that the very word Pagan is the same as the word Peasant. We may say that this art is only artificiality; but it is not a love of the artificial. On the contrary, it is in its very nature only the failure of nature-worship, or the love of the natural.

For the shepherds were dying because their gods were dying. Paganism lived upon poetry; that poetry already considered under the name of mythology. But everywhere, and especially in Italy, it had been a mythology and a poetry rooted in the countryside; and that rustic religion had been largely responsible for the rustic happiness. Only as the whole society grew in age and experience, there began to appear that weakness in all mythology already noted in the chapter under that name. This religion was not quite a religion. In other words, this religion was not quite a reality. It was the young world's riot with images and ideas like a young man's riot with wine or love-making; it was not so much immoral as irresponsible; it had no foresight of the final test of time. Because it was creative to any extent it was credulous to any extent. It belonged to the artistic side of man, yet even considered artistically it had long become overloaded and entangled. The family trees sprung from the seed of Jupiter were a jungle rather than a forest; the claims of the gods and demi-gods seemed like things to be settled rather by a lawyer or a professional herald than by a poet. But it is needless to say that it was not only in the artistic sense that these things had grown more anarchic. There had appeared in more and more flagrant fashion that flower of evil that is really implicit in the very seed of nature-worship, however natural it may seem. I have said that I do not believe that natural worship necessarily begins with this particular passion; I am not of the De Rougemont school of scientific folk-lore. I do not believe that mythology must begin with eroticism. But I do believe that mythology must end in it. I am quite certain that mythology did end in it. Moreover, not only did the poetry grow more immoral, but the immorality grew more indefensible. Greek vices, oriental vices, hints of the old horrors of the Semitic demons began to fill the fancies of decaying Rome, swarming like flies on a dung heap. The psychology of it is really human enough to anyone who will try that experiment of seeing history from the inside There comes an hour in the afternoon when the child is tired of 'pretending'; when he is weary of being a robber or a Red Indian. It is then that he torments the cat. There comes a time in the routine of an ordered civilisation when the man is tired at playing at mythology and pretending that a tree is a maiden or that the moon made love to a man. The effect of this staleness is the same everywhere; it is seen in all drug-taking and dram-drinking and every form of the tendency to increase the dose. Men seek stranger sins or more startling obscenities as stimulants to their jaded sense. They seek after mad oriental religions for the same reason. They try to stab their nerves to life, if it were with the knives of the priests of Baal. They are walking in their sleep and try to wake themselves up with nightmares.

At that stage even of paganism therefore the peasant songs and dances sound fainter and fainter in the forest. For one thing the peasant civilisation was fading, or had already faded from the whole countryside. The Empire at the end was organised more and more on that servile system which generally goes with the boast of organisation, indeed it was almost as senile as the modern schemes for the organisation of industry. It is proverbial that what would once have been a peasantry became a mere populace of the town dependent for bread and circuses; which may again suggest to some a mob dependent upon doles and cinemas. In this as in many other respects the modern return to heathenism has been a return not even to the heathen youth but rather to the heathen old age. But the causes of it were spiritual in both cases; and especially the spirit of paganism had departed with its familiar spirits. The heat had gone out of it with its household gods, who went along with the gods of the garden and the field and the forest. The Old Man of the Forest was too old; he was already dying. It is said truly in a sense that Pan died because Christ was born. It is almost as true in another sense that men knew that Christ was born because Pan was already dead. A void was made by the vanishing of the whole mythology of mankind, which would have asphyxiated like a vacuum if it had not been filled with theology. But the point for the moment is that the mythology could not have lasted like a theology in any case. Theology is thought, whether we agree with it or not. Mythology was never thought, and nobody could really agree with it or disagree with it. It was a mere mood of glamour and when the mood went it could not be recovered. Men not only ceased to believe in the gods, but they realised that they had never believed in them. They had sung their praises; they had danced round their altars. They had played the flute; they had played the fool.

So came the twilight upon Arcady and the last notes of the pipe sound sadly from the beechen grove. In the great Virgilian poems there is already something of the sadness; but the loves and the household gods linger in lovely lines like that which Mr. Belloc took for a test of understanding; incipe parve puer risu cognoscere matrem. But with them as with us, the human family itself began to break down under servile organisation and the herding of the towns. The urban mob became enlightened; that is it lost the mental energy that could create myths. All round the circle of the Mediterranean cities the people mourned for the loss of gods and were consoled with gladiators. And meanwhile something similar was happening to that intellectual aristocracy of antiquity that had been walking about and talking at large ever since Socrates and Pythagoras. They began to betray to the world the fact that they were walking in a circle and saying the same thing over and over again. Philosophy began to be a joke; it also began to be a bore. That unnatural simplification of everything into one system or another, which we have noted as the fault of the philosopher, revealed at once its finality and its futility. Everything was virtue or everything was happiness or everything was fate or everything was good or everything was bad; anyhow, everything was everything and there was no more to be said; so they said it. Everywhere the sages had degenerated into sophists; that is, into hired rhetoricians or askers of riddles. It is one of the symptoms of this that the sage begins to turn not only into a sophist but into a magician. A touch of oriental occultism is very much appreciated in the best houses. As the philosopher is already a society entertainer, he may as well also be a conjurer.

Many moderns have insisted on the smallness of that Mediterranean world; and the wider horizons that might have awaited it with the discovery of the other continents. But this is an illusion, one of the many illusions of materialism. The limits that paganism had reached in Europe were the limits of human existence; at its best it had only reached the same limits anywhere else. The Roman stoics did not need any Chinamen to teach them stoicism. The Pythagoreans did not need any Hindus to teach them about recurrence or the simple life or the beauty of being a vegetarian. In so far as they could get these things from the East, they had already got rather too much of them from the East. The Syncretists were as convinced as Theosophists that all religions are really the same. And how else could they have extended philosophy merely by extending geography? It can hardly be proposed that they should learn a purer religion from the Aztecs or sit at the feet of the Incas of Peru. All the rest of the world was a welter of barbarism. It is essential to recognise that the Roman Empire was recognised as the highest achievement of the human race; and also as the broadest. A dreadful secret seemed to be written as in obscure hieroglyphics across those mighty works of marble and stone, those colossal amphitheatres and aqueducts. Man could do no more.

For it was not the message blazed on the Babylonian wall, that one king was found wanting or his one kingdom given to a stranger. It was no such good news as the news of invasion and conquest. There was nothing left that could conquer Rome; but there was also nothing left that could improve it. It was the strongest thing that was growing weak. It was the best thing that was going to the bad. It is necessary to insist again and again that many civilisations had met in one civilisation of the Mediterranean sea; that it was already universal with a stale and sterile universality. The peoples had pooled their resources and still there was not enough. The empires had gone into partnership and they were still bankrupt. No philosopher who was really philosophical could think anything except that, in that central sea, the wave of the world had risen to its highest, seeming to touch the stars. But the wave was already stooping; for it was only the wave of the world.

That mythology and that philosophy into which paganism has already been analysed had thus both of them been drained most literally to the dregs. If with the multiplication of magic the third department, which we have called the demons, was even increasingly active, it was never anything but destructive. There remains only the fourth element or rather the first; that which had been in a sense forgotten because it was the first. I mean the primary and overpowering yet impalpable impression that the universe after all has one origin and one aim; and because it has an aim must have an author. What became of this great truth in the background of men's minds, at this time, it is perhaps more difficult to determine. Some of the Stoics undoubtedly saw it more and more clearly as the clouds of mythology cleared and thinned away; and great men among them did much even to the last to lay the foundations of a concept of the moral unity of the world. The Jews still held their secret certainty of it jealously behind high fences of exclusiveness; yet it is intensely characteristic of the society and the situation that some fashionable figures, especially fashionable ladies, actually embraced Judaism. But in the case of many others I fancy there entered at this point a new negation. Atheism became really possible in that abnormal time; for atheism is abnormality. It is not merely the denial of a dogma. It is the reversal of a subconscious assumption in the soul; the sense that there is a meaning and a direction in the world it sees. Lucretius, the first evolutionist who endeavoured to substitute Evolution for God, had already dangled before men's eyes his dance of glittering atoms, by which he conceived cosmos as created by chaos. But it was not his strong poetry or his sad philosophy, as I fancy, that made it possible for men to entertain such a vision. It was something in the sense of impotence and despair with which men shook their fists vainly at the stars, as they saw all the best work of humanity sinking slowly and helplessly into a swamp. They could easily believe that even creation itself was not a creation but a perpetual fall, when they saw that the weightiest and worthiest of all human creations was falling by its own weight. They could fancy that all the stars were falling stars; and that the very pillars of their own solemn porticos were bowed under a sort of gradual deluge. To men in that mood there was a reason for atheism that is in some sense reasonable. Mythology might fade and philosophy might stiffen; but if behind these things there was a reality, surely that reality might have sustained things as they sank. There was no God; if there had been a God, surely this was the very moment when He would have moved and saved the world.

The life of the great civilisation went on with dreary industry and even with dreary festivity. It was the end of the world, and the worst of it was that it need never end. A convenient compromise had been made between all the multitudinous myths and religions of the Empire; that each group should worship freely and merely live a sort of official flourish of thanks to the tolerant Emperor, by tossing a little incense to him under his official title of Divus. Naturally there was no difficulty about that; or rather it was a long time before the world realised that there ever had been even a trivial difficulty anywhere. The members of some Eastern sect or secret society or other seemed to have made a scene somewhere; nobody could imagine why. The incident occurred once or twice again and began to arouse irritation out of proportion to its insignificance. It was not exactly what these provincials said; though of course it sounded queer enough. They seemed to be saying that God was dead and that they themselves had seen him die. This might be one of the many manias produced by the despair of the age; only they did not seem particularly despairing. They seem quite unnaturally joyful about it, and gave the reason that the death of God had allowed them to eat him and drink his blood. According to other accounts God was not exactly dead after all; there trailed through the bewildered imagination some sort of fantastic procession of the funeral of God, at which the sun turned black, but which ended with the dead omnipotence breaking out of the tomb and rising again like the sun. But it was not the strange story to which anybody paid any particular attention; people in that world had seen queer religions enough to fill a madhouse. It was something in the tone of the madmen and their type of formation. They were a scratch company of barbarians and slaves and poor and unimportant people; but their formation was military; they moved together and were very absolute about who and what was really a part of their little system; and about what they said. However mildly, there was a ring like iron. Men used to many mythologies and moralities could make no analysis of the mystery, except the curious conjecture that they meant what they said. All attempts to make them see reason in the perfectly simple matter of the Emperor's statue seemed to be spoken to deaf men. It was as if a new meteoric metal had fallen on the earth; it was a difference of substance to the touch. Those who touched their foundation fancied they had struck a rock.

With a strange rapidity, like the changes of a dream, the proportions of things seemed to change in their presence. Before most men knew what had happened, these few men were palpably present. They were important enough to be ignored. People became suddenly silent about them and walked stiffly past them. We see a new scene, in which the world has drawn its skirts away from these men and women and they stand in the centre of a great space like lepers. The scene changes again and the great space where they stand is overhung on every side with a cloud of witnesses, interminable terraces full of faces looking down towards them intently; for strange things are happening to them. New tortures have been invented for the madmen who have brought good news. That sad and weary society seems almost to find a new energy in establishing its first religious persecution. Nobody yet knows very clearly why that level world has thus lost its balance about the people in its midst; but they stand unnaturally still while the arena and the world seem to revolve round them. And there shone on them in that dark hour a light that has never been darkened; a white fire clinging to that group like an unearthly phosphorescence, blazing its track through the twilights of history and confounding every effort to confound it with the mists of mythology and theory; that shaft of light or lightning by which the world itself has struck and isolated and crowned it; by which its own enemies have made it more illustrious and its own critics have made it more inexplicable; the halo of hatred around the Church of God.

PART II

ON THE MAN CALLED CHRIST

THE GOD IN THE CAVE

This sketch of the human story began in a cave; the cave which popular science associates with the cave-man and in which practical discovery has really found archaic drawings of animals. The second half of human history, which was like a new creation of the world, also begins in a cave. There is even a shadow of such a fancy in the fact that animals were again present; for it was a cave used as a stable by the mountaineers of the uplands about Bethlehem; who still drive their cattle into such holes and caverns at night. It was here that a homeless couple had crept underground with the cattle when the doors of the crowded caravanserai had been shut in their faces; and it was here beneath the very feet of the passers-by, in a cellar under the very floor of the world, that Jesus Christ was born. But in that second creation there was indeed something symbolical in the roots of the primeval rock or the horns of the prehistoric herd. God also was a Cave-Man, and had also traced strange shapes of creatures, curiously coloured, upon the wall of the world; but the pictures that he made had come to life.

A mass of legend and literature, which increases and will never end, has repeated and rung the changes on that single paradox; that the hands that had made the sun and stars were too small to reach the huge heads of the cattle. Upon this paradox, we might almost say upon this jest, all the literature of our faith is founded. It is at least like a jest in this, that it is something which the scientific critic cannot see. He laboriously explains the difficulty which we have always defiantly and almost derisively exaggerated; and mildly condemns as improbable something that we have almost madly exalted as incredible; as something that would be much too good to be true, except that it is true. When that contrast between the cosmic creation and the little local infancy has been repeated, reiterated, underlined, emphasised, exulted in, sung, shouted, roared, not to say howled, in a hundred thousand hymns, carols, rhymes, rituals, pictures, poems, and popular sermons, it may be suggested that we hardly need a higher critic to draw our attention to something a little odd about it; especially one of the sort that seems to take a long time to see a joke, even his own joke. But about this contrast and combination of ideas one thing may be said here, because it is relevant to the whole thesis of this book. The sort of modern critic of whom I speak is generally much impressed with the importance of education in life and the importance of psychology in education. That sort of man is never tired of telling us that first impressions fix character by the law of causation; and he will become quite nervous if a child's visual sense is poisoned by the wrong colours on a golliwog or his nervous system prematurely shaken by a cacophonous rattle. Yet he will think us very narrow-minded, if we say that this is exactly why there really is a difference between being brought up as a Christian and being brought up as a Jew or a Moslem or an atheist. The difference is that every Catholic child has learned from pictures, and even every Protestant child from stories, this incredible combination of contrasted ideas as one of the very first impressions on his mind. It is not merely a theological difference. It is a psychological difference which can outlast any theologies. It really is, as that sort of scientist loves to say about anything, incurable. Any agnostic or atheist whose childhood has known a real Christmas has ever afterwards, whether he likes it or not, an association in his mind between two ideas that most of mankind must regard as remote from each other; the idea of a baby and the idea of unknown strength that sustains the stars. His instincts and imagination can still connect them, when his reason can no longer see the need of the connection; for him there will always be some savour of religion about the mere picture of a mother and a baby; some hint of mercy and softening about the mere mention of the dreadful name of God. But the two ideas are not naturally or necessarily combined. They would not be necessarily combined for an ancient Greek or a Chinaman, even for Aristotle or Confucius. It is no more inevitable to connect God with an infant than to connect gravitation with a kitten. It has been created in our minds by Christmas because we are Christians, because we are psychological Christians even when we are not theological ones. In other words, this combination of ideas has emphatically, in the much disputed phrase, altered human nature. There is really a difference between the man who knows it and the man who does not. It may not be a difference of moral worth, for the Moslem or the Jew might be worthier according to his lights; but it is a plain fact about the crossing of two particular lights, the conjunction of two stars in our particular horoscope. Omnipotence and impotence, or divinity and infancy, do definitely make a sort of epigram which a million repetitions cannot turn into a platitude. It is not unreasonable to call it unique. Bethlehem is emphatically a place where extremes meet.

Here begins, it is needless to say, another mighty influence for the humanisation of Christendom. If the world wanted what is called a non-controversial aspect of Christianity, it would probably select Christmas. Yet it is obviously bound up with what is supposed to be a controversial aspect (I could never at any stage of my opinions imagine why); the respect paid to the Blessed Virgin. When I was a boy a more Puritan generation objected to a statue upon my parish church representing the Virgin and Child. After much controversy, they compromised by taking away the Child. One would think that this was even more corrupted with Mariolatry, unless the mother was counted less dangerous when deprived of a sort of weapon. But the practical difficulty is also a parable. You cannot chip away the statue of a mother from all round that of a new-born child. You can not suspend the new-born child in mid-air; indeed you cannot really have a statue of a new-born child at all. Similarly, you cannot suspend the idea of a new-born child in the void or think of him without thinking of his mother. You cannot visit the child without visiting the mother; you cannot in common human life approach the child except through the mother. If we are to think of Christ in this aspect at all, the other idea follows as it is followed in history. We must either leave Christ out of Christmas, or Christmas out of Christ, or we must admit, if only as we admit it in an old picture, that those holy heads are too near together for the haloes not to mingle and cross.

It might be suggested, in a somewhat violent image, that nothing had happened in that fold or crack in the great grey hills except that the whole universe had been turned inside out. I mean that all the eyes of wonder and worship which had been turned outwards to the largest thing were now turned inward to the smallest. The very image will suggest all that multitudinous marvel of converging eyes that makes so much of the coloured Catholic imagery like a peacock's tail. But it is true in a sense that God who had been only a circumference was seen as a centre; and a centre is infinitely small. It is true that the spiritual spiral henceforward works inwards instead of outwards, and in that sense is centripetal and not centrifugal. The faith becomes, in more ways than one, a religion of little things. But its traditions in art and literature and popular fable have quite sufficiently attested, as has been said, this particular paradox of the divine being in the cradle. Perhaps they have not so clearly emphasised the significance of the divine being in the cave. Curiously enough, indeed, tradition has not very clearly emphasised the cave. It is a familiar fact that the Bethlehem scene has been represented in every possible setting of time and country, of landscape and architecture; and it is a wholly happy and admirable fact that men have conceived it as quite different according to their different individual traditions and tastes. But while all have realised that it was a stable, not so many have realised that it was a cave. Some critics have even been so silly as to suppose that there was some contradiction between the stable and the cave; in which case they cannot know much about caves or stables in Palestine. As they see differences that are not there, it is needless to add that they do not see differences that are there. When a well-known critic says, for instance, that Christ being born in a rocky cavern is like Mithras having sprung alive out of a rock, it sounds like a parody upon comparative religion. There is such a thing as the point of a story, even if it is a story in the sense of a lie. And the notion of a hero appearing, like Pallas from the brain of Zeus, mature and without a mother, is obviously the very opposite of the idea of a god being born like an ordinary baby and entirely dependent on a mother. Whichever ideal we might prefer, we should surely see that they are contrary ideals. It is as stupid to connect them because they both contain a substance called stone as to identify the punishment of the Deluge with the baptism in the Jordan because they both contain a substance called water. Whether as a myth or a mystery, Christ was obviously conceived as born in a hole in the rocks primarily because it marked the position of one outcast and homeless. Nevertheless it is true, as I have said, that the cave has not been so commonly or so clearly used as a symbol as the other realities that surrounded the first Christmas.

And the reason for this also refers to the very nature of that new world. It was in a sense the difficulty of a new dimension. Christ was not only born on the level of the world, but even lower than the world. The first act of the divine drama was enacted, not only on no stage set up above the sight-seer, but on a dark and curtained stage sunken out of sight; and that is an idea very difficult to express in most modes of artistic expression. It is the idea of simultaneous happenings on different levels of life. Something like it might have been attempted in the more archaic and decorative medieval art. But the more the artists learned of realism and perspective, the less they could depict at once the angels in the heavens and the shepherds on the hills, and the glory in the darkness that was under the hills. Perhaps it could have been best conveyed by the characteristic expedient of some of the medieval guilds, when they wheeled about the streets a theatre with three stages one above the other, with heaven above the earth and hell under the earth. But in the riddle of Bethlehem it was heaven that was under the earth.

There is in that alone the touch of a revolution, as of the world turned upside down. It would be vain to attempt to say anything adequate, or anything new, about the change which this conception of a deity born like an outcast or even an outlaw had upon the whole conception of law and its duties to the poor and outcast. It is profoundly true to say that after that moment there could be no slaves. There could be and were people bearing that legal title, until the Church was strong enough to weed them out, but there could be no more of the pagan repose in the mere advantage to the state of keeping it a servile state. Individuals became important, in a sense in which no instruments can be important. A man could not be a means to an end, at any rate to any other man's end. All this popular and fraternal element in the story has been rightly attached by tradition to the episode of the Shepherds; the hinds who found themselves talking face to face with the princes of heaven. But there is another aspect of the popular element as represented by the shepherds which has not perhaps been so fully developed; and which is more directly relevant here.

Men of the people, like the shepherds, men of the popular tradition, had everywhere been the makers of the mythologies. It was they who had felt most directly, with least check or chill from philosophy or the corrupt cults of civilisation, the need we have already considered; the images that were adventures of the imagination; the mythology that was a sort of search; the tempting and tantalising hints of something half-human in nature; the dumb significance of seasons and special places. They had best understood that the soul of a landscape is a story and the soul of a story is a personality. But rationalism had already begun to rot away these really irrational though imaginative treasures of the peasant; even as systematic slavery had eaten the peasant out of house and home. Upon all such peasantries everywhere there was descending a dusk and twilight of disappointment, in the hour when these few men discovered what they sought. Everywhere else Arcadia was fading from the forest. Pan was dead and the shepherds were scattered like sheep. And though no man knew it, the hour was near which was to end and to fulfil all things; and though no man heard it, there was one far-off cry in an unknown tongue upon the heaving wilderness of the mountains. The shepherds had found their Shepherd.

And the thing they found was of a kind with the things they sought. The populace had been wrong in many things; but they had not been wrong in believing that holy things could have a habitation and that divinity need not disdain the limits of time and space. And the barbarian who conceived the crudest fancy about the sun being stolen and hidden in a box, or the wildest myth about the god being rescued and his enemy deceived with a stone, was nearer to the secret of the cave and knew more about the crisis of the world, than all those in the circle of cities round the Mediterranean who had become content with cold abstractions or cosmopolitan generalisations; than all those who were spinning thinner and thinner threads of thought out of the transcendentalism of Plato or the orientalism of Pythagoras. The place that the shepherds found was not an academy or an abstract republic, it was not a place of myths allegorised or dissected or explained or explained away. It was a place of dreams come true. Since that hour no mythologies have been made in the world. Mythology is a search.

We all know that the popular presentation of this popular story, in so many miracle plays and carols, has given to the shepherds the costumes, the language, and the landscape of the separate English and European countrysides. We all know that one shepherd will talk in a Somerset dialect or another talk of driving his sheep from Conway towards Clyde. Most of us know by this time how true is that error, how wise, how artistic, how intensely Christian and Catholic is that anachronism. But some who have seen it in these scenes of medieval rusticity have perhaps not seen it in another sort of poetry, which it is sometimes the fashion to call artificial rather than artistic. I fear that many modern critics will see only a faded classicism in the fact that men like Crashaw and Herrick conceived the shepherds of Bethlehem under the form of the shepherds of Virgil. Yet they were profoundly right; and in turning their Bethlehem play into a Latin Eclogue they took up one of the most important links in human history.

Virgil, as we have already seen, does stand for all that saner heathenism that had over-thrown the insane heathenism of human sacrifice; but the very fact that even the Virgilian virtues and the sane heathenism were in incurable decay is the whole problem to which the revelation to the shepherds is the solution. If the world had ever had the chance to grow weary of being demoniac, it might have been healed merely by becoming sane. But if it had grown weary even of being sane, what was to happen, except what did happen? Nor is it false to conceive the Arcadian shepherd of the Eclogues as rejoicing in what did happen. One of the Eclogues has even been claimed as a prophecy of what did happen. But it is quite as much in the tone and incidental diction of the great poet that we feel the potential sympathy with the great event; and even in their own human phrases the voices of the Virgilian shepherds might more than once have broken upon more than the tenderness of Italy 'Incipe, parve puer, risu cognoscere matrem' They might have found in that strange place all that was best in the last traditions of the Latins; and something better than a wooden idol standing up for ever for the pillar of the human family; a household god. But they and all the other mythologists would be justified in rejoicings that the event had fulfilled not merely the mysticism but the materialism of mythology. Mythology had many sins; but it had not been wrong in being as carnal as the Incarnation. But something of the ancient voice that was supposed to have rung through the graves, it could cry again, 'We have seen, he hath seen us, a visible god.' So the ancient shepherds might have danced, and their feet have been beautiful upon the mountains, rejoicing over the philosophers. But the philosophers had also heard.

It is still a strange story, though an old one, how they came out of orient lands, crowned with the majesty of kings and clothed with something of the mystery of magicians. That truth that is tradition his wisely remembered them almost as unknown quantities, as mysterious as their mysterious and melodious names; Melchior. Caspar, Balthazar. But there came with them all that world of wisdom that had watched the stars in Chaldea and the sun in Persia; and we shall not be wrong if we see in them the same curiosity that moves all the sages. They would stand for the same human ideal if their names had really been Confucius or Pythagoras or Plato. They were those who sought not tales but the truth of things, and since their thirst for truth was itself a thirst for God, they also have had their reward. But even in order to understand that reward, we must understand that for philosophy as much as mythology, that reward was the completion of the incomplete.

Such learned men would doubtless have come, as these learned men did come, to find themselves confirmed in much that was true in their own traditions and right in their own reasoning. Confucius would have found a new foundation for the family in the very reversal of the Holy Family; Buddha would have looked upon a new renunciation, of stars rather than jewels and divinity than royalty. These learned men would still have the right to say, or rather a new right to say, that there was truth in their old teaching. But after all these learned men would have come to learn. They would have come to complete their conceptions with something they had not yet conceived; even to balance their imperfect universe with something they might once have contradicted. Buddha would have come from his impersonal paradise to worship a person. Confucius would have come from his temples of ancestor-worship to worship a child.

We must grasp from the first this character in the new cosmos; that it was larger than the old cosmos. In that sense Christendom is larger than creation; as creation had been before Christ. It included things that had not been there; it also included the things that had been there. The point happens to be well illustrated in this example of Chinese piety, but it would be true of other pagan virtues or pagan beliefs. Nobody can doubt that a reasonable respect for parents is part of a gospel in which God himself was subject in childhood to earthly parents. But the other sense in which the parents were subject to him does introduce an idea that is not Confucian. The infant Christ is not like the infant Confucius; our mysticism conceives him in an immortal infancy. I do not know what Confucius would have done with the Bambino had it come to life in his arms as it did in the arms of St. Francis. But this is true in relation to all the other religions and philosophies; it is the challenge of the Church. The Church contains what the world does not contain. Life itself does not provide as she does for all sides of life. That every other single system is narrow and insufficient compared to this one; that is not a rhetorical boast; it is a real fact and a real dilemma. Where is the Holy child amid the Stoics and the ancestor worshippers? Where is Our Lady of the Moslems, a woman made for no man and set above all angels? Where is St. Michael of the monks of Buddha, rider and master of the trumpets, guarding for every soldier the honour of the sword? What could St. Thomas Aquinas do with the mythology of Brahminism, he who set forth all the science and rationality and even rationalism of Christianity? Yet even if we compare Aquinas with Aristotle, at the other extreme of reason, we shall find the same sense of something added. Aquinas could understand the most logical parts of Aristotle; it is doubtful if Aristotle could have understood the most mystical parts of Aquinas. Even where we can hardly call the Christian greater, we are forced to call him larger. But it is so to whatever philosophy or heresy or modern movement we may turn. How would Francis the Troubadour have fared among the Calvinists, or for that matter among the Utilitarians of the Manchester School? Yet men like Bossuet and Pascal could be as stern and logical as any Calvinist or Utilitarian. How would St. Joan of Arc, a woman waving on men to war with the sword, have fared among the Quakers or the Doukhabors or the Tolstoyan sect of pacifists? Yet any number of Catholic saints have spent their lives in preaching peace and preventing wars. It is the same with all the modern attempts at Syncretism. They are never able to make something larger than the Creed without leaving something out. I do not mean leaving out something divine but something human; the flag or the inn or the boy's tale of battle or the hedge at the end of the field. The Theosophists build a pantheon; but it is only a pantheon for pantheists. They call a Parliament of Religions as a reunion of all the peoples; but it is only a reunion of all the prigs. Yet exactly such a pantheon had been set up two thousand years before by the shores of the Mediterranean; and Christians were invited to set up the image of Jesus side by side with the image of Jupiter, of Mithras, of Osiris, of Atys, or of Ammon. It was the refusal of the Christians that was the turning-point of history. If the Christians had accepted, they and the whole world would have certainly, in a grotesque but exact metaphor, gone to pot. They would all have been boiled down to one lukewarm liquid in that great pot of cosmopolitan corruption in which all the other myths and mysteries were already melting. It was an awful and an appalling escape. Nobody understands the nature of the Church, or the ringing note of the creed descending from antiquity, who does not realise that the whole world once very nearly died of broadmindedness and the brotherhood of all religions.

Here it is the important point that the Magi, who stand for mysticism and philosophy, are truly conceived as seeking something new and even as finding something unexpected. That tense sense of crisis which still tingles in the Christmas story and even in every Christmas celebration, accentuates the idea of a search and a discovery. The discovery is, in this case, truly a scientific discovery. For the other mystical figures in the miracle play; for the angel and the mother, the shepherds and the soldiers of Herod, there may be aspects both simpler and more supernatural, more elemental or more emotional. But the wise Men must be seeking wisdom, and for them there must be a light also in the intellect. And this is the light; that the Catholic creed is catholic and that nothing else is catholic. The philosophy of the Church is universal. The philosophy of the philosophers was not universal. Had Plato and Pythagoras and Aristotle stood for an instant in the light that came out of that little cave, they would have known that their own light was not universal. It is far from certain, indeed, that they did not know it already. Philosophy also, like mythology, had very much the air of a search. It is the realisation of this truth that gives its traditional majesty and mystery to the figures of the Three Kings; the discovery that religion is broader than philosophy and that this is the broadest of religions, contained within this narrow space. The Magicians were gazing at the strange pentacle with the human triangle reversed; and they have never come to the end of their calculations about it. For it is the paradox of that group in the cave, that while our emotions about it are of childish simplicity, our thoughts about it can branch with a never-ending complexity. And we can never reach the end even of our own ideas about the child who was a father and the mother who was a child.

We might well be content to say that mythology had come with the shepherds and philosophy with the philosophers; and that it only remained for them to combine in the recognisation of religion. But there was a third element that must not be ignored and one which that religion for ever refuses to ignore, in any revel or reconciliation. There was present in the primary scenes of the drama that Enemy that had rotted the legends with lust and frozen theories into atheism, but which answered the direct challenge with something of that more direct method which we have seen in the conscious cult of the demons. In the description of that demon-worship, of the devouring detestation of innocence shown in the works of its witchcraft and the most inhuman of its human sacrifice, I have said less of its incorrect and secret penetration of the saner paganism; the soaking of mythological imagination with sex; the rise of imperial pride into insanity. But both the indirect and the direct influence make themselves felt in the drama of Bethlehem. A ruler under the Roman suzerainty, probably equipped and surrounded with the Roman ornament and order though himself of eastern blood, seems in that hour to have felt stirring within him the spirit of strange things. We all know the story of how Herod, alarmed at some rumour of a mysterious rival, remembered the wild gesture of the capricious despots of Asia and ordered a massacre of suspects of the new generation of the populace. Everyone knows the story; but not everyone has perhaps noted its place in the story of the strange religions of men. Not everybody has seen the significance even of its very contrast with the Corinthian columns and Roman pavement of that conquered and superficially civilised world. Only, as the purpose in his dark spirit began to show and shine in the eyes of the Idumean, a seer might perhaps have seen something like a great grey ghost that looked over his shoulder; have seen behind him filling the dome of night and hovering for the last time over history, that vast and fearful face that was Moloch of the Carthaginians; awaiting his last tribute from a ruler of the races of Shem. The demons also, in that first festival of Christmas, feasted after their own fashion.

Unless we understand the presence of that enemy, we shall not only miss the point of Christianity, but even miss the point of Christmas. Christmas for us in Christendom has become one thing, and in one sense even a simple thing. But like all the truths of that tradition, it is in another sense a very complex thing. Its unique note is the simultaneous striking of many notes; of humility, of gaiety, of gratitude, of mystical fear, but also of vigilance and of drama. It is not only an occasion for the peacemakers any more than for the merry-makers; it is not only a Hindu peace conference any more than it is only a Scandinavian winter feast. There is something defiant in it also; something that makes the abrupt bells at midnight sound like the great guns of a battle that has just been won. All this indescribable thing that we call the Christmas atmosphere only hangs in the air as something like a lingering fragrance or fading vapour from the exultant explosion of that one hour in the Judean hills nearly two thousand years ago. But the savour is still unmistakable, and it is something too subtle or too solitary to be covered by our use of the word peace. By the very nature of the story the rejoicings in the cavern were rejoicings in a fortress or an outlaw's den; properly understood it is not unduly flippant to say they were rejoicings in a dug-out. It is not only true that such a subterranean chamber was a hiding-place from enemies; and that the enemies were already scouring the stony plain that lay above it like a sky. It is not only that the very horse-hoofs of Herod might in that sense have passed like thunder over the sunken head of Christ. It is also that there is in that image a true idea of an outpost, of a piercing through the rock and an entrance into an enemy territory. There is in this buried divinity an idea of undermining the world; of shaking the towers and palaces from below; even as Herod the great king felt that earthquake under him and swayed with his swaying palace.

That is perhaps the mightiest of the mysteries of the cave It is already apparent that though men are said to have looked for hell under the earth, in this case it is rather heaven that is under the earth And there follows in this strange story the idea of an upheaval of heaven. That is the paradox of the whole position; that henceforth the highest thing can only work from below. Royalty can only return to its own by a sort of rebellion. Indeed the Church from its beginnings, and perhaps especially in its beginnings, was not so much a principality as a revolution against the prince of the world. This sense that the world had been conquered by the great usurper, and was in his possession, has been much deplored or derided by those optimists who identify enlightenment with ease. But it was responsible for all that thrill of defiance and a beautiful danger that made the good news seem to be really both good and new. It was in truth against a huge unconscious usurpation that it raised a revolt, and originally so obscure a revolt. Olympus still occupied the sky like a motionless cloud moulded into many mighty forms; philosophy still sat in the high places and even on the thrones of the kings, when Christ was born in the cave and Christianity in the catacombs. In both cases we may remark the same paradox of revolution; the sense of something despised and of something feared The cave in one aspect is only a hole or corner into which the outcasts are swept like rubbish; yet in the other aspect it is a hiding-place of something valuable which the tyrants are seeking like treasure. In one sense they are there because the innkeeper would not even remember them, and in another because the king can never forget them. We have already noted that this paradox appeared also in the treatment of the early Church. It was important while it was still insignificant, and certainly while it was still impotent. It was important solely because it was intolerable; and in that sense it is true to say that it was intolerable because it was intolerant. It was resented, because, in its own still and almost secret way, it had declared war. It had risen out of the ground to wreck the heaven and earth of heathenism. It did not try to destroy all that creation of gold and marble; but it contemplated a world without it. It dared to look right through it as though the gold and marble had been glass. Those who charged the Christians with burning down Rome with firebrands were slanderers; but they were at least far nearer to the nature of Christianity than those among the moderns who tell us that the Christians were a sort of ethical society, being martyred in a languid fashion for telling men they had a duty to their neighbors, and only mildly disliked because they were meek and mild.

Herod had his place, therefore, in the miracle play of Bethlehem because he is the menace to the Church Militant and shows it from the first as under persecution and fighting for its life. For those who think this a discord, it is a discord that sounds simultaneously with the Christmas bells. For those who think the idea of the Crusade is one that spoils the idea of the Cross, we can only say that for them the idea of the Cross is spoiled; the idea of the cross is spoiled quite literally in the cradle. It is not here to the purpose to argue with them on the abstract ethics of fighting; the purpose in this place is merely to sum up the combination of ideas that make up the Christian and Catholic idea, and to note that all of them are already crystallised in the first Christmas story. They are three distinct and commonly contrasted things which are nevertheless one thing; but this is the only thing which can make them one. The first is the human instinct for a heaven that shall be as literal and almost as local as a home. It is the idea pursued by all poets and pagans making myths; that a particular place must be the shrine of the god or the abode of the blest; that fairyland is a land; or that the return of the ghost must be the resurrection of the body. I do not here reason about the refusal of rationalism to satisfy this need. I only say that if the rationalists refuse to satisfy it, the pagans will not be satisfied. This is present in the story of Bethlehem and Jerusalem as it is present in the story of Delos and Delphi; and as it is not present in the whole universe of Lucretius or the whole universe of Herbert Spencer. The second element is a philosophy larger than other philosophies; larger than that of Lucretius and infinitely larger than that of Herbert Spencer. It looks at the world through a hundred windows where the ancient stoic or the modern agnostic only looks through one. It sees life with thousands of eyes belonging to thousands of different sorts of people, where the other is only the individual standpoint of a stoic or an agnostic. It has something for all moods of man, it finds work for all kinds of men, it understands secrets of psychology, it is aware of depths of evil, it is able to distinguish between ideal and unreal marvels and miraculous exceptions, it trains itself in tact about hard cases, all with a multiplicity and subtlety and imagination about the varieties of life which is far beyond the bald or breezy platitudes of most ancient or modern moral philosophy. In a word, there is more in it; it finds more in existence to think about; it gets more out of life. Masses of this material about our many-sided life have been added since the time of St. Thomas Aquinas. But St. Thomas Aquinas alone would have found himself limited in the world of Confucius or of Comte. And the third point is this; that while it is local enough for poetry and larger than any other philosophy, it is also a challenge and a fight. While it is deliberately broadened to embrace every aspect of truth, it is still stiffly embattled against every mode of error. It gets every kind of man to fight for it, it gets every kind of weapon to fight with, it widens its knowledge of the things that are fought for and against with every art of curiosity or sympathy; but it never forgets that it is fighting. It proclaims peace on earth and never forgets why there was war in heaven.

This is the trinity of truths symbolised here by the three types in the old Christmas story; the shepherds and the kings and that other king who warred upon the children. It is simply not true to say that other religions and philosophies are in this respect its rivals. It is not true to say that any one of them combines these characters; it is not true to say that any one of them pretends to combine them. Buddhism may profess to be equally mystical; it does not even profess to be equally military. Islam may profess to be equally military; it does not even profess to be equally metaphysical and subtle. Confucianism may profess to satisfy the need of the philosophers for order and reason; it does not even profess to satisfy the need of the mystics for miracle and sacrament and the consecration of concrete things. There are many evidences of this presence of a spirit at once universal and unique. One will serve here which is the symbol of the subject of this chapter; that no other story, no pagan legend or philosophical anecdote or historical event, does in fact affect any of us with that peculiar and even poignant impression produced on us by the word Bethlehem. No other birth of a god or childhood of a sage seems to us to be Christmas or anything like Christmas. It is either too cold or too frivolous, or too formal and classical, or too simple and savage, or too occult and complicated. Not one of us, whatever his opinions, would ever go to such a scene with the sense that he was going home. He might admire it because it was poetical, or because it was philosophical, or any number of other things in separation; but not because it was itself. The truth is that there is a quite peculiar and individual character about the hold of this story on human nature; it is not in its psychological substance at all like a mere legend or the life of a great man. It does not exactly in the ordinary sense turn our minds to greatness; to those extensions and exaggerations of humanity which are turned into gods and heroes, even by the healthiest sort of hero-worship. It does not exactly work outwards, adventurously, to the wonders to be found at the ends of the earth. It is rather something that surprises us from behind, from the hidden and personal part of our being; like that which can some times take us off our guard in the pathos of small objects or the blind pieties of the poor. It is rather as if a man had found an inner room in the very heart of his own house, which he had never suspected; and seen a light from within. It is as if he found something at the back of his own heart that betrayed him into good. It is not made of what the world would call strong materials; or rather it is made of materials whose strength is in that winged levity with which they brush us and pass. It is all that is in us but a brief tenderness that is there made eternal; all that mean no more than a momentary softening that is in some strange fashion become a strengthening and a repose; it is the broken speech and the lost word that are made positive and suspended unbroken; as the strange kings fade into a far country and the mountains resound no more with the feet of the shepherds; and only the night and the cavern lie in fold upon fold over something more human than humanity.

THE RIDDLES OF THE GOSPEL

To understand the nature of this chapter, it is necessary to recur to the nature of this book. The argument which is meant to be the backbone of the book is of the kind called the reductio ad absurdum. It suggests that the results of assuming the rationalist thesis are more irrational than ours; but to prove it we must assume that thesis. Thus in the first section I often treated man as merely an animal, to show that the effect was more impossible than if he were treated as an angel. In the sense in which it was necessary to treat man merely as an animal, it is necessary to treat Christ merely as a man. I have to suspend my own beliefs, which are much more positive; and assume this limitation even in order to remove it. I must try to imagine what would happen to a man who did really read the story of Christ as the story of a man; and even of a man of whom he had never heard before. And I wish to point out that a really impartial reading of that kind would lead, if not immediately to belief, at least to a bewilderment of which there is really no solution except in belief. In this chapter, for this reason, I shall bring in nothing of the spirit of my own creed; I shall exclude the very style of diction, and even of lettering, which I should think fitting in speaking in my own person. I am speaking as an imaginary heathen human being, honestly, staring at the Gospel story for the first time.

Now it is not at all easy to regard the New Testament as a New Testament. It is not at all easy to realise the good news as new. Both for good and evil familiarity fills us with assumptions and associations; and no man of our civilisation, whatever he thinks of our religion, can really read the thing as if he had never heard of it before. Of course it is in any case utterly unhistorical to talk as if the New Testament were a neatly bound book that had fallen from heaven. It is simply the selection made by the authority of the Church from a mass of early Christian literature. But apart from any such question there is a psychological difficulty in feeling the New Testament as new. There is a psychological difficulty in seeing those well-known words simply as they stand and without going beyond what they intrinsically stand for. And this difficulty must indeed be very great; for the result of it is very curious. The result of it is that most modern critics and most current criticism, even popular criticism, makes a comment that is the exact reverse of the truth. It is so completely the reverse of the truth that one could almost suspect that they had never read the New Testament at all.

We have all heard people say a hundred times over, for they seem never to tire of saying it, that the Jesus of the New Testament is indeed a most merciful and humane lover of humanity, but that the Church has hidden this human character in repellent dogmas and stiffened it with ecclesiastical terrors till it has taken on an inhuman character. This is, I venture to repeat, very nearly the reverse of the truth. The truth is that it is the image of Christ in the churches that is almost entirely mild and merciful. It is the image of Christ in the Gospels that is a good many other things as well. The figure in the Gospels does indeed utter in words of almost heart-breaking beauty his pity for our broken hearts. But they are very far from being the only sort of words that he utters. Nevertheless they are almost the only kind of words that the Church in its popular imagery ever represents him as uttering. That popular imagery is inspired by a perfectly sound popular instinct. The mass of the poor are broken, and the mass of the people are poor, and for the mass of mankind the main thing is to carry the conviction of the incredible compassion of God. But nobody with his eyes open can doubt that it is chiefly this idea of compassion that the popular machinery of the Church does seek to carry. The popular imagery carries a great deal to excess the sentiment of 'Gentle Jesus, meek and mild.' It is the first thing that the outsider feels and criticises in a Pieta or a shrine of the Sacred Heart. As I say, while the art may be insufficient, I am not sure that the instinct is unsound. In any case there is something appalling, something that makes the blood run cold, in the idea of having a statue of Christ in wrath. There is something insupportable even to the imagination in the idea of turning the corner of a street or coming out into the spaces of a marketplace, to meet the petrifying petrifaction of that figure as it turned upon a generation of vipers, or that face as it looked at the face of a hypocrite. The Church can reasonably be justified therefore if she turns the most merciful face or aspect towards men; but it is certainly the most merciful aspect that she does turn. And the point is here that it is very much more specially and exclusively merciful than any impression that could be formed by a man merely reading the New Testament for the first time. A man simply taking the words of the story as they stand would form quite another impression; an impression full of mystery and possibly of inconsistency; but certainly not merely an impression of mildness. It would be intensely interesting; but part of the interest would consist in its leaving a good deal to be guessed at or explained. It is full of sudden gestures evidently significant except that we hardly know what they signify; of enigmatic silences; of ironical replies. The outbreaks of wrath, like storms above our atmosphere, do not seem to break out exactly where we should expect them, but to follow some higher weather-chart of their own. The Peter whom popular Church teaching presents is very rightly the Peter to whom Christ said in forgiveness, 'Feed my lambs.' He is not the Peter upon whom Christ turned as if he were the devil, crying in that obscure wrath, 'Get thee behind me, Satan.' Christ lamented with nothing but love and pity over Jerusalem which was to murder him. We do not know what strange spiritual atmosphere or spiritual insight led him to sink Bethsaida lower in the pit than Sodom. I am putting aside for the moment all questions of doctrinal inferences or expositions, orthodox or otherwise; I am simply imagining the effect on a man's mind if he did really do what these critics are always talking about doing; if he did really read the New Testament without reference to orthodoxy and even without reference to doctrine. He would find a number of things which fit in far less with the current unorthodoxy than they do with the current orthodoxy. He would find, for instance, that if there are any descriptions that deserved to be called realistic, they are precisely the descriptions of the supernatural. If there is one aspect of the New Testament Jesus in which he may be said to present himself eminently as a practical person, it is in the aspect of an exorcist. There is nothing meek and mild, there is nothing even in the ordinary sense mystical, about the tone of the voice that says 'Hold thy peace and come out of him.' It is much more like the tone of a very business-like lion-tamer or a strong-minded doctor dealing with a homicidal maniac. But this is only a side issue for the sake of illustration; I am not now raising these controversies; but considering the case of the imaginary man from the moon to whom the New Testament is new.

Now the first thing to note is that if we take it merely as a human story, it is in some ways a very strange story. I do not refer here to its tremendous and tragic culmination or to any implications involving triumph in that tragedy. I do not refer to what is commonly called the miraculous element; for on that point philosophies vary and modern philosophies very decidedly waver. Indeed the educated Englishman of to-day may be said to have passed from an old fashion, in which he would not believe in any miracles unless they were ancient, and adopted a new fashion in which he will not believe in any miracles unless they are modern. He used to hold that miraculous cures stopped with the first Christians and is now inclined to suspect that they began with the first Christian Scientists. But I refer here rather specially to unmiraculous and even to unnoticed and inconspicuous parts of the story. There are a great many things about it which nobody would have invented, for they are things that nobody has ever made any particular use of; things which if they were remarked at all have remained rather as puzzles. For instance, there is that long stretch of silence in the life of Christ up to the age of thirty. It is of all silences the most immense and imaginatively impressive. But it is not the sort of thing that anybody is particularly likely to invent in order to prove something; and no body so far as I know has ever tried to prove anything in particular from it. It is impressive, but it is only impressive as a fact; there is nothing particularly popular or obvious about it as a fable. The ordinary trend of hero-worship and myth-making is much more likely to say the precise opposite. It is much more likely to say (as I believe some of the gospels rejected by the Church do say) that Jesus displayed a divine precocity and began his mission at a miraculously early age. And there is indeed something strange in the thought that he who of all humanity needed least preparation seems to have had most. Whether it was some mode of the divine humility, or some truth of which we see the shadow of the longer domestic tutelage of the higher creatures of the earth. I do not propose to speculate; I mention it simply as an example of the sort of thing that does in any case give rise to speculations, quite apart from recognised religious speculations. Now the whole story is full of these things. It is not by any means, as baldly presented in print, a story that it is easy to get to the bottom of. It is anything but what these people talk of as a simple Gospel. Relatively speaking, it is the Gospel that has the mysticism and the Church that has the rationalism. As I should put it, of course, it is the Gospel that is the riddle and the Church that is the answer. But whatever be the answer, the Gospel as it stands is almost a book of riddles.

First, a man reading the Gospel sayings would not find platitudes. If he had read even in the most respectful spirit the majority of ancient philosophers and of modern moralists, he would appreciate the unique importance of saying that he did not find platitudes. It is more than can be said even of Plato. It is much more than can be said of Epictetus or Seneca or Marcus Aurelius or Apollonius of Tyana. And it is immeasurably more than can be said of most of the agnostic moralists and the preachers of the ethical societies; with their songs of service and their religion of brotherhood. The morality of most moralists ancient and modern, has been one solid and polished cataract of platitudes flowing for ever and ever. That would certainly not be the impression of the imaginary independent outsider studying the New Testament. He would be conscious of nothing so commonplace and in a sense of nothing so continuous as that stream. He would find a number of strange claims that might sound like the claim to be the brother of the sun and moon; a number of very startling pieces of advice; a number of stunning rebukes; a number of strangely beautiful stories. He would see some very gigantesque figures of speech about the impossibility of threading a needle with a camel or the possibility of throwing a mountain into the sea. He would see a number of very daring simplifications of the difficulties of life; like the advice to shine upon everybody indifferently as does the sunshine or not to worry about the future any more than the birds. He would find on the other hand some passages of almost impenetrable darkness, so far as he is concerned, such as the moral of the parable of the Unjust Steward. Some of these things might strike him as fables and some as truths; but none as truisms. For instance, he would not find the ordinary platitudes in favour of peace. He would find several paradoxes in favour of peace. He would find several ideals of non-resistance, which taken as they stand would be rather too pacific for any pacifist. He would be told in one passage to treat a robber not with passive resistance, but rather with positive and enthusiastic encouragement, if the terms be taken literally; heaping up gifts upon the man who had stolen goods. But he would not find a word of all that obvious rhetoric against war which has filled countless books and odes and orations; not a word about the wickedness of war, the wastefulness of war, the appalling scale of the slaughter in war and all the rest of the familiar frenzy; indeed not a word about war at all. There is nothing that throws any particular light on Christ's attitude towards organised warfare, except that he seems to have been rather fond of Roman soldiers. Indeed it is another perplexity, speaking from the same external and human stand point, that he seems to have got on much better with Romans than he did with Jews. But the question here is a certain tone to be appreciated by merely reading a certain text; and we might give any number of instances of it.

The statement that the meek shall inherit the earth is very far from being a meek statement. I mean it is not meek in the ordinary sense of mild and moderate and inoffensive. To justify it, it would be necessary to go very deep into history and anticipate things undreamed of then and by many unrealised even now; such as the way in which the mystical monks reclaimed the lands which the practical kings had lost. If it was a truth at all, it was because it was a prophecy. But certainly it was not a truth in the sense of a truism. The blessing upon the meek would seem to be a very violent statement; in the sense of doing violence to reason and probability. And with this we come to another important stage in the speculation. As a prophecy it really was fulfilled; but it was only fulfilled long afterwards. The monasteries were the most practical and prosperous estates and experiments in reconstruction after the barbaric deluge; the meek did really inherit the earth. But nobody could have known anything of the sort at the time--unless indeed there was one who knew. Something of the same thing may be said about the incident of Martha and Mary; which has been interpreted in retrospect and from the inside by the mystics of the Christian contemplative life. But it was not at all an obvious view of it; and most moralists, ancient and modern, could be trusted to make a rush for the obvious. What torrents of effortless eloquence would have flowed from them to swell any slight superiority on the part of Martha; what splendid sermons about the Joy of Service and the Gospel of Work and the World Left Better Than We Found It, and generally all the ten thousand platitudes that can be uttered in favour of taking trouble--by people who need take no trouble to utter them. If in Mary the mystic and child of love Christ was guarding the seed of something more subtle, who was likely to understand it at the time? Nobody else could have seen Clare and Catherine and Teresa shining above the little roof at Bethany. It is so in another way with that magnificent menace about bringing into the world a sword to sunder and divide. Nobody could have guessed then either how it could be fulfilled or how it could be justified. Indeed some freethinkers are still so simple as to fall into the trap and be shocked at a phrase so deliberately defiant. They actually complain of the paradox for not being a platitude.

But the point here is that if we could read the Gospel reports as things as new as newspaper reports, they would puzzle us and perhaps terrify us much more than the same things as developed by historical Christianity. For instance, Christ after a clear allusion to the eunuchs of eastern courts, said there would be eunuchs of the kingdom of heaven. If this does not mean the voluntary enthusiasm of virginity, it could only be made to mean something much more unnatural or uncouth. It is the historical religion that humanises it for us by experience of Franciscans or of Sisters of Mercy. The mere statement standing by itself might very well suggest a rather dehumanised atmosphere; the sinister and inhuman silence of the Asiatic harem and divan. This is but one instance out of scores; but the moral is that the Christ of the Gospel might actually seem more strange and terrible than the Christ of the Church.

I am dwelling on the dark or dazzling or defiant or mysterious side of the Gospel words, not because they had not obviously a more obvious and popular side, but because this is the answer to a common criticism on a vital point. The freethinker frequently says that Jesus of Nazareth was a man of his time, even if he was in advance of his time; and that we cannot accept his ethics as final for humanity. The freethinker then goes on to criticise his ethics, saying plausibly enough that men cannot turn the other cheek, or that they must take thought for the morrow, or that the self-denial is too ascetic or the monogamy too severe. But the Zealots and the Legionaries did not turn the other cheek any more than we do, if so much. The Jewish traders and Roman tax-gatherers took thought for the morrow as much as we, if not more. We cannot pretend to be abandoning the morality of the past for one more suited to the present. It is certainly not the morality of another age, but it might be of another world.

In short, we can say that these ideals are impossible in themselves. Exactly what we cannot say is that they are impossible for us. They are rather notably marked by a mysticism which, if it be a sort of madness, would always have struck the same sort of people as mad. Take, for instance, the case of marriage and the relations of the sexes. It might very well have been true that a Galilean teacher taught things natural to a Galilean environment; but it is not. It might rationally be expected that a man in the time of Tiberius would have advanced a view conditioned by the time of Tiberius; but he did not. What he advanced was something quite different; something very difficult; but something no more difficult now than it was then. When, for instance, Mahomet made his polygamous compromise we may reasonably say that it was conditioned by a polygamous society. When he allowed a man four wives he was really doing something suited to the circumstances, which might have been less suited to other circumstances. Nobody will pretend that the four wives were like the four winds, something seemingly a part of the order of nature; nobody will say that the figure four was written for ever in stars upon the sky But neither will anyone say that the figure four is an inconceivable ideal; that it is beyond the power of the mind of man to count up to four; or to count the number of his wives and see whether it amounts to four. It is a practical compromise carrying with it the character of a particular society. If Mahomet had been born in Acton in the nineteenth century, we may well doubt whether he would instantly have filled that suburb with harems of four wives apiece. As he was born in Arabia in the sixth century, he did in his conjugal arrangements suggest the conditions of Arabia in the sixth century. But Christ in his view of marriage does not in the least suggest the conditions of Palestine of the first century. He does not suggest anything at all, except the sacramental view of marriage as developed long afterwards by the Catholic Church. It was quite as difficult for people then as for people now. It was much more puzzling to people then than to people now. Jews and Romans and Greeks did not believe, and did not even understand enough to disbelieve, the mystical idea that the man and the woman had become one sacramental substance. We may think it an incredible or impossible ideal; but we cannot think it any more incredible or impossible than they would have thought it. In other words, whatever else is true, it is not true that the controversy has been altered by time. Whatever else is true, it is emphatically not true that the ideas of Jesus of Nazareth were suitable to his time, but are no longer suitable to our time. Exactly how suitable they we to his time is perhaps suggested in the end of his story.

The same truth might be stated in another way by saying that if the story be regarded as merely human and historical, it is extraordinary how very little there is in the recorded words of Christ that ties him at all to his own time. I do not mean the details of a period, which even a man of the period knows to be passing. I mean the fundamentals which even the wisest man often vaguely assumes to be eternal. For instance, Aristotle was perhaps the wisest and most wide-minded man who ever lived. He founded himself entirely upon fundamentals, which have been generally found to remain rational and solid through all social and historical changes. Still, he lived in a world in which it was thought as natural to have slaves as to have children. And therefore he did permit himself a serious recognition of a difference between slaves and free men. Christ as much as Aristotle lived in a world that took slavery for granted. He did not particularly denounce slavery. He started a movement that could exist in a world with slavery. But he started a movement that could exist in a world without slavery. He never used a phrase that made his philosophy depend even upon the very existence of the social order in which he lived. He spoke as one conscious that everything was ephemeral, including the things that Aristotle thought eternal. By that time the Roman Empire had come to be merely the orbis terrarum, another name for the world. But he never made his morality dependent on the existence of the Roman Empire or even on the existence of the world. 'Heaven and earth shall pass away, but my words shall not pass away.'

The truth is that when critics have spoken of the local limitations of the Galilean, it has always been a case of the local limitations of the critics. He did undoubtedly believe in certain things that one particular modern sect of materialists do not believe. But they were not things particularly peculiar to his time. It would be nearer the truth to say that the denial of them is quite peculiar to our time. Doubtless it would be nearer still to the truth to say merely that a certain solemn social importance, in the minority disbelieving them, is peculiar to our time. He believed, for instance, in evil spirits or in the psychic healing of bodily ills; but not because he was a Galilean born under Augustus. It is absurd to say that a man believed things because he was a Galilean under Augustus when he might have believed the same things if he had been an Egyptian under Tutenkamen or an Indian under Gengis Khan. But with this general question of the philosophy of diabolism or of divine miracles I deal elsewhere. It is enough to say that the materialists have to prove the impossibility of miracles against the testimony of all mankind, not against the prejudices of provincials in North Palestine under the first Roman Emperors. What they have to prove, for the present argument, is the presence in the Gospels of those particular prejudices of those particular provincials. And, humanly speaking, it is astonishing how little they can produce even to make a beginning of proving it.

So it is in this case of the sacrament of marriage. We may not believe in sacraments, as we may not believe in spirits, but it is quite clear that Christ believed in this sacrament in his own way and not in any current or contemporary way. He certainly did not get his argument against divorce from the Mosaic law or the Roman law or the habits of the Palestinian people. It would appear to his critics then exactly what it appears to his critics now; an arbitrary and transcendental dogma coming from nowhere save in the sense that it came from him. I am not at all concerned here to defend that dogma; the point here is that it is just as easy to defend it now as it was to defend it then. It is an ideal altogether outside time; difficult at any period; impossible at no period. In other words, if anyone says it is what might be expected of a man walking about in that place at that period, we can quite fairly answer that it is much more like what might be the mysterious utterance of a being beyond man, if he walked alive among men.

I maintain therefore that a man reading the New Testament frankly and freshly would not get the impression of what is now often meant by a human Christ. The merely human Christ is a made-up figure, a piece of artificial selection, like the merely evolutionary man. Moreover there have been too many of these human Christs found in the same story, just as there have been too many keys to mythology found in the same stories. Three or four separate schools of rationalism have worked over the ground and produced three or four equally rational explanations of his life. The first rational explanation of his life was that he never lived. And this in turn gave an opportunity for three or four different explanations, as that he was a sun-myth or a corn-myth, or any other kind of myth that is also a monomania. Then the idea that he was a divine being who did not exist gave place to the idea that he was a human being who did exist. In my youth it vas the fashion to say that he was merely an ethical teacher in the manner of the Essenes, who had apparently nothing very much to say that Hillel or a hundred other Jews might not have said; as that it is a kindly thing to be kind and an assistance to purification to be pure. Then somebody said he was a madman with a Messianic delusion. Then others said he was indeed an original teacher because he cared about nothing but Socialism; or (as others said) about nothing but Pacifism. Then a more grimly scientific character appeared who said that Jesus would never have been heard of at all except for his prophecies of the end of the world. He was important merely as a Millenarian like Dr. Cumming; and created a provincial scare by announcing the exact date of the crack of doom. Among other variants on the same theme was the theory that he was a spiritual healer and nothing else; a view implied by Christian Science, which has really to expound a Christianity without the Crucifixion in order to explain the curing of Peter's wife's mother or the daughter of a centurion. There is another theory that concentrates entirely on the business of diabolism and what it would call the contemporary superstition about demoniacs, as if Christ, like a young deacon taking his first orders, had got as far as exorcism and never got any further. Now, each of these explanations in itself seems to me singularly inadequate; but taken together they do suggest something of the very mystery which they miss. There must surely have been something not only mysterious but many-sided about Christ if so many smaller Christs can be carved out of him. If the Christian Scientist is satisfied with him as a spiritual healer and the Christian Socialist is satisfied with him as a social reformer, so satisfied that they do not even expect him to be anything else, it looks as if he really covered rather more ground than they could be expected to expect. And it does seem to suggest that there might be more than they fancy in these other mysterious attributes of casting out devils or prophesying doom.

Above all, would not such a new reader of the New Testament stumble over something that would startle him much more than it startles us? I have here more than once attempted the rather impossible task of reversing time and the historic method; and in fancy looking forward to the facts, instead of backward through the memories. So I have imagined the monster that man might have seemed at first to the mere nature around him. We should have a worse shock if we really imagined the nature of Christ named for the first time. What should we feel at the first whisper of a certain suggestion about a certain man? Certainly it is not for us to blame anybody who should find that first wild whisper merely impious and insane. On the contrary, stumbling on that rock of scandal is the first step. Stark staring incredulity is a far more loyal tribute to that truth than a modernist metaphysic that would make it out merely a matter of degree. It were better to rend our robes with a great cry against blasphemy, like Caiaphas in the judgement, or to lay hold of the man as a maniac possessed of devils like the kinsmen and the crowd, rather than to stand stupidly debating fine shades of pantheism in the presence of so catastrophic a claim. There is more of the wisdom that is one with surprise in any simple person, full of the sensitiveness of simplicity, who should expect the grass to wither and the birds to drop dead out of the air, when a strolling carpenter's apprentice said calmly and almost carelessly, like one looking over his shoulder: 'Before Abraham was, I am.'

THE STRANGEST STORY IN THE WORLD

In the last chapter I have deliberately stressed what seems to be nowadays a neglected side of the New Testament story, but nobody will suppose, I imagine, that it is meant to obscure that side that may truly be called human. That Christ was and is the most merciful of judges and the most sympathetic of friends is a fact of considerably more importance in our own private lives than in anybody's historical speculations. But the purpose of this book is to point out that something unique has been swamped in cheap generalisations; and for that purpose it is relevant to insist that even what was most universal was also most original. For instance, we might take a topic which really is sympathetic to the modern mood, as the ascetic vocations recently referred to are not. The exaltation of childhood is something which we do really understand; but it was by no means a thing that was then in that sense understood. If we wanted an example of the originality of the Gospels we could hardly take a stronger or more startling one. Nearly two thousand years afterwards we happen to find ourselves in a mood that does really feel the mystical charm of the child; we express it in romances and regrets about childhood, in Peter Pan or The Child's Garden of verses. And we can say of the words of Christ with so angry an anti-Christian as Swinburne:--

'No sign that ever was given
To faithful or faithless eyes
Showed ever beyond clouds riven
So clear a paradise.

Earth's creeds may be seventy times seven
And blood have defiled each creed
But if such be the kingdom of heaven
It must be heaven indeed.'

But that paradise was not clear until Christianity had gradually cleared it. The pagan world, as such, would not have understood any such thing as a serious suggestion that a child is higher or holier than a man. It would have seemed like the suggestion that a tadpole is higher or holier than a frog. To the merely rationalistic mind, it would sound like saying that a bud must be more beautiful than a flower or that an unripe apple must be better than a ripe one. In other words, this modern feeling is an entirely mystical feeling. It is quite as mystical as the cult of virginity; in fact it is the cult of virginity. But pagan antiquity had much more idea of the holiness of the virgin than of the holiness of the child. For various reasons we have come nowadays to venerate children, perhaps partly because we envy children for still doing what men used to do; such as play simple games and enjoy fairy-tales. Over and above this, however, there is a great deal of real and subtle psychology in our appreciation of childhood; but if we turn it into a modern discovery, we must once more admit that the historical Jesus of Nazareth had already discovered it two thousand years too soon. There was certainly nothing in the world around him to help him to the discovery. Here Christ was indeed human; but more human than a human being was then likely to be. Peter Pan does not belong to the world of Pan but the world of Peter.

Even in the matter of mere literary style, if we suppose ourselves thus sufficiently detached to look at it in that light, there is a curious quality to which no critic seems to have done justice. It had among other things a singular air of piling tower upon tower by the use of the a fortiori; making a pagoda of degrees like the seven heavens. I have already noted that almost inverted imaginative vision which pictured the impossible penance of the Cities of the Plain. There is perhaps nothing so perfect in all language or literature as the use of these three degrees in the parable of the lilies of the field; in which he seems first to take one small flower in his hand and note its simplicity and even its impotence; then suddenly expands it in flamboyant colours into all the palaces and pavilions full of a great name in national legend and national glory; and then, by yet a third overturn, shrivels into nothing once more with a gesture as if flinging it away ``and if God so clothes the grass that today is and tomorrow is cast into the oven—how much more" It is like the building of a good Babel tower by white magic in a moment and in the movement of a hand; a tower heaved suddenly up to heaven on the top of which can be seen afar off, higher than we had fancied possible, the figure of man; lifted by three infinities above all other things, on a starry ladder of light logic and swift imagination. Merely in a literary sense it would be more of a masterpiece than most of the masterpieces in the libraries; yet it seems to have been uttered almost at random while a man might pull a flower. But merely in a literary sense also, this use of the comparative in several degrees has about it a quality which seems to me to hint of much higher things than the modern suggestion of the simple teaching of pastoral or communal ethics. There is nothing that really indicates a subtle and in the true sense a superior mind so much as this power of comparing a lower thing with a higher and yet that higher with a higher still; of thinking on three planes at once. There is nothing that wants the rarest sort of wisdom so much as to see, let us say, that the citizen is higher than the slave and yet that the soul is infinitely higher than the citizen or the city. It is not by any means a faculty that commonly belongs to these simplifiers of the Gospel; those who insist on what they call a simple morality and others call a sentimental morality. It is not at all covered by those who are content to tell everybody to remain at peace. On the contrary, there is a very striking example of it in the apparent inconsistency between Christ's sayings about peace and about a sword. It is precisely this power which perceives that while a good peace is better than a good war, even a good war is better than a bad peace. These far-flung comparisons are nowhere so common as in the Gospels; and to me they suggest something very vast. So a thing solitary and solid, with the added dimension of depth or height, might tower over the flat creatures living only on a plane.

This quality of something that can only be called subtle and superior, something that is capable of long views and even of double meanings, is not noted here merely as a counterblast to the commonplace exaggerations of amiability and mild idealism. It is also to be noted in connection with the more tremendous truth touched upon at the end of the last chapter. For this is the very last character that commonly goes with mere megalomania; especially such steep and staggering megalomania as might be involved in that claim. This quality that can only be called intellectual distinction is not, of course, an evidence of divinity. But it is an evidence of a probable distaste for vulgar and vainglorious claims to divinity. A man of that sort, if he were only a man, would be the last man in the world to suffer from that intoxication by one notion from nowhere in particular, which is the mark of the self-deluding sensationalist in religion. Nor is it even avoided by denying that Christ did make this claim. Of no such man as that, of no other prophet or philosopher of the same intellectual order, would it be even possible to pretend that he had made it. Even if the Church had mistaken his meaning, it would still be true that no other historical tradition except the Church had ever even made the same mistake. Mahomedans did not misunderstand Mahomet and suppose he was Allah. Jews did not misinterpret Moses and identify him with Jehovah. Why was this claim alone exaggerated unless this alone was made. Even if Christianity was one vast universal blunder, it is still a blunder as solitary as the Incarnation.

The purpose of these pages is to fix the falsity of certain vague and vulgar assumptions; and we have here one of the most false. There is a sort of notion in the air everywhere that all the religions are equal because all the religious founders were rivals, that they are all fighting for the same starry crown. It is quite false. The claim to that crown, or anything like that crown, is really so rare as to be unique. Mahomet did not make it any more than Micah or Malachi. Confucius did not make it any more that Plato or Marcus Aurelius. Buddha never said he was Bramah. Zoroaster no more claimed to be Ormuz than to be Ahriman. The truth is that, in the common run of cases, it is just as we should expect it to be, in common sense and certainly in Christian philosophy. It is exactly the other way. Normally speaking, the greater a man is, the less likely he is to make the very greatest claim. Outside the unique case we are considering, the only kind of man who ever does make that kind of claim is a very small man; a secretive or self-centered monomaniac. Nobody can imagine Aristotle claiming to be the father of gods and men, come down from the sky; though we might imagine some insane Roman Emperor like Caligula claiming it for him, or more probably for himself. Nobody can imagine Shakespeare talking as if he were literally divine; though we might imagine some crazy American crank finding it as a cryptogram in Shakespeare's works, or preferably in his own works. It is possible to find here and there human beings who make this supremely superhuman claim. It is possible to find them in lunatic asylums; in padded cells; possibly in strait waistcoats. But what is much more important than their mere materialistic fate in our very materialistic society, under very crude and clumsy laws about lunacy, the type we know as tinged with this, or tending towards it, is a diseased and disproportionate type; narrow yet swollen and morbid to monstrosity. It is by rather an unlucky metaphor that we talk of a madman as cracked; for in a sense he is not cracked enough. He is cramped rather than cracked; there are not enough holes in his head to ventilate it. This impossibility of letting in daylight on a delusion does sometimes cover and conceal a delusion of divinity. It can be found, not among prophets and sages and founders of religions, but only among a low set of lunatics. But this is exactly where the argument becomes intensely interesting; because the argument proves too much. For nobody supposes that Jesus of Nazareth was that sort of person. No modern critic in his five wits thinks that the preacher of the Sermon on the Mount was a horrible half-witted imbecile that might be scrawling stars on the walls of a cell. No atheist or blasphemer believes that the author of the Parable of the Prodigal Son was a monster with one mad idea like a cyclops with one eye. Upon any possible historical criticism, he must be put higher in the scale of human beings than that. Yet by all analogy we have really to put him there or else in the highest place of all.

In, fact, those who can really take it (as I here hypothetically take it) in a quite dry and detached spirit, have here a most curious and interesting human problem. It is so intensely interesting, considered as a human problem, that it is in a spirit quite disinterested, so to speak, that I wish some of them had turned that intricate human problem into something like an intelligible human portrait. If Christ was simply a human character, he really was a highly complex and contradictory human character. For he combined exactly the two things that lie at the two extremes of human variation. He was exactly what the man with a delusion never is; he was wise; he was a good judge. What he said was always unexpected; but it was always unexpectedly magnanimous and often unexpectedly moderate. Take a thing like the point of the parable of the tares and the wheat. It has the quality that unites sanity and subtlety. It has not the simplicity of a madman.

It has not even the simplicity of a fanatic. It might be uttered by a philosopher a hundred years old, at the end of a century of Utopias. Nothing could be less like this quality of seeing beyond and all round obvious things, than the condition of the egomaniac with the one sensitive spot on his brain. I really do not see how these two characters could be convincingly combined, except in the astonishing way in which the creed combines them. For until we reach the full acceptance of the fact as a fact, however marvellous, all mere approximations to it are actually further and further away from it. Divinity is great enough to be divine; it is great enough to call itself divine. But as humanity grows greater, it grows less and less likely to do so. God is God, as the Moslems say; but a great man knows he is not God, and the greater he is the better he knows it. That is the paradox; everything that is merely approaching to that point is merely receding from it. Socrates, the wisest man, knows that he knows nothing. A lunatic may think he is omniscience, and a fool may talk as if he were omniscient. But Christ is in another sense omniscient if he not only knows, but knows that he knows.

Even on the purely human and sympathetic side, therefore, the Jesus of the New Testament seems to me to have in a great many ways the note of something superhuman; that is of something human and more than human. But there is another quality running through all his teachings which seems to me neglected in most modern talk about them as teachings; and that is the persistent suggestion that he has not really come to teach. If there is one incident in the record which affects me personally as grandly and gloriously human, it is the incident of giving wine for the wedding-feast. That is really human in the sense in which a whole crowd of prigs, having the appearance of human beings, can hardly be described as human. It rises superior to all superior persons. It is as human as Herrick and as democratic as Dickens. But even in that story there is something else that has that note of things not fully explained; and in a way here very relevant. I mean the first hesitation, not on any ground touching the nature of the miracle, but on that of the propriety of working any miracles at all, at least at that stage; 'my time is not yet come.' What does that mean? At least it certainly meant a general plan or purpose in the mind, with which certain things did or did not fit in. And if we leave out that solitary strategic plan, we not only leave out the point of the story, but the story.

We often hear of Jesus of Nazareth as a wandering teacher, and there is a vital truth in that view in so far as it emphasises an attitude towards luxury and convention which most respectable people would still regard as that of a vagabond. It is expressed in his own great saying about the holes of the foxes and the nests of the birds, and, like many of his great sayings, it is felt as less powerful than it is, through lack of appreciation of that great paradox by which he spoke of his own humanity as in some way collectively and representatively human; calling himself simply the Son of Man; that is, in effect, calling himself simply Man. It is fitting that the New Man or the Second Adam should repeat in so ringing a voice and with so arresting a gesture the great fact which came first in the original story, that man differs from the brutes by everything, even by deficiency; that he is in a sense less normal and even less native; a stranger upon the earth. It is well to speak of his wanderings in this sense and in the sense that he shared the drifting life of the most homeless and hopeless of the poor. It is assuredly well to remember that he would quite certainly have been moved on by the police and almost certainly arrested by the police for having no visible means of subsistence. For our law has in it a turn of humour or touch of fancy which Nero and Herod never happened to think of, that of actually punishing homeless people for not sleeping at home.

But in another sense the word 'wandering' as applied to his life is a little misleading. As a matter of fact, a great many of the pagan sages and not a few of the pagan sophists might truly be described as wandering teachers. In some of them their rambling journeys were not altogether without a parallel in their rambling remarks. Apollonius of Tyana, who figured in some fashionable cults as a sort of ideal philosopher, is represented as rambling as far as the Ganges and Ethiopia, more or less talking all the time. There was actually a school of philosophers called the Peripatetics; and most even of the great philosophers give us a vague impression of having very little to do except to walk and talk. The great conversations which give us our glimpses of the great minds of Socrates or Buddha or even Confucius often seem to be parts of a never-ending picnic; and especially, which is the important point, to have neither beginning nor end. Socrates did indeed find the conversation interrupted by the incident of his execution. But it is the whole point and the whole particular merit, of the position of Socrates that death was only an interruption and an incident. We miss the real moral importance of the great philosopher if we miss that point; that he stares at the executioner with an innocent surprise, and almost an innocent annoyance, at finding anyone so unreasonable as to cut short a little conversation for the elucidation of truth. He is looking for truth and not looking for death. Death is but a stone in the road which can trip him up. His work in life is to wander on the roads of the world and talk about truth for ever. Buddha, on the other hand, did arrest attention by one gesture; it was the gesture of renunciation, and therefore in a sense of denial. But by one dramatic negation he passed into a world of negation that was not dramatic; which he would have been the first to insist was not dramatic. Here again we miss the particular moral importance of the great mystic if we do not see the distinction; that it was his whole point that he had done with drama, which consists of desire and struggle and generally of defeat and disappointment. He passes into peace and lives to instruct others how to pass into it. Henceforth his life is that of the ideal philosopher; certainly a far more really ideal philosopher than Apollonius of Tyana; but still a philosopher in the sense that it is not his business to do anything but rather to explain everything; in his case, we might almost say, mildly and softly to explore everything. For the messages are basically different. Christ said 'Seek first the kingdom, and all these things shall be added unto you.' Buddha said 'Seek first the kingdom, and then you will need none of these things.'

Now compared to these wanderers the life of Jesus went as swift and straight as a thunderbolt. It was above all things dramatic; it did above all things consist in doing something that had to be done. It emphatically would not have been done, if Jesus had walked about the world for ever doing nothing except tell the truth. And even the external movement of it must not be described as a wandering in the sense of forgetting that it was a journey. This is where it was a fulfilment of the myths rather than of the philosophies; it is a journey with a goal and an object, like Jason going to find the Golden Fleece, or Hercules the golden apples of the Hesperides. The gold that he was seeking was death. The primary thing that he was going to do was to die. He was going to do other things equally definite and objective; we might almost say equally external and material. But from first to last the most definite fact is that he is going to die. No two things could possibly be more different than the death of Socrates and the death of Christ. We are meant to feel that the death of Socrates was, from the point of view of his friends at least, a stupid muddle and miscarriage of justice interfering with the flow of a humane and lucid, I had almost said a light philosophy. We are meant to feel that Death was the bride of Christ as Poverty was the bride of St. Francis. We are meant to feel that his life was in that sense a sort of love-affair with death, a romance of the pursuit of the ultimate sacrifice. From the moment when the star goes up like a birthday rocket to the moment when the sun is extinguished like a funeral torch, the whole story moves on wings with the speed and direction of a drama, ending in an act beyond words.

Therefore the story of Christ is the story of a journey, almost in the manner of a military march; certainly in the manner of the quest of a hero moving to his achievement or his doom. It is a story that begins in the paradise of Galilee, a pastoral and peaceful land having really some hint of Eden, and gradually climbs the rising country into the mountains that are nearer to the storm-clouds and the stars, as to a Mountain of Purgatory. He may be met as if straying in strange places, or stopped on the way for discussion or dispute; but his face is set towards the mountain city. That is the meaning of that great culmination when he crested the ridge and stood at the turning of the road and suddenly cried aloud, lamenting over Jerusalem. Some light touch of that lament is in every patriotic poem; or if it is absent, the patriotism stinks with vulgarity. That is the meaning the stirring and startling incident at the gates of the Temple, when the tables were hurled like lumber down the steps, and the rich merchants driven forth with bodily blows; the incident that must be at least as much of a puzzle to the pacifists as any paradox about non resistance can be to any of the militarists. I have compared the quest to the journey of Jason, but we must never forget that in a deeper sense it is rather to be compared to the journey of Ulysses. It was not only a romance of travel but a romance of return; and of the end of a usurpation. No healthy boy reading the story regards the rout of the Ithacan suitors as anything but a happy ending. But there are doubtless some who regard the rout of the Jewish merchants and money changers with that refined repugnance which never fails to move them in the presence of violence, and especially of violence against the well-to-do. The point, here however, is that all these incidents have in them a character of mounting crisis. In other words, these incidents are not incidental. When Apollonius the ideal philosopher is brought before the judgement-seat of Domitian and vanishes by magic, the miracle is entirely incidental. It might have occurred at any time in the wandering life of the Tyanean; indeed, I believe it is doubtful in date as well as in substance. The ideal philosopher merely vanished, and resumed his ideal existence somewhere else for an indefinite period. It is characteristic of the contrast perhaps that Apollonius was supposed to have lived to an almost miraculous old age. Jesus of Nazareth was less prudent in his miracles. When Jesus was brought before the judgement-seat of Pontius Pilate, he did not vanish. It was the crisis and the goal; it was the hour and the power of darkness. It was the supremely supernatural act, of all his miraculous life, that he did not vanish.

Every attempt to amplify that story has diminished it. The task has been attempted by many men of real genius and eloquence as well as by only too many vulgar sentimentalists and self-conscious rhetoricians. The tale has been retold with patronising pathos by elegant sceptics and with fluent enthusiasm by boisterous best-sellers. It will not be retold here. The grinding power of the plain words of the Gospel story is like the power of mill-stones; and those who can read them simply enough will feel as if rocks had been rolled upon them. Criticism is only words about words; and of what use are words about such words as these? What is the use of word painting about the dark garden filled suddenly with torchlight and furious faces? 'Are you come out with swords and staves as against a robber? All day I sat in your temple teaching, and you took me not.' Can anything be added to the massive and gathered restraint of that irony; like a great wave lifted to the sky and refusing to fall? 'Daughters of Jerusalem, weep not for me but weep for yourselves and for your children.' As the High Priest asked what further need he had of witnesses, we might well ask what further need we have of words. Peter in a panic repudiated him: 'and immediately the cock crew; and Jesus looked upon Peter, and Peter went out and wept bitterly.' Has anyone any further remarks to offer. Just before the murder he prayed for all the murderous race of men, saying, 'They know not what they do'; is there anything to say to that, except that we know as little what we say? Is there any need to repeat and spin out the story of how the tragedy trailed up the Via Dolorosa and how they threw him in haphazard with two thieves in one of the ordinary batches of execution; and how in all that horror and howling wilderness of desertion one voice spoke in homage, a startling voice from the very last place where it was looked for, the gibbet of the criminal; and he said to that nameless ruffian, 'This night shalt thou be with me in Paradise'? Is there anything to put after that but a full stop? Or is anyone prepared to answer adequately that farewell gesture to all flesh which created for his Mother a new Son?

It is more within my powers, and here more immediately to my purpose, to point out that in that scene were symbolically gathered all the human forces that have been vaguely sketched in this story. As kings and philosophers and the popular element had been symbolically present at his birth, so they were more practically concerned in his death; and with that we come face to face with the essential fact to be realised. All the great groups that stood about the Cross represent in one way or another the great historical truth of the time; that the world could not save itself. Man could do no more. Rome and Jerusalem and Athens and everything else were going down like a sea turned into a slow cataract. Externally indeed the ancient world was still at its strongest; it is always at that moment that the inmost weakness begins. But in order to understand that weakness we must repeat what has been said more than once; that it was not the weakness of a thing originally weak. It was emphatically the strength of the world that was turned to weakness and the wisdom of the world that was turned to folly.

In this story of Good Friday it is the best things in the world that are at their worst. That is what really shows us the world at its worst. It was, for instance, the priests of a true monotheism and the soldiers of an international civilisation. Rome, the legend, founded upon fallen Troy and triumphant over fallen Carthage, had stood for a heroism which was the nearest that any pagan ever came to chivalry. Rome had defended the household gods and the human decencies against the ogres of Africa and the hermaphrodite monstrosities of Greece. But in the lightning flash of this incident, we see great Rome, the imperial republic, going downward under her Lucretian doom. Scepticism has eaten away even the confident sanity of the conquerors of the world. He who is enthroned to say what is justice can only ask: 'What is truth?' So in that drama which decided the whole fate of antiquity, one of the central figures is fixed in what seems the reverse of his true role. Rome was almost another name for responsibility.

Yet he stands for ever as a sort of rocking statue of the irresponsible. Man could do no more. Even the practical had become the impracticable. Standing between the pillars of his own judgement-seat, a Roman had washed his hands of the world.

There too were the priests of that pure and original truth that was behind all the mythologies like the sky behind the clouds. It was the most important truth in the world; and even that could not save the world. Perhaps there is something overpowering in pure personal theism; like seeing the sun and moon and sky come together to form one staring face. Perhaps the truth is too tremendous when not broken by some intermediaries divine or human; perhaps it is merely too pure and far away. Anyhow it could not save the world; it could not even conquer the world. There were philosophers who held it in its highest and noblest form; but they not only could not convert the world, but they never tried. You could no more fight the jungle of popular mythology with a private opinion than you could clear away a forest with a pocket-knife. The Jewish priests had guarded it jealously in the good and the bad sense. They had kept it as a gigantic secret. As savage heroes might have kept the sun in a box, they kept the Everlasting in the tabernacle. They were proud that they alone could look upon the blinding sun of a single deity; and they did not know that they had themselves gone blind. Since that day their representatives have been like blind men in broad daylight, striking to right and left with their staffs, and cursing the darkness. But there has been that in their monumental monotheism that it has at least remained like a monument, the last thing of its kind, and in a sense motionless in the more restless world which it cannot satisfy. For it is certain that for some reason it cannot satisfy. Since that day it has never been quite enough to say that God is in his heaven and all is right with the world, since the rumour that God had left his heavens to set it right.

And as it was with these powers that were good, or at least had once been good, so it was with the element which was perhaps the best, or which Christ himself seems certainly to have felt as the best. The poor to whom he preached the good news, the common people who heard him gladly, the populace that had made so many popular heroes and demigods in the old pagan world, showed also the weaknesses that were dissolving the world. They suffered the evils often seen in the mob of the city, and especially the mob of the capital, during the decline of a society. The same thing that makes the rural population live on tradition makes the urban population live on rumour. Just as its myths at the best had been irrational, so its likes and dislikes are easily changed by baseless assertion that is arbitrary without being authoritative. Some brigand or other was artificially turned into a picturesque and popular figure and run as a kind of candidate against Christ. In all this we recognise the urban population that we know, with its newspaper scares and scoops. But there was present in this ancient population an evil more peculiar to the ancient world. We have noted it already as the neglect of the individual, even of the individual voting the condemnation and still more of the individual condemned. It was the soul of the hive; a heathen thing. The cry of this spirit also was heard in that hour, 'It is well that one man die for the people.' Yet this spirit in antiquity of devotion to the city and to the state had also been in itself and in its time a noble spirit. It had its poets and its martyrs; men still to be honoured for ever. It was failing through its weakness in not seeing the separate soul of a man, the shrine of all mysticism; but it was only failing as everything else was failing. The mob went along with the Sadducees and the Pharisees, the philosophers and the moralists. It went along with the imperial magistrates and the sacred priests, the scribes and the soldiers, that the one universal human spirit might suffer a universal condemnation; that there might be one deep, unanimous chorus of approval and harmony when Man was rejected of men.

There were solitudes beyond where none shall follow. There were secrets in the inmost and invisible part of that drama that have no symbol in speech; or in any severance of a man from men. Nor is it easy for any words less stark and single-minded than those of the naked narrative even to hint at the horror of exaltation that lifted itself above the hill. Endless expositions have not come to the end of it, or even to the beginning. And if there be any sound that can produce a silence, we may surely be silent about the end and the extremity; when a cry was driven out of that darkness in words dreadfully distinct and dreadfully unintelligible, which man shall never understand in all the eternity they have purchased for him; and for one annihilating instant an abyss that is not for our thoughts had opened even in the unity of the absolute; and God had been forsaken of God.

They took the body down from the cross and one of the few rich men among the first Christians obtained permission to bury it in a rock tomb in his garden; the Romans setting a military guard lest there should be some riot and attempt to recover the body. There was once more a natural symbolism in these natural proceedings; it was well that the tomb should be sealed with all the secrecy of ancient eastern sepulture and guarded by the authority of the Caesars. For in that second cavern the whole of that great and glorious humanity which we call antiquity was gathered up and covered over; and in that place it was buried. It was the end of a very great thing called human history; the history that was merely human. The mythologies and the philosophies were buried there, the gods and he heroes and the sages. In the great Roman phrase, they had lived. But as they could only live, so they could only die; and they were dead.

On the third day the friends of Christ coming at daybreak to the place found the grave empty and the stone rolled away. In varying ways they realised the new wonder; but even they hardly realised that the world had died in the night. What they were looking at was the first day of a new creation, with a new heaven and a new earth; and in a semblance of the gardener God walked again in the garden, in the cool not of the evening but the dawn.

THE WITNESS OF THE HERETICS

Christ founded the Church with two great figures of speech; in the final words to the Apostles who received authority to found it. The first was the phrase about founding it on Peter as on a rock; the second was the symbol of the keys. About the meaning of the former there is naturally no doubt in my own case; but it does not directly affect the argument here save in two more secondary aspects. It is yet another example of a thing that could only fully expand and explain itself afterwards, and even long afterwards. And it is yet another example of something the very reverse of simple and self-evident even in the language, in so far as it described a man as a rock when he had much more the appearance of a reed.

But the other image of the keys has an exactitude that has hardly been exactly noticed. The keys have been conspicuous enough in the art and heraldry of Christendom; but not everyone has noted the peculiar aptness of the allegory. We have now reached the point in history where something must be said of the first appearance and activities of the Church in the Roman Empire; and for that brief description nothing could be more perfect than that ancient metaphor. The Early Christian was very precisely a person carrying about a key, or what he said was a key. The whole Christian movement consisted in claiming to possess that key. It was not merely a vague forward movement, which might be better represented by a battering-ram. It was not something that swept along with it similar or dissimilar things, as does a modern social movement. As we shall see in a moment, it rather definitely refused to do so. It definitely asserted that there was a key and that it possessed that key and that no other key was like it; in that sense it was as narrow as you please. Only it happened to be the key that could unlock the prison of the whole world; and let in the white daylight of liberty.

The creed was like a key in three respects; which can be most conveniently summed up under this symbol. First, a key is above all things a thing with a shape It is a thing that depends entirely upon keeping its shape. The Christian creed is above all things the philosophy of shapes and the enemy of shapelessness. That is where it differs from all that formless infinity, Manichean or Buddhist, which makes a sort of pool of night in the dark heart of Asia; the ideal of uncreating all the creatures. That is where it differs also from the analogous vagueness of mere evolutionism, the idea of creatures constantly losing their shape. A man told that his solitary latchkey had been melted down with a million others into a Buddhistic unity would be annoyed. But a man told that his key was gradually growing and sprouting in his pocket, and branching into new wards or complications, would not be more gratified.

Second, the shape of a key is in itself a rather fantastic shape. A savage who did not know it was a key would have the greatest difficulty in guessing what it could possibly be. And it is fantastic because it is in a sense arbitrary. A key is not a matter of abstractions; in that sense a key is not a matter of argument. It either fits the lock or it does not. It is useless for men to stand disputing over it, considered by itself; or reconstructing it on pure principles of geometry or decorative art. It is senseless for a man to say he would like a simple key; it would be far more sensible to do his best with a crowbar. And thirdly, as the key is necessarily a thing with a pattern, so this was one having in some ways a rather elaborate pattern. When people complain of the religion being so early complicated with theology and things of the kind, they forget that the world had not only got into a hole, but had got into a whole maze of holes and corners. The problem itself was a complicated problem; it did not in the ordinary sense merely involve anything so simple as sin. It was also full of secrets, of unexplored and unfathomable fallacies, of unconscious mental diseases, of dangers in all directions. If the faith had faced the world only with the platitudes about peace and simplicity some moralists would confine it to, it would not have had the faintest effect on that luxurious and labyrinthine lunatic asylum. What it did do we must now roughly describe; it is enough to say here that there was undoubtedly much about the key that seemed complex, indeed there was only one thing about it that was simple. It opened the door.

There are certain recognised and accepted statements in this matter which may for brevity and convenience be described as lies. We have all heard people say that Christianity arose in an age of barbarism. They might just as well say that Christian Science arose in an age of barbarism. They may think Christianity was a symptom of social decay, as I think Christian Science a symptom of mental decay. They may think Christianity a superstition that ultimately destroyed a civilisation, as I think Christian Science a superstition capable (if taken seriously) of destroying any number of civilisations. But to say that a Christian of the fourth or fifth centuries was a barbarian living in a barbarous time is exactly like saying that Mrs. Eddy was a Red Indian. And if I allowed my constitutional impatience with Mrs. Eddy to impel me to call her a Red Indian, I should incidentally be telling a lie. We may like or dislike the imperial civilisation of Rome in the fourth century; we may like or dislike the industrial civilisation of America in the nineteenth century; but that they both were what we commonly mean by a civilization no person of commonsense could deny if he wanted to. This is a very obvious fact but it is also a very fundamental one; and we must make it the foundation of any further description of constructive Christianity in the past. For good or evil, it was pre-eminently the product of a civilised age, perhaps of an over-civilised age. This is the first fact apart from all praise or blame; indeed I am so unfortunate as not to feel that I praise a thing when I compare it to Christian Science. But it is at least desirable to know something of the savour of a society in which we are condemning or praising anything; and the science that connects Mrs. Eddy with tomahawks or the Mater Dolorosa with totems may for our general convenience be eliminated. The dominant fact, not merely about the Christian religion, but about the whole pagan civilisation, was that which has been more than once repeated in these pages. The Mediterranean was a lake in the real sense of a pool; in which a number of different cults or cultures were, as the phrase goes, pooled. Those cities facing each other round the circle of the lake became more and more one cosmopolitan culture. On its legal and military side it was the Roman Empire, but it was very many-sided. It might be called superstitious in the sense that it contained a great number of varied superstitions; but by no possibility can any part of it be called barbarous.

In this level of cosmopolitan culture arose the Christian religion and the Catholic Church; and everything in the story suggests that it was felt to be something new and strange. Those who have tried to suggest that it evolved out of something much milder or more ordinary have found that in this case their evolutionary method is very difficult to apply. They may suggest that Essenes or Ebionites or such things were the seed; but the seed is invisible; the tree appears very rapidly full-grown; and the tree is something totally different. It is certainly a Christmas tree in the sense that it keeps the kindliness and moral beauty of the story of Bethlehem; but it was as ritualistic as the seven-branched candlestick, and the candles it carried were considerably more than were probably permitted by the first prayer-book of Edward the Sixth. It might well be asked, indeed, why any one accepting the Bethlehem tradition should object to golden or gilded ornament since the Magi themselves brought gold, why he should dislike incense in the church since incense was brought even to the stable. But these are controversies that do not concern me here. I am concerned only with the historical fact, more and more admitted by historians, that very early in its history this thing became visible to the civilisation of antiquity; and that already the Church appeared as a Church; with everything that is implied in a Church and much that is disliked in a Church. We will discuss in a moment how far it was like other ritualistic or magical or ascetical mysteries in its own time. It was certainly not in the least like merely ethical and idealistic movements in our time. It had a doctrine; it had a discipline; it had sacraments; it had degrees of initiation, it admitted people and expelled people; it affirmed one dogma with authority and repudiated another with anathemas. If all these things be the marks of Antichrist, the reign of Antichrist followed very rapidly upon Christ.

Those who maintain that Christianity was not a Church but a moral movement of idealists have been forced to push the period of its perversion or disappearance further and further back. A bishop of Rome writes claiming authority in the very lifetime of St. John the Evangelist; and it is described as the first papal aggression. A friend of the Apostles writes of them as men he knew and says they taught him the doctrine of the Sacrament, and Mr. Wells can only murmur that the reaction towards barbaric blood-rites may have happened rather earlier than might be expected. The date of the Fourth Gospel, which at one time was steadily growing later and later, is now steadily growing earlier and earlier; until critics are staggered at the dawning and dreadful possibility that it might be something like what it professes to be. The last limit of an early date for the extinction of true Christianity has probably been found by the latest German professor whose authority is invoked by Dean Inge. This learned scholar says that Pentecost was the occasion for the first founding of an ecclesiastical, dogmatic, and despotic Church utterly alien to the simple ideals of Jesus of Nazareth. This may be called, in a popular as well as a learned sense, the limit. What do professors of this kind imagine that men are made of? Suppose it were a matter of any merely human movement, let us say that of the conscientious objectors. Some say the early Christians were Pacifists; I do not believe it for a moment; but I am quite ready to accept the parallel for the sake of the argument. Tolstoy or some great preacher of peace among peasants has been shot as a mutineer for defying conscription; and a little while afterwards his few followers meet together in an upper room in remembrance of him. They never had any reason for coming together except that common memory; they are men of many kinds with nothing to bind them, except that the greatest event in all their lives was this tragedy of the teacher of universal peace. They are always repeating his words, revolving his problems, trying to imitate his character. The Pacifists meet at their Pentecost and are possessed of a sudden ecstasy of enthusiasm and wild rush of the whirlwind of inspiration, in the course of which they proceed to establish universal Conscription, to increase the Navy Estimates, to insist on everybody going about armed to the teeth and on all the frontiers bristling with artillery; the proceedings concluded with the singing of 'Boys of the Bulldog Breed' and 'Don't let them scrap the British Navy.' That is something like a fair parallel to the theory of these critics; that the transition from their idea of Jesus to their idea of Catholicism could have been made in the little upper room at Pentecost. Surely anybody's commonsense would tell him that enthusiasts who only met through their common enthusiasm for a leader whom they loved, would not instantly rush away to establish everything that he hated. No, if the 'ecclesiastical and dogmatic system' is as old as Pentecost it is as old as

Christmas. If we trace it back to such very early Christians we must trace it back to Christ.

We may begin then with these two negations. It is nonsense to say that the Christian faith appeared in a simple age; in the sense of an unlettered and gullible age. It is equally nonsense to say that the Christian faith was a simple thing; in the sense of a vague or childish or merely instinctive thing. Perhaps the only point in which we could possibly say that the Church fitted into the pagan world, is the fact that they were both not only highly civilised but rather complicated. They were both emphatically many-sided; but antiquity was then a many-sided hole, like a hexagonal hole waiting for an equally hexagonal stopper. In that sense only the Church was many-sided enough to fit the world. The six sides of the Mediterranean world faced each other across the sea and waited for something that should look all ways at once. The Church had to be both Roman and Greek and Jewish and African and Asiatic. In the very words of the Apostle of the Gentiles, it was indeed all things to all men. Christianity then was not merely crude and simple and was the very reverse of the growth of a barbaric time. But when we come to the contrary charge, we come to a much more plausible charge. It is very much more tenable that the Faith was but the final phase of the decay of civilisation, in the sense of the excess of civilisation; that this superstition was a sign that Rome was dying, and dying of being much too civilised. That is an argument much better worth considering; and we will proceed to consider it.

At the beginning of this book I ventured on a general summary of it, in a parallel between the rise of humanity out of nature and the rise of Christianity out of history. I pointed out that in both cases what had gone before might imply something coming after; but did not in the least imply what did come after. If a detached mind had seen certain apes it might have deduced more anthropoids; it would not have deduced man or anything within a thousand miles of what man has done. In short, it might have seen Pithecanthropus or the Missing Link looming in the future, if possible almost as dimly and doubtfully as we see him looming in the past. But if it foresaw him appearing it would also foresee him disappearing, and leaving a few faint traces just as he has left a few faint traces; if they are traces. To foresee that Missing Link would not be to foresee Man, or anything like Man. Now this earlier explanation must be kept in mind; because it is an exact parallel to the true view of the Church; and the suggestion of it having evolved naturally out of the Empire in decay.

The truth is that in one sense a man might very well have predicted that the imperial decadence would produce something like Christianity. That is, something a little like and gigantically different. A man might very well have said, for instance, 'Pleasure has been pursued so extravagantly that there will be a reaction into pessimism. Perhaps it will take the form of asceticism;

men will mutilate themselves instead of merely hanging themselves.' Or a man might very reasonably have said, 'If we weary of our Greek and Latin gods we shall be hankering after some eastern mystery or other; there will be a fashion in Persians or Hindoos.' Or a man of the world might well have been shrewd enough to say, 'Powerful people are picking up these fads; some day the court will adopt one of them and it may become official.' Or yet another and gloomier prophet might be pardoned for saying, 'The world is going down-hill; dark and barbarous superstitions will return, it does not matter much which. They will all be formless and fugitive like dreams of the night.'

Now it is the intense interest of the case that all these prophecies were really fulfilled; but it was not the Church that fulfilled them. It was the Church that escaped from them, confounded them, and rose above them in triumph. In so far as it was probable that the mere nature of hedonism would produce a mere reaction of asceticism it did produce a mere reaction of asceticism. It was the movement called Manichean and the Church was its mortal enemy. In so far as it would have naturally appeared at that point of history, it did appear; it did also disappear, which was equally natural. The mere pessimist reaction did come with the Manichees and did go with the Manichees But the Church did not come with them or go with them; and she had much more to do with them going than with their coming. Or again, in so far as it was probable that even the growth of scepticism would bring in a fashion of eastern religion, it did bring it in; Mithras came from far beyond Palestine out of the heart of Persia, bringing strange mysteries of the blood of bulls. Certainly there was everything to show that some such fashion would have come in any case but certainly there is nothing in the world to show that it would not have passed away in any case. Certainly an Oriental fad was something eminently fitted to the fourth or fifth century; but that hardly explains it having remained to the twentieth century, and still going strong. In short, in so far as things of the kind might have been expected then, things like Mithraism were experienced then; but it scarcely explains our more recent experiences. And if we were still Mithraists merely because Mithraic head-dresses and other Persian apparatuses might be expected to be all the rage in the days of Domitian, it would almost seem by this time that we must be a little dowdy.

It is the same, as will be suggested in a moment, with the idea of official favouritism. In so far as such favouritism shown towards a fad was something that might have been looked for during the decline and fall of the Roman Empire, it was something that did exist in that Empire and did decline and fall with it. It throws no sort of light on the thing that resolutely refused to decline and fall; that grew steadily while the other was declining and falling; and which even at this moment is going forward with fearless energy, when an other aeon has completed its cycle and another civilisation seems almost ready to fall or to decline.

Now the curious fact is this; that the very heresies which the early Church is blamed for crushing testify to the unfairness for which she is blamed. In so far as something deserved the blame, it was precisely the things that she is blamed for blaming. In so far as something was merely a superstition, she herself condemned that superstition. In so far as something was a mere reaction into barbarism, she herself resisted it because it was a reaction into barbarism. In so far as something was a fad of the fading empire, that died and deserved to die, it was the Church alone that killed it. The Church is reproached for being exactly what the heresy was repressed for being The explanations of the evolutionary historians and higher critics do really explain why Arianism and Gnosticism and Nestorianism were born--and also why they died. They do not explain why the Church was born or why she has refused to die. Above all, they do not explain why she should have made war on the very evils she is supposed to share.

Let us take a few practical examples of the principle; the principle that if there was anything that was really a superstition of the dying empire, it did really die with the dying empire; and certainly was not the same as the very thing that destroyed it. For this purpose we will take in order two or three of the most ordinary explanations of Christian origins among the modern critics of Christianity. Nothing is more common, for instance, than to find such a modern critic writing something like this: 'Christianity was above all a movement of ascetics, a rush into the desert, a refuge in the cloister, a renunciation of all life and happiness; and this was a part of a gloomy and in human reaction against nature itself, a hatred of the body, a horror of the material universe, a sort of universal suicide of the senses and even of the self. It came from an eastern fanaticism like that of the fakirs and was ultimately founded on an eastern pessimism, which seems to feel existence itself as an evil.'

Now the most extraordinary thing about this is that it is all quite true; it is true in every detail except that it happens to be attributed entirely to the wrong person. It is not true of the Church; but it is true of the heretics condemned by the Church. It is as if one were to write a most detailed analysis of the mistakes and misgovernment of the ministers of George the Third, merely with the small inaccuracy that the whole story was told about George Washington; or as if somebody made a list of the crimes of the Bolshevists with no variation except that they were all attributed to the Czar. The early Church was indeed very ascetic in connection with a totally different philosophy; but the philosophy of a war on life and nature as such really did exist in the world, if the critics only knew where to look for it.

What really happened was this. When the Faith first emerged into the world, the very first thing that happened to it was that it was caught in a sort of swarm of mystical and metaphysical sects, mostly out of the East; like one lonely golden bee caught in a swarm of wasps. To the ordinary onlooker, there did not seem to be much difference, or anything beyond a general buzz; indeed in a sense there was not much difference so far as stinging and being stung were concerned. The difference was at only one golden dot in all that whirring gold-dust had the power of going forth to make hives for all humanity; to give the world honey and wax or (as was so finely said in a context too easily forgotten) 'the two noblest things, which are sweetness and light.' The wasps all died that winter; and half the difficulty is that hardly anyone knows anything about them and most people do not know that they ever existed; so that the whole story of that first phase of our religion is lost. Or, to vary the metaphor, when this movement or some other movement pierced the dyke between the east and west and brought more mystical ideas into Europe, it brought with it a whole flood of other mystical ideas besides its own, most of them ascetical and nearly all of them pessimistic. They very nearly flooded and over-whelmed the purely Christian element. They came mostly from that region that was a sort of dim borderland between the eastern philosophies and the eastern mythologies, and which shared with the wilder philosophers that curious crave for making fantastic patterns of the cosmos in the shape of maps and genealogical trees. Those that are supposed to derive from the mysterious Manes are called Manichean; kindred cults are more generally known as Gnostic; they are mostly of a labyrinthine complexity, but the point to insist on is the pessimism; the fact that nearly all in one form or another regarded the creation of the world as the work of an evil spirit. Some of them had that Asiatic atmosphere that surrounds Buddhism; the suggestion that life is a corruption of the purity of being. Some of them suggested a purely spiritual order which had been betrayed by the coarse and clumsy trick of making such toys as the sun and moon and stars. Anyhow all this dark tide out of the metaphysical sea in the midst of Asia poured through the dykes simultaneously with the creed of Christ; but it is the whole point of the story that the two were not the same; that they flowed like oil and water. That creed remained in the shape of a miracle; a river still flowing through the sea. And the proof of the miracle was practical once more; it was merely that while all that sea was salt and bitter with the savour of death, of this one stream in the midst of it a man could drink.

Now that purity was preserved by dogmatic definitions and exclusions. It could not possibly have been preserved by anything else If the Church had not renounced the Manicheans it might have become merely Manichean. If it had not renounced the Gnostics it might have become Gnostic. But by the very fact that it did renounce them it proved that it was not either Gnostic or Manichean. At any rate it proved that something was not either Gnostic or Manichean; and what could it be that condemned them, if it was not the original good news of the runners from Bethlehem and the trumpet of the Resurrection? The early Church was ascetic, but she proved that she was not pessimistic, simply by condemning the pessimists. The creed declared that man was sinful, but it did not declare that life was evil, and it proved it by damning those who did. The condemnation of the early heretics is itself condemned as something crabbed and narrow; but it was in truth the very proof that the Church meant to be brotherly and broad. It proved that the primitive Catholics were specially eager to explain that they did not think man utterly vile; that they did not think life incurably miserable; that they did not think marriage a sin or procreation a tragedy. They were ascetic because asceticism was the only possible purge of the sins of the world; but in the very thunder of their anathemas they affirmed for ever that their asceticism was not to be anti-human or anti-natural; that they did wish to purge the world and not destroy it. And nothing else except those anathemas could possibly have made it clear, amid a confusion which still confuses them with their mortal enemies. Nothing else but dogma could have resisted the riot of imaginative invention with which the pessimists were waging their war against nature; with their Aeons and their Demiurge, their strange Logos and their sinister Sophia. If the Church had not insisted on theology, it would have melted into a mad mythology of the mystics, yet further removed from reason or even from rationalism; and, above all yet further removed from life and from the love of life. Remember that it would have been an inverted mythology, one contradicting everything natural in paganism; a mythology in which Pluto would be above Jupiter and Hades hang higher than Olympus; in which Brahma and all that has the breath of life would be subject to Seeva, shining with the eye of death.

That the early Church was itself full of an ecstatic enthusiasm for renunciation and virginity makes this distinction much more striking and not less so. It makes all the more important the place where the dogma drew the line. A man might crawl about on all fours like a beast because he was an ascetic. He might stand night and day on the top of a pillar and be adored for being an ascetic, but he could not say that the world was a mistake or the marriage state a sin without being a heretic. What was it that thus deliberately disengaged itself from eastern asceticism by sharp definition and fierce refusal, if it was not something with an individuality of its own; and one that was quite different? If the Catholics are to be confused with the Gnostics, we can only say it was not their fault if they are. And it is rather hard that the Catholics should be blamed by the same critics for persecuting the heretics and also for sympathising with the heresy.

413

The Church was not a Manichean movement if only because it was not a movement at all. It was not even merely an ascetical movement, because it was not a movement at all. It would be nearer the truth to call it the tamer of asceticism than the mere leader or loosener of it. It was a thing having its own theory of asceticism, its own type of asceticism, but most conspicuous at the moment as the moderator of other theories and types. This is the only sense that can be made, for instance, of the story of St. Augustine. As long as he was a mere man of the world, a mere man drifting with his time, he actually was a Manichean. It really was quite modern and fashionable to be a Manichean. But when he became a Catholic, the people he instantly turned on and rent in pieces were the Manicheans. The Catholic way of putting it is that he left off being a pessimist to become an ascetic. But as the pessimists interpreted asceticism, it ought to be said that he left off being an ascetic to become a saint. The war upon life, the denial of nature, were exactly the things he had already found in the heathen world outside the Church, and had to renounce when he entered the Church. The very fact that St. Augustine remains a somewhat sterner or sadder figure than St. Francis or St. Teresa only accentuates the dilemma. Face to face with the gravest or even grimmest of Catholics, we can still ask, 'Why did Catholicism make war on Manichees, if Catholicism was Manichean?'

Take another rationalistic explanation of the rise of Christendom. It is common enough to find another critic saying, 'Christianity did not really rise at all; that is, it did not merely rise from below; it was imposed from above. It is an example of the power of the executive, especially in despotic states. The Empire was really an Empire; that is, it was really ruled by the Emperor. One of the Emperors happened to become a Christian. He might just as well have become a Mithraist or a Jew or a Fire-Worshipper; it was common in the decline of the Empire for eminent and educated people to adopt these eccentric eastern cults. But when he adopted it, it became the official religion of the Roman Empire; and when it became the official religion of the Roman Empire, it became as strong, as universal and as invincible as the Roman Empire. It has only remained in the world as a relic of that Empire; or, as many have put it, it is but the ghost of Caesar still hovering over Rome.' This also is a very ordinary line taken in the criticism of orthodoxy, to say that it was only officialism that ever made it orthodoxy. And here again we can call on the heretics to refute it.

The whole great history of the Arian heresy might have been invented to explode this idea. It is a very interesting history often repeated in this connection; and the upshot of it is in that in so far as there ever was a merely official religion, it actually died because it was merely an official religion; and what destroyed it was the real religion. Arius advanced a version of Christianity which moved, more or less vaguely, in the direction of what we should call Unitarianism; though it was not the same, for it gave to Christ a curious intermediary position between the divine and human. The point is that it seemed to many more reasonable and less fanatical; and among these were many of the educated class in a sort of reaction against the first romance of conversion. Arians were a sort of moderates and a sort of modernists. And it was felt that after the first squabbles this was the final form of rationalised religion into which civilisation might well settle down. It was accepted by Divus Caesar himself and became the official orthodoxy; the generals and military princes drawn from the new barbarian powers of the north, full of the future, supported it strongly. But the sequel is still more important. Exactly as a modern man might pass through Unitarianism to complete agnosticism, so the greatest of the Arian emperors ultimately shed the last and thinnest pretense of Christianity; he abandoned ever Arius and returned to Apollo. He was a Caesar of the Caesars; a soldier, a scholar, a man of large ambitions and ideals; another of the philosopher kings. It seemed to him as if at his signal the sun rose again. The oracles began to speak like birds beginning to sing at dawn; paganism was itself again; the gods returned. It seemed the end of that strange interlude of an alien superstition. And indeed it was the end of it, so far as there was a mere interlude of mere superstition. It was the end of it, in so far as it was the fad of an emperor or the fashion of a generation. If there really was something that began with Constantine, then it ended with Julian.

But there was something that did not end. There had arisen in that hour of history, defiant above the democratic tumult of the Councils of the Church, Athanasius against the world. We may pause upon the point at issue; because it is relevant to the whole of this religious history, and the modern world seems to miss the whole point of it. We might put it this way. If there is one question which the enlightened and liberal have the habit of deriding and holding up as a dreadful example of barren dogma and senseless sectarian strife, it is this Athanasian question of the Co-Eternity of the Divine Son. On the other hand, if there is one thing that the same liberals always offer us as a piece of pure and simple Christianity, untroubled by doctrinal disputes, it is the single sentence, 'God is Love.' Yet the two statements are almost identical; at least one is very nearly nonsense without the other. The barren dogma is only the logical way of stating the beautiful sentiment. For if there be a being without beginning, existing before all things, was He loving when there was nothing to be loved? If through that unthinkable eternity He is lonely, what is the meaning of saying He is love? The only justification of such a mystery is the mystical conception that in His own nature there was something analogous to self-expression; something of what begets and beholds what it has begotten. Without some such idea, it is really illogical to complicate the ultimate essence of deity with an idea like love. If the moderns really want a simple religion of love, they must look for it in the Athanasian Creed. The truth is that the trumpet of true Christianity, the challenge of the charities and simplicities of Bethlehem or Christmas Day never rang out more arrestingly and unmistakably than in the defiance of Athanasius to the cold compromise of the Arians. It was emphatically he who really was fighting for a God of Love against a God of colourless and remote cosmic control; the God of the stoics and the agnostics. It was emphatically he who was fighting for the Holy Child against the grey deity of the Pharisees and the Sadducees. He was fighting for that very balance of beautiful interdependence and intimacy, in the very Trinity of the Divine Nature, that draws our hearts to the Trinity of the Holy Family. His dogma, if the phrase be not misunderstood, turns even God into a Holy Family.

That this purely Christian dogma actually for a second time rebelled against the Empire, and actually for a second time refounded the Church in spite of the Empire, is itself a proof that there was something positive and personal working in the world, other than whatever official faith the Empire chose to adopt. This power utterly destroyed the official faith that the Empire did adopt. It went on its own way as it is going on its own way still. There are any number of other examples in which is repeated precisely the same process we have reviewed in the case of the Manichean and the Arian. A few centuries afterwards, for instance, the Church had to maintain the same Trinity, which is simply the logical side of love, against another appearance of the isolated and simplified deity in the religion of Islam. Yet there are some who cannot see what the Crusaders were fighting for; and some even who talk as if Christianity had never been anything but a form of what they call Hebraism coming in with the decay of Hellenism. Those people must certainly be very much puzzled by the war between the Crescent and the Cross. If Christianity had never been anything but a simpler morality sweeping away polytheism, there is no reason why Christendom should not have been swept into Islam. The truth is that Islam itself was a barbaric reaction against that very humane complexity that is really a Christian character; that idea of balance in the deity, as of balance in the family, that makes that creed a sort of sanity, and that sanity the soul of civilisation. And that is why the Church is from the first a thing holding its own position and point of view, quite apart from the accidents and anarchies of its age. That is why it deals blows impartially right and left, at the pessimism of the Manichean or the optimism of the Pelagian. It was not a Manichean movement because it was not a movement at all. It was not an official fashion because it was not a fashion at all. It was something that could coincide with movements and fashions, could control them and could survive them.

So might rise from their graves the great heresiarchs to confound their comrades of to-day. There is nothing that the critics now affirm that we cannot call on these great witnesses to deny. The modern critic will say lightly enough that Christianity was but a reaction into asceticism and anti-natural spirituality, a dance of fakirs furious against life and love. But Manes the great mystic will answer them from his secret throne and cry, 'These Christians have no right to be called spiritual; these Christians have no title to be called ascetics, they who compromised with the curse of life and all the filth of the family. Through them the earth is still foul with fruit and harvest and polluted with population. Theirs was no movement against nature, or my children would have carried it to triumph; but these fools renewed the world when I would have ended it with a gesture.' And another critic will write that the Church was but the shadow of the Empire, the fad of a chance Emperor, and that it remains in Europe only as the ghost of the power of Rome. And Arius the deacon will answer out of the darkness of oblivious 'No, indeed, or the world would have followed my more reasonable religion. For mine went down before demagogues and men defying Caesar; and around my champion was the purple cloak and mine was the glory of the eagles. It was not for lack of these things that I failed. And yet a third modern will maintain that the creed spread only as a sort of panic of hell-fire; men everywhere attempting impossible things in fleeing from incredible vengeance; a nightmare of imaginary remorse; and such an explanation will satisfy many who see something dreadful in the doctrine of orthodoxy. And then there will go up against it the terrible voice of Tertullian, saying, 'And why then was I cast out; and why did soft hearts and heads decide against me when I proclaimed the perdition of all sinners; and what was this power that thwarted me when I threatened all backsliders with hell? For none ever went up that hard road so far as I; and mine was the Credo Quia Impossible.' Then there is the fourth suggestion that there was something of the Semitic secret society in the whole matter; that it was a new invasion of the nomad spirit shaking a kindlier and more comfortable paganism, its cities and its household gods; whereby the jealous monotheistic races could after all establish their jealous God. And Mahomet shall answer out of the whirlwind, the red whirlwind of the desert, 'Who ever served the jealousy of God as I did or left him more lonely in the sky? Who ever paid more honour to Moses and Abraham or won more victories over idols and the images of paganism? And what was this thing that thrust me back with the energy of a thing alive; whose fanaticism could drive me from Sicily and tear up my deep roots out of the rock of Spain? What faith was theirs who thronged in thousands of every class a country crying out that my ruin was the will of God; and what hurled great Godfrey as from a catapult over the wall of Jerusalem, and what brought great Sobieski like a thunderbolt to the gates of Vienna? I think there was more than you fancy in the religion that has so matched itself with mine.'

Those who would suggest that the faith was a fanaticism are doomed to an eternal perplexity. In their account it is bound to appear as fanatical for nothing, and fanatical against everything. It is ascetical and at war with ascetics, Roman and in revolt against Rome, monotheistic and fighting furiously against monotheism; harsh in its condemnation of harshness; a riddle not to be explained even as unreason. And what sort of unreason is it that seems reasonable to millions of educated Europeans through all the revolutions of some sixteen hundred years? People are not amused with a puzzle or a paradox or a mere muddle in the mind for all that time. I know of no explanation except that such a thing is not unreason but reason; that if it is fanatical it is fanatical for reason and fanatical against all the unreasonable things. That is the only explanation I can find of a thing from the first so detached and so confident, condemning things that looked so like itself, refusing help from powers that seemed so essential to its existence, sharing on its human side all the passions of the age, yet always at the supreme moment suddenly rising superior to them, never saying exactly what it was expected to say and never needing to unsay what it had said; I can find no explanation except that, like Pallas from the brain of Jove, it had indeed come forth out of the mind of God, mature and mighty and armed for judgement and for war.

THE ESCAPE FROM PAGANISM

The modern missionary, with his palm-leaf hat and his umbrella, has become rather a figure of fun. He is chaffed among men of the world for the ease with which he can be eaten by cannibals and the narrow bigotry which makes him regard the cannibal culture as lower than his own. Perhaps the best part of the joke is that the men of the world do not see that the joke is against themselves. It is rather ridiculous to ask a man just about to be boiled in a pot and eaten, at a purely religious feast, why he does not regard all religions as equally friendly and fraternal. But there is a more subtle criticism uttered against the more old-fashioned missionary; to the effect that he generalises too broadly about the heathen and pays too little attention to the difference between Mahomet and Mumbo-Jumbo. There was probably truth in this complaint, especially in the past; but it is my main contention here that the exaggeration is all the other way at present. It is the temptation of the professors to treat mythologies too much as theologies; as things thoroughly thought out are seriously held. It is the temptation of the intellectuals to take much too seriously the fine shades of various schools in the rather irresponsible metaphysics of Asia. Above all it is their temptation to miss the real truth implied in the idea of Aquinas contra Gentiles or Athanasius contra mundum.

If the missionary says, in fact, that he is exceptional in being a Christian, and that the rest of the races and religions can be collectively classified as heathen, he is perfectly right. He may say it in quite the wrong spirit, in which case he is spiritually wrong. But in the cold light of philosophy and history, he is intellectually right. He may not be right minded, but he is right. He may not even have a right to be right, but he is right. The outer world to which he brings his creed really is some thing subject to certain generalisations covering all its varieties, and is not merely a variety of similar creeds. Perhaps it is in any case too much of a temptation to pride or hypocrisy to call it heathenry. Perhaps it could be better simply to call it humanity. But there are certain broad characteristics of what we call humanity while it remains in what we call heathenry. They are not necessarily bad characteristics; some of them are worthy of the respect of Christendom; some of them have been absorbed and transfigured in the substance of Christendom. But they existed before Christendom and they still exist outside Christendom, as certainly as the sea existed before a boat and all round a boat; and they have as strong and as universal and as unmistakable a savour as the sea.

For instance, all real scholars who have studied the Greek and Roman culture say one thing about it. They agree that in the ancient world religion was one thing and philosophy quite another, there was very little effort to rationalise and at the same time to realise a real belief in the gods. There was very little pretense of any such real belief among the philosophers. But neither had the passion or perhaps the power to persecute the others save in particular and peculiar cases; and neither the philosopher in his school nor the priest in his temple seems ever to have seriously contemplated his own concept as covering the world. A priest sacrificing to Artemis in Calydon did not seem to think that people would some day sacrifice to her instead of to Isis beyond the sea; a sage following the vegetarian rule of the Neo-Pythagoreans did not seem to think it would universally prevail and exclude the methods of Epictetus or Epicurus. We may call this liberality if we like; I am not dealing with an argument but describing an atmosphere. All this, I say, is admitted by all scholars; but what neither the learned nor the unlearned have fully realised, perhaps, is that this description is really an exact description of all non-Christian civilisation today; and especially of the great civilisations of the East. Eastern paganism really is much more all of a piece, just as ancient paganism was much more all of a piece, than the modern critics admit. It is a many-coloured Persian Carpet as the other was a varied and tessellated Roman pavement; but the one real crack right across that pavement came from the earthquake of the Crucifixion.

The modern European seeking his religion in Asia is reading his religion into Asia. Religion there is something different; it is both more and less. He is like a man mapping out the sea as land; marking waves as mountains; not understanding the nature of its peculiar permanence. It is perfectly true that Asia has its own dignity and poetry and high civilisation. But it is not in the least true that Asia has its own definite dominions of moral government, where all loyalty is conceived in terms of morality; as when we say that Ireland is Catholic or that New England was Puritan. The map is not marked out in religions, in our sense of churches. The state of mind is far more subtle, more relative, more secretive, more varied and changing, like the colours of the snake. The Moslem is the nearest approach to a militant Christian; and that is precisely because he is a much nearer approach to an envoy from western civilisation. The Moslem in the heart of Asia almost stands for the soul of Europe. And as he stands between them and Europe in the matter of space so he stands between them and Christianity in the matter of time. In that sense the Moslems in Asia are merely like the Nestorians in Asia. Islam, historically speaking, is the greatest of the Eastern heresies. It owed something to the quite isolated and unique individuality of Israel; but it owed more to Byzantium and the theological enthusiasm of Christendom. It owed something even to the Crusades. It owed nothing whatever to Asia. It owed nothing to the atmosphere of the ancient and traditional world of Asia, with its immemorial etiquette and its bottomless or bewildering philosophies. All that ancient and actual Asia felt the entrance of Islam as something foreign and western and warlike, piercing it like a spear.

Even where we might trace in dotted lines the domains of Asiatic religions, we should probably be reading into them something dogmatic and ethical belonging to our own religion. It is as if a European ignorant of the American atmosphere were to suppose that each 'state' was a separate sovereign state as patriotic as France or Poland; or that when a Yankee referred fondly to his 'home town' he meant he had no other nation, like a citizen of ancient Athens or Rome. As he would be reading a particular sort of loyalty into America, so we are reading a particular sort of loyalty into Asia. There are loyalties of other kinds; but not what men in the West mean by being a believer, by trying to be a Christian, by being a good Protestant or a practising Catholic. In the intellectual world it means something far more vague and varied by doubts and speculations. In the moral world it means something far more loose and drifting. A professor of Persian at one of our great universities, so passionate a partisan of the East as practically to profess a contempt for the West, said to a friend of mine: 'You will never understand oriental religions, because you always conceive religion as connected with ethics. This kind has really nothing to do with ethics.' We have most of us known some Masters of the Higher Wisdom, some Pilgrims upon the Path to Power, some eastern esoteric saints and seers, who had really nothing to do with ethics. Something different, something detached and irresponsible, tinges the moral atmosphere of Asia and touches even that of Islam. It was very realistically caught in the atmosphere of Hassan; and a very horrible atmosphere too. It is even more vivid in such glimpses as we get of the genuine and ancient cults of Asia. Deeper than the depths of metaphysics, far down in the abysses of mystical meditations under all that solemn universe of spiritual things, is a secret, an intangible and a terrible levity. It does not really very much matter what one does. Either because they do not believe in a devil, or because they do believe in a destiny, or because experience here is everything and eternal life something totally different, but for some reason they are totally different. I have read somewhere that there were three great friends famous in medieval Persia for their unity of mind. One became the responsible and respected Vizier of the Great King; the second was the poet Omar, pessimist and epicurean, drinking wine in mockery of Mahomet; the third was the Old Man of the Mountain who maddened his people with hashish that they might murder other people with daggers. It does not really much matter what one does.

The Sultan in Hassan would have understood all those three men; indeed he was all those three men. But this sort of universalist cannot have what we call a character; it is what we call a chaos. He cannot choose; he cannot fight; he cannot repent; he cannot hope. He is not in the same sense creating something; for creation means rejection. He is not, in our religious phrase, making his soul. For our doctrine of salvation does really mean a labour like that of a man trying to make a statue beautiful; a victory with wings. For that there must be a final choice, for a man cannot make statues without rejecting stone. And there really is this ultimate unmorality behind the metaphysics of Asia. And the reason is that there has been nothing through all those unthinkable ages to bring the human mind sharply to the point; to tell it that the time has come to choose. The mind has lived too much in eternity. The soul has been too immortal, in the special sense that it ignores the idea of mortal sin. It has had too much of eternity, in the sense that it has not had enough of the hour of death and the day of judgement. It is not crucial enough; in the literal sense that it has not had enough of the cross. That is what we mean when we say that Asia is very old. But strictly speaking Europe is quite as old as Asia; indeed in a sense any place is as old as any other place. What we mean is that Europe has not merely gone on growing older. It has been born again.

Asia is all humanity; as it has worked out its human doom. Asia, in its vast territory, in its varied populations, in its heights of past achievement and its depths of dark speculation, is itself a world; and represents something of what we mean when we speak of the world. It is a cosmos rather than a continent. It is the world as man has made it; and contains many of the most wonderful things that man has made. Therefore Asia stands as the one representative of paganism and the one rival to Christendom. But everywhere else where we get glimpses of that mortal destiny, they suggest stages in the same story. Where Asia trails away into the southern archipelagoes of the savages, or where a darkness full of nameless shapes dwells in the heart of Africa, or where the last survivors of lost races linger in the cold volcano of prehistoric America, it is all the same story; sometimes perhaps later chapters of the same story. It is men entangled in the forest of their own mythology; it is men drowned in the sea of their own metaphysics. Polytheists have grown weary of the wildest of fictions. Monotheists have grown weary of the most wonderful of truths. Diabolists here and there have such a hatred of heaven and earth that they have tried to take refuge in hell. It is the Fall of Man; and it is exactly that fall that was being felt by our own fathers at the first moment of the Roman decline. We also were going down that side road; down that easy slope; following the magnificent procession of the high civilisations of the world.

If the Church had not entered the world then, it seems probable that Europe would be now very much what Asia is now. Something may be allowed for a real difference of race and environment, visible in the ancient as in the modern world. But after all we talk about the changeless East very largely because it has not suffered the great change. Paganism in its last phase showed considerable signs of be coming equally changeless. This would not mean that new schools or sects of philosophy would not arise; as new schools did arise in Antiquity and do arise in Asia. It does not mean that there would be no real mystics or visionaries; as there were mystics in Antiquity and are mystics in Asia. It does not mean that there would be no social codes, as there were codes in Antiquity and are codes in Asia. It does not mean that there could not be good men or happy lives, for God has given all men a conscience and conscience can give all men a kind of peace. But it does mean that the tone and proportion of all these things, and especially the proportion of good and evil things, would be in the unchanged West what they are in the changeless East. And nobody who looks at that changeless East honestly, and with a real sympathy, can believe that there is anything there remotely resembling the challenge and revolution of the Faith.

In short, if classic paganism had lingered until now, a number of things might well have lingered with it; and they would look very like what we call the religions of the East. There would still be Pythagoreans teaching reincarnation, as there are still Hindus teaching reincarnation. There would still be Stoics making a religion out of reason and virtue, as there are still Confucians making a religion out of reason and virtue. There would still be Neo-Platonists studying transcendental truths, the meaning of which was mysterious to other people and disputed even amongst themselves; as the Buddhists still study a transcendentalism mysterious to others and disputed among themselves. There would still be intelligent Apollonians apparently worshipping the sun-god but explaining that they were worshipping the divine principle; just as there are still intelligent Parsees apparently worshipping the sun but explaining that they are worshipping the deity. There would still be wild Dionysians dancing on the mountain as there are still wild Dervishes dancing in the desert. There would still be crowds of people attending the popular feasts of the gods, in pagan Europe as in pagan Asia. There would still be crowds of gods, local and other, for them to worship. And there would still be a great many more people who worshipped them than people who believed in them. Finally there would still be a very large number of people who did worship gods and did believe in gods; and who believed in gods and worshipped gods simply because they were demons. There would still be Levantines secretly sacrificing to Moloch as there are still Thugs secretly sacrificing to Kalee. There would still be a great deal of magic; and a great deal of it would be black magic. There would still be a considerable admiration of Seneca and a considerable imitation of Nero; just as the exalted epigrams of Confucius could coexist with the tortures of China. And over all that tangled forest of traditions growing wild or withering would brood the broad silence of a singular and even nameless mood; but the nearest name of it is nothing. All these things, good and bad, would have an indescribable air of being too old to die.

None of these things occupying Europe in the absence of Christendom would bear the least likeness to Christendom. Since the Pythagorean Metempsychosis would still be there, we might call it the Pythagorean religion as we talk about the Buddhist religion. As the noble maxims of Socrates would still be there, we might call it the Socratic religion as we talk about the Confucian religion. As the popular holiday was still marked by a mythological hymn to Adonis, we might call it the religion of Adonis as we talk about the religion of Juggernaut. As literature would still be based on the Greek mythology, we might call that mythology a religion, as we call the Hindu mythology a religion. We might say that there were so many thousands or millions of people belonging to that religion, in the sense of frequenting such temples or merely living in a land full of such temples. But if we called the last tradition of Pythagoras or the lingering legend of Adonis by the name of a religion, then we must find some other name for the Church of Christ.

If anybody says that philosophic maxims presented through many ages, or mythological temples frequented by many people, are things of the same class and category as the Church, it is enough to answer quite simply that they are not. Nobody thinks they are the same when he sees them in the old civilisation of Greece and Rome; nobody would think they were the same if that civilisation had lasted two thousand years longer and existed at the present day; nobody can in reason think they are the same in the parallel pagan civilisation in the East, as it is at the present day. None of these philosophies or mythologies are anything like a Church; certainly nothing like a Church Militant. And, as I have shown elsewhere, even if this rule were not already proved, the exception would prove the rule. The rule is that pre-Christian or pagan history does not produce a Church Militant; and the exception, or what some would call the exception, is that Islam is at least militant if it is not Church. And that is precisely because Islam is the one religious rival that is not pre-Christian and therefore not in that sense pagan. Islam was a product of Christianity; even if it was a by-product; even if it was a bad product. It was a heresy or parody emulating and therefore imitating the Church. It is no more surprising that Mahomedanism had something of her fighting spirit than that Quakerism had something of her peaceful spirit. After Christianity there are any number of such emulations or extensions. Before it there are none.

The Church Militant is thus unique because it is an army marching to effect a universal deliverance. The bondage from which the world is thus to be delivered is something that is very well symbolised by the state of Asia as by the state of pagan Europe. I do not mean merely their moral or immoral state. The missionary, as a matter of fact, has much more to say for himself than the enlightened imagine even when he says that the heathen are idolatrous and immoral. A touch or two of realistic experience about

Eastern religion, even about Moslem religion, will reveal some startling insensibilities in ethics; such as the practical indifference to the line between passion and perversion. It is not prejudice but practical experience which says that Asia is full of demons as well as gods. But the evil I mean is in the mind. And it is in the mind wherever the mind has worked for a long time alone. It is what happens when all dreaming and thinking have come to an end in an emptiness that is at once negation and necessity. It sounds like an anarchy, but it is also a slavery. It is what has been called already the wheel of Asia; all those recurrent arguments about cause and effect or things beginning and ending in the mind, which make it impossible for the soul really to strike out and go anywhere or do anything. And the point is that it is not necessarily peculiar to Asiatics; it would have been true in the end of Europeans--if something had not happened. If the Church Militant had not been a thing marching, all men would have been marking time. If the Church Militant had not endured a discipline, all men would have endured a slavery.

What that universal yet fighting faith brought into the world was hope. Perhaps the one thing common to mythology and philosophy was that both were really sad; in the sense that they had not this hope even if they had touches of faith or charity. We may call Buddhism a faith; though to us it seems more like a doubt. We may call the Lord of Compassion a Lord of Charity, though it seems to us a very pessimist sort of pity. But those who insist most on the antiquity and size of such cults must agree that in all their ages they have not covered all their areas with that sort of practical and pugnacious hope. In Christendom hope has never been absent; rather it has been errant, extravagant, excessively fixed upon fugitive chances. Its perpetual revolution and reconstruction has at least been an evidence of people being in better spirits. Europe did very truly renew its youth like the eagles; just as the eagles of Rome rose again over the legions of Napoleon, or we have seen soaring but yesterday the silver eagle of Poland. But in the Polish case ever revolution always went with religion. Napoleon himself sought a reconciliation with religion. Religion could never be finally separated even from the most hostile of the hopes; simply because it was the very source of the hopefulness. And the cause of this is to be found simply in the religion itself. Those who quarrel about it seldom even consider it in itself. There is neither space nor place for such a full consideration here; but a word may be said to explain a reconciliation that always recurs and still seems to require explanation.

There will be no end to the weary debates about liberalising theology, until people face the fact that the only liberal part of it is really the dogmatic part. If dogma is incredible, it is because it is incredibly liberal. If it is irrational, it can only be in giving us more assurance of freedom than is justified by reason. The obvious example is that essential form of freedom which we call free-will. It is absurd to say that a man shows his liberality in denying his liberty. But it is tenable that he has to affirm a transcendental doctrine in order to affirm his liberty. There is a sense in which we might reasonably say that if man has a primary power of choice, he has in that fact a super-natural power of creation, as if he could raise the dead or give birth to the unbegotten. Possibly in that case a man must be a miracle; and certainly in that case he must be a miracle in order to be a man; and most certainly in order to be a free man. But it is absurd to forbid him to be a free man and do it in the name of a more free religion.

But it is true in twenty other matters. Anybody who believes at all in God must believe in the absolute supremacy of God. But in so far as that supremacy does allow of any degrees that can be called liberal or illiberal, it is self-evident that the illiberal power is the deity of the rationalists and the liberal power is the deity of the dogmatists. Exactly in proportion as you turn monotheism into monism you turn it into despotism. It is precisely the unknown God of the scientist, with his impenetrable purpose and his inevitable and unalterable law, that reminds us of a Prussian autocrat making rigid plans in a remote tent and moving mankind like machinery. It is precisely the God of miracles and of answered prayers who reminds us of a liberal and popular prince, receiving petitions, listening to parliaments and considering the cases of a whole people. I am not now arguing the rationality of this conception in other respects; as a matter of fact it is not, as some suppose, irrational; for there is nothing irrational in the wisest and most well-informed king acting differently according to the action of those he wishes to save. But I am here only noting the general nature of liberality, or of free or enlarged atmosphere of action. And in this respect it is certain that the king can only be what we call magnanimous if he is what some call capricious. It is the Catholic, who has the feeling that his prayers do make a difference, when offered for the living and the dead, who also has the feeling of living like a free citizen in something almost like a constitutional commonwealth. It is the monist who lives under a single iron law who must have the feeling of living like a slave under a sultan. Indeed I believe that the original use of the word suffragium, which we now use in politics for a vote, was that employed in theology about a prayer. The dead in Purgatory were said to have the suffrages of the living. And in this sense, of a sort of right of petition to the supreme ruler, we may truly say that the whole of the Communion of Saints, as well as the whole of the Church Militant, is founded on universal suffrage.

But above all, it is true of the most tremendous issue; of that tragedy which has created the divine comedy of our creed. Nothing short of the extreme and strong and startling doctrine of the divinity of Christ will give that particular effect that can truly stir the popular sense like a trumpet; the idea of the king himself serving in the ranks like a common soldier. By making that figure merely human we make that story much less human. We take away the point of the story which actually pierces humanity; the point of the story which was quite literally the point of a spear. It does not especially humanise the universe to say that good and wise men can die for their opinions; any more than it would be any sort of uproariously popular news in an army that good soldiers may easily get killed. It is no news that King Leonidas is dead any more than that Queen Anne is dead; and men did not wait for Christianity to be men, in the full sense of being heroes. But if we are describing, for the moment, the atmosphere of what is generous and popular and even picturesque, any knowledge of human nature will tell us that no sufferings of the sons of men, or even of the servants of God, strike the same note as the notion of the master suffering instead of his servants. And this is given by the theological and emphatically not by the scientific deity. No mysterious monarch, hidden in his starry pavilion at the base of the cosmic campaign, is in the least like that celestial chivalry of the Captain who carries his five wounds in the front of battle.

What the denouncer of dogma really means is not that dogma is bad; but rather that dogma is too good to be true. That is, he means that dogma is too liberal to be likely. Dogma gives man too much freedom when it permits him to fall. Dogma gives even God too much freedom when it permits him to die. That is what the intelligent sceptics ought to say; and it is not in the least my intention to deny that there is something to be said for it. They mean that the universe is itself a universal prison; that existence itself is a limitation and a control; and it is not for nothing that they call causation a chain. In a word, they mean quite simply that they cannot believe these things; not in the least that they are unworthy of belief. We say not lightly but very literally, that the truth has made us free. They say that it makes us so free that it cannot be the truth. To them it is like believing in fairyland to believe in such freedom as we enjoy. It is like believing in men with wings to entertain the fancy of men with wills. It is like accepting a fable about a squirrel in conversation with a mountain to believe in a man who is free to ask or a God who is free to answer. This is a manly and a rational negation for which I for one shall always show respect. But I decline to show any respect for those who first of all clip the wings and cage the squirrel, rivet the chains and refuse the freedom, close all the doors of the cosmic prison on us with a clang of eternal iron, tell us that our emancipation is a dream and our dungeon a necessity; and then calmly turn round and tell us they have a freer thought and a more liberal theology.

The moral of all this is an old one; that religion is revelation. In other words it is a vision, and a vision received by faith; but it is a vision of reality. The faith consists in a conviction of its reality. That, for example, is the difference between a vision and a day-dream. And that is the difference between religion and mythology. That is the difference between faith and all that fancy-work, quite human and more or less healthy, which we considered under the head of mythology. There is something in the reasonable use of the very word vision that implies two things about it; first that it comes very rarely, possibly that it comes only once; and secondly that it probably comes once and for all. A day-dream may come every day. A day-dream may be different every day. It is something more than the difference between telling ghost-stories and meeting a ghost.

But if it is not a mythology neither is it a philosophy. It is not a philosophy because, being a vision, it is not a pattern but a picture. It is not one of those simplifications which resolve everything into an abstract explanation; as that everything is recurrent; or everything is relative; or everything is inevitable; or everything is illusive. It is not a process but a story. It has proportions, of the sort seen in a picture or a story; it has not the regular repetitions of a pattern or a process; but it replaces them by being convincing as a picture or a story is convincing. In other words, it is exactly, as the phrase goes, like life. For indeed it is life. An example of what is meant here might well be found in the treatment of the problem of evil. It is easy enough to make a plan of life of which the background is black, as the pessimists do; and then admit a speck or two of star-dust more or less accidental, or at least in the literal sense insignificant. And it is easy enough to make another plan on white paper, as the Christian Scientists do, and explain or explain away somehow such dots or smudges as may be difficult to deny. Lastly it is easiest of all perhaps, to say as the dualists do, that life is like a chess-board in which the two are equal, and can as truly be said to consist of white squares on a black board or of black squares on a white board. But every man feels in his heart that none of these three paper plans is like life; that none of these worlds is one in which he can live. Something tells him that the ultimate idea of a world is not bad or even neutral; staring at the sky or the grass or the truths of mathematics or even a new-laid egg, he has a vague feeling like the shadow of that saying of the great Christian philosopher, St. Thomas Aquinas, 'Every existence, as such, is good.' On the other hand, something else tells him that it is unmanly and debased and even diseased to minimise evil to a dot or even a blot. He realizes that optimism is morbid. It is if possible even more morbid than pessimism. These vague but healthy feelings, if he followed them out, would result in the idea that evil is in some way an exception but an enormous exception; and ultimately that evil is an invasion or yet more truly a rebellion. He does not think that everything is right or that every thing is wrong, or that everything is equally right and wrong. But he does think that right has a right to be right and therefore a right to be there, and wrong has no right to be wrong and therefore no right to be there. It is the prince of the world; but it is also a usurper. So he will apprehend vaguely what the vision will give to him vividly; no less than all that strange story of treason in heaven and the great desertion by which evil damaged and tried to destroy a cosmos that it could not create. It is a very strange story and its proportions and its lines and colours are as arbitrary and absolute as the artistic composition of a picture. It is a vision which we do in fact symbolise in pictures by titanic limbs and passionate tints of plumage; all that abysmal vision of falling stars and the peacock panoplies of the night. But that strange story has one small advantage over the diagrams. It is like life.

Another example might be found, not in the problem of evil, but in what is called the problem of progress. One of the ablest agnostics of the age once asked me whether I thought mankind grew better or grew worse or remained the same. He was confident that the alternative covered all possibilities. He did not see that it only covered patterns and not pictures; processes and not stories. I asked him whether he thought that Mr. Smith of Golder's Green got better or worse or remained exactly the same between the age of thirty and forty. It then seemed to dawn on him that it would rather depend on Mr. Smith; and how he chose to go on. It had never occurred to him that it might depend on how mankind chose to go on; and that its course was not a straight line or an upward or downward curve, but a track like that of a man across a valley, going where he liked and stopping where he chose, going into a church or falling down in a ditch. The life of man is a story; an adventure story; and in our vision the same is true even of the story of God.

The Catholic faith is the reconciliation because it is the realisation both of mythology and philosophy. It is a story and in that sense one of a hundred stories; only it is a true story. It is a philosophy and in that sense one of a hundred philosophies; only it is a philosophy that is like life. But above all, it is a reconciliation because it is something that can only be called the philosophy of stories. That normal narrative instinct which produced all the fairy tales is something that is neglected by all the philosophies--except one. The Faith is the justification of that popular instinct; the finding of a philosophy for it or the analysis of the philosophy in it. Exactly as a man in an adventure story has to pass various tests to save his life, so the man in this philosophy has to pass several tests and save his soul. In both there is an idea of free will operating under conditions of design; in other words, there is an aim and it is the business of a man to aim at it; we therefore watch to see whether he will hit it. Now this deep and democratic and dramatic instinct is derided and dismissed in all the other philosophies. For all the other philosophies avowedly end where they begin; and it is the definition of a story that it ends differently; that it begins in one place and ends in another. From Buddha and his wheel to Akhen Aten and his disc, from Pythagoras with his abstraction of number to Confucius with his religion of routine, there is not one of them that does not in some way sin against the soul of a story. There is none of them that really grasps this human notion of the tale, the test, the adventure; the ordeal of the free man. Each of them starves the story-telling instinct, so to speak, and does something to spoil human life considered as a romance; either by fatalism (pessimist or optimist) and that destiny that is the death of adventure; or by indifference and that detachment that is the death of drama; or by a fundamental scepticism that dissolves the actors into atoms; or by a materialistic limitation blocking the vista of moral consequences; or a mechanical recurrence making even moral tests monotonous; or a bottomless relativity making even practical tests insecure. There is such a thing as a human story; and there is such a thing as the divine story which is also a human story; but there is no such thing as a Hegelian story or a Monist story or a relativist story or a determinist story; for every story, yes, even a penny dreadful or a cheap novelette, has something in it that belongs to our universe and not theirs. Every short story does truly begin with creation and end with a last judgement.

And that is the reason why the myths and the philosophers were at war until Christ came. That is why the Athenian democracy killed Socrates out of respect for the gods; and why every strolling sophist gave himself the airs of a Socrates whenever he could talk in a superior fashion of the gods; and why the heretic Pharaoh wrecked his huge idols and temples for an abstraction and why the priests could return in triumph and trample his dynasty under foot; and why Buddhism had to divide itself from Brahminism, and why in every age and country outside Christendom there has been a feud for ever between the philosopher and the priest. It is easy enough to say that the philosopher is generally the more rational; it is easier still to forget that the priest is always the more popular. For the priest told the people stories; and the philosopher did not understand the philosophy of stories. It came into the world with the story of Christ.

And this is why it had to be a revelation or vision given from above. Any one who will think of the theory of stories or pictures will easily see the point. The true story of the world must be told by somebody to somebody else. By the very nature of a story it cannot be left to occur to anybody. A story has proportions, variations, surprises, particular dispositions, which cannot be worked out by rule in the abstract, like a sum. We could not deduce whether or no Achilles would give back the body of Hector from a Pythagorean theory of number or recurrence; and we could not infer for ourselves in what way the world would get back the body of Christ, merely from being told that all things go round and round upon the wheel of Buddha. A man might perhaps work out a proposition of Euclid without having heard of Euclid; but he would not work out the precise legend of Eurydice without having heard of Eurydice. At any rate he would not be certain how the story would end and whether Orpheus was ultimately defeated. Still less could he guess the end of our story; or the legend of our Orpheus rising, not defeated from, the dead.

To sum up; the sanity of the world was restored and the soul of man offered salvation by something which did indeed satisfy the two warring tendencies of the past; which had never been satisfied in full and most certainly never satisfied together. It met the mythological search for romance by being a story and the philosophical search for truth by being a true story. That is why the ideal figure had to be a historical character, as nobody had ever felt Adonis or Pan to be a historical character. But that is also why the historical character had to be the ideal figure; and even fulfil many of the functions given to these other ideal figures; why he was at once the sacrifice and the feast, why he could be shown under the emblems of the growing vine or the rising sun. The more deeply we think of the matter the more we shall conclude that, if there be indeed a God, his creation could hardly have reached any other culmination than this granting of a real romance to the world. Otherwise the two sides of the human mind could never have touched at all; and the brain of man would have remained cloven and double; one lobe of it dreaming impossible dreams and the other repeating invariable calculations. The picture-makers would have remained forever painting the portrait of nobody. The sages would have remained for ever adding up numerals that came to nothing. It was that abyss that nothing but an incarnation could cover; a divine embodiment of our dreams; and he stands above that chasm whose name is more than priest and older even than Christendom; Pontifex Maximus, the mightiest maker of a bridge.

But even with that we return to the more specially Christian symbol in the same tradition; the perfect pattern of the keys. This is a historical and not a theological outline, and it is not my duty here to defend in detail that theology, but merely to point out that it could not even be justified in design without being justified in detail—like a key. Beyond the broad suggestion of this chapter I attempt no apologetic about why the creed should be accepted. But in answer to the historical query of why it was accepted and is accepted, I answer for millions of others in my reply; because it fits the lock, because it is like life. It is one among many stories; only it happens to be a true story. It is one among many philosophies; only it happens to be the truth. We accept it; and the ground is solid under our feet and the road is open before us. It does not imprison us in a dream of destiny or a consciousness of the universal delusion. It opens to us not only incredible heavens but what seems to some an equally incredible earth, and makes it credible. This is the sort of truth that is hard to explain because it is a fact; but it is a fact to which we can call witnesses. We are Christians and Catholics not because we worship a key, but because we have passed a door; and felt the wind that is the trumpet of liberty blow over the land of the living.

THE FIVE DEATHS OF THE FAITH

It is not the purpose of this book to trace the subsequent history of Christianity, especially the later history of Christianity; which involves controversies of which I hope to write more fully elsewhere. It is devoted only to the suggestion that Christianity, appearing amid heathen humanity, had all the character of a unique thing and even of a supernatural thing. It was not like any of the other things; and the more we study it the less it looks like any of them. But there is a certain rather peculiar character which marked it henceforward even down to the present moment, with a note on which this book may well conclude.

I have said that Asia and the ancient world had an air of being too old to die. Christendom has had the very opposite fate. Christendom has had a series of revolutions and in each one of them Christianity has died. Christianity has died many times and risen again; for it had a God who knew the way out of the grave. But the first extraordinary fact which marks this history is this: that Europe has been turned upside down over and over again; and that at the end of each of these revolutions the same religion has again been found on top. The Faith is always converting the age, not as an old religion but as a new religion. This truth is hidden from many by a convention that is too little noticed. Curiously enough, it is a convention of the sort which those who ignore it claim especially to detect and denounce. They are always telling us that priests and ceremonies are not religion and that religious organisation can be a hollow sham, but they hardly realise how true it is. It is so true that three or four times at least in the history of Christendom the whole soul seemed to have gone out of Christianity; and almost every man in his heart expected its end. This fact is only masked in medieval and other times by that very official religion which such critics pride themselves on seeing through. Christianity remained the official religion of a Renaissance prince or the official religion of an eighteenth-century bishop, just as an ancient mythology remained the official religion of Julius Caesar or the Arian creed long remained the official religion of Julian the Apostate. But there was a difference between the cases of Julius and of Julian; because the Church had begun its strange career. There was no reason why men like Julius should not worship gods like Jupiter for ever in public and laugh at them for ever in private. But when Julian treated Christianity as dead, he found it had come to life again. He also found, incidentally, that there was not the faintest sign of Jupiter ever coming to life again. This case of Julian and the episode of Arianism is but the first of a series of examples that can only be roughly indicated here. Arianism, as has been said, had every human appearance of being the natural way in which that particular superstition of Constantine might be expected to peter out. All the ordinary stages had been passed through; the creed had become a respectable thing, had become a ritual thing, had then been modified into a rational thing; and the rationalists were ready to dissipate the last remains of it, just as they do to-day. When Christianity rose again suddenly and threw them, it was almost as unexpected as Christ rising from the dead. But there are many other examples of the same thing, even about the same time. The rush of missionaries from Ireland, for instance, has all the air of an unexpected onslaught of young men on an old world, and even on a Church that showed signs of growing old. Some of them were martyred on the coast of Cornwall; and the chief authority on Cornish antiquities told me that he did not believe for a moment that they were martyred by heathens but (as he expressed it with some humour) 'by rather slack Christians.'

Now if we were to dip below the surface of history, as it is not in the scope of this argument to do, I suspect that we should find several occasions when Christendom was thus to all appearance hollowed out from within by doubt and indifference, so that only the old Christian shell stood as the pagan shell had stood so long. But the difference is that in every such case, the sons were fanatical for the faith where the fathers had been slack about it. This is obvious in the case of the transition from the Renaissance to the Counter-Reformation. It is obvious in the case of a transition from the eighteenth century to the many Catholic revivals of our own time. But I suspect many other examples which would be worthy of separate studies.

The Faith is not a survival. It is not as if the Druids had managed somehow to survive somewhere for two thousand years. That is what might have happened in Asia or ancient Europe, in that indifference or tolerance in which mythologies and philosophies could live for ever side by side. It has not survived; it has returned again and again in this Western world of rapid change and institutions perpetually perishing. Europe, in the tradition of Rome, was always trying revolution and reconstruction; rebuilding a universal republic. And it always began by rejecting this old stone and ended by making it the head of the corner; by bringing it back from the rubbish-heap to make it the crown of the capitol. Some stones of Stonehenge are standing and some are fallen; and as the stone falleth so shall it lie. There has not been a Druidic renaissance every century or two, with the young Druids crowned with fresh mistletoe, dancing in the sun on Salisbury Plain. Stonehenge has not been rebuilt in every style of architecture from the rude round Norman to the last rococo of the Baroque. The sacred place of the Druids is safe from the vandalism of restoration.

But the Church in the West was not in a world where things were too old to die; but in one in which they were always young enough to get killed.

The consequence was that superficially and externally it often did get killed; nay, it sometimes wore out even without getting killed. And there follows a fact I find it somewhat difficult to describe, yet which I believe to be very real and rather important. As a ghost is the shadow of a man, and in that sense the shadow of life, so at intervals there passed across this endless life a sort of shadow of death. It came at the moment when it would have perished had it been perishable. It withered away everything that was perishable. If such animal parallels were worthy of the occasion we might say that the snake shuddered and shed a skin and went on, or even that the cat went into convulsions as it lost only one of its nine-hundred-and-ninety-nine lives. It is truer to say, in a more dignified image, that a clock struck and nothing happened; or that a bell tolled for an execution that was everlastingly postponed.

What was the meaning of all that dim but vast unrest of the twelfth century; when, as it has been so finely said, Julian stirred in his sleep? Why did there appear so strangely early, in the twilight of dawn after the Dark Ages, so deep a scepticism as that involved in urging nominalism against realism? For realism against nominalism was really realism against rationalism, or something more destructive than what we call rationalism. The answer is that just as some might have thought the Church simply a part of the Roman Empire, so others later might have thought the Church only a part of the Dark Ages. The Dark Ages ended as the Empire had ended, and the Church should have departed with them, if she had been also one of the shades of night. It was another of those spectral deaths or simulations of death. I mean that if nominalism had succeeded, it would have been as if Arianism had succeeded, it would have been the beginning of a confession that Christianity had failed. For nominalism is a far more fundamental scepticism than mere atheism. Such was the question that was openly asked as the Dark Ages broadened into that daylight that we call the modern world. But what was the answer? The answer was Aquinas in the chair of Aristotle, taking all knowledge for his province; and tens of thousands of lads down to the lowest ranks of peasant and serf, living in rags and on crusts about the great colleges, to listen to the scholastic philosophy.

What was the meaning of all that whisper of fear that ran round the west under the shadow of Islam, and fills every old romance with incongruous images of Saracen knights swaggering in Norway or the Hebrides? Why were men in the extreme west, such as King John if I remember rightly, accused of being secretly Moslems, as men are accused of being secretly atheists? Why was there that fierce alarm among some of the authorities about the rationalistic Arab version of Aristotle? Authorities are seldom alarmed like that except when it is too late. The answer is that hundreds of people probably believed in their hearts that Islam would conquer

Christendom; that Averroes was more rational than Anselm; that the Saracen Culture was really, as it was superficially, a superior culture. Here again we should probably find a whole generation, the older generation, serve doubtful and depressed and weary. The coming of Islam would only have been the coming of Unitarianism a thousand years before its time. To many it may have seemed quite reasonable and quite probable and quite likely to happen. If so, they would have been surprised at what did happen. What did happen was a roar like thunder from thousands and thousands of young men, throwing all their youth into one exultant counter-charge, the Crusades. It was the sons of St. Francis, the Jugglers of God, wandering singing over all the roads of the world; it was the Gothic going up like a flight of arrows; it was the waking of the world. In considering the war of the Albigensians, we come to the breach in the heart of Europe and the landslide of a new philosophy that nearly ended Christendom for ever. In that case the new philosophy was also a very new philosophy; it was pessimism. It was none the less like modern ideas because it was as old as Asia; most modern ideas are. It was the Gnostics returning; but why did the Gnostics return? Because it was the end of an epoch, like the end of the Empire; and should have been the end of the Church. It was Schopenhauer hovering over the future; but it was also Manichaeus rising from the dead; that men might have death and that they might have it more abundantly.

It is rather more obvious in the case of the Renaissance, simply because the period is so much nearer to us and people know so much more about it. But there is more even in that example than most people know. Apart from the particular controversies which I wish to reserve for a separate study, the period was far more chaotic that those controversies commonly imply. When Protestants call Latimer a martyr to Protestantism, and Catholics reply that Campion was a martyr to Catholicism, it is often forgotten that many who perished in such persecutions could only be described as martyrs to atheism or anarchism or even diabolism. That world was almost as wild as our own; the men wandering about in it included the sort of man who says there is no God, the sort of man who says he is himself God, the sort of man who says something that nobody can make head or tail of. If we could have the conversation of the age following the Renaissance, we should probably be shocked by its shameless negations. The remarks attributed to Marlowe are probably pretty typical of the talk in many intellectual taverns. The transition from Pre-Reformation to Post-Reformation Europe was through a void of very yawning questions; yet again in the long run the answer was the same. It was one of those moments when, as Christ walked on the water, so was Christianity walking in the air.

But all these cases are remote in date and could only be proved in detail. We can see the fact much more clearly in the case when the paganism of the Renaissance ended Christianity and Christianity unaccountably began all over again. But we can see it most clearly of all in the case which is close to us and full of manifest and minute evidence; the case of the great decline of religion that began about the time of Voltaire. For indeed it is our own case, and we ourselves have seen the decline of that decline. The two hundred years since Voltaire do not flash past us at a glance like the fourth and fifth centuries or the twelfth and thirteenth centuries. In our own case we can see this oft-repeated process close at hand; we know how completely a society can lose its fundamental religion without abolishing its official religion; we know how men can all become agnostics long before they abolish bishops. And we know that also in this last ending, which really did look to us like the final ending, the incredible thing has happened again; the Faith has a better following among the young men than among the old. When Ibsen spoke of the new generation knocking at the door, he certainly never expected that it would be the church-door.

At least five times, therefore, with the Arian and the Albigensian, with the Humanist sceptic, after Voltaire and after Darwin, the Faith has to all appearance gone to the dogs. In each of these five cases it was the dog that died. How complete was the collapse and how strange the reversal we can only see in detail in the case nearest to our own time.

A thousand things have been said about the Oxford Movement and the parallel French Catholic revival; but few have made us feel the simplest fact about it; that it was a surprise. It was a puzzle as well as a surprise; because it seemed to most people like a river turning backwards from the sea and trying to climb back into the mountains. To have read the literature of the eighteenth and nineteenth centuries is to know that nearly everybody had come to take it for granted that religion was a thing that would continually broaden like a river, till it reached an infinite sea. Some of them expected it to go down in a cataract of catastrophe, most of them expected it to widen into an estuary of equality and moderation; but all of them thought its returning on itself a prodigy as incredible as witchcraft. In other words, most moderate people thought that faith like freedom would be slowly broadened down, and some advanced people thought that it would be very rapidly broadened down, not to say flattened out. All that world of Guizot and Macaulay and the commercial and scientific liberality was perhaps more certain than any men before or since about the direction in which the world is going. People were so certain about the direction that they only differed about the pace. Many anticipated with alarm, and a few with sympathy, a Jacobin revolt that should guillotine the Archbishop of Canterbury or a Chartist riot that should hang the parsons on the lampposts. But it seemed like a convulsion in nature that the Archbishop instead of losing his head should be looking for his mitre; and that instead of diminishing the respect due to parsons we should strengthen it to the respect due to priests. It revolutionised their very vision of revolution; and turned their very topsyturveydom topsyturvey.

In short, the whole world being divided about whether the stream was going slower or faster became conscious of something vague but vast that was going against the stream. Both in fact and figure there is something deeply disturbing about this, and that for an essential reason. A dead thing can go with the stream, but only a living thing can go against it. A dead dog can be lifted on the leaping water with all the swiftness of a leaping hound; but only a live dog can swim backwards. A paper boat can ride the rising deluge with all the airy arrogance of a fairy ship, but if the fairy ship sails up stream it is really rowed by the fairies. And among the things that merely went with the tide of apparent progress and enlargement there was many a demagogue or sophist whose wild gestures were in truth as lifeless as the movement of a dead dog's limbs wavering in the eddying water; and many a philosophy uncommonly like a paper boat, of the sort that it is not difficult to knock into a cocked hat. But even the truly living and even life-giving things that went with that stream did not thereby prove that they were living or life-giving. It was this other force that was unquestionably and unaccountably alive; the mysterious and unmeasured energy that was thrusting back the river. That was felt to be like the movement of some great monster; and it was none the less clearly a living monster because most people thought it a prehistoric monster. It was none the less an unnatural, an incongruous, and to some a comic upheaval; as if the Great Sea Serpent had suddenly risen out of the Round Pond--unless we consider the Sea Serpent as more likely to live in the Serpentine. This flippant element in the fantasy must not be missed, for it was one of the clearest testimonies to the unexpected nature of the reversal. That age did really feel that a preposterous quality in prehistoric animals belonged also to historic rituals; that mitres and tiaras were like the horns or crests of antediluvian creatures; and that appealing to a Primitive Church was like dressing up as a Primitive Man.

The world is still puzzled by that movement; but most of all because it still moves. I have said something elsewhere of the rather random sort of reproaches that are still directed against it and its much greater consequences; it is enough to say here that the more such critics reproach it the less they explain it. In a sense it is my concern here, if not to explain it, at least to suggest the direction of the explanation; but above all, it is my concern to point out one particular thing about it. And that is that it had all happened before; and even many times before.

To sum up, in so far as it is true that recent centuries have seen an attenuation of Christian doctrine, recent centuries have only seen what the most remote centuries have seen. And even the modern example has only ended as the medieval and pre-medieval examples ended. It is already clear, and grows clearer every day, that it is not going to end in the disappearance of the diminished creed; but rather in the return of those parts of it that had really disappeared. It is going to end as the Arian compromise ended, as the attempts at a compromise with Nominalism and even with Albigensianism ended. But the point to seize in the modern case, as in all the other cases is that what returns is not in that sense a simplified theology; not according to that view a purified theology; it is simply theology. It is that enthusiasm for theological studies that marked the most doctrinal ages; it is the divine science. An old Don with D. D. after his name may have become the typical figure of a bore; but that was because he was himself bored with his theology, not because he was excited about it. It was precisely because he was admittedly more interested in the Latin of Plautus than in the Latin of Augustine, in the Greek of Xenophon than in the Greek of Chrysostom. It was precisely because he was more interested in a dead tradition than in a decidedly living tradition. In short, it was precisely because he was himself a type of the time in which Christian faith was weak. It was not because men would not hail, if they could, the wonderful and almost wild vision of a Doctor of Divinity.

There are people who say they wish Christianity to remain as a spirit. They mean, very literally, that they wish it to remain as a ghost. But it is not going to remain as a ghost. What follows this process of apparent death is not the lingerings of the shade; it is the resurrection of the body. These people are quite prepared to shed pious and reverential tears over the Sepulchre of the Son of Man; what they are not prepared for is the Son of God walking once more upon the hills of morning. These people, and indeed most people, were indeed by this time quite accustomed to the idea that the old Christian candle-light would fade into the light of common day. To many of them it did quite honestly appear like that pale yellow flame of a candle when it is left burning in daylight. It was all the more unexpected, and therefore all the more unmistakable, that the seven branched candle-stick suddenly towered to heaven like a miraculous tree and flamed until the sun turned pale. But other ages have seen the day conquer the candle-light and then the candle-light conquer the day. Again and again, before our time, men have grown content with a diluted doctrine. And again and again there has followed on that dilution, coming as out of the darkness in a crimson cataract, the strength of the red original wine. And we only say once more to-day as has been said many times by our fathers: 'Long years and centuries ago own fathers or the founders of our people drank, as they dreamed, of the blood of God. Long years and centuries have passed since the strength of that giant vintage has been anything but a legend of the age of giants. Centuries ago already is the dark time of the second fermentation, when the wine of Catholicism turned into the vinegar of Calvinism. Long since that bitter drink has been itself diluted; rinsed out and washed away by the waters of oblivion and the wave of the world. Never did we think to taste again even that bitter tang of sincerity and the spirit, still less the richer and the sweeter strength of the purple vineyards in our dreams of the age of gold. Day by day and year by year we have lowered our hopes and lessened our convictions; we have grown more and more used to seeing those vats and vineyards overwhelmed in the water-floods and the last savour and suggestion of that special element fading like a stain of purple upon a sea of grey. We have grown used to dilution, to dissolution, to a watering down that went on for ever. But 'Thou hast kept the good wine until now.'

This is the final fact, and it is the most extraordinary of all. The faith has not only often died but it has often died of old age. It has not only been often killed but it has often died a natural death; in the sense of coming to a natural and necessary end. It is obvious that it has survived the most savage and the most universal persecutions from the shock of the Diocletian fury to the shock of the French Revolution. But it has a more strange and even a more weird tenacity; it has survived not only war but peace. It has not only died often but degenerated often and decayed often; it has survived its own weakness and even its own surrender. We need not repeat what is so obvious about the beauty of the end of Christ in its wedding of youth and death. But this is almost as if Christ had lived to the last possible span, had been a white-haired sage of a hundred and died of natural decay, and then had risen again rejuvenated, with trumpets and the rending of the sky. It was said truly enough that human Christianity in its recurrent weakness was sometimes too much wedded to the powers of the world; but if it was wedded it has very often been widowed. It is a strangely immortal sort of widow. An enemy may have said at one moment that it was but an aspect of the power of the Caesars; and it sounds as strange to-day as to call it an aspect of the Pharaohs. An enemy might say that it was the official faith of feudalism; and it sounds as convincing now as to say that it was bound to perish with the ancient Roman villa. All these things did indeed run their course to its normal end; and there seemed no course for the religion but to end with them. It ended and it began again.

'Heaven and earth shall pass away, but my words shall not pass away.' The civilisation of antiquity was the whole world: and men no more dreamed of its ending than of the ending of daylight. They could not imagine another order unless it were in another world. The civilization of the world has passed away and those words have not passed away. In the long night of the Dark Ages feudalism was so familiar a thing that no man could imagine himself without a lord: and religion was so woven into that network that no man would have believed they could be torn asunder. Feudalism itself was torn to rags and rotted away in the popular life of the true Middle Ages; and the first and freshest power in that new freedom was the old religion. Feudalism had passed away, and the words did not pass away. The whole medieval order, in many ways so complete and almost cosmic a home for man, wore out gradually in its turn and here at least it was thought that the words would die. They went forth across the radiant abyss of the Renaissance and in fifty years were using all its light and learning for new religious foundations, new apologetics, new saints. It was supposed to have been withered up at last in the dry light of the Age of Reason; it was supposed to have disappeared ultimately in the earthquake of the Age of Revolution. Science explained it away; and it was still there. History disinterred it in the past; and it appeared suddenly in the future. To-day it stands once more in our path; and even as we watch it, it grows.

If our social relations and records retain their continuity, if men really learn to apply reason to the accumulating facts of so crushing a story, it would seem that sooner or later even its enemies will learn from their incessant and interminable disappointments not to look for anything so simple as its death. They may continue to war with it, but it will be as they war with nature; as they war with the landscape, as they war with the skies. "Heaven and earth shall pass away, but my words shall not pass away." They will watch for it to stumble; they will watch for it to err; they will no longer watch for it to end. Insensibly, even unconsciously, they will in their own silent anticipations fulfil the relative terms of that astounding prophecy; they will forget to watch for the mere extinction of what has so often been vainly extinguished; and will learn instinctively to look first for the coming of the comet or the freezing of the star.

Conclusion: The Summary of This Book

I have taken the liberty once or twice of borrowing the excellent phrase about an Outline of History; though this study of a special truth and a special error can of course claim no sort of comparison with the rich and many-sided encyclopedia of history, for which that name was chosen. And yet there is a certain reason in the reference: and a sense in which the one thing touches and even cuts across the other. For the story of the world as told by Mr. Wells could here only be criticised as an outline. And, strangely enough, it seems to me that it is only wrong as an outline. It is admirable as an accumulation of history; it is splendid as a store-house or treasure of history; it is a fascinating disquisition on history; it is most attractive as an amplification of history; but it is quite false as an outline of history. The one thing that seems to me quite wrong about it is the outline; the sort of outline that can really be a single line, like that which makes all the difference between a caricature of the profile of Mr. Winston Churchill and of Sir Alfred Mond. In simple and homely language, I mean the things that stick out; the things that make the simplicity of a silhouette. I think the proportions are wrong; the proportions of what is certain as compared with what is uncertain, of what played a great part as compared with what played a smaller part, of what is ordinary and what is extraordinary, of what really lies level with an average and what stands out as an exception.

I do not say it as a small criticism of a great writer, and I have no reason to do so; for in my own much smaller task I feel I have failed in very much the same way. I am very doubtful whether I have conveyed to the reader the main point I meant about the proportions of history, and why I have dwelt so much more on some things than others. I doubt whether I have clearly fulfilled the plan that I set out in the introductory chapter; and for that reason I add these lines as a sort of summary in a concluding chapter. I do believe that the things on which I have insisted are more essential to an outline of history than the things which I have subordinated or dismissed. I do not believe that the past is most truly pictured as a thing in which humanity merely fades away into nature, or civilisation merely fades away into barbarism, or religion fades away into mythology, or our own religion fades away into the religions of the world. In short I do not believe that the best way to produce an outline of history is to rub out the lines. I believe that, of the two, it would be far nearer the truth to tell the tale very simply, like a primitive myth about a man who made the sun and stars or a god who entered the body of a sacred monkey. I will therefore sum up all that has gone before in what seems to me a realistic and reasonably proportioned statement; the short story of mankind.

In the land lit by that neighbouring star, whose blaze is the broad daylight, there are many and very various things motionless and moving. There moves among them a race that is in its relation to others a race of gods. The fact is not lessened but emphasised because it can behave like a race of demons. Its distinction is not an individual illusion, like one bird pluming itself on its own plumes; it is a solid and a many-sided thing. It is demonstrated in the very speculations that have led to its being denied. That men, the gods of this lower world, are linked with it in various ways is true; but it is another aspect of the same truth. That they grow as the grass grows and walk as the beasts walk is a secondary necessity that sharpens the primary distinction. It is like saying that a magician must after all have the appearance of a man; or that even the fairies could not dance without feet. It has lately been the fashion to focus the mind entirely on these mild and subordinate resemblances and to forget the main fact altogether. It is customary to insist that man resembles the other creatures. Yes; and that very resemblance he alone can see. The fish does not trace the fish-bone pattern in the fowls of the air; or the elephant and the emu compare skeletons. Even in the sense in which man is at one with the universe it is an utterly lonely universality. The very sense that he is united with all things is enough to sunder him from all.

Looking around him by this unique light, as lonely as the literal flame that he alone has kindled, this demigod or demon of the visible world makes that world visible. He sees around him a world of a certain style or type. It seems to proceed by certain rules or at least repetitions. He sees a green architecture that builds itself without visible hands; but which builds itself into a very exact plan or pattern, like a design already drawn in the air by an invisible finger. It is not, as is now vaguely suggested, a vague thing. It is not a growth or a groping of blind life. Each seeks an end; a glorious and radiant end, even for every daisy or dandelion we see in looking across the level of a common field. In the very shape of things there is more than green growth; there is the finality of the flower. It is a world of crowns. This impression, whether or not it be an illusion, has so profoundly influenced this race of thinkers and masters of the material world, that the vast majority have been moved to take a certain view of that world. They have concluded, rightly or wrongly, that the world had a plan as the tree seemed to have a plan; and an end and crown like the flower. But so long as the race of thinkers was able to think, it was obvious that the admission of this idea of a plan brought with it another thought more thrilling and even terrible. There was someone else, some strange and unseen being, who had designed these things, if indeed they were designed. There was a stranger who was also a friend; a mysterious benefactor who had been before them and built up the woods and hills for their coming, and had kindled the sunrise against their rising, as a servant kindles a fire. Now this idea of a mind that gives a meaning to the universe has received more and more confirmation within the minds of men, by meditations and experiences much more subtle and searching than any such argument about the external plan of the world. But I am concerned here with keeping the story in its most simple and even concrete terms; and it is enough to say here that most men, including the wisest men, have come to the conclusion that the world has such a final purpose and therefore such a first cause. But most men in some sense separated themselves from the wisest men, when it came to the treatment of that idea. There came into existence two ways of treating that idea, which between them made up most of the religious history of the world. The majority, like the minority, had this strong sense of a second meaning in things; of a strange master who knew the secret of the world. But the majority, the mob or mass of men, naturally tended to treat it rather in the spirit of gossip. The gossip, like all gossip, contained a great deal of truth and falsehood. The world began to tell itself tales about the unknown being or his sons or servants or messengers. Some of the tales may truly be called old wives' tales; as professing only to be very remote memories of the morning of the world; myths about the baby moon or the half-baked mountains. Some of them might more truly be called travellers' tales; as being curious but contemporary tales brought from certain borderlands of experience; such as miraculous cures or those that bring whispers of what has happened to the dead. Many of them are probably true tales; enough of them are probably true to keep a person of real commonsense more or less conscious that there really is something rather marvellous behind the cosmic curtain. But in a sense it is only going by appearances; even if the appearances are called apparitions. It is a matter of appearances—and disappearances. At the most these gods are ghosts; that is, they are glimpses. For most of us they are rather gossip about glimpses. And for the rest, the whole world is full of rumours, most of which are almost avowedly romances. The great majority of the tales about gods and ghosts and the invisible king are told, if not for the sake of the tale, at least for the sake of the topic. They are evidence of the eternal interest of the theme; they are not evidence of anything else, and they are not meant to be. They are mythology or the poetry that is not bound in books--or bound in any other way.

Meanwhile the minority, the sages or thinkers, had withdrawn apart and had taken up an equally congenial trade. They were drawing up plans of the world; of the world which all believed to have a plan. They were trying to set forth the plan seriously and to scale. They were setting their minds directly to the mind that had made the mysterious world; considering what sort of a mind it might be and what its ultimate purpose might be. Some of them made that mind much more impersonal than mankind has generally made it; some simplified it almost to a blank; a few, a very few, doubted it altogether. One or two of the more morbid fancied that it might be evil and an enemy; just one or two of the more degraded in the other class worshipped demons instead of gods. But most of these theorists were theists: and they not only saw a moral plan in nature, but they generally laid down a moral plan for humanity. Most of them were good men who did good work: and they were remembered and reverenced in various ways. They were scribes; any their scriptures became more or less holy scriptures. They were law-givers; and their tradition became not only legal but ceremonial. We may say that they received divine honours, in the sense in which kings and great captains in certain countries often received divine honours. In a word, wherever the other popular spirit, the spirit of legend and gossip could come into play, it surrounded them with the more mystical atmosphere of the myths. Popular poetry turned the sages into saints. But that was all it did. They remained themselves; men never really forgot that they were men, only made into gods in the sense that they were made into heroes. Divine Plato, like Divus Ceasar, was a title and not a dogma. In Asia, where the atmosphere was more mythological, the man was made to look more like a myth, but he remained a man. He remained a man of a certain social class or school of men, receiving and deserving great honour from mankind. It is the order or school of the philosophers; the men who have set themselves seriously to trace the order across any apparent chaos in the vision of life. Instead of living on imaginative rumours and remote traditions and the tail-end of exceptional experiences about the mind and meaning behind the world, they have tried in a sense to project the primary purpose of that mind a priori. They have tried to put on paper a possible plan of the world; almost as if the world were not yet made.

Right in the middle of all these things stands up an enormous exception. It is quite unlike anything else. It is a thing final like the trump of doom, though it is also a piece of good news; or news that seems too good to be true. It is nothing less than the loud assertion that this mysterious maker of the world has visited his world in person. It declares that really and even recently, or right in the middle of historic times, there did walk into the world this original invisible being; about whom the thinkers make theories and the mythologists hand down myths; the Man Who Made the World. That such a higher personality exists behind all things had indeed always been implied by all the best thinkers, as well as by all the most beautiful legends. But nothing of this sort had ever been implied in any of them. It is simply false to say that the other sages and heroes had claimed to be that mysterious master and maker, of whom the world had dreamed and disputed. Not one of them had ever claimed to be anything of the sort. Not one of their sects or schools had even claimed that they had claimed to be anything of the sort. The most that any religious prophet had said was that he was the true servant of such a being. The most that any visionary had ever said was that men might catch glimpses of the glory of that spiritual being; or much more often of lesser spiritual beings. The most that any primitive myth had even suggested was that the Creator was present at the Creation. But that the Creator was present at scenes a little subsequent to the supper-parties of Horace, and talked with tax-collectors and government officials in the detailed daily life of the Roman Empire, and that this fact continued to be firmly asserted by the whole of that great civilisation for more than a thousand years--that is something utterly unlike anything else in nature. It is the one great startling statement that man has made since he spoke his first articulate word, instead of barking like a dog. Its unique character can be used as an argument against it as well as for it. It would be easy to concentrate on it as a case of isolated insanity; but it makes nothing but dust and nonsense of comparative religion.

It came on the world with a wind and rush of running messengers proclaiming that apocalyptic portent, and it is not unduly fanciful to say that they are running still. What puzzles the world, and its wise philosophers and fanciful pagan poets, about the priests and people of the Catholic Church is that they still behave as if they were messengers. A messenger does not dream about what his message might be, or argue about what it probably would be; he delivers it as it is. It is not a theory or a fancy but a fact. It is not relevant to this intentionally rudimentary outline to prove in detail that it is a fact; but merely to point out that these messengers do deal with it as men deal with a fact. All that is condemned in Catholic tradition, authority, and dogmatism and the refusal to retract and modify, are but the natural human attributes of a man with a message relating to a fact. I desire to avoid in this last summary all the controversial complexities that may once more cloud the simple lines of that strange story; which I have already called, in words that are much too weak, the strangest story in the world. I desire merely to mark those main lines and specially to mark where the great line is really to be drawn. The religion of the world, in its right proportions, is not divided into fine shades of mysticism or more or less rational forms of mythology. It is divided by the line between the men who are bringing that message and the men who have not yet heard it, or cannot yet believe it.

But when we translate the terms of that strange tale back into the more concrete and complicated terminology of our time, we find it covered by names and memories of which the very familiarity is a falsification. For instance, when we say that a country contains so many Moslems, we really mean that it contains so many monotheists; and we really mean, by that, that it contains so many men; men with the old average assumption of men--that the invisible ruler remains invisible. They hold it along with the customs of a certain culture and under the simpler laws of a certain law-giver; but so they would if their law-giver were Lycurgus or Solon. They testify to something which is a necessary and noble truth; but was never a new truth. Their creed is not a new colour; it is the neutral and normal tint that is the background of the many-coloured life of man. Mahomet did not, like the Magi, find a new star; he saw through his own particular window a glimpse of the great grey field of the ancient starlight. So when we say that the country contains so many Confucians or Buddhists, we mean it contains so many pagans whose prophets have given them another and rather vaguer version of the invisible power; making it not only invisible but almost impersonal. When we say that they also have temples and idols and priests and periodical festivals, we simply mean that this sort of heathen is enough of a human being to admit the popular element of pomp and pictures and feasts and fairy-tales. We only mean that Pagans have more sense than Puritans. But what the gods are supposed to be, what the priests are commissioned to say, is not a sensational secret like what those running messengers of the Gospel had to say. Nobody else except those messengers has any Gospel; nobody else has any good news; for the simple reason that nobody else has any news.

Those runners gather impetus as they run. Ages afterwards they still speak as if something had just happened. They have not lost the speed and momentum of messengers; they have hardly lost, as it were, the wild eyes of witnesses. In the Catholic Church, which is the cohort of the message, there are still those headlong acts of holiness that speak of something rapid and recent; a self-sacrifice that startles the world like a suicide. But it is not a suicide; it is not pessimistic; it is still as optimistic as St. Francis of the flowers and birds. It is newer in spirit than the newest schools of thought; and it is almost certainly on the eve of new triumphs. For these men serve a mother who seems to grow more beautiful as new generations rise up and call her blessed. We might sometimes fancy that the Church grows younger as the world grows old.

For this is the last proof of the miracle; that something so supernatural should have become so natural. I mean that anything so unique when seen from the outside should only seem universal when seen from the inside. I have not minimised the scale of the miracle, as some of our wilder theologians think it wise to do. Rather have I deliberately dwelt on that incredible interruption, as a blow that broke the very backbone of history. I have great sympathy with the monotheists, the Moslems, or the Jews, to whom it seems a blasphemy; a blasphemy that might shake the world. But it did not shake the world; it steadied the world. That fact, the more we consider it, will seem more solid and more strange. I think it a piece of plain justice to all the unbelievers to insist upon the audacity of the act of faith that is demanded of them. I willingly and warmly agree that it is, in itself, a suggestion at which we might expect even the brain of the believer to reel, when he realised his own belief. But the brain of the believer does not reel;

it is the brains of the unbelievers that reel. We can see their brains reeling on every side and into every extravagance of ethics and psychology; into pessimism and the denial of life; into pragmatism and the denial of logic; seeking their omens in nightmares and their canons in contradictions; shrieking for fear at the far-off sight of things beyond good and evil, or whispering of strange stars where two and two make five. Meanwhile this solitary thing that seems at first so outrageous in outline remains solid and sane in substance. It remains the moderator of all these manias; rescuing reason from the Pragmatists exactly as it rescued laughter from the Puritans. I repeat that I have deliberately emphasised its intrinsically defiant and dogmatic character. The mystery is how anything so startling should have remained defiant and dogmatic and yet become perfectly normal and natural. I have admitted freely that, considering the incident in itself, a man who says he is God may be classed with a man who says he is glass. But the man who says he is glass is not a glazier making windows for all the world. He does not remain for after ages as a shining and crystalline figure, in whose light everything is as clear as crystal.

But this madness has remained sane. The madness has remained sane when everything else went mad. The madhouse has been a house to which, age after age, men are continually coming back as to a home. That is the riddle that remains; that anything so abrupt and abnormal should still be found a habitable and hospitable thing. I care not if the sceptic says it is a tall story; I cannot see how so toppling a tower could stand so long without foundation. Still less can I see how it could become, as it has become, the home of man. Had it merely appeared and disappeared, it might possibly have been remembered or explained as the last leap of the rage of illusion, the ultimate myth of the ultimate mood, in which the mind struck the sky and broke. But the mind did not break. It is the one mind that remains unbroken in the break-up of the world. If it were an error, it seems as if the error could hardly have lasted a day. If it were a mere ecstasy, it would seem that such an ecstasy could not endure for an hour. It has endured for nearly two thousand years; and the world within it has been more lucid, more level-headed, more reasonable in its hopes, more healthy in its instincts, more humorous and cheerful in the face of fate and death, than all the world outside. For it was the soul of Christendom that came forth from the incredible Christ; and the soul of it was common sense. Though we dared not look on His face we could look on His fruits; and by His fruits we should know Him. The fruits are solid and the fruitfulness is much more than a metaphor; and nowhere in this sad world are boys happier in apple-trees, or men in more equal chorus singing as they tread the vine, than under the fixed flash of this instant and intolerant enlightenment; the lightning made eternal as the light.

APPENDIX I: ON PREHISTORIC MAN

On re-reading these pages I feel that I have tried in many places and with many words, to say something that might be said in one word. In a sense this study is meant to be superficial. That is, it is not meant as a study of the things that need to be studied. It is rather a reminder of the things that are seen so quickly that they are forgotten almost as quickly. Its moral, in a manner of speaking, is that first thoughts are best; so a flash might reveal a landscape; with the Eiffel Tower or the Matterhorn standing up in it as they would never stand up again in the light of common day. I ended the book with an image of everlasting lightning; in a very different sense, alas, this little flash has lasted only too long. But the method has also certain practical disadvantages upon which I think it well to add these two notes. It may seem to simplify too much and to ignore out of ignorance. I feel this especially in the passage about the prehistoric pictures; which is not concerned with all that the learned may learn from prehistoric pictures, but with the single point of what anyone could learn from there being any prehistoric pictures at all. I am conscious that this attempt to express it in terms of innocence may exaggerate even my own ignorance. Without any pretence of scientific research or information, I should be sorry to have it thought that I knew no more than what was needed, in that passage, of the states into which primitive humanity has been divided. I am aware, of course, that the story is elaborately stratified; and that there were many such stages before the Cro-Magnon or any peoples with whom we associate such pictures. Indeed recent studies about the Neanderthal and other races rather tend to repeat the moral that is here most relevant. The notion noted in these pages of something necessarily slow or late in the development of religion, will gain little indeed from these later revelations about the precursors of the reindeer picture-maker. The learned appear to hold that, whether the reindeer picture could be religious or not, the people that lived before it were religious already; burying their dead with the significant signs of mystery and hope. This obviously brings us back to the same argument; an argument that is not approached by any measurement of the earlier man's skull. It is little use here to compare the head of the man with the head of the monkey, if it certainly never came into the head of the monkey to bury another monkey with nuts in his grave to help him towards a heavenly monkey house. Talking of skulls, I am also aware of the story of the Cro-Magnon skull that was much larger and finer than a modern skull. It is a very funny story; because an eminent evolutionist, awakening to a somewhat belated caution, protested against anything being inferred from one specimen. It is the duty of a solitary skull to prove that our fathers were our inferiors. Any solitary skull presuming to prove that they were superior is felt to be suffering from swelled head.

APPENDIX II: ON AUTHORITY AND ACCURACY

In this book which is merely meant as a popular criticism of popular fallacies, often indeed of very vulgar errors, I feel that I have sometimes given an impression of scoffing at serious scientific work. It was however the very reverse of my intentions. I am not arguing with the scientist who explains the elephant, but only with the sophist who explains it away. And as a matter of fact the sophist plays to the gallery, as he did in ancient Greece. He appeals to the ignorant, especially when he appeals to the learned. But I never meant my own criticism to be an impertinence to the truly learned. We all owe an infinite debt to the researches, especially the recent researches, of single minded students in these matters; and I have only professed to pick up things here and there from them. I have not loaded my abstract argument with quotations and references, which only make a man look more learned than he is; but in some cases I find that my own loose fashion of allusion is rather misleading about my own meaning. The passage about Chaucer and the Child Martyr is badly expressed; I only mean that the English poet probably had in mind the English saint; of whose story he gives a sort of foreign version. In the same way two statements in the chapter on Mythology follow each other in such a way that it may seem to be suggested that the second story about monotheism refers to the Southern Seas. I may explain that Atahocan belongs not to Australasian but to American savages. So in the chapter called "The Antiquity of Civilisation," which I feel to be the most unsatisfactory, I have given my own impression of the meaning of the development of Egyptian monarchy too much, perhaps, as if it were identical with the facts on which it was formed as given in works like those of Professor J. L Myres. But the confusion was not intentional; still less was there any intention to imply, in the remainder of the chapter, that the anthropological speculations about races are less valuable than they undoubtedly are. My criticism is strictly relative; I may say that the pyramids are plainer than the tracks of the desert; without denying that wiser men than I may see tracks in what is to me the trackless sand.

THE END

451

48146727R00258

Made in the USA
Middletown, DE
12 June 2019